The RISE OF

AMERICAN COOPERATIVE ENTERPRISE:

1620-1920

The

RISE OF

**The Interstate
Printers & Publishers, Inc.**

Danville, Illinois

Joseph G. Knapp

AMERICAN COOPERATIVE ENTERPRISE:

1620-1920

Library of Congress
catalog card number: 77-77564

To   **Edwin G. Nourse**

Dean of Scholars
in American Cooperative Enterprise

FOREWORD

In a foreword one may be personal, and it has seemed to me that readers might like to know how the author got involved in this field, and how this book came to be written. My story goes back to the fall of 1920 when I took a course in agricultural cooperation and credit at the University of Illinois under Professor Ivan Wright. My main recollection of this course is that for textbooks we used *Cooperation in Agriculture* (1913) by G. Harold Powell, and *How To Cooperate and Double Profits* (1915) by Clarence Poe. In those days cooperation was considered a coming thing, but there was little organized information available on the subject.

My interest in cooperatives was sharpened by the agricultural depression which began to influence my own affairs in 1921, and the dramatic crusade of Aaron Sapiro to organize agriculture along big business lines which was then attracting nationwide attention. When opportunity came to me in 1924, as a Fellow of the Food Research Institute at Stanford University, to select a subject for my doctoral dissertation, I chose for study the pool marketing of wheat.

To obtain a background for this study I made field excursions to examine the operations of the great agricultural cooperatives in California. In this way, I became acquainted with the California Fruit Growers Exchange (now Sunkist Growers), and the California Walnut Growers Association (now Diamond Walnut Growers), and other important California cooperatives. These field trips inspired my first writing on cooperation.

I spent the summer of 1925 gathering at first hand information on the operations of the wheat pools in the United States and Canada. Fortunately the dissertation was prepared under the direction of Dr. Joseph S. Davis who brought home to me that scholarship to be effective requires not only enthusiasm but infinite patience.

My work for the doctoral degree was not completed in 1926 when I was invited by Dr. Edwin G. Nourse of the Institute of Economics (now incorporated in the Brookings Institution) to come to Washington,

D. C., to work with him on a study of livestock marketing cooperatives, a subject of great interest to both of us. This was a tremendous opportunity for a budding agricultural economist with an interest in cooperatives for Dr. Nourse was then, as he is today, the Dean of cooperative theorists in the United States. He understood why and how cooperatives were important as part of our economic life. I found especially congenial his belief that to understand an economic institution one must know its history. In the book that resulted from our study, *The Cooperative Marketing of Livestock*, there is this statement written by Dr. Nourse in the Introduction, to which I fully subscribe:

> The natural scientist has found that he must examine the lower forms of life as a preliminary to the study of the more complex. It is equally necessary that any really adequate study of the complicated economic institutions of today be grounded thoroughly in the evolutionary process of which they are merely the latest stage. Cooperation is much too complex an economic and social institution to flourish on mere enthusiasm. It must be grounded on patient and fearless study of its past as well as its present manifestations and disinterested discussion of the issues on their merits.

Being in Washington in the mid-1920's was a fortunate experience for a neophyte in the field of cooperative enterprise. Agricultural cooperation was in the national spotlight. The Division of Cooperative Marketing, established by the Cooperative Marketing Act of 1926, was shaping up with the gifted leadership of its chief, Chris L. Christensen, who was well versed in the long history of Danish cooperation. Forces were then gathering for the passage of the Agricultural Marketing Act of 1929 which provided for an all-out effort to fashion strong national marketing cooperatives with the guidance and support of a Federal Farm Board. Most important to me, the American Institute of Cooperation, founded in 1925, was then establishing itself as a national forum for cooperative discussion and planning under the intellectual direction of Dr. Nourse, Chairman of its program committee. I was thus at the very center of things in what Charles W. Holman, long-time Secretary of the American Institute of Cooperation, was later to term "The Golden Age of Cooperation in America." Through working with Nourse and Holman I soon came to know many of the leaders—Richard Pattee, Walton Peteet, John D. Miller, M. W. Thatcher, Charles C. Teague, Carl Williams, C. O. Moser, Forrest Ketner, and John Brandt—who, for example were then shaping the course of cooperative advancement.

In the fall of 1929, with our book on the cooperative marketing of livestock largely completed and with my doctoral thesis accepted by Stanford University, I was ready for a new adventure. This came in an opportunity to take charge of teaching, extension, and research in marketing and cooperative subjects at North Carolina State College, now North Carolina State University. My five years at Raleigh from 1929 to

1934, the years of the Great Depression, convinced me that the main hope for agriculture lay in the better organization of farmers. I was caught up in the efforts of the Federal Farm Board to help build a strong cooperative for desperately pressed tobacco growers. Concurrently, I became involved in the drive to consolidate cooperative purchasing efforts in North Carolina by the formation of a state-wide purchasing cooperative. As secretary of the organizational committee for this proposed organization I was able to help bring into being the Farmers Cooperative Exchange—the F. C. X.—which has since become one of the major cooperatives in the nation.

With the reorganization of federal agricultural agencies in the early days of the New Deal I was invited in the summer of 1934 to join the staff of the Cooperative Division in the newly formed Farm Credit Administration to develop a research, service, and educational program for cooperative purchasing associations. This was a pleasing opportunity, for cooperative purchasing was then entering its period of most rapid growth, and it gives one satisfaction to be in on the ground floor. In this work I was able to work intimately on practical problems with the great pioneers in this development—H. E. Babcock, James A. McConnell, Quentin Reynolds, W. G. Wysor, Harvey Hull, Marvin Briggs, Howard Cowden, Murray Lincoln, Clark Brody, H. S. Agster, Emil Syftestad, E. G. Cort, John Lawler, Harry Beernink, Clyde Edmunds, Charles Baker, C. H. Becker, Lloyd Marchant, M. G. Mann, D. W. Brooks, Charles McNeil, and many others.

The mid-1930's were exciting years to be back in Washington, D. C. The Banks for Cooperatives were being organized and the research, service, and educational program of the government with cooperatives, which had been absorbed by the Federal Farm Board, was being reinstated and strengthened in the Farm Credit Administration. The Rural Electrification Administration was being set up to serve the electric cooperatives, then in their infancy. The credit unions were being encouraged by national legislation and sentiment for consumers' cooperation was building up, sparked by the popularity of Marquis Childs's book, Sweden—The Middle Way, which found in cooperatives a solution for many economic problems. It was a period of cooperative euphoria, when the future just around the corner seemed bright.

It was then that I began to think about writing a book on cooperative purchasing associations to search out the lessons of their experience. I was impressed by their vision and accomplishments and it seemed to me that they were giving a new dimension to the concept of cooperative enterprise. My work during World War II further convinced me of the need for an in-depth study of these associations. With the close of the war the Brookings Institution gave me the opportunity to do what

I had in mind and the Farm Credit Administration granted me two leaves of absence for six-month periods in 1945 and 1946 for this purpose.

As I began to dig into the roots of cooperative purchasing I found them so entangled with those of other forms of cooperation that I could not unravel them without studying the whole cooperative plant. Irresistably, I found myself broadening my inquiry with the concurrence of Dr. Nourse, whose disposition has always been to go to first causes. Thus, the study grew into an examination of the evolution and status of cooperative enterprise in the United States.

With active administrative responsibilities in government I was unable to complete this project in the time allowed, so it was put aside until it could be given more research and reflective consideration. Moreover, since the cooperatives then were changing rapidly under many influences it seemed wise to let these changes proceed further before completing the book. So while working on current cooperative affairs I kept building my files and gathering pertinent information. One major advantage came from this postponement. My position as Administrator of the Farmer Cooperative Service from 1953 to 1966 enriched my opportunity to observe almost all aspects of cooperative development.

When I settled down to complete the book in 1966, free from official responsibilities, I found that the subject could not be encompassed in one volume. The natural division point was 1920 for before that year cooperative enterprise was finding itself. From then on it began to expand and widen its sphere of influence. The present volume I call *The Rise of American Cooperative Enterprise* for this book examines the evolution of cooperative enterprise in the United States from its origins to the time when it represented an articulate and promising institution. A second volume in preparation, to be called *The Advance of American Cooperative Enterprise*, will deal with the great amplification of cooperative development during the years from 1920 to 1970. Together these two volumes will comprise a history of cooperative enterprise in the United States.

In *The Rise of American Cooperative Enterprise* I have tried to tell the story of how cooperative enterprise grew up naturally and spontaneously in many areas and under differing conditions in response to economic and social problems. This book will make clear that the great cooperatives of today did not spring into existence by government fiat. Although assistance from the government in the form of research, education, laws, and credit has been of great value our modern cooperatives represent the product of years of cumulative effort by millions of people. This background has made them experimental, innovative, and pragmatic.

I am presenting this volume in five parts. Part One covers the years from 1620 to 1896, when cooperative enterprise was gaining a foothold in the United States. Part Two enquires into the economic, social, and political factors favorable to cooperative enterprise that were active from 1897 to 1920. Parts Three, Four, and Five examine the substantial progress of different forms of cooperative enterprise during those years. The final chapter, "The End of the Beginnings," evaluates cooperative enterprise in 1920, the year that marked the close of the period of establishment and the starting of the modern period of expansion and development.

Joseph G. Knapp

Bethesda, Maryland
June 1969

AUTHOR'S ACKNOWLEDGEMENTS

I am indebted to many colleagues and associates for their encouragement and counsel in the preparation of this book, but four names may well come at the head of this list.

First comes Dr. Henry C. Taylor, pioneer and historian of agricultural economics and one of the founders of the American Institute of Cooperation. His understanding of the nature of cooperation and its importance for agriculture and his faith in my work in this field have been an inspiration and a support.*

Even before Dr. Taylor organized the Bureau of Agricultural Economics, Charles J. Brand, as first Chief of the Office of Markets, inaugerated the program to improve the marketing of farm products through cooperative associations. He took a lively interest in my early work on this book and was of unfailing encouragement.

George E. Farrand, the innovative lawyer who helped fashion the California Fruit Growers Exchange (now Sunkist Growers) and many of the other California cooperative associations, was generous with essential information and beneficial advice, and helpful criticism of early chapters in their first draft.

The long-continued interest and help I have received from Dr. Edwin G. Nourse, Vice-President of the Brookings Institution and later the first Chairman of the Council of Economic Advisers, is gratefully acknowledged in the Foreword and at various places throughout the book.

Of others who have helped to bring this study to fruition, I would especially thank my long-time colleague, Kelsey B. Gardner, who has read all of the manuscript with a critical but friendly eye. I wish also to thank the following for their review and suggestions on certain chapters: Martin A. Abrahamsen, I through IV; Wayne D. Rasmussen, I through IX; Robert B. Tootell, VI and VII; William I. Myers, VI, VII, and XXII; Florence Parker, XXI; and David Angevine, XXI and XXII.

---

*Dr. Taylor died on April 28, 1969, while this book was in production.

Many others, who cannot here be named, have also provided helpful information or other assistance.

I wish also to record here my sincere appreciation to The Cooperative Foundation, and a number of associated cooperatives and persons, for a generous grant that has helped me meet typing, travel, and other incidental research expenses. I am indebted also to many cooperative associations for their confidence in this book as expressed by advance orders to ensure its publication.

OTHER BOOKS BY JOSEPH G. KNAPP

The Cooperative Marketing of Livestock
[with Edwin G. Nourse]
(1931)

The Hard Winter Wheat Pools:
An Experiment in Agricultural Marketing Integration

(1933)

E. A. Stokdyk: Architect of Cooperation

(1953)

Seeds That Grew:
A History of the Cooperative Grange League Federation Exchange

(1960)

Farmers in Business

(1963)

Great American Cooperators

[with associates]
(1967)

TABLE OF CONTENTS

The RISE OF
AMERICAN COOPERATIVE ENTERPRISE

1620-1920

Part One

PROBINGS

In the first four chapters of this book, cooperative enterprise is traced from its informal beginnings in early colonial days down to the time when it was fairly well rooted as a form of business in a vigorous expanding nation. By 1896, the great period of settlement and westward expansion was over and the general structure of our economic system was largely formed.

The first chapter reaches from the Mayflower Compact to the Civil War—which Charles and Mary Beard characterized as "the second American Revolution." In the two centuries and more covered by this chapter, the pattern for later cooperative development began to emerge.

The next three chapters examine how cooperative enterprise took on form and substance in the turbulent period of economic and social change ushered in by the Civil War. Buoyant enthusiasm was being tempered by economic realities. In 1896, cooperation was on the threshold of its modern development.

The entire period from 1620 to 1896 for cooperatives was one of search and experiment. It can be characterized as a time of probings when much was learned but little of a tangible nature was accomplished.

Chapter I

EARLY EXPLORATIONS

In the 240 years from the settlement of New England to the opening of the Civil War, cooperation as a method of social and economic organization was feeling its way, adjusting to a developing environment, experimenting in new techniques. It was a time of discovery, with new lands, new people, new problems, and new solutions. A vigorous young nation was emerging and moving lustily toward maturity.

Colonial Origins

When the Pilgrims came to America in 1620, they were by compact a cooperative organization bound together to meet the vicissitudes of an unknown and unsettled country.[1] In their primitive surroundings, the Pilgrims soon found that mutual help in building and maintaining homes was indispensable, and this conclusion was encouraged by the religious teachings of their church and their democratic form of government by town meetings. The concept of mutuality was also suited to their first industry—fishing, in which fishermen pooled labor and risk and shared in the catch of cod and mackerel.[2]

The New England settlers also brought with them the English system of common fields and fences which was in itself an embryonic form of cooperation. The early practice in this regard has been described as follows:

> The tillage and mowing land of the community was laid out in common fields, which were surrounded by common fences. The fence, of posts and rails with a ditch before it, was constructed and kept in repair by holders of allotments within the fields, each man being responsible for a certain length of fence in proportion of the extent of his allotment. It ought to be noted here that although tillage was carried on in a common field, it was not tillage in common. Every settler cultivated his own allotment; he was, however, under restriction as to choice of crops and date of harvest.[3]

5

In this period, a strong communal spirit, fostered by the vicissitudes of living, manifested itself in forms of cooperation which were often of a compulsory nature. This is shown by a law passed by the Massachusetts Bay Colony in 1646:

> Because the harvest of hay, corn, flax, and hemp comes usually so near together that much loss can hardly be avoided, it is ordered and decreed by this court, that the constable of every town, upon request made to him, shall require artificers or handicraftsmen, meet to labor, to work by the day for their neighbors needing him, in mowing, reaping, and inning thereof, and that those whom they help shall duly pay them for their work, and if any person so required shall refuse, or the constable neglect his office herein, they shall each of them pay to the use of the poor of the town double so much as such a day's work comes unto; provided no artificer, etc., shall be compelled to work for others while he is necessarily attending on like business of his own.[4]

Such forms of "compulsory" cooperation gradually gave way to "voluntary" cooperation of groups of settlers in heavy tasks, as, for instance, in log rolling bees, corn husking bees, etc., which soon became a significant feature of colonial agriculture in the North, and as the pioneers moved westward, they took their "habits of group cooperation" with them.[5]

This tendency of Americans to work together on common problems greatly impressed our first foreign visitors:

> It is necessary to remark, that in the early part of the settlement of a country like this, a great number of things occur necessary to be done, which require the united strength of numbers to effect. In those parts, money cannot purchase for the new settler the required aid; but that kind and generous feeling which men have for each other, who are not rendered callous by the possession of wealth, or the dread of poverty, comes to his relief: his neighbors, even unsolicited, appoint a day when as a *frolic,* they shall, for instance, build him a house. On the morning of the appointed day they assemble, and divide themselves into parties, to each of which is assigned its respective duty; one party cuts down trees, another lops and cuts them to proper lengths, a third is furnished with horses and oxen, and drags them to the spot designed for the site of the house; another party is employed in making *shingles* to cover the roof, and at night all the materials are ready upon the spot; and on the night of the next day, he and his family sleep in their new habitation. No remuneration is expected nor would it be received. It is considered the performance of a duty, and only lays him under the obligation to discharge the debt by doing the same to subsequent settlers. But this combination of labour in numbers, for the benefit of one individual, is not confined to the newcomer only, it occurs frequently in the course of a year amongst the old settlers, with whom it is a continued bond of amity, and social intercourse, and in no part of the world is good *neighborship* found in greater perfection than in the western territory, or in America generally.[6]

There was little opportunity for more complex forms of cooperation to develop since self-sufficient agriculture and household industry were dominant throughout the colonial period.[7] While commercial trade was beginning to arise in such cities as Philadelphia, New York, and Boston, the country store continued to be the principal commercial establishment in the small towns and villages:

> In every village there were one or more country stores with a varied stock generally described as European and West India goods. Under the first head were included a few pieces of imported dress goods, crockery, glassware, powder and shot, and bars of iron and steel. The West India goods were salt, molasses, rum and other liquors, indigo, spices, and sugar.
>
> Practically all the transactions at the country stores were by barter, for "hard" money was scarce, and paper currency depreciated so rapidly as to be but a poor medium of exchange. The storekeeper took in exchange for his goods a great variety of farm products—butter, cheese, flaxseed, tow cloth, grain, provisions, potash, feathers, and beeswax. There was as yet little specialization in marketing functions, and so the storekeeper usually undertook on his own responsibility the resale of his miscellaneous purchases in the seaports, or if he lived on the coast or on a river, he might be himself a shipowner and exporter.[8]

With industry still in the household or handicraft stage, there was no large urban class of wage workers, and thus little need or opportunity for cooperation to develop in buying and selling commodities. This explains why cooperation as a form of business enterprise first arose in the field of fire insurance.

The Emergence of Mutual Fire Insurance

Fire has always been a disaster to property owners and from the time of the first settlement it has been unwritten law that neighbors should help each other not only in preventing and fighting fires[9] but in sharing part of the loss that might be occasioned by a fire. Early records indicate that it was an established custom for neighbors to take up a collection to help any of their number who had suffered a serious fire loss.

The seriousness of fire loss attracted the attention of Benjamin Franklin as early as 1735, when he recommended various measures for preventing fires "as an ounce of prevention is worth a pound of cure."[10]

The following year, Franklin and four friends founded the pioneer Union Fire Company as an association for mutual assistance in fighting fires. Each member agreed to furnish his own fire fighting apparatus—"six leather buckets," as well as "two stout linen bags" for use in holding property saved at a fire which might be in danger of theft.[11] This company became the model for many similar volunteer fire-fighting companies which have been a feature of American life down to the present day,[12] and the direct progenitor of the first successful mutual fire insurance company to be established in this country.

If neighbors could organize cooperatively to protect their homes from fire loss, why could they not "chip in" to a fund which could be used to meet losses which any of the group might suffer by fire? This type of thinking led the members of the Union Fire Company in February 1750 to raise 200 pounds for "A fund for an Insurance Office to make up the Damage that may Arise by Fire among this Company." The next step is recorded in the minutes of the company of August 26, 1751:

> A Proposal from Benjamin Franklin relating to the consideration of the late scheme for Insurance of Houses being read, Requesting that this Company would appoint two of their Members to attend such Persons as may be appointed by the other several Fire Companies to meet at the Standard in Market Street on the 7th day of the 7th Month next, to Consider such Matters as they think will tend most to the Utility of Ye Inhabitants in General. They have accordingly appointed Benjamin Franklin and Phillip Syng to attend as aforesaid which they Consent to."[13]

This resulted in the formation of the Philadelphia Contributionship for the Insurance of Houses from Loss by Fire on March 25, 1752, the first names recorded on the Deed of Settlement following that of the Lieutenant Governor of the Province of Pennsylvania being those of Benjamin Franklin and Phillip Syng, the other member of the special committee from the Union Fire Company.[14]

The plan of the Contributionship was patterned on "The Amicable Contributionship, and Hand-in-Hand Fire Office," which was established in London in 1696.[15] Its most interesting features were:

> 1. The insurance policies were for seven years.
> 2. The premium was "the deposit of a sum, the use of interest of which during the policy belonged to the company."
> 3. "The payment of the deposit and the signature of the deed of settlement made the assured a member of the company . . ."
> 4. "The personal liability of the members for losses, beyond their own deposits, was half as much more, in case a single fire, beginning in one house and damaging one or more houses, should sweep away all the funds of the Company."
> 5. "The concern was managed *for the profit and loss of the members*, interest being allowed to them on their deposits, in proportion to the whole amount received by the Company, and a proportion of the losses and expenses charged to them, and the balance settled at the expiration of the policy."[16]

The last provision, which followed the example of the Amicable Contributionship, proved to be a cardinal defect in the scheme, since it prohibited the accumulation of a fund that would give stability to the company. After two years of experience, this became apparent, with the result that the deed was unanimously changed by the following stipulation: "That the interest arising from the stock should be carried to one common account, to answer the contingent charges of the company, and all losses and damages that might happen to same."[17] Otherwise this plan, with minor alterations, has been continued by the Philadelphia Contributionship to the present day.[18]

The actual operation of the company was simple. For example, members made a deposit of 20 shillings in the hundred pounds for brick and stone houses in good condition, or at the rate of 1 per cent. This deposit was all that was required during the life of the policy, unless an assessment should be required by a general fire disaster. The directors took their responsibilities seriously, and they conscientiously considered all claims for loss and similar problems. It is of interest that in order to insure attendance at directors' meetings a fine of one shilling was imposed for tardiness and double that amount for absence from a meeting. In 1764, the fund which had accumulated from these fines was invested in milestones to assist the wayfarer along the highways running out of the city.

The success of the Philadelphia Contributionship encouraged the formation of a number of similar mutual fire insurance companies prior to the formation of the first stock company in 1794. There were some 10 mutual fire insurance companies in existence by 1800 as compared with 4 companies organized on a stock basis.[19] Thus, it was in the field of mutual insurance that the cooperative form of business enterprise first took definite form in the United States.

The Industrial Awakening

Although the Industrial Revolution began to influence the character of American economic life shortly after the Revolutionary War, these changes did not encourage the development of cooperative associations until the factory system began to grow following Hamilton's famous report on Manufactures in 1791.[20]

This situation, which gave rise to the emergence of an urban population working for wages, resulted in the first significant experiment in industrial cooperation, when the Journeymen Cordwainers of Philadelphia in 1806 undertook to become their own employers by opening a warehouse to market at wholesale and retail the boots and shoes manufactured by the organization's members.[21]

The embargo and the War of 1812, by concentrating attention on the necessity and desirability of internal development, accentuated industrial expansion, and encouraged the construction of improved roads, turnpikes, canals, and railroads to facilitate the opening of the West. With these developments came various types of specialized middlemen, particularly of the commission agent type, while separate wholesalers began to take the place of the general merchant who had formerly performed both wholesale and retail functions.[22]

These new conditions encouraged a rapid growth in population, and cities sprang up rapidly after 1820 with the extension of factory methods of manufacturing. The population in 1790 was less than 4,000,000. By 1860, it was over 31,000,000. In 1790, there were only six cities having a population of 8,000 inhabitants or more. By 1860, there were 141 cities of this size.

During this period, little occurred in the way of industrial cooperation until in the 1830's a wave of enthusiasm for cooperative workshops struck the workingmen's associations which were just beginning to become an important factor in industrial life. This movement culminated in Philadelphia where, in 1836, the cabinet makers ware-room was one of the largest furniture stores in the city, while the cordwainers and hand loom weavers had "opened cooperative manufactories," and the tailors, booters, and saddlers were preparing to open cooperative shops to distribute their own wares.[23] Of interest here is the following resolution of the Philadelphia Trades Union reported in the National Laborer, June 11, 1836:

> Resolved, that the cooperation society recently established by the Cordwainers, Ladies Branch, and the store which they have opened at No. 40 Arcade, is a striking evidence that they have become acquainted with the only means of securing a just reward for their labor, and that this union cheerfully recommends said establishment to the patronage of all connected with or interested in the advancement of those who earn their bread in the sweat of their brow, and particularly to those females who desire to see their husbands and brothers obtain sufficient wages to keep the female part of their families from the drudgery of factories, workshops, and all other contaminating and debasing female employments.[24]

At that time, the National Laborer was vigorously urging the National Trades Union to foster cooperation by raising a fund for use in helping start cooperatives and insure them against loss, and in October the following resolution was offered by the Committee on Cooperation of the National Trades Union:

> Resolved, that the Trades' Unions, Trades' Societies, and mechanics of all branches in the United States and elsewhere, be requested to take measures to investigate the subject of Cooperation, and that meetings be held by all the unions and Societies represented in this Union, at which the subject may be

fully discussed, as it is the opinion of the Committee, that until a system of Cooperation is adopted by which the producers of wealth may also be its possessors, and consequently enjoy its benefits, that the great burden of the evils of which we so justly complain, will never be removed.

Resolved, that it is the opinion of this Convention, that if Trades' Unions and Trade Societies were to apply their funds to the establishing of Cooperation in Societies suffering aggression, instead of exhausting their funds by supporting strikes, a much more permanent benefit would be rendered.[25]

The heart was taken out of these promising experiments by the panic of 1837 and the ensuing period of hard times, which brought failure to all but the strongest firms, and this experience dampened the confidence of workingmen in industrial cooperation until it was to rise again in the 1860's.

Building and Loan Associations

The rapid growth of cities with the rise of working-class solidarity was also favorable to the development of another form of cooperative enterprise—the building and loan association. Although the first association of this type was formed in Philadelphia in 1831,[26] such organizations did not become general until 1850, when they were formed in increasing numbers as a protest against high rents, under the slogan, "Do your own land lording."

Under the general plan worked out, members contributed funds in weekly installments to a common pool from which members who wished to build could borrow. The interest paid by the borrowers for capital to build homes was paid to the lenders. Thus these associations were, in effect, mutual savings banks to facilitate home ownership. At first they were strictly local and mutual in character with the members meeting together for business purposes.[27]

The achievements of these associations in making possible the ownership of homes did much to gain recognition for the cooperative movement in the latter half of the eighteenth century.[28]

Agricultural Beginnings

More progress was being made at that time in the organization of farmers. Starting with the creation of the Philadelphia Society for Promoting Agriculture in 1785, many similar societies were formed to foster improved agricultural techniques. Dominated by "gentlemen farmers," their principal achievement was in the field of agricultural education.[29]

Of more practical importance were the numerous "county societies" which were patterned on the Berkshire Agricultural Society formed in 1810. The county societies attempted to attract the working farmers "through their hearts" rather than through their heads, primarily through the holding of cattle shows, machinery exhibits, and fairs. The climax of this movement came between 1820 and 1825 when there were hundreds of such societies, with thousands of members in New England and the eastern seaboard states. To some extent, they were furthered by the falling level of prices which followed the War of 1812 since at that time farmers were beginning to feel dependent upon commercial outlets.

> With vague hopes they turned for relief to the county societies, but in the ... campaign for better farming, the farmers found little comfort. What they wanted to know was not how to grow greater crops and fatter animals (irrespective of cost), but how and where to sell what they already had produced.[30]

Although the county societies were not able to give the help that was most desired, they did perform a needed function in stimulating better farming methods which raised the professional standards of the industry. Of perhaps more importance, they gave "rise to a new community of interests among farmers and increased their feeling of importance as an economic group."[31]

Manifestations of cooperation in marketing farm products closely followed the trend toward commercial farming. As early as 1820, a group of Ohio farmers "associated together for the purpose of sending their produce to market. Their first attempt was the marketing of hogs. These were put into the custody of representatives of the company and driven to Sandusky, where they were slaughtered, the pork being packed and shipped by boat to Montreal."[32] In 1822, the farmers of southeastern Pennsylvania "attempted to remedy unsatisfactory marketing conditions by a bold experiment in cooperation. Believing that the Philadelphia brewers had combined to keep down the price of barley, the farmers determined to brew their own grain and erected a building for the purpose in the city. The venture did not prove successful, and after a few years the plant was sold and the enterprise was abandoned." An even more ambitious program was formulated by Maine wool growers in 1833 and 1834.

> Complaining of false market rumors circulated by buyers, and of the lack of warehouse facilities, they formulated a program of reform measures which sounds strangely modern. They demanded a decrease in the number of middlemen, and proposed to establish an agency for the collection and dissemination of market information. They planned also to build warehouses where small lots of wool might be deposited as security for loans to the growers, and they

urged united action in holding wool for a minimum price of 50 cents a pound. There seems to be no evidence that the ambitious program was ever carried out or that the organization had more than a brief existence.[33]

While none of these early experiments took root, they are significant in showing how the transition from self-sufficient to commercial agriculture caused farmers to turn naturally to cooperative measures. There was more opportunity for such ventures to establish themselves a few decades later after the new system had become widespread.[34]

Farmers' Mutual Fire Insurance Companies

The growing tendency of farmers to work together on common problems expressed itself with more effect in the promotion of farmers' mutual fire insurance companies, somewhat similar to those already established in urban centers. Starting shortly after 1820 in New England, "the movement spread from one community to another," until by 1860 more than 100 were functioning in the northern states, scattered from Maine to Missouri. In general, they were incorporated under special charters, which prescribed in detail the methods of operation and government.[35]

The most successful of these early companies was the Hartford County Mutual Fire Insurance Company, chartered in 1831. Unlike some of the other mutuals of that period, it did not rely on assessments to cover losses sustained by members but from the first lived on its low rate of premium income. The method of operation pursued by this company can best be explained by an example. On a dwelling house in the country valued at $1,000, the premium charge (for which it was liable in the event of assessments) at 6 per cent would amount to $60.00. Of this, the member was required to pay in "one year's premium" amounting to 3⅓ per cent, or $2.00 upon becoming a member plus $1.00 fee for policy and application. This fund of $3.00 would provide insurance for a three-year period, when a fee of 25 cents would provide renewal for another three years. At the end of six years, the $3.25 put in would have given insurance protection of $1,000 for six years; or in other words, the member would have obtained insurance at the rate of 5.4 cents per hundred dollars per annum. Over a longer period of time, the rate would be diminished with every renewal.[36]

Some of the farmer mutuals of this period charged higher rates and refunded overcharges to members. The Hartford from the beginning attempted to charge rates just sufficient to cover costs so as to give the member the immediate advantage of low-cost insurance.

The contribution of these early farmers' mutual fire insurance companies to the development of other forms of agricultural cooperation in the United States has been pronounced. By demonstrating how the cooperative form of organization could be used by farmers to meet their insurance needs, the mutuals gave encouragement to the formation of various types of cooperatives designed to meet other common problems. Moreover, their carefully drawn charters served as patterns which could be used in drawing up the organization plans for other forms of cooperative association. Of equal importance, these mutuals served as valuable training schools for cooperators in business methods and democratic management. John Daniels, in *Cooperation, the American Way* (New York: Covici-Friede, 1938, p. 126), has aptly referred to them as "the primary school of American cooperation."

Mutual Insurance on Factories and Lives

The success of the farmers' mutual fire insurance companies encouraged the formation of similar companies to insure factories. In 1835, Zachariah Allen, a far-seeing textile manufacturer, established in Providence, Rhode Island, a mutual fire insurance company devoted exclusively to insuring factories. This organization met an economic need in the rapidly growing manufacturing industry of the Northeast and by 1860 eight factory mutuals of this type were in existence.[37]

In the early 1840's, economic conditions were favorable for the development of mutual life insurance companies. The depression following 1837 had made the sale of stock in life insurance companies almost impossible and this gave a great impulse to the use of the mutual form of organization. The first company of this type to establish itself was the Mutual Life Insurance Company of New York, which ranks today as the eleventh largest life insurance company in the United States. This company was formed under a special act of the New York state legislature passed in 1842. Its charter, often referred to as "the Magna Carta of life insurance in America," provided that:

> In conformity with the principle of mutuality, every policyholder was to become a member of the Company—the Company was to be theirs. The corporate powers of the Company were to be exercised by a board of thirty-six trustees, nine of whom were to be chosen from among the policyholders ... The president was to be elected from among the policyholders by the trustees. This was veritably government of the people and by the people ... Government was also for the people. The charter, stipulated that premiums fixed by the trustees, should be paid by all policyholders into a common fund and that from this fund benefits should be paid ...[38]

When the Mutual Life came into being in 1843, "a new era in life insurance was inaugurated, an era that was characterized by the placing of life insurance on a scientific and mutual basis."[39] By 1850, following the lead of the Mutual Life Insurance Company, several more companies—which were to become prominent in the life insurance field—were organized on the principle of mutuality.[40]

The Associationist Impulse

The changing economic environment which followed in the wake of the Industrial Revolution gave rise to a spirit of unrest which found expression in various attempts to create a new form of society based on the principle of brotherly love rather than on the search for profits.[41] Such experiments, by serving as a testing ground for cooperative theories and practices, cleared the way for many subsequent cooperative developments.

The New Harmony colony. Among these experiments, none is of more interest than that conceived by Robert Owen, who in 1825 planted his famous "New Harmony" community in Indiana to demonstrate the theory that men could fashion a society on the principles of cooperation.

To carry out his plan, Owen acquired a tract of 20,000 acres which included a going community that had been developed by the Rappists, a religious sect. The facilities for the experiment were already available. There were dwelling houses for the settlers, four large buildings to serve as community houses, a granary, and a church. There was also a silk factory, a woolen mill, saw mill, brick yard, distillery, oil mill, and dye works.

Owen already had a good reputation as a philanthropist in England when he came to this country in 1825 to get the new colony under way, and, according to Podmore, "The New World was prepared to welcome both the man and his doctrines." On his way to New Harmony he delivered two addresses in the "Hall of Representatives" at Washington "before distinguished audiences, which included the President of the United States and several members of the Cabinet, Judges, Members of Congress, and other persons of importance" on his "doctrine of the influence of circumstances on belief and character" and his plans for the New Harmony project.[42]

Attracted by the announcement of Owen's plan, hundreds of persons were in New Harmony awaiting his arrival. In addressing this group on April 25, 1825, Owen declared: "New Harmony, the future

name of this place, is the best half-way house I could procure for those
who are going to travel this extraordinary journey with me." Owen
was realistic enough to believe that the community would have to go
through a preliminary stage before it could function as a full "community
of equality." The first Committee on Management was largely appointed
by Owen, with the proviso that later the members would elect their own
governing committee. Under the plan,

> The members accepted no pecuniary liability. They were to bring with
> them their own furniture and effects; they were to work under the direction
> of the committee, at some trade or occupation; a credit was to be set against
> each name at the public store for the amount of useful work done; and
> against this credit a debit was entered for goods supplied. At the end of the
> year the balance would be placed to the credit of the member; but he was not
> at liberty to withdraw any part of it in cash, without the consent of the
> committee. He could, however, leave the Society at a week's notice, and with-
> draw his balance.[43]

With the community launched, Owen returned to England in August,
leaving in charge his son William, who immediately reported difficulties
in organizing the nondescript membership: "We have been much puz-
zled to know what to do with those who profess to do anything and
everything; they are perfect drones, and can never be satisfied here.
We have got rid of a good many such, although we still have a few left."[44]

In January 1826, Robert Owen came back to America full of enthusiasm, bringing with him an assorted collection of social experimenters
and men of science. When he arrived in New Harmony, he decided that it
would now be possible for the colony to draw up a permanent constitution.
He therefore summoned a general meeting of the residents who selected
a committee of seven to draw up the Constitution, which was adopted on
February 5, 1826. Henceforth, the colony was to be known as the New
Harmony Community of Equality. The heart of the Constitution was in
Article II which declared:

> All the members of the Community shall be considered as one family,
> and no one shall be held in higher or lower estimation on account of occupa-
> tion.
> There shall be similar food, clothing, and education, as near as can be,
> furnished for all according to their ages and, as soon as practicable, all shall
> live in similar houses, and in all respects be accommodated alike.
> Every member shall render his or her best service for the good of the whole.

In the words of Podmore:

> Thus, the Society at one step emerged from the chrysalis stage of modified
> individualism into the winged glory of pure communism ... in the new Society
> there was to be no discrimination between one man's labour and another's;
> nor any buying and selling within the bounds of the community. Each man

was to give of his labour according to his ability and to receive food, clothing, and shelter according to his needs.[45]

It was soon found that the members of the community could not live up to the high ideals set by the founder and the Constitution, and various members of the colony began to withdraw into little communities of their own. By April 1828, even Owen was convinced that the experiment was a failure. In his final address to a public meeting of the inhabitants of New Harmony, he declared:

> This last experiment has made it evident that families trained in the individual system, founded as it is upon superstition, have not acquired those moral qualities of forbearance and charity for each other which are necessary to promote full confidence and harmony among all the members, and without which communities cannot exist . . . My intention now is to form such arrangements on the estate of Harmony as will enable those who desire to promote the practice of the Social System to live in separate families on the individual system, and yet to unite their general labour, or to exchange labour for labour on the most beneficial terms for all, or to do both or neither as their feelings and apparent interest may influence them.

Looking back on the experiment, it is not difficult to see that it was doomed from the first. The people who became members could not be carefully selected, and its basis was sentimental rather than economic. Under Owen's scheme, there was no penalty for idleness and no reward for industry and thus no outlet for ambition. As Podmore remarked:

> Such a system might work in a golden age, when mankind, finding all their material wants satisfied, should have realized the universal human brotherhood, and left themselves free to turn their thoughts to the things of the spirit. But in a society which had found that the good things of the world are not enough to go round, and whose members had been trained each to snatch as large a share as he could, the great dream was too great . . .[46]

And yet it is not possible to say that New Harmony was a failure. It was an experiment in social organization that has had a permanent influence on the development of practical cooperative thought. The idealism that gave rise to New Harmony gave a vision to other cooperative experiments. Its failure only demonstrated that any permanent cooperative organization must take into account people as they come, that effective cooperatives must be founded on their ability to serve common needs as well as on idealistic motives; that the interests of the members of a cooperative organization must be homogeneous, and that a careful plan must be set up in advance for sound government on democratic principles. The New Harmony colony, by demonstrating such facts, encouraged others to search out more workable methods for achieving their aims.

Labor exchange stores. An interesting offshoot of Owenism was the "equity" or "exchange of labour for labour store" which Josiah Warren opened in Cincinnati in 1827 following his disillusionment with collectivism as practiced at New Harmony. Warren's plan "which was designed to enable small producers to barter their wares indirectly" attempted to value all goods in terms of the amount of labor time employed in producing them.

> ... The estimates of the time cost, of articles having been obtained from those whose business it is to produce them, are always exposed to view, so that it may be readily ascertained, at what rate any article will be given and received. He who deposits an article, which by our estimate costs ten hours labour, receives any other articles, which, together with the labour of the keeper in receiving and delivering them, costs ten hours, or, if the person making the deposit does not wish at that time, to draw out any article, he receives a Labour Note for the amount, with this note he will draw out articles, or obtain the labour of the keeper, whenever he may wish to do so.[47]

While Warren's store was to some extent dependent upon group support, it was primarily a personal enterprise. From a cooperative standpoint, his idea was carried further by some of his followers who, in 1828, established the "Producers' Exchange of Labour for Labour Association" in Philadelphia. The constitution of this pioneer experiment in merchandising included such cooperative features as democratic control by members, full disclosure of information, operation on a time cost of service basis and equal responsibility for expenses.[48]

As it was soon found impracticable to confine the operations of the association to barter transactions, the name was changed to "Producers' Exchange Association" and provision was made for the sale of articles on commission. In this way, the association gradually became a cash store through which workers sold their own wares.[49]

The Phalanxes. About 1840, the ideas of the French social philosopher, Charles Fourier, were vigorously promoted in this country by Albert Brisbane and Horace Greeley. Fourier favored the establishment of planned communities or "phalanxes." His plan was somewhat less idealistic than that of Owen in that it provided for individualized reward for labor and the payment of interest for the use of capital.

Of the 33 phalanxes which were formed in the United States during the 1840's, the one of most interest from a cooperative standpoint was the Wisconsin Phalanx in Fond-du-lac country which continued in existence from 1845 to 1850.[50] "By a clause in the charter of the Phalanx, the increase in the annual appraisal of all property, real and personal of the Phalanx, exceeding the cost, was to be yearly divided or credited one fourth to stock (capital) and the remaining three-fourths to labor, in such manner as the by-laws should provide."[51] In 1849, the Phalanx had in operation a grist mill and a saw mill. There was a stone school house, a blacksmith's shop, and dwellings of workers.

The principal reason for its failure was presented in a statement subscribed to by the membership on November 13, 1849:

> Our charter contains a radical error. It is not just nor expedient to credit stock yearly with one-fourth of the net increase, in the annual appraisement of the property ... We are now firmly of opinion that no dividend whatever in the nature of interest, should be allowed to capital. Brotherhood and usury cannot co-exist. Their tendencies are opposite and hostile. One or the other must finally sink under the antagonism. Besides, families uniting in industrial co-operation, should include in their compact the principle of mutual guaranteeism, so that no deserving brother or sister may suffer from want caused by sickness or other casuality. The constitution of the Wisconsin Phalanx includes no such principle of guaranteeism, but it includes an extravagant form of usury, awarding to capital yearly, the one fourth part of the increase in the annual appraisement of all property, real and personal, of the Phalanx, exceeding the cost and the last appraisement. When it is considered that the labor of the Phalanx consisted chiefly in building, and in agricultural occupations, not requiring a great outlay of capital in machinery, it is manifest that this feature of injustice in the charter would eventually, if not corrected, prove fatal, by running the property into the hands of a few, and those not always the most industrious and deserving.[52]

Brook Farm. The best known of all associationist experiments occurred at Brook Farm, near Boston, where in 1842 a little group of New England intellectuals ("Transcendentalists") including George Ripley, Margaret Fuller, Waldo Emerson, and Nathaniel Hawthorne, founded a community based on common ownership and labor. According to Parrington:

> Brook Farm grew out of the impact of the Industrial Revolution upon the social conscience of New England. Industrialism and social speculation were contemporary developments. How these consequences affected more sensitive and intelligent minds—men like William Henry Channing, Theodore Parker, and George Ripley—is suggested by their eager talk of mutualism, association, cooperation, as potential cures for the growing ills of competition ...[53]

The Brook Farm Colony differed from the other associationist efforts in its insistence on the free participation of the individual. When it became necessary to allot tasks to keep the project going, the faith of the founders departed. This led to reorganization as a Phalanx in 1844, and in this form the colony continued until 1846.

Brook Farm's significance was in the realm of ideas. By highlighting the communal weaknesses of utopianistic colonies, while forcing attention on the economic and social problems of the period, it gave encouragement to less grandiose and more practical schemes of cooperation.

The Mormons and cooperative irrigation. The development of co-

operative irrigation arrangements by the Mormons was the most permanent cooperative achievement of any of these communal groups.[54]

When the Mormon pathfinders moved down into the Salt Lake Valley
on July 21, 1847, they found themselves in an arid land which could
not support crops without irrigation, and they immediately set to work to
build dams "to irrigate the soil." Under the plan of settlement:

> When the Mormon Church authorities determined upon a new coloniza-
> tion project, a location was selected, leaders were appointed from among the
> ones experienced in colonization; and a sufficiently large body of colonists to
> protect themselves against the Indian menace and to construct irrigation canals
> were called to locate the new town. They were expected to move in a body,
> and did so.[55]

Generally, the colonies were set up on a village community basis
since a compact settlement was necessary in order to afford protection
from the Indians, and give access to the meeting house which served
as a religious and community center. The plan of settlement therefore
provided that each settler would have a lot in the central community
and plots of land in the area surrounding the village. Fair apportionment
was obtained through dividing the land immediately surrounding the
village into 5 or 10-acre plots. Then, "just beyond the area divided into
5 or 10-acre lots, the irrigable land was divided into 10-acre farms,
20-acre farms and finally in a few cases into 40-acre farms." The amount
of land permitted to each man "was limited according to the needs of
those dependent on him."

This plan of settlement presupposed a high degree of cooperation
among the members of the community, and the equity of the arrangements gave a good basis for cooperative action. Many of the Mormon
settlements provided for a common herd ground, the use of which was
made available to all members of the community. Moreover, the building of canals for irrigation was "as a rule, a community or cooperative
undertaking because not only the welfare but the very existence of the
community depended upon its success."[56]

The actual work of constructing the canals was largely performed by
the settlers working as a group. Each settler also accepted responsibility
for helping in the work of cleaning and repairing the canals which had
to be performed each spring.

In effect, the Mormon irrigation systems were operated on true cooperative lines in that they provided settlers with irrigation service on a
cost-of-service basis. According to Thomas, they "were built by the farmers, and operated by the farmers." This early plan of cooperative irrigation which has been described as "the first scientific irrigation system

in America," was the prototype of the many mutual irrigation companies which are now found throughout the arid western states.[57]

The Protective Union Stores

The first significant trial of cooperative purchasing in the cities came with the establishment of the first Protective Union Store in Boston on October 6, 1845.[58] The origin of this store can be traced back to 1840 when John Kaulback, a Boston tailor, started a buying club to bolster up attendance at the weekly meetings of his labor union.[59] Under Kaulback's plan, members of the union each contributed certain amounts for the purchase of required items and these were then divided at the weekly meetings. Encouraged by the success of this "dividing store," as the buying clubs of this sort were called, the group proceeded to go into store-keeping as the first division of the Workingmen's Protective Union which was established at the time with Mr. Kaulback, Treasurer.

Under the constitution of the Workingmen's Protective Union, "divisions" or stores were to be formed by no less than 15 who would agree to be governed by the Constitution.[60] Membership was to be open to "any person of good moral character, capable of earning a livelihood. . . who does not use intoxicating drinks as a beverage." Each prospective member was to apply for admission and be accepted into membership upon "receiving two-thirds of all the votes cast . . . signing the Constitution, paying an initiation fee of Three Dollars" and agreeing to pay a monthly assessment of 25 cents. Each Division was to be governed by a president, a vice president, recording secretary, corresponding secretary, steward, treasurer, a board of commerce, and a visiting committee, all of whom were to be elected annually by ballot, on separate tickets. The fraternal character of the Workingmen's Protective Union is indicated by the duties set forth for the visiting committees, which were to visit sick members, "and let no means whatever be unexerted that may tend in the slightest to alleviate the brother's sufferings."

The business affairs of each division were to be under the supervision of a board of commerce, whose duties were set forth as follows:

It shall be the duty of the Board of Commerce to transact all mercantile affairs of the Division. They shall introduce all new members to the Division in the most social manner, who have complied with the requisitions of the Constitution; and shall audit the Records, Accounts, and Bills of the Secretary, Steward, and Treasurer, and make a report of the same at least once in three months, and a summary of a report at the expiration of the year. All bills must be signed by at least two of them, before being paid, and at intervals of the Division's meetings they shall have such a general inspection of its affairs, as its interest may demand. (Art. XI)

The plan for financing the union was set forth as follows:

> The money received as Initiation fee shall constitute a standing fund,
> three fifths of which may be invested in fuel and groceries, or such other
> objects as the Division may deem best. The money arising from the assessments,
> interest on the standing fund, and donations, shall constitute a general fund,
> which shall be devoted to the use of sick members ... (Art. XV)

> In the ratio that the funds arise to hundreds of dollars it shall be the
> duty of the Treasurer to make known the fact to the Division, when a member
> shall be appointed to deposit each hundred in his own name, which member
> shall give a written acknowledgement of the same to the Treasurer and the
> acknowledgement, with the Bank Book shall be kept by the Treasurer, subject
> to the order of the Division. This fund shall not be drawn upon except by vote
> of the Division, and an order to be valid must be signed by the President and
> Recording Secretary. (Art. XVI)

The arrangement in the previous paragraph represents an ingenious
device for safeguarding against improper use of funds since there was
then no general corporation law under which limited liability associations
could be formed.

The Workingmen's Protective Union grew slowly and in January
1847, when a Supreme Division was organized, there were only 12
divisions, of which 10 were located in Massachusetts. From then on
progress was rapid, and by October, the session of the Supreme Division
was represented by 25 divisions having 1,993 members. In January 1849,
the Workingmen's Protective Union took the name New England Protective Union, and the Supreme Division became the Central Division.
Following a report of a special committee appointed "to carry out that
part of the Constitution that referred to the organization of industry,"
the committee on trade in July 1849 was instructed to provide a suitable
depot for the deposit and exchange of products and goods. The following
excerpts from the report of this committee give a vivid picture of the
spirit and aspirations of this group, and show how it was independently
coming to conclusions similar to those reached by the Rochdale Society
of Equitable Pioneers in England in 1844:

> It is evident that to stop with simply succeeding in the trading department
> merely, we shall not have accomplished the one-half of the object of our
> association. Let us for a moment review the proceedings of our society. We
> commenced with this one *grand idea*, the elevation of the laboring classes.
> The dollars was to us of minor importance—humanity and not mercenary
> were our motives.
>
> We were poor (a crime in civilized society); we were ignorant to a
> *great extent* of the arts and intrigues of trade, but saw enough to induce the
> undertaking of an experiment and with faith in God and the right, we com-
> menced our work by the purchase of a box of soap and one-half box of tea.
>
> Some dozen or more persons commenced in an upper chamber over the
> Boylston market (a modest place in these times of extravagance, October 6,

1845). From that time we have never ceased to work, and the result has been success—success of the grandest import; it is no longer an idle dream, an experiment, but a common-sense system of conducting trade . . .

Brothers, shall we content ourselves with the miserable idea of merely saving a few dollars, and say we have found enough? Future generations, aye, the uprising generation, is looking to us for nobler deeds. Shall we disappoint them? No! by all that is great and good, let us trust in the truth of organized industry. Time, undoubtedly, must intervene before great results can be expected to accrue from a work of this character. We must proceed from combined stores to combined shops, from combined shops to combined houses, to joint ownership in God's earth, the foundation that our edifice must stand upon.[61]

The report of the committee on trade in July 1850 shows that the union stores were then operating on a cost-plus basis and exerting a beneficial influence on competitive conditions:

> Your committee believe that the system adopted by the union of distributing goods on the cost principle, that is, adding to the original cost just sufficient to cover all expenses, to be correct, and that by the steady cooperation of the divisions in concentrating the funds in one agency, the foundation will be laid for a better and more equitable system of commerce, which will secure to the laborer the products of his industry.
>
> That our institution has proved beneficial to the whole community where divisions have been established, is acknowledged in all sections of New England, as the tendency has been to induce the working class to adopt the cash system, and the traders, in their endeavors to compete with the divisions, have been obliged to come into the market with the cash instead of purchasing on credit.

Up to this time the agent had largely financed operations out of his own pocket. As trade began to increase, the secretary of the Central Division issued a circular which urged that the "subdivisions deposit a certain percentage of their capital with the committee on trade, in order to assist the agent in his purchases."

The growth of the New England Protective Union during the next few years is shown by the fact that the number of divisions stood at 106 at the end of 1850 and 403 in October 1852, while the total sales reported by 167 of the divisions for the year ending October 1, 1852, amounted to $1,696,825.

As the union grew, it became increasingly aware of the necessity for sound business procedures. This is shown by the following view expressed in the 1852 annual report of the board of government:

> The future of protective union depends upon *men*. Especially should all its offices be filled with those who combine practical business talent with enlarged views of human rights and human duties. We want no mere fanatics to lead us on to nothingness—persons who ridicule the plainest truths of political economy because above the reach of their mental vision, and deny the existence of the very stars because they cannot see them at noon-day.

In January 1853, a bitter controversy developed within the union arising over the amount of commission paid to John Kaulback, the general agent. As a result, a rival organization—which later took the name The American Protective Union—arose under the leadership of Mr. Kaulback while the Central Division of the New England Protective Union was reorganized under Albert Wright as president. Overtones of this unfortunate experience are clearly discernible in the next report of the New England Protective Union which clearly shows that a valuable lesson in realism was being digested:

> Personal ambition and preferences, and party rivalry, should not be suffered to invade and disturb our deliberations. Our institution was not established to confer favors, but to secure rights; not to build up sinecures, but protect all useful members of the community from the unjust exactions of modern commerce.
>
> The history of the past warns us to guard well our institutions against the schemes of self-aggrandisement and personal aspiracy (sic.). All popular governments and associations, however correct their principles or however honest their supporters may be, are liable to be invaded by ambition and love of power . . .
>
> It is to be regretted that some of the divisions are disposed to adopt the policy of joint-stock companies, of selling goods at considerable advances and declaring dividends among the shareholders from the proceeds, thus perverting the original purposes of the union. The design of the Protective Union is not to make, but to save, money, and the profits which, under the old system of trade went to swell the coffers of the exchanger and speculator, belong, under the new, to those who buy the goods.

The schism practically destroyed the New England Protective Union as a social force, although it continued for a few years as a significant "cooperative effort on the joint-stock plan for the concentration of trade." This is indicated by the fact that the business volume amounted to almost a million dollars for each of the years 1855 and 1856. The report of the board of government in October 1856 disclosed a breaking away from the social principles on which the union was founded, and in September 1857 its epitaph as an effective force was printed as follows in the Journal of the Protective Union:

> The management of union stores, we regret to say, has not always fallen into competent and judicious hands, a circumstance not unheard of in connection with all human enterprises; and in consequence therefore distrust, dissentions, embarrassments, adoption of the credit system, and finally "selling out and closing up" have followed.
>
> The most grievous hindrance to the success of union stores, thus far, has been the employment of incompetent, unfaithful and scheming managers and clerks—often men destitute of correct business habits, unfriendly to the principles and objects of the organization, and given to trickery and craft. Stores, under such management, will soon break away from the safeguards of the system, and gradually run into the old channels of trade and the

adoption of the credit system, with all their uncertain and ruinous consequences, and finally "blow up," as they ought, being nothing but shams.

The seceding branch of the New England Protective Union was less motivated by cooperative idealism than by practical business considerations. In effect, the American Protective Union was a forerunner of the chain store system, with control being in the central agency rather than in the local division. Like the parent Union, the American adhered to the principle of temperance, membership being restricted to "persons of good moral character who do not use or vend intoxicating drinks." The American "stores" did not, however, restrict their trade to members but sold "to any party making prompt pay on an amount of profit equivalent to cover all necessary expenses and incidental liabilities in conducting the affairs of the institution."

In attempting to handle goods "at a specified profit on their cost," the American "stores" fixed the markings on each article regardless of the ability of the article to sustain the price. In 1859, a special committee recommended that a discriminating policy be used in applying the percentage. Furthermore, the difficulties of the cost-plus method of operation caused the committee to question the desirability of hauling "so close in the wind of philanthropy as always to be endangered by the breakers of deficiency, or, by some misfortune, to dash on the rocks of bankruptcy." This committee also looked forward to the time when an annual dividend could be paid since "in any social or pecuniary enterprise (a dividend) appears to possess almost the property of an electric spark, dispensing vitality and energy."

In the middle 1850's, the divisions or agencies of the American were widespread throughout New England and New York. During this period its annual volume of trade amounted to about one and a half million dollars.

The foregoing record shows that both the New England Protective Union and American Protective Union were gradually disintegrating during the closing years of the decade.[62] The disintegration was no doubt hastened by the panic of 1857 and by the preoccupation of the people in the intense political discussions which preceded the Civil War.[63]

By 1860, many of the member stockholders in the local divisions had sold out their interests to the storekeeper, who continued operations on his own account, although many of the Protective Union stores continued to operate for many years. A study made in 1913, by the Russell Sage Foundation found two of these original stores still operating on much the same basis as when they were founded.[64]

The Farmers' Protective Associations

While the Protective Union stores were expanding through the more settled sections of the East, the farmers of the frontier were setting up their own forms of protective association.

In Iowa and Minnesota such associations grew from the way these states had been settled in the 1830's in disregard to laws forbidding settlement upon unsurveyed land. To safeguard their holdings, the settlers formed "voluntary land leagues or claim associations. These organizations prescribed a uniform size for the 'claims' in their respective districts ... Records were carefully kept, and the transfer of claims was permitted ... For several years tens of thousands of pioneer farmers held their homes upon no other title than that given by membership in what we may call cooperative land associations." When the government eventually surveyed the land and sold it at auction to the highest bidder, the members of these associations "turned out in force and bid in each parcel of land at the minimum price of one dollar and a quarter per acre. Effective means were used to prevent outside bidders from bidding."[65] With the achievement of their aims, these associations then ceased existence as spontaneously as they had arisen.

The next cooperative effort of the Western pioneers grew out of the "exactions" taken by merchants for marketing their produce or for providing them with supplies. This development has been well described in the following way by one who was an active participant:

> Dating from about the year 1848, there was a general feeling among the farmers throughout Illinois that they were not receiving the just reward of their labor. The country was settling up, and the cost of transporting produce to St. Louis and Chicago, the principal distributing points, over the common roads was so great that it left the farmer little or nothing to carry back to his family. The country villages were few and far between. Railroads had not been built ... The construction of railroads began, but before these were in operation (1852) a feeling of awakening had so grown upon the popular mind that Farmers' Clubs began organizing, though, at first, more to discuss matters of cultivation than anything else.
>
> In 1852, the exactions of the country merchants, or middle men, as they were even then called, came in for a great share of the blame, and justly, beyond a doubt. They were the protected monopolists, who, by the force of their cohesion, controlled prices, and, while they grew rich themselves, oppressed the farmers.[66]

While the coming of the railroads temporarily improved the farmers' situation, the feeling that relief must be had finally gained such strength that a general convention or congress was called, and held at Centralia, on September 15, 1858. This congress in its platform declared:

We believe that in union there is strength, and that in union alone can the necessarily isolated conditions of farmers be so strengthened as to enable them to cope, on equal terms, with men whose callings are, in their very nature, a permanent and self-created combination of interests. To achieve this general end, the following "Plan of Operations" was set forth:

First. The formation of Farmers' Clubs wherever practical, the object of which shall be to produce concert of action on all matters connected with their interests.

Second. The establishment, as far as possible, of the ready pay system in all pecuniary transactions.

Third. The formation of wholesale purchasing and selling agencies in the greatest centers of commerce, so that producers may, in a great measure, have it in their power to save the profits of the retailers.

Fourth. The organization of such a power as to insure the creation of a national agricultural bureau, the main object of which shall be an annual or semi-annual census of all our national products, and the collection and dissemination of valuable seeds, plants, and facts.

Fifth. The election of producers to all places of public trust and honor the general rule, and the election of non-producers the exception.[67]

The promise of this almost modern program was cut short by the Civil War which not only consumed the interests and imagination of the people but also brought to farmers a short period of abnormal demand for their products, at inflated prices.

Status of Cooperation in 1860

On the eve of the Civil War the best rooted form of cooperative enterprise was the Farmers Mutual Insurance Company. At that time there were well over a hundred associations of this type located principally in New England, the Middle Atlantic states, and as far west as Illinois. In the Far West, the Mutual Irrigation Associations were becoming established, particularly in Utah, while in the eastern cities the building and loan associations which had caught hold during the 1850's were gaining in popularity and were rapidly perfecting their methods. Little remained of the Protective Union Store movement in 1860 except a few isolated stores. Likewise, the interest in producers' cooperative associations had died down and was practically dormant, while the few farmers' associations engaged either in cooperative marketing or cooperative purchasing were yet of only local importance. The idea of working together was, however, well established. When farmers, for example, had a problem in common, such as that which led to the claim associations in the 1840's they were quick to associate together for their mutual benefit.

While the tangible gains of cooperation were not impressive, much valuable experience had been accumulated. The failures of the associationists, while dampening enthusiasm for Utopian schemes, had taught that cooperation to succeed must be set up on a practical basis. The dissolution of the Protective Union Stores had shown the importance of capital accumulation, the weakness of selling commodities on a near cost basis, the value of regional organization, and the importance of competent and reliable direction. While there was yet no cooperative movement in the modern sense there was beginning to develop an understanding of the fact that cooperatives can only succeed where there is a felt economic need, sound membership understanding, and good management.

Chapter II

URBAN EXPERIMENTATION

With the Civil War came a great change in the industrial life of the United States which was to have a marked effect on the character of urban cooperative development. Significant economic factors were at work—the opening of the West by the railroads, the expansion of world markets by the steamboat and the transatlantic cable, a steady rise in population favored by immigration, and technological improvements which tremendously increased the efficiency of manufacturing.[1] These conditions intensified the use of the corporation form of enterprise as a means of amassing capital and favored industrial integration by means of trusts.[2] The need for markets also revolutionized marketing methods by bringing in the traveling salesman, aggressive advertising of branded merchandise, the general adoption of the one-price policy, the department store, the mail-order house, and the chain store.[3] With these changes, the number of wage workers steadily increased in the cities, and national unions arose to protect their interests. The extent of the change that occurred in the industrial life of the nation from 1860 to 1900 is portrayed by the following facts from census or other official data.

	1860	1900	% Increase
United States population	31,443,000	75,995,000	142
Places of 8,000 or more population	141	547	288
Population of places of 8,000 or more	5,072,000	25,018,000	393
Railroad mileage	30,626	198,964	550
Patents issued	4,778	26,499	455
Total United States wealth	$16.2 billion	$88.5 billion	448
Gainful workers in United States	12,925,000*	29,073,000	125
" " " agriculture	6,850,000*	10,912,000	59
" " " trade	878,000*	3,085,000	251
" " " transportation and communication	540,000*	1,952,000	261
" " " manufacturing	2,643,000*	7,199,000	172

*for 1870

29

Infiltration of the Rochdale Idea

Although the now famous Rochdale Society of Equitable Pioneers had been formed in England in 1844, there is no evidence that it had any significant influence on American cooperative thinking prior to about 1859 when Horace Greeley, editor of the *New York Tribune*, brought out an American edition of George Jacob Holyoake's *Self-Help by the People—The History of the Rochdale Pioneers*.

This little book was unique in many ways. It not only had a story to tell, but the story was so simply and completely told that it was in reality a practical guide book on cooperative organization. *Self-Help by the People* charmingly and persuasively showed how a group of 28 workingmen carefully planned and then established their cooperative association. It also gave the Society's rules and plan of operation and emphasized its major cooperative contribution—the patronage refund method by which supplies were sold at market prices and savings returned to purchasers in proportion to the volume of their patronage. The value of this method of cooperative operation, moreover, was demonstrated by giving the record of the Rochdale Society from 1844 through 1857. If Holyoake's book is examined in the light of the conditions of the 1860's, some idea is obtained of the impact that it made on Americans who had an interest in the possibilities of cooperative organization.

The first Rochdale-type associations. The panic of 1857 and the depression which followed nearly eliminated the emerging local labor unions. With the rise in the cost of living growing out of war conditions, they again began to spring up in industrial centers. Much interest was also expressed for cooperation and this led to the formation of a number of associations. Of these the Union Cooperative Association No. 1 of Philadelphia, organized in December 1862, was apparently the first to test out Rochdale methods on American soil. This association procured the constitution and other documents direct from the Rochdale Society and on them modeled its own rules for a store which was opened in April 1864. While the store got off to a good start and adhered "to the rigid old Rochdale system," it soon got into difficulties due to hasty expansion, and this brought on its failure in November 1866. As Thomas Phillips, the principal founder, later explained:

> Everything at this time looked promising. Sales, membership and stock were increasing. Public meetings were held and every effort made to establish the store at the new stand. But the cry that the store must go to the people, instead of the people must come to the store, was the loudest, and consequently branches No. 1, 2, and 3 were established. Trade and membership did not increase in proportion to the outlay. Profits ceased. Business fell off and

Branch No. 1 was closed, being located among a class of people who cared not for co-operation. The summer soldiers and sunshine cooperators began to withdraw their stock and throw a wet blanket over the concern.[4]

While the store did not survive its weaknesses, it performed during its life an important function in popularizing Rochdale methods in America. While enthusiasm was still high, Phillips, over the name of "Worker," contributed to the columns of *Fincher's Trades' Review*, the national labour weekly, a series of enthusiastic letters in which he explained the Rochdale plan and enlarged upon the possibilities of co-operation in America. Twice during the first year, to meet urgent demands for information, *Fincher's Trades' Review* found it necessary to reprint in full the rules of the Rochdale Equitable Pioneers' Society, then beginning its twentieth year in England. This propaganda led to the organization of some 30 similar cooperative grocery stores by early 1866 when "the movement had extended until practically every important industrial town between Boston and San Francisco had some kind of distributive cooperation."[5]

With the decline in prices immediately following the war, conditions became less favorable for cooperative stores, although a number were started during the postwar period, especially in New England. These very conditions, however, were favorable to the development of cooperative workshops of various kinds. Disappointed by strike actions, the unions turned to "productive cooperation."[6]

The Cooperative Workshops

That cooperation was well accepted in labor circles by 1866 is shown by the following resolution of the first National Labor Congress:

> Resolved, that in cooperation we recognize a sure and lasting remedy for the abuses of the present industrial system, and hail with delight the organization of cooperative stores and workshops in this country, and would urge their promotion in every section of the country and in every branch of business.[7]

At this congress a committee was appointed to prepare an address to the workingmen of America on the objectives of the National Labor Union. This address declared:

> The question of cooperative stores and cooperative associations for trading and manufacturing purposes has the widest bearing and effect upon the condition of the workingmen ... The committee cannot too strongly urge upon the workingmen of this country the advantage—almost necessity even—of establishing cooperative stores. The example of Rochdale shows how easily they may do so, and when extended to every manufacture and trade, as they

easily may, the workingmen will cease to contribute to the support of those
who do not of themselves contribute anything to the products of labor.[8]

Although the labor organizations continued to encourage cooperative
stores, their main interest was turning to producers' cooperation as a
means through which workingmen could secure the full fruits of their
labors. Members of practically all of the leading trades including "the
bakers, coach-makers, collar-makers, coal miners, shipwrights, machinists
and blacksmiths, nailers, foundry workers, ship-carpenters, and caulkers,
glassblowers, hatters, boiler-makers, plumbers, iron-rollers, tailors, printers,
needle women, and moulders," started cooperative workshops in the three
years following the war. The most interesting of these experiments was
that of the Molders' International Union which encouraged the formation
of some 11 cooperative stove factories during the years 1866-1868.[9]

An interesting by-product of this early interest in cooperation was
the enactment of the first state cooperative laws: Michigan, 1865;
Massachusettts, 1866; Pennsylvania, 1868; Minnesota, 1870. While these
laws were simple in character and went little further than existing corporation laws, they significantly recognized the mutual character of cooperative business enterprise.[10]

However, results did not come up to expectations. Self-employment
brought many problems for which the groups were ill-trained—problems
in financing, management, merchandising, and even in labor relations—
and, as a result, the workshops generally lasted only a few years. While
this encouraged the labor groups to place more confidence in strikes—
which were proving effective with the improved economic conditions
following 1868—a considerable sentiment for cooperative workshops continued to persist. The Knights of St. Crispin (the shoemakers), for
example, declared in 1869: "The present demand of the Crispin is steady
employment and fair wages, but his future is self-employment."[11] Cooperative workshops were also encouraged by the National Labor Union,[12]
which flourished for several years prior to the panic of 1873, and by the
Industrial Brotherhood from 1873 to 1875 before it gave way to the
Sovereigns of Industry and the Knights of Labor.

With the ebbing of confidence in cooperative workshops, attention
again centered on cooperative stores.[13] Direction to this new emphasis was
to be given by the Sovereigns of Industry.

The Sovereigns of Industry

Impressed by the contemporary accomplishments of the Patrons of
Husbandry—the Grange—William H. Earle conceived the idea of form-

ing an order not restricted to farmers but open to "all persons of good character engaged in industrial pursuits." Earle thereupon invited sympathetic persons to consult with him at Springfield, Massachusetts, on January 6, 1874, where after "eight days and nights" of discussion the National Council of the Order of Sovereigns of Industry was established with a preamble, constitution, and ritual.[14]

The preamble set forth the Sovereigns' spirit and purposes in the following way:

> By all the wise and kindly measures it can command, it will present organized resistance to the organized encroachment of the monopolies and other evils of the existing industrial and commercial system. It will try to establish a better system of economical exchanges and to promote, on a basis of equity and liberty, mutual fellowship and cooperative action among the producers and consumers of wealth throughout the earth. We wage no wars with persons or classes, but only with wrongs, discords and hardships, which have existed too long. We most earnestly deprecate hatred, jealousy or envy between classes, and call on all people to be of one mind in the spirit of justice. We abhor every scheme of agrarianism or violence, and shall use only such instrumentalities as are sanctioned by demonstrated principles of moral philosophy and social science, the universal interests of humanity, and a philanthropy rising impartially above all distinctions of class, sex, creed, race or nationality.[15]

The plan of organization provided for local or subordinate councils, state councils, and a national council and as soon as organization was effected the local councils undertook cooperative buying. The common arrangement was for members to pool their orders—covered by cash deposits—through an agent who obtained goods for them at wholesale prices. This simple procedure, which required no operating capital, yielded substantial savings under the "high retail prices of that period," with the result that the Sovereigns began to spread rapidly through New England and into the Middle Atlantic states.

While many of the local councils continued to operate as "dividing stores," a number soon began to establish regular stores, first on the "Springfield" and then on the "Rochdale" plan of organization. Under the Springfield plan, goods were sold "at a price sufficient to allow of profits not exceeding 2 per cent on gross sales." The immediate growth of the Springfield Association was so great as to "bewilder the directors." Sales in 1876 amounted to $135,000 and membership reached 3,000. But the success was only temporary. "By attempting to sell at cost, and claiming thus to undersell every other store in town, a fierce competition, pronounced by wholesale dealers at that time to be the fiercest in all Massachusetts, was engendered. Some rivals would offer sugar below cost, trusting to profits on other goods to recompense themselves. Others undersold the Sovereigns on other staples." This use of loss leaders gradually broke down the loyalty of the members and trade began a rapid decline. Even this difficult problem might have been solved had the organization been constructed on a sound business foundation. As it was, the arrangement for control by trustee stockholders—who had no direct financial interest—could not achieve efficient management. An attempt to remedy the situation by reorganizing on the Rochdale plan in 1878 came too late for resuscitation, and in January 1879 the corporation collapsed.[16]

From the beginning, the less dramatic Rochdale plan of cooperation apparently had many adherents among the Sovereigns, for in 1876 a committee recommended that the Rochdale principles be accepted as the basis for cooperation within the order. Even before this the National Council through its lecturer John Orvis was aggressively promoting a "Rochdale" plan for the organization and management of cooperative stores "to secure uniformity among the councils." The National Council summarized this plan as follows:

1. Allow but one vote to a shareholder, without regard to the number of shares held.
2. Shares to draw a minimum rate of interest.
3. Dividends to be made only on purchases, and that quarterly.
4. Every member of the order entitled to full dividends on purchases, provided the directors may retain such dividends in their discretion, until the same shall amount to at least one share of stock.
5. Shares not to exceed $5 each, unless required otherwise by statute.
6. Dividends to non-members one-half the profits on their purchases.
7. Sell at current prices—the same price to members of the order and the general public—thus disarming opposition.
8. Look after the interests of the store as strictly as if the store were on individual property.
9. Choose persons worthy of your confidence for managers—then give them your hearty support.[17]

While a number of the Sovereign stores had started on the Springfield plan, the support of the order was rapidly shifting to the Rochdale method during 1875. "In December 1875, one hundred and one councils reported that they had in practice some methods of supplying members with goods," and "of these, twenty-six councils distributed goods at cost, twenty gave dividends on purchases."

Although the Sovereigns as an organization declined in strength rapidly after 1876, the Rochdale stores organized by the Sovereigns continued to prosper. In 1877, "next to Springfield, the ten Sovereign stores doing the largest business were all organized on the Rochdale plan." These 10 stores then had a combined capital of $28,100, and a trade volume of $341,000.[18] Several of these stores carried on for many years, and thus perpetuated the cooperative contribution of the Sovereigns.[19]

The break-up of the Sovereigns, which finally occurred in 1879, while partly due to internal weaknesses consequent to its rapid growth, was more fundamentally due to the period of hard times which set in following the panic of 1873. This was a period of intense commercial competition marked by a volume of commercial failures never before known in the life of the country. Many of the Sovereigns found themselves unemployed and unable to continue as members, while a spirit of pessimism pervaded those who could give it their support.[20] As long as times were good, workingmen could buy and pay cash. With hard times they were forced to seek credit. This explains why many of the Sovereign stores turned from strictly cash principles to sale on credit, and their resulting failure.[21]

The primary cooperative contribution of the Sovereigns was the emphasis which it gave to cooperative distribution and its demonstration of "Rochdale" superiority to "Springfield," "joint-stock," or "cost-of-service" schemes.[22] By popularizing the Rochdale principles from Maine to Minnesota, the Sovereigns paved the way for the next wave of cooperative experimentation.

The Knights of Labor

While the Knights of Labor originated in 1869, it was not until 1878 that it blossomed out as a national labor organization.[23] In that year it took over the program of the defunct Industrial Brotherhood, including its plank calling "for the establishment of cooperative institutions, productive and distributive." However, the real keynote on cooperation was given by Terrence V. Powderly, the Grand Master Workman, at the annual convention in September 1880. Powderly declared:

> Organization once perfected, what must we do? I answer, study the best means of putting your organization to some practical use by embarking in a system of cooperation, which will eventually make every man his own master—every man his own employer; a system which will give the laborer a fair proportion of the products of his toil ... The enthusiasm of the hour will avail us nothing, and cooperation requires every Washington of labor to be up and doing. The laboring man needs education in this great social question, and the best minds of the Order must give their precious thought to this system. There is no good reason why labor cannot, through cooperation, own and operate mines, factories and railroads. By cooperation alone can a system of colonization be established in which men may band together for the purpose of securing the greatest good to the greatest number, and place the man who is willing to toil upon his own homestead."[24]

At the session held the following year definite steps were taken to put these views into effect by making provision in the constitution for a cooperative fund. This fund was to be accumulated through monthly payments of 10 cents per male worker and 5 cents per female worker. In return for such contributions, certificates of stock were to be issued which would give holders an equal share "of all profits arising from the investment of funds." By this time, the order was successfully conducting a number of strikes, and apparently any amounts collected in the cooperative fund were diverted to this use.

At the New York session in 1882, all affairs "relating to cooperation" were entrusted to a "Cooperative Board of Five" which was elected at that time. This Board apparently proved ineffective, for it was replaced with new members the following year.

The period from 1879 to 1882 had been one of prosperity in which strike action had proved effective in securing wage increases. With a recession in 1882, strikes proved less satisfactory and "cooperation increased its following tremendously." This interest was manifest in the establishment of "either merchandising stores or coal shafts" by a number of Knights of Labor locals, and in a demand for a more aggressive national program which encouraged the national organization to purchase a coal mine at Cannelburg, Indiana, "with the idea of selling coal at reduced prices to the members."[25]

By 1884, "the rank and file, which had hitherto been indifferent, now seized upon the idea with enthusiasm," and, as a result, the order adopted a decentralized plan of encouraging cooperative ventures through the locals, in contrast to the "plan of centralization," which had hitherto been recommended. Under this plan all kinds of productive enterprises were locally undertaken. Some were set up and managed as stock companies. Others were organized and managed by the local or district assemblies. With this turn in psychology, the Cooperative Board in its report for 1884 urged:

> 1. That in establishing our cooperative institutions we must not forget that men reared under the conditions of wage-service cannot jump at once to the much higher level of cooperation ... Therefore, it seems that in our institutions we must preserve that feature of the wage-system which calls upon the man to put forth his best exertions, and to put them forth harmoniously, or be stricken from the pay-roll.
>
> 2. That individual incentive must be provided. It seems that although the desire for social honor may be a motive force with many, yet, after all, the material benefits are the most generally desired, and that, therefore, gradations of wages must be retained.
>
> 3. That the executive officers must be endowed with ample power to discipline refractory members—of course always subject to appeal.

4. That the executive officers be amply endowed with authority to select the men best adapted to the work in hand.

The enthusiasm for cooperation continued unabated during 1885, for in that annual session Powderly remonstrated:

> Many of our members grow impatient and unreasonable because every avenue of the Order does not lead to cooperation. This is a wrong impression and is calculated to do injury to the very movement they advocated. We cannot make men; we must take them as we find them . . . The great fault with a great many cooperators is that they advocate the establishment of cooperative institutions on too large a scale . . . They hang a millstone around their necks in the beginning, and it eventually pulls them down until . . . confidence in cooperation is destroyed . . . Workingmen are not businessmen by any means; and as long as we continue the question of getting a few cents more in the day for labor done, and neglect to look after the matter of investing the money we do get to the best advantages . . . we will continue to be ignorant of the laws by which business is governed.

In keeping with Powderly's views, the general Cooperative Board began to promote programs of education and co-ordination. It issued a model constitution and set of by-laws adaptable to the needs of local associations and proceeded to publish statements "on the dangers and pitfalls in cooperative ventures, such as granting credit, poor management, etc." A bulletin by John Samuel, "How to Organize Cooperative Societies" (1886), became the handbook of the Order on cooperative enterprises. To achieve better coordination the label of the Knights of Labor was to be restricted to goods made by accredited cooperatives. At this time the Central Cooperative Board was flooded with calls for financial assistance. This finally tried the patience of the secretary of the board who in a notice to the members of the order cried out as follows:

> The Cooperative Board would require the resources of some of our millionaires to be sufficient for the demands upon them; and the calls for a visit to see and examine this and that, from the Atlantic to the Pacific, would take the time of several Secretaries. Kind friends and dear brethren, this thing of expecting help in starting a carp pond, a dairy, or a machine shop, is a great mistake. The Cooperative Fund would soon become a nuisance as well as a nonentity. Halt! Give us a rest, in the name of Brotherhood and humane charity. If you have printed plans of cooperative stores or shops, or other enterprises, send me a copy; if you have ideas of value, please forward them; or if you think the present cooperative law, as found in the Constitution, can be amended, send us your propositions. But do not look for aid such a long way from home. If your plans are feasible, the best place to look for help must be near home. Self-help is the surest as well as the best help . . . I must respectfully give notice that I am utterly unable to grant help in any way to parties wishing loans from the Cooperative Fund.[26]

The cooperative efforts of the Knights reached highwater mark in

1887 when, in addition to a number of cooperative stores, there were some 135 cooperative productive enterprises of various sorts scattered throughout the nation. Of these, more than half were mines, cooperage plants, shoe or clothing factories, foundries, and soap works, and most were conducted on a small scale, the average investment per establishment being about $10,000.

The vitality of the movement was gone by 1888, although some of the better established enterprises continued to function for several years. A number of causes can be given for the decline of interest, but in the main it reflected a change in labor psychology throughout the nation. Labor had become disillusioned with ameliorative measures and was turning to strong collective bargaining action under the rapidly rising American Federation of Labor. The membership in the Knights which had stood at 700,000 in 1886 declined to 222,000 in 1888 and to 100,000 in 1890.[27]

Cooperation in production and collective bargaining were found to be antithetical. "When the cooperators lowered the price of their product in order to build up a market, the wages of the workers who continued to work for private employers were immediately affected for the worse. Hence the Order, when it endeavored to practice both cooperation and trade unionism, was driving its teams in opposite directions."[28] Moreover, the promises made for cooperative production were not being realized in practice. Many cooperative enterprises were failing due to lack of full cooperation on the part of members, boycotts by suppliers of raw materials, inability to obtain financial backing, difficulties in marketing products produced, and weaknesses of management. This was a time of economic depression and rapid technological change when only the strongest firms could survive.

The experience of the Knights of Labor has exerted a great influence on American cooperative development. Never again was there to be such confidence reposed by workingmen in self-employment. However, by effectively demonstrating the weaknesses of such enterprises the Knights helped to center attention on the possibilities of cooperation in distribution.

While the Knights encouraged cooperative stores, their major interest had been in productive cooperation. This was natural in that the workingmen under the conditions of the time were primarily concerned with finding a method of organization that would assure steady employment at a fair wage.

Not all of the vision of the Knights of Labor was lost. The enthusiasm that was engendered promoted careful study of the possibilities and potential usefulness of the cooperative form of organization. In this way, a fund of literature was created on sound and unsound methods of cooperation. The Knights of Labor also taught another important lesson in showing that cooperation and labor unionism cannot be harnessed in one organization—that cooperation must be furthered as a means to an end, rather than as a supplement to other objectives.

Independent Growth

All of the great waves of urban cooperative enthusiasm had so far been generated from central labor organizations—in the 1840's and 1850's by the New England and American Protective Unions, in the 1860's by the National Labor Union and other labor groups, in the 1870's by the Sovereigns of Industry, and in the 1880's by the Knights of Labor. None of these movements had been able to consolidate cooperative efforts over wide areas in central federations, although all had given lip service to this as an ultimate objective.

With the extension of cooperation in the 1870's and 1880's a growing number of cooperators came to look upon cooperation as a method of doing business on its own merits, rather than as an adjunct to labor organizations.[29]

By 1881, this new philosophy was given expression in a little book by Charles Barnard, *Cooperation as a Business.* Barnard gave his conception of cooperation in these modern words: "Cooperation has been often confounded with socialism, communism, and other vicious fancies . . . It simply means business."

In presenting his book, Barnard declared that his aim was to "briefly consider cooperation from its commercial and economic aspect . . . It is not the intention to describe any social experiments whatever, but to show how certain people saved money to build a home, buy groceries, and insure their children's lives."[30]

Barnard felt that American efforts at cooperation had failed "chiefly from the wrong methods," and that fortunately the ground had been cleared "by the failure and extinction of badly designed societies," so that "we can now begin fair and at the right end. In place of starting stores here and there and permitting each to struggle along in ignorance of right methods and each other, it has been proposed to form, first, a central board, whose duty it should be to point the way and assist each and all by bringing them together for mutual aid and council" (p. 117).

Barnard described the Central Cooperative Board (New York City) which had been established "purely as an advisory body" to promote:

1. Sound principles of business economy.
2. Honesty in the production of profits, with equity in the division of profits as a sound basis of business morality.
3. The principle of buying and selling for cash, combined with one price for all customers, as a means of encouraging thrift and economy as a personal habit.
4. Cooperation in business undertakings, to enable large numbers of people, who save money in small sums, to create safe and profitable investments for their money when saved, and to utilize such capital in the business of supplying their common wants. (p. 118)

The board had at that time prepared model cooperative by-laws which followed the Rochdale pattern (pp. 119-39). However, little in the way of permanent development came from the Central Cooperative Board, for it was not even referred to in the comprehensive surveys made a few years later under the direction of Professor Richard T. Ely of Johns Hopkins University.

Of more practical importance was the American Sociologic Society which actively promoted cooperation in the middle 1880's by means of a little periodical, *The Sociologic and Cooperative News*. This society, which had been formed in 1882 "for the propagation of the principles of cooperation or 'mutual helpfulness' among the people of this country" sponsored in 1886 the formation of a National Cooperative Board to collect and diffuse cooperative information, and this led, in 1887, to the issuance of a quarterly journal, *The Cooperative News*. The Sociologic Society, during this period, was offering for sale at 3 cents each or 25 cents a dozen pamphlets with such titles as: *The Philosophy of Cooperation; The Birth and Growth of the Rochdale System of Cooperation; Five Reasons Why I Am a Cooperator; The Lower Law of Competition and the Higher Law of Cooperation; How to Form a Cooperative Society; Dividend—What It is and How It is Made;* and *Studies for Beginners in Cooperation.*[31]

Such educational propaganda was quite influential in bringing cooperative ideas and methods to the attention of the "Intellectuals" of the period, and this assisted in freeing cooperation from its dependence on the labor movement. It was at this time that college cooperative societies were first formed to enable students and faculty members to buy at cost, books and similar supplies. The Harvard Cooperative Society, founded in 1882, served as the model for similar societies at Yale, 1885, and Massachusetts Institute of Technology, 1886.[32]

The growing interest in cooperation in the middle 1880's is suggested by the fact that in Massachusetts, the state legislature directed the Bureau of Statistics of Labor "to prepare and publish for distribution a pamphlet descriptive of the history, methods, and present condition of co-operative distribution in Great Britain." This pamphlet, written under the direction of Commissioner Carroll D. Wright,[33] provided an excellent analysis of cooperative distribution not only in Great Britain, but also in France, Germany, Denmark, Sweden, Italy, and many other countries. It concluded with the following views:

> Whatever hope and future promise may rest in cooperation, it is not as a scheme for remedying all the evils which many feel to be inherent in the present industrial organization that this plan of cooperative distribution is to be recommended. It may be a help, however. As a method of capital-saving it affords the groundwork of a system of cooperative production, which might be made safe and remunerative so far as the market for product could be assured by the demands of the stores themselves. Such an assured market would materially relieve the cooperative producers from the struggle which must always be before them in any effort to secure a market in competition with private manufacturers. Taken for what it is, it has been of great benefit to the working classes in Great Britain, and under similar social conditions might be equally beneficial elsewhere . . . Much of the need for these stores is also met in our larger towns by enterprising private concerns who put before the public the best goods at low cash prices. But still there is no doubt that in many towns the same financial benefits might accrue to any society formed and conducted on the Rochdale plan, the work being modified in some respects to meet local requirements, and to conform to the needs of American communities. The experiment is one easily tried, not involving loss, if carefully managed, and the results, if successful, well worth the effort.

In the same year (1886) the *Second Biennial Report of the Wisconsin Bureau of Labor and Industrial Statistics* devoted 195 pages to a discussion of cooperation. In introducing the report, the Commissioner of Labor Statistics, Frank A. Flower, stated that:

> So far as the writer is aware . . . the report [on] cooperation embraces more facts than any volume yet put forth in America . . . My hope in giving so much space to the subject was to induce workingmen, union, and assemblies to turn their attention from strikes, denunciation of capital, boycotts, politics, bickerings and agitation, to the more productive and laudable business of saving money and building up material interests of their own through the medium of cooperative effort . . . Cooperation, shorn of the absurd and utopian features given to it by hare-brained theorists and crazy world-reformers, can be made to lighten the burdens and cheer the pathways of life in many ways.

Cooperation as a form of independent business organization was also given strong academic encouragement in 1887 by the publication of a series of monographs by the newly formed American Economic Association on the status of cooperation in various parts of the United States. These were published, with additional material, in book form the following year by Johns Hopkins University under the title *Cooperation in the United States.*[34]

In the preface of this book, Professor Ely, who had directed the studies, declared:

> The present work makes it clear that we have in this country as remarkable instances of success in cooperation as can be found in Europe. The Minneapolis coopers are of as much significance as the Rochdale pioneers . . . It is to be hoped that the well-worn illustrations of cooperation found in old textbooks may, in American newspapers and periodicals, make way for these fresher . . . and more valuable experiments.

The writings of other prominent economists were also reflecting a growing interest in cooperation, particularly in the field of production. John Bates Clark in his *Philosophy of Wealth* (1886) declared:

> Such is the aim of cooperation. It is the principle of solidarity in a new field. The great consolidations now in process are for belligerent ends; this is for an amicable end. The organization of capital, on the one hand, and that of labor, on the other, enable these agents to fight a good battle over the division of products; co-operation allays strife, and enables them to expend their whole energy in creating products . . . co-operation . . . merges two classes which are now in hostile attitude (p. 183).

It is significant that Clark did not look upon the Rochdale form of cooperative store as true cooperation, since "the essential principle of true cooperation is its obliteration of dividing lines in industrial society. Workmen become, by means of it, employers of their own labor, and distribution (in sharing wealth produced), the cause of strife, is conducted on a new plan. To this result the Rochdale enterprise contributes nothing." Moreover, he did not feel that American conditions were favorable for the success of Rochdale cooperation. "That similar experiments have been less successful in this country is, in part, due to the fact that they are less needed ... Competition is here sharper, and retail shops are better than in England. It is less easy for a store established on the new plan to attract customers." However, he maintained that "such an enterprise should be started" when "conditions are favorable" (pp. 190-93).

The advance of cooperation for itself alone was further stimulated in 1891 by Herbert Myrick's book, *How to Cooperate—A Manual for Cooperators.* Myrick looked upon cooperation as "the true way out of the evils that now affect both producers and consumers." While he directed his book primarily to farmers, he kept in view "the wants of the toiling masses in town and city, factory, store, and mine." He focused his attention on *how* rather than the *wherefore* of cooperation, since he felt that "less theory and more practice is the great need of cooperation." To Myrick, cooperation was "not a scheme whereby vision-ary enthusiasts can reform the world" nor "a new plan of *transacting business*." Rather it was "a different method of *dividing the fruits* of industry—to labor rather than to capital," and it was "by no means independent of the every-day principles that underlie success in any undertaking or business."[35]

The book carefully examined a number of the most significant cooperative developments in the United States and pointed out the lessons that could be derived from this experience. Of particular useful-ness was the appendix of about 100 pages which contained the rules and by-laws of the Rochdale Equitable Pioneers, as well as those of nine American cooperative stores of various types, a descriptive Direc-tory of Cooperative Enterprises, a review of Laws Relative to Coopera-tion in the Respective States, and a Bibliography of Cooperation.

Myrick's common sense view was that farmers and wage earners—producers and consumers—needed to grasp the possibilities of coopera-tion. He favored starting cooperatives in a small way, since "a start of the right kind, under the humblest auspices is far better than more pretentious and usually injudicious effort." He likewise stressed the importance of proper management, holding that "the future holds no inducement for poorly or mismanaged cooperation."

Like Barnard, Myrick favored more communication between co-operators and held that the great need was to get all "distributive" societies together in a "comprehensive union." Then he thought that it might be feasible for all types of cooperatives, distributive and produc-tive, to hold a Cooperative Congress at the World's Fair to be held in Chicago in 1893 and thus "immensely stimulate the progress of true cooperative literature." He ended his book by saying: "The *future of cooperation* is thus fraught only with good to the individual and to the state. Its star is in the ascendancy and nothing can stay its course."[36]

Nothing came of Myrick's hope for a cooperative congress at the World's Fair, but a Cooperative Union of America was set up in 1895 through the efforts of Professor Francis G. Peabody, of Harvard Univer-sity, and other cooperative well-wishers. Its declared object was the promotion in America of the Rochdale plan of cooperation. It was open to all persons in sympathy who could become members for one dollar a year. Moreover, a cooperative society, trade union, or like organization could become a member by paying an annual fee equal to and not less than two cents for each of its members. Largely through its excellent official magazine, *The American Cooperative News*, and its annual meetings, the union did much to encourage cooperative development prior to its collapse in 1899. James Ford, writing some dozen years later, said: "This experience proved the hollowness of a cooperative federation which is forced upon existing societies from without and is not the democratic expression of their own realization of the necessity of federation.[37]

Another attempt to establish a national cooperative body, stemming from Kansas, occurred in 1896 at the St. Louis Populist Convention. Although this resulted in the formation of the American Co-operative Union, it had no real support from cooperatives and proved abortive from the start.[38]

Appraisal, 1896

The years 1894, 1895, and 1896, following the panic of 1893, marked the close of the epoch of hard times which had prevailed with minor interruption since the panic of 1873. These were the years of Coxey's march of the unemployed on Washington, of the bitter strike and bloodshed at Pullman, and of Bryan's Cross of Gold speech.[39] The long downward trend in prices following the Civil War had finally reached bottom and conditions favorable for a long period of better times were imperceptibly forming. The year 1896 thus provides a good vantage point from which to examine the growth made by urban cooperation since 1860.

In 1896, the residue of urban cooperative achievement, other than in the building and loan associations, in mutual fire and life insurance companies, and in mutual savings banks, was to be found principally in the field of cooperative distribution, for the many experiments in cooperative production had largely run their course. Except for a few "only moderately successful" cooperative cooper shops in Minneapolis, Bemis found "scarcely anything of the kind" existing in America.[40]

While the record in cooperative distribution was not striking, there were tangible gains to report. In New England, Bemis found that "while six of the stores that had a trade of $134,000 in 1886 are now closed, the trade of the remaining 13 of those in existence in the former period has grown from $479,900 to $978,951.48 and nine new stores report a trade of $251,409.49. The total cooperative trade in New England, almost entirely on the Rochdale plan, is thus over twice as great as ten years ago" (p. 615). The "total cooperative trade" outside of New England "was about $900,000 in 1895, as contrasted with about $1,000,000 in 1886," although Bemis felt that a survey as complete as that made in 1886 might reveal a small growth (p. 615). The associations that were functioning in 1896 were making a good showing, the average rate of dividend for 20 New England Rochdale stores in 1895 being 6.8 per cent and for 13 outside of New England 3.5 per cent. Bemis concluded: "Any business house that could make both ends meet the past year is to be congratulated. It is a fair record, therefore, that these cooperative societies present" (pp. 619-20).

The most striking achievement in cooperative growth since 1860 had, however, been made by the building and loan associations. An exhaustive study by the U. S. Commissioner of Labor in 1893 disclosed that the total dues paid in plus the profits on the same, then amounted to $450,667,594. The report then said: "A business represented by this great sum, conducted quietly, with little or no advertising, and ... with the experienced banker in charge, shows that the common people in their own way, are quite competent to take care of their savings."[41]

Taking everything into consideration, the principal cooperative gain since 1860 was in understanding and realism. Cooperation was no longer being urged as a solution for all social and economic problems. At last, free of labor domination and well grounded in tested Rochdale methods, it was beginning to gain recognition as a distinct form of business enterprise usable by any urban group to further their individual interests as members.

Now, let us turn to consideration of the progress of cooperation among farmers during this same period.

Chapter III

THE AGRARIAN GROUNDSWELL

The revolution in agriculture—ushered in by the Civil War—cleared the ground for the development of agricultural cooperation, and by the end of the century it had become well rooted in the United States.

Up to 1860, the farmer largely had relied upon his own resources to produce for the needs of his family and nearby markets. By 1890, a pronounced transformation to commercial and capitalistic farming had occurred. In that year, an agricultural publicist could say:

> The farmer of today is a dependent, locked in the industrial chain; a producer, simply—a manufacturer, if you please, of raw products, which are fashioned by other hands into their final forms for consumption. He depends upon distant centers for markets for his raw products, and he draws the finished products from the same distant centers.[1]

A combination of forces had brought about this significant change in the farmer's economic position. Of these the most important were: a great expansion of land in farms, encouraged by the Homestead Act of 1862 and the westward extension of railroads; a steady cheapening of costs of agricultural production through improvements in farm machinery and technical progress; and a continuous growth of commercial market outlets made possible by rapid population growth—stimulated by immigration, urbanization of industry, and improved methods of communication and transportation.[2]

With the rapid expansion and mechanization of farms, output increased "by leaps and bounds," and this increased supply exerted a downward pressure on farm prices, which was further aggravated by the decline in the general price level which followed the Civil War.

The farmer, however, would not accept the theory that his troubles were entirely due to overproduction and deflation.[3] He blamed much of his plight on an unfair system of "interchange," whereby he was forced to pay excessive toll in marketing his products, and excessive prices for his purchased supplies; and he was vehement in his resentment of all "monopolists" and "middlemen." As the farmer saw his condition, he was "fleeced both coming and going."[4]

Unable individually to protect himself against exploitation from industry which was rapidly becoming organized in corporations and combinations, the farmer turned for relief to economic cooperation as a counter method of organization, first under the auspices of the Grange and then through the Farmers' Alliance movement. "Let us organize" became the battle cry.[5]

Cooperation and the Granger Movement

While cooperative efforts among farmers had been sporadic up to the close of the Civil War, conditions became ripe for its national development with the leadership of the Patrons of Husbandry, popularly known as the Grange.[6]

When O. H. Kelley founded the Grange as a fraternal order for farmers in 1866 he did not conceive of it as an instrument for economic power but hoped that it would serve "to restore kindly feelings" between the people of the North and South.[7] As this social motivation was not strong enough to sustain the interest of farmers, especially in view of their serious economic difficulties, cooperation for economic relief was soon turned to as one of the purposes of the order.[8]

The earliest cooperative activity under Grange auspices apparently developed in Minnesota during 1868, and led to the appointment of a state business agent in the spring of 1869.[9] Soon the idea spread to other states. By 1870, the growing popularity of cooperative buying impelled the National Grange to issue a circular which contained the following paragraph:

> Subordinate Granges are requested, as part of their work, to communicate freely with the National Grange, on any matter which they may deem of interest or value to the Order at large. Information relative to machinery, tools, seeds, etc., which they may have tested either in favor of or otherwise, and whenever they desire any information relative to crops, stock, plants, seeds, machinery, advertisements, or any subject whatever, *the same will be given, if possible to be obtained, by applying to the Secretary of the National Grange. All information given to the National is the property of the Subordinate Granges, and will be freely imparted to them.*[10]

By 1871, the terms "cooperation" and "down with monopoly" were proving "popular watchwords," and when the annual meeting was held in January 1872, cooperation had become a dominant motive of the Order. At that meeting the report of Secretary Kelley contained the following statement:

The education and social features of our Order offer inducement to
some to join, but the majority desire pecuniary benefits—advantages in
purchase of machinery, and sales of produce. To bring all the Granges into
direct communication, and to devise a system of cooperation, devolves upon
the National Grange. But until its membership is much increased, we must
wait patiently the appearance of our new Moses, who is to present the
coveted plan.[11]

Up to this time the growth of the Grange had been slow. With
the acceptance of cooperation as the main feature of the order, membership began to increase rapidly. This is shown by the fact that 1,105
new granges were organized during 1872, which made altogether 1,362
at the end of the year.[12]

Evolution of early buying plans. The earliest Grange activity in
cooperative buying was a grass-roots growth of "concentration of trade"
plans, similar to those which had preceded the promotion of Protective
Union Stores about 1840 (see Chapter I). The arrangements were
simple, the Grangers agreeing to give a local merchant their exclusive
cash patronage in return for substantial reductions in prices. This
method usually worked well for a short time and then broke down when
other merchants lowered their prices to meet the competition.[13]

The weakness of the "concentration of trade" plans soon led local
Granges to employ their own business agents to by-pass the local merchants.[14]

Under these plans, as they developed by trial and error, each local
Grange had its own representative or agent who—usually on a volunteer
basis—assembled orders and placed them with wholesale merchants or
manufacturers. It was not long before the advantage of having a state
grange business agent became evident, since this would keep the local
granges from bidding against each other and result in the building up
of larger volumes on which better discounts could be obtained. As
noted, the Minnesota Grange appointed a state business agent as early
as 1869, presumably with the idea that the agent would be able to
make deals in behalf of the local Grangers and keep them informed
on desirable buying opportunities.

By 1873, the practice of employing local and state business agents
had become general, although there was little uniformity in methods
followed. In some cases, the state agents were paid a salary, but the
general practice was to pay the agent on a commission basis. Generally,
the agent did not engage in active merchandising, although in Iowa and
several other states, the agent occasionally purchased goods outright
and then sold them to local Grange agents who in turn sold them to
members.

The more common practice was to have the local Grange send in its orders to the state agent, who thereupon placed a "combined order" with a manufacturer or wholesale merchant. In this connection, special attempts were made to concentrate orders in certain periods of the year, especially in the spring as substantial discounts could be obtained when goods were shipped in carlots to one local point. As a protection against dishonesty or other cause of loss agents, both local and state, who handled cash were customarily required to furnish adequate bond. At first cash was generally required with each order both by the local and state agents, but later this requirement was allowed to lapse. In some cases, a discount of 10 per cent was granted to induce cash trading.

This arrangement, which was primarily a collective bargaining plan, worked well for commodities that could be purchased in bulk quantities such as reapers, threshers, sewing machines, dried fruit, flour, sugar, etc. But it was not adapted to the needs of farmers for the many miscellaneous items required in every-day life.[15] About 1873, the system at the local points began to give way to the establishment of stores—organized as simple joint stock companies with stock holding being restricted to Grangers—which would carry a stock of merchandise and have samples available of other goods that could be ordered on demand. By this time the state agent system was also beginning to show weakness, due to the rise of a class of wholesale merchants who were willing to give Grangers special considerations. In Illinois, for example, certain merchants were quoting wholesale prices to local Grange agents as early as 1872; and it was in this way that the first mail order house—the firm of Montgomery Ward—got its start, through making a specialty of Grange orders.[16]

While the Grange business agency system was not suited to the permanent needs of Grangers, it at least demonstrated the power of organized action. During the years 1873 and 1874, while enthusiasm was at its highest, significant savings were achieved. In Iowa, for illustration, the Grange claimed that its agents in 1873 had done a purchasing business of 5 million dollars, with a saving of at least 15 per cent on family supplies and 20 per cent on agricultural implements.[17] Of more permanent benefit were the results achieved in forcing commercial concerns to lower prices and improve their services to farmers in general.

Grange farm machinery manufacturing experience. The early success of cooperative purchasing through business agents encouraged the manufacture of farm implements.

Just at this time the treasuries of the national and state granges were overflowing with money, which had been collected from dispensations and dues. How better could these funds be invested than in independent Grange factories which could be used to "smash" the "Harvester Ring," the "Plow Ring," and other combinations which were adverse to the interests of farmers? So at least reasoned the leading Patrons; and when the order was once embarked in this direction, all sorts of schemes for Grange manufacturing made their appearance.[18]

The first attempt of this kind was tried out in Nebraska as early as 1872 when the state Grange arranged to have a "header" manufactured for its members. The Grangers were thus able to obtain a header for $150 while the standard headers were selling at from $225 to $300; and "as a consequence the price of all sorts of harvest machinery was reduced over the state, railroads gave better service on machinery of eastern manufacture, and everything seemed to indicate that the Grange had made a wise move." This experience then led the Nebraska Grange to attempt the manufacture of a cultivator at Platsmouth where "about twice as many were manufactured as could be sold." A net loss of about $5,000 resulted, which effectively curbed the confidence of the Nebraska Grangers in all forms of business cooperation.[19]

The most ambitious manufacturing undertaking originated in Iowa where the state agent in 1873 "found it practically impossible to induce the manufacturers of harvesters to sell to the Order at wholesale rates." This encouraged the state agent, in cooperation with the National Grange, to obtain the patent for the Werner "Harvester" for $1,000 under an agreement that $2.00 would be paid as royalty for each machine made. Arrangements were then entered into for its manufacture at foundries in various places in Iowa, Minnesota, and Nebraska. At first results were promising as 250 machines were furnished to Grangers at $140 each, or at about half the prevailing price for harvesters. However, some of the machines proved to be defective, and others were received from the factories too late to be used in the harvest so that the net result was a loss to the state granges involved.[20]

The highest pitch of manufacturing fever was reached during the summer of 1874. Encouraged by the apparent success being attained in manufacturing the Werner Harvester, the Executive Committee of the National Grange "conceived the design of having practically all machinery used by farmers manufactured under the auspices of the Grange." Patents were bought up either by the National Grange or by state granges "on all sorts of implements; cultivators, seeders, hay racks, a combined reaper and mower, and so on; and care was not always taken to have the machines thoroughly tested or to be sure that the patents were valid."[21]

While various manufacturing enterprises were started in many states, few got into actual operation due to difficulties involved in raising capital or in making satisfactory arrangements for management.[22] The early enthusiasm aroused by extravagant reports of success in manufacturing in Iowa was rapidly dissipated when word got around that this program was showing unmistakable signs of failure.

Critics of cooperation have long maintained that these early efforts of the Grange in the field of manufacturing demonstrated that manufacturing could not be efficiently carried on by cooperative associations. The facts suggest a different interpretation. These early ventures were only embryonic cooperative structures. As such, they showed that technical organization of cooperatives had not developed far enough to support such undertakings. This was recognized by many of the Grangers themselves, and it was partly due to the prevalence of this sentiment that the Grange turned to the more conservative Rochdale methods of cooperation from this point onward.

The swing to Rochdale cooperation. As noted, many local joint-stock cooperative stores had been established under Grange auspices in 1873 and 1874. They apparently developed normally in response to a local demand for a store which would be financed by and operated for Grangers. In most of them, shares of stock could be obtained at reasonable cost and to democratize control a limit was generally placed on the number of shares that could be held. The general plan was to sell merchandise at cost plus a nominal amount to cover expenses.

From the beginning these stores brought on intense competition from local merchants who were quick to lower their prices to hold trade. The arrangement thus had the same weakness as the method of centering trade on one store in that after a short period of initial success there were no advantages to the Grange member that he could not get other places. Moreover, the provision for voting by shares of stock owned set up a conflict between those who desired a profit on their investment and those who desired merchandise at the lowest possible cost.

The dissatisfaction with these joint-stock stores, as they were called, was voiced by the Master of the Grange, at the St. Louis meeting of the Grange in February 1874. He said: "The subject of cooperative stores is one in which subordinate Granges have manifested much interest, but the want of definite information as to the most approved and successful plan of conducting them, has prevented their general establishment." He then urged the preparation of "a careful and elaborate plan for such stores, using therefore the abundant materials which the experience of the Rochdale and other societies afford." He concluded: "This would be hailed with delight by thousands of Patrons, who are now groping in the dark." In keeping with this sentiment the Executive Committee was "instructed to devise some safe plan for cooperative stores for the information of members of the Order."[23]

The plan when presented at the Louisville sessions in November 1875 appeared to be just what the disillusioned Grangers were looking for. Here was a method that had well served the Rochdale weavers which could be applied with much if not equal success by the farmers of the United States.

Let us briefly examine the report of this committee which was destined to become one of the most influential documents in the history of American cooperation.[24] It was introduced by the following "Advice to members": (1) All cooperative associations should become incorporated; (2) care should be taken that all records, accounts and vouchers are properly kept; (3) expose dishonesty and punish fraud; (4) buy as far as practicable from the producer and manufacturer, and sell to the consumer, if possible; (5) never depart from the principle of buying and selling for cash; (6) take account of stock and make settlements quarterly; (7) neither fear nor court competition; (8) choose only men of undoubted integrity and ability for your officers, and then give them your confidence.

This "Advice" was followed by a "Preface" which emphasized the significance of the system being proposed.

> Practical cooperation does not necessarily imply buying by wholesale and distributing at cost, neither does its success depend upon buying from the producer and selling to the consumer. These are principles of trade to be generally commended. But successful cooperation is based upon the policy of investing the profits of trade for the benefit of the purchaser.
>
> If a number of persons, collectively, buy a stock of goods and distribute them to each other at wholesale or cost prices, there is no substantial evidence of profit, but an invariable creation of prejudice throughout the mercantile community. If, however, the same party dispose of their wares to themselves and others at usual retail rates, and invest the profits in favor of those who purchase, the transaction is at once pronounced legitimate and laudable, and rapid accumulation of profit is the result.

Following a brief illustration designed to show how rapidly profits would accumulate, the Preface closed with this optimistic note:

> It is not an extravagant assertion that in all mercantile transactions an exchange is seldom if ever made for less than ten per cent profit. Hence successful cooperation is dependent upon quick exchange for *cash*, and *cash only*, and not upon wholesale buying, or large marginal profits to secure extended credit.

The heart of the report consisted of a set of model cooperative "rules" which were simply the Rules of the Rochdale Equitable Pioneers adapted to meet the rural needs of the Grangers.[25] Their most significant provisions were expressed as follows:

OBJECT. The object of this Association is to establish and maintain general trade in merchandise, farm products, and machinery, for the mutual benefit of the shareholders and customers.

MEMBERS. Any member of the Order of Patrons of Husbandry in good standing may become a member of this Association by subscribing and paying for at least one share therein, and by signing his name and place of residence to these rules. But no Patron shall continue a member unless he purchases goods from this Association to the amount of twenty dollars per year.

CAPITAL. The capital of this Association shall be_____dollars, and shall be raised in shares of five dollars each, which shall not be transferable except to members of this Association.

NUMBER OF SHARES. No member shall hold more than one hundred shares in the capital of this Association.

PROFITS. The net profits of all business carried on by said Association, after paying the expenses of management, making the proper reduction in value of fixed stock, and paying the interest on the capital thereof as aforesaid, shall from time to time be applied by vote of the Association at the quarterly meeting of the Association, either to increase the capital or business of the Association, or for any educational or provident purposes authorized by the Association, and the remainder shall be divided among those who have purchased goods from this Association during the preceding quarter (to non-members one half the proportion of members) in proportion to the amount of purchases during the quarter.

MANAGEMENT OF BUSINESS. The Directors shall have the general management and supervision of the business of the Association; shall appoint the salesmen and other employes; and shall assign to them such duties and compensation as the Directors may think fit.

CASH TRADING. The business of the Association shall be conducted for cash. All persons trading with this Association shall be furnished with checks representing the amount of their purchases.

INVESTMENT. This Association may invest such portions of its surplus capital in any wholesale Co-operative Association as the Association may determine, notice of the same having been given in writing at a previous regular meeting; and such investment shall be made under the supervision of the Directors.

VOTING. At all meetings of the Association or of the Directors each member shall have one vote only.

Application of the Rochdale plan. The Grange gave its enthusiastic support to the new plan which was quietly brought to the attention of the thousands of local Granges, then spread throughout the nation, and according to Aiken, who was a member of the Grange Executive Committee at that time, the rules, based upon the Rochdale system, were "greedily clutched at by the order."[26] As a result, "hundreds" of new associations were soon formed, or stock companies reorganized on this plan. Of these, most were formed for purchasing, although many were designed for cooperative marketing.

For a short period almost the entire effort of the Grange was devoted to the development of cooperation along the Rochdale line. This enthusiasm in 1875 and 1876 caused the Grange to entertain an elaborate plan for reciprocal trading with the cooperatives of England, under which American Grange cooperatives would supply farm products to English cooperatives while the English cooperatives would supply the Grange cooperatives with various manufactured products. After protracted negotiations, during which an official representative of the Grange spent several months in England, the Committee on Cooperation proposed the formation of an Anglo-American Cooperative Company. However, for various reasons, the proposal was turned down by a vote of 24 to 18.[27]

With the general acceptance of the Rochdale plan the Grange also withdrew its support to the various commission agency schemes which were in general proving unsatisfactory. The official views of the National Grange were made unmistakably clear on this matter in the 1877 report of its Executive Committee:

> During the past fiscal year your Committee have had an opportunity of examining, and have made much inquiry and investigation into the system of agencies adopted by the several states, and are warranted in their judgment in advising the discontinuance of any one now in existence. Honest competition is what we want, but not as commission-houses. There have been more failures than successes with our Grange agencies, and how long the successful few are able to maintain themselves is unknown to those who patronize them. Were they established upon the principles embodied in the rules promulgated two years ago by the National Grange, every customer would possess some tangible evidence of their efficiency, and to that extent would their permanency and solvency be beyond question? Your Committee would recommend to the National Grange that they use every effort to encourage among Patrons the establishment of retail and wholesale stores upon the strictest principles of cooperation, and discourage the building up of commissioner or salaried agencies.[28]

While information is unfortunately not available on the number of Grange cooperative stores established on the Rochdale plan, the abundant references to them in the literature of the period suggest that they were at least given a trial in almost every state, and that perhaps as many as 500 were organized during the 10 years from 1875 to 1885. It is significant that many of these associations continued to function even after the Grange as an organization had lost much of its initial vitality.

Perhaps the most successful application of the Rochdale rules occurred in Kansas where the Johnson County Cooperative Association was organized at Olathe in June 1876. The immediate success of this store was "phenomenal" and this led to the establishment of some 20 or 30 similar stores in the state.[29] As late as 1913 this store was referred to as the "largest cooperative store in the United States." At that time a survey of its 35 years of operation disclosed that it had done a total business of $8,413,314, and had made "net profits" of $515,421.[30]

Cooperation on the Rochdale plan also had a remarkable growth in Texas following the organization of the Texas Cooperative Association at Galveston in July 1878. This association, which was the first large cooperative wholesale federation to operate with any degree of success in this country,[31] reached its peak about 1887 when it was credited with having a total purchasing volume of about $500,000 in addition to significant cotton marketing operations. At that time it was serving 132 Grange stores which were together doing an aggregate retail volume estimated at $1,612,812.[32]

Under its by-laws (1) any cooperative association of the Patrons of Husbandry or subordinate Grange could become a member by purchase of a $5 share of stock; (2) management was vested in the board of directors elected by members; (3) each member was limited to one vote; (4) members were restricted to a fixed number of shares of stock, interest on paid-up stock was limited to 10 per cent per annum; (5) distribution of profits was in accordance with the amount of business furnished.[33]

The decline of this association, starting about 1884 was due to three principal factors: (1) inability to keep on a cash basis, (2) gravitation of control to stockholders who were interested in making profits on capital, and (3) competition with the more vital Texas Farmers' Alliance movement (to be discussed later in this chapter). Moreover, as an organization, it suffered from lack of adequate capital, and was handicapped in rendering service by its wide territory which resulted in a high cost of distribution. As Hunt remarked: "The local store managers were perfectly human and insisted upon buying where they pleased, and where they could get the best bargains, and the best bargains were not always found at the Galveston headquarters."[34]

Regardless of the numerous setbacks, which proved that the Rochdale plan was not a panacea for all cooperative problems, the Grange's support of it did not waver. Ten years after the plan had been adopted, the Committee on Cooperation said: "As regards business cooperation, your committee knows of no other system or plan better adapted to the wants of our people than the Rochdale, as recommended by the National Grange. The history of the plan has been fraught with such wonderful results, that we deem it unwise to offer any other."[35]

Grange activities in cooperative marketing and insurance. From the first, the Grange had supported cooperation in marketing as well as in purchasing.[36] While the state Grange business agents gave most of their attention to purchasing, they also assisted in finding markets for the surplus products of the local Granges. And in many instances, the state Granges arranged to center the marketing of grain, poultry, and livestock, or other products through accredited commission firms. From 1872 to 1875 a large number of farmers' elevators and shipping stations of one kind or another were also formed by the local Grangers, mostly on a stock company basis. Moreover, many plants for processing farm products were also established, such as "grist mills, cheese and butter factories, linseed oil factories, starch factories, pork-packing establishments, and even hemp factories."[37]

When it was found in 1875 that the Rochdale methods could be adapted to the marketing of farm products, there was a trend to this method of organization, although it never caught hold as it did in purchasing.

In 1876, the interest of the Grangers in marketing was evidenced by a number of petitions urging the National Grange to set up wool and tobacco warehouses. This led to the formulation of the following definite Grange policy on cooperative marketing:

> Now it is the unanimous judgment of your committee that the National Grange recommend to our members who are specially interested in the tobacco product and the wool product, or indeed any other product, that they themselves form associations on the cooperative principle, and select the center where they wish to concentrate their trade, choose their own officers and managers, make their own rules and regulations as nearly in conformity with the plan of co-operation adopted by the National Grange at this session as possible, for, bear in mind, the principles of cooperation are as well adapted to the commission business as to the wholesale or retail business.[38]

The Grange also actively promoted the growth of mutual fire insurance companies, and this resulted in a significant increase in the number of such organizations during the 1870's.[39] Other forms of cooperative enterprise encouraged by the Grange were mutual life insurance companies, building and loan associations, banks, and mutual irrigation companies.

Thus the Granger movement gave a very decided encouragement to the promotion of all forms of agricultural cooperation and helped to pave the way for its future development.

The Grange contribution. Looking backward, it is easy to see that the Grange might have had more permanent success in its cooperative efforts if the Rochdale principles of cooperative organization had been applied in 1873 or early 1874, when the enthusiasm of the Grangers was at its highest. However, when the plan was adopted in the fall of 1876. the force of the movement was waning,[40] and many Grangers had lost their confidence in cooperation through unfortunate experiences with joint-stock stores. Moreover, at that time business conditions had begun to improve slightly following the panic of 1873 and farmers were less inclined to turn to cooperation for relief.

Even though the achievements of the Grangers in cooperation fell far short of their ambitions, they may be given credit for the following highly significant cooperative contributions. The Grangers (1) grasped the significance of cooperation as a method of self-help and popularized the idea throughout the nation; (2) proved the power of cooperative action in purchasing, marketing, and other activities; (3) demonstrated the value of the Rochdale principles of organization, and showed that they could be applied to marketing as well as in purchasing operations; (4) pointed out the necessity of—and showed possibilities of—whole-sale regional cooperative organization; (5) educated farmers in sound cooperative techniques such as the importance of cash trading, adequate capital, and membership support, and the necessity of good management; (6) emphasized the fact that sound cooperative organization must precede ambitious projects as shown by the farm machinery and wholesaling ventures; (7) brought cooperation to the attention of the public as a method of business organization; (8) taught the limitations of cooperation as well as its possibilities, and thus helped channel its development along practical lines.

The Granger movement thus prepared the cooperative seedbed for the gathering forces of the second great farm protest movement—the Farmers' Alliance.

The Alliance Impetus

The Farmers' Alliance movement, which swept the rural sections of the nation from 1887 to 1890, did not directly stem from the Grange, for, in fact, the power and prestige of the Grange retarded its early growth.

The motivation of the Alliance was primarily economic.[41] It grew and flourished during a period when the price level was steadily falling. Farmers who had rapidly acquired land and improvements on mortgages and credit, and this represented a large fraction of the farmers of the West since the new settlers had little capital, found themselves compelled to repay their debts with steadily appreciating dollars.[42] While the prices of agricultural machinery and other manufactured products had fallen somewhat since the Grangers had forced a reduction, the decline was far less than that of farm products. The farmer was caught in the middle between low prices for his products and relatively high-priced supplies and his distress was further aggravated by a heavy debt burden. On the other hand, industry was apparently thriving, through tariff protection on manufactured products and the effective use of the corporation and trust forms of organization. The farmer, discontented by his growing debts, and his inability to get adequate financial assistance from the then inflexible banking system, with decreasing prices for his crops and confronted by organized business groups in selling his products or in purchasing supplies, naturally attributed his weakness to lack of organization and turned to cooperation as a means of relief.

Students of the Alliance trace its origins back to the farmers' Clubs which sprang up spontaneously in the 1840's, 1850's, and 1860's in the pioneer settlements of the West and the Southwest. These clubs were apparently first organized for mutual protection against "land sharks," who contrived to get possession of land homesteaded or otherwise acquired by farmers, and gangs of cattle and horse thieves.[43] Later these protective societies and clubs gradually undertook social and other activities, and then it was a natural step for them to undertake cooperative buying and selling. While the Grange had absorbed many of these organizations, a number had retained their independence, and with the decline of the Grange after 1876 they again increased in number and significance.

> One of the most interesting was the Iowa Farmers' Protective Association which was formed in 1881 to combat the "barbed wire trust." At that time the demand for barbed wire was very strong, amounting to about 200 million pounds a year in Iowa. This led one concern to buy up all of the patents with the result that "retail prices were advanced—about three cents a pound more than the previous year, an increase of 40 per cent. This margin was equivalent to an annual tax of $5,000,000, or $6,000,000 upon the farmers of the single state of Iowa." Confronted by this situation, the Farmers Protective Association was quickly set up "to supply its members and others with barbed wire," and with the membership fee fixed at $1.00 there were soon several thousand members. The association then entered into an agreement to have barbed wire made for its members at a "free factory," where no patent royalty was paid. This resulted in a long and bitter legal struggle in which the farmers obtained the support of the state legislature. The secretary of the association writing in January 1887 said: "The victory of the farmers in this contest has been more complete than the most sanguine anticipated. Barbed wire has sold at all points in Iowa for the past three years at from four to six cents a pound, or less than half the price fixed upon it by the combination when the Farmers' Association was organized, and it is as low as it can be manufactured at the present time." The "farmers' factory" was chiefly valuable as a regulator of prices. According to the secretary: "The

amount of wire made by the farmers' factory would have supplied but a small portion of what was demanded, but it was sold direct to the user, and every dealer in the towns of Iowa, knowing that his customers could send and get their wire from Des Moines at the advertised price, demanded of the combination that they furnish him with wire so that he could compete with the farmers' factory. The farmers' factory has dictated the price on wire fencing during the past five years." The secretary attributed much of the success of the organization—which incidentally had been formed with the support of the Iowa Farmers' Alliance—to the experience which farmers had gained in the Granger movement.[44]

As a movement, the Farmers' Alliance had a somewhat confused beginning. It did not develop from a promotional center but grew from the ground up from several organizing spores.[45] Its lifeline can be traced from a Kansas protective association which was started about 1874. The plans of this Kansas organization were transplanted to local communities in Texas and New York where the seed grew into two independent but organically similar Alliance movements which were never completely merged. Of the two, the Texas movement was by far the more virile and through a series of consolidations starting in 1887 under the brilliant leadership of C. W. Macune it had covered the South by 1888, and by 1890 through further consolidations and confederations it had become almost national in scope, with some two million adherents. On the other hand, the "New York" Alliance movement expanded throughout the West and Northwest where it became strongest in Illinois, Iowa, and Minnesota. In 1890, this branch of the Alliance, popularly called the Northwestern Alliance, had perhaps 400,000 members.[46]

Early cooperative methods. The earliest efforts in cooperative purchasing associated with the Alliance movement were comparable to those first used by the Grange. A common arrangement was for a local Alliance to work out a deal with a local merchant under which special terms were given Alliance members in return for their assured trade.[47]

However, as it was impossible to enforce such arrangements or restrict their benefits to Alliance members, the local Alliances soon turned their energies to the organization of joint-stock stores for purchasing and of elevators and cotton sales yards for marketing their agricultural products.[48] With the formation of such local organizations for buying and selling, there soon developed a demand for assistance from the state organization.

Dr. C. W. Macune—who was to become the dominating national leader of the Farmers' Alliance Movement—gave direction to this sentiment at the meeting of the State Alliance in January 1887. Macune said:

The order has grown in the last year and a half from 700 alliances to about 3500 ...; and perhaps the most potent argument ... has been the individual benefits that would accrue from concentration of trade in purchasing supplies, and the bulking of products when offered for sale ... This body should take effective and adequate steps to support and assist, to direct and concentrate, the efforts being made by county Alliances to regulate and reform the system of purchasing supplies and sale of products.[49]

With the appointment of Macune as the state business agent on March 1, 1887, steps were immediately taken to achieve a co-ordinated program. The response to this leadership was so favorable that in August the state Alliance established the Farmers' Alliance Exchange of Texas as a means of achieving even better results. This had a profound influence on the future activities of the Farmers' Alliance, for the Texas Exchange became the model for similar state business agencies which were functioning throughout the South and Middle West by 1890.

The Texas State Exchange. The Farmers' Alliance Exchange of Texas —Macune's brain child—was incorporated with an authorized capital of $500,000, divided into 25 shares of $20,000 each. The 25 stockholders were to serve as trustees for the members of the Farmers' State Alliance, and were to be elected by them at the annual sessions of the state Alliance. The actual capital was to be raised by an assessment of $2 for each Alliance member. The exchange was to be managed by a board of three (later increased to seven) who were to be generally responsible to the stockholders. The declared purpose of the Exchange was set forth as follows: "To negotiate the sale of cotton and other products, and stock, and such other property, personal, real, or mixed, as may be desired by the members of the Farmers' State Alliance of Texas; also, the purchase of all such commodities, machinery, and other things as may be desired."[50]

Upon organization, the trustee stockholders immediately employed Macune as business manager and made arrangements to establish headquarters at Dallas upon the invitation of a group of businessmen who offered a cash subsidy of $10,000 and a rent-free building.

At the beginning, the Exchange confined its efforts to the handling of cotton and grain and to the procurement of farm implements. Cotton and grain were sold "after the plan of a regular commission house" while implements "were procured and furnished at good discounts by centering the trade direct to a wholesale dealer." However, business was soon "extended to the buying and selling of dry goods, groceries, and general supplies." At this time, enthusiasm ran high, "amounting to almost a universal conviction that financial salvation was come." All kinds of optimistic developments were anticipated—cotton and woolen mills, implement and wagon factories, a printing plant, and even an Alliance university.[51]

This exuberance, plus the need for a program that would improve the lot of the tenant cotton producers who were being throttled by the prevalent time merchant credit system, resulted in the adoption of a highly ingenious credit scheme in November 1887. Designed to permit farmers to purchase supplies upon the security of their cotton crops, it represented an attempt to employ the "time merchant system" in behalf of Alliance members. To achieve this end, members of each sub-Alliance were to pledge cotton worth three times as much as the amount of credit that would be involved in furnishing them supplies. The several members of each sub-Alliance were then to execute a joint note to cover the value of the estimated amount of supplies required. These joint notes were to be used by the Exchange as collateral security in financing the acquisition of merchandise and were to be liquidated when the cotton represented by the pledge was sold through the Exchange.

In effect, this scheme attempted to finance both the farmer and his exchange through the anticipated sale of the members' cotton. It might have been used effectively if the Exchange had been more strongly financed and thus able to guarantee from its own resources the payment of the notes. However, if the Exchange had been adequately financed to begin with, it would not have required the use of the notes. As it was, the impracticability of the plan soon became evident. In the first place, the notes were slow to come in so that the plans for the orderly distribution of merchandise could not be adequately worked out. Then it proved impossible to get banks or commercial firms to accept the notes except at great discounts, with the result that the manager could not use the notes as security for funds required to purchase merchandise to supply the needs of the members. Confronted with this financial dilemma, the business manager and the directors charged that there was a conspiracy to crush the Exchange by the bankers, wholesale merchants, implement dealers, and manufacturers. Although there was no doubt cause for this view since the plans of the Exchange if successful would have materially affected the pecuniary interests of these groups, it is more to the point that the Exchange's difficulties were internal in that it was undertaking to do a very large volume of business on very little paid-in capital. This was recognized too late. Although a frantic effort was made to get members to pay up their capital assessments, this netted only $50,000 which was insufficient in view of the extensive operations being carried on.[52]

Although the Exchange was reorganized without the "note plan" and under different management, it was not able to recapture the confidence of the farmers of Texas and, in 1889, after 20 months, it was unable to continue operations.[53]

The Georgia plan. In his Shreveport, Louisiana, address, October 12, 1887, to the newly born "National Alliance," Macune pointed out that the National Farm Alliance and Cooperative Union of America had been formed with "one great battle-cry of cooperation as the universal principle upon which all could unite." He therefore recommended "that this body promote some plan of universal cooperation ... whereby each sub, county and state alliance shall have an agent, and that a national agent be chairman of a board composed of the different state agents."[54]

As rapidly as state alliances were formed throughout the Cotton Belt, business agents were therefore appointed, and in May 1888, the business agents of the organized states met for the purpose of organizing a state business agents association. At this meeting a model plan for state exchanges was developed, and this plan was largely followed in the establishment of state exchanges in Georgia, Alabama, Florida, North Carolina, South Carolina, Tennessee, and Arkansas. (Mississippi already had a state exchange organized on the Texas plan in February 1888.) Of these, the most successful was the Farmers' Alliance Exchange of Georgia which continued operations until 1893.[55]

The declared purposes of the Georgia Exchange were:

> To conduct a general mercantile business; to act as agent for the purchase and sale of all kinds of farm and orchard products, and general forwarding agent for all kinds of commodities; to erect, manage, and operate warehouses, stock-yards, grain elevators, packing establishments; to manufacture guano and other fertilizers; and all such other enterprises as may be found necessary or advisable to profit and betterment.[56]

The Georgia Exchange plan differed from the Texas plan primarily in that it placed responsibility and control in the county alliances rather than in the individual Alliance members. On the basis of his Texas experience, Macune felt that this provided a much more satisfactory arrangement since it tied the county alliances more definitely into the program and gave the local Alliance members a greater feeling of direct responsibility. The Georgia plan thus combined both federated and centralized features of regional organization. Although it was centralized organically for operating purposes, it was decentralized in the sense that each county unit was made directly responsible for control and support.

The Dakota plan. While the state exchange plan was being developed in Texas, members of the independent "Northwest Alliance" were setting up the Dakota Farmers' Alliance Company. This organization, with headquarters at Aberdeen, South Dakota, was incorporated in July 1887 with an authorized capital of $200,000 divided into shares of $10 each—but each Alliance member was restricted to 50 shares.

The method of operation was to pool orders from local Alliances through county branch agencies and then contract with firms for supplies to fill these orders. As far as possible the company bought direct from "mines and factories." For example, a five-year contract was drawn for the entire output of a wagon factory, and the wagons were branded "The Alliance." The company attempted to operate on a low margin so as to give Alliance members merchandise at the lowest possible prices, and in 1888 the margin was about 2.5 per cent on first cost.

The principal supplies handled were for use in farm operations. This is shown by a report on the operations of the company for 1888 when sales totaled $343,000. In that year the company distributed: 1,525,565 pounds of binding twine; 700 barrels of machine oil; 200 buggies; 173 mowing machines; 70 sets of harness; 11 cars of barbed wire; 7 cars of seeders and drillers; 6 cars of farm wagons; 5 cars of corn cultivators; 4 cars of harrows; 3 cars of plows; 3 cars of hay rakes. Coal was also an important item. In 1889, the company coal contract was for 2,000 car loads, "the largest by far ever made in the Dakotas." The savings of farmers through the company's operations were estimated at 25 per cent.[57]

The Kansas plan. Another significant "Northwestern Alliance" business organization was the Kansas Alliance Exchange Company, organized in August 1889. The plan of the Kansas Company was apparently influenced by the Georgia plan of organization, which had been widely publicized in Alliance circles. In 1889, Kansas Alliance groups were veering toward the National Alliance, which it officially joined in December 1889. Its authorized capital was $500,000, divided into 100,000 shares of $5.00 each. Stock was sold both to sub-alliances and to individual Alliance members, but no Alliance or individual could own more than 50 shares of stock. Each sub-alliance was entitled to the election of one trustee stockholder who was to represent the Alliance at the meeting of the trustee stockholders for the county, and he was entitled to as many votes as were represented by the stockholders of the sub-Alliance. Moreover, each individual stockholder was also entitled to vote (either in person or by proxy) at the county meeting of trustee stockholders in proportion to his holdings of stock.

The principal activity at the county meetings of sub-Alliance and individual stockholders was the election of the "county trustee stock-holder" who was authorized "to represent the stock held in that county in the State meeting of trustee stockholders of the corporation" and who was entitled to vote in proportion to the shares of stock which he represented. The county trustee stockholders were the official representatives of the Exchange in the county Alliances, and they elected the board of directors of seven which was given complete control over the business affairs of the corporation. The Exchange combined the functions of a wholesale purchasing association with those of a sales agency for farm products. Among the most important supplies purchased for farmers were farming implements, vehicles, and machinery, groceries, barbed wire and binding twine, while grain and livestock were the principal products marketed. The following quotation throws light on the price policy followed: "In 1891, its sale of binding twine reached over one hundred car loads, the twine being sold uniformly at the same price to all—one-half per cent per pound above cost at retail and one-fourth cent above cost to local cooperative stores."[58]

According to a contemporary authority, the division of profits was "a little peculiar," 40 per cent of the net profit going to capital, the other 60 per cent going to dividends or rebates to purchasers. The dividend was payable in cash to shareholders while in the case of Alliance members who were not shareholders, it was passed to their credit against shares of stock.

The Kansas plan thus had several modern cooperative features. It provided in a detailed way for direct control by individuals either through their ownership of stock or through their membership in sub-Alliances. It also recognized the importance of providing for the distribution of savings on a patronage as well as on a stock basis. Moreover, its by-laws represented an advance in arrangements for business management.[59]

Other Alliance activities. While the state Exchanges were the most spectacular forms of Alliance cooperative activity, there were many other significant cooperative developments. In many states, for example, business agents on the old Grange pattern assisted local Alliance groups in pooling orders for supplies or in marketing their products. In 1889 and 1890, the volume of such business amounted to several million dollars annually.[60]

A number of specialized terminal marketing agencies were also developed under Alliance auspices. The most important of these was the American Livestock Commission Company which was formed in March 1889 by the State Alliances of Kansas, Nebraska and Missouri, and the Kansas State Grange. It opened offices at Chicago, Kansas City, East St. Louis, and Omaha, and in 1890 sold livestock valued at over $2.5 million. This association was quite successful at the start, and "this success aroused the opposition of other commission firms on the grounds that the American was operating contrary to the anti-rebate rule of the livestock exchanges. The latter therefore refused to grant the privilege of membership to the cooperative organization or to allow their members to deal with it. This handicapped the American Livestock Commission Company so severely that it ceased operations entirely in 1891."[61]

The operations of the Exchanges, business agents, and terminal marketing agencies gave encouragement to the promotion of many local stores, elevators, and shipping associations. Some of these were based on the Rochdale plan but the majority were simply stock companies owned by Alliance members. The Alliance also encouraged cooperative insurance. According to Hicks: "Cooperative fire, hail, and life insurance was tried out by the Dakota Alliance and by a few others with good results temporarily; and in 1890 a National Alliance Aid Association, operating on the Dakota plan was opened in Washington, D.C.[62]

The cooperative philosophy of the Alliance. It is not commonly appreciated that the cooperative philosophy of the Alliance was radically different from that of the Grangers. Macune made this clear at the annual meeting of the Alliance held at Meridian, Mississippi, in December 1888:

> This plan is pure and simple cooperation, with no joint-stock features whatever, and differs from similar plans before introduced in several important particulars. It is calculated *to benefit the whole class,* and not simply those who have surplus money to invest in capital stock; it does not aspire to, and is not calculated to be a business for profit in itself, *but is intended to be strictly auxiliary and supplemental to the farming efforts.* Another distinctive feature of the exchange plan is that, instead of encouraging a number of independent stores scattered over the country, each in turn to fall a prey to the opposition, whenever they shall think it of sufficient importance to concentrate a few forces against it—*this plan provides for a strong central State head,* and places sufficient capital stock there to make that the field for concentrating the fight of the opposition, and a bulwark of strength and refuge for the local store efforts.[63]

In effect, Macune and the other Alliance leaders turned their backs on Rochdale cooperation as being inadequate for their needs.[64]

> The plan of business inaugurated by the Exchange was a great innovation upon the established usages and customs of the country ... The people had been for twenty years taught the Rochdale system of conducting stores, and as it had for its object an entirely different purpose from that taught by the Alliance, the Exchange could not use that plan, and therefore was compelled to undertake the difficult task of introducing a new system, and combating

the opposition from within the order, of many who were wedded to the
Rochdale plan of joint-stock (miscalled co-operative) stores . . .

To make his point clear, Dunning showed by example how a Rochdale type store would operate in a local community so as to benefit its
members primarily, and then continued:

> Now had an Alliance store been started in the place of the Rochdale
> store, in the same town, at that time, with a like capital, different conditions
> would have prevailed, and a very different result would have ensued. The
> Alliance store would have said: "We are strictly auxiliary to the farming
> effort, and therefore will not charge the membership the usual profits of
> merchants, and then return it to them as dividends. We will let them keep
> the profits in their pockets, by selling them the goods at the cost of laying
> them down here and handling. The people will thereby be able to make their
> money go farther towards paying the expenses of the farming effort . . ."
> [Thus] the gain from the business of the Alliance store would accrue to the
> general public in the shape of reduced prices; and, as nine-tenths of the
> people of the county were farmers, nine-tenths of the gains would accrue
> to agriculture.[65]

The Alliance leaders in thus rejecting the Rochdale objectives as
being too limited for the needs of farmers, gave a new direction to
cooperative thinking which may be called *the industry* rather than *the
individual* approach. The Alliance leaders emphasized the basic importance of having strong central organizations as they saw their problem as being regional in scope. They therefore stressed the significance
of developing a plan which could be applied over wide territories so
as to make the full power of farmers felt.[66] Under the Alliance plan, the
local agency became an instrumentality or service center for the state
program—a unit in a chain system. Thus, the Alliance state business
agencies were the prototype of the large centralized farm cooperatives
of a later date—in which the ultimate control is directly vested in individual members rather than in federated member associations. As
such, they left a heritage of experience which has had a great influence
on subsequent cooperative development.[67]

The decline of the Alliance. Although the cooperative activities of
the Alliance helped the farmers, they were not capable of controlling
the economic forces which were relentlessly bearing down on the agricultural industry. It was natural, therefore, for the Alliance leaders,
supported by the mass emotion of farmers, to turn their energies to
political remedies. For a time Macune and other Alliance leaders resisted all forms of political action, but the demand for assistance gradually became irresistible as the hard times in the late 1880's increased
in severity.[68]

There is a fair possibility that the state exchanges might have developed into permanent cooperative organizations had the National Alliance not become deeply involved in politics at this time. When the energies of the Alliance were absorbed by political measures after 1890, this completely drained it of vital interest in self-help cooperation, and brought on its rapid disintegration as a general farmers' organization.

Lessons from Alliance experience. The Alliance, in groping for a cooperative plan which would fit the current needs of American farmers, made a significant advance over much of the earlier Granger effort, and greatly influenced the character of subsequent cooperative thinking.

Perhaps the greatest cooperative contribution was the demonstration by the state exchanges of the possibilities of strong large-scale organizations in purchasing and marketing. The Grange had emphasized the importance of local associations and their federation to form wholesale organizations. The Alliance conceived of regional associations with local service centers and individual memberships, and thus gave support to the theory of development from the "top down" rather than from the "bottom up."

The Alliance also made a contribution by placing emphasis on the fact that a cooperative's success should be measured by its ability to improve the economic condition of its members as a group, rather than as separate individuals. This fraternal concept of "cooperative solidarity" was later to find expression in the formation of "non-stock member associations," and in the commodity marketing movement.

The Alliance can also be given credit for seeing the importance of giving members savings direct through low-price policy on commodities purchased or higher prices on products marketed, rather than in patronage dividends. However, the experience of the Alliance also showed that such policies could not be administered by weakly financed or poorly supported organizations.

The experience of the Alliance was also replete with business lessons useful for later cooperators. For example, the state exchanges and marketing agencies demonstrated that one of the principal causes of cooperative failure is inadequate membership capital and over-expansion; that a cooperative merchandising organization should avoid becoming involved in supplementary banking or credit operations; that good management and membership education are indispensable to permanent cooperative success. Most important of all, the Alliance experience offered an inescapable lesson that cooperatives cannot become engaged in political controversy without jeopardizing their strength as economic organizations. For many years following the collapse of the Alliance, the wistful refrain could be heard in farm circles, "Politics killed the Alliance."

The Agrarian Heritage

The Grangers and the Alliancemen, in their efforts to meet their economic problems through the use of cooperative organization, left a rich heritage of cooperative experience to oncoming generations of farmers. They clearly perceived the possibilities of cooperative organization as a method peculiarly suited to the collective needs of the "family-sized farm" and rooted this idea deep in the consciousness of the rural community. While many of the cooperatives which they formed died young, those that survived became "pilot plants" for more effective associations yet to come. Even those cooperatives that failed had their value to the farmers of that time in such ways as in improving marketing and merchandising methods, in lowering margins, in curbing credit abuses, in raising quality standards, and in increasing economic and business knowledge. Altogether, these cooperative efforts exerted a highly valuable corrective influence on the "materialistic" economic and political forces of the time and thus on the subsequent character of American life.

During this period, while the Grangers and the Alliancemen were attempting to fashion their cooperative systems, many independent cooperative associations were also developing spontaneously. This story will be told in Chapter IV.

Chapter IV

GROWTH OF INDEPENDENT
AGRICULTURAL COOPERATIVES

Chapter I told how farmers prior to 1860 had formed a number of agricultural cooperative associations for such purposes as finding markets, reducing costs of farming, or protecting themselves from "land sharks." Such developments continued during and after the Civil War, not as parts of a movement, but as independent group efforts of farmers to improve their lot—and they would have continued with or without the support of the Grange or Alliance movements.

A continuation of this independent growth of cooperatives will be described in this chapter. Although at times it became temporarily intermingled with the Granger and Farmers' Alliance movements, even during these periods a certain degree of independence was maintained. Beginning in the 1880's, however, this independent movement began increasingly to take on a character of its own in various parts of the country. Separate cooperative marketing developments began to be discernible in the dairying, grain, and fruit industries in which emphasis was placed on the cooperative performance of business operations essential to farmers' welfare. As this chapter will show, a significant residue of such cooperative achievement had accumulated by 1896.

The Extension of Dairy Cooperation

Cooperative or associated dairying for cheese making was becoming established in New York state by 1860. Following the Civil War, this "system of associated dairies" spread rapidly in New England and Canada, and by 1872 it reached as far west as Kansas. It was known as the "American System of Dairying" since "its peculiarities are so well adapted to the genius of our people as to give it a distinctive character of nationality." The distinguishing characteristic of the American system was the "constant effort to reduce the whole art and practice of dairying to a science... The great result sought is to make associated capital pay better than non-associated capital... It is adopting the rule to farming that has been found successful in commerce and merchandising."[1]

The general plan of organization and operation was described as follows by the President of the New York State Cheese Manufacturers Association in 1864:

> Within a brief period several operations have been formed for making cheese under the general manufacturing law of New York. The stock is divided into small shares, and generally distributed as much as may be among the dairymen of the neighborhood, with a view of creating a general desire for the success of the institution, and enlisting efforts to secure patronage. The concerns of the association are managed by a board of management, beyond the annual election of the trustees... The actual cost of conducting the company's business is charged to the patrons in a general account, with a percentage on the amount of capital stock sufficient to pay interest on the investment and cover the wear and tear of fixtures. In this account credits are given for all monies received for cheese, whey, and other produce, and the balance apportioned among the dairymen according to the amount of milk furnished by each.[2]

While some of the cooperative cheese factories manufactured butter, there was also a considerable growth of cooperative creameries exclusively devoted to butter making. In the formation of factories a crude, but effective, membership agreement was employed. The recommended form of agreement in 1871 read as follows:

> We, the undersigned, residents of the town of _____, hereby agree to enter into association for the purpose of erecting and operating a cheese and butter factory at _____, in said town. And we severally and individually bind ourselves by these presents, on or before the first day of _____, 1871, to pay to our regularly appointed building committee, the several sums set opposite our names, for the purpose of building and furnishing said factory, And it is understood and agreed that when said factory shall have been completed and opened for work, each member of the association is to patronize it by delivering milk for one year in proportion to the number of cows set opposite our names. The manufactured product of said milk is to be sold by the regularly appointed agent of the association, and each member to receive his share of the sales in proportion to the quantity of milk delivered, less the cost of manufacturing, etc. The above not to be binding unless the sum of $4,000 and the milk of 400 cows are subscribed.[3]

Local cooperative cheese factories and creameries were thus well established in the United States before the Grangers began to give general encouragement to all forms of agricultural cooperative organization in the early 1870's.[4]

With the encouragement of cooperation by the Grangers, hundreds of local cooperative cheese factories and creameries were formed in the 1870's, and the movement continued in the 1880's with the support of the Northwestern Farmers' Alliance. In 1891, Myrick said: "It is safe to estimate that sixty percent of the cheese made in factories in the United States is the product of cooperative effort."[5]

The creamery promotion period. The introduction of the centrifugal cream separator in 1879 gave a great impetus to the commercial manufacture of "creamery" butter since the new method not only saved much labor over the old gravity system but also took all of the cream instead of three quarters and produced it at any degree of thickness.[6]

While this energized the formation of many cooperative creameries on a sound basis, it likewise gave rise to a wave of promotional activity by "professional promoters," which resulted in the establishment of hundreds of local cooperative creameries in Iowa, Indiana, Illinois, and other mid-western states, destined to failure. The peak of this promotional activity which started about 1885 was reached in the early 1890's, and "by 1893, there were enough idle promoted creameries to represent $7,000,000 in investment, but which were neither usable nor salable."[7]

While through most of the Midwest, the sound development of cooperative creameries was being demoralized by the unscrupulous efforts of promoters who were primarily interested in selling creamery equipment, in Minnesota their efforts were arrested by the vigorous efforts of Professor T. L. Haecker who had come to the University of Minnesota in 1891. Haecker, an earnest advocate of cooperative creameries, brought the resources of the university to the assistance of Minnesota farmers. He succeeded in thwarting the promoters and in establishing large numbers of cooperative creameries on an efficient operating basis. To insure their sound operation, he started a school for butter making at the University in 1892 which was instrumental in raising the quality level of Minnesota butter production. Largely as a result of Haecker's aggressive educational program, several hundred efficient cooperative creameries were functioning in Minnesota by 1896.[8]

The trial period for collective bargaining. With the growth of cities, there had gradually developed a dealer system of milk distribution which divorced fluid milk producers from direct contact with consumers. This placed farmers at the mercy of unscrupulous dealers who, by agreement among themselves, could fix the prices paid to producers at little more than cost of production.[9]

The first organized dairymen's protest against this system came in 1883 in New York when 800 farmers of Orange County who were shipping milk to New York City formed an association to protect their prices. This led to a meeting with the dealers at which the farmers demanded three and a half cents a quart at the railroad depots as compared with the three cents then paid. The city retail price was then 10 cents. As no agreement could be reached, the dairymen at a mass meeting passed a resolution to stop all milk shipments the next night. After three days of strike, "the farmers secured nearly all of the increase demanded." While this informal association had bettered conditions it was soon recognized that a "wider organization" was required to prevent the flooding of the New York market and this led in 1889 to the formation of an organization called the Five States Milk Producers' Union to unite producers in New York, New Jersey, Connecticut, Massachusetts and Pennsylvania.[10]

Although the ambitious plans of this organization to furnish milk direct to consumers were not carried out, its accomplishments were material, especially "in uniting scattered farms and acting as an agent through which their claims might be stated and pressed in dealing with the Milk Exchange."[11] In 1898, the Union gave way to the Five States Milk Producers' Association which was the forerunner of the present Dairymen's League.

Similar marketing problems led to the organization of dairymen supplying other urban markets. The Boston Milk Producers' Union, the antecedent of the New England Milk Producers' Association was organized in 1886; while the United Milk Producers' Association was formed by dairymen to supply the Philadelphia market in 1887.[12] By 1896, the practice of collective bargaining through milk producers' associations had become fairly well established at a number of principal markets, although the principle was not completely recognized as a right of agricultural producers until the Capper-Volstead Act was passed in 1922.[13]

The Farmers' Elevator Struggle

As the railroads began to extend their lines into the heavy grain-producing areas tributary to Chicago, Milwaukee, and St. Louis, the cumbersome and expensive method of handling grain in sacks rapidly yielded to bulk handling through local and terminal elevators. This facilitated the movement of a large volume of grain within a short period following the harvest, and encouraged rapid sale by farmers who were hard pressed for cash and who, moreover, had no adequate facilities for storage at home.

The development of local elevators was accelerated by the railroads who were anxious to increase tonnage hauled on their lines. In general, the railroads built the elevators and leased them to individual operators. In other cases, they encouraged the building of privately owned elevators by providing at a nominal charge sites along their rights of way and by giving exclusive privileges, special rates, or rebates on shipments.[14]

At the terminal markets, storage was controlled by a few large operators who worked closely with the railroads. In 1869, all of the elevators in Milwaukee were controlled by one man while in 1872, "eight men working together controlled all the storage in Chicago." Out of these conditions, networks of specially favored wheat buying "rings" or syndicates began to develop which were soon able to smother effectively any competition in local markets.[15]

The collusion of the railroads, the elevator interests, and grain-buying combinations placed the farmers in an intolerable position. The Grange was the voice of their protest, which expressed itself in demands for the state regulation of the grain trade, the divorcement of railroads from elevator holdings, and in the establishment of farmers' elevators.

The first Iowa movement. In Iowa, the first cooperative elevator to be formed in the face of this almost insuperable opposition was started at Blairstown in 1867 or 1868. This was followed by the organization of the "Farmers' Union Elevator" at Brooklyn in 1869 and the St. Angstar Protective Association in 1871.

From 1872 on, the Granger influence was evidenced by the title "Patrons' Joint Stock Company" which began to appear at this time. This first movement reached its high-water mark in 1874 with 14 elevators formed. A total of 42 associations were started in Iowa during the decade. Practically all of these early elevators were organized as stock companies with farmers as members. However, they were cooperative in intention and to a large extent they operated as cooperatives.[16]

With the weakening of the Granger movement in 1875, most of these elevators went out of existence for they were unable to meet the competition of the more strongly financed and better managed commercial elevators favored by the terminal elevators and railroads.[17] Furthermore, as marketing conditions improved after the panic of 1873, there was less pressure for such elevators.

While none of the first Iowa elevators lived for more than a few years, not all of this effort was wasted for "it was a valuable first lesson showing the farmers what could be accomplished when they did pull together." The experience also emphasized "that a very definite and efficient business organization was needed to produce results."[18]

The attack on line elevator domination. The next wave of interest in cooperative elevators came in the middle 1880's as a protest against the exactions of the "line elevators" which had become dominant since the first line of elevators was formed in 1873. The line elevators combined the operating advantages of large-scale organization with those of ruthless power. They were able to obtain special concessions from railroad and terminal handling agencies, and were able to buy off any serious competition that might arise.[19]

The line elevators were natural descendants of the "wheat rings." As the railroads divested themselves of elevator holdings these were acquired by strong individuals or firms, who then used their power to obtain control of other elevators.[20]

From 1876 to 1885, the development of line elevators in Minnesota fostered by the Minneapolis Millers' Association, supplemented the control which its members had through line elevators by means of contracts with other elevators. According to one authority, "no marketing organization in Minnesota has ever been so widely and so persistently considered a monopoly as the Millers' Association.[21]

Farmers were naturally embittered by the control over their industry, and this caused them in the early 1880's to turn for protection to the Farmers' Alliance which was beginning to take form in Iowa and Minnesota. At first the Alliance had little influence, but by 1885 it had become an effective reform movement. This led the Alliance to sponsor legislative acts in Minnesota and other states designed to eliminate railroad discrimination and free the terminal markets from the domination of the elevator interests. While these acts did not entirely correct the situation, they did achieve a significant improvement. As Miss Larson has observed:

> The reform movement which started in 1885 . . . accomplished considerable that has been of great importance in the Minnesota wheat trade. The distinctly laissez faire attitude of the state was changed to a comprehensive policy of supervision and interference.[22]

Finding, however, that legislative action was powerless to bring about improvement in local markets dominated by the line elevators, Minnesota farmers began again in 1885 to form cooperative elevators. "Its coming at that time must be attributed largely to the railroad act of that year, which required impartial granting of elevator sites."[23] Six elevators were established in 1885, five in 1886, one in 1887, and one in 1888. Most of these elevators were Alliance supported, and, in general, they were small concerns—often only flat warehouses—with capacities of from 3,500 to 30,000 bushels. Each member had one vote regardless of share holdings, and no dividends were declared.[24]

While these elevators had little direct influence, they were the harbingers of a permanent cooperative elevator movement, which began to gather real strength about 1889.

The increased interest in cooperative elevators at that time, which extended into the Dakotas, was marked by a new philosophy which held that farmers should also establish elevators in terminal markets. The first project of this type was a Dakota concern, the Scandinavian Farmers' Elevator Syndicate. Although not strictly a farmers' company, it was accepted by the National Alliance as a successful type of farmers' organization. Unable to obtain membership in the Minneapolis Chamber of Commerce and actively opposed by the elevators, it soon collapsed.

A more ambitious organization was the Alliance Elevator Company started by Red River farmers in 1890. It planned to secure a capital of $2 million, to build terminal warehouses at Minneapolis and Duluth and to establish lines of locals. Although an elevator was secured at Minneapolis, it failed within the year due to incompetent management and the boycott of the established trade. Another organization of the same type was the Northwestern Farmers' Protective Association which "secured small elevators at West Superior and Duluth, and had a few local cooperatives as members." The most successful was, however, the Grain Growers' Association, which placed its emphasis on the building of local elevators as a basis for later terminal operation. These early attempts at terminal operation all proved abortive, primarily because they lacked the support of strong, well-established local organizations.[25] The answer to this problem was to come from Iowa.

The second Iowa movement. While the second cooperative elevator movement in Iowa was less spectacular in conception than that of Minnesota, it was to have more permanent influence. As recorded by Nourse, the second elevator movement spread very slowly from two or three points of origin in north central and northwestern Iowa. New companies learned methods of organization and operation from the elevators already established in nearby towns, and the whole group fought its way against determined opposition of the line and independent companies.[26]

While many of these early elevators failed within a few years, several attained permanent status: Marcus in 1887, Rockwell in 1889, Rockford in 1891, and Park Valley in 1892. The problem of the cooperative elevator in "combatting a powerful organization of private grain interests already in possession of the field,"[27] was formidable, and it is doubtful whether the effort would have succeeded had it not been for the invention of an ingenious device—"the maintenance clause," described by Nourse as follows: "The idea back of the maintenance clause is simply that if farmers set up an elevator company of their own, they must definitely bind themselves to support it."[28]

The way in which this device was discovered and applied makes one of the most interesting chapters in the history of American cooperation.[29]

On the day that the Rockwell Cooperative Society opened its doors for business in April 1889, "it began buying wheat at 4 cents per bushel above the previous local quotations and selling coal at $2 less per ton and lumber at $5 less per thousand feet." Whereupon, "the private elevator (a member of a line concern) immediately raised its grain price 3 cents above the farmers' elevator price." This tactic of over-bidding a cooperative elevator until it had drained away its supporting membership began immediately to wean members away from their own elevators and it "looked as though the new company might suffer swift eclipse."[30]

After struggling for a year to meet this worsening situation, Norman Densmore, the president, proposed a by-law providing that the members should pay a fixed charge per bushel on all grain sold, whether thru their own company or to others. This charge was to go for the maintenance of their own elevator to give them a fair market outlet when others might not be quoting such favorable prices. The by-law "decreed that a member failing to pay an outside commission within thirty days was to be notified by the board; and, if at the expiration of sixty days, such commission were still unpaid, there would be issued a second notice that carried with it suspension of said member from the benefits of member-ship until such commission was paid."

The success of this measure, after its enactment on June 7, 1890, was immediate, for the maintenance clause (then commonly called the penalty clause), "baffled the wisdom of those whose self-interest had caused them to overbid the market, until they had demoralized the trade and exhausted the funds of those farmers' organizations which had hitherto attempted to establish themselves in the local grain trade."[31] But victory did not come without a struggle. As Refsell has written:

> With the untried penalty clause as the only weapon upon which they could rely, the farmers of Rockwell entered the fight against the line com-panies. The latter tried their old method of outbidding the farmers' company. This, however, did not bring about the ruin of the company as it had done in previous instances. Other plans were also tried, but proved to be equally unavailing. The competition continued as fiercely as ever until finally the

ingenuity of the line elevator companies was exhausted and they abandoned the struggle in despair. The fight had been so severe, however, that it was only the extraordinary determination of the farmers, and their willingness to impose upon themselves a sufficient tax, in the form of the penalty mentioned above, to support their own organization, which permitted the farmers' elevator company to live through its struggle. One observer has described the incident in the following words: "There in Rockwell, a little village of less than five hundred souls, was waged one of the fiercest commercial battles ever fought on American soil, every trick of trade known to the modern political jackal and commercial bandit was tried and failed, and a final and complete victory won by the farmers of Cerro Gordo County."[32]

Within a short period this by-law was copied by many of the other farmers' elevators in the state, and, by 1900, it had become standard for farmers' elevators in Illinois and other nearby states. The Rockwell elevator thus was of particular significance as a cooperative model, since like the Rochdale Society of England, it was soon able to show remarkable achievements.[33] With good management it was able to issue $10 dividend certificates by March 2, 1892, and by the tenth year its grain and side-line supply business reached $365,740.[34]

The Rockwell Society, and most of the other farmers' elevators of this period, were stock companies. As such they were generally cooperative in conception, and controlled by farmers through the one-member, one-vote principle. While the distribution of savings according to patronage was increasing, this had not yet become widespread.[35]

The Emergence of Fruit and Vegetable Marketing Associations

Cooperative marketing of fruits has grown naturally with the growth of commercial fruit production. Perhaps this is explained by the fact that fruit industry was characterized by local over-expansion and periods of glutted markets, which caused farmers to see the advantages of joint action in finding markets, in methods of sale, and in community standardization of product. At any rate there are many early instances of cooperative marketing of such products which seem to have arisen out of the needs of growers for improvement of their local marketing conditions, rather than from any outside pressure of a general farmers' organization.

The first cooperative fruit and vegetable marketing association of record was the Fruit Growers' Union formed at Hammonton, New Jersey, in 1867. Little is known of this organization during its first 17 years of existence. Apparently it was "better than nothing ... as it brought the farmers together at least once a year, and helped somewhat in marketing facilities, and to some extent in buying heavy supplies in bulk."[36]

Then, in 1884, it was reorganized and incorporated as the Fruit Growers' Union and Cooperative Society, Ltd. Its certificate of association declared that, "The objects of this society shall be to arrange the methods for shipping and selling fruit and other products of the soil, and to protect the interests of shippers; to conduct a store for the sale of general merchandise, to its members and others."

Capital stock was set at $50,000 divided into 10,000 shares with a par value of $5.00. Any person "satisfactory to the officers" could "become a member by paying an entrance fee of one dollar, subscribing for one or more shares of stock, and agreeing to the provisions of this certificate and the bylaws of this society." After providing for payment of annual interest at the rate of 6 per cent on stock, and a contingent fund equal to 5 per cent of net savings, dividends were to be "paid to members and purchasers . . . provided that purchasers who are not members shall receive one-half the rate of dividend paid to members." Stock could be issued to members "in payment of any dividend made from profits accruing from shipments or sales of fruit or produce." These provisions show the influence of Rochdale thinking as then spread by the Granger movement.

Rather comprehensive information on this association is available for the period from 1885 through 1890. During these six years, the number of members grew from 233 to 519; net assets from $8,454 to $36,034; and total savings from $712 to $11,430. The business operations were carried on through two departments (1) the shipping, or marketing department, and (2) the store department which undertook "to carry all lines of goods." Of special interest here is the shipping department which in 1891 was "supported by a three-tenths per cent rebate paid it by the produce merchants out of their 10 per cent commission on sales." During the shipping season the department employed "two clerks, five loaders, and six dispatch-carriers."[37]

The general weaknesses which were to bring about the society's downfall in 1897 were diagnosed as follows by Myrick:

> The people and locality are not specially adapted to co-operation. There is not as much social intercourse among these people as is common in many other places. The farmers are mostly intelligent, but not extraordinarily so . . . The weakest point in the whole affair is the growing dependence upon the manager, who is constantly overworked . . . While the books are well kept, an unsparing audit is specially necessary in a country society to maintain the *esprit de corps* and strict adherence to best business principles . . . To this may be added the dangers of the credit allowed. No institution can be perfect, and aside from these points there is little to criticize.[38]

A number of somewhat similar fruit and vegetable marketing associations were formed in the 1870's and 1880's in various parts of the country. Of these—other than those in California which are discussed in the next section—the most significant were: (1) the New Jersey Cranberry Growers Association; (2) the Delaware Fruit Exchange; (3) the Chautauqua-Erie Grape Cooperatives; (4) the Florida Fruit Exchange.[39]

1. The New Jersey Cranberry Growers Association was organized in 1872 "to aid the growers in obtaining crop and market information . . . and to enlarge the markets at home and abroad . . . The association adopted standard packages (and) made a shipment of cranberries to England accompanied with directions for cooking." In 1895, the Jersey growers joined with some Massachusetts growers to form the Growers Cranberry Company, and about the same time some Massachusetts growers organized the Cape Cod Cranberry Sales Company. These early experiments eventually led to the American Cranberry Exchange formed in 1911.[40]

2. The Delaware Fruit Exchange was organized in 1881, with headquarters at Wyoming, the heart of the peach region. In 1891, Myrick looked upon this organization as a model for similar enterprises:

> The Delaware Fruit Exchange shows what can be done in this single line. Until its advent, growers shipped their peaches to the large markets to be sold on commission. The result was that frequently the markets were glutted and the prices received did not cover the cost of transportation, baskets and sellers commission. The prices were very uneven, there was great loss in failure to return packages, and the profits were largely consumed by the commission merchants' charges.[41]

3. The earliest cooperative effort in the Chautauqua-Erie Grape Belt of New York occurred in 1880 when a number of growers started joint shipments on consignment to Philadelphia. This led to the formation of the Chautauqua Grape Growers Shipping Association in the winter of 1885-86.[42] This Association started operations in 1886 with 180 members, and shipped in that year 103 cars. The following year the by-laws were tightened and a trademark was adapted. As the main revenue came from rebates received from railroads, then not considered illegal, "it was provided that any grower who failed to ship all his grapes through the association should thereby forfeit his share in this rebate fund, as it was called."[43] At the start of the third year another reorganization provided for representation on the board of directors for growers who had joined the association from other townships. Also a membership fee of one dollar was required with a charge of 1 cent per basket. Shipments were to be pooled every three days and returns made on the basis of the

average price received for the pool. However, after one year's trial the pooling agreement was abandoned.[44]

The Association continued until 1891 when it was disbanded "to make way for the first attempt at complete belt-wide cooperation," which followed with the formation of the Chautauqua and North East Grape Association in early 1892. By that time, several other shipping associations had been formed on the pattern of the pioneer association, and it was deemed desirable to co-ordinate them in one organization so as to have "monopoly power." Its objectives as stated in its articles of incorporation were as follows:

> to supply a uniform grade of fruit at prices that shall afford the greatest possible profit to the grower; to sell on track as much, and consign as little fruit as possible; to induce the railroads to grant a lower classification and more reasonable freight rates on grapes, and to adopt some plan whereby cars shall be guarded or else sealed more effectively to prevent theft in transit; if other similar unions are formed in other grape sections, to act in conjunction with them; *to divide and classify the whole territory of the United States so that overloading of the markets may be prevented and each section secure fruit according to its requirments.*[45]

The Chautauqua and North East Grape Association was incorporated with a capital stock of $10,000, with shares of $5.00 which could be sold only to *bona fide* growers on the basis of not more than one share for every 16 acres. The actual control of the organization was highly centralized under a general manager, with branch managers at shipping points. A written membership contract required the grower to ship all his Concord grapes through the Association, and provided that a penalty of one cent a basket for the grower's crop should be paid in the event of its violation.

The Association during its first season held contracts with 2,000 growers and shipped 1,841 cars of grapes, or about 72 per cent of all shipments for the area. The third year a disgruntled group formed a separate association, and shipments declined to 1,131 cars or about 30 per cent of the total shipments. Having failed "in its avowed aim of controlling the entire grape crop of the region," the Association finally dissolved in January 1895, leaving in its wake several newly formed local shipping associations. It was on the basis of this experience that a second belt-wide association was formed in 1897, the Chautauqua and Erie Grape Company. It provided for local associations to be affiliated into a central organization, and was truly cooperative although it was "forced by inadequate laws to masquerade under the guise of the ordinary stock company plan."[46] This organization continued to function until 1919 when it became the Erie Grape Growers' Cooperative Association, Inc.

4. The Florida Fruit Exchange was formed by orange growers in 1885. Five years later, the president of the organization could report:

> We have much reason to be gratified by the present position and prospects of the Exchange. Five years ago . . . the whole marketing of the products of our growers was then in the hands of commission merchants . . . The auction system in the great markets of the East, which we adopted and have since adhered to, was made the subject of violent denunciation, until experience had demonstrated the correctness of our position.[47]

In the spring of 1889, the Exchange was strengthened by the organization of an Orange Growers' Union which began shipping fruit through the Exchange, and for a number of years steady progress was made. In 1894, it started a program for central packing houses, and three were built. When the Exchange failed in 1895 it was from causes outside of its control—the heavy freezes of December 1894 and February 1895, which almost obliterated the need for a marketing agency for some 10 years.[48]

While these cooperative developments were in themselves significant, the most spectacular development of such associations was to come in California.

Beginnings of Cooperation in the California Fruit Industry

During the 1880's and 1890's, California became an experimental laboratory for cooperative techniques, and out of this experience came many of the methods which have characterized American cooperatives in the twentieth century. California was then a new country, unfettered by custom, in which commercial agriculture was rapidly expanding. Located far from eastern markets and thus easily victimized by dealers and commission agents, the goal of finding a profitable outlet for crops produced, early led growers to associated action. At first, results were slow and fumbling, then as lessons were learned a solid foundation was constructed on which later building could take place.

The California Fruit Union. The rapid development of deciduous fruit in California and the growing problem of disposing of it profitably in distant markets resulted in the formation of the California Fruit Union, with headquarters at Sacramento, in November 1885.[49] Authorized capital was fixed at $250,000 with shares of one dollar each which were to be subscribed for by fruit growers on the basis of one share per acre of bearing fruit.

Although at the outset the organizers had resisted dealer representation in the association, after one year of experience an attempt was made to harmonize interests of growers and buyers by permitting buyers to join the Union upon subscribing for 200 shares of stock. While this led to conflict within the organization, it was apparently necessary under the prevailing marketing customs and relationships of the time.[50]

Soon after the Union commenced operations it entered into a contract with one firm as its exclusive eastern sales agent, although it had been formed with the idea that it would deal with responsible fruit firms in different eastern markets. By this action the growers hoped to eliminate competition with the only "strong rival organization in the field." However, this "likewise created the fear that it would endanger the ... attempt to build up a strong growers' association because the shipping company employed as sole agent could firmly entrench itself and leave the cooperative weak."[51]

This plan not proving satisfactory, the Union in April 1887 appointed agents at various eastern centers who were "to handle no fruit not shipped through the Union." This change also was in accord with the adoption of the auction plan of sale at a number of markets following reports made by Harris Weinstock in 1886 on the desirability of this method already in use for the sale of imported oranges, and then being tried out by the Florida Fruit Exchange.[52]

The Union's plan for local membership organization is of particular interest, since it led to the formation of many local fruit growers' associations. Simply, it provided for the use of branch unions at each important shipping point. "These were not members as organizations, but rather organizations of Union stockholders located in the several localities."[53] The members of these branches elected a manager who supervised shipments and other local arrangements. In general, his salary and expenses were met "by his commissions on the box lumber, wrapping paper, nails, etc., which he furnished to the members, obtaining the same through the central union."[54]

From the standpoint of business volume, the Union had a satisfactory career prior to its retirement as a fruit shipping association in March 1894. In 1890, its out-of-state shipments had reached 68 million pounds and, by 1893, they were 160 million pounds. The decision to cease operations was partly due to the increasing California fruit production which flooded eastern markets then demoralized by business depression.[55] More fundamentally, the passing of the Union was due to its failure to live up to its original promise as a growers' association. By 1894, it had "become a little more than a glorified clearing house," and a desire was beginning to develop for a new start on entirely different lines. This led eventually to the formation of the present California Fruit Exchange (1903), although in the interim the place of the Union was partly taken by the California Fruit Growers and Shippers Association formed in February 1895, on a plan which has been credited with being "the first clearing-house in the California fresh-deciduous fruit industry."[56]

The experience of the California Fruit Union was significant in many respects. For one thing, it demonstrated that the interests of growers and shippers could not be entirely harmonized. It also showed the possibilities of large-scale organization, and taught growers many valuable lessons in marketing. Moreover, it did much to develop local associations—necessary for strong regional organization—and introduced them to the advantages of joint purchase of supplies. At least by 1896, the deciduous fruit growers of California had cut their cooperative eye-teeth.[57]

The Origins of the California Fruit Growers Exchange System

The development of the commercial citrus industry in California really got started in the 1870's following the completion of the transcontinental railroad systems which made eastern markets accessible and the introduction of the navel orange, which was found to be especially adapted to California conditions. By 1881, there were 484,227 bearing orange trees and 62,130 bearing lemon trees in the state.[58]

With the commercial development of the industry there arose a coterie of dealers who purchased and packed the growers' fruit, and then shipped it to eastern markets.

> At first the system of dealer purchase, imperfect though it was, returned profits both to the grower and dealer, but as the supply increased, business proved less remunerative and more uncertain. Also there was no understanding between the buyers as to distribution among the eastern markets, and glutting and undersupply followed .... By 1885, the shipments had increased to about 1,000 carloads and the marketing conditions had become unbearable."[59]

The first stirrings of a cooperative nature came in October 1885 when citrus growers at a meeting in Los Angeles passed a resolution which maintained "that unless some united action was taken for improved methods in the sale of their fruit, they would soon lose their homes."

This sentiment soon resulted in the organization of the Orange Growers' Protective Union of Southern California. Declaring that its cornerstone was "intelligent distribution," The Orange Growers' Protective Union proceeded to send representatives East who were to "sell, regulate and distribute and do all services as required of them . . ." On December 22, 1885, the following policy was adopted: "That it is the sense of this board of directors that the Orange Growers' Protective Union should not enter into entangling alliances with fruit dealers, but should avail themselves, when proper, of the facilities that they may have to offer, bearing in mind that the Union is one of growers and for the interests of growers."[60]

On February 12, 1886, a contract was adopted by which the grower members promised to pay to the Protective Union

> two and one-half cents upon every box of oranges or lemons which I may ship or sell, whether such shipment or sale is made by myself personally, or through the Orange Growers Protective Union, or otherwise . . . The money paid under the foregoing contract is for the purpose of funds to defray the expenses of the corporation, incurred by it in carrying out the purposes for which it was formed.[61]

For a few years the Protective Union gave beneficial results. This is shown by the report of its secretary after two years of operation:

> The work done by the Orange Growers' Protective Union of Southern California offers a good example of the benefits of co-operation as applied to fruit growing . . . Oranges for several years brought such low prices that it did not pay to produce them . . . The Union [has] shipped over 1,000 carloads, at an increased price, amounting to over one-fourth of a million dollars to the members, as well as securing saving in freight that alone paid all the expenses of the Union and returned $23 per car as a dividend to members shipping through the Union. The present year the Union adopted a resolution not to ship on commission but to sell here at home. The result has been that nearly all the oranges of members have been sold at most satisfactory prices.[62]

The failure of the Union soon after this statement was made has been attributed to many causes: lack of cooperation from growers, weaknesses in internal organization, lack of packing facilities and local organization, bitter opposition from speculative shippers.[63] Whatever the causes of failure a beginning had been made.

Other abortive attempts were made to organize the orange industry, but they were "founded on incorrect principles in that the interests of growers and packers, . . . represented in these bodies, are inherently diverse. . . . Real progress was not made until the growers realized the incompatibility of the two elements and began to operate exclusively as growers' organizations."[64] The permanent foundation of the California

Fruit Growers Exchange came from more humble origins, although these industry-wide efforts helped condition the minds of growers to the need of an effective form of large-scale organization.

It was at Pachappa, a little community near Riverside, that the exchange system began to evolve under the leadership of T. H. B. Chamblin, who has been dubbed the "father of the Exchange." Here, the Pachappa Orange Growers Association got started in the late 1880's when 11 neighbors "banded themselves together and agreed to sell their fruit in a pool."[65] For the first two years the fruit was sold to a fruit packer. Then, until the association started its own packing in 1895, fruit was packed under contract by a local packer. The membership contract in 1893 fully set forth this arrangement and the responsibilities of members.[66]

The experience of the Pachappa association soon led Chamblin, its secretary and manager, to the conclusion that the bankruptcy of the industry "could only be averted through a general organization on a cooperative pooling basis, embracing all the orange growing districts in Southern California." As a first step toward achieving this aim, Chamblin developed a plan for the organization of the Riverside district which was adopted by prominent orange growers and businessmen in April 1893. This resulted in the organization of 10 local associations, and "the first district exchange," known as the "Riverside Fruit Exchange."

Chamblin's plan had provided for the formation of local associations, which would each "establish a purely local brand without individual or company name attached, under which the fruit embraced in each Association shall be packed respectively." Packing was to be done by local associations either on contract or under their own management. Selling was to be done under a system of brokerage, and orders were to be "prorated among the Associations so as to keep the fruit moving proportionately." The proceeds of sales of fruit were "to be distributed pro rata from time to time as the management of each association may direct." To achieve the desired ends, a central office was to be established, "where all telegrams and correspondence shall be delivered, and where the said managers (of locals) shall meet daily and transact the necessary business . . ."[67]

To effectuate the plan a membership contract was approved on May 5, 1893, which contained the following important provisions:

> We, the undersigned, orange growers of Riverside, California being desirous of having our fruit handled in a manner substantially as set forth in the foregoing plan for marketing Riverside oranges, do, for such purpose, hereby severally constitute and appoint the Riverside Fruit Exchange, a corporation organized under the laws of the State of California, *our sole agent and convey*

to said corporation the entire crop of oranges that may be grown upon our respective ranches for the season 1893-94.

We and each of us hereby agree to become members of some one of the associations referred to in said paper and to be hereafter formed for the purpose of packing our said fruit upon the community plan as above outlined, and when so packed to be turned over to said corporation for the purpose above stated. We and each of us further agree that all expense incurred by said corporation in marketing said fruit shall be paid out of the proceeds of the sale of said fruit prorata according to the amount furnished by each of said associations respectively, and we each of us agree *to accept for our crops our pro rata share of the net proceeds of the sales of fruit furnished by the associations to which we may respectively belong, after deducting cost of packing, selling and other necessary expenses....* This contract to be in force when in the judgment of the board of directors of said corporation ninety per cent of the Riverside crop shall be substantially under control as outlined.[68]

While this plan was maturing, another staunch little group of growers at Claremont were coming to somewhat similar conclusions, which led them in January 1893 to form The Claremont California Fruit Growers' Association under the leadership of P. J. Dreher. This association immediately undertook to do its own packing under its own brand "Indian Hill" as it was the declared intention "to build up a reputation for its fruits by grading and shipping the very best under a special brand and the inferior fruits as second grade." The Claremont association saw the need of conducting its business "with the jobbing trade direct" and the success of this method during the first year led to its general adoption when the complete exchange system was developed.[69]

From 1890 to 1893, while the Riverside and Claremont groups were maturing their plans, the orange industry of California was passing through a period of serious depression due to a startling increase in production combined with an unsatisfactory marketing system. These were the infamous "red ink years," in California citrus history, when year end losses were more common than gains.[70]

By April 1893, with conditions unendurable throughout the southern California citrus industry, a meeting of orange growers was held in Los Angeles to develop some plan of action. The committee appointed at this meeting, recommended the formation of eight districts (along the lines of the Riverside Exchange plan) and the organization of local associations within each district, each to do its own packing under its own local brand. In addition to a central office for each district, there was to be an executive committee for southern California composed of one member for each district, which was to have charge of matters affecting all the districts. Under this plan, district and local associations were formed during the summer of 1893, prior to the formal adoption of this plan on August 29, 1893.[71]

The plan, when put into effect for the 1893-94 season, met with immediate acceptance, and by December 1894, the executive board of the exchanges "stated that the exchanges positively controlled four-fifths of the orange crop of southern California." For the 1894-95 season, it was estimated that shipments by districts "totaled 4,190 carloads, or 89.4 per cent of the actual total orange shipments for the season." However, in the following year, shipments fell to 2,574 cars, or only 36.7 per cent of the actual shipments. The decline was largely due to a reaction from over-enthusiasm, disappointment in not being able to develop an efficient system overnight, and the development of new unorganized orange-producing regions.[72]

While the district exchange system was at the height of its first popularity in the fall of 1895, Southern California Fruit Exchange was incorporated to take over the functions of the executive board, and with this change the California exchange system of marketing became reasonably well established. However, a period of testing had to take place before the California Fruit Growers Exchange system was finally perfected in 1903. (See Chapter XIII.)

The California Dried Fruit and Nut Associations

Other cooperatives were developing in California during the 1880's and 1890's while the California Fruit Growers Exchange system was taking shape. Of these, the most significant to later cooperative development, were the dried fruit associations for marketing such products as raisins, prunes, and apricots, and the nut associations. The problems in marketing such crops were similar to those which prevailed in the citrus industry. Production was increasing rapidly and the commercial marketing methods which grew up were not designed to serve the best interests of producers. Most of the production was in localized areas favorable for the operation of cooperative associations.

The earliest of these associations was the California Dried Fruit Association organized in September 1888 "to develop the dried fruit, nut, and raisin interests." It apparently gave early satisfaction, which led to the formation of a separate organization for raisin growers in 1892—the California State Raisin Growers' Association. This organization, with the support of packers and dealers, attempted to set a minimum price for raisins, but this proved unsuccessful. About this time a number of local cooperative packing houses were started, but by 1894 all but two had fallen "into the hands of the commission packers by sale or lease."[73] The permanent development of cooperation in the raisin industry did not come until the California Raisin Association was formed in 1898.

The earliest association for marketing prunes and other dried fruit in the Santa Clara Valley, then the principal area of production, was the West Side Fruit Union which started operations in the fall of 1891. "The plan accepted the principle of bringing the fruit for drying to the drying grounds of the Society, thus concentrated the fruit for shipment in car-load lots, and so performing one of the functions of the local dryer." Since it was difficult to sell the fruit of each member separately, the Union adopted a pooling plan by which his fruit was graded and a receipt given for the quantity of each grade delivered. Sales were made "as if the product [were] of one owner. At the end of the season each owner received in payment for each grade of his fruit the average price received during the season for that grade. As the season went on, and sales were made, growers received money on account as was required: final settlement was made when all was sold."[74]

The idea of pooling being new, only 17 of the 80 stockholders gave their support during the first year.[75] But the results were so encouraging "that the next year nearly one-half of the stockholders had the full courage of their convictions, and marketed through the association." With a short crop, prices went higher and "the whole Santa Clara Valley went wild over the profits of the prune business and the profits of cooperation."[76]

In the spring of 1892, a mass meeting of fruit growers instituted a committee to effect an organization for the entire district tributary to San Jose. This resulted in the organization of the Santa Clara County Fruit Exchange, which opened in May 1893 with five member cooperative associations, and a "substantial warehouse" at San Jose. For a few years the plan worked well but the independence of the local associations precluded consolidation of efforts. The problem was not to be solved until 1916 when the California Prune and Apricot Growers, Inc., was established.

Another of the early California cooperatives was the Los Nietos and Ranchita Walnut-growers Association, organized in 1887, by about 20 walnut growers in Los Angeles County. For a considerable period it was the sole society of this type, but with increasing production others were formed until by 1898 nearly all growers belonged to one of seven associations, as yet not federated. In 1905 these associations were joined together in a central organization called the Executive Committee of Southern California Walnut Associations. The original society by 1898 had 220 members who shipped over 200 cars of walnuts.[77]

The Significance of California Experience

By 1896, California farmers—by trial and error—had established a pattern of cooperative action that was to be more fully developed in the next two decades, and extended throughout the United States.[78] To the California farmer, cooperation was a means to an end. His problem was one of finding profitable outlets for his crops grown in specialized producing areas. To meet this problem joint action by large groups of farmers was essential. In cooperation he found and developed a method by which the growers of an entire area, far distant from markets, could be so organized as to achieve the advantages of large-scale management in the marketing of their specialized crops, while preserving their independence as individual producers.

In fashioning his cooperative associations, the California farmer developed what may be called a membership philosophy. He saw himself as a member of an economic organization representing his complete interest rather than as a stockholder in a jointly conducted enterprise. The cooperative became an extension of his farm—his exclusive marketing agency.

Looking upon cooperation as a part of his business, the California farmer sought to attract the most competent managers as a means of obtaining the maximum in efficient service. While in other areas, cooperative managers were recompensed largely by satisfactions from serving a worthy cause, in California it was early established that an adequate salary was essential to efficient managerial service.[79]

In approaching cooperation as a form of business, the California cooperators likewise made many contributions in cooperative techniques —such as in membership agreements, pooling, and federation. By proving that this approach yielded economic benefits to members, cooperation was directed toward efficiency as a goal of performance.

Livestock and Cotton Developments

While the richest veins of cooperative experience during this period are found in the dairy, grain, and fruit industries, there were other significant developments related to livestock and cotton.

Livestock. In Chapter III, reference was made to the formation in 1889 of the American Livestock Commission Company under the joint sponsorship of the Farmers Alliance and the Grange. An earlier instance not tied to a general farm organization, the Goodlettsville, Tennessee, Lamb Club, was organized in 1877 to enable growers to market their lamb crop. This association started to function on an auction basis, but this was supplemented by joint shipments when local auction prices were unsatisfactory.[80]

Another early association which continued to function for many years was the Farmers Shipping Association of Superior, Nebraska, formed in 1882, as a protest against the wide margins taken by the local buyers, and the custom of "lumping off" stock without weighing it. Many obstacles failed to stop this organization—difficulty in getting cars from the railroads or use of scales, and price bribes offered members—and eventually it became the only shipper in the field. A number of similar cooperative shipping associations were formed in Kansas, Iowa, and other states prior to 1896, sometimes with and sometimes independently of Farmers' Alliance or similar organization support.[81]

Cotton marketing. The Civil War left the cotton growers of the South impoverished and tied to a credit system that restricted their freedom in marketing. This made the cotton farmers receptive to any program that promised to improve their economic condition.

The earliest cooperative cotton program came from the Grange in 1873 when state Granges of Alabama and Mississippi arranged to deal with established agents. The Alabama State Grange had an agent in New York City, while the Mississippi State Grange had one in Liverpool. "Grange activities in those two states involved concentrating cotton in leased warehouses, financing shipments, and grading as well as actual selling."[82] However, little was heard of these operations after 1875. The cotton marketing program of the Texas Cooperative Association proved more effective during the middle 1880's but was of no permanent importance. An even more ambitious cotton program was advanced by the National Farmers' Alliance following the experience of the Texas Alliance State Exchange in 1887 and 1888 and for several years a considerable amount of cotton was marketed through state Alliance exchanges or state agents.[83] As in the case of the Grange, these efforts likewise had little permanent cooperative significance, although they apparently brought immediate benefits to members and had some influence in temporarily bettering commercial marketing practices.

The problem of cotton producers was one of steadily increasing supply with almost constantly declining prices. Any marketing program which could not control supply could thus not give permanent satisfaction. The growers themselves vaguely realized this and in 1879 a group formed the Mississippi Valley Cotton Planters' Association which for some three years promoted remedial measures including crop reduction. In the 1890's, a somewhat similar organization, the Southern

Cotton Growers Association, promoted the raising of cotton prices by a reduction of acreage.

Such mass efforts to control the one-crop cotton economy through reduction of supply were to be given new life by the Southern Cotton Growers Protective Association and the Farmers' Union in the first decade of the next century, and by the commodity marketing philosophy which became prevalent throughout the South about 1920.

Early Independent Cooperative Purchasing Efforts

Most of the cooperative purchasing by farmers during the period from 1860 to 1896 has been described in connection with the Grangers and Farmers' Alliance movements. There were, however, some independent developments which should be briefly described.

The earliest association of this type was formed on December 25, 1863, at Riverhead, New York, as a farmers' club. In 1866, the society was incorporated as the Riverhead Town Agricultural Society, and, in 1868 or 1869, a purchasing agent was elected to purchase Peruvian guano for the club. Each farmer who wished to purchase paid cash, and the agent then chartered a vessel to bring guano from New York to the Jamesport wharf. The agent's commission was 1.5 per cent. For a few years after 1872 the society was replaced by a Grange, but following this period it continued to operate for many years. In 1887, the society adopted its own fertilizer formula and got bids from fertilizer companies for its manufacture. This is the earliest known instance of specification buying by a cooperative. At one time sales reached 2,100 tons.[84]

Most of the cooperative purchasing carried on independently of the Grange and Alliance movements grew up as a "side-line" activity of cooperative marketing organizations. In fact, the term "side-line" does not adequately convey the significance of such operations in many of the early associations, for as L. S. Tenney remarked at the American Institute of Cooperation in 1925, "Many . . . were held together through adding the function of cooperative buying."[85] This increased the services rendered by the association while it reduced costs for capital and management. In some cases, as we have seen for the Fruit Growers' Union and Co-operative Society, the "side-line" purchasing activity was carried on as a separate department. The store of this society in 1890 was "a splendid three-story structure" designed for the sale of feed, hay, agricultural implements, wooden ware, harness, groceries, clothing and similar items.[86]

The store sold "at fair retail prices" after a period of "savage" price cutting which reduced dividends to 6 per cent. Patrons were given a slip containing the names, prices, and amounts of the articles purchased as a basis for dividend payments. "In a dividend book are posted up the monthly totals of the purchasers' slips, the quarterly dividend on which is credited on his account if he owes, or otherwise paid in cash."[87]

In general, the purchasing operations of marketing associations were confined to items needed in farm production. The cooperative elevators, fruit associations, and creameries early found that these bulk supplies could easily be handled in connection with marketing operations. In this regard, the pioneer experience of the Rockwell Cooperative Society of Iowa is of special interest.

Soon after the Rockwell Cooperative was started in 1891, it began to handle farm machinery on a 2 per cent margin to members and a 10 per cent margin to non-members. This led to so much dissention that after a few years it was discontinued. Of more significance was the incursion into lumber and coal operations. In 1893, the lumber and coal business in that area was highly controlled by two chains of lumber yards which divided territory by each taking alternate towns. In this way they were able to keep out competition by setting local prices at different levels. To keep out competition, prices were fixed so low at Rockwell that farmers from Mason City came there to buy. The members of the Rockwell Society, fully aware of the way in which this system was worked to the disadvantage of farmers, decided to boycott the "chains" yard at any price, and, in 1893, started their own yard. The battle between the two yards continued until finally—some 10 years later—the cooperative bought out its competitor and "built a fine, large lumber shed on the site of this battle for cooperation." Besides lumber and coal, the Society during its early years also handled coffee, sugar, paint, and oil which could be carried in the office and store room.[88]

Aside from the side-line purchasing carried on for members by marketing associations there was in 1896 little specialized farm supply purchasing, except through a few state Grange business agents who bought certain bulk supplies for local groups of grangers. We shall see in later discussions that it was only when farmers began to purchase larger quantities of specialized supplies for their farming operations that the need and opportunity for separate cooperative purchasing associations became apparent.

The Spread of Mutual Irrigation Associations

With the agricultural development of the arid West, cooperative irrigation associations continued steadily to increase in number and importance. In 1860, mutual irrigation associations had been limited to a number of informal associations in Utah and a few in California. By the end of the century, there were at least 1,218 associations rendering service throughout the western states.[89]

With the expansion of irrigation, the early informal associations were gradually replaced by incorporated companies of water users. In Utah, for example, "the growing independence of individual members of irrigation communities led to various reasons for the desirability of incorporation. One of the most impelling reasons was the need for a quick, simple method of enforcing collection of assessments. The sale of capital stock on which the assessment was delinquent provided such a remedy." The way in which incorporation grew is shown by the following statement:

> Between 1865 and 1880 most of the organizing that took place was under the irrigation district act, which had been designated as "an act to incorporate irrigation companies." Prior to 1880 a few companies were incorporated under the general incorporation act of 1870, but it was not until the water law of 1880 called attention to the fact that companies might incorporate for irrigation purposes that the organization of such corporations really began. In the 80's and 90's many of the canals that had been controlled by informal associations and irrigation districts passed to the corporation plan, and the trend has continued to the present time.[90]

The importance of irrigation and the desire to free it of private domination even before 1870 impelled California farmers to "promote a general irrigation law which would establish public rights and abolish private wrongs." This led in 1887 to the Wright Irrigation District Law which was designed "to enable a certain number of those owning dry land to act together and force others to take part with them in a community organization which would be empowered to acquire water, construct irrigation works and assess the cost of all the property benefited.[91] While legal obstruction kept this law from being effectively applied prior to 1897, such water districts of a semi-cooperative character have since become an important part of community irrigation organization in California and in other states.[92]

During this period while the district form of organization was being promoted—and contested in the courts—there was a significant growth in the number of mutual irrigation associations which were operated on true cooperative lines, not only in California but also in the other western states. This growth was to serve as the basis for a much more extensive development after 1900.

The Expansion of Farmers' Mutual Fire
Insurance Companies

Well rooted by 1860, farmers' mutual fire insurance companies continued to expand in numbers and significance with the westward extension of agriculture. By the end of the century there were at least 1,400 associations of this type serving farmers in some 40 states.[93]

While many of the farmers' mutual fire insurance associations formed prior to 1896 were promoted in connection with the Grange and Farmers' Alliance movements, the great majority were organized by independent groups of farmers to meet specific local needs. Of importance was the encouragement given by special state laws.[94] As early as 1857, the state of New York recognized these associations by placing "upon its statute books a separate chapter authorizing the organization and prescribing the method of operation of farmers' mutual fire insurance companies. In the 20 or 30 years following the enactment of this law in New York, many other states enacted [somewhat similar laws]."[95]

Another factor, which accounted for much of the progress in the last two decades of the century, was the formation of state associations of farm mutuals. By 1900, such state associations had been formed in 17 states from New York to Kansas.[96]

Status of Agricultural Cooperatives in 1896

In this chapter we have traced the growth of cooperation as an independent self-help business movement among farmers. By 1896, such business cooperation was well established. Although many of the cooperatives formed since 1860 were no longer in existence, there was a considerable number of healthy associations which were steadily growing in strength. In the dairy industry, cooperative creameries and cheese plants were widespread and fluid milk bargaining associations were growing in importance. Cooperative elevators—after a 30-year struggle—were at last rooted by the maintenance clause. Fruit marketing associations, particularly in California, had found effective forms of organization which were attaining an increasing degree of growers' support. While less progress had been made by livestock producers, they also were finding how cooperative shipping associations and terminal sales agencies could be used for their protection in marketing. In 1896, cooperative purchasing was less popular than cooperative marketing—partly due to disillusionment from the hasty expansion forced by the Grange and the Alliance, and partly due to the awakening of farmers to their marketing problems. While the number of cooperative stores and specialized supply purchasing cooperatives was not large, experience was being gained, particularly in bulk purchasing of farm supplies as a side activity of marketing associations. More progress had been made by mutual irrigation companies and farmers' mutual fire insurance companies, which were then widespread and steadily growing in number and business efficiency.

While much of this cooperative development was sporadic and unrelated, cooperation as a form of business organization, adapted to the needs of farmers, had to a considerable extent become articulate. This was apparent in the growing use of the corporation form of organization, and in the embryonic development of distinctive business practices adapted to the needs of cooperative business operation such as pooling, patronage refunds, and membership agreements. Increasing emphasis was being placed on management, accounting, and membership administration. Moreover, agricultural cooperation was becoming recognized legally as a method of business organization by state cooperative laws and court decisions.[97]

Part Two

FORMATIVE FORCES

In Part One we traced the growth of cooperative enterprise in the United States from the Pilgrim fathers to 1896. We saw how cooperative organization naturally arose as a method through which individuals made mutual adjustments to meet various kinds of economic needs. As other forms of business organization became more complex, we found that the cooperative form of enterprise also took on a more formal character, especially in agriculture.

We now come to an examination of how cooperatives evolved to meet the many new economic and social problems that arose during the period from 1897 to 1920. During these 24 years, the pattern for modern cooperative enterprise was largely made. The dominant area of development was in agriculture which then had a much larger place in the economy than it has today. In fact, agriculture provided a laboratory for the testing of cooperative ideas and methods that could then be adapted to other parts of the economy. The character of cooperative development in other areas was thus molded largely on the lessons learned by cooperatives in serving farmers and rural people.

To understand better this dynamic situation we will consider in Part Two the new institutions and other forces that were giving encouragement and direction to cooperative growth.

Chapter V

THE INFLUENCE OF
NEW RURAL FORCES

The period from 1897 to 1920 witnessed a revolutionary change in the character of the farming industry and in the relationship of agriculture to the economy as a whole. This change was the result of a combination of interacting forces. Their nature and the way in which they contributed support to the emerging cooperative movement will be discussed in this chapter.

Basic Economic and Technical Changes

During the period under review, the long transformation of American agriculture from "a simple, pioneer, and largely self-sufficing occupation into a modern business organized on a scientific, capitalistic, and commercial basis" was largely completed.[1] The interrelated factors—economic, technical, and social—which together brought about this fundamental change in the character of the agricultural industry, are briefly examined here from the standpoint of their effect on the growth of cooperative enterprises.

The closing of the frontier. "Up to the end of the nineteenth century we were still in the stages of exploitative development of a rapidly expanding—not to say overexpanded—land domain."[2] With the closing of the frontier—officially recognized by the Census in 1890— there was a shift toward more intensive farming. To express this in a slightly different way, with the wide open plains largely filled, attention was forced on methods of best utilizing land already in farms. This gave a new stability to the farm population, for it was no longer so easy to pull up stakes and go West. To make a success of farming it was now necessary to improve farming efficiency on available land. The greater stability of farming in turn encouraged the growth of cooperative enterprise, for cooperation is both a social and economic form of organization, dependent upon community stability.

With land limited, the application of capital to agricultural production steadily increased. This took the form of increasing expenditures for farm machinery and equipment and for such farm production supplies as fertilizer, insecticides, seed, and feed. Up to 1896, the farmers' annual bill for supplies used in production was relatively unimportant. By 1920, the supply bill had come to represent about 25 per cent of gross farming receipts. As the bill for farm supplies increased, farmers naturally turned to cooperative purchasing as a means of decreasing this cost.

The upswing in prices. The changeover from extensive to intensive farming was fortunately lubricated by a change which occurred about this time in basic economic conditions.

The period from 1873 to 1896 was marked by a general decline in the level of prices. Starting in 1897, the price level began a long upward climb which did not come to a full stop until the postwar crash of 1920.[3] While in the period from 1865 to 1896, the decline in the prices of farm products roughly paralleled the general price decline, from 1897 to 1920 the prices of farm products went up a bit more rapidly than other prices. Thus, in these years, the purchasing power of farm products increased slightly as the prices of farm products rose.[4]

During much of this period, the output of farm production was expanding to meet the needs of a growing urban population and a strong demand from Europe, while unit costs of farm production were declining due to better farm management with improved farm machinery. Likewise farmers were benefited by more favorable freight rates resulting from the increasing competition among carriers which were growing in efficiency.

Expanding production, with more favorable prices, infused a new spirit into farm life. The deep pessimism which had pervaded agricultural circles during the 1880's and early 1890's gave way to confidence. The growing feeling of agricultural well-being was perhaps best expressed in the later reports of Secretary Wilson. In 1912 he said:

> Most productive of all agricultural years in this country has been 1912. The earth has produced its greatest annual dividend. The prices at the farm are generally profitable, and will continue the prosperity that farmers have enjoyed for years ... During the last 16 years the farmer has steadily increased his wealth production year by year, with the exception of 1911 ... If the wealth produced on farms in 1899 be regarded as 100, the wealth produced 16 years ago, or in 1896, is represented by 84, and the wealth produced in 1912 by 202.1.[5]

With the improvement in farmers' income there came a great rise in rural living standards. For the first time in their lives farmers were able to do many things that had been denied them before. They were able to build and equip better homes and improve their farm facilities. They were in increasing numbers able to send their boys and girls to college. They were able to support better roads and better schools and buy more books, newspapers, and magazines. All of these things altered rural social attitudes and made farmers appreciative of higher living standards. This new sentiment had a definite stimulating effect upon measures that would sustain and expand the prosperity being enjoyed, and thus it served as a promotive force for agricultural cooperation.[6]

The expansion of business combinations. Another economic factor that greatly encouraged the expansion of cooperation was the rapid increase in the number and power of business combinations of all types following the improvement of business conditions in 1897.[7]

Confronted by large corporate organizations on every side, farmers increasingly became convinced that their own economic salvation was dependent upon their ability to develop counter forms of organization adapted to their own requirements. This desire to emulate the power of the big business corporation and obtain for themselves the advantages of large-scale organization and operation while preserving their economic and social independence was thus a powerful factor favorable to the development of cooperative organizations.[8]

The growth of urban markets. As the nation became more and more industrial in character, the proportion of the population living in the cities steadily increased. The extent of this change is shown by the fact that the percentage of the population living in places of 8,000 or more increased from 32.9 in 1900 to 43.8 in 1920, the number of such places increasing during these 20 years from 547 to 924. The rural population, including places with a population of less than 2,500, fell from 60.0 per cent of the total population in 1900 to 48.6 per cent in 1920.

The trend toward urbanization made farmers increasingly dependent upon commercial marketing agencies, unless they were to perform this service for themselves cooperatively. As farmers studied their marketing problems with these two alternatives in view, they became more and more convinced that they could obtain more efficient services through their own agencies. Thus the intensification of the farmers' marketing problem brought about by greater urbanization caused them to turn increasingly to cooperative marketing methods.

The great immigrant influx. The millions of immigrants of various nationalities who came to this country in the period from 1880 to 1910 had a marked influence on the social character of our rural population which was reflected in the cooperative movement. Although many immigrants found employment in industrial and commercial occupations, a large number settled on farms.

In their problems of adjustment to their new environment, the immigrants tended to settle in nationality blocs known as "colonies." Thus, by 1900, there were German, Russian, Scandinavian, Italian, Portuguese, and similar colonies scattered throughout most of the United States. With a high degree of racial, lingual, and religious cohesion, these groups naturally formed simple cooperative organizations for procuring supplies, for marketing their products, or for meeting similar problems.[9] Moreover, many of these immigrants, especially those from the Scandinavian countries who settled in large numbers in Minnesota and adjoining states, brought with them experience in cooperative organization that was quickly applied to the conditions of their new environment.[10]

Altogether, this injection of immigrants into our rural population greatly stimulated the adoption of cooperation. Moreover, as the clanishness of the immigrant groups gradually diminished with the process of Americanization, a heritage of cooperative methods was carried over into the rural community as a whole.

The coming of power farming. In 1897, agriculture was largely dependent upon the horse for power. The gas engine was coming into use for automobiles, but few were used by farmers before 1912 when the Model-T began to come on the market in quantity and at a reasonable price.[11]

Rapid technological improvements in automobile engines greatly encouraged the development of stationary gas engines which could be used on farms as a source of power for all kinds of farm work—in turning grindstones, in running washing machines, in operating hay forks, in lighting buildings, and similar ways. From 1910 to 1920, many thousands of gasoline or stationary gasoline engines were put to such uses on farms, increasing the efficiency of farm operations while reducing the drudgery and loneliness of farm living, thus giving farm families more leisure time to study their economic problems, and participate in cooperative activities. The full revolutionary effect of mechanical power in farming did not become apparent until about 1910. By then, the trend, to be nurtured by the war, had become irresistible.[12]

Progress was slow in the adoption by farmers of tractors and trucks until the war years. Then there was a rapid jump in their use with the demand for greater production coincident with a shortage of manpower. The tractor soon began to change the whole farm machinery industry. Plows, harrows, disks, and other farm implements were soon adapted to the tractor, although this development was just getting well underway by 1920. While the change in motive power was transforming the character of farm machinery, improvements were taking place in other types of equipment. The cream separator, which had become indispensable by 1900, was being steadily improved. Moreover, the milking machine was becoming a practical farm tool, and mechanical incubators were increasingly supplementing the mother hen.

The use of mechanical power in farming promoted the development of cooperative enterprise in many ways. It cut down the time of farm operations so that farmers had more time to attend meetings and to consider their economic and social problems. The use of complicated machinery also increased technical knowledge and encouraged more business-like farm thinking. By increasing output, machinery also encouraged farmers to examine the possibilities of cooperative methods for sale of farm products.

The advance in the biological sciences. Progress in the biological sciences likewise increased the productivity of farming during this period. New varieties of plants were developed or adapted to various growing conditions. Improved plant breeding techniques greatly increased yields. Methods of insect control were perfected.

Similar advances were made in livestock production. Starting about 1900 great strides were made in the science of animal breeding, while nutritional studies greatly increased feeding efficiency. Progress was also made in controlling livestock disease through tuberculin testing, tick eradication, hoof-and-mouth disease quarantines, and similar measures.

The total effect of these developments—which were quickly transmitted to farmers through the farmers' institutes, the agricultural colleges, the farm press, and similar agencies, were almost as significant as the improvements in farm machinery. They expanded the farmers' knowledge of his business and made him alert to improvement. By making possible larger yields through scientific principles, they called attention to the need and possible use of similar principles applied to the management of the farm as a whole. Moreover, in many cases, the adoption of biological improvements was dependent upon group action. For example, plant and animal breeding improvement was found to be largely dependent upon community effort. Cow-testing associations, breeding improvement associations, crop improvement associations, and similar organizations required collective as well as individual acceptance. Participation in such joint production activities disciplined farmers in cooperative action.[13]

The good roads movement. Another factor which facilitated cooperative organization was the good roads movement. As early as 1892, the U. S. Department of Agriculture had undertaken studies in road construction and maintenance. With the inauguration of rural free mail delivery service in 1896—which called attention to the primitive roads then serving farmers—such work was greatly encouraged. About this time a national crusade for better rural roads began to gather strength. As Dearing has explained:

> The rural economy was [then] restricted by eighteenth century standards of mobility in an era when the urban population was reaping the direct benefits of modernized technology and organization. There arose a national undercurrent of pressure for adjustments that would enable the rural population to share in the new ways of life emerging from industrialization. Road reform was hit upon as one of the most direct and obvious methods of achieving this objective.[14]

The pressure for better roads heightened with the widespread adoption of the automobile about 1910, and both state and national governments responded. By 1921, there were 387,457 miles of "surfaced" roads as compared with 153,330 miles in 1904, an increase of over 150 per cent.[15]

The good roads movement, plus the coming of the automobile, greatly facilitated the development of effective cooperative associations. The automobile enabled farmers to attend farm meetings and keep in close touch with each other and, along with the truck, widened the area of service available from cooperative associations. This made possible greater operating efficiency for cooperatives through an expansion of their operations.[16]

Rural free delivery. Prior to 1896, farmers were isolated by the lack of a regular mail service. In that year, rural free delivery service was begun, and within a few years, the great majority of farmers were being served regularly at their farms. It is difficult to appreciate the change that this made in the character of farm life. It brought farmers letters, newspapers, and magazines which stimulated their interest in community and national problems, and in methods of raising their standards of living. From the standpoint of cooperative organization it afforded a mechanism by which farmers could be called together to meetings and kept informed on cooperative matters. It made possible the ready dissemination of cooperative literature and thus expanded knowledge and interest in the cooperative form of enterprise.[17]

The rural telephone. Cooperative development was also favored by the telephone which began to spread in rural districts about 1895. Through the use of the telephone, farmers could be brought together on short notice on matters of mutual interest, and they could be kept informed on matters of general concern. The desire to have telephone service in itself resulted in cooperative activity. Almost spontaneously, farmers began to form telephone companies and within a few years thousands of farmers were being served by them. The telephone cooperatives demonstrated that farmers by joining together could obtain services which were denied them as individuals. Membership in telephone cooperatives taught many people—not otherwise disposed toward cooperative endeavor—the advantage of cooperation when applied to their own needs.

The spread of scientific methods. Up to the end of the century, farming was not generally looked upon as a business, and it was commonly held that almost anyone could farm with little "book learning." Starting about 1900 and encouraged by the swing to more intensive farming, the science of farm management began to develop somewhat parallel to the earlier growth of scientific management in the industrial field. The early farm management men were concerned with finding out the best farm techniques, the best combinations of crops and livestock, the best arrangement of farms, the best layout of farm buildings, and similar things which would bring about the most productive utilization of land, labor, and capital in the farming enterprise.[18] As better farm management practices grew, it had a definite influence on the character of farm thinking. For example, attention to farm management and farm cost accounting made farmers more conscious of the importance of business methods, and this ripened them for cooperative development. Moreover, it was obvious that there were many problems in farming that extended beyond the boundaries of an individual farm. As farmers studied their farms to make them more efficient, they became more and more aware of the weakness of their marketing methods, and to improve their marketing methods they soon found that cooperative action provided the only technique under their full control. Thus there was a definite relationship between better farm management, more efficient production, better marketing, and cooperation.

The Educational Advance

Improvements in rural education also greatly contributed to the growth of agricultural cooperation. Until about 1900, rural standards of education were unbelievably low. The country school was usually a one-room building where children of all ages were taught simultaneously. As teaching standards under such conditions were low and discipline was hard to keep, little was learned except a smattering of the three R's.[19]

One of the obstacles in improving rural schools lay in their inaccessibility to many students. Better roads helped, but real progress did not come until about 1910 when the automobile and the publicly supported school bus began to make possible the effective consolidation of schools.[20]

The consolidated schools not only resulted in a great improvement in educational efficiency; they also broke down community barriers and widened the areas of community action. Both of these factors encouraged the growth of cooperative organizations.[21]

By 1896, the land-grant colleges, together with the associated agricultural experiment stations and the U.S. Department of Agriculture, were providing a nation-wide system of publicly supported college education backed up by agencies for research. In the period under review, great progress was made in extending the scope and character of this system. The number of agricultural college students showed a marked increase, and, at the same time, the teaching program was enriched by a wider variety of courses and by higher standards of instruction and scholarship.

The expansion and improvement of agricultural college education had a permanent effect on cooperative advancement by raising the quality of available rural leadership. Not only were an increasing number of cooperative managers and employees trained in such institutions but respect for professional training was greatly increased as college education became more common.

During these years a great program of extension education for rural people was growing up through the efforts of the state departments of agriculture and the land-grant colleges, supported by the federal government through the U.S. Department of Agriculture. This first took form in the farmers' institutes which, by 1900, were "a recognized part of governmental machinery." With increasing state and federal aid, the influence of the institutes was greatly expanded, the number of institutes increasing from 2,722 in 1902 to 8,861 in 1914, while attendance increased during these years from some 800,000 to over 3,000,000.[22]

During this period the farmers' institutes played a significant role in encouraging the formation of agricultural cooperative associations. Although the institute programs largely reflected the interest that was then prevalent in making two blades of grass grow where one had grown before, marketing and farm management problems were increasingly considered. As a result, many cooperative elevators, creameries, and similar associations grew out of institute activity. Of perhaps more significance to the cooperative movement was the fact that these institutes encouraged farmers to think and work together on their problems. They brought to them knowledge of what other groups were doing under similar conditions, and this tended to break down rural isolation and pave the way for cooperative action.

With the passage of the Smith-Lever Act in 1914, which gave national recognition to the county agent system of extension work, the institutes ebbed in importance, although for many years they continued to be an important force for rural enlightenment.

The beginnings of the county agent system of extension go back to 1903 when Seaman A. Knapp of the U. S. Department of Agriculture devised a program of demonstration teaching for Texas cotton farmers which was designed to resist the advance of the Mexican boll weevil.

Knapp's plan was simple. He undertook to get selected farmers to follow certain simple methods of farming—deeper plowing, better seed, systematic crop rotation with winter cover crops, etc.—as a means of demonstrating to the other farmers in the neighborhood that these methods would give desired results. The farms selected were called "demonstration farms." In time, nearby farmers agreed to follow the methods being used by the "demonstrators" and to report their results at the end of the season. These farmers were designated "cooperators." Thus, the program as a whole soon became known as "Farmers Cooperative Demonstration Work."[23]

Within a few years, the "cooperative demonstration farm" idea had spread throughout the Southern states as a means of teaching farmers more productive agricultural methods. At first the work was carried on by travelling specialists of the Department of Agriculture, but it was soon found that more permanent benefits could be achieved through having the work performed by a resident agent assigned to a county.

Encouraged by the support given by the Country Life Commission in 1909, and the growing record of satisfaction with the work being performed, the system—which from 1910 on included "home agents" to provide a demonstration teaching service for farm women[24]—continued to expand with the support of the Rockefeller-endowed General Education Board, railroads, local commercial clubs, farmers' organizations, and state and local governments. As a result, the number of county and home agents increased until there were about 1,350 in 1914 when the Smith-Lever Act was passed, and of these more than 80 per cent were in the South.[25]

The nation-wide system of extension work provided for under this act was just getting well established when the war came in 1917. Then it was found that the county and home demonstration agents could perform an indispensable war service through promoting greater production and better conservation of foods and clothing. As a result, "between the spring day when we declared war in 1917 and Armistice Day, 1918, . . . the number of male county agents increased from 1,400 to 2,400 . . . [while some] 1,100 new home demonstration agents were born of the First World War."[26]

The pioneers in county agent work had been primarily concerned with showing farmers how they could raise crops and livestock more efficiently. However, as the worth of this program was demonstrated, farmers turned to the county agents for advice and assistance on their other problems, particularly those relating to farm management and marketing. Within a short while, the county agents thus became general farm advisers on all kinds of problems relating to farming—technical, economic, and social—and the organizing centers for rural activities.

The development of associations to help support and promote the program of county agents occurred almost simultaneously with their coming and from these, as we shall see in Chapter XI, the nation-wide Farm Bureau movement eventually arose. Thus, the county agent system of extension brought with it an "organizing" factor which was to exert a great influence on the spread of agricultural cooperation.

The original county agent program was primarily a method of adult education. It was soon found that much could be gained in improving farm practices through working with farm boys. As a result, the county agents began in 1909 to develop boys' clubs through which youths could be taught better farming practices through participation in group activities under capable direction. In many instances, such club work served as a training school in cooperation.[27]

Although the club projects sponsored by the county and home agents represented an important step in improving the agricultural education of rural boys and girls—for club work for girls soon followed that for boys—it was felt that they did not go far enough. For many years, a demand had been growing for a national system of agricultural education for boys and girls. This demand was recognized in 1917 with the passage of the Smith-Hughes Act, which provided federal support for the teaching of agriculture in rural high schools of the nation.[28]

Thus, within a generation, almost a new day had arrived in rural education. During this period, primary and secondary education had been revolutionized by the beginning of school consolidation and by the provision for special instruction in agriculture in the high schools of the nation. Moreover, the colleges had kept pace with the advance in primary and secondary education through improvements in facilities and in the character of instruction. To cap all, there had grown up a great system of adult education for rural people through the federal-state extension service. These developments, by raising both the intellectual and social caliber of rural life, had a highly stimulating effect on the growth of cooperative activity.

In this chapter we have endeavored to show how many vital new rural forces were providing a foundation for a great forward surge in agricultural cooperation. With this background, let us examine how rural cooperation was significantly advanced by the Country Life Movement.

Chapter VI

THE CONTRIBUTION OF THE
COUNTRY LIFE MOVEMENT

With the increasing industrialization of American life, those interested in rural welfare feared that the city was being favored to the neglect of the country, and that vast farming areas were in danger of becoming rural slums. There was a real basis for this concern. The evidence of a disparity in favor of city living standards was apparent on every hand, and particularly in the decline of land values and the abandonment of farms. As Nourse has observed: "At the opening of the twentieth century American agriculture stood in just the same subservient position to American industrialism that the colonies had occupied toward England a century and a quarter before."[1]

This anxiety over the dwindling economic and social importance of agriculture in our national life found expression in the Country Life Movement, which represented an attempt to protect the values of rural life from the encroachments of industrialism.[2] To some extent, this agitation was but another manifestation of the spirit of reform which dominated American life from 1897 to 1917. It was the era of the "muck-rakers," who burned the evils of unbridled materialism into the consciousness of the American people, and of the "progressives" who endeavored "to devise new political techniques and administrative agencies that sought to insure a more effective operation of democracy."[3]

The Country Life Commission

The Country Life Movement was vague and undefined until August 10, 1908, when President Theodore Roosevelt gave it form by appointing the Country Life Commission with Dean Liberty Hyde Bailey of Cornell University as chairman.

The other original members of the Commission were: Henry Wallace, the founder and editor of *Wallace's Farmer* (and the father of Secretary of Agriculture, Henry C. Wallace, and the grandfather of Secretary of Agriculture, Henry A. Wallace); Kenyon L. Butterfield, president of the Massachusetts Agricultural College; Gifford Pinchot, chief forester, U.S.D.A., and chairman of the National Commission on Conservation; and Walter Hines Page, editor of *World's Work* and a trustee of the General Education Board. After the Commission was set up, President Roosevelt added as members, Charles S. Barrett, president of the Farmers' Educational and Cooperative Union, and William A. Beard, the editor of the *Great Western Magazine* of Sacramento, California.[4]

President Roosevelt's interest in improving country life grew naturally from his deep interest in the conservation of forest and agricultural resources.[5] In fact, it was Gifford Pinchot, the leader of the conservationist movement, who actually suggested the formation of the Country Life Commission. In his *Autobiography,* Roosevelt tells of his growing interest in rural welfare as evidenced by conversations with Senator Tom Watson, Charles S. Barrett, Henry Wallace, L. H. Bailey, and Kenyon Butterfield, and then proceeds:

> One man from whose advice I especially profited was not an American, but an Irishman, Sir Horace Plunkett. In various conversations he described to me and my close associates the reconstruction of farm life which had been accomplished by the Agricultural Organization Society of Ireland, of which he was the founder and the controlling force; and he discussed the application of similar methods to the improvements of farm life in the United States. In the spring of 1908, at my request, Plunkett conferred on the subject with Garfield [James Rudolph Garfield, then Secretary of the Interior] and Pinchot, and the latter suggested to him the appointment of a Commission on Country Life as a means for directing the attention of the Nation to the problems of the farm, and for securing the necessary knowledge of the actual conditions of life in the open country. After long discussion a plan for a Country Life Commission was laid before me and approved. (pp. 413-14.)

President Roosevelt officially acknowledged his indebtedness to Plunkett in a letter from the White House dated March 2, 1909, addressed to the British Ambassador, Lord Bryce:

> You have, I know, followed with keen interest the work of the Country Life Commission which has pointed the way, I think, to a better handling of country problems and a more satisfying life on the farms. But I do not know how far you are acquainted with the origin of the movement in the United States. Of course I have been interested for many years in farm life, and especially in the tasks and troubles of the women on the farm. But my interest did not reach the point of action until I began to follow what was being accomplished through the farmers' cooperative movement in Ireland. My old friend, Horace Plunkett, whom I saw on his periodical journeys to America, kept me informed of the Irish agricultural situation and of the movement for

better living on the farms in Ireland. We Americans owe much to Ireland and
to Plunkett in the work we have been trying to do in the United States, and
before I leave the Presidency I want to acknowledge our debt and to send
through you my thanks for the help we have had; and not only my thanks, but
the thanks of every man who knows what has been done, and sees the need
and the sure results of this great movement to help the men and women
who feed the nation and stand at the foundation of its greatness and its
progress.[6]

In his letter asking Bailey to serve as chairman of the Country
Life Commission, President Roosevelt declared:

> No nation has ever achieved permanent greatness unless the greatness
> was based on the well-being of the great farm class, the men who live on the
> soil; for it is upon their welfare, material and moral, that the welfare of the
> rest of the nation ultimately rests. . . . The farmers have hitherto had less than
> their full share of public attention along the lines of business and governmental
> life. There is too much belief among all our people that the prizes of life be
> away from the farm. I am therefore anxious to bring before the people of the
> United States the question of securing better business and better living on the
> farm, whether by cooperation between farmers for buying, selling, and bor-
> rowing; by promoting governmental advantages and opportunities in this coun-
> try; or by any other legitimate means . . . My immediate purpose in appointing
> this Commission is to secure from it such information and advice as will
> enable me to make recommendations to Congress upon this extremely im-
> portant matter.

The Commission set to work with great vigor. With the cooperation of the U. S. Department of Agriculture, some 550,000
questionnaires were immediately dispatched to farmers, county clerks,
rural ministers, township crop reporters, and other similar persons
in rural communities requesting answers on 12 specific questions, of
which the following were typical: "Have the farmers in your neighborhood satisfactory facilities for doing their business in banking, credit,
insurance, etc.? Are farmers and their wives in your neighborhood
satisfactorily organized to promote their mutual buying and selling
interest?" Following each question were the sub-questions: "(a) Why?
(b) What suggestions have you to make?" To these inquiries, about
115,000 persons replied "mostly with care and with every evidence of
good faith." Supplementing the questionnaires the Commission from
November 9 to December 22 held hearings at 30 places in all parts
of the country which were well attended by leaders in rural and
community activities.[7] Another helpful source of information was the
numerous reports from "school house meetings" which were called at
the suggestion of the President. Through these means the Commission
quickly was able to feel the aggregate rural pulse of the nation.[8]

The President transmitted the report of the Commission in a
special message to Congress on February 9, 1909, which was keynoted

by the sentence: "There are three main directions in which the farmers can help themselves: namely, better farming, better business, and better living on the farm."[9]

To achieve these ends, the President held that "the introduction of effective agricultural cooperation throughout the United States is of the first importance. Where farmers are organized cooperatively, they not only avail themselves much more readily of business opportunities and improved methods, but it is found that the organizations which bring them together in the work of their lives are used also for social and intellectual advancement." He went on to say:

> The cooperative plan is the best plan of organization wherever men have the right spirit to carry it out. Under this plan any business undertaking is managed by a committee; every man has one vote and only one vote; and everyone gets profits according to what he sells or buys or supplies. It develops individual responsibility and has a moral as well as a financial value over any other plan.[10]

The report of the Commission, as drafted by Chairman Bailey,[11] set forth the deficiencies in country life and urged a number of specific remedies such as "encouragement of a system of extension work"; "a thorough investigation by experts of the middleman system"; establishment of "effective and economical highway systems" and "a system of parcel post and postal savings banks." With regard to cooperation, the report said: "There must be a vast enlargement of voluntary organized effort among farmers themselves... We have only begun to develop business co-operation in America." The report maintained that:

> It is of the greatest consequence that the people of the open country should learn to work together, not only for the purpose of forwarding their economic interests and of competing with other men who are organized, but also to develop themselves and to establish an effective community spirit. This effort should be a genuinely cooperative or common effort in which all the associated persons have a voice in the management of the organization and share proportionately in its benefits.

Many other expressions in the report reflected a great faith in the power of well-designed and democratically managed cooperatives to serve economic needs of farmers and rural communities. This emphasis impressed Clayton S. Ellsworth who has perceptively observed:

> The Commission leaned heavily upon the formation of cooperatives to shore up the economic low spots of country life. Cooperatives of all kinds were recommended, ranging from the simplest voluntary club organized for recreational purposes to credit, telephone and electricity. Cooperatives might well attempt to establish prices and to control production. Although the success of the cooperatives would depend ultimately upon the ability of private in-

dividuals, the Commission hinted that cooperatives would probably have to be stimulated and protected by federal and state laws.[12]

While Congress refused to publish the report for general distribution, the findings of the Commission soon began to have a stimulating effect on the formation of cooperative associations.[13] For the first time agricultural cooperation had been endorsed by a president of the United States, and by a governmental committee of high standing. The fact that the report was suppressed no doubt intensified its influence in agricultural circles, and this "served to initiate the modern country-life movement with its progressing constructive investigations and studies and its more systematic and efficient organization."[14]

The attention aroused by the report was reflected in the agricultural journals during 1909, particularly in *Wallace's Farmer,* under the editorship of Henry Wallace. In the issue of December 17, 1909, an article on "The Country Life Commission," declared: "One of the surprising things to us is that the interest of the common people— the people of the open country—in the Country Life Commission . . . will not die . . . The interest that was thus awakened seems to continue and increase . . ." When the first Henry Wallace said this the pervasive impact of the Report of the Country Life Commission was just beginning to take hold. In the next 10 years—as we will see as this story unfolds— many accomplishments in agricultural legislation and organization could be credited to its stimulative effect. Probably no government document has achieved more in bringing about constructive laws and desirable social action in the United States over a long period of years, and the report continues to exert a beneficial influence in our national life.[15]

Formulation of a Cooperative Program

While President Roosevelt and the Country Life Commission had recognized the necessity of cooperative organization among farmers, they had not formulated a definite program for encouraging its development. This need was recognized by Sir Horace Plunkett.

Taking the formula which Mr. Roosevelt adopted—better farming, better business, and better living—as the basis for a program of rural improvement, Plunkett maintained: "There must be one important change in the order of procedure—'better business' must come first."[16]

To Plunkett the key to better business, and thus to better farming and better living, was the effective use of cooperative organization. He therefore proposed the formation of an American Agricultural Organization Society—somewhat similar to the Irish Agricultural Organization Society—as an educational body to promote the spread of cooperation along sound lines, and a Country Life Institute which "would be, in effect, a Bureau of Research or Rural Social Economy." At the head of the list of questions that the Institute might study Plunkett placed "the influence of cooperative methods (a) on the productive efficiency of rural communities, and (b) on the development of a social country life."[17]

Plunkett's suggestions, which focused attention on the recommendations of the Country Life Commission with regard to cooperation, contributed materially to the growing interest in this subject by the agricultural colleges and the U. S. Department of Agriculture. His influence no doubt also gave support to the establishment in 1913 of the Rural Organization Service in the U. S. Department of Agriculture under the direction of Dr. Thomas N. Carver.

In the same year Plunkett was successful in launching an Agricultural Organization Committee of America under the presidency of Gifford Pinchot. Others on the committee were Dr. Charles McCarthy of Wisconsin, Charles S. Barrett of Georgia, Senator Peter Norbeck of South Dakota, Laurence Godkin of New York, and Henry C. Wallace of Iowa. With a grant of $5,000 from Andrew Carnegie this committee undertook to train leaders for cooperative organization work in the United States. Under this modest program two men who later attained prominence as American cooperative leaders—Charles W. Holman and Charles A. Lyman—were separately sent to Ireland to study under Plunkett's direction the methods of the Irish Agricultural Organization Society. As we shall see later in this chapter, this committee was supplanted by the National Agricultural Organization Society which was formed with Plunkett's blessing in 1915.[18]

The Campaign for Cooperative Credit

In one field, the report of the Country Life Commission had fallen on especially fertile soil. Even before the report had been issued there had arisen a demand for a better system of rural credit to meet the needs of a growing commercialization of agriculture and provide a means of helping to offset the traditional drain on capital from rural areas. This had been intensified by the monetary panic of 1907 which had awakened farmers to their credit subserviency under the existing national banking system. The Commission's report which suggested that "a method of cooperative credit would undoubtedly prove of great service" fed the fire and within a few years a cooperative system of credit was being demanded by farm groups from coast to coast. In the following chapter, we will show how this pressure for better cooperative credit services culminated in the passage of the Federal Farm Loan Act of 1916 and the promotion of credit unions, both rural and urban. Here it is significant to point out that the interest in cooperative credit reform gave impetus to the formation of the American Commission on Agricultural Cooperation and Rural Credit in Europe, and that the significant findings of this Commission after its comprehensive study of European cooperative institutions in 1913 carried further the cooperative ideas set forth in the report of the Country Life Commission and vigorously espoused by Sir Horace Plunkett. Thus, the American Commission's report was in the nature of a sequel to the report of the Country Life Commission. Both were impregnated with the same spirit of rural reform.[19]

The National Conferences on Marketing and Farm Credits

In April 1913, just prior to the embarkation of the American Commission for Europe, the first of a series of four annual conferences on marketing and farm credits was held in Chicago. Although these conferences did not directly stem from the Country Life Movement, they were an offshoot of the interest in improved marketing and credit facilities for farmers which had been aroused by the report of the Country Life Commission.

The first national conference was called by a group of farm journal publishers who were concerned with the paradox of "the high cost of living" while many farmers were not obtaining "profitable returns on labor and investment." The founder of the conference was Frank P. Holland, publisher of *Farm and Ranch* and *Holland's Magazine*. His former associate, Charles W. Holman, by serving as secretary for the first and subsequent conferences, gave these four conferences an organizational continuity. Holman traced the interest of Colonel Holland back to 1911 when *Farm and Ranch,* under Holland's editorship, began to promote the Texas Social Center movement which was clearly derived from the interest aroused in community organization by the Country Life Commission. This led Holland to a study of agricultural cooperation, and, in 1912, he sent Holman to find out about the cooperatives in Oklahoma, Colorado, Utah, southern California, and Oregon. Colonel Holland in the meantime had called a conference on marketing at Dallas and this gave him the idea of a national conference.

Holman attributes the success of the first Chicago conference to the fact that everybody—especially the representatives of the rival farm journals—came to see what was going on.[20]

The keynote of the first conference—which was attended by most of the outstanding agricultural leaders of the time—was sounded by President Van Hise of the University of Wisconsin: "The keywords of the solution of the industrial situation of the farmer are cooperation among themselves, cooperation with the consumer for their mutual benefit, and this in order to eliminate the great wastes of the existing distributing system and thus secure efficiency."

This conference succeeded in focusing national attention on the role that cooperative business organizations could perform in helping solve the farmers' marketing and credit problems. Naturally the recommendations of the Conference, which represented the best agricultural thought in the nation, carried great weight. The principal recommendations were as follows:

> That the National government should establish a bureau or other effective agency for the study of the problems of marketing and for the distribution of information as to conditions and needs and national methods of meeting these needs;
> That the several state governments should in similar manner, take up the study of this problem . . .;
> That we favor organized cooperation, both of consumers and producers, under proper supervision, to promote efficient distribution, economical marketing, and reduce expenses between producers and consumers; also organized cooperation, properly supervised, for securing more advantageous systems of rural credit.

Acting upon the instruction of the Conference, a committee presented these and other resolutions to the President of the United States, the Secretary of Agriculture, and various senators and representatives. The main objective of the committee was to secure the creation "of a bureau of markets in the Department of Agriculture with an appropriation of $1,000,000 a year."

At this strategic time, the Office of Markets was being established in the Department of Agriculture. Thus, the recommendation of the Conference gave material encouragement to the new administration in developing this program.

The subject of the second conference, held in April 1914, was "Cooperation and the need of careful consideration of the reports of the American Agricultural Commission." The first conference had provided for the holding of a second conference the following year "under the auspices of the agricultural press," and it was agreed that "the work of this body should be perpetuated under the name of the National

Conference on Marketing and Farm Credits." The resolutions of this conference urged "legislation which will properly modify the existing Sherman law to the end that proper and reasonable protection and regulation be extended to co-operative organizations, whether they be of consumers or producers, and to the end that such organizations be fully protected and encouraged thereby." Another resolution "heartily" endorsed "the passage by several legislatures of true cooperative laws based upon the one man, one vote basis" and urged "the necessity of promoting such laws in every state of the union."

The third conference, held in the late fall of 1915, with Sir Horace Plunkett as its guest, centered attention "on how to do the things that all are agreed must be done." Two very important steps were taken: (1) Provision was made for continuing the National Conference of Marketing and Farm Credits "as an open forum of discussion of the problems that surround the production, distribution, and financing of the American farm and the American farm products." (2) Provision was made for the organization of an American Agricultural Organization Society "to promote the cooperative organization of farmers, etc." Plunkett in his opening address had concluded: "I come now to the one definite constructive suggestion that I have to offer to the Conference . . . That is to form a national organization movement to carry out the organization of agricultural cooperative societies."

A new point of view permeated the fourth conference—held on December 4-9, 1916—which was attended by 2,000 persons who were claimed to represent over 2 million farmers. The preceding three conferences had achieved many of their objectives in rural marketing and credit reform and the National Agricultural Organization Society was just getting under way. The fourth congress gave its attention to practical procedures for accomplishing cooperative objectives.[21] As a result there were more talks made by managers and officers of cooperative organizations and relatively few contributions from general agricultural leaders. The cooperative movement as such was beginning to express itself. This was evidenced by the formation of the National Cooperative Milk Producers Federation during this conference—an organization destined to exert a powerful influence for cooperative advancement in the years to come.[22]

The fourth conference was the last to be held owing to the entry of the United States into World War I. When the war was over, the role of the conferences as cooperative forums was eventually to be assumed by the American Institute of Cooperation in 1925.

The National Agricultural Organization Society

As instructed by the Third National Conference on Marketing and Farm Credits, the National Agricultural Organization Society—the N.A.O.S.—was launched in January 1916 with temporary headquarters at Madison, Wisconsin. It started with a small corps of organizers, legal counsel, and a clerical staff which were financed by funds transferred from the Plunkett-sired Agricultural Organization Committee, and a further contribution of $20,000 from Carnegie. The Society was, however, designed to be "an entirely democratic self-sustaining body" supported by affiliation fees and service charges.

The purposes of the N.A.O.S. were expressed as follows in its Provisional Constitution and By-Laws:

(a) To cooperate with central bodies and local branches of societies or other associations, for the promotion of "Better farming, better business, and better living."

(b) To organize agriculture and other rural industries in the United States on cooperative lines.

(c) To examine into the methods of production and distribution of farm products with a view of evolving a system of greater economy and efficiency in handling and marketing the same.

(d) To encourage and promote the cooperative organization of farmers and of those engaged in allied industries for mutual help in the distribution, storing, and marketing of produce.

(e) To aid in the economical transfer of agricultural produce from the producer to consumer.

(f) To supply instructors and lecturers upon the subject of cooperation among farmers, auditing and accounting experts and legal advice in matters relating to organization.

(g) To issue reports, pamphlets and instructions that will help in spreading knowledge of the best means of rural betterment and organization.

(h) To encourage and cooperate with educational institutions, federal and state departments, societies, educational centers, etc., in all efforts to solve the questions of rural life, rural betterment and agricultural finance and marketing and distribution of produce and the special application of the facts and methods discovered to the conditions existing among the farmers of America and to the solution of the problem of increasing cost of living.

(i) To investigate the land conditions and land tenure with a view to working out better, more equitable and fairer systems of dealing with this problem so vital to the social and economic well-being of the country.

(j) To call from time to time such conferences or conventions as will carry out the above mentioned objects.[23]

The first efforts of the N.A.O.S. were directed toward providing cooperative associations with legal advice on problems of organization and operation, and in encouraging the enactment of "workable laws governing the problem of cooperative societies." In addition, several general studies were undertaken while assistance was also rendered several associations on various operating problems.[24] With our entry into the war early in 1917, it was necessary to abandon this program, and the N.A.O.S. "went out of existence." After the war the need for this type of work was less apparent. By then the federal and state governments and the land-grant colleges had increased their educational and technical assistance to agricultural cooperatives, and general farm and cooperative organizations were increasingly rendering effective service for agricultural cooperatives.

Let us now examine in Chapter VII how the deep-seated demand of farmers for rural credit reform brought forth cooperative institutions to serve better their financial needs. While this development was related to the Country Life Movement, it was in itself an energizing force for cooperative advancement. The importance of its achievements justifies separate treatment.

Chapter VII

THE COMING OF COOPERATIVE
FINANCING INSTITUTIONS

In Chapter VI we showed how the drive for farm credit relief was intertwined with the advancing country life movement. In this chapter we will describe the coming of the Federal Farm Loan System and the somewhat related rise of credit unions. These emerging cooperative credit institutions had a significant contemporary influence on other forms of cooperative enterprise.

The Background Situation

Farmers had long been discontented with their weak credit position and it had been a major factor in the "Populist Revolt" of the 1880's and 1890's.[1] As Murray R. Benedict has observed: "The mortgage credit facilities available to farmers had been a sore subject with them for decades ... Interest rates were high, loans were limited to short periods, and many abuses existed, such as excessive charges for renewal of loans, repetitious title searches, and avaricious foreclosure in times of credit stringency."[2] Moreover, farmers were also dissatisfied with short-term credit facilities for operating purposes. They found it difficult to obtain adequate supplies of credit at reasonable cost for crop and livestock production.[3]

For many years farmers had grumbled but they could find no way of improving their borrowing situation. With the gradual improvement in commodity and farm land prices following the upswing in prices after 1896 they became more conscious of their handicaps in borrowing money for land purchase and production, and remedies were demanded. Some relief was provided by an amendment of the National Banking Act of 1900 which stimulated the organization of country banks but this did not satisfy the broad credit needs of farmers. We saw in the preceding chapter how the Country Life Commission gave emphasis to the farmers' credit problems in 1909. This reflected a sentiment that had been building up for many years.

The farmers' credit needs were also emphasized by the monetary panic of 1907 which disclosed the structural weaknesses of our national banking system. This event set in motion forces that were to culminate in the passage of the Federal Reserve Act of 1913. The drive for banking and currency reform also directed attention to the unique financial problems of farmers. The National Monetary Commission set up by Congress to develop plans for a more satisfactory national banking and currency system, gathered a great amount of information on all aspects of the monetary problem. One of its reports issued in 1910 explained and looked with favor on the "landschaft" mortgage credit system in Germany and this stimulated much interest in the possible adoption of a like system in the United States.

No one understood and appreciated the seriousness of the farmers' credit problem more than David Lubin who had long been involved in agricultural and commercial operations in California (see Chapter IV). His experience convinced him that greater access to a supply of farm credit on reasonable terms was the most serious problem confronting agriculture in the United States. Moreover, his extensive travels in Europe during the 1890's gave him confidence that European cooperative credit institutions could be wisely adapted to the needs of American farmers. His convictions were strengthened in the early 1900's when he visited various European countries in his campaign to establish the International Institute of Agriculture. On October 29, 1907, he wrote to President Theodore Roosevelt as follows: "My studies and observations in Europe make me feel that the Raiffeisen and Schultze-Delitsch system of cooperative credit associations would lift the Southern producer of cotton and tobacco from the payment of ten to one hundred percent interest, entailed by the crop lien credit system, and give him money at six percent. Your assistance is needed to aid in causing associations to be started in each cotton and tobacco state."

After the Institute became a fact in 1908, Lubin, as the American delegate, could devote more attention to this subject and in the next few years he kept up an incessant campaign to draw attention to the credit needs of American farmers and the usefulness of European experience to help meet them. Lubin was a natural propagandist and he took full advantage of his post in the International Institute of Agriculture to promote his views. With his encouragement the cooperative bureau of the Institute issued a report in 1910 on cooperative credit institutions in Europe. This document gave Lubin just what he needed to bring European experience to the attention of American farm and business leaders, and he mailed it to them by the thousand.[4] His propaganda paid off in the autumn of 1911 when he received a letter from the Secretary of the Southern Commercial Congress[5] inviting him to take part in its convention to be held in May 1912 in Nashville, Tennessee. According to his biographer: "Lubin was a past master in the art of seizing a straw and coverting it into a solid prop. He was at that time searching for a means of focussing the interest aroused in cooperative credit and directing it into channels of achievement, and he saw in this letter Providence supplying the means."[6] Lubin replied at once and persuaded the Congress to set up a special conference on farm finance during the Congress, under his leadership. After a week of discussion at the conference he was able to get a resolution adopted which instructed the Southern Commercial Congress to assemble a commission comprised of two delegates from each state as well as delegates from the Canadian provinces to study European credit and cooperative systems and methods. In the words of Farm Credit Administration Governor Robert B. Tootel: "This was a crucial point in the movement for a rural credit system in the United States. It marked the beginning of an action program."[7]

The job of getting delegates selected from the states and Canadian provinces and making all arrangements for this work was turned over to Clarence J. Owens, the Executive Secretary of the Congress, with offices in Washington, D. C. This was a big undertaking and as 1912 was an election year it was deemed desirable to delay sending the commission to Europe until 1913 after the new administration could take office. While the delegates were being selected from the various states and plans were being made for its work, the Southern Commercial Congress carried on a campaign of publicity and education for improvement of farm credits in America. In the presidential campaign then under way the Southern Commercial Congress sought and was successful in getting an endorsement of the commission idea in the planks of the Republican and Democratic Parties.[8]

The plank of the Democratic Party read as follows:

Of equal importance with the question of currency reform is the question of rural credits or agricultural finance. Therefore, we recommend that an investigation of agricultural credit societies in foreign countries be made, so that it may be ascertained whether a system of rural credits may be devised suitable to conditions in the United States . . . (Democratic Convention, July 2, 1912)

The plank of the Republican Party maintained that:

It is as important that financial machinery be provided to supply the demands of farmers for credit as it is that the banking and currency system be
reformed in the interest of general business. Therefore, we recommend and
urge an authoritative investigation of agricultural credit societies and corporations in other countries and the passage of state and federal laws for
the establishment and capable supervision of organizations having their
purpose the loaning of funds to farmers. (Republican Convention June 22,
1912)

The idea of the commission was also strongly endorsed by such
government, business, and agricultural organizations as the House of
Governors, the American Association of Commercial Executives, the
Chamber of Commerce of the United States, the Farmers' Educational
and Cooperative Union of America, and the National Grange.

President Taft's interest in rural credit reform had been demonstrated
even before the Nashville conference was held. In the spring he
directed the American embassies and ministries in Europe to gather
information on "the forms and effectiveness of rural organizations," in
their respective countries. The information so assembled was prepared
in report form by Myron T. Herrick, then Ambassador to France, and
was released on October 11, 1912.[9] A copy of the report was sent to the
governors of the states with a letter from President Taft approving its
recommendations and inviting the governors to a special conference on
the subject which was held at the White House on December 7, 1912.

The sponsors of the American Commission from the beginning saw
the desirability of getting governmental support for its work and undertook to get the Commission officially endorsed by the U. S. Congress. To
achieve this end it was proposed that the U. S. Congress set up a companion commission to cooperate and work jointly with the independently
organized American Commission. In order that the appointment of the
Commission would not be made by a lame duck president, action in
Congress was deferred until the closing days of the Taft administration.
Then in the agricultural appropriation act for the coming year Congress
made provision for the appointment of a United States Commission: "To
cooperate with the American Commission assembled under the auspices
of the Southern Commercial Congress to investigate and study in
European countries, cooperative land-mortgage banks, cooperative rural
credit unions, and similar organizations and institutions devoting their
attention to the promotion of agriculture and the betterment of rural
conditions." This measure was signed by President Taft on his last day
in office, March 4, 1913.

On the day he took office President Wilson appointed the seven
members of the United States Commission. They were: Duncan U.
Fletcher, Florida, Chairman; John Lee Coulter, Minnesota, Secretary;

Thomas P. Gore, Oklahoma; Ralph W. Moss, Indiana; Kenyon L. Butterfield, Massachusetts; Clarence J. Owens, Maryland; and Harvie Jordan, Georgia.

Of these Butterfield had been an influential member of the Country Life Commission while Coulter had actively assisted the Country Life Commission in its work. Clarence J. Owens, the Executive Director of the Southern Commercial Congress, and Harvie Jordan were well known as progressive agricultural leaders. Senator Fletcher was then President of the Southern Commercial Congress, while Messrs. Gore and Moss were Congressmen. These appointments were important as it was felt that legislation might result from the enquiry.

Before the commissions left for Europe the United States Commission decided that it should confine itself to the problem of rural credit and leave to the American Commission the preparation of a report that would cover all aspects of agricultural cooperation. Furthermore, to harmonize the work of the commissions the American Commission accepted as members the members of the United States Commission. Thus the two commissions were integrated to study cooperation and credit in Europe and their instructions and membership gave continuity to the work of the Country Life Commission.[10]

Soon after the plan of the American Commission was agreed upon Lubin began to make advance arrangements for its work in Europe, and by the time of the appointment of the United States Commission, arrangements for its itinerary and methods of investigation were largely completed. Secretary of State, William Jennings Bryan, gave the Commissions official status by requesting that all diplomatic officers in Europe further their work to the extent possible. With arrangements completed, the American and United States Commissions sailed from New York on April 26, to return in late July.

Before the departure of the Commission, Dr. Clarence Owens, Director General of the American Commission, reported relative to the plans of the American Commission at the first National Conference on Marketing and Farm Credits in Chicago on April 10, 1913. He made it clear that the Commission's principal objective was to find a basis for essential farm credit legislation. He quoted with approval a letter he had recently received from David Lubin:

> The questions affecting the mode of procedure on cooperative production and distribution, while they will have their place in the enquiry, are, nevertheless of minor importance in the scheme. By far the most important question before the American Commission is that of how the American farmer can obtain the money. That question has largely been settled in some countries by government agency. But no such settlement of the case is pos-

sible in the United States. The United States is far removed from sympathy
with paternalism. If money is to be obtained there, it must be had without re-
course to governmental sources.

Now how are the farm assets of the United States to be rendered available
for this purpose in the form of liquid security? How are these assets to
be converted into a form of security which would render them as liquid and
as safe as United States bonds, and marketing at about as low a rate of
interest? . . . These are the questions that confront the American Commission; these are the questions that it will have to take up, digest, elaborate
and place in suitable form for adaptation in the United States . . . .

In view of the great demand that had been aroused for farm credit
legislation, Dr. Owens was concerned that no hasty action be taken
before the American Commission could make its report. "I assert most
emphatically that we have not in available form for farmers of the
United States, the material explaining the cooperative systems of Europe
and their practical adaptation to the economic conditions that prevail in
America."[11]

While the Commissions were in Europe and while they were preparing their reports, the attention of farmers was centered on how they
would be affected by the proposed Federal Reserve Act. It is necessary
to consider how this important law influenced the campaign for a better
farm credit system.

The Federal Reserve Act Brings Relief

The subject of general banking and currency reform was of major
concern to the nation while interest was developing in better methods for
financing farmers. This was one of the major campaign issues in the
Presidential Election of 1912 and it became a legislative matter in 1913,
following President Wilson's inauguration.

The National Monetary Commission, which reported in 1912, recommended the establishment of a central banking system similar to that
of various European countries, but this plan was assailed as a reversion to
the Bank of the United States closed by President Andrew Jackson, and
as a measure designed by the "powerful money trust." Wilson had made
clear during his campaign that he favored an entirely different approach
to banking and currency reform, and he came to office with plans well
worked out for a system of 12 federal reserve banks controlled by a
Federal Reserve Board in Washington, D. C.

In his campaign Wilson had not ignored the interest of farmers in
a banking system that would be better adapted to their needs. In his
acceptance speech of August 2, 1912, he said: "No mere banker's plan

will meet the requirements, no matter how honestly conceived. It should be a merchants' and farmers' plan as well, elastic in the hands of those who use it as an indispensable part of their daily business." Farmers generally agreed that general banking and currency legislation should be the first order of business. This sentiment was reflected in the resolutions of the first National Conference on Marketing and Farm Credits (April 8-10, 1913), which termed general reform in our currency, banking, and credit systems to be a "national necessity."

During the legislative struggle that culminated in the enactment of the Federal Reserve Act, on December 23, 1913, farming interests were partly successful in incorporating into the act some recognition of their special needs.[12]

Of most importance to farmers, the new Federal Reserve Act made eligible for rediscount agricultural paper with a maturity up to six months, while other commercial paper was made eligible for rediscount only to three months. The act also permitted national banks to extend credit on real estate mortgage security with a maturity up to five years. These provisions went part way toward meeting farmers' demands for improved credit machinery, and, incidentally, the system of Federal Reserve Banks provided a precedent for the establishment of a like system of Federal Land Banks, in 1916, to provide farmers with an amortized system of long-time mortgage financing.

The Federal Reserve System was really the first step in bringing credit reform to agriculture. As Dr. John D. Black later said: "The Federal Reserve system liberalized markedly the sources of credit for agriculture."[13] Others have called attention to the fact that the Federal Reserve System fostered the growth of small country banks capable of giving farmers more adequate machinery for personal credit and short-time loans.[14]

While the passage of the Federal Reserve Act was welcomed, it did not bring instant jubilation to the farmers. They saw it as a step in the right direction, but they maintained that it would not meet their major problem—long-term farm loans. President Wilson recognized this fact in his first message to Congress on December 2, 1913, when he said: "I present to you . . . the urgent necessity that special provision be made also for financing the credit needed by the farmers of the country. The pending currency bill [soon to be the Federal Reserve Act] does the farmers a great service. It puts them upon an equal footing with other businessmen and masters of enterprise, as it should, and upon its passage they will find themselves quit of many of the difficulties which now hamper them in the field of credit." But this was not enough.

Wilson contended that farmers needed and should obtain legislation that would make their "own abundant and substantial credit resources available as a foundation for joint, concerted, local action in their own behalf in securing the capital they must use."[15]

Just after the Federal Reserve Act was passed, the reports of the American and United States Commissions were issued as public documents.

The Findings of the Commissions

The American and United States Commissions returned with great respect for the accomplishments of European farmers, both in credit and cooperation. Moreover, they now had a more realistic understanding of the difficulties that would be involved in adapting foreign methods to American conditions.

A joint report of the two commissions brought together the materials collected during the inquiry (Senate Document 214, 63rd Congress, 1st Session, 1913). This volume of over 900 pages entitled "Information and Evidence" contained the basic information gathered by both commissions and it included significant statements presented by such outstanding cooperative leaders as Signor Luigi Luzzati of Italy and Sir Horace Plunkett of Ireland. With regard to this collection of source materials, the American Commission in its report declared: "It is doubtful whether so much valuable first-hand material on the subject of agricultural credit and agricultural cooperation in general has ever been brought together, in any language." This question remained: How was this mass of material to be used? Both commissions published separate reports, but the report of the United States Commission confined itself to rural credit and was in the form of a report to Congress (Senate Document 380, 63rd Congress, 2nd Session, 1914). The report of the American Commission was addressed to "the American people" and was entitled "Agricultural Cooperation and Rural Credit in Europe" (Senate Document 261, Parts I and II, 63rd Congress, 2nd Session, 1914).

The observations and recommendations of the American Commission —which also represented the general views of the United States Commission—were presented in the form of a majority report (Part I). This report which reflected the highly professional competence of the drafting committee, dealt with all aspects of cooperative organization and cooperative credit and was considered within this framework. By placing emphasis on the broad principles of cooperative organization, rather than on any one kind or type, the American Commission did much to encourage all forms of cooperative enterprise in the United States. It carried much further the ideas which were but sketchily presented in the Report of the Country Life Commission. It is therefore essential that we deal briefly with the general cooperative findings of the American Commission as a background for the specific recommendations made by the Commission on agricultural credit. The Commission declared in its majority report:

> The person who goes among European farmers for the first time will be impressed with the fact that cooperation is the most important thing about European agriculture . . . It is really astonishing to see the extent to which the farmers, particularly small farmers, have accomplished results which would have been impossible if each farmer had depended upon himself (Part I, p. 9).

The Commission continued: "We cannot borrow European cooperative methods indiscriminately. The only wise method is to take what seems best from Europe, adapt it to our conditions, and 'try it out.' "

It is not possible here to present in full the views presented in this extraordinary document which had so much influence on the subsequent development of cooperative enterprise in the United States. However, it should be noted, that the observations of the Commission were broad in scope, while intensely practical. Of particular interest were the views of the Commission on how the government might assist farmers in the development of cooperative institutions. On this, the Commission declared:

> (1) The Government, as representing all the people, should do all such a Government can do on behalf of better farm practice, better farm business, and better farm life—insofar as this betterment is to the advantage of all the people; (2) In general, however, the Government should do nothing that can effectively be done by individual farmers, or by the farmers collectively through voluntary aid. It is highly important to develop self-help. The "cooperative spirit" is vital to the success of cooperative effort and this spirit is best engendered by the work of voluntary agencies of social service; (3) The Government, however, may take the lead temporarily in many movements, in order to stimulate interest and to show how progress may best be secured; (4) Where there is practically unanimous agreement on the part of the people that a certain type of effort is essential for the good of the whole people, it is highly proper that the Government should be the agency to perform the service. (pp. 27-28)

The Commission thus held that the government can "investigate," "interpret," "inform," "advise," and "demonstrate"—but "not participate in the farmer's business nor direct their community life." These general views reflected the great influence of Horace Plunkett on members of the Commission, for Ireland, under his leadership, then served as a cooperative demonstration of intense interest to the members of the Commission.

The Commission offered a number of special observations on rural credit in European countries:

> (1) Agricultural credit in the greater part of Europe ranks as high as, or even higher than, commercial credit ... (2) Land-mortgage credit ranks as high as, or higher than, industrial credit ... Land loans for the most part are paid upon the amortization plan, so that the obligation will be discharged in from 30 to 60 years ... (3) Rural credit societies and land-mortgage associations are often fostered by government grants, loans or special privileges. (4) Commercial banks and land-mortgage banks of private capital are not in antagonism with these government-fostered institutions ... (p. 18)

One of the principal sections of the report dealt with the important question: "Shall the Government Help in Rural Credit?" On this, the Commission was of the opinion "that our American problem of rural credit should be worked out without Government aid." Support for this opinion was found in European experience. "One of the great lessons learned in Europe is that in the long run the farmers succeed best when they help themselves. Whenever they become dependent on the Government they keep looking to the Government for more aid" (p. 13). The Commission then went on to say:

> It is sometimes urged that the Government should loan money directly to farmers at a very low rate of interest. A low rate of interest is not so much the great need of farmers as more capital, under better conditions, at *fair* interest. Everything should be done to give the farmer an equal opportunity with other businessmen in securing capital ... In other words, the Government should help bring about a better system of rural credit by legislation, but not by subsidy. (p. 14)

The Commission gleaned several features of an adequate system of long-term rural credit from European experience which it considered applicable to American conditions. It found a long period of credit needed, and amortization of loans an absolute essential, with issuance of land-mortgage bonds on collective security and for a localized area. The Commission concluded that:

> A system of land-mortgage banks would seem to be the best way for the farmers of America to gain greater facilities for long term credit. Whether these should be state institutions or should be chartered under a national law may be open to question. The Commission is inclined to coincide with the views of the United States Commission favoring a national law and charter and supervision, with operations of the land-mortgage banks in any state restricted to that state. (p. 15)

In its general conclusions, the commission spelled out its views more fully: "In order that there would be a uniform and nation-wide system of long-term credit, it would seem wise to secure the enactment of a federal law permitting the organization of farm land banks, either on the joint-stock or the cooperative plan, authorized to issue long time bonds secured by farm mortgages, required to do business on a narrow margin of profit, to allow payment of principal on the amortization plan, and carefully and fully supervised by the Federal Government" (pp. 28-29).

On short-term rural credit the Commission recognized the valuable work being done by the Raiffeisen and similar cooperative credit societies of Europe, and pointed with approval to the rural credit unions being formed along similar lines in various American states. The Commission then said: "A tremendously important question faces the American people at the outset in endeavoring to secure a better system of rural credit, both real and personal. Shall this credit be developed by profit-making banks or through the cooperation of the borrowers—that is, by the farmers themselves?" The Commission concluded that:

> The European experience seems to indicate that the cooperative form of furnishing credit is likely to be the ultimate method in America, for the very simple reason that credit will be furnished by private joint-stock financial institutions only for profit to the institution, whereas, under cooperative credit the members get the profits. Moreover, it is difficult for a great financial system to adapt itself to the needs of the men of small means; but it is they who are most numerous and, in the long run, most important. Hence, there should be provided opportunity and encouragement for the development of cooperative institutions to supply credit to the farmer—that is, institutions for members rather than for outsiders. This observation applies both to the question of long-term credit and the question of short-term credit... (p. 18)

Six members of the Commission took vigorous exception to the views in the majority report favorable to the encouragement of short-term cooperative credit associations—although they expressed general agreement with other recommendations in the majority report. Their minority report asked the question:

> Is it wise at the present time to encourage farmers, as is done in the majority report, to believe that they can find relief from their financial difficulties by cooperative systems of credit which have admittedly succeeded in Europe because of the peculiar conditions existing there? Is there not danger that farmers may be induced to "try out" systems which cannot succeed under our conditions, and thus lead them into much more serious difficulties? (p. 7)

The report then said:

> Cooperation and the ability to cooperate must be a process of development,

of evolution, and of growth. Is it not vital and essential that where farmers desire to cooperate they should experiment first in matters that concern them alone and in which there is the smallest degree of risk, such as cooperative buying and selling, cooperative creameries, cow testing associations, breeding circuits, etc.? It seems resonable that only by this means can farmers of this country acquire that degree of education in cooperative effort that would warrant the introductions of this system into the more intricate phases of their business; this step to be taken, if deemed necessary, only after a demonstrated success in the more rudimentary branches. (p. 7)

Later there is this paragraph:

It is well here to call attention to the fact that our country banks are strong in number and resources, and are largely owned by the farmers themselves. The currency law, just enacted [The Federal Reserve Act] will place country banks in a stronger position than ever to serve their respective farming communities and it is believed will make a new system of banking unnecessary and expensive to establish with problematical outcome. (p. 10)

The report therefore proposed:

that the farmers cooperate with the stockholders of banks in rural communities . . . in the organization in their respective localities of small unit land-mortgage associations, capitalized in proportion to the needs of their respective communities—minimum capital $10,000. Each association to be organized upon the share capital plan, cooperative . . . or non-cooperative—as might be desired.

The report of the United States Commission which dealt exclusively with credit, simply amplified the general views of the American Commission and presented a draft law which was later introduced into Congress as the Fletcher-Moss Bill. Thus, the reports of the Commissions set the stage for a modest program to provide long-term credit on an amortized basis through a system of joint-stock land banks. While there was much sentiment for a cooperative plan, there was little agreement on how it could be accomplished.

While the most direct effect of the reports of the American and United States Commissions was the stimulation that they gave to farm credit legislation, they provided great encouragement to the sound development of agricultural cooperation of all types. For example, committees were set up by governors of various states to determine agricultural needs, at the instance of the American Commission. The reports of these committees which indicated the interest then prevalent in various forms of agricultural cooperation were published as Part 3 of Senate Document 214. Moreover, the reports gave support to the work of the newly organized "Office of Markets" and "Rural Organization Service." They gave backing to the Conferences on Marketing and Farm Credits, and they encouraged the agricultural colleges in getting programs of research and extension for cooperatives under way. They also provided a fund of information on cooperatives for college class use. But, most important of all, they stimulated leadership. The members of the Commissions went home to their communities in the United States with a new vision of what could be accomplished by cooperative means in their own country, and in many cases these men took the lead in cooperative endeavors. Thus the reports of the Commission served as a sequel to the Report of the Country Life Commission. They were impregnated with the same spirit of rural reform.

The Struggle for a Federal Farm Loan Act

With the passage of the Federal Reserve Act in December 1913, and the submission of the reports of the American and United States Commissions in January 1914, the stage was set for action on the farmers' mortgage credit problem. Moreover, in anticipation of legislative activity the Department of Agriculture had begun studies to determine the nature and scope of the farmers' credit needs, and the Committees on Banking and Currency of the Senate and House of Representatives had started hearings on the farmers' mortgage and short-term credit problems.

This situation was brought to a focus by the Fletcher-Moss Bill, introduced in Congress in January 1914 by Senator Duncan U. Fletcher of Florida, and by Congressman Ralph W. Moss of Indiana, who were members of the two commissions. Although the individual members of the commissions were not in full agreement on what kind of a rural credit plan to favor, the commissions gave their official endorsement to the Fletcher-Moss Bill which therefore became known as the "Commission Bill." It proposed the organization under federal charter of land-mortgage associations, either cooperative or private, with a minimum capital of $10,000, which would be authorized to issue bonds.

While acceptable to mortgage bankers and other banking interests, the Fletcher-Moss Bill was strongly opposed by agricultural interests who felt that it was a banker's rather than a farmer's bill, and it soon became apparent that it could not be enacted.[16] Support began to grow in the House and Senate Banking and Currency Committees for an entirely different plan that would utilize local cooperative credit associations and provide for a system of Federal Farm Loan Banks, somewhat on the pattern of the recently established Federal Reserve Banks. Advocates of this approach found expression in the Hollis-Buckley Bill, introduced on May 12, 1914, in the Senate by Senator Henry R. Hollis of New Hampshire, and in the House by Congressman Robert J. Buckley of Ohio. These men were chairmen of the Rural Credits sub-committees of the Senate and House, and so their bill came to be referred to as the "Committee Bill." This bill proposed the establishment of a system of Federal Land Banks under a Federal Farm Loan Board which would serve cooperative land bank associations patterned on the "landschaft" type of association in vogue in Europe. However, the Committee Bill was not satisfactory to the proponents of the Commission Bill, nor was it acceptable to a significant group who desired an outright grant of federal funds to help farmers on their long-term financing problems. There ensued a legislative deadlock for a period of nearly two years, during which it was questioned whether any bill acceptable to the three factions could be passed. During this period, scores of long-term farm credit bills were introduced but none captured overwhelming support. According to Governor Tootel: "In the 63rd Congress, 30 bills and two joint resolutions were introduced in the Senate; and 68 bills and eight joint resolutions were introduced in the House, all proposing agricultural credit legislation. Each of them involved one or a combination of three quite different philosophies," which may be designated as favoring private enterprise, cooperative enterprise, or direct loans by the federal government.[17]

The Marketing and Credits Conference of 1915 reflected the confusion that then existed among farm leaders as to the type of bill they desired. Men like Lubin and Herrick were frustrated and expressed little faith in a government solution of the problem. Herrick said: "The farm-credits movement whose simple but grand objects originally were cooperative banking and long-term mortgaging, has taken on such paternalistic and socialistic tendencies that it likely will be written in history as the farmers' state-aid craze."[18] The Conference in its resolution said:

> We are confident that with the undoubted sentiment for better credit facilities expressed in no uncertain tone by the farmers of the country, Congress will enact at this session some legislation along the line of rural credit. But this conference goes on record as endorsing only such legislation as will provide for the soundest valuation and the most careful maintenance of true educational values, and only such legislation as is based upon *self-help, careful auditing, a sound amortization plan, and the cooperative principle* of organization for rural credit banks.[19]

The impasse was eventually broken in the spring of 1915 when the whole subject was referred to a joint congressional committee. After several months, this committee solved the problem by incorporating the views of all opposing parties, although the dominant influence was the thinking expressed in the Hollis-Buckley Bill. In effect it provided for two distinct systems of long-term credit—one based upon the cooperative approach, while the other embraced the private enterprise principle.

The compromise measure finally became law on July 17, 1916, as the Federal Farm Loan Act. In reporting out the bill on May 8, 1916, House Committee Report No. 630 said:

> The bill reported, therefore, whatever its obligations to successful foreign systems, provides for a *distinctively American System* of rural credits and endeavors to embody . . . the best thought which the thorough discussions of the past years have developed with reference to rural credits legislation.[20]

President Wilson, in signing the Act, was jubilant. He held that it "would introduce business methods into farm finance, bring order out of chaos, reduce the cost of handling farm loans, place upon the market mortgages which would be a safe investment for private funds, attract into agricultural operations a fair share of the capital of the Nation and lead to a reduction of interest."[21]

Herbert Myrick, who had long fought for better rural credit and other farm causes, felt that the new Federal Farm Loan System had "potentialities of transcendent importance to the American people," and that "the new statute may prove to be epochal in its economic and social benefits." He went so far as to declare "The Act is the Magna Charta of American farm finance."[22]

The Character of the Federal Farm Loan System

The Federal Farm Loan Act provided for a dual system of farm mortgage banks. The Federal Land Banks with their supporting farm loan associations were to be cooperative in nature while the joint-stock land banks were to be organized and operated as private enterprises.[23] This dual system was justified on the grounds that the two types of banks would serve two distinct classes of farmers. According to C. W. Thompson, who served as Department of Agriculture advisor in shaping up the Act, it was the intent of Congress "to meet two distinct credit needs." On this he said:

> Some farmers are already in a position to furnish satisfactory security, while others are greatly in need of improvement in this respect. The federal land bank system, with its farm-loan associations, is designed for those farmers who are in need of improvement in their security as well as in the form of their credit obligations and the facilities for marketing them. The joint-stock land banks are intended for such farmers as are able to furnish adequate security and are interested in obtaining loans on better terms with as few restrictions as possible. A clear understanding of the distinction here drawn between the two classes of farmers must be kept in mind in order to appreciate the purpose of providing for two distinct land bank systems.[24]

While the government was to provide initial capital for the establishment of the Federal Land Banks, no financial assistance was deemed necessary for the joint-stock land banks. However, the Federal Farm Loan Act provided that government capital in the Federal Land Banks would be retired as soon as conditions would warrant. Farmer borrowers were to become owners of the Federal Land Banks through the requirement that they purchase stock equal to 5 per cent of their loan. There was no stock ownership requirement as a prerequisite to borrowing from the joint-stock land banks which were organized and owned by non-farmers who invested in them with the intent of making a profit.

As Thompson pointed out: "Clearly, the use of public funds thus proposed must rest on the performance of a recognized service, such as the general improvement of agriculture . . ." Later he said: "These banks were designed for farmers and not for capitalistic owners of farm lands."[25]

The Federal Land Banks were to be directed by boards of directors responsible largely to the farm loan associations, which were to be cooperative organizations controlled by their stockholder members. It was appreciated that setting up of the farm loan associations would be difficult for they called for the formation of cooperatives organized from the top down. Thus the whole success of the Federal Land Banks would depend upon the willingness of farmers to embrace the system. As Congressman Buckley, one of the major architects of the Act, said:

> Cooperation is relatively new to the American farmer, and we often hear it said that he will not take kindly to a system which forces his co-operation with his neighbors, and makes known to them the details of his land-mortgage operations.

But he was confident that the new plan would take hold, because of the benefits it would give farmers such as the return to them of "whatever profits may arise from the operation of the system." It was his conviction that "There is every reason to believe that the actual operation of the system will provide an object lesson in the benefits of farmers' cooperation," and that, "The Farm Loan Act marks the beginning of a great and valuable cooperation among farmers hitherto unknown and believed to be impossible."[26]

The Federal Farm Loan Act thus represented an innovation in government assistance to agriculture. The power of government was to be employed to get the cooperative features of the land bank system into operation not only through financial assistance but through the processes of education. It set a precedent which was to be drawn on in the later development of other parts of the Farm Credit System, in the development of rural electric cooperatives under the Rural Electrification Act of 1935, the home loan banks, and other credit programs after that date.

Just after the Act was passed, Edwin G. Nourse said: "The Federal Farm Loan Act ... provides a thoroughly American device of making the investment capital of the whole country accessible to the farmer for land mortgage purposes. If this machinery can be coupled up with vigorous, self-reliant, and cooperative activity on the part of those who need credit in their agricultural enterprises, we may hope in time to see a large part of the difficulties of this transition era disappear."[27]

Installation of the Federal Farm Loan System

The Federal Farm Loan Act was favorably received by farmers. The members of the new Federal Farm Loan Board were carefully selected and they moved with caution and firmness in getting the new program under way. As instructed by the Act, an effective educational program was immediately developed to explain how the new system would work to the advantage of farmers.

About six months after the Federal Farm Loan Act was passed the Fourth National Conference on Marketing and Farm Credits was held (December 1916). Interest in the new system was then very high and the attendance at the conference reached nearly 2,000. One of the features of this gathering was consideration of how the new Farm Loan Act would work. Mr. James B. Morman, who had been employed by the Board as editor of publications gave a full exposition of how the program was being developed. He said:

> This act sets forth two systems, a cooperative system and an individual-istic or capitalistic system. The cooperative system is outlined by means of 12 federal land banks ... These federal land banks will deal with what is known as national farm loan associations. These associations are groups of farmers . . . Standing over against this is the capitalistic plan. The law provides for the establishment of joint stock land banks. These are supposed to be organized by capitalists, but the objects of these joint stock land banks are precisely the same as the federal land banks. They are to make mortgage loans and to make mortgage loans only.

One of the first actions of the Board had been to decide that no joint-stock land bank would be chartered until the federal land bank system had been instituted. Morman explained that this decision was made because "The Board felt that if the joint stock land banks were granted charters they would come in and occupy the field to the detriment of the farmers." Morman felt that the "problem of problems" before farmers was to organize the national farm loan associations and get them into operation so as to "reap the benefits of this great act."[28]

The Conference went on record in favor of the new system in a resolution which declared:

> The said Federal Farm Loan Act offers the first and only effective system for the proper financing of the farmers of the country on long time mortgage loans at low rates of interest and easy payments ... We heartily recommend to the farmers of the United States the Federal Farm Loan Act and urge upon them that they make the fullest use of the same. And we especially endorse the national farm loan associations as providing the best means of which farmers can avail themselves of the benefits of the law.[29]

During 1917, the Federal Farm Loan Board carried on an aggressive program to get the national farm loan associations established and into operation. A number of readable circulars were issued by the Board to explain how farm loan associations could be easily formed and managed.[30] The U. S. Department of Agriculture also gave the new system all possible encouragement through the Federal Extension Service, and county agents were directed to assist farmers in establishing national farm loan associations. The Department also published Farmers Bulletin 792, by C. W. Thompson, "How the Federal Farm Loan Act Benefits the Farmer" (January 1917), to serve as a guide and handbook. As a result of this general campaign—supported by the national farm organizations and farmers cooperative associations, the loans of the 12 land banks totalled $29,824,655 by November 30, 1917.[31]

During the next few years the system—both cooperative and capitalistic—rapidly expanded. Loans outstanding of the Federal Land Banks grew to $156 million by the end of 1918, and to $295 million by the end of 1919, while loans outstanding of the joint-stock land banks grew to $8 million by the end of 1918 and to $60 million by the end of 1919.[32] Although progress was brought to a standstill in 1920 by a law suit that clouded the constitutionality of the Federal Farm Loan Act until it was cleared by the Supreme Court on February 28, 1921, there was no doubt that the system had taken root.

The Development of Credit Unions in the United States

Over 100 years ago the credit union movement in the United States got its inspiration from the work of the cooperative credit societies established in Germany. The success of these organizations, established by Herman Schultze of Delitzsch in 1852 and by William Raiffeisen in 1864, soon became known in this country through immigrants from Germany or through reports by American scholars, such as Richard T. Ely, who recognized the importance of such societies in an article on the German cooperative credit unions in the *Atlantic Monthly* for February 1881. The Schultze-Delitzsch societies served primarily workingmen in towns and cities while the Raiffeisen societies served those in rural communities.

The credit union idea is simple. A credit union is a cooperative banking association in which individual members place their savings to be used in making loans to borrowing members. The borrower pays a modest rate of interest which provides a reasonable return to those who lend their money.[33]

Charles Barnard's book, *Cooperation as a Business*, published in 1881, contained a chapter on "The People's Banks" which described "the system of cooperative banking that is now known under the name of Schultze-Delitzsch credit unions." Barnard saw great opportunities for similar cooperative banks in the United States. Soon afterwards, in 1892, the U.S. Department of Agriculture published a bulletin by Edward T. Peters on *Cooperative Associations in Certain European Countries*, as Report No. 3 of the Division of Statistics. This bulletin provided comprehensive information on the Schultze-Delitzsch, Raiffeisen and Italian credit societies. In introducing this bulletin, J. R. Dodge, Statistician, said: "These people's banks have a success that justifies their existence, as they fill a virtual vacuum in banking opportunities for the agricultural and industrial classes." Herbert Myrick, in his book, *How To Cooperate*, published in 1891, pointed out that "credit unions—so successful in Germany and Italy—afford the best model" for cooperative banking. He observed: "The credit union, or people's bank, in Europe is almost as old as the Rochdale system of distributive cooperation in England, though unlike the latter it has as yet secured no foothold in this country" (p. 201). Two main reasons may be given for the slow adoption of the credit union idea in this country. Unlike Germany and other European countries, people were not settled in relatively close permanent communities. Moreover, Americans at this time were generally more interested in making money than in saving it. With the closing of the frontier and the coming of new rural forces as described in Chapter V, conditions became more favorable for the formation of credit union organizations by farmers. Somewhat similar new urban forces also were making credit unions more practicable for workingmen in towns and cities.

Mention has been made of the pioneer work of David Lubin in

fostering the Raiffeisen plan for American farmers at the turn of the century. However, credit unions were to come to this country via Canada where the first credit union in the Western Hemisphere was formed in 1900. It is important to understand how this organization came into being, and how the idea grew.

In 1885, Alphonse Desjardins, a young journalist of Levis, Quebec, was attracted to the problem of usury through the revelations of law suits which indicated that "poor borrowers" were "obliged to pay to infamous usurers rates of interest amounting to several hundred per cent for most insignificant loans." Desjardins began his search to find the best possible solution for this problem, and during the next 15 years he gathered pertinent information from Europe and elsewhere. Above all, he was influencd by the experience of the Raiffeisen and Schultze-Delitzsch societies in Germany. In developing his plan for people's banks, Desjardins recognized that the Schultze-Delitszch and Raiffeisen models from Germany would have to be modified to take into account "the decided hostility of our people to anything like wide, and therefore, more or less unlimited liability." To quote him further:

> I adopted in Canada an entirely new regime similar to the prevailing system of the savings banks of the New England States, where there is no capital stock, the depositors alone providing the funds and enjoying to the fullest extent the right to withdraw their money almost at will . . . The main idea of this system is exactly the same as is to be found in the uncapitalized savings banks of the United States, but with this most commendable feature, that the funds thus accumulated are utilized to meet the needs of the very classes from which the customers of these banks are drawn.[34]

Fortified by his studies and encouraged by letters from European cooperative authorities, Desjardins was at last ready to undertake his great experiment in his little home town of Levis, near the old city of Quebec, and, in December 1900, he established *La Caisse Populaire de Levis* (The People's Bank of Levis). The enterprise included two rural parishes, for he desired to see how the "institution" would work for both laborers and farmers. The start was not auspicious, for according to Desjardins "the first installment paid was a dime and the total first collection amounted to only $26."[35] However, the idea caught hold and in a few years *La Caisse Populaire de Levis* was a conspicuous success. Within five years, 150 similar cooperative people's banks had sprung up in French Canada.

Naturally the idea also attracted attention among French Canadians living in New England and in 1909, with the advice of Desjardins, a credit union was established in Manchester, New Hampshire. But of more importance to the development of credit unions in the United

States was an investigation into the operations of professional money lenders who were victimizing factory workers in Boston—ordered in 1908 by Pierre Jay, the Massachusetts Banking Commissioner. As a result of the findings, Jay invited Desjardins to assist in drawing up a bill to legalize credit unions in Massachusetts. This bill, with the support of the innovating and public-spirited Boston merchant, Edward A. Filene, became law on May 21, 1909, and the Massachusetts Credit Union Act became the foundation for the development of credit unions in the United States.[36] The first credit union to be formed under the Massachusetts law was organized by Herbert Myrick in 1910 for workers in his publishing plant in Springfield.

At about this time the Jewish Agricultural and Industrial Aid Society began to promote credit unions for Jewish farmers and in the next few years several were formed and operated successfully.[37]

The credit union idea was further popularized in 1910 by Hector MacPherson's University of Chicago doctoral dissertation, *Cooperative Credit Associations of the Province of Quebec*. This drew attention to the great opportunity for credit union development in the United States.

Thus, the credit union idea was beginning to take hold while attention was being directed to the rural credit problem by Lubin, Herrick, Myrick, and others. It was significant that President Taft gave his support to credit unions in the White House Conference in December 1912. The American and United States Commissions, in their studies of cooperation and credit in Europe, also did much to popularize the Raiffeisen and other credit union plans. One of the members of the American Commission, John Sprunt Hill, a prominent North Carolina banker, admittedly went to Europe to "find Raiffeisen." Having found Raiffeisen he came back determined to put the idea to work, and with his support a North Carolina Credit Union Act was passed in 1915 that dealt directly with the establishment of rural credit unions.[38]

While the struggle for long-term rural credit legislation went on, the proponents of credit unions continued to press for state and national credit union legislation. This interest in credit unions was reflected in the discussions of the Third National Conference on *Rural Credits and Cooperation* in the late fall of 1915, and in an analysis of existing state laws for the organization of credit unions undertaken in 1916 by the Department of Agriculture's Office of Markets and Rural Organization. This led to the drafting of a model state law for credit unions in 1917 and official promotion of such organizations.[39]

As noted, the first state credit union law was promoted mainly to provide urban workers with a dependable source of low cost credit.

Soon afterwards the Russell Sage Foundation found in credit unions an ideal instrument to combat the predatory practices of loan sharks and, with telling effect, it began to promote their formation by supplying information and guidance.[40] A Credit Union Primer, by Arthur H. Ham and Leonard G. Robinson, issued in 1914, was one of its most effective publications.[41] Largely as a result of the Foundation's extension campaign, credit union laws were passed in New York and several other states and a number of credit unions were formed—mostly for urban workers.

The interest building up in credit unions was somewhat arrested by the wave of prosperity induced by World War I, although a considerable number of credit unions were formed in the war and postwar years. By 1920, credit unions had become established as practical forms of cooperative banking for farmers and urban workers in factories and offices.[42]

Thus, from 1900 to 1920, substantial progress was recorded in both rural and urban credit cooperation. During this period the foundations were laid for the cooperative Farm Credit System of the present day which was to bring with it important impacts on the nature and operation of farmer cooperatives. In these two decades was laid the broad base for the tremendous expansion of urban and rural credit unions that was to come in the next few decades.

Chapter VIII

FEDERAL GOVERNMENT ENCOURAGEMENT

Up to this point we have said little of the growing support that was coming to farmer cooperatives from the federal and state governments. To some extent this aid arose naturally as a reaction to the various forces described in Chapter V. It also reflected a determination to improve rural life through the organization of the farmers themselves as reflected in the Country Life Movement.

Prior to 1900, government agencies had contributed little specific aid to the growth of cooperatives in agriculture. In the next 20 years, rural people increasingly turned to the government for assistance on their increasingly complex business problems, and this brought forth a growth of federal and state agricultural agencies. The response of these agencies to this demand, in the form of direct assistance to cooperatives came through the related services of the U.S. Department of Agriculture, the state agricultural colleges, and the state departments of agriculture or similar state agencies. In this chapter we will trace the development of such assistance through the federal government.

By 1896, the U.S. Department of Agriculture had made marked advances toward becoming a great agricultural laboratory and educational center, and farmers had come to expect from it any service that might assist them. The Department then was occupied in a myriad of activities for the promotion of agricultural welfare, as indicated by the report of the Secretary for 1896 which revealed that some 376 publications aggregating 6,561,700 copies had been issued "principally for gratuitous circulation." Most of these related to technical agricultural problems, although a few dealt with such broad topics as *The World's Market for American Products* and *Agricultural Educational Methods*.[1]

While the Department was a much simpler organization in 1896 than it has subsequently become, its structure was already complex. At that time, its principal administrative units were the Weather Bureau and the Bureau of Animal Industry; the Offices of Experiment Stations, of Fiber Investigations, and of Public Road Inquiries; the Divisions of Chemistry, Entomology, Biological Survey, Forestry, Botany, Vegetable Physiology and Pathology, Agrostology, Pomology, Agricultural Soils, Publications, Statistics, Accounts and Disbursements, Gardens and Grounds; and a Section of Foreign Markets. The Department's appropriation for 1896 amounted to $2,583,750, although this included $720,000 which was paid directly to the experiment stations by the Treasury.

While it is true that the interests of the Department were still dominated by problems related to plant and animal production, economic problems of agriculture were beginning to claim attention. In his report for 1896, Secretary J. Sterling Morton said:

> Agricultural colleges and experiment stations are teaching the science of agriculture. But they are not generally teaching farm economics and the importance of markets. Science is constantly showing the farmer how to increase the annual product per acre in cereals and other staples, but the great question confronting each tiller of the soil is how to secure satisfactory remuneration for the results of his toil. In view of this, it is a legitimate function of the Department of Agriculture to place before the farmers of the United States as many facts and figures relative to markets as it is possible to obtain.

Under the long reign of James Wilson, as Secretary of Agriculture (1897-1913), the Department was to have an outstanding growth. During this period basic research was increased, many regulatory functions were undertaken, and extension work was systematically developed through farmers' institutes, and later by farm and home demonstration agents. Beginnings were made in effective farm management and marketing work and agricultural cooperation was directly encouraged as a method of increasing the effectiveness of such efforts.

First Work With Cooperatives

Although the U.S. Department of Agriculture was primarily interested in the physical productivity of agriculture during the early years of the new century, the growing business problems of agriculture caused an increasing amount of attention to be given to problems of farm management and marketing. One of the earliest indications of this new interest was the surveys begun by W. J. Spillman in 1902, and the establishment of an office of farm management in the Bureau of Plant Industry in 1905. Soon afterward the Department also began to recognize the importance of marketing and agricultural cooperation.[2]

In 1908, Secretary Wilson devoted two pages of his annual report to an appraisal of cooperative developments in agriculture since 1896. He found that farmers cooperatives in the United States had developed enormously during the period under review, and that more than half of the 6,100,000 farms were represented in "economic cooperation." He concluded: "Contrary to his reputation, the farmer is a great organizer, and he has achieved remarkable and enormous successes in many lines of economic co-operation in which the people of other occupations have either made no beginning at all or have nearly, if not completely, failed."[3]

In his report the following year, Secretary Wilson again gave cooperation his support:

> One of the most promising tendencies of the day is the spirit of co-operation and mutual helpfulness which is beginning to manifest itself among the producers of truck crops. The successful organization and working of cooperative marketing companies or exchanges by farmers have proved the possibility as well as the desirability of a system of marketing which shall have headquarters at the point of distribution.

The *U.S.D.A. Yearbook of Agriculture, 1909,* contained an article by Frank Andrews of the Division of Production and Distribution of the Bureau of Statistics on "Methods and Costs of Marketing" which pointed out that:

> The number of farmers' cooperative associations through which produce is marketed is increasing constantly ... Two of the important results of cooperation in marketing have been the shipment of better grades of fruits and vegetables, and the command by the farmers of a greater influence in the market on account of large quantities of produce being controlled by a single authority (p. 172).

In his 1910 report, Secretary Wilson said: "It is plain that the farmer is not getting an exorbitant price for his products, and that the cost of distribution—to the consumer—is the problem ... for treatment." He went on:

> Farmers' cooperative selling associations are numerous in this country, but cooperative buying associations among the people of the cities and homes are few. Aside from buying associations maintained by farmers, hardly any exist in this country. It is apparent, therefore, that the consumer has much to do to work out his own solution with regard to the prices that he pays (p. 26).

In the same year, a very significant pioneer article was contributed to the *U.S.D.A. Yearbook of Agriculture, 1910,* by G. Harold Powell of the Bureau of Plant Industry—"Cooperation in the Handling and Marketing of Fruit." This was the first serious analysis of cooperative procedure to be made by the federal government. According to Powell:

> The cooperative method has brought about large economies in the purchase of supplies, in the cost of preparing the fruit for shipment, and in

the charges for distribution and sale. It has improved the methods of fruit
packing and grading enormously. It has sometimes doubled the net returns
to the individual grower . . . (pp. 391-406).

The expanding interest of the Department of Agriculture in agricultural marketing and cooperation was expressed in 1911 by Frank Adams
in a *Yearbook* article, "The Reduction of Waste in Marketing," and in
1912, by L. C. Corbett, horticulturist of the Bureau of Plant Industry
who contributed to the *Yearbook*—"A Successful Method of Marketing
Vegetable Products"—an article which was largely devoted to a description
of "the cooperative system." It was held that: "Experience has
demonstrated that the results derived from true cooperation are sufficiently
important from a commercial standpoint to justify the method even
though no other results were obtained." (p. 358) In the same volume,
Charles J. Brand, physiologist in charge of Cooperative Cotton Handling
and Marketing Investigations, Bureau of Plant Industry, in discussing
"Improved Methods of Handling and Marketing Cotton," likewise gave
careful consideration to the ways in which farmers through cooperative
organization could improve their business practices. Brand closed his
article with this sentence: "Well organized responsible cooperative growing and handling associations, acting in concert with the other elements
of the cotton trade, can ultimately bring about improvements that will
save millions of dollars." (p. 462) These various contributions made
by personnel of the U.S.D.A. prior to 1913 were symptoms of a growing
awareness of the importance of agricultural cooperation which were to
find fuller expression with the establishment of an Office of Markets in
May 1913.

The Establishment of the Office of Markets

Although there had been a considerable amount of attention given
to marketing in connection with various activities of the U.S.D.A., this
was largely sporadic prior to the establishment of the Office of Markets
in 1913. The steps leading up to this important action are significant.

The support of Congress for marketing work was first expressed in
the 1911 Appropriation Act for the Department of Agriculture.[4] The
Secretary was authorized "to investigate the cost of food supplies at the
farm and to the consumer and to disseminate the results of such
investigations in whatever manner he may deem best." This authority
was expressly continued in the corresponding act for 1912. But "no real
results were obtained" as no funds were made available to implement
the authorization.[5]

In the following year, Congress went further by including the following provision in the Appropriation Act for 1913:

> And the Secretary of Agriculture be and he is hereby directed to secure from the various branches of the department having authority to investigate such matters, reports relative to systems of marketing farm products, cooperative or otherwise, in practice in various sections of the United States and of the demand for such products in various trade centers, and shall make such recommendations to Congress relative to further investigations of these questions and the dissemination of such information, as he shall deem necessary.

In compliance with this order Secretary Wilson, in December 1912, transmitted to Congress a comprehensive statement entitled "Systems of Marketing Farm Products and Demand for such Products at Trade Centers."[6] This "epoch-making" report "reviewed existing commercial systems in some detail, presented statements by managers of large firms and associations, outlined marketing investigations already undertaken in various bureaus of the Department, discussed the functions of a possible 'Division of Markets' in the Department of Agriculture, and made specific recommendations regarding the proposed duties and the proper limitations of such a division."[7] With regard to "associative marketing," the report said: "The cooperative marketing association, if properly organized, equipped, supported, and managed, affords the best means for the sale of many products of the farm, among which fruits and vegetables are conspicuous." (p. 18) It held that:

> A division of markets could perform excellent service in helping farmers to help themselves to organize marketing associations . . . A division of markets, equipped with a corps of competent field agents, could get into touch with farmers for the purpose of promoting the organization of marketing associations wherever the farmers request assistance or information; the agent could meet the assembled farmers and practically organize them if they desired. It can hardly be doubted that this service can be successfully performed and, eventually, with results greatly beneficial to farmers. The traveling field agents also could perform good service in examining into the affairs of weak and unsuccessful marketing associations and advise changes in their improvement (p. 21).

By the spring of 1913, the insistent demand for agricultural marketing legislation had expressed itself in a number of bills favoring the establishment of a Division of Markets or similar action. This led to a modest beginning. "After considerable debate and numerous conferences, in which many elaborate schemes were proposed and discussed, wiser counsel finally prevailed, and it was decided merely to insert an item in the agricultural appropriation bill for 1914, under which tentative work might begin in a rather independent way."[8]

The clause in the Appropriation Bill (signed by President Taft on March 4, 1913) as finally approved read as follows:

> To enable the Secretary of Agriculture to acquire and to diffuse among the people of the United States useful information on subjects connected with the marketing and distributing of farm products, and for the employment of persons and means necessary in the city of Washington and elsewhere, there is hereby appropriated the sum of $50,000, of which sum $10,000 shall be immediately available.[9]

This legislation gave Secretary David Franklin Houston, who became secretary when the new administration came in on March 4, an immediate opportunity to develop marketing work in accordance with the insistent demand that economic and social problems of agriculture be given more attention. As a first step, a departmental conference was held "primarily to discuss plans for ... carrying into effect the provision in the agricultural appropriation bill."[10] A second conference was held on April 29, 1913, to "secure the views of experts and others in the problem of organizing and conducting a marketing service in the Department of Agriculture."[11] At this conference the Secretary gave his views on how the authority given could best be used. He felt that work in marketing could be classified into four lines: organized marketing, market news service, methods and cost of distribution, and transportation. At this conference a number of influential recommendations were offered by G. Harold Powell, who had recently resigned from the Department of Agriculture (1912) to become general manager of the highly successful California Fruit Growers Exchange. Powell maintained "that the government should not provide a crutch for the farmer to lean on when he can walk without it."

Moreover he felt that any program should be developed "cautiously and slowly." His views are worth quoting in some detail.

> The department's work in this field must grow as a result of experience, just as cooperative organization grows, for as soon as the department begins to collect information that will influence distributing and marketing practices, it will undoubtedly meet the antagonism of many of the agencies already in the field, because if designed to encourage the business organization of farmers it will tend to eliminate the unnecessary cost of distribution and to simplify the methods of placing the farmers' products before the American consumer and consequently will abolish these agencies. There are but few experts in crop distribution and marketing in this country, and they cannot be created suddenly by legislation, and unless the department can obtain trained men who have a practical knowledge of the matter in hand it can become involved in controversies which could easily endanger the usefulness of the services it may perform.

He therefore suggested:

One of the first steps in this direction would be to assist the farmers in organizing their industries along lines that are sound from the social, economic, and agricultural point of view by setting forth the correct principles of organization. It might also make a careful study of existing organizations with a view to setting forth the principles governing the voting of members, payment of dividends, limitation of membership, and other questions essential to a successful farmers' business organization.[12]

In incubating plans for the new Office of Markets, it was recognized that its success would largely depend upon the person designated as chief. Perhaps the man most commonly favored for the job was G. Harold Powell, who was recognized both within and without government circles as the best fitted by experience and temperament for getting the work underway. Powell was, however, unwilling to give up his challenging post as general manager of the California Fruit Growers Exchange.

There were several possible candidates interested in marketing investigations, within the Department. Among them were Dr. William J. Spillman, who was then in charge of farm management, and Charles J. Brand, who had been making cotton marketing studies in the Bureau of Plant Industry. To determine their relative fitness, these men were asked each to submit a statement as to how they would proceed to organize the new work. The statement submitted by Brand on May 5 so fully met the Secretary's views that on May 17 he was asked to put his plans into effect. Brand's memorandum thus provided the working plan for the new program.[13]

Plan of the Office of Markets

In his memorandum, Brand declared:

> There is no one principle, the correct application of which will cure our present difficulties in distribution and marketing. The problem as a whole is one of articulation. . . . Certain specific and almost elementary things can be taken up at once which may be expected to produce immediate results. Beyond this, the facts will have to be determined and we must then proceed with these as a basis.

Brand outlined the following six sub-projects for early attention:

A. The Study and Promulgation of Market Grades and Standards

B. Cooperative Marketing

> This sub-project would include (1) Promotion of marketing organizations and assistance to existing organizations; (2) a compilation of laws, state and national, affecting organized production. This is very necessary.

C. Surveys of Supply and Demand and Organization of Consumers
This work would include surveys of consumption and market possibilities in definite localities and educational and organization work
among consumers . . .

D. Study of Methods and Cost of Distribution
This would include: (1) Study of existing cooperative organizations
for marketing farm products together with a determination of cost and
general advantages and disadvantages of this method. (2) An investigation of present commercial methods of distribution, prices received by
the producer, cost of transportation, storage, etc.; changes of ownership or possession between producer and consumer, accumulated
charges, costs, and ultimate prices and profits at each step in the
process by individual products or classes of products. This would give
a true measure of the benefits to be obtained by the general introduction of the cooperative method.

E. Study of Transportation Problems and Assistance to Producing Organizations in Securing Suitable Transportation Facilities

F. Market News Service for Perishable Products

In concluding his memorandum Brand admitted that this program
was "very ambitious and difficult," but he pointed out that "it scarcely
outlines the great problem of economic waste in the handling and
marketing of farm products."

To implement his proposed plan, Brand offered a scheme of staff
organization which would utilize the $50,000 available for the work of
the Office of Markets. Six key professional positions were provided for:
(1) an organization specialist; (2) a transportation specialist; (3) an
officer in charge of market surveys; (4) a specialist in the marketing of
perishable crops; (5) a law and reference clerk; and (6) an expert
bookkeeper and auditor to devise "accounting systems for cooperative
producers and consumers." The specific qualifications required for each
of these positions were set forth in an accompanying letter to Dr. Beverly
T. Galloway, assistant Secretary of Agriculture (May 5, 1913).

In this letter Brand pointed out that:

The work must be definitely practical and not academic. The point of
view in tackling the problem must be that of the common man—the
small producer and the average consumer. The officers connected with the
work must cultivate a deep personal familiarity with the classes of persons
to be helped and with the problems involved in helping them. The human
and economic rather than the laboratory and statistical point of view must
rule . . . The immediate ideal in all of the work will be to take up first those
activities that promise to give the most immediate beneficial results. . . The
success of the whole work will depend on getting men who will do sound,
earnest team work and I believe they can be gotten.

While the Department was getting its plans for an Office of Markets
under way, a grant from the General Education Board made possible
the immediate establishment of a Rural Organization Service. The way

in which this agency promoted the Department's program for the advancement of cooperative organization can well be considered at this point.

The Contribution of the Rural Organization Service

The scope of the Department's program in marketing was admittedly restricted by its small appropriation. In the early spring of 1913 this problem came to the attention of the General Education Board—which was then assisting in the support of the extension service—and resulted in a grant from that body to the department of $30,000 "for the study of co-operation, including rural credits and the general organization of rural communities for economic, social and educational purposes." The Department agreed to place a director in charge of this work, and Dr. Thomas Nixon Carver of Harvard University was selected by the Secretary with the concurrence of the General Education Board. In this way the Rural Organization Service was established even before arrangements could be completed for the new Office of Markets.[14]

This situation might have resulted in jurisdictional friction, had it not been for the harmonious working relationship that rapidly grew up between Carver and Brand, when the latter assumed charge of the Office of Markets. As we have noted, Brand was primarily interested in practical issues, while Carver was more concerned with the social aspects of cooperation. When the General Education Board terminated its support at the end of the year, the work of the Rural Organization Service was absorbed by the Office of Markets.[15]

Although the Rural Organization Service had a short life as a (privately supported) government agency, it exerted a considerable influence on the future cooperative work of the Department. By emphasizing the great significance of the cooperative form of organization, Carver helped to broaden the scope of the Department's studies in the field, especially in purchasing and credit.[16] The rural Organization Service also performed a useful transitory service in promoting sound principles of cooperative organization and management in the interim before the work would be more adequately implemented by the Office of Markets.[17]

Development of Cooperative Work

In the discussion which follows attention is focused on the work directly related to agricultural cooperation. From the beginning, the Office of Markets gave attention to many marketing problems not related to cooperation as is suggested by the Secretary's classification which follows. Within a few years the work of the Office in market news service, in promulgation of grades and standards, and in regulation activities dwarfed the specific attention given to cooperative organization. While much of the work was of a general character, it indirectly benefited the growth of cooperation through making conditions more suitable for cooperative growth.

Following his appointment as Chief on May 16, 1913, Brand began to develop comprehensive plans "relating to the scope and nature of the investigational" work to be undertaken and to assemble "the nucleus of a scientific staff" based on special Civil Service examinations.[18]

The work of the Office was thus well under way on December 1, 1913, when Secretary Houston made his first annual report. He said:

> Heretofore the Department of Agriculture has, of necessity, concerned itself mainly with problems of production ... We have been suddenly brought face to face with the fact that in many directions further production waits on better distribution and that the field of distribution presents problems which raise in very grave ways the simple issue of justice ... As difficult as are the problems of production, they are relatively simple as compared with those of distribution ... The department has given assistance here and there in the past; it is prepared to give further assistance and information now.[19]

"The Department," the Secretary continued "has arranged its marketing investigations under five important subdivisions: (1) Marketing surveys, methods and costs ... (2) Transportation and storage problems ... (3) City marketing and distribution investigations ... (4) Study and promulgation of market grades and standards ... (5) Co-operative production and marketing investigations." (p. 22)

The interest of the Secretary in cooperation was expressed in a special section of the report which asserted: "It is clear that before the problems of marketing, the individual farmer, acting alone, is helpless. Nothing less than concerted action will suffice. Cooperation is essential." His attitude, however, was tempered with caution:

> Cooperation can not result in an organization which shall attempt to establish a closed market to fix prices. . . Furthermore, it is desirable that such concerted action shall proceed from below upward. . . Experience shows that the best results are secured only when the members of such a cooperative society are those who are bona fide producers. . . [Cooperatives] are of all sorts and descriptions; some are truly cooperative, others are clearly exploited. Some operate on principles that are sound; others on principles that are obviously bad. A form helpful to one undertaking is not necessarily the best for another . . . There are many facts to be ascertained.

We desire to know and to estimate the various sorts of enterprises afoot in order to be able to give the people information concerning the principles and practices of the best forms of cooperation.[20]

In view of the recognition which had been given cooperative organization as a desirable means of improving the farmers' methods of marketing in the discussion which had preceded the establishment of the Office of Markets it is not surprising that immediate attention was directed to this subject. The work with cooperatives which was begun on October 1, 1913, was divided into two parts—a survey of agricultural cooperative marketing organizations and a study of the systems of accounting and auditing for such organizations.

With regard to the general work with cooperatives, Brand reported in 1914:

> This project has aimed to strengthen associations already organized and to make their work more efficient, to guide new associations along safe and businesslike methods and away from the common mistakes of such enterprises, to arouse public interest in the spirit of cooperation, and to emphasize the essentials for successful application of that principle to the farmers' business.[21]

Brand reported that information had been obtained on over 7,000 organizations in the survey of cooperative agricultural marketing organizations, and that studies had been started on accounting forms and descriptions of accounting systems being used for fruit and produce associations, grain elevators, creameries, and produce exchanges. Plans had also been made for the preparation of uniform systems of accounting for cooperative warehouses, canneries, creameries, cotton gins, and meat packing plants, and for the recommendation of systems of auditing, plans for financing, and methods of business practice for these organizations. A general accounting bulletin for cooperative agricultural marketing associations had also been submitted for publication.

From the beginning, the Office of Markets endeavored to correlate its work with the marketing work already under way in other divisions of the Department of Agriculture and to develop working relationships with agricultural agencies in the states. For example, the first report of the Chief of the Office of Markets indicated that:

> Cooperative relationships have also been established with the University of Minnesota, the State Dairy and Food Commission of that State, and the Dairy Division of the Bureau of Animal Industry in an investigation of the methods and costs of handling and marketing butter, with special reference to the business of the cooperative creameries in Minnesota (p. 326).

The Office of Markets was also beginning to give leadership in cooperative education. In the hearings on the Agricultural Appropriation

Bill for the following year, Brand called attention to the need of publications on cooperation for use in educational work. He continued: "We are outlining so far as we can and assisting professors in the colleges and universities who are coming to us in outlining courses in co-operation and marketing. That, in a way, answers the question as to teaching the younger generation. We are meeting with some success in those outlines, and a few State universities are now using them."[22]

The work of the Office of Markets expanded rapidly. For the year ending June 30, 1915, its appropriation rose to $200,000, while $40,000 was separately appropriated to continue the work started by the Rural Organization Service. The staff which numbered 83 on July 1, 1914, had grown to 219 by July 1, 1915.[23]

The second annual report of the Chief of the Office of Markets—which by that time had become the "Office of Markets and Rural Organization"—disclosed significant accomplishments in assisting cooperatives. The survey of cooperative organizations which had been started the previous year was being continued. Information had been assembled on some 11,000 cooperative or semi-cooperative associations, but of these "only about one-sixth [were] truly cooperative." It was found that most of the so-called cooperatives were "governed and profits paid on the basis of capital invested . . ." Moreover, most of these were "held together by a loosely drawn membership agreement, with penalty clauses that were clearly illegal." To remedy these weaknesses, the Office of Markets had undertaken to assist "many of these capitalistic associations" in reorganizing "on the basis of no capital stock, non-profit, and payment of patronage dividends, with a one-vote membership control." Moreover, "a membership agreement which bases all sales upon a legally drawn power of attorney [had] been prepared so as to give more stability to farm selling organizations."

Altogether, the survey of cooperation in the United States had found that it was "far more prevalent than is generally believed, though not upon as strong a business basis as is needed." The Office of Markets thus felt that it was on the right track in its endeavor "to strengthen existing organizations and to guide new associations as far as practicable so that they may serve their members more effectively and avoid the many difficulties and failures which have resulted in the past from lack of experience and foresight."

In undertaking to assist in the proper organization of cooperatives, the Office of Markets had found that in a majority of the states "it was necessary to organize under the regular corporation law, which makes no provision for the distribution of profits on the basis of the amount of sales and purchases made by the farmer with the organization." The Office of Markets in collaboration with the Office of the Solicitor was therefore aiding state authorities in drafting new state laws which would provide adequately for cooperative development. Finding that one of the greatest weaknesses of existing cooperative associations lay in their accounting systems and methods, and general business practices, the Office of Markets had set up a special project, "Marketing Business Practice," and under it steps immediately had been taken to devise accounting systems suitable for various types of cooperative enterprises— elevators, fruit and produce organizations, livestock shipping associations, rural creameries, and cooperative retail stores (pp. 366-70).

The Office of Markets had also found that "first-hand knowledge of the individual problems of cooperative organizations is essential for giving the most helpful service." Representatives of the Office were, therefore, giving direct personal assistance to existing and prospective organizations in Maine, Michigan, Oregon, Colorado, Kentucky, and many more states. As noted, the Office of Markets appreciated from the beginning that there was a dearth of sound printed information on cooperative marketing and purchasing which could be placed in the hands of farmers for their own study. With little delay publications on the following subjects had been prepared and initial supplies were soon exhausted: *Cooperative Purchasing of Farm Supplies, Cooperative Organization Business Methods, Cooperative Marketing and Financing of Market Associations, A System of Accounts for Farmers' Cooperative Elevators, A System of Accounting for Cooperative Fruit Associations.*

Work of the Rural Organization Service (now merged with the Office of Markets) was being developed in the fields of rural credit, insurance, and communication. In rural credit, a subject of great current interest, field assistance had been rendered "in perfecting an organization agreement for farm-mortgage credit improvement among the members of a cotton-growers' association in Arkansas," and a bulletin, "How Farmers May Improve Their Personal Credit," had been issued. Investigations in agricultural insurance, begun in February 1915, included surveys of mutual fire, hail, windstorm, and livestock insurance companies. A preliminary study was also made of farmers' mutual telephone companies and some aid had been extended in this field. Other work in rural organization included several community surveys designed to further "constructive organization work," a study of county fairs to improve their community usefulness, and a preliminary review of organization work among farm women.

The work of the Office of Markets and Rural Organization expanded greatly during the next fiscal year ending June 30, 1916, due partly to the absorption of marketing activities which had been performed by other agencies within the Department but more particularly to new regulatory and administrative responsibilities placed in the Office by new legislation.[24] By this time, the work relating to cooperation was well established. Secretary Houston opened his report for the year ending June 30, 1916, by saying: "The half of agriculture embracing the marketing of farm products, rural finance, and rural organization has strikingly occupied attention during the last three and one-half years." He held that the Department possessed "the largest and best trained and supported staff of experts dealing with the distribution of agricultural commodities and rural organization to be found anywhere in the world."

The report of the Chief of the Office of Markets and Rural Organization for 1916 reflected a broadening of the work already under way with respect to cooperative marketing and purchasing. Emphasis was still being directed toward the improvement of business practices. By the end of the fiscal year systems of accounting had been devised for cooperative elevators, fruit and produce associations, livestock shipping associations, creameries, cooperative stores, and cotton warehouses. A bulletin, "Patronage Dividends in Cooperative Grain Companies," was being used by a large number of elevators "for declaring and prorating patronage dividends" (p. 387). The Office (with the active collaboration of the Office of the Solicitor) was also busily engaged in drafting "proposed laws to encourage cooperation" (p. 385).

In rural organization, assistance was being given on the formation of credit unions while "the most practical methods of operation of farmers' mutual insurance companies" were being studied. The preliminary survey of farmers' telephone companies, now completed, was being used as the basis for helping farmers with this form of organization.

A significant development during the year came from the decision to coordinate state and federal marketing activities. As a foundation for this anticipated development, a survey of state marketing activities was made and a report issued under the title, "Results of a Survey of Marketing Activities throughout the United States."

The year ending June 30, 1917, marked the publication of the first government bulletin to provide complete statistical information on cooperative purchasing and marketing organizations among farmers in the United States. Another highly significant publication was the draft of a proposed state cooperative law which was issued as Service and Regulatory Announcement No. 20: Suggestions for a state law designed to conform to Section 6 of the Clayton Act.[25]

The Office was continuing its emphasis on the development and installation of standard accounting systems for cooperatives. It was also assisting in the "formation of auditing associations in North Dakota and Kansas which were formed for the purpose of conducting periodic audits for all business associations holding membership with the object of limiting the annual expense for this service and of securing comparative statistics in similar lines of business operation." In rural credit, a digest had been made of existing state laws relating to credit unions preliminary to the drafting of a model state law (in collaboration with the Office of the Solicitor) providing for the incorporation and supervision of cooperative credit associations or credit unions. Moreover, a bulletin had been issued on "The Organization and Management of a Farmers' Mutual Fire Insurance Company," while a digest had also been made of the laws relating to farmers' mutual fire insurance.

The most significant new development during the year was the establishment of formal cooperation with the states in marketing work. Under the plan which was developed, field agents of the Office of Markets worked in cooperation with state market bureaus, extension divisions of agricultural colleges, commissions of agriculture, and other state agents under cooperative agreements developed by the Office and cooperating agencies. The report of the Chief indicated that much of the work then being carried on in the states was related to the formation and assistance of various types of agricultural cooperative associations. He called attention to the fact that the Office had actively conducted work in 18 states during the year.

Cooperative Work During and After World War I

When the Office of Markets and Rural Organization officially became the Bureau of Markets on July 1, 1917, the emphasis of its work was naturally "placed upon those phases of work ... which would be most directly helpful to the nation in successfully prosecuting the war with Germany." This brought a curtailment of demonstrational and service work and an all-out effort to use existing knowledge and experience to obtain more "efficient distribution and conservation of food products."

Although investigational work was curtailed, several important cooperative bulletins were completed and published during the year— *Cooperative Organization By-Laws, System of Accounting for Fruit Shipping Organizations, Marketing Practices of Wisconsin and Minnesota Creameries.* Although the work in cooperative credit, insurance, and telephone associations was also slowed up during the year, a model state law for "credit associations or credit unions" was prepared in collaboration with the Office of the Solicitor. While the war brought about an expansion in the importance of the state agents in marketing, their work with cooperatives was overshadowed by demands made on their time by officials of the Food Administration and the State Councils of Defense. During the year, 27 states cooperated with the Bureau in this program.

A development of particular interest relating to cooperative purchasing arose from the designation of the Bureau of Markets (January 1918) as the agency to purchase and distribute nitrate of soda "at cost to farmers"—a war measure required to increase production. In this work for which an appropriation of $10 million was made the Bureau enlisted the help of the county agents who obtained orders from farmers and arranged for distribution through country nitrate distributors. Brand has described this arrangement in these words:

> As time was so short and no special machinery of distribution could be set up for the purpose of insuring a quick and equitable distribution, the federal supervisor of nitrate distribution utilized the county-agent system of the Extension Service which was just then developing at its greatest rate. . . In cooperation with the county agents a county distributor was selected for each county or each group of counties where the amount to be distributed warranted such action. . . Shipments were made to the county nitrate distributors on "order notify" bills of lading with sight drafts attached. The county distributors collected from farmers purchasing the nitrate and also distributed the nitrate on arrival.[26]

In many instances, this resulted in the formation of local fertilizer purchasing associations to serve as "distributors," as the small margins allowed did not attract many commercial dealers. According to D. S. Murph, who was in charge of the project under Brand, "The county agents were the only agencies who could put over a plan quickly as a necessary war measure. The nitrate of soda plan really put the county agents into the co-operative purchasing of fertilizer" (interview of October 27, 1945).

In his postwar annual report for the year ending June 30, 1919, Secretary Houston again affirmed his confidence in agricultural cooperation:

> Particularly must the Federal and State agencies omit nothing to promote farmers' cooperative associations along right lines. . . The rational program would seem to be to expand these activities, which have clearly demonstrated their value, to follow the scent as it were, and further to develop the machinery through which increased assistance may be furnished. There should be in every state one or more trained market specialists of the Department of Agriculture, working in cooperation with the proper state authority, to stimulate cooperative enterprises and to aid farmers in their marketing work by helpful suggestions as to plans and methods. These experts could very

effectively aid the extension workers. County agents generally have the assistance of specialists in many other lines, but at present they have not the requisite aid in distribution. They cannot be expected to be expert in all agricultural matters or to be omniscient. The department is requesting increased funds to make this extension possible and will take the necessary action promptly if the appropriations are made.

The report of the new chief of the Bureau of Markets, George Livingston, who succeeded Brand as of June 30, 1919, indicated that work with cooperatives, while continuing, had been seriously interrupted by the loss of technical men through resignation, enlistment in the military service, or assignment to other war work.

However, work had been completed on a uniform classification of accounts for creameries and a tentative system of accounting for purchasing agents and cooperative stores was prepared. With the promulgation of official grain grades, inaugurated and administered by the Bureau, it had been found necessary to revise and reissue the bulletin on bookkeeping for country elevators. A model state law was drawn up for farmers' mutual fire insurance companies, and a bulletin was issued—*Prevailing Plans and Practices of Farmers' Mutual Fire Insurance Companies.*

The program of the state agents in marketing was being conducted in 22 states. By this time the bulk of the work of the Bureau in assisting in the formation and improvement of cooperative associations had been assigned to these state representatives of the Bureau.

The responsibility of the Bureau in distributing nitrate of soda continued into the spring of 1919 and essentially the same plan of distribution was followed as in 1918. Altogether some 153,000 tons was distributed during the year with a saving to farmers estimated at over $2 million.[27]

While this operation was undertaken as a war measure, it served as a gigantic demonstration of the possibilities of cooperative purchasing and it had a very definite promotive effect on the cooperative purchasing of fertilizer. It also forced county agents into joint purchasing activity and led farmers in the future to demand that the government continue such assistance.[28]

No abatement of interest in marketing or in cooperative marketing followed the resignation of Secretary Houston. In transmitting his annual report for the year ending June 30, 1920, E. G. Meredith asserted:

We must omit no effort to improve our marketing machinery and practices and to furnish necessary market information to the farmer so that he may take full advantage of modern business methods in the distribution of his commodities . . . The department recognizes fully the importance of the co-

operative movement and its potentialities for good in the general marketing
scheme. . . This work should be extended and developed. (pp. 14-15)

The report of the Chief of the Bureau of Markets indicated, however,
that work with cooperatives had become routine, with much of the work
of the Bureau transferred to the state agents in marketing. Some
indications of the work of these agents is indicated by the following
statement in the Chief's report:

> While complete figures are not available relative to the work of the
> agents in marketing, those at hand show that they assisted producers to
> form 183 marketing organizations, including 50 livestock shipping associations;
> 57 fruit and vegetable associations; 12 credit unions; and 19 federations of
> existing associations (p. 557).

The period of vigorous promotion of cooperative enterprises by the
Bureau of Markets had passed.[29] The following year (1921) a reorgani-
zation was to combine the Bureau of Markets with the Bureau of Crop
Estimates and in 1922 the work was to be merged into a newly formed
Bureau of Agricultural Economics.

Chapter IX

ASSISTANCE FROM THE STATES

The same forces that nurtured the first work of the federal government with cooperatives also had a like influence in the states. In this chapter we will examine the way in which the agricultural colleges and state departments of agriculture got involved in the study and promotion of agricultural cooperation. To a large extent this work supplemented that being performed by the federal government.[1]

The Contribution of the State Colleges

For some time farm leaders had urged the state agricultural colleges to give more assistance to farmers on their economic problems, particularly those related to marketing. Although a few institutions, notably Cornell University and the University of Wisconsin, had started work in agricultural economics early in the 1900's, little came of this demand for assistance on marketing problems prior to 1909 when it was brought to public attention by the findings of the Country Life Commission. As we shall see, the educational ferment which followed the Commission's report encouraged several of the colleges to develop courses of instruction relating to marketing and rural organization. The interest of the colleges in this subject was shown by the 1911 report of the Land-Grant College Committee on Instruction in Agriculture, which declared:

> The time has arrived when the discussion of economic problems should be differentiated from . . . the farm practice subjects . . . It seems desirable to use the term *rural economics* as applicable to the general field of economics in its relation to agriculture and rural communities . . . Besides the more general courses on rural economics, there will undoubtedly be an increasing number of courses treating of various subdivisions of this subject, in addition to farm management. Such for example would be courses in farm accounting, cooperation and credit, farm labor, markets and marketing, taxation, etc. . . . Your committee is deeply impressed with the importance of developing strong

courses in rural economics and sociology and the other subjects just referred
to. These all involve the human element in agricultural and country life.[2]

It is with this background that we turn to a consideration of how
specialized courses on cooperation began to arise in the curricula of
agricultural colleges.

Massachusetts State College. The first college course specifically
devoted to cooperation was given at Massachusetts State College in 1910
by Alexander E. Cance. This course was described as follows in the
Massachusets Agricultural College Catalogue for 1909-10:

> COOPERATION IN AGRICULTURE: This course contemplates a some-
> what comprehensive view of the history, principles and social relations of
> agricultural organization, for profit.
>
> Part I. *The Business Aspects of Cooperation.* (1) Survey of the develop-
> ment and progress, the methods and economic results of farmers' organizations
> and great cooperative movements in the past; (2) the phases of business
> organization of agriculture abroad, and the present aspects and tendencies
> in the United States; (3) the principles underlying successful cooperative
> endeavor among farmers, and practical working plans for cooperative as-
> sociation as illustrated by the operations of successful cooperative enterprises,
> with particular reference to perishable products.
>
> Part II. *Social Aspects.* This . . . part treats of the social conditions
> necessary to successful cooperation; the effects of cooperation on character,
> e. g. on individualism, conservatism; the relation of cooperation to political
> achievement—; the influence of cooperation in begetting a community
> consciousness; and the effect of organization on class status.

The Country Life Commission made clear that the agricultural colleges had a responsibility for providing training in the field of rural
organization. The leader of this point of view among the Commissioners
was Kenyon L. Butterfield, president of Massachusetts State College.
Casting around in the fall of 1908 for someone who was fitted by training
and experience to give instruction in this field, Butterfield obtained the
services of Alexander E. Cance who had recently received his doctor's
degree from the University of Wisconsin. This brought Cance in close
touch with the work of the Country Life Commission for he was called
upon by Butterfield to assist in summarizing and editing the questionnaires received from thousands of rural people from all parts of the
country. With regard to this work, Cance later said: "One section of
the questionnaire dealt with farmer organizations for business purposes,
and I learned then what the farmers in a good many parts of the
country were asking for."[3] Just prior to this Cance had been engaged
in making a study of immigrant agricultural communities in the United
States for the Congressional Committee on Immigration. This work had

enabled him to visit most of the immigrant communities east of the Mississippi and he had been "much impressed with the things they were inclined to do cooperatively."

With regard to the inception of this first course, Cance observed:

> The course in Cooperation . . . was an integral part of a comprehensive curriculum in Rural Social Science first outlined by Kenyon Butterfield, and amended by conference with his staff and other men interested and active in the social growth of country life . . . The Country Life Movement had a great deal to do with the organization of this course . . . As a matter of fact, the whole atmosphere here was permeated with the ideal of rural betterment; better business and better living for rural people. It was being discussed and considered practically for the first time, as you know. The two sides of Country Life went together. Whether the farmers' prosperity or the farmers' improved social life should come first or was really the end of country betterment was more of a question in New England than in the West.

On the basis of his studies, Cance advocated business organization for farmers. He said: "I . . . maintained at the time as against Butterfield that farmers could be better represented politically and could organize with more effect on a business basis than on a social basis. . ."

When the course was outlined Cance was afraid that not enough material could be mustered to give "a substantial college course," but he soon found plenty for his needs. Although no up-to-date text on American cooperative experience was available, there was a considerable amount of fragmentary material that could be drawn on for teaching purposes. Fortunately, C. R. Fay's valuable book, *Cooperation at Home and Abroad,* had just been published in England (1908) and this provided a comprehensive analysis of European experience in both agricultural and industrial cooperation. There was also available a considerable amount of information on consumers' cooperation in England and on agricultural cooperation in Ireland.[4]

The plan of giving the course in two parts with separate instructors for the business and social aspects of agricultural cooperation was soon dropped as material on the social side was found "rather meager." The course was then continued as "Business Cooperation in Agriculture."

The interest of President Butterfield did not stop with resident instruction, for in 1912 the college "hired a man in Extension Service, E. S. Morgan, to help organize communities for social purposes." At first this work—which contributed to the formation of cooperatives to meet economic needs—met with resistance from the Legislature, but in time its importance became recognized.[5]

The work of the college in sponsoring business cooperation soon began to bear fruit with the formation of local cooperative exchanges, which sprang up in considerable numbers following the enactment of a new cooperative law in 1913 and the publication of an Extension Service Bulletin, "The Farmers' Cooperative Exchange," by Alexander E. Cance in 1914.

New York. The College of Agriculture of Cornell University, then under the stimulating influence of Dean Liberty Hyde Bailey, was the next college to offer a full course devoted to cooperation. This two-hour, one-term course, given first in 1911-12 by George N. Lauman under the title "Cooperation," was described as follows: "A study of the principles and testing of cooperation, with special reference to agricultural conditions prevailing in the United States." This course was given annually until 1919-20 although the description was changed in 1916 to emphasize the economic aspects of the subject.[6]

The introduction of this course grew naturally from the interest that Dean Bailey had inspired in the socio-economic aspects of agriculture. With regard to the specific conditions leading up to "the beginning of instruction [at Cornell] in marketing and cooperation," Bailey later said:

> The field began to be visualized very early in my career here, and it took definite shape when I sent George F. Warren to Wayne County to investigate the marketing condition in the apple business; and the field enlarged as he went later to Orleans and Chautauqua County. George N. Lauman was long my assistant and later attained a full professorship. He was always interested in the economic and social side of agriculture, and I think he was the first to give a regular course in the subject to students. Where the suggestion for this course came from I cannot recall and perhaps it is not important, except that I hope Lauman may have the credit for starting the work. There was no outside pressure for such a course.[7]

Bailey's broad interest in agricultural cooperation was evident in the attention given to the subject in the *Cyclopedia of American Agriculture* under his editorship. In introducing the chapter, "Business Organization in Agriculture" in the volume on *Farm and Opportunity* (Volume IV., 1909), Bailey said:

> A cooperative organization is an open group in which all participants share and share alike in proportion to their contribution, and in which the directorate is created genuinely by the parties to the association. It is a membership group. Fully cooperative associations are often not able to do business as effectively as the close or capitalistic associations, because they are likely to lack strong leadership, because there is little opportunity for any one member to acquire wealth, and because we have not yet learned how. Theoretically, the cooperative business society is preferable, because it is natively democratic, and should be the means of educating its members and developing the com-

munity. The very fact that it does not offer great money reward for any one person is the best reason for its existence; it is altruistic rather than selfish, working for the good of all rather than a few. Its chief effect is educational. Real and effective cooperative organization is possible only in a highly developed society, because it thrives in proportion as mere self-interest recedes.

Bailey went on to say:

Counting all the business associations that exist among farmers, the number is great and the membership is legion . . . There has been no careful study of such organizations by any supervising authority, and therefore no direction to them. They need to be studied as carefully as do methods of crop-growing and animal-breeding, in order that helpful co-ordination and development may be suggested.

The emphasis of Lauman's course in cooperation reflected his view, and that of Dean Bailey, that cooperation should be an important problem for study in the field of rural economy, which he defined as the "great body of questions of an economic nature that lies beyond the individual farm and farmers." Lauman believed that "rural economy" should be concerned with the "farmer and the farm in their relation to the community in general."

Although Cornell was one of the first colleges to provide instruction in agricultural cooperation, little was effectively done to promote cooperative organization through research studies prior to 1922.[8]

Wisconsin. A third center of early college work in cooperation developed in Wisconsin with the establishment of a chair in "cooperation" in January 1913. At this time Wisconsin was gaining national attention for its "progressiveness" under the political leadership of Robert M. La-Follette, and under the educational guidance of Charles R. Van Hise, president of the University of Wisconsin.[9]

To understand the situation which gave birth to the course, it is necessary to realize that for several years a strong agitation for cooperative organization had been carried on by the Wisconsin Society of Equity which then had attained a considerable political influence.[10]

The Equity had early attracted the support of Charles McCarthy, the head of the Wisconsin Legislative Reference Library and the driving force behind the Wisconsin Board of Public Affairs,[11] and through these agencies McCarthy was able to exert effective influence on the character of cooperative development in Wisconsin. It is also significant that McCarthy's interest in agricultural cooperation was greatly stimulated by his close friendship with Sir Horace Plunkett who had collaborated with him in drafting the Wisconsin Cooperative Act of 1911. Of McCarthy, Plunkett said in 1915: "I never met a man with whose aims I seemed to have so much in common."[12]

The Wisconsin Board of Public Affairs had been set up in 1910 to make "basic studies relating to the human and social welfare of the State," and one of the first subjects to attract its attention was cooperation. At the request of the Board, John F. Sinclair of the Legislative Reference Library undertook a comprehensive study of cooperation which in 1912 was issued by the board in four parts: (1) Agricultural Cooperatives; (2) Cooperative Credit; (3) Municipal Markets; (4) Distributive or Store Cooperation.

In this study, Sinclair came to the conclusion "That the time has now arrived for the state of Wisconsin to take an active interest in directing the cooperative movement within its borders." He recommended that a new Division of Cooperation be created under the general supervision of the Board of Regents. It was to be placed in the General Extension Department of the University rather than in the Extension Department of the Agricultural College, since "to be effective, the division should not only be of service to those of our people who live on the farm and in the small town, important as this field is, but such a division should minister also to the 900,000 of our people who live in cities of 2,500 and over."[13]

McCarthy on July 11, 1912, supplemented "Sinclair's recommendation" by proposing:

> (1) That we should teach marketing and cooperative methods in the short course in the University; (2) That we should make some arrangements for the teaching of the same in rural schools of the state; and (3) that we should have some paper or publication which would tell monthly or perhaps quarterly exactly what the cooperative agricultural storehouses had, their prices, etc., so that the people in the city who wish to have stores of this kind would know from whom to buy in the state, and so that the progress of the movement be well marked; and (4) that we should provide for cooperative credit units . . ."[14]

While Sinclair's recommendations, plus those of McCarthy, did not lead to legislative action, they did emphasize the importance of cooperation in the state, and the need for a more aggressive policy with respect to cooperation by the University.

It was largely as a result of this stimulation that the Board of Regents of the University of Wisconsin established a professorship in cooperation in the Department of Agricultural Economics headed by Dr. Henry C. Taylor.[15] Dr. Taylor secured approval for the appointment to this post of Benjamin H. Hibbard, then professor at Iowa State College, who began his work on January 1, 1913.[16]

Even prior to the establishment of the chair in cooperation the University had been brought into connection with cooperatives through the Board of Public Affairs. At the request of the Board, which was aroused by the complaints of cheese producers, the Department of Agricultural Economics had undertaken an analysis of cheese marketing conditions in the state. The report on this study, presented in person to the Board by Dr. Taylor, gave consideration to the use of cooperation as a remedy for exising cheese marketing conditions. While this report was "conservative," it provided a careful analysis of facts necessary for the establishment of a sound cooperative program and set the mold for a number of marketing studies undertaken by the University during the next few years.[17] The conclusions of this bulletin are of so much interest as an expression of the then current cooperative philosophy of the University that they are here given in some detail:

> The marketing of cheese is not so simple as we may have supposed when this study was undertaken . . . It is unquestionably true that the present system is not faultless . . . But in any effort to improve the present system great care should be taken. No institution which is performing efficiently an important function for a fair price should be attacked. Where excessive charges are being made, two methods are available for establishing fair charges. The first of these is cooperation; the second is state regulation. The first is valuable locally, the second for state-wide questions. What are the opportunities for improving the marketing of cheese by cooperation and state regulation?

> Some of the unsatisfactory phases of the present system of marketing cheese are local, hence there is a field for cooperation. There is opportunity for joint action on the part of the patrons of each factory, if organized for the purpose of providing for the manufacture and sale of cheese. This does not necessitate the ownership of a factory. A cheese-maker who owns a factory may be hired to manufacture the cheese. The essential thing is that the patrons control the marketing of their product with a view of eliminating the temptation to dishonesty in this process. No farmer would hire a man to do his threshing for so much per bushel and give the thresherman the exclusive privilege of selling the grain. Why then should a group of farmers who pool their milk and hire a man to make cheese, leave to the cheese-maker the business of disposing of the product? . . .

> The first duty of the state is to learn more of the present system of marketing as a basis of popular education on questions relating to the disposal of farm products. The state will then be in a position to furnish timely information regarding methods of marketing and the condition of the market, and to regulate any unjust acts or charges which may arise in the marketing of the products.

During 1911 and 1912 there was some disagreement between the University as represented by Dean Russell and Dr. Taylor and the McCarthy-Equity group, who favored more aggressive action. McCarthy was continuously prodding Taylor to "get in and learn cooperation." In a memorandum, "The Development of Research and Education in Agricultural Co-operation and Marketing at the University of Wisconsin 1910-20," Taylor recalls the following conversation that he had with

McCarthy when the cheese marketing study was just being started (1912): "I said to McCarthy 'We do not know enough about the marketing of cheese as yet to act intelligently.' McCarthy replied, 'Get to doing something and you'll learn a lot faster.'" Taylor in looking back conceded that he was somewhat conservative but he attributed this to his fear that McCarthy and the Equity were wanting action in advance of understanding.[18]

In January 1913 an agreement was reached with McCarthy under which the University would "educate but not directly stimulate" the formation of cooperative organizations. This remained the policy of the University for the next five years. Then in 1918 Taylor took the position that "the time was ripe for the college to become somewhat more aggressive in the question of dealing directly with farmers on the subject of co-operation."[19]

Minnesota. Early in the century the subject of cooperation was attracting much attention in the state of Minnesota. For several years Dr. John A. Williams, head of the Department of Economics at the University, had shown a sympathetic interest in cooperatives, and in 1909-10 information on cooperation was included in courses in agricultural economics taught by John Lee Coulter. It was this experience that encouraged Coulter to prepare his *Cooperation Among Farmers* (1911) as a textbook on the subject. When Coulter left the University in 1910 no attention was apparently given to cooperation until 1912 when Professor Carl W. Thompson included it in his course in agricultural economics. In the following year, this work was taken over by L. D. H. Weld, who devoted considerable attention to cooperative marketing in his seminar on agricultural economics. An interesting by-product of this seminar was a university bulletin entitled *Studies in the Marketing of Farm Products* (1915) by Weld and his graduate students. This bulletin contained research studies relating to cooperative marketing. One of these was a report "Cooperative Potato Marketing in Minnesota" by O. B. Jesness.

The first Minnesota research in agricultural cooperation thus was a product of Professor Weld's seminar. A number of general studies soon followed, the first being a survey of cooperative development in Minnesota.[20]

From research, it was not long before the college undertook extensive encouragement through the provision of short courses for cooperative managers, and other employees, and by direct assistance to cooperatives on their problems of organization and operation. Much of the work was carried on as a joint project with representatives of the Office of Markets.

Nebraska, Oregon, Kentucky. With the establishment of the Office of Markets, the interest aroused by the conferences on marketing and farm credits and by the reports of the American Commission, several other colleges in 1914 began to give instruction in agricultural coopera- tion. Among these were the University of Nebraska, Oregan State Col- lege, and the University of Kentucky.

The origin of the course at the University of Nebraska in 1913 has been explained as follows by H. C. Filley, its founder:

> I attended the first national conference on marketing and farm credits that was held in Chicago and decided that there was a need for the teaching of marketing . . . I sketched a course to be given the next year without having any very definite idea concerning the textbook or other material that I could use in the course. A few weeks before the course would begin I happened to secure a copy of Powell's *Cooperation in Agriculture.* As a result, the course was primarily a course in cooperative marketing . . .[21]

The inauguration of a course in "Cooperation" at Oregon State Col- lege in the college year 1913-14 was largely due to the interest of Pro- fessor Hector McPherson. His attention had been aroused from 1907 to 1909 while he was a student in Germany. This had led him to prepare a doctoral thesis at the University of Chicago on *Cooperative Credit Societies in Quebec* (1911) and this in turn resulted in his selection as one of the members of the American Commission to study cooperation and rural credit in Europe. Convinced that cooperative action was es- sential to an improvement of agricultural conditions, McPherson intro- duced the course on Cooperation, which was continued for several years with little change. The catalogue description of the course shows the influence of McPherson's background:

> This course takes up the origin and development of the cooperative move- ment in Europe and its introduction into the United States. It sets forth the general principles underlying the economic and social activities of co- operative associations. Then, following this, the different types of organization, the methods by which they are formed, their working plans in different enter- prises, and the factors which determine their success or failure, will be studied in detail. The store, the factory, the dairy and cow testing associations, the credit organization, etc., will be taken up systematically, and the advantages and difficulties of cooperation will in each case receive careful analysis.

Under McPherson's stimulus the college also began at this time actively to assist cooperative organization through research and exten- sion activities carried on in cooperation with the Office of Markets.

In 1914, the University of Kentucky offered its first course in agricultural cooperation under the title "Cooperation and Marketing," with Charles E. Bohannon as instructor. The character of this course is shown by its description in the University catalog 1914-15:

> The purpose of this course is to put the student in touch with the principles underlying cooperation and the science of marketing. A detailed study will be made of the rise and development of the various forms of agricultural cooperation in Europe and America, including cooperative buying, cooperative stores, cooperative marketing, general farmers' organizations, and rural credits. An attempt will be made to ascertain the essentials of successful cooperative effort along each of the lines studied, especially attention will be given to marketing and cooperation in Kentucky.

For some years Kentucky farmers had been greatly interested in cooperative marketing as applied to tobacco and this led in 1916 to the establishment of a cooperative bureau in the experiment station.[22]

By 1915 special instruction in agricultural cooperation was thus recognized in at least seven of the state agricultural colleges, while research and extension work related to agricultural cooperation was also becoming well established. As we now will see, the importance of agricultural cooperation was gaining concurrent recognition in state departments of agriculture.

Encouragement from State Marketing Departments

Spurred by the creation of the Office of Markets in the Department of Agriculture in 1913, and encouraged by the sentiment in favor of better marketing practices displayed at the national conferences on marketing and farm credits, a number of the states undertook to improve agricultural marketing conditions through the establishment of state marketing divisions or departments.[23]

By 1915 the director of the newly formed Idaho Department of Farm Markets declared before the National Conference on Marketing and Farm Credits: "The State assistance to marketing idea has come to stay, and I am confident that within a very short time most of the states in the Union will be conducting such departments." At this same conference the state marketing officers present formed a National Association of State Marketing Officials while the resolutions of the conference strongly urged all states to create marketing departments "at the earliest time."[24]

These early state marketing departments generally worked in close cooperation with the newly formed federal Office of Markets and with the extension and research departments of the state agricultural col-

leges.[25] Although they differed considerably in objectives and character
they all had as their major aim the improvement of agricultural marketing methods through cooperatives or other means. These departments
were commonly required by law to investigate and promote efficient
distribution, to gather and disseminate market information, and to develop and make effective standard grades for agricultural products.

The State Market Commission of California. The most significant of
the state marketing programs from the standpoint of influence on cooperative development was undertaken in California under the aggressive leadership of Colonel Harris Weinstock, as State Market Director.[26]

Weinstock had been appointed late in 1914 under an act providing
for a "State Commission Market" which gave wide discretionary powers
to the State Market Director. Building upon the successful experience
of the California Fruit Growers' Exchange and other California cooperative marketing organizations, Weinstock immediately undertook to
establish "cooperative marketing combinations under government patronage, but without enforced control."[27] As Nourse has pointed out, he
"aspired to work out a program under which each of the important lines
of production in the State would be integrated into a single marketing
organization." Thus, "so far as public manifestations were concerned,
the commodity marketing movement began with the appointment of
Colonel Harris Weinstock."[28]

Immediately upon taking office, Colonel Weinstock issued a general
statement "to the people of California" (Dec. 1, 1915) in which he
declared:

> To me, as State Market Director, has been assigned the task of working
> out some scientific system of selling which will enable the producer to sell
> at a fair price everything which he can raise, and which will at the same
> time enable the consumer to purchase it for less than he now pays ... The
> hope that I have in mind, along the lines of remedying existing marketing
> evils, lies among other lines, in the utilization on the one hand of existing
> machinery for the distribution of farm productions and, on the other hand,
> to aiding and directing the producers scientifically to do their own marketing.
> The state will have performed its highest function, in my opinion, when
> it will have aided the producer to help himself. It is simply necessary for
> the California farmer to get hold of the "know-how" to produce the highest
> possible marketing results. This "know-how," in my opinion, can best be
> acquired by collective action on the part of the California producers ...
> Singly and alone I can, of course, hope to do very little. My chief success
> must come from winning and holding the earnest and hearty cooperation of
> the producers and distributors; without their support, failure is inevitable;
> with their support wonders can be accomplished. The present is the first
> Market Commission created in California and I am the first Market Director
> ever appointed in California. I have no precedents to guide me. The work
> right from the first hour must be creative and constructive in character.[29]

Armed with a written opinion obtained from the Department of
Justice "to the effect that cooperative associations among farmers for
marketing their products might be formed in such a way as not to
violate the anti-trust laws,"[30] Weinstock proceeded to organize cooperatives among growers of the various specialty crops.

The Market Commission followed no set rule in setting up cooperative marketing associations, the plan for each organization being
based upon a study of the underlying conditions. Some were established
on a non-stock membership basis. Others were formed with capital stock.
One general idea was, however, common to all—that the association
would control a sufficient fraction of the crop to be marketed to influence selling prices.[31] To achieve such control, enforceable membership
agreements were devised running for various periods of time and a considerable fraction of the growers of the crops to be marketed were required to sign them before they would become effective.

The first marketing association to be promoted by Weinstock, the
California Peach Growers, Inc., was largely patterned on the plan of
the California Raisin Growers which had been formed in 1911. In an
address to the Peach Growers Association promotion committee, November 20, 1915 (his first official statement as Market Director), Weinstock
declared: "Unless you can follow the lines so successfully demonstrated
by the raisin growers, there can be little or no hope for the future of
the California dried peach industry."[32]

Producers were required to sign marketing agreements for a period
of five years which would give the trustees of the association full jurisdiction over the crops to be marketed. To insure efficient operations,
these contracts were to be effective only after a certain proportion of
the growers had signed them.[33]

One of the difficulties recognized by Weinstock in getting this plan
accepted was the unwillingness of growers "to place the marketing of
their crops for a period of five years into the hands of seven directors
at this time unknown." To give growers confidence, Weinstock therefore
proposed "that the trustees of the proposed Peach Growers Association
elect as one of the proposed seven directors of the association a state
representative to be nominated by the Market Director, approved by
the Governor, and elected by the proposed 25 trustees." This "public
director" was to occupy "substantially the same position as does a state
bank examiner in the supervision of State banks." He was to attend all
meetings and report any weakness to the Market Director who, in
turn, was to take any steps necessary to afford "the fullest protection
to the absent stockholders or subscribers, thus tending to secure wise,

honest, and economic management." This provision for a public director soon became a standard feature of the associations promoted by Colonel Weinstock as Market Director.[34]

A considerable number of later prominent cooperative marketing associations were soon established in accordance with Weinstock's views, among them being the California Prune and Apricot Growers, Inc., and the Poultry Producers of Central California, Inc. These various organizations served as laboratories for testing out the theory of "commodity marketing" which was to be broadcast over the nation in the early 1920's by Aaron Sapiro, the attorney who drafted most of the legal documents used by the organizations promoted by the Market Commission.[35]

Weinstock did not confine his efforts to the organization of cooperative marketing associations. Shortly after he had taken office he proposed the organization of two state "bureaus of distribution," one for citrus and one for deciduous fruits. The proposed bureaus of distribution were modeled on the plan for cantaloupes in the Imperial Valley then being "successfully conducted by the Federal Office of Markets." They were designed for the purpose of co-ordinating the marketing efforts of all agencies whether cooperative or private.[36] Although there was a considerable measure of grower support for these plans, they were effectively opposed by the managements of the California Fruit Growers' Exchange (citrus) and of the California Fruit Exchange (deciduous), who considered them unnecessary and disruptive to their present organized efforts.[37]

Although it was charged that Weinstock exceeded his authority in his cooperative promotion efforts,[38] his program was so popular with the farmers of the state that it was sustained in 1917 when a revised Act was passed, "which provided in express terms for all of the things which the director had been doing for the great part of the two preceding years." By this Act the State Market Commission was given authority:

> To act as advisor for producers and distributors when requested, assisting them in economical and efficient distribution of any such products at fair prices.

> To gather and disseminate impartial information concerning supply, demand, prevailing prices, and commercial movements, including common and cold storage of any such products.

> To promote, assist and encourage the organization and operation of cooperative and other associations and organizations for improving the relations and services among producers, distributors and consumers of any such products, and to protect and conserve the interests of the producers and consignors of such products.

To foster and encourage cooperation between producers and distributors of any such products, in the interest of the general public.

To foster and encourage the standardizing, grading, inspection, labelling, handling, storage and sale of any such products.

To act as a mediator or arbitrator, when invited by both parties, in any controversy or issue, that may arise between producers and distributors of any such products.

To certify, for the protection of owners, buyers or creditors, when so requested, warehouse receipts for any such products, verifying quantities and qualities thereof, and to charge for such service fees sufficient to make the service at least self-supporting.

To issue labels bearing the seal of the state market commission on request of the producer, packer, canner or distributor, for any such products, for which state labels have not otherwise been authorized by law, under such rules and regulations as the director may deem necessary and to charge for such labels such fees as in the judgment of the state market director may be proper.

To act on behalf of the consumers of any such products in conserving and protecting their interests in every practicable way.

To improve, broaden and extend in every practicable way, the distribution and sale of any such California products throughout the markets of the world.

To promote in the interest of the producer, the distributor, and consumer, economical and efficient distribution and marketing of all or any agricultural, fishery, dairy and farm products produced, grown, raised, caught, manufactured or processed within the state of California.

It shall be within the province of the state market director, hereinafter provided for, to determine and decide, when, where and to what extent, existing conditions render it necessary or advisable to carry out any or all the purposes of this act and he is herewith granted power and authority to carry out any or all of said purposes.

Although the State Market Director promoted all of these objectives, he directed his primary attention to the organization of strong cooperatives. To Weinstock, David Lubin, and Aaron Sapiro, these objectives were all interrelated. As Nourse has noted:

These men looked upon California as a great and varied producing plant with a large and diversified commercial surplus which called for skillful merchandising in the markets of this country and abroad. Each commodity line represented to them a department of the whole State's business, and they believed that the interest of these commodity groups could be dealt with effectively only if each were brought together under some co-ordinated leadership which should provide for adequate standardization and inspection of the product, the dissemination of information, the provision of adequate credit, and skillful distribution of the production in all available markets. The State Market Commission was conceived as the official promoter and guide of such organization along cooperative lines.[39]

However, with the establishment of strong cooperative marketing associations for most of the California specialty crops, the need for Weinstock's services became less apparent and resentment gradually set in toward his "paternalistic policies." This was heightened by his attempt to organize a California Federation of Farmers Cooperative Associations to increase the effectiveness of cooperative action. Although this organization was established in the spring of 1917 with Aaron Sapiro as its secretary, it never succeeded in getting the support of the California Fruit Growers Exchange and other important organizations which had not been set up through the efforts of the State Market Director.[40] Moreover, the special problems brought about by the war forced the State Market Commission to give more consideration to routine duties of standardization and inspection. After 1918 Weinstock was less aggressive although he continued as State Market Director until March 1920. The following year the Legislature abolished the State Market Commission and transferred its functions to the State Department of Agriculture.

What then were the lessons from this experience? To what extent did it affect the character of evolving cooperative development? Unquestionably, it established the idea that a state government could accept responsibility in helping to organize and direct cooperative activity as a matter of broad public policy. This encouraged other states to give more direct encouragement to cooperative development. On the other hand, this experience also showed how easily state assistance could develop into a bureaucratic form of control, and this served as a warning on the dangers of paternalism. Of more direct importance was the fact that the California State Market Commission provided a seedbed for nurturing the philosophy of "commodity marketing," and a laboratory for trying it out under varying conditions and situations. Out of this experience came the pattern for the commodity marketing movement to be spread nationally and internationally by Aaron Sapiro in the early 1920's.

Chapter X

FARM ORGANIZATION STIMULATION—
The Farmers' Union, the Equity, and the M.F.A.

Four general farm organizations gave significant encouragement to cooperative business in the period from 1896 to 1920—the Farmers' Union, the Society of Equity, the Grange, and the emerging Farm Bureau. Of less national significance, but comparable in its general encouragement to cooperative enterprise was the Missouri Farmers Association. The part that each played in directly advancing cooperatives is examined in this and the following chapter. Moreover, all of these organizations gave support to legislation and governmental action which created conditions more favorable to cooperative development. They deserve a large share of the credit for the legislation which made possible better roads, better schools, and better marketing conditions. They also fostered legislation which specifically facilitated the formation of cooperative associations and assured their legal position.

The Farmers' Union

In 1902, two new general farm organizations began to promote cooperation among farmers in the South and Midde West. The first, the Farmers' Educational and Cooperative Union of America, originated in Texas; while the second, the American Society of Equity, started in Indiana.

The Farmers' Union was patterned largely on the defunct Farmers' Alliance, and like the Alliance it centered attention on the organization of cooperative associations. In fact, as one student of farm organization has said: "The Farmers' Union took up cooperation where the Farmers' Alliance dropped it."[1]

From Texas the Farmers' Union quickly spread into Oklahoma, Arkansas, and Louisiana, and from there it moved eastward until by 1905 it had covered the Cotton Belt. From then until about 1912 the bulk of the Union's strength was in the South, although during 1907 and 1908 active state branches were formed in California, Oregon, and Washington.

The cotton-holding plan. During its early life the Union was mainly concerned with measures designed to raise the price of cotton. As part of this program, cotton warehouses were established at local handling centers to enable farmers to store and hold their cotton for fixed "minimum" prices.[2] When the peak of this development had been reached in 1909, there were some 1,500 local warehouses scattered throughout the South, although most of them were established as farmers' stock companies rather than as true cooperative organizations.

In the first years of the holding movement the Farmers' Union gave little attention to cotton marketing. However, it soon became apparent to Union officials that a program was needed for the sale of cotton on a quality basis through the local warehouses. The question naturally arose, What good were the warehouses without a plan for marketing the stored cotton on a quality basis? By 1906 Union officials in Texas began to see how the warehouses could be used as a foundation for a cooperative selling agency. This placed the Union leaders in a dilemma. The Union had the storage facilities, the cotton, and the vision of great possibilities, but it knew little about the cotton marketing business. A question from a young farmer brought a practical solution to this problem: "Why can't farmers be taught to grade and class cotton?"

Obtaining the services of an experienced cotton buyer as teacher, some 64 farm men and boys were assembled by the Union in Dallas for a 10-week period to learn cotton classing. The results were surprisingly good—to the consternation of scoffing regular cotton dealers, who had belittled the experiment. In 1907 the number of students in the school jumped to 163.[3] In this year a similar school was established by the Union in Alabama, and in 1908 one was established in Georgia.

With trained personnel it was now possible to develop state-wide programs. In Texas, the Farmers' Union Cotton Company was formed in November 1906 to sell direct to spinners, with the local Farmers' Union warehouses to serve as assembling units. Another large-scale organization, the Farmers' Union Cotton Company of Memphis, was organized in 1907 with even broader aims, and it opened offices in Liverpool and Manchester, England. In Georgia, the Union Consolidated Warehouse

Company which was designed to render marketing as well as storage
service was established in 1908. However, none of these over-ambitious
companies long survived due to their weak financial structures, inexperienced managements, and lack of strong supporting local associations.[4]

The problem of making the warehouse program more effective for
marketing purposes was a constant concern of Union officials.[5] This
impelled the president of the Union in 1908 to request the formulation
of a "practical and systematic plan" for getting the warehouses to cooperate. In the plan that was devised by O. T. Ladson in response to
this request, it was pointed out:

> While the Farmers Union warehouses, under separate ownership and
> management, are of great benefit, yet it is also true that much greater benefits
> can be secured by federating such warehouses into state and interstate
> central companies . . . One of the main causes for low prices of cotton is
> because too much cotton is "dumped" on the market in the early fall months,
> instead of being held back, and sold out as the world needs and demands
> it . . .
>
> By federating all the Farmers Union warehouses in each state, and forming
> state central companies, these central companies, having such great financial
> strength, would quickly attain high commercial ratings, and warehouse
> receipts or certificates, guaranteed by such central companies, would be re-
> garded as A-1 security or collateral, in any bank in the United States . . . The
> forming of such strong central companies will have to *precede* the forming and
> successful operation of central *selling companies* . . . Of course, to successfully
> carry out these plans will require a great deal of sound business sense. It will
> require loyalty and confidence and cooperation of the membership now owning
> such warehouses, as well, also, of the rank and file of the entire membership.
> The most experienced men should be placed at the head of such central
> companies, and every responsible officer and agent should be required to give
> fidelity bonds. The central companies should arrange to borrow the needed
> funds, and no favoritism should be shown to one warehouse or locality more
> than to others, in the distribution of borrowed money . . . It is impossible . . .
> to more than briefly outline plans of this character. In order to make these
> central companies successful, the loyalty, confidence, and support of your
> membership *must be forthcoming*, otherwise, such plans will result in failure.[6]

This interesting plan—which incidentally throws light on the weakness of the existing warehouse and marketing operations—would have
done much, if conscientiously followed, to provide the basis for an effective cotton marketing program. However, little support for it was
found as it was somewhat ahead of the existing state of organizational
experience.

Spread of cooperative buying. During its first few years the energies
of the Farmers' Union were largely concentrated on the improvement
of cotton prices and little encouragement was given to cooperative buying. Its leaders were fearful of repeating the mistakes attributed to the

Grange and the Alliance, and they tried to preserve the Union as a sellers' organization. This attitude was well expressed by the president of the Texas State Union in 1907: "The Grange and Alliance sought to cheapen the farmers' plows, sugar and clothing; the Union seeks to get the maximum price for his cotton and potatoes."[7]

Nevertheless, it was not long before cooperation in buying began to grow in significance. At first—as with the Grange—trade of Union members was centered with selected firms. Then as the movement grew, the old Grange plan of state business agents reappeared along with the establishment of local stores owned by Farmers' Union members.[8]

Cooperative purchasing through the Union was more successful in Georgia than in the other southern states, probably due to the effective leadership and good business management of J. G. Eubanks, the state business agent.[9] Starting in 1906, Eubanks built up a very extensive system of local business agents through which supplies could be distributed to farmers so as to give them the advantage of "milling or harvest rates on flour" and "carlot" rates on local purchases of goods. The success of these efforts led the Georgia Farmers' Union in 1907 to set up a farm implement plant as well as a fertilizer factory—The Union Phosphate Company. It was claimed in 1909 that the latter saved Georgia farmers $180,000 on their fertilizer purchases in 1908.[10]

Dissatisfaction with the state local business agent plan led to the formation of more and more local purchasing and marketing associations throughout the South. After 1910, North Carolina became the center of Farmers' Union cooperative development in the South. Here the state Union established a business office in 1909 which did a business of $231,626 in 1910, principally in the distribution of fertilizer. This development was soon resisted by the fertilizer companies which offered special prices to local Unions, with the result that soon more business was done through the local and county Unions than through the state office. In 1912, the executive committee undertook to handle the fertilizer business through a committee of its own members to offset this situation. While most of the cooperative business of the Farmers' Union in North Carolina was done through the county Unions and the locals, there were many separate organizations also formed by Union members. These were principally stores, cotton warehouses and cotton gins followed in number by telephone lines, creameries, mills, and factories.[11]

The shift to the West. After 1910 the Union began to recede rapidly in the South (except in North Carolina and Virginia) and to some extent in the Far West, and to swell in the Central West, particularly in Kansas, Nebraska, and Iowa. By 1919, over one-half the membership was concentrated in these three states, while in 1910 more than three-fourths of the membership had been located in the southern states.

The expansion which occurred in the Far West after 1907 and in the Central West after 1912 was based almost entirely upon the development of cooperative enterprises of the Rochdale type. While at first the major emphasis was given to group purchasing and the organization of cooperative stores, it was not long before Farmers' Union elevators and livestock shipping associations began to grow rapidly in number. With little delay the state Unions began to promote wholesale exchanges for marketing and purchasing. The first association of this type was the Tri-State Terminal Warehouse Company which was incorporated in 1911 to serve as the marketing agent for local Farmers' Union grain marketing companies of Washington, Oregon, and Idaho.[12] Its capital stock was held by individual farmers and local farm companies. With offices in Seattle, Portland, and Spokane, the Tri-State operated from 1911 to 1921. During this period it consistently paid dividends on stock of about 10 per cent annually, while acquiring ownership of about a score of county warehouses and elevators.

It is of interest that the Washington State Farmers' Union first introduced "commodity marketing" from California into the Pacific Northwest, from where it spread to the wheat-growing areas of the central states. In December 1919, at the invitation of the Farmers' Union of Washington, Aaron Sapiro presented a plan for the cooperative marketing of wheat based upon the experience of prune growers in California.[13] As a result of Sapiro's talk, the Union created a committee "to prepare the plans and work out all the details for such an organization to market grain." As reported by A. C. Adams:

> Outstanding wheat farmers, whether Farmers Union men or not, were selected to serve on the committee, which promptly organized and got under way with Sapiro retained as counsel. A similar committee was created for Idaho, likewise sponsored by the Union. While the Idaho committee comprised a separate group of individuals, the two committees worked in union and frequently as one group. The secretary of the Washington State Farmers Union served as trustee for both committees, handling all the funds and maintaining appropriate records.

This led to the formal incorporation of the Washington Wheat Growers Association in August 1920, and to the incorporation of the Idaho Wheat Growers Association a month later. The two organizations functioned as one with a common business office in Spokane, with A. C. Adams as Secretary.[14]

The Tri-State Terminal Warehouse Company did not long survive the adoption of the pool plan which was designed to bring all wheat producers into one organization so as to achieve orderly marketing. Although an attempt was made to reorganize the company after the pool plan had failed to give satisfaction, this proved unsuccessful. The Tri-State Terminal Warehouse Company was thus a casualty of the new marketing philosophy introduced by Sapiro. If it had not been for "his contagious enthusiasm, leaders would undoubtedly have continued with the Tri-State plan with probable increasing support from the country as prices went lower and farmers grew worse off with no other method offered."[15]

Kansas and Nebraska expansion. Of more permanent significance was the Union's growth in Kansas and Nebraska and adjoining states which started about 1910. The primary object in these states was expressed in the preamble of the Nebraska State Union formed in December 1913: "To obtain a better and more direct market for all products of the farm, and to eliminate increasing expense in buying our supplies." Within a few years there were scores of Farmers' Union cooperative enterprises—mostly stores, elevators, and livestock shipping associations—operating in this general region.[16]

To serve these local enterprises terminal marketing and purchasing agencies were formed: The State Farmers' Union Exchange of Omaha, Nebraska in 1914, and the Farmers' Union Jobbing Association of Kansas City, Missouri, in 1915. Similar exchanges were soon formed to serve local Union cooperatives in Colorado, South Dakota, and Iowa.

The mushroom growth of cooperative livestock shipping associations (some of which were related to cooperative elevators and stores) also led to the formation of Farmers' Union livestock commission companies in several terminal markets—Omaha, 1917; St. Joseph, 1917; Sioux City, 1918; Kansas City, 1918; Denver, 1919.[17]

The Farmers' Union contribution. While the Grange supported cooperative enterprise as a general policy, the Farmers' Union made it the cornerstone of its program.

During the years from 1902 to 1920, the Farmers' Union's cooperative philosophy passed through two stages. Up to about 1908 the emphasis was placed on the raising of cotton prices through the holding campaigns. As experience proved the futility of these efforts, the Union turned to the more conservative program of building local and terminal cooperative enterprises. In the absence of satisfactory state cooperative laws, these enterprises were at first organized as farmers' stock corporations. With the passage of state laws of the Rochdale type—an action sponsored by state farmers' unions—the Union enterprises increasingly took the Rochdale form. Undoubtedly the Farmers' Union can be given much credit for stimulating the early growth of many soundly conceived and practically operated cooperative organizations.

The Society of Equity

While the Farmers' Union was emerging in Texas, the American Society of Equity was gestating in Indiana. In many ways, both were but different manifestations of the same impulse toward organization. The founder of the equity was J. A. Everitt, the editor of a farm magazine in Indianapolis. As early as 1901 Everitt had begun to urge the need for a powerful farmers' organization capable of fixing prices on important farm crops. The reception to this propaganda was so favorable that "in October (1902) he announced that the Society was to be organized, and charter members were urged to sign up."[18] Some two months later, on December 24, the American Society of Equity was granted its charter under the laws of Indiana.

The Society was established on a broadly democratic basis, under a provision in its articles of incorporation for the election of officers and directors by popular vote at the annual meeting. All farmers and "friends of agriculture" could be members upon paying a membership fee of $1.00 and dues of $1.00 a year. While individual members were not required to be members of local unions, such unions were recommended "for local affairs, social features, and assisting each other to hold crops." To facilitate the formation of local unions, a constitution and by-laws for governing local unions was drawn up which required an individual to sign an application for membership in which he agreed "to follow the reasonable advice of the Society regarding crops, prices, and so forth."[19]

The philosophy of the Equity. The Bible of the Equity movement was *The Third Power,* published by Everitt in 1903. The key to this little book was its title. The *third power* was to be the power of organized agriculture. In Everitt's words: "There is some danger today lest we forget that there are three factors in production—land, labor and capital ... We thus have the three powers—money power, organized labor, and the farmer. And the question is as to the necessity of making the third power a real power."[20]

Everitt saw "combinations, cooperation and trusts in almost every branch of industry," while the farmers had "yet to draw the lesson." Others had "something to say about the prices at which they will sell

their commodities" but the farmer allowed "others to make prices for
him." In fact, Everitt maintained:

> All he is supposed to know under the present system is how to work sixteen
> hours a day and the road to market. When he gets there he finds a man
> who tells him how much his produce is worth, and if he wants to take
> something home with him he is told the price of that also. He has no
> organization, and no method of bringing pressure to bear on those who buy
> from him ... This arbitrary fixing of prices destroys the independence of the
> greatest class of our citizens—the farmers—and is more tyrannical than
> were the taxes imposed by George III.[21]

Therefore, said Everitt: 'From every point of view ... It is imperative that the farmers should organize, not for political, but for busines
reasons."[22]

The organization which was to "make the Third Power a real power"
was the American Society of Equity—which was "not a farmers' society
only, but an American society—that is [one] for all good Americans
who want to see better conditions prevail on the farm. It is not a benefit
society, but an equity society [since] benefits are always for an individual or class, while equity is for all."[23]

No elaborate program of organization was called for. This was emphasized by the following italicized paragraph in the "official plan" of
the Society:

> *Remember, it will not be necessary for each person to be told when to
> sell any crop. The plan contemplates that each owner of produce, wherever
> situated, shall supply the markets through the regular channels with all they
> will take at the minimum price, and stop selling the moment the buyers won't
> take more. There need be no fear that buyers will be out of the market long,
> because the world must have your goods all the time. They cannot do without
> them a month, nor a week, nor even a day. The price can be made and
> maintained as soon as this society has a million members. Then other millions
> will ask the price also.*[24]

Prices were to be controlled by organized farmers determining the
rate of flow to the market: According to Everitt: "All that is necessary. . .
to make prices on the farm is to control that part, which, at times,
overstocks the market, and which fixes prices on all."[25]

Everitt never gave his full enthusiasm to the promotion of cooperative associations, although he looked with favor on cooperative
elevators and warehouses as an adjunct to the Equity's program for
holding products off the market. Everitt favored farm storage as more
desirable.

> I claim the best place to hold grain is on the farm in a good safe,
> vermin-proof granary ... The next best way is to have a community ele-
> ator" (pp. 99-100) ... After the first declared object of the Equity in its

articles of incorporation: "To obtain profitable prices for all products of the farm, garden and orchard," came the following: "To build and maintain elevators, warehouses, and cold storage houses ... so that farm produce may be held for an advantageous price, instead of passing into the hands of middlemen or trusts.[26]

Like Sapiro in later years, he felt that, "without the ability to make equitable—profitable—prices, they [the cooperatives] will still be at the mercy of the trusts, speculators and gamblers."[27]

Everitt was not only concerned with raising the prices of products produced by farmers. He likewise felt that farmers should have something to say about the prices which they paid for supplies. He did not advocate cooperative buying as a means of lowering prices,[28] but relied more on the force of organized power through boycott. He declared:

> The farmers propose to take the field in a campaign for lower prices on the things they buy where lower prices should prevail, and they are going to use a force the operation of which will be irresistible . . . If a farmer were able to say to the thresher that he would pay five or four cents, and that no farmer in the United States would pay a cent more, and if this was an equitable price, he would get his threshing done for four or five cents. This is the position in which the American Society of Equity would place every farmer in the country with reference to buying.[29]

The wheat-holding campaigns. The first test of the Equity idea was made in May 1903 when the first of the farmers "Hold your Wheat" bulletins was issued from Equity headquarters. Growers were urged to hold for $1.00 per bushel on the Chicago market—a price which was considered fair on the basis of "visible supply" and "cost-of-production" factors. Although the campaign was launched on a rising market, the Equity took full credit for bringing the price up. This "achievement" naturally enhanced its prestige, and led to a great expansion in Equity membership.[30]

In 1904, the Equity's holding price on wheat was fixed at $1.20, while similar price-fixing campaigns were inaugurated for beans, oats, barley, timothy hay, cotton, corn, potatoes, and tobacco. However, wheat still "received the lion's share of attention." The results in holding wheat were almost as spectacular in 1904 as they had been in 1903 and this gave increased support to the holding philosophy. Although the price for 1905 was again set at $1.00 little was accomplished in arresting the decline which had set in.

By spring of 1906, extreme measures seemed necessary, and the Equity promoted a farmers' strike—which was simply the holding campaign advocated in more drastic form. While prices were not raised, the Equity took credit for cushioning the fall.[31]

By this time the experience with the holding campaigns had demonstrated the need for a stronger marketing program. It was being urged that the Equity should take full responsibility for marketing all farm crops and that growers should be required to sign marketing agreements. "Cooperative warehouses, elevators, and cold storage plants were endorsed, and for perishable crops canning and preserving factories were to be erected."[32]

The year 1908 marked the high point of the Equity attempt to control the wheat crop. With "dollar wheat" the objective, a comprehensive program was worked out which required binding pledges from farmers in six states—North Dakota, South Dakota, Minnesota, Nebraska, Kansas, and Oklahoma. With trained organizers, the pledging campaign was vigorously pushed. While this campaign was on, the price of wheat reached a dollar—due primarily to the weather which greatly reduced the crop. While this no doubt lessened the intensity of the drive, still thousands of farmers signed the pledges, particularly in North Dakota and Kansas.[33]

The need for marketing agencies to handle the pledged grain led the Equity in July 1909 to establish a grain growers marketing department which was to arrange for marketing on the principal terminal markets. This move which had considerable promise was blighted by the internal conflict which developed in the Equity soon after the plan was adopted. As will be shown later, the only area where a significant operation developed was in the Northwest—following the establishment of the Equity Cooperative Exchange.

Looking back on the wheat-holding campaigns, it is easy to disparage their effectiveness. While it is true that no great proportion of the total wheat crop was ever held, yet the program did retard somewhat the immediate disposal of wheat after harvest, and this may have exerted some influence on the market price. It is of more significance that the idea appealed to the farmers psychologically. The fact that tens of thousands joined the campaigns year after year in the belief that they could influence the price cannot be denied. This increased their spirit of independence and encouraged them to work together. No doubt, this force gave much encouragement to the rising cooperative elevator movement. At least, the popularity of the wheat-holding campaigns of 1903 and 1904 served to get the Equity under way as a farmers' organization.

War on the tobacco trust. The "grower monopoly" gospel of the Equity fell on fertile soil in Kentucky where tobacco growers were being ground mercilessly by the "tobacco trust."[34] As early as 1901 conditions in the tobacco districts had become so bad that restriction of acreage and tobacco pooling had become popular topics of discussion. When the American Tobacco Company was reorganized in October 1904 so as to effectuate better its control over the domestic industry[35] the resentment of growers could no longer be restrained, and growers began to flock to the Equity—which was being credited with success in its wheat-holding campaigns—as a last hope for relief.

The first pooling association to be formed was almost a mass uprising. Led by a wealthy planter, Felix G. Ewing, some 6,000 farmers assembled at Guthrie on September 24, 1904, and formed without delay the Dark Tobacco District Planters' Protective Association for the purpose of raising tobacco prices from 5 or 6 to 11 cents a pound. Immediately some 40,000 tobacco growers in the "Black Patch" of Kentucky and Tennessee joined the association, and those who did not join voluntarily were soon intimidated into membership by their neighbors. The control over the special type of tobacco grown only in this area was so tight that the American Tobacco Company, the principal buyer, paid the price, and this greatly enhanced the prestige of the Equity.[36]

In the more important burley district an even greater victory was achieved through the formation at Winchester in January 1907 of the Burley Tobacco Society on the pattern developed by the Planters' Protective Association.[37]

To insure that the association would not be declared illegal under the provisions of Kentucky's constitution, the Equity leaders had secured the enactment of a law which declared that any number of persons could lawfully "combine, unite, or pool, any or all of the ... farm products raised by them, for the purpose of classifying, grading, storing, holding, selling, or disposing of same ... for the purpose of obtaining a greater or higher price thereof than they sought or could obtain or receive by selling said crops separately or individually."[38]

As anticipated, the Burley Society was vigorously resisted. The "trust" fought the Burley Association with every weapon available: through control of newspapers, by applying pressure on bankers, by paying special prices to the timid or those financially harrassed. Even a "fake cooperative" was launched to cause confusion and wean away support for "the pool." The trust stopped at nothing to break the pooling arrangement[39]; and as the American Tobacco Company was practically the sole buyer of burley tobacco, crops were stored but not sold for two years. The determination not to sell unless at their own prices, caused the growers who were loyal to the association to take strenuous measures to maintain grower solidarity. This gave rise to the night-riding episodes of 1906 and 1907 which have become famous in American history and legend. The purpose and significance of "night riding" has been well described by Anna Youngman:

> The farmer trained by his association to see that his best interests lay in joint selling, was resolved to see that his neighbor should also recognize its benefits. Just as long as the latter did not do so, he made doubtful the success of the association, because, as a matter of course, any pooling agreement is strong only in proportion to the relative completeness of its control. The campaign of education, conducted under the auspices of authority, brought in some recalcitrants. But there were still "hill-billies" in plenty—an epithet analogous to that of the "scabs" of labor-union terminology . . . "The hill-billy" was profiting at the expense of his neighbors, but not for long. His neighbors proceeded to organize secret bands, first to threaten him, next to destroy his property, finally to whip, and if need were to kill him . . . There set in the era of night riding—an institution having historical precedents in the Ku-Klux Klans of the post-Civil War period, and finding immediate antecedents in the lynching bees of our modern civilization. As a result of the coercive measures adopted by the night riders, there has been an incidental property loss, in the Black Patch alone, estimated at $1,000,000 . . . The situation in the Blue Grass district has, generally speaking, been less serious in character . . . However deplorable has been the loss of life and the destruction of property, resulting in a public demoralization bordering on anarchy, the fact remains that it was only by the aid of night-riding that the farmers held their ground against the trust and the "regie" buyers.[40]

After two years of futile holding in the face of a growing public disfavor for night riding, the burley growers determined to eliminate, or "cut out," the production of the 1908 crop. This was largely effected by the persuasion of influential planters who organized themselves as the "Peaceful Riders by Day" to call on farmers at their homes and obtain their pledges of support. Confronted by this persistence, which severely reduced the 1908 crop, the American Tobacco Company finally yielded and agreed to pay the prices asked.[41]

Although the tobacco growers had won a remarkable victory, it proved impossible to hold the organizations together. The victory had been won, but farmers were unwilling to go through a similar grim struggle in the future. Moreover, conditions had been temporarily improved and tobacco prices for a few years were more satisfactory.

Despite the virtual collapse of the movement in 1909, a very significant benefit resulted from this experience. Nothing could have more forcibly drawn attention to the inequitable methods of the tobacco trust, and this forced a measure of improvement in merchandising methods. With the decline of the pooling movement the auction method of sale increased rapidly. While not free of abuse, the auction system at least brought buying and selling into public view. Moreover, the success of the pool had left a threat that growers could organize again should conditions warrant and this temporarily gained for growers a certain measure of respect.[42]

A more tangible gain resulted in the form of 17 warehouses which were built from funds collected by the Burley Society from growers' sales.[43]

Some years later Hibbard held that the growers "undoubtedly gained a much stronger position as bargainers than they would have had without the pooling episode."[44]

Conflict and schism. With growth and expansion, discontent began to develop with the original plan of organization and particularly with Everitt's all powerful position in the society. In May 1905 Everitt attempted to stem this rising sentiment by proclaiming a new constitution which provided for "county-unions" and "for a definite scheme of representation at the annual conventions." These reforms did not satisfy the delegates to the 1905 convention who revised the constitution by adding state unions who were to have control over Equity activities within states.[45]

However, Everitt's leadership was not severely challenged prior to the 1906 convention when a faction led by M. Wes Tubbs, the national secretary, obtained support for the Rochdale type of cooperative marketing as well as for the development of a plan of association with organized labor "to the end that consumers may secure the necessities of life at equitable prices."[46] Everitt sharply opposed these measures, as weakening to the crop-holding objectives of the Equity. This led to a bitter controversy which finally resulted in Everitt's eclipse at the 1907 convention.

With a new slate of officers the Equity was completely reorganized on the basis of local, state, departmental, and district unions. Nevertheless, the Society continued to disintegrate except in the northwestern states of Wisconsin, Minnesota, the Dakotas, and Montana—where it continued to be strong for a number of years.[47] Although those who got control had advocated a vigorous program of cooperative marketing, they were not able to deliver one that was "definite and satisfactory,"[48] and as a result, those who were discontented formed in 1910 another organization, The Farmers' Equity Union, which gave its full attention to the promotion of cooperative enterprises.

Although the unity of the Equity movement was broken in 1907, it had set in motion forces which were greatly to promote agricultural cooperation during the next 10 years. After 1907 the real strength of the

Equity movement centered in the Wisconsin Society of Equity, the Equity Central Exchange, and the offshoot of the parent society, The Farmers' Equity Union.

The Wisconsin Society of Equity. From its beginning, the Equity movement in Wisconsin was aligned with the Progressive Movement headed by Robert M. LaFollette.

> Many of the farmers who assisted in the progressive upheaval believed that what was accomplished in the political field could likewise be accomplished in the economic. In essence, the LaFollette movement had blazed the trail for the economic organization that was to follow—The Equity and La-Follette movements had two things in common: first, they attracted their first substantial support in the western and northwest portions of the State; and second, they were antimonopolistic in philosophy. According to LaFollette, monopoly and graft were the corrupting influences in government; to the Equity these identical forces in the form of middlemen, boards of trade, bankers, and railroad interests were responsible for depressed agricultural prices. Both were fighting on a common ground but were utilizing different methods of attack.[49]

The farmers of Wisconsin were first attracted to the Equity by the "hold-your-wheat" campaigns of 1903 and 1904 and by a similar program to raise the price of potatoes by means of a "nation-wide strike." Although these and similar efforts to fix prices of farm products did not develop into permanent organizations, they were responsible for the establishment of a number of elevators and storage warehouses for potatoes, wool, tobacco, and other products which continued to function as cooperative marketing organizations. Combined with them in many instances were livestock shipping associations, while many also performed a side-line supply purchasing service.

From the time that the Wisconsin Society of Equity was formed in 1906, steady progress was made in the promotion of all kinds of cooperative enterprises. By 1914, the Wisconsin Society of Equity—with some 12,000 members—had become a powerful agency for stimulating cooperative activity of all kinds and during the next few years hundreds of various kinds of local cooperative associations were established.[50] In 1920, when the Wisconsin Society of Equity attained its greatest strength with some 40,000 members, there were 400 local cooperative purchasing and selling organizations, bearing the Equity name.[51]

While the Wisconsin Society of Equity gave first attention to the promotion of marketing associations, cooperative purchasing was not neglected. As the Equity took the position that purchasing should be carried on as a joint activity with marketing operations, rather than as a separate venture, a large proportion of the elevators and warehouses

were thus both marketing and purchasing associations. Purchasing operations were given specific assistance by the business department of the
Society which purchased for the locals such commodities as feeds, flour,
twine, and coal. The extent of this business, though the business department handled on a brokerage basis, reached $2,500,000 in 1920.[52]

Aside from the short-lived pooling organizations, the Equity associations in Wisconsin were mostly Rochdale in character. The formation
of associations on this basis was facilitated by the enactment—with
Equity support—of the Wisconsin Cooperative Law of 1911, which became the pattern for similar "Rochdale" laws in several other states.[53]

The Equity Cooperative Exchange. In Wisconsin, as we have seen,
the Equity generated a general cooperative movement. To the west in
Minnesota and the Dakotas, the Equity influence concentrated on the
problem of improving the methods of wheat marketing.

In this area, the hold-your-wheat campaigns had had their greatest
strength.[54] When they failed to raise prices—due to the inherent weakness
of the plan as well as its inability to finance those who held their wheat—
there was left a strong nucleus of Equity members who were firm in
their determination to correct the abuses of the Minneapolis grain market. This led to the organization of the Equity Cooperative Exchange at
Minneapolis in 1908 as part of a general plan of the Grain Growers
Department of the American Society of Equity "to organize the grain
growers on as many terminal markets of the nation as possible."[55]

The idea that the terminal market was the key to the solution of
the wheat marketing problem dated back to the early 1890's, as we
saw in chapter IV. A later effort of the same type had been the formation in 1902 of the short-lived Minnesota Farmers' Exchange, which
had failed through inability to gain a seat on the powerful Minneapolis
Chamber of Commerce.

The plan of organization was simple. Capital stock was issued to
farmers at $50 a share, and it paid interest of 8 per cent per year. The
balance of any earnings was "prorated back to the shippers of grain."
Each stockholder was restricted to one vote regardless of the number of
shares held. In effect, the organization was simply a farmer-owned cooperative commission firm.[56]

Although the Equity Cooperative Exchange was formed in 1908,
it was not incorporated until 1911 under the laws of North Dakota "for
the purchase and sale of grain on consignment on a one-vote per stockholder basis."[57] Moreover, the progress of the Exchange did not really
get started until August 1, 1912, when George Loftus—"an aggressive

and uncompromising foe of the organized grain trade"—became sales manager. Taking advantage of the bitter and ill-advised attacks being made on the Exchange by the Minneapolis Chamber of Commerce, Loftus succeeded in developing a tremendous farm support behind the Exchange program. Volume of wheat marketed through it increased from 1.8 million bushels in 1911-12 to 3 million bushels, and in the first four months of 1914-15, it amounted to 6.5 million bushels.[58]

Although the business methods of the Exchange were far from satisfactory due to the stress placed on propaganda rather than on operating performance, the fact remains that the Exchange had a program which struck a responsive chord among the discontented wheat growers of the Northwest.[59]

The Equity Cooperative Exchange was a significant organization for two reasons. In the first place it was the first terminal grain marketing association to become established in the Central West. By doing so, in the face of powerful opposition, attention was directed to the possibilities of such associations. In the second place, the Exchange "sought to organize the farmers on the basis of crop produced. By so doing, its leaders were pursuing a realistic course, for experience had revealed that the 'farming class' was a heterogeneous group consisting of farmers with differing and frequently antagonistic interests, and that the success of a marketing organization depended primarily on the ability to bring together producers of identical crops with identical problems."[60]

In 1918 the Exchange operated commission selling agencies at St. Paul and Superior and a terminal elevator of 300,000-bushel capacity at St. Paul. In that year "it established a line of elevators by selling enough of its capital stock at points where elevators were located at least to pay for the cost of the elevator." However, "these local elevators [were] treated as regards earnings as independent units, although all [were] owned by the Equity Cooperative Exchange and controlled from the central office at St. Paul." In 1922 the Equity owned 80 of these elevators located in the Dakotas and Minnesota. As a result of large losses incurred in these local elevator operations with the decline of wheat prices during 1920 and 1921, the Exchange was forced into bankruptcy in 1923. The remnants of the Exchange were largely absorbed by the growing Farmers' Union movement in the Northwest.[61]

The Farmers' Equity Union. When the Farmers' Equity Union broke away from the American Society of Equity in 1910 under the leadership of C. D. Drayton, it adopted an entirely different organizational approach. It discarded the plan of local, state, and departmental unions in favor of local cooperative business exchanges. Under the Farmers' Equity Union plan, "A local union and a local exchange [were] one and the same organization."[62]

The Farmers' Equity Union immediately began to promote the establishment of local cooperative creameries, elevators, stores, and similar enterprises along certain railroad rights-of-way with the intention of serving them through the establishment of central exchanges, rather than individuals, and any savings were to be repaid to them, in the same way that local exchanges repaid their savings to their individual members. In fact, the whole system was designed on the Rochdale plan of organization and federation.

The first central exchange was formed in 1916—the Farmers' Equity Union Grain Company of Kansas City—to market the grain of Equity Union local exchanges, then operating in Kansas, Nebraska, and Colorado. In addition to grain marketing, with incidental cooperative purchasing of farm supplies, the Equity early gave its attention to the organization of cooperative creameries, particularly "along the centralized pattern," where cream was gathered from a considerable area, either through cream stations or by direct shipment and manufactured at a central point. Such associations were usually formed in areas where there was not enough production to support local creameries. The first organization of this type (Equity Union Creameries, Inc.) was established at Aberdeen, South Dakota, in February 1916. This was soon followed by the organization of the Farmers Equity Cooperative Creamery Association at Orleans, Nebraska, in January 1917, and one at Lima, Ohio, in 1919.

Although the methods of the Farmers' Equity Union were not spectacular, they resulted in the establishment of many sound cooperative enterprises.

Significance of the Equity movement. The national encouragement given by the Equity movement to cooperative development has been inadequately recognized, largely due to the fact that the Equity, like the Farmers' Alliance, failed to survive as a farmers' organization.

Yet it cannot be denied that the first significant achievements in commodity pooling were made by the Equity, and that the enthusiasm for holding crops engendered by the Equity resulted in the formation of hundreds of cooperative elevators and warehouses.

As confidence in crop holding weakened, the Equity increasingly relied on the formation of cooperative business organizations. In Wisconsin, we have seen how an entire state was permeated by the cooperative doctrine of the Equity. This resulted in rooting cooperative methods so firmly that they have never been dislodged in the agricultural programs of that state.

The Equity movement, also, can be given much credit for its experimentation with large-scale organizations. The Equity Exchange, for many years, was a beacon light showing how farmers could organize over a wide area for marketing purposes. In a similar way, the regionals established by the Equity Union—which have persisted to the present—made a valuable contribution by the stress that was placed on organization in accordance with economic rather than political values.

For these reasons, the American Society of Equity, and its offshoots, cannot be ignored in any attempt to trace the development of cooperative institutions in the United States.

The Missouri Farmers Association

The same forces which spawned the Farmers' Union and the Equity brought forth the Missouri Farmers Association in 1917. William Hirth, its founder, as a young man was an ardent supporter of the Farmers' Alliance in the early 1890's, and he determined then to carry forward the aspirations of the Alliance and the Grange through the development of strong cooperative organizations. To expound his views he established a farm journal in 1908, *The Missouri Farmer and Breeder,* which became *The Missouri Farmer* in 1912. In 1913 Hirth began to espouse the formation of farm clubs with an article "Time for Farmers to Get Together." The farm club idea took hold and soon there were scores of them formed. As Ray Derr has said: "Farmers in various parts of Missouri were beginning again to consider the cooperative idea . . . The spark of hope was still burning—only its fanning by a zealot was needed to cause it to burst into flames." Hirth recognized this opportunity.

In 1917 the farm club coalesced in the establishment of a statewide organization—The Missouri Farmers Association—which was primarily concerned with the promotion of farmers' cooperative business activities. During the next two years the M. F. A. gathered strength, and in 1919 it was able to get enacted a state law which facilitated the organization of cooperative associations. By 1920 the organization claimed to represent some 60,000 farmers and 2,500 farm clubs. By then the M.F.A. had become the dominant voice of farmers in Missouri, and it was the counterpart to the Wisconsin Society of Equity in Wisconsin or one of the strong state farmers' unions.[63]

Chapter XI

FARM ORGANIZATION STIMULATION—

The Grange and the Farm Bureau

In the preceding chapter we examined how the Farmers' Union and the Equity movements influenced the character of cooperative growth starting about 1902. Of equal importance during this period was the stimulation given cooperation by the Grange and Farm Bureau movements.

The Revitalized Grange

With the collapse of the Farmers' Alliance following its absorption by the Populist Party, the National Grange again began to grow. While there were only 132,000 Grange members in 1896, by 1910 there were 425,000 and by 1915 the number had increased to 540,000. While the Grange, at the peak of its first development was spread over the South as well as over the North, the new growth occurred almost exclusively in the northern, middle western, and far western states.

New cooperative policies. By 1896 the Grange had lost much of its old crusading spirit for cooperation as a method of economic and social reform. While cooperation was still espoused, it had become subordinate in importance to the broad social and economic objectives of the order.[1] The attitude of the Grange toward cooperation at this time is shown by the following passage from the report of the Grange Committee on Cooperation in 1897:

> The history of cooperative movements having demonstrated beyond question that the only permanently successful schemes have been those which have adhered strictly to the Rochdale system, we believe that the National Grange will do well to reaffirm its advocacy of the Rochdale plan.[2]

The interest in cooperation began to revive from this point onward,

194

although the early enthusiasm was never entirely recaptured. In 1900, the Master of the National Grange declared: "There is a general demand for enlarging the scope and benefits of intelligent and conservative cooperation." In the following year the Committee on Cooperation held that it was "not practicable for the National Grange to perfect a plan of cooperation which would be satisfactory or profitable to all sections of the country." It was therefore recommended that each state adopt such plans as would best serve its interests. By this time more and more cooperatives were being established by farmers for specific purposes—elevators, creameries, shipping associations, and so forth. The Grange recognized their independent characters and wisely urged its members to join with other farmers wherever sound cooperative enterprises could be developed. This constructive attitude on the part of the Grange is shown in the report of the Committee on Cooperation for 1903 which recommended that the order "give its support and encouragement to every legitimate cooperative enterprise that has for its purpose the betterment of agricultural conditions, . . ."

In 1905 the Committee on Cooperation, finding that cooperative bureaus of information were functioning satisfactorily in some states, recommended this program for wider adoption. In that year the reports for several states showed that Grange mutual insurance plans were widespread and that cooperative buying and selling was steadily growing. The Michigan State Grange reported: "Our trade contract system is proving eminently successful. We are now carrying trade arrangements with some 40 different business houses. The aggregate business done for this year will amount to nearly $400,000."[3] During the next few years, most of the important state Granges encouraged cooperative marketing and purchasing through state business agents or by similar devices.

In 1909 the Committee on Cooperation further expressed itself with regard to Grange participation in cooperative organizations:

> Your committee would recommend that individual members form cooperative or state associations, such as mutual fire insurance companies, establish feed stations or exchanges for the purpose of pooling all farm supplies in a wholesale way, also take up the matter of selling the staple crops of our farms . . . All business associations should be established on sound business principles and managed by honest men with large experience and qualifications, and all transactions should be conducted on a cash basis. The Order of Patrons of Husbandry, subordinate Pomona, state, or national grange should not be involved as an organization in any of these enterprises.

In 1912, the Committee noted that "practical cooperation is arousing nation-wide interest" and urged the adoption of uniform cooperative laws. In that year reference was made to the organization of a state Grange exchange in Pennsylvania and to the New York plan for developing car door purchasing through Grange agents.

No significant change in Grange policy with respect to cooperation occurred during the war years. It was a period of experimentation, with each state Grange following the type of cooperative program that appeared best. In general the Granges encouraged group purchasing and incidental marketing through local and state business agents, as in Ohio, although in some states, as in New York, this system was giving way to the establishment of separate business corporations for buying and selling.

Following the war the increased interest in cooperation forced the Grange to reconsider its position with regard to cooperation. In its 1919 convention, the report of the Committee on Cooperation declared:

> Your committee has gone over the reports of the Cooperative Committee covering a period of the last twenty years to get an idea of what has been the sentiment expressed in these reports. They are good reading, and through them all runs a clear note of a stronger development in cooperation. We wish to strengthen this idea if possible, and to suggest a plan of action for the National Grange, which so far has not been strongly expressed, as most of the suggestions seem to be for state, Pomona and subordinate Granges.
>
> There is a strong feeling in the subordinate Granges that the National Grange has not taken the lead as it should in this valuable part of Grange development. Your committee believes the time has come when we can no longer refrain from taking an active part in what we have recommended for over fifty years.
>
> Every subordinate Grange should have its business agent, alive and alert, studying conditions and cooperating with the other agents of the County, making a strong unit of the County and the County units uniting in making the State the great clearing house for furnishing supplies and marketing produce; the State uniting through the National Grange or men chosen by it, until the vast and greatest industry of all should act as one man.[4]

When the National Grange convened in November 1920, farmers were in a determined mood following the precipitous decline of agricultural prices which had commenced in May, while there had been as yet no commensurate decline in non-agricultural prices. This increased their interest in more aggressive forms of cooperation, and encouraged them to work together for their common interests. This change of circumstances was reflected in the report of the Committee on Cooperation:

> The American farmer is thoroughly sick and tired of conditions that make it impossible for him to have a voice in determining what he is to receive for the product of his toil. They are tired of developing millionaire grain gamblers, meat packers and food distributors, while tenantry increases and the boys and girls leave the farm by the thousands. The American farmer is

never radical, but he is conservatively progressive, and when once aroused can be relied upon to take action for the welfare of agriculture and the nation.

Most farmers and all farm organizations have been giving lipservice at the shrine of cooperation for more than a generation. The time is at hand when the welfare of agriculture and the life of the nation demand definite, constructive and foward-looking progress in this direction ... individualism and personal selfishness must give way to cooperative effort and community spirit; and the first essential step is the planting of the Grange or some similar organization into the rural communities of the nation ... Next in importance must come a complete development of our commodity organizations. Agriculture must organize around meat, milk, grain, fruit, etc., for the sake of efficiency. Equal in importance to this is the necessity of having these organizations strongly financed, and the farmers must be willing to pay, for these various groups will not interfere with each other's success. Legislation may be necessary to protect the producer and the consumer in the development of the movement.[5]

The Grange committee fully recognized that its objectives required closer cooperation with other farmers' organizations. It commended the formation of the Grange League Federation under which the buying agencies in New York were united "in a strong incorporated company with abundant capital," saying: "This plan will make for efficiency, where local conditions warrant, and where the organizations composing the whole are of about equal size and character."

But the greatest cooperative interest of the Grange was then in marketing. In the view of the Committee:

All other questions take minor place when compared with our great marketing problems. The Committee of Seventeen (appointed by the American Farm Bureau Federation) seemingly represents all the rural interests in the grain-producing states. We recommend, therefore, no definite plan of cooperative grain marketing at the present time, awaiting the action of this committee.[6]

To facilitate the formation of strong cooperative associations the Committee moreover recommended "the passage by Congress of legislation guaranteeing the right of collective bargaining and cooperative marketing of farm products" and urged the "passage of comprehensive, cooperative legislation by the federal government and uniform cooperative laws by the states." It also declared: "Plans must be made for the proper short-time financing of the farmer during the movement of grain and food products, permitting their marketing in an orderly manner as the market demands."[7]

Grange cooperative contributions in various states. The foregoing discussion indicates that the National Grange considered the development of cooperative enterprises—at least up to 1919—to be largely a state or local Grange matter. As a result there was considerable variation in the extent of cooperative development and in the methods followed among the important Grange states.

The experience in Ohio, one of the leading states in Grange membership, was fairly typical. The way in which cooperation was conducted by the Grange in Ohio during this period was described as follows:

> Practically every subordinate grange has a business agent, whose duty it is to attend to such collective buying and selling as its members may decide to do. The buying by subordinate granges may be done independently by each, or it may be done through the state business agent, depending on where the best quotations are secured or the quickest or best services offered. The State Grange has for many years been getting quotations on such supplies as lime, fertilizer, coal, binder twine, and other commodities needed by its members. Such quotations are obtained on the basis of the quantity of goods which it is estimated the members will take. These quotations are then sent to the business agents of the various subordinate granges who present them to the members at later meetings. It is then left to the members to decide whether they will accept the offers, whether they will buy collectively elsewhere, or whether they will buy collectively at all. When a local grange decides to take advantage of prices quoted to the State Grange, its business agent may send the orders to the state business agent, who in turn orders from the companies which have made the best quotations. More frequently, however, the local business agent sends the orders directly to such companies.[8]

In New England, Grange cooperative efforts apparently reached a peak in the years from 1908 to 1911 with the formation of state Grange purchasing agencies in all the New England states with the exception of Rhode Island.[9] At this time most of the New England local Granges apparently were purchasing in one form or another. There was also a nucleus of local Grange stores of which some dated back to early Grange days. This activity served to promote interest in the possibilities of a buying federation for New England.[10] As will be shown in Chapter XIX, the Eastern States Farmers' Exchange, which was formed in 1918 as a regional purchasing association for New England, with Grange endorsements, represented a culmination of this sentiment.

In New York, the first enthusiasm for cooperation was never entirely lost, and in 1901, a number of stores started by the Grange were still functioning. About this time local Granges again began to undertake joint buying with the result that this was a common Grange function by 1912. In that year the state Grange appointed a committee on cooperation which recommended:

> That the New York State Grange enter into a contract with some reliable parties to conduct a business of supplying members of the Grange, through a representative selected by a subordinate or Pomona Grange, or a regularly organized Grange "Cooperative Association," with farm supplies that

can be handled in car lots, on a cash basis, and to be delivered to any railroad station in the state.

In accordance with this resolution an agreement was entered into with a private firm by which supply purchasing business would be carried on under the name, New York State Grange Purchasing Agency. All kinds of supplies were purchased—"feeds, fertilizers, flour, seeds, coal, lime, tile, groceries, and fencing."

The unsatisfactory character of this arrangement led the New York State Grange in 1918 to set up its own buying corporation—the New York Grange Exchange—formed on a one-man, one-vote basis with an authorized capital stock of $100,000 divided into 10,000 shares at $10 each which were restricted to Grange members. Unfortunately, the Exchange commenced operations with only a small portion of the authorized capital paid in and with an ambitious program that required both experienced management and a considerable amount of working capital. Although the Exchange was able to perform services of value in purchasing certain supplies, seeds, and other materials, it was not set up on a strong enough basis to achieve permanence. Moreover, it found itself almost immediately in a trade war with established fertilizer companies and other large concerns which undertook to cut prices and give concessions for the purpose of stopping the growth of the new organization.[11]

Recognizing that the needs of New York farmers required a buying organization which would have the support of all farm groups, the New York State Grange early in 1920 joined with the Dairymen's League and the newly formed State Farm Bureau Federation in establishing the Grange League Federation Exchange which thus merged the cooperative buying activities then being separately conducted by the three organizations. (See Chapter XX.)

Another center of Grange cooperative development began to develop in the Pacific Northwest following World War I. It was significant in that it paved the way for the formation in 1920 of the Grange Cooperative Wholesale. In 1919, the Washington State Grange in its report to the National Grange declared: "We have a system of merchandising which we call the 'warehouse system.' It is unique in being an organization different from all other systems, and is growing and developing by leaps and bounds." The following year the state report claimed that it had "60 warehouses in the state doing several millions of business annually." It was also reported that the Grange was then encouraging cooperative efforts in all lines of farming endeavor—a great cooperative wheat selling agency, and similar ventures. Enthusiasm of the time was reflected in the following sentence: "Altogether cooperative efforts are developing fast with us, with glowing prospects for the future."

The Grange contribution. This brief analysis of Grange cooperative policy and achievement from 1896 to 1920 suggests that the Grange contributed materially to the growing cooperative movement. While the total extent of the cooperative business done through the Grange or its agencies was not impressive, the training in cooperative thinking and methods given by the Grange did much to provide leadership for the new cooperative forces. Of particular importance was the policy followed by the Grange in aligning itself with other groups to achieve cooperative objectives that could not be encompassed by the Grange alone. The Grange not only encouraged its members to participate in the formation and operation of strong cooperative organizations independent of the Grange, but even welcomed the coming of another general farm organization—the American Farm Bureau—as a necessary business organization for agriculture.

The obligation which many of the large cooperatives had to the Grange for this farsighted policy was well expressed in December 1920 by Richard Pattee, then secretary of the New England Milk Producers Association:

> Publicly and privately (wrote Pattee), I have stated my opinion that the success of the NEMPA was in many ways due to the Grange. I heartily believe that is true. For three years I traveled all over New England, trying to get the milk producers to organize. Wherever I found a strong Grange, I had the least difficulty in getting milk producers to join our association. Usually I could depend on the Grange officers for help and Grange meetings were splendid opportunities to preach the doctrine of collective bargaining. State granges endorsed and recommended the NEMPA to their members and Grange halls were placed at our disposal without charge. Grange officials have always responded heartily to all calls for assistance and the influence of the organization has helped us in many ways in all the states.
>
> I used to think the Grange itself should undertake much of the work that special organizations like ours are now doing. I now see that there should be specially organized and directed movements to conduct certain lines of work, and in the development of such organizations the influence of the Grange, its years of teaching and preaching organization and cooperation, have been the most powerful aid possible. It has been the Mother Organization. Many worthwhile and successful efforts have been made possible by the Grange, some of which, alas, do not realize their debt to the splendid old order that for over half a century has been building up the sentiment, developing the leadership and laying the foundation for the work that was to follow.[12]

The Coming of the Farm Bureau

The fourth of the farm organizations to influence the growth of cooperation during this period—the Farm Bureau—grew out of the agricultural extension movement. In Chapter V, we described how the county agent system grew naturally from the demonstration methods promoted by Seaman A. Knapp and the farm management extension efforts of W. J. Spillman. As the county agent work developed, the desirability of working with and through groups of farmers became apparent. At first such cooperation between the agents and farmers was informal in character. Gradually, there emerged formal associations designed for the express purpose of furthering the work of county agents. These gradually became known as county Farm Bureaus.

The earliest Farm Bureau was established in Broome County, New York, in 1911 through the joint efforts of the Binghamton, New York, Chamber of Commerce, the Delaware and Lackawanna Railroad, and the Office of Farm Management of the Bureau of Plant Industry. Together these three agencies provided funds for the employment of a county agent who would work in close cooperation with a farm "bureau" in the Chamber of Commerce.[13]

To make his work more effective, the county agent soon proceeded to appoint community chairmen throughout the territory served, with the result that the county-wide form of organization was soon rooted in the local communities. With the enactment of a state law in 1912, which provided support for farm improvement work, other counties began to develop Farm Bureaus designed to have local farmer membership and control. While the Broome County farmers had enjoyed friendly relations with the Chamber of Commerce, the desirability of having an independent organization of their own led them to reorganize first as the "Farm Improvement Association of Broome County" in October 1913, and then one year later as "The Broome County Farm Bureau."

While the Broome County Farm Bureau is generally regarded as the first county Farm Bureau, there were somewhat similar organizations in other states. "Probably the first real farmer organization similar to later farm bureaus was organized in Pettis County, Missouri, in 1912, and began financial cooperation with the Missouri College of Agriculture and the United States Department of Agriculture in 1913."[14]

When the Smith-Lever Act was passed in 1914, the desirability of having supporting organizations through which the county agents could most effectively carry on their work was well established, with the result that they expanded with the encouragement thus given to the county agent movement. In fact, "The organization of county farm bureaus was enthusiastically promoted by federal and state extension leaders and by county agents in the northern and western states. It was made a prerequisite condition before the installation of a county agent in many states."[15]

With the passage of the Emergency Food Production Act in August 1917—providing more federal funds for county agent work—the number of county agents jumped from 542 on July 1, 1917, to 1,133 on June 30, 1918, and the number of county Farm Bureaus increased from 516 to 791. On the later date approximately 290,000 farmers were embraced in county Farm Bureau membership.[16]

As the county Farm Bureaus became established as county agent auxiliaries, representatives of the county Farm Bureaus were commonly invited to attend state conferences of county agents held at the agricultural colleges. This practice which started in Vermont in October 1914 was followed in New York in November, and in Illinois in February 1915.[17] This soon led to the formation of state federations of county Farm Bureaus. The first organizations of this type were set up in Missouri (November 1915) and in Massachusetts (May 1915).[18]

In the beginning the sole purpose of the state organizations had been to further the program of agricultural extension work. In 1916, a change began to appear in the objectives of such state Farm Bureau organizations with the formation in March of the Illinois Agricultural Association (the Illinois Federation of County Agricultural Associations) for the frank purpose of engaging in business and political activity.[19]

The purpose of the new organization was stated specifically in its constitution as follows:

To promote the general interests of agriculture by studying the methods of production and distribution of farm products *with the view of working out a system of greater economy and efficiency in handling and marketing the same;* to encourage the production, marketing, and distribution of livestock, *to encourage and promote the co-operative organization of farmers* and of those engaged in the secondary industries or mutually helping in a more efficient organization of the business of agriculture; to publish and issue when deemed advisable, reports, bulletins, and instructions generally which will help in spreading knowledge of the best means of rural betterment and organization; to effect a system of effective cooperation between the several county farm bureaus throughout the State for "better farming, better business, and better living;" to encourage and cooperate with educational institutions, departments, societies, and the several local organizations in all efforts to solve the questions relative to rural betterment and agricultural science; *to cooperate where necessary in the purchase of seed, fertilizers, and such other commodities* as may from time to time seem necessary and advisable; *to make a thorough study of all legislative matters and use our influence in securing the enactment of wise legislation and the defeat of unwise legislation.* In short, the Illinois Agricultural Association is formed for the purpose of promoting cooperation between the several county farm bureaus of the state and the members of such bureaus, increasing their efficiency and extending their usefulness. *It is intended to secure cooperative action in advancing the common purposes of its members; uniformity and equity in business and laws and proper consideration and concentration upon questions affecting the financial, commercial, and civic interests of the State.*[20]

Following the leadership of Illinois, other state Farm Bureau organizations as they were formed (New York, 1917; West Virginia, 1918; Iowa, 1918; Ohio, 1919; Michigan, 1919) began to concern themselves with business cooperation and agricultural legislation, in spite of efforts made by the Office of Extension Work, north and west, to restrict their activities to the promotion of educational work in cooperation with the county agents. As a result there had grown up by 1919 a network of nine state Farm Bureau organizations, all pledged to the support of agricultural extension work through county agents—but holding divergent views with respect to the economic and political functions that such organizations should perform.

At this juncture, in February 1919, the president of the New York State Federation of County Farm Bureau Associations called a meeting of representatives of 12 states at Ithaca, New York, for the declared purpose of forming a national federation of Farm Bureaus:

(1) To provide the nation with some sane organization thoroughly representative of agriculture throughout the entire United States, which might speak for the farmers of the entire country; (2) to take advantage of a nationwide organization—the farm bureau—which promises great possibilities of usefulness in developing a program which will reach the entire country and which will bring into action the strongest farmers of the country.[21]

At the Ithaca meeting a committee was appointed "to outline a plan of procedure designed to effect a national organization." This committee recommended that a meeting be held at Chicago in November "to perfect such an organization," and that in the meantime additional state federations should be formed.[22]

As the time for the Chicago meeting approached, enthusiasm for a national federation gained momentum, and many additional federations were formed. The following quotations show the vitality of the movement at that time:

Interest in agricultural circles worked up to a high heat. The possibility of creating a great, new national farmers' organization on a basis different from anything that had preceded and with elements of strength never before possible, was suddenly borne home alike in professional agricultural circles and to the practical farmer. It was recognized by all that here was a sleeping giant that might be awakened to full power almost immediately.[23]

The time was ripe for a farmer movement. The Non-Partisan League was flourishing in the Northwest. The Equity was doubling its membership in Wisconsin. The Farmers' Union was making good headway in various sections. Even so, there were too many farmers who did not belong to these organizations, and too many who for some reason or other would not have joined any one of them. However, here was ready for use in every state of the Union, almost in every county, a group already in a sense united, and for a common purpose. Why not vitalize the skeleton by putting some flesh and blood with it and make a farmers' society already nation-wide, and give action and virility to a body not now functioning in a large or comprehensive manner.[24]

When the Chicago meeting convened on November 12 with approximately 500 delegates and visitors present from some 30 states "the atmosphere was surcharged with a feeling of electric tenseness." Farm Bureau leaders in the Middle West hoped to use "the new organization as an instrument to solve their marketing problems on a nationwide cooperative plan." Those from the East, South, and West who favored a more conservative course feared that the powerful Midwest group "was determined to put through a program of . . . commercial radicalism."[25]

For a time it appeared that the interests of the two factions could not be harmonized, but gradually an acceptable compromise was worked out. Under the constitution of the proposed organization—which would be temporary until ratified by 12 states—the American Farm Bureau Federation was designed:

> to correlate and strengthen the state farm bureaus and similar state organizations of the several states in the national federation, to promote, protect, and represent the business, economic, social, and educational interests of the farmers of the nation, and to develop agriculture.[26]

When the ratification conference was held at Chicago in March 1920, opposition to commercial activities had largely died down, and the temporary constitution was ratified by 28 states. The spirit of the new organization as it started forth on its permanent career was voiced by Henry C. Wallace, then editor of *Wallace's Farmer*:

> This federation must get to work at once on a real business program if it is to justify its existence. *That doesn't mean turning the work over to committees of farmers, either. Every line of work must be in charge of experts.* The best qualified men in the United States should be hired to manage each of the various lines of work. This federation must not degenerate into an educational or social institution. It must be made the most powerful business institution in the country.[27]

The American Farm Bureau Federation wasted no time in getting under way as a national organization. With liberal financial backing, the executive committee immediately set up "departments of transpor-

tation, trade relations, distribution, statistics, legislation, and cooperation."[28]

The growth of Farm Bureau cooperative activities. In the foregoing
section, we have shown how the Farm Bureau came into being and
rapidly attained national status as a general farmers' organization. We
are now concerned with the way in which this movement became
more and more concerned with the promotion of cooperative activities.

As already described, the county Farm Bureaus were originally designed for the purpose of furthering educational programs of the county
agents—particularly in improving farming methods and practices. It
was soon found that this program was too limited to attract continuous
farm support. Farmers who paid dues to Farm Bureaus which helped
support the work of county agents saw no reason why the Farm Bureaus
should not perform supply buying and marketing services.

The county agents were not slow in responding to such demands.
They were sympathetic to the farmers' need for better purchasing and
marketing service and they welcomed this opportunity to pay their way
by being economically useful. However, it was not long before the increasing amount of buying and marketing business transacted by the
Farm Bureaus with county agent assistance began to draw fire from
business concerns who charged that this represented an unfair incursion of government in business. This forced the Secretary of Agriculture
to state in a letter dated March 24, 1914, the following policy with
respect to the assistance which might properly be given by government
workers to farmers in their buying and marketing operations.

> It is a legitimate and proper part of the work of this department, in fact
> its duty, to furnish farmers with information which will enable them to
> develop greater efficiency in all respects, including the securing of their sup-
> plies and marketing their products . . . In no case is any actual business what-
> ever transacted for him individually or collectively. Whenever and wherever
> farmers through machinery of their own are developing greater agricultural
> or business efficiency, we shall use the means of education at our disposal
> with perfect freedom in bringing the methods of such organizations or com-
> munities to the attention of others. In the carrying out of this policy, we
> endeavor at all times and in all matters to act in perfect fairness to all
> interests concerned, whether producer, middleman, or consumer.[29]

Under the Secretary's statement county agents could encourage cooperative activity but not engage in direct business operations for
farmers. Thus, county agents were left free to work with county Farm
Bureaus in an educational way on their cooperative problems—a situation
which emphasized the separate significance of the county Farm Bureaus.
As Kile pointed out:

If the practice of cooperative buying was to be continued, it must be done by the farmers themselves. Here was a definite job for the farm bureau, separate and distinct from its duties arising out of its relationship to the county agent for demonstration and educational purposes. In a sense, it made the farm bureau an absolute necessity in the county.[30]

By January 1914 the county Farm Bureaus had already begun to develop on a common pattern which was in accord with the Secretary's view. This was clearly indicated in an address of the New York State Director of Farm Bureaus. He said:

There are some misconceptions as to the functions and the real purposes of the Farm Bureau. The greatest is that this institution has as its principal function the giving of advice. Farmers to whom this idea has been advanced have very properly resented it and opposed a local bureau development along this line. It is true . . . that [this service] forms a part of every county agent's work . . . (b) this kind of work alone would not justify the expense and the effort put into a county Farm Bureau . . .

As the leaders of the movement . . . [national and state] conceive the functions of the Farm Bureau, they are, in order of their importance as follows: (1) the federation and organization of all the agricultural forces of the county to a common purpose; (2) agricultural leadership in its broad sense; (3) organization of cow testing, seed improvement, and similar associations; (4) the organization of buying and selling agencies for supplies and products; (5) the study of the local economic conditions of the county with the viewpoint of affirming or improving, as the case may be, the local farm management and farm practice of the county; (6) the demonstration of better methods of farm management and practice; (7) the giving of personal advice to farmers on farm practice and management.

All these functions should be exercised with the point of view of increasing the financial profitableness of farming within the county by increasing the net income of farmers, and of making country life and work increasingly worthwhile in the larger sense.[31]

As the Farm Bureaus were built around the county agents, the latter were expected to further these objectives. In particular, they were to provide leadership in organizing farmers to help themselves on their common problems. This was made clear in the following excerpts from the same address:

In New York State, almost every community feels the need of cooperation. Many communities are now ready to cooperate. What is needed more than any other thing is leadership. A qualified man is wanted who can give a portion of his time and energy to developing and organizing cooperative associations, with the help of the State Superintendent and others interested in this phase of work. Such a man cannot exercise this leadership alone, but he may be the agent of individuals or forces in a county who need just this man's help and energy.

No small part of the county agent's work, as I view it, is the organization of associations for the improvement of various phases of the county's farming. In several counties a number of cow-testing associations have been promoted and organized by the county agents with the institutions of the State. A very successful potato seed improvement association has been organized in one of the counties.

A phase of the county agent's work, which is a most popular one with farmers but one in which great care has to be exercised, is the organization of buying and selling agencies for the securing of supplies and the disposition of products. It is a legitimate function for the county agent to encourage and to promote such organizations, when it can be clearly shown that they benefit the farming community as a whole. This is a matter, however, in which much judgment should be exercised. It seems wise to handle this work by means of committees of the Farm Bureau Associations or by means of subsidiary co-operating companies. The county agent should never be asked or permitted to handle funds or to hold office in any organization for buying or selling for profit. He may, however, at all times advise as to methods, and counsel with committees and directors when his advice is sought.[32]

Although the county agents were expected to further the formation and proper operation of cooperative associations—while not serving as the business agents for such organizations—it was difficult to draw the line between educational assistance and direct participation. The problem involved in keeping county agents from directly participating in cooperative marketing and purchasing activity made this a common subject for discussion at college and extension workers conferences from 1914 to 1920. The views of the Department of Agriculture on the problem in 1917—while the country was at war—were set forth as follows by Bradford Knapp, who was then in charge of extension work in the South:

I believe that this particular problem of the marketing of farm products and the purchasing of farm supplies is the hardest nut the extension worker has to crack. The principles involved are easy of application in the vast field of extension work but difficult of application in this particular type of extension work . . .

The county agent or other extension worker must remember that his work will be effective in direct proportion as he gets other people to do things and it will be unsuccessful in proportion as he assumes responsibilities himself which might be undertaken by other persons under his leadership. He is a teacher, an inspirer of activities upon the part of the people. He must lead them, educate them, teach them and train them to do things for themselves . . .

The county agent should be understood to be therefore, a public officer having to do with instruction, leadership and, possibly, with the perfecting of organizations. He shall ardently and fearlessly advocate the formation of cooperative enterprises in the interest of a more efficient agriculture. I believe in county agents helping organizations and influencing people to organize for business purposes, to teach and train them in their work, always keeping before his own mind and the minds of the people with whom he deals that he has a definite object in view, namely to get them to do something for their own good and not to do something himself. If we keep that in mind, then I feel sure that the relationship which exists between the extension workers on the one hand and the cooperative buying and selling organizations on the other, will be a thoroughly satisfactory one.[33]

With our entry into World War I and the consequently increased responsibilities placed on county agents in increasing food production, the problem of "keeping the county agents out of business" became even more difficult. As True has explained:

> The extraordinary conditions growing out of the war, and the participation of the United States therein, led the extension forces to do many things which they would not ordinarily do in time of peace. The urgent desire of many farmers to improve their economic conditions by cooperative action brought about a general inclination of the county agents to engage directly in the transaction of business for the cooperatives which they had assisted in forming.[34]

To clarify completely the Department's position on this matter Dr. True, the director of the State Relations Service, issued an order in 1918 which forbade county agents to engage directly in any business activity.[35] This ruling, in effect, again emphasized the importance of county Farm Bureaus as organizations which could perform business services unobtainable through county agents. As the federal official in charge of county-agent work in the northern and western states had expressed this:

> The Farm Bureau, while largely a development imposed by necessity in the furtherance of county-agent work, is really possessed of broader powers than the county agent, and may engage in many activities which would not be proper for the county agent as a public official to undertake.[36]

While some of the county Farm Bureaus were thus engaging directly in cooperative buying and marketing, a somewhat different conception of the role of Farm Bureaus with relationship to cooperative enterprise was developing in those areas where such activity was already widespread. Here the county Farm Bureaus either actively aided in the formation of separate cooperatives or sought to unify and strengthen the efforts of existing cooperatives but did not engage themselves in cooperative activity.[37]

Throughout most of the country, the following view was commonly held about 1919 when the American Farm Bureau Federation was formed. "Essentially the county Farm Bureau is a chamber of agriculture, corresponding in many of its functions with a city chamber of commerce."[38] The view of Professor Walter F. Handschin of Illinois Agricultural College throws light on the thinking of most Farm Bureau leaders at that time. He saw the Farm Bureau as a pervasive cooperative influence—rather than as a specific cooperative organization.[39]

Evolution of Farm Bureau cooperative programs in selected states. In the preceding section we have seen how the Farm Bureau movement acquired a distinctive role with respect to the rapidly growing cooperative movement. Further light on this important development can be obtained by examining the growth of Farm Bureau cooperative activities in four focal states—New York, Mississippi, California, and Illinois.

New York. As we have observed, the Farm Bureau movement in New York early divorced itself from actual business operations. It was generally held by Farm Bureau and extension leaders that the Farm Bureau should be an educational organization primarily. Nevertheless, in following out this policy the Farm Bureaus were brought into constant relationship with the rapidly rising cooperative movement in the state, and this eventually led the New York State Farm Bureau Federation to participate in the formation of an organization which was to become for many years the largest cooperative purchasing and marketing association in the United States—the Cooperative Grange League Federation Exchange—popularly known as the G. L. F.

At about the same time that the Grange in New York was entering into a statewide cooperative purchasing program, the county Farm Bureaus began to develop an improved seed program which eventually resulted in a limited amount of cooperative seed purchasing through county Farm Bureaus. The reorganized Dairymen's League likewise had become interested in the cooperative purchasing of feed as a sideline to its marketing operations.

Fearing that these incipient developments might lead to competitive purchasing associations, the leaders of the three organizations decided to merge all purchasing operations, in 1920, so as to form one strong independent organization. In this way the Farm Bureau became one of the sponsoring organizations of the G. L. F.[40]

Mississippi. In the South, where significant cooperative buying and marketing organizations had not been able to establish themselves, it was very difficult for county agents to refrain from engaging in cooperative buying and marketing. Farmers could not see why the county agents should not help them on their buying and marketing problems, as well as on their problems of crop production. The way in which the Farm Bureau got involved in cooperative marketing work in Mississippi (which may be taken as typical for several southern states) has been described by Charles McNeil, a longtime leader of Farm Bureau work in that state:

> In the spring of 1915, County Agent Rich organized a 4-H pig club in Yazoo County, and in November of that year he shipped the pigs grown by these club boys in the first cooperative shipment of hogs ever moved from Mis-

sissippi. That was the beginning of cooperative marketing in Mississippi under the new regime . . . This program was so successful that the farmers in Yazoo County immediately demanded that they be rendered the same service, and thus cooperative marketing of livestock and miscellaneous commodities was inaugurated in Mississippi.[41]

Even with the development of county and state Farm Bureau organizations in the South, it was difficult for the county agent and state extension workers to follow a "hands off" policy in business matters. This was not entirely their fault as a vacuum then existed in southern agricultural leadership which almost compelled county agents to assist actively such organizations if they were to provide service for farmers. This "paternal role" of the county agent to some extent was to continue in the South for many years.

California. The early cooperative experience of the Farm Bureau in California is of particular interest in view of the then already highly developed use of cooperation in that state. The first county Farm Bureau in California was organized in Humboldt County in 1914 through the efforts of the state extension service. By 1919 there were "no less than 35." These county farm Bureaus early began

to extend their functions beyond the field of education, [as] it was felt that they could serve their members to greater advantage by interesting themselves and representing their members in such matters as cooperative marketing of farm products, purchasing of farm supplies, legislative work affecting agriculture, irrigation and drainage projects and power rates. Such work was undertaken by the county farm bureaus as separate organizations [as] the Agricultural Extension Service never associated itself with the farm-bureau organization in any activities not of a purely educational nature.[42]

The first cooperative marketing experience came in February 1917 with the establishment of a cooperative hog auction market by the marketing committee of the Kern County Farm Bureau. Results were so satisfactory that the plan quickly spread to adjoining counties, and this led to the federation of such operations in seven counties as the Farm Bureau Marketing Association in October 1918. About this time a number of county Farm Bureaus also established associations or departments for cooperative marketing and purchasing. Thus cooperation was well rooted in the county Farm Bureaus when the California Farm Bureau Federation was formed in October 1919.[43]

Illinois. In view of the position of leadership early assumed by Illinois in the Midwest Farm Bureau movement, it is of particular interest to see how the Illinois program developed its distinctive economic and political character. Illinois served as the laboratory in which were developed the aggressive Farm Bureau programs to be undertaken in 1920 and 1921.[44]

The beginnings of the Farm Bureau movement in Illinois can be traced back to the winter of 1910-11 when a "soil and crop improvement" association was organized and incorporated in DeKalb County to support the work of an "agricultural specialist." Soon afterwards a similar association was formed in Kankakee County, and by June 1914 there were 14 "soil and crop improvement" associations in the state.[45] At first these early associations were "regarded solely as agencies of production" in the limited sense indicated by their names but within a short time their interests widened to cover the entire question of the organization and management of the whole farm."[46] For example, work of a cooperative nature naturally developed from the growing use of limestone and phosphate rock, brought about by the activities of the association.

> With the organization of the farm bureaus the amounts of limestone and phosphate increased very rapidly in most counties . . . Practically all of this material was purchased in carload lots . . . Since little of these materials were used, there were almost no local dealers handling them . . . Under these conditions, it was only natural that the farm advisers and the farm bureaus should order the materials for their members.[47]

Such experience led to cooperative purchasing of seed and other farm supplies which could be handled in bulk quantities.[48]

Soon after the county soil and crop improvement associations were well established, sentiment developed for joining them together for mutual benefit in a state organization. This led to the organization of the Illinois Agricultural Association by a group of farm advisers, not then called county agents, and farmers at a meeting held at the University of Illinois in January 1916.

The activities of the association were largely confined to legislative work during the war years as "Illinois farmers were too busy growing crops to devote much attention to organization." However, the close of the war brought a "multitude of pressing farm problems" which gave a new vitality to the association and led to its reorganization at Peoria in January 1919 on a basis which "made it the strongest and best financed farm organization in the world." A five-dollar individual membership fee was adopted and a drive for membership begun. By December 8, 1919 (or one month after the A.F.B.F. organization meeting), there were 40,511 members.[49]

At the Peoria meeting various committees were set up to examine the problems confronting farmers and to develop constructive programs for their solution. Immediate interest was centered on the improvement of marketing methods for livestock and corn through the appointment of strong committees, staffed with the best men available and assured of adequate financial support.

There soon developed a tremendous enthusiasm for the forceful program undertaken at Peoria. When the association held its next annual meeting in Peoria in January 1920, President H. J. Sconce claimed that the association comprised "the 'cream' of the American farmer [and] will be the greatest force for advancement and perpetuating the great ideals of agriculture that we have." While his view was exuberant, this was the spirit of the new movement. A groundswell of organizational fervor was again forming among farmers not unlike that headed by the Grange in the early 1870's. Significantly, Dean Eugene Davenport, the eminent agriculturist of the University of Illinois, struck the chord for this sentiment by saying: "The Farm Bureaus and their federations, state and national, constitute at once the most progressive, the most rational, the most representative, and the most powerful organization ever devised by farmers."[50]

The Farm Bureau in 1920. When the American Farm Bureau Federation stepped forth in 1920, its attitude toward cooperation was still in a formative state. As a "business organization for agriculture," it could not ignore the importance of cooperative organization, while as an "educational organization" it could not confine its interests to any single line of action. It sought more efficient production as well as more efficient marketing and purchasing by integrating the efforts of farmers with those of public institutions. As Clifford Gregory who was active in creating the American Farm Bureau Federation later wrote: "The new movement had vitality. It was composed chiefly of farmers who were aggressively trying to improve their lot by becoming better producers."[51]

This chapter has shown how cooperatives benefited from the support of the Grange and Farm Bureau in the years prior to 1920. In Part III we will examine the general development of cooperative marketing enterprises during this period.

Part Three

COOPERATIVE MARKETING
PROGRESS

From 1897 to 1920 farmers learned how to form, operate, and manage cooperative marketing and purchasing associations. This helped bring a new day in agriculture. Louis M. Hacker recognizes this in his interpretative book. The World of Andrew Carnegie *(1968): "From 1897 on, the skies began to brighten; as more and more intensive farming replaced extensive; as reliance upon the domestic market replaced the foreign; as devices of self-help—farm cooperatives—made for improved and orderly marketing, the utilization of surpluses, mass purchasing of supplies and implements parts."*

In this part of our study we will examine the growth of cooperative marketing for various agricultural commodities. Attention will be focused on the experience of organizations that took the lead in demonstrating what cooperation in marketing could accomplish. Of particular interest will be the remarkable achievements of the California Fruit Growers Exchange, now Sunkist Growers, Inc., which by 1920 had become the model for cooperative marketing organizations throughout the world.

In Part Three we will see how cooperative marketing grew by federation from local communities to wide geographic areas. We will see also how the modern centralized form of cooperative marketing organization came into existence.

Chapter XII

THE EXPANSION OF COOPERATIVE
MARKETING

In Chapter IV we saw how various kinds of farmers' cooperative marketing associations had become established by 1896. Local cooperative creameries, cheese factories, and elevators were then fairly common in the Middle West while fruit marketing associations were gaining strength in California, Florida, and other fruit-producing areas. Moreover, several experiments had been made in regional federation, the most promising being those of the citrus growers in southern California. The formation of bargaining associations for marketing fluid milk had also been attempted, but in 1896 their future was clouded by doubt of their legality. At this point, we shall examine how these embryonic developments expanded during the next 24 years of rising prices. By 1920, cooperative marketing had come almost into full flower.

Although statistics disclose a great growth in the extent of cooperative marketing from 1897 to 1920, both in number of associations and in business volume, they cannot make clear the significant character of this development. To find this we must study the unfolding of cooperative marketing enterprise in various fields of agricultural industry.

Dairymen's Marketing and Manufacturing Associations

From 1897 to 1920 dairymen made great progress in developing cooperative marketing associations adapted to their economic requirements. By 1920 the lines of direction had been found and permanent building of strong cooperatives could be safely undertaken.

Cooperative creameries. No form of cooperative marketing enterprise was so well established by 1896 as cooperative creameries and cheese factories. On this foundation the number of such organizations steadily increased until in 1920 there were almost 3,000 associations of this type, located largely in such leading dairy states as Wisconsin, Minnesota, and New York. However, there were also many in other parts of the country.

Most of the local cooperative creameries and cheese factories changed little in character during this period although there was a marked improvement in accounting and business practices after 1914, due to the assistance of the state agricultural colleges, the federal Office of Markets, and the state departments of agriculture. There was also some strengthening of these organizations due to the failure of the weaker ones and the consequent concentration of volume among those that remained.

About 1900 the cooperative creameries were confronted by a new kind of competition in the form of commercial centralizer creameries which collected cream from wide areas for butter manufacture at a central location. These central plants were able to operate with large volumes and thus get the advantages of low-cost operation. The centralizers also gained marketing advantages through having large quantities of product for sale under standard trade marks. This made possible the development of marketing channels direct to retailers with resulting reductions in wholesaling and jobbing costs.[1]

Most of the local cooperative creameries felt the competition of centralizers more in marketing than in their creamery operations for, in general, they were located in concentrated dairy regions which provided an adequate supply of milk from members to insure economical butter production. The local creameries also had an advantage in that the quality of butter made from fresh cream generally commanded a price premium over the butter produced by the centralizers. However, as the centralizers found ways to improve the quality of their product there was a gradual reduction in such premiums.

The first effort of the cooperative creameries to meet the competition of centralizers came in 1907 with the formation of the Minnesota Cooperative Dairy Association, designed to serve as a sales agency for the local creameries on the terminal markets. This was a loosely formed organization whose principal significance lay in the training which it gave creameries in working together on a common problem. This experience taught that any program of effective federation for marketing would need to be based upon the development and maintenance of uniform and high standards in butter manufacture.[2]

Recognizing that the principal need of the cooperative dairies was a uniform product to permit proper merchandizing, the Dairy Extension Department of the University of Minnesota began in 1918 to undertake a program designed to get the cooperative creameries within certain counties to federate in county organizations for the manufacture of a more standardized product. As this movement gained in momentum it was guided toward the formation of a state-wide federation of cooperative creameries, and in 1921 the Minnesota Cooperative Creamery Association—later to be known by its Land O'Lakes brand—was formed with over one-half of the 645 cooperative creameries in the state enrolled as stockholder members.[3]

While the cooperative creameries in the central states were slowly moving toward federation, a somewhat comparable development was occurring in the Far West. In 1910, the Dairymens' Cooperative Creamery of Tulare County, California, undertook to sell its butter under the trade name "Challenge" through an established butter dealer in Los Angeles. When this arrangement failed to give satisfaction, the association, in January 1911, joined with the Riverdale Cooperative Creamery of adjacent Fresno County in launching their own distributing house in Los Angeles as the Challenge Cream and Butter Company. After several years of struggle, during which the Challenge trademark was established in the Los Angeles area, the two member creameries were joined in 1917 by the well-established Danish Creamery Association of Fresno County which had long enjoyed a premium on the Los Angeles market for the high quality of its butter. At this time the company was reorganized as a cooperative federation and became The Challenge Cream and Butter Association.[4]

While Minnesota cooperative creameries were taking their first steps in federation, leaders of the Equity Union in the Dakotas and Nebraska were proceeding to establish cooperative centralizer associations. These men saw no reason why the general methods of the commercial centralizers could not be adapted to their needs—where milk production did not warrant the operation of strong local creamery associations.[5] As noted in Chapter X, the first association of this type was opened at Aberdeen, South Dakota, in 1916 and its success soon led to the establishment of a similar association at Orleans, Nebraska.

Under the plan followed, a patron became a shareholder out of the dividend savings from his cream shipments. The membership thus embraced the farmers who might be located several hundred miles from the plant to which cream was shipped. In many communities, members were organized in cream shipping associations to facilitate economical collection and transportation to the central plant.[6]

While several cooperative centralizers succeeded in establishing themselves on a permanent basis in widely scattered areas of low milk production, the idea never took root in the heart of the Dairy Belt—where federation of cooperative creameries was a more logical development. However, these cooperative centralizers effectively demonstrated that the cooperative form of organization was sufficiently flexible to permit it to obtain the operating advantages of corporate competitors while maintaining the democratic advantages of cooperative operation.

Cheese factories. Most of the cooperative cheese factories, like the cooperative creameries, undertook little responsibility for marketing the product which they manufactured. However, the movement toward federation for marketing got started as early as 1904 when several farmers' cheese factories in Tillamook County, Oregon, jointly employed a sales manager to market their product in various West Coast cities. The success of this plan led nine of the factories in 1909 to organize the Tillamook County Creamery Association. An inspector was engaged to supervise the quality of cheese made in each factory, and this resulted in a more uniform product of better quality which, under the trademark "Tillamook," soon enjoyed an enviable position throughout the West.

Although the Association was originally set up to promote the manufacture of better cheese, it soon became in fact their joint sales agency. As the plan gave satisfaction, other local cheese factories joined until in 1921 the federation embraced 25 and marketed for them almost seven million pounds of cheese. Strictly speaking, the Tillamook County Creamery Association was not a 100 per cent cooperative association, for a few privately owned creameries were member organizations. Yet the organization was operated in a cooperative manner and its accomplishments were widely heralded in cooperative circles. The experience of the Tillamook Association thus proved of influence as a demonstration of the value of federation.[7]

While the Tillamook Association was becoming established, a sentiment for stronger organization was stirring among the cooperative cheese factories of Wisconsin. For many years, the Wisconsin cheese producers had resented the unfair conditions under which their cheese was marketed. In 1912, the complaints were so general that the Wisconsin Board of Public Affairs directed the University of Wisconsin to make a study of the cheese industry of Wisconsin. Before this study could be completed, the cheese producers of Sheboygan County, ably led by State Senator Henry Kumrey, established the Sheboygan County Cheese Producers Federation with a membership of 45 local cheese factories.[8]

When the Federation opened for business in April 1914, it was handicapped by lack of established market outlets and bitter opposition of the established cheese trade. Gradually the Federation developed its own regular customers and, in 1917, it decided that it would be in a stronger position if it changed its name to Wisconsin Cheese Producers' Federation and widened its membership to cover the state. By 1919, some 120 member associations were marketing over 14 million pounds of cheese through the Federation. Although it did not attempt to market its product under one trademark, it undertook to raise the quality of cheese produced by its member associations through a vigorous educational program.

By 1920, the Wisconsin Cheese Producers' Federation had become one of the outstanding examples of successful cooperative federation in the central states, and its plan of operation was being widely used as an example to encourage the formation of federations for the marketing of butter, grain, and other products.[9]

Fluid milk distribution. In Chapter IV we described the first efforts of fluid milk producers to bargain collectively with city distributors. With the expansion of cities, the distributors grew in power and the need for sturdy organizations to represent the farmers' interests became apparent. The developments in the New York "milk shed" well illustrate the way in which strong regional milk marketing organizations finally became established.

The Five State Milk Producers' Union, described in Chapter IV, was reorganized in 1898 as the Five State Milk Producers Association, but it was unable to achieve any real standing as a spokesman for the dairy farmer. Before its demise, the milk producers of Orange County, New York, had organized themselves in 1903 under Grange auspices as the United Dairymen and this experience led to the formation of the Dairymen's League in 1907, as an unincorporated regional organization designed to represent all the dairy farmers dependent upon the New York City market.

Under the League's plan, it would not commence to function until it had secured members owning 50,000 cows—a goal not reached until 1910. From then on the League membership grew, but little was achieved as a marketing organization until the fall of 1916 when the rising costs of milk production occasioned by conditions growing out of the European war forced its Executive Committee to set what it considered to be a fair price for milk. When the distributors refused to pay this price, a boycott was called.

The time was ripe for a movement. To the surprise of many instead of only 13,000 responding to the information that their milk had not been sold, practically all or a very large proportion of the dairy farmers all over that territory, who were selling to distributors, suddenly found that they did not care to sell their milk either, and the war was on and it continued for eleven days, at the expiration of which time our friends, the distributors, were good enough to reconsider their former resolution and thought that they could deal with the organization, and did so, and a contract was arrived at.[10]

While the Dairymen's League was firmly established by this action, there was little opportunity for collective bargaining during the next two years as prices were determined by the Food Administration. With the discontinuance of federal control early in 1919, producers again were forced to boycott the dealers to obtain what they thought was a fair price. This boycott or "strike" which was finally won after 18 days so enhanced the League's prestige that its membership rose to 75,000 farmers. At this time it was appreciated by the leaders of the League that boycotts or strikes, no matter how effective, could not permanently solve the marketing problem, for the abnormal demands of war had brought into being a large milk surplus which could not all be sold in fluid form. A careful study of the problem indicated that a strong marketing organization equipped with local plants and processing facilities was required. The problem then confronting the association was later presented as follows by one of the League's leaders:

> [The existing] contract simply clothed the organization with a bargaining power and did not create the organization as a cooperative marketing agent. The result was that the organization could only go out and bargain with distributors for a price, and having reached an agreement as to a price, it had performed its principal function ... Under our ... contract we could not name one price to condensaries and another to fluid milk dealers for the reason that the condensaries, paying the farmers direct, would result in adjoining farmers receiving different prices, depending upon whether the milk went into a condensary or into the city, and as all milk would actually seek the highest priced market, it would throw the entire marketing system out of adjustment ... Therefore, it became evident that our organization must be reorganized, and new contracts obtained from the farmers that would clothe the association with powers, as a marketing agent, to collect the proceeds of all sales, blend them, and so distribute them among producers as equity [might] determine.[11]

To accomplish the ends desired, a new organization was formed— after long deliberation and study—to supplant the Dairymen's League. This organization, the Dairymen's League Cooperative Association, Inc., was to function only after 50,000 marketing contracts had been signed—a goal which was not reached until May 1921. The principal clause of this contract read as follows:

The producer, wishing to avail himself of the facilities to be furnished for marketing his milk and dairy products when the association is equipped for same, hereby appoints the association his sales agent and as such grants to it full power and authority to sell said milk in the fluid state, or in its discretion to manufacture the same into such products as it may from time to time determine, and to sell such manufactured products, the proceeds of all such sales to be blended into one fund and distributed as hereinafter provided.

One of the other clauses required the producer to deliver his milk "to such shipping stations or other plants as the Association may from time to time direct." This provision was "attacked by the enemies of the plan as a contract by which the farmer mortgaged his farm herd and his wife and children."[12]

To achieve the aims of the Association, which called for a substantial investment in operating facilities, provision was made in the by-laws for a comprehensive revolving fund system of financing. This plan provided for capital formation through deductions made from the members' monthly milk checks which were evidenced annually by Certificates of Indebtedness, yielding 6 per cent interest, due in five years or payable earlier at the discretion of the board of directors. After the initial five-year period, the association would be adding to its capital monthly and retiring a part of its capital each year.[13]

While the milk producers of the New York region were organizing their marketing system somewhat similar developments were taking place in other parts of the country. The abnormal market conditions which had brought on the New York boycott resulted in similar producer boycotts in the same year at Boston, Pittsburgh, Cincinnati, and Chicago, and these were all more or less successful in establishing milk marketing associations.[14] Most of these associations were formed primarily for bargaining purposes, but in several instances distributive functions were soon undertaken as in the case of the Dairymen's League.

Of the early associations of the bargaining type, the most ambitious was the New England Milk Producers Association (the NEMPA) which was organized to serve as a bargaining organization for milk producers on a New England-wide basis. The principal founder of NEMPA pointed out that it was set up on the theory "that the dairymen should be organized to a problem and not to a remedy."[15] Although NEMPA was centralized in form, the membership functioned through local associations which were granted a considerable amount of control. Thus the milk producers in the vicinity of any of the secondary New England milk markets negotiated contracts for sale of their milk through their own sales committees—although the program as a whole was co-ordinated through the New England Milk Producers Association.

Another significant bargaining-type association was formed at the end of the war by milk producers serving the Baltimore markets. This association was the first to make practical use of "the base-surplus plan"—an innovation in marketing procedure that has exerted a considerable influence on the development of national agricultural policy.

To appreciate the significance of this plan it is essential to realize that one of the most difficult problems in operating a fluid milk bargaining association on certain markets resulted from the severe fluctuations in fluid milk production. During part of the year production was scarcely adequate to meet consumer demands for milk in fluid form. In other periods production was so flush that part of the milk produced had to be diverted to by-product uses which yielded much lower returns. The officials of the Maryland State Dairymen's Association, soon after its formation as a bargaining association, recognized that its success was dependent upon some plan which would regularize milk production throughout the year so as to insure an adequate supply at all times while reducing surpluses that demoralized prices. The solution to this problem was found in the "base-surplus plan" adopted in the fall of 1918. Under this plan each producer was given a base—or a definite share of the fluid milk market—depending upon his production of milk in the fall months when production was at the low point during the year. On this amount of base production the producer was paid the base price in every month of the year while for any surplus over this base a lower surplus price was paid. This scheme thus penalized the production of surplus milk when it was not needed, while it encouraged an increase in production during the customary months of shortage.[16]

The base-surplus plan was a contribution of first importance to the success of milk bargaining associations and within a few years modified base-surplus plans were being successfully used at Philadelphia and in a number of other markets.[17]

While most of the fluid milk associations which undertook marketing functions expanded from earlier bargaining forms of organization, the Twin-City Milk Producers Association was established almost outright in 1916 as a bargaining and marketing organization. The conditions of this flush producing area were considerably different from those found near the urban centers in the East. Any plan for fluid milk marketing required the use of local facilities so that surplus milk could be held back at country points for processing. The Association, therefore, proceeded to acquire local facilities which could process milk at the point of production so that it would not converge on the central markets and upset prices. A pooling method was devised under which the member was paid the average price received for milk by the Association regardless of the way in which it was used. At first the Association endeavored to operate with rented facilities, but experience soon indicated that it was essential for the Association to own its own local and central processing plants.[18]

The rapid growth of large fluid milk associations which embraced a large share of the milk producers supplying important urban markets was viewed with alarm by many who feared that these associations would operate as producers' monopolies. As a result, the organized dairymen were soon harrassed by many legal impediments, and, in several instances, they were prosecuted under state anti-trust laws as being in restraint of trade.

As long as their legal standing was questioned it was difficult for such organizations to carry on normal business operations. For example, it was almost impossible to obtain adequate membership capital to provide for needed processing plants as long as the continuation of the organization was in doubt. It was also appreciated that the support of the general public was being undermined by allegations made against the producers' organizations. Under these circumstances, it soon became the primary objective of the dairy cooperatives to obtain national legislation which would make clear the farmer's right to organize for his economic advancement and protection.

The spearhead of this thrust for recognition was the National Milk Producers Federation which was organized following the 1916 National Conference on Marketing and Farm Credits as an organization to represent the broad interests of fluid milk marketing associations. (See Chapter VI). Working with other farm organizations, support was finally obtained for legislation which adequately protected the farmers' right to organize cooperatively and removed the fear of prosecution under the Sherman Act.[19] In this way, the efforts of the dairy cooperatives to secure national recognition of their rights to organize cooperatively served not only themselves but all similar groups of organized farmers.

Thus, by 1920, cooperation was well established in all branches of the dairy industry. Cooperative creameries and cheese factories were then being knit together into well-articulated marketing systems while the farmers who supplied fluid milk for direct consumption had found systems of marketing organization that permitted them to deal successfully with the large distributing interests which were entrenched in the large urban centers. Moreover, the struggle to achieve legal standing had built support for forthcoming national legislative recognition of the cooperative form of enterprise.

The Organization of the Grain Growers

In Chapter IV we described the way in which the farmers of Rockwell, Iowa, made use of the "maintenance clause" to secure a firm foothold for the cooperative elevator movement. By 1900, the number of cooperative elevators scattered throughout the grain-producing belt exceeded 100, and the movement was slowly gaining strength.

This development was not looked upon with indifference either by the established line or independent local elevators. By 1895 these two groups, who "had come to consider themselves as the 'regular' dealers entitled to the whole of the grain business,"[20] began to form strong state grain dealers' associations and by 1900 such organizations were functioning in practically all of the principal grain-producing states. At first the state grain dealers' associations were opposed particularly to "scoop shovelers"[21] but as the cooperative elevators began to increase in number, they also received disapproval.

To stop the growth of cooperative elevators, the state grain dealers' associations in 1901 threatened to boycott any terminal receivers of grain at Chicago who accepted shipments from "irregular firms." As commission firms were afraid to lose the patronage of the more numerous "regular" elevators, they promptly established a boycott against cooperative elevators, and their grain stood on the track at the terminal markets or piled up in their elevators "for want of an outlet." Fortunately, the grain dealers' associations were defied by two commission firms in Chicago who saw a profitable source of business with the growing number of cooperative elevators, and this eventually broke the boycott.[22]

The state farmers' grain dealers' associations. The opposition of the state grain dealers' associations proved a blessing in disguise, for it convinced grain farmers that they had to develop a marketing system under their own control. According to Farlow:

> The boycott actually stimulated the farmers' elevator movement. Farmers throughout the Middle West accepted the challenge and entered into an earnest fight in defense of their right to improve marketing conditions. Cooperation was not only an economic necessity but an expression of class consciousness as well.[23]

Seeing the organized power of the state grain dealers' associations, the farmers' elevators began to form themselves into state farmers' grain dealers' associations. The first organizations of this type were established in Nebraska and Illinois in the spring of 1903, and in Iowa in 1904.[24] Similar associations were formed in Minnesota and South Dakota in 1907, in North Dakota in 1911, in Kansas in 1913, and in Ohio and Indiana in 1916. Although the first organizations were largely defensive in character, they soon found that they could render many constructive services for their member elevators such as representing their interests in legislative and legal matters; in negotiations with carriers or terminal receivers designed to obtain lower transportation or handling charges and better service; in helping them with problems of organization and operation; in such matters as incorporation, accounting, auditing, insurance, selection of managers, bonding of employees, and collection of damage claims. Almost immediately these state farmers' elevators' associations thus became the vital centers for mobilizing and directing a vigorous farmers' elevator movement.

With the cooperative elevators integrated through their state associations, the latter began to work together on common problems and thus the movement soon became integrated nationally. An effective instrument for national coordination was the *American Cooperative Journal* which was issued with the official endorsement of the state farmers' grain dealers' associations from 1906 to 1911, when it was purchased by them and made their official organ.[25] From then on the *American Cooperative Journal* was for many years the outstanding cooperative publication serving American farmers.[26] It was full of write-ups designed to improve the cooperative and business practices of the farmers' elevators and other forms of cooperative enterprise. It emphasized incessantly the need for better accounting, better management,[27] and more team work among elevators and other groups in handling common problems. Largely through its influence in acquainting the various state associations of their mutual needs, the state farmers' grain dealers' associations joined together in 1912 to form the National Council of Farmers Cooperative Associations, which in 1920 became The Farmers National Grain Dealers Association. Thus, bound together, through their overhead organizations and the *American Cooperative Journal* as an effective mouthpiece, the local cooperative elevators were at last fully articulated as a national movement.

As farmers' elevators began to demonstrate their power, they grew rapidly not only in number but also in internal strength. The boycott had aroused a remarkable spirit of class loyalty and this was maintained by the persistent opposition of the organized grain dealers. As the elevators improved their cooperative and operating techniques, they were able to provide increasing economic benefits in the form of patronage refunds and added services, such as the purchase of farm supplies. With less need for using the maintenance clause as a means of ensuring loyalty, it gradually dwindled in significance. As one of the pioneers in the Rockwell society later wrote:

> The success of the "penalty clause" in a measure brought its own reward in the form of the loyalty with which it imbued its members. The "clause" itself gradually faded from the picture; and the means became obscured by the end attained. It had been the means of breaking through the solid ranks of opposition to cooperative grain marketing on a successful scale in the local markets of the grain belt. State laws were enacted suited to cooperative needs; and now the more eminently successful societies found a patronage dividend sufficient to maintain loyalty in their membership.[28]

From stock companies to cooperative associations. We have noted that the first cooperative elevators were largely organized as stock companies under general corporation laws since there were at that time no adequate statutes which provided specifically for the incorporation of cooperative enterprises. This condition imposed a severe handicap to cooperative development, since it was difficult to establish and maintain effective cooperative associations under the general corporation laws which in many instances provided for control and division of savings in accordance with shares of stock held. As a result, many of the farmers' elevators set up under such laws could scarcely be considered true cooperative associations although various means were used to make them as cooperative in character as possible, such as "limitations upon the holding and transfer of stock and the exercise of control of the company through the voting privilege."[29]

This impediment to effective cooperative growth became increasingly apparent as farmers gained more and more cooperative experience. Obviously they could not build strong cooperative organizations under laws which encouraged them to operate in a non-cooperative manner. As Powell, writing in 1913, said:

> Under the corporation laws of most of the states, it is generally impossible to organize a business agricultural association on a non-profit cooperative basis . . . In stock corporations formed for pecuniary profit, the voting power of the member is proportional to the number of shares held by each member . . . This is a right fixed by the statute. The right to sell and transfer the stock is incident to the ownership. It is also a statutory right and not subject to the control of the corporation . . . The ordinary corporation law is therefore inadequate to meet the requirements of the farmers' cooperative organization . . . The membership in these associations is confined exclusively to producers and should not be transferrable except under rules legally provided by the associations. These restrictions are non-enforceable under the United States Corporation laws.[30]

Recognizing this limitation to their efforts, farmers and their leaders (as organized in general farm organizations or through state cooperative organizations such as farmers' grain dealers' associations) turned to the state legislatures for relief, and quickly secured the enactment of laws designed to facilitate cooperation along Rochdale lines.[31]

The new cooperative laws soon began to exert a profound effect on the character of the farmers' elevator movement through the formation of many new associations or the reorganization of many old ones, in accordance with their provisions. As a result of this change there was a rapid increase in the practice of distributing savings according to patronage. In 1914, the Office of Markets and Rural Organization found that only 26 per cent of the farmers' elevators in the North Central states were operating on the patronage refund plan, while in 1918, only four years later, the Federal Trade Commission found that 61 per cent of the farmers' elevators in this territory were distributing savings on this basis.[32]

In the task of modifying their legal structures—and necessarily their business practices—so as to make them conform to the new legal statutes, the elevators drew heavily on the assistance of their state associations, as well as on the general farm organizations. Fortunately the Office of Markets and Rural Organization, which was just becoming established when this conversion began to take place, was in position to assist materially in this work, especially in cooperation with the state agricultural colleges and state marketing agencies.[33]

Cooperative sales agencies. In an earlier chapter we described how farmers endeavored to establish cooperative sales agencies in the terminal grain markets as early as the 1880's. Little of permanent significance except the lessons of experience came from these efforts, although they focused farmers' attention on the need for such organizations. To some extent the holding campaigns of the Equity retarded cooperative efforts in terminal marketing by encouraging farmers to feel that they could maintain prices by controlling the flow of grain to the terminal markets.

However, as the farmers' elevator movement gained momentum, and the holding movement disclosed its weaknesses, attention became increasingly centered on the problem of marketing at the terminals. We have already described how this led to the formation of the Equity Cooperative Exchange in 1911, the Tri-State terminal operations in the Pacific Northwest and the Farmers' Union-sponsored commission firms on the Kansas City, Hutchinson, and Omaha grain markets. None of these organizations represented true federations of local elevators. Rather, they were commission sales agencies set up by general farm organizations to serve local farmers' elevators affiliated with them. Although there were several instances of cooperative terminal grain selling by 1920, it could not be said that they integrated the efforts of the local elevator associations in any comprehensive marketing sense.

Looking back over the period from 1896 to 1920, we can see that great progress was made in cooperative grain marketing, particularly at the local markets. Although there was less significant progress in forming regional grain marketing associations, a good foundation for such efforts had been laid by the work of the farmers state grain dealers' associations and the terminal sales agencies.

Cooperative Achievements in Livestock Marketing

Only a few livestock shipping associations had been formed prior to 1897. Starting about 1904, they began to expand in number with the result that there were about 600—centered largely in the North Central states—when the state of rapid expansion opened in 1917. The number had increased to over 1,800 by the end of 1920.

The livestock shipping associations were an expression of farmers' discontent with the prevailing "country buyer" system of livestock marketing. Farmers saw no reason for paying exorbitant charges for the service of assembling their livestock and consigning it to terminal markets when they could so easily perform this task and more to their satisfaction through cooperative effort.[34]

To a great extent the growth of livestock shipping associations was encouraged by the success with which farmers' elevators had rapidly established themselves in the same general territory. If farmers could build elevators and ship their grain cooperatively in the face of the united opposition of the grain trade, why could they not perform for themselves another important function with little or no capital expenditure? Significantly, cooperative livestock shipping naturally developed in many instances as a side-line elevator activity.[35]

Only modest effort was required in forming a typical livestock shipping association. After interest had been aroused by a few leaders, an organization meeting was held and at this time the constitution and by-laws were adopted, the directors elected, and the manager appointed. Generally a membership fee of $1.00 was required, but this was often collected as a deduction from market receipts. Few of the first associations were incorporated, but after the enactment of "Rochdale" cooperative laws, incorporation became increasingly common with shares generally fixed at the nominal price of $1.00.

Operation of a livestock shipping association presented little difficulty. In most cases the "manager became the association" subject to intermittent supervision from the board of directors. When farmers had livestock to ship they notified the manager who arranged for cars, and the shipment was consigned to terminal market receivers. The livestock of each farmer was so marked that sales returns could be made to each individual owner. Only a minimum of expense pooling and accounting for sales proceeds was required.[36]

As the shipping associations gained volume and experience, their methods were gradually modified. Accounting records were improved, member responsibilities were clarified, and methods of management and operation were systematized.[37]

Overhead service organizations. As livestock shipping associations grew in number and scope, a need arose for overhead service organizations that would perform for them services comparable to those rendered by the state farmers' grain dealers' associations for farmers' elevators—particularly in standardization of accounting forms, in legislative representation, and in handling transportation problems. This need first expressed itself in 1915 with the formation of the Minnesota Central Cooperative Livestock Shipping Association as a federation of local shipping associations. Similar service associations were in process of formation in Iowa, Illinois, Indiana, Ohio, and Michigan in 1919 when their development was arrested, except in Iowa, by the establishment of cooperative livestock marketing departments in connection with the emerging state Farm Bureau federations.[38]

In Iowa, the strength of the independent shipping associations expressed itself early in 1920 in their federation as the Iowa Cooperative Livestock shippers. From then on, except in Minnesota and Iowa, where the shipping associations were strongly federated in their own independent state associations, shipping association developments were increasingly dominated by the livestock marketing activities carried on as Farm Bureau programs.

In Minnesota and Iowa, the state livestock shipping associations in 1920 were reaching out to perform necessary marketing functions for member associations. In Minnesota, this expressed itself in 1921 in the formation of the Central Cooperative Commission Association as a marketing agency for the shipping associations.[39] In Iowa, where livestock was shipped less exclusively to one principal market, the marketing efforts of the Iowa Livestock Shippers were largely directed toward assisting the local shipping associations in selecting the best market outlets.[40]

Cooperative sales agencies. During the period when the livestock shipping associations were growing in number, cooperative livestock commission sales agencies were becoming established on the terminal markets, more or less independently of the shipping associations. As noted in Chapter IV, cooperative sale of livestock on terminal markets first attracted support in 1889. Thereafter the idea of cooperative sales agencies slumbered for 15 years, to be awakened in 1905 by the formation of the Cooperative Livestock Commission Company. Although this agency was sponsored by the American National Livestock Association, the Corn Belt Meat Producers' Association, and other educational and protective organizations of livestock producers, it failed in 1909 through lack of effective supporting organizations of livestock producers at the shipping point.

By 1916, the conditions which had caused the failure of the earlier commission firms had been largely changed with the increase in cooperative livestock shipping associations, and by the growth of the Equity and Farmers' Union, as effective advocates of agricultural cooperation. Both of these organizations had sponsored the formation of livestock shipping associations, along with elevators and other forms of cooperative enterprise. It was thus natural for them to turn their attention to the formation of sales facilities to serve these shipping associations on the terminal markets. In the case of the Equity, the cooperative sale of livestock was first undertaken in 1916, as a division activity of the Equity Cooperative Exchange at South St. Paul. Although this operation was quite successful, it was subject to criticism by livestock producers since patronage refunds were distributed on the total volume of grain and livestock business, and this resulted in using the savings of the livestock division to offset the losses incurred in grain marketing and other activities.[41]

The first of the Farmers' Union livestock commission firms was established at Omaha in April 1917, soon after the livestock division of Equity Cooperative Exchange began business, and within a few years Farmers' Union commission firms were operating at St. Joseph, Sioux City, Kansas City, and Denver. These organizations could be set up at little cost since no extensive facilities were required and with a good volume of livestock assured from the cooperative shipping associations they were able to return substantial amounts in patronage refunds.

Cooperative livestock packing associations. While the enthusiasm for livestock shipping associations was high, a group of shrewd promoters began to interest farmers in the possibilities of developing their own livestock packing plants. The first of these pseudo-cooperative packing plants was started at LaCrosse, Wisconsin, in 1914 and by 1920 some 13 plants of this type had been formed in Wisconsin and nearby states. None was soundly conceived and none achieved any degree of success, and as a result this experience cost farmers several millions of dollars. On the constructive side, these failures had a chastening effect on those who felt that cooperative organizations could be successfully formed without a full examination of the economic problems involved. Farmers found again that there was no easy road to successful cooperation organization.[42]

Thus, by 1920, cooperative-livestock marketing was well established, with effective local shipping associations and terminal sales agencies—both supported by strong farmers' organizations or by strong service organizations of livestock shippers. On the other hand, experience to that date with cooperative packing plants had been discouraging.

The Cooperative Awakening of Cotton and Tobacco Growers

The significant efforts of farmers to establish cotton and tobacco cooperatives early in the century under the aegis of the Farmers' Union and the Equity crop-holding movements have been examined in Chapter X. Athough this experience did not lead to the formation of any lasting cooperative associations it had a pronounced influence on the character of later cooperative developments related to these two important farm commodities.

Community efforts toward better cotton marketing. After 1910 when the cotton growers were somewhat disillusioned over the prospects of being able to control supply through cooperative arrangements, interest began to develop in less dramatic solutions of their marketing problem. By this time the extension philosophy of Seaman A. Knapp was bearing fruit. Farmers were beginning to examine their problems from the standpoint of ways in which they themselves might help in their solution, and workers in the U. S. Department of Agriculture were not slow to take advantage of this new attitude.

It was at this time that Dr. O. F. Cook, who was then in charge of cotton-breeding investigations in the Bureau of Plant Industry, began his crusade for the establishment of one-variety cotton communities—following careful studies of the cotton farmer's problem. In 1911, Dr. Cook declared: "The American cotton industry presents unusual opportunities for improvement through community organization. Many important advantages are not to be realized by individual farmers working alone but require the united action of entire cotton-growing communities ..." He continued:

> Cotton growers have been urged to organize in order to reduce production or to secure higher prices by withholding the crop from the market. But there are other and more positive objectives to be gained. An occasional period of low prices is not as serious a danger to the cotton industry of the United States as continued high prices that stimulate a rapid development of cotton culture in other countries. A well established foreign competition means an ultimate reduction or restriction of prices ... The only adequate protection against foreign competition is to improve our own industry by growing better cotton and by growing it more cheaply than other countries are able to do, notwithstanding the lower wages of farm labor.

To meet this need, Dr. Cook urged the formation of one-variety cotton-improvement associations to standardize the production for local areas. He maintained that the organization of cotton growing communities to study and remove the present obstacles to progress would place the American cotton industry on a much firmer basis in relation to foreign competition. He also believed that such cooperative improvement in the quality of the crop would lead to the formation of a complete cooperative marketing system. He saw cooperative ginning as a natural accompaniment to community improvement in the quality of cotton production, and, looking to the future, he declared: "there is no fundamental reason why cooperative ginneries, compressors, and oil mills should not be conducted for the advantage of agricultural communities in the same way as creameries, canneries, packing houses and other cooperative enterprises."[43]

While Dr. Cook was promoting one-variety cotton communities, Charles J. Brand, also in the Bureau of Plant Industry, began studies to determine how methods of handling and marketing cotton could be improved.[44]

The first results of Brand's work were reported in the *U.S.D.A. Yearbook of Agriculture, 1912*. Here he maintained that "the individual farmer can rarely sell a few bales of cotton as advantageously as a community organization could sell uniform lots of 50 or more bales," or "afford to construct the necessary warehouses," or "as readily secure needed credit and many other things which organizations would bring within his reach."

Brand cited the great achievements of the California citrus fruit growers in giving "the country better fruit without increasing the cost to the consumer," while improving the economic position of the growers. He then declared that "the cotton growers of the South have the same need if not a greater need to organize for the purpose of marketing their product to the best advantage." Brand recommended a "true cooperative plan of organization" with each person having but one vote and with division of expenses and profits made purely on the basis of the amount of business done with or through the organization. He foresaw that "probably in most cases it will pay ultimately for organizations to own their own gins, warehouses, seedhouses and possibly oil mills, obliging all members of the organization largely to have their work done at their own ginnery and sold through their own selling agency." He was definitely opposed to crop holding as being "bad economics and probably wholly indefensible." Like Cook, he feared that "any widespread movement to try to bring about excessively high or fixed prices will certainly result in the stimulation of cotton culture in foreign countries and ultimate restriction of the market for American cotton."[45] Brand's views were supported the following year by a significant bulletin issued by the newly formed Office of Markets which described prevailing cotton-marketing methods in Oklahoma.[46]

The ideas espoused by Cook and Brand were first tried out by a group of cotton growers at Scott, Arkansas, who in 1912 formed the Scott Cotton Growers Association whose constitution set forth the following objectives: "(1) To produce cotton from pure seed; (2) to secure uniformity in ginning; (3) to sell cotton in even running lots; (4) to deal as nearly directly with the mills as possible; (5) to act in co-operation with the United States Department of Agriculture toward accomplishing these objects, and to take such further action as may be practicable to produce better cotton and improve the prevailing methods of handling and marketing same."

The membership fee was set at 10 cents a bale and there were to be fees of 50 cents per bale for selling cotton and 50 cents per ton for selling cotton seed. In the beginning, a pooling of sales proceeds was attempted but this soon gave way to sale on a separate basis for each member. However, a system of fines imposed upon members selling outside the Association helped to keep the program intact.

The Association was immediately successful and sales during 1914 amounted to $488,347. In the first year savings "ranged as high as $5 a bale of cotton and $4 per ton of seed." With good management this Association served to show what might be accomplished in community cooperative-cotton marketing and a few other associations were modeled somewhat on it. The Scott Association continued operations until 1922 when it was absorbed in the larger efforts of the Arkansas Cotton Growers Cooperative Association.[47]

Emergence of cooperative gins. While the Scott Association was establishing itself, there was a continuing interest in the formation of cooperative cotton warehouses and cooperative gins. It will be recalled that the Farmers' Union had promoted cotton warehouses essential to an effective holding movement. Most, however, were formed as farmers' joint-stock companies and, like other organizations of this type, they were soon owned and controlled by a few individuals. Even though this early experience had proven unsatisfactory it was recognized that "a well organized system of cotton warehouses would be of the greatest assistance to the farmer," and farmers were urged to "form cooperative associations and build their own warehouses."[48] However, few successful associations of the warehouse type were formed prior to 1920.

We have already mentioned the establishment of early cooperative gins by farmers associated with the Farmers' Union. Most of these gins were farmer-owned, joint-stock gins and in most instances they soon were in the hands of a few individuals. This experience "excited considerable feeling among farmers against cooperative ginning and particularly against cooperative ginning organizations formed on a capital stock basis."[49]

The sad experience of cotton growers in attempting to form and operate cooperative gins or warehouses under Texas statutes led them to secure the enactment of a non-stock cooperative law in 1917, which became known as the "Society Law."[50] With the enactment of this law, a number of "society" gins were soon organized in north Texas.[51] These associations had a number of interesting features. They were formed with no capital stock, no savings could be paid out if the association was in debt, equities were non-transferrable, only farmers could be members, and only one vote was permitted each member. As one observer has said, they were "semi-fraternal organizations, somewhat like churches."[52] Although these associations proved generally successful they were handicapped by lack of financial and operating flexibility.

Oklahoma farmers were likewise experimenting with the formation of cooperative gins following the enactment of a state cooperative law in 1919 which provided for cooperative stock associations set up along Rochdale lines. The first successful association, which was the forerunner of many more, was established in Johnson County in July 1919. Although this association was formed for the specific purpose of ginning cotton, it was also authorized by its by-laws to "engage in such other lines incident to said business as may be, from time to time, designated by the directors, which shall include the right to acquire, own, and operate cotton and cottonseed warehouses, compresses, cottonseed-oil mills and such other plant or plants as may be necessary to reduce cottonseed and products to the most refined state for commercial use."

The trend toward cooperation. Cotton farmers were gradually learning how to build cooperative cotton marketing institutions in the years from 1912 to 1920. In the later year there were a number of one-variety cotton growing communities, which had been established with government encouragement, and there were several successful cooperative gins, warehouses, and cotton marketing enterprises in operation. Just at this time conditions following World War I began to give a new direction to cooperative cotton marketing efforts. To understand this situation we must realize that under war conditions cotton prices soared to new levels in 1918 and 1919, and that this situation gave concern to cotton growers who feared a severe price recession. Shocked by the immediate drop in cotton prices following the cessation of hostilities in November 1918, and fearful of a severe postwar decline, a mixed assortment of plantation owners, bankers, merchants, and warehousemen formed the American Cotton Association in May 1919.[53] This organization was somewhat similar in character to the earlier Southern Cotton Association, for acreage reduction as a means of controlling redundant supplies was its first objective. However, there were many in its membership who felt that a fundamental improvement in the cotton marketing system was essential for the long run interests of the industry, so they proposed a comprehensive program of cooperative organization. The story of what resulted in 1920 must be deferred to Volume II of this history.

Tobacco growers mark time. Following the virtual collapse of the tobacco holding movement in 1910, as described in Chapter X, there was little significant interest in cooperative marketing of tobacco for the next decade. During this time the loose-leaf system of marketing was becoming established in the wake of the federal court decree in 1911 which dissolved the "tobacco trust," and for a time there was little complaint of market domination. During 1915 the Kentucky Agricultural Experiment Station made an exhaustive study of tobacco marketing which found that the loose-leaf system was "the most economically efficient system yet devised for marketing burley tobacco in central Kentucky. This study saw little opportunity for significant cooperative action."[54] Moreover, the war clearly increased the demand for tobacco with the result that farmers were not discontented with prices received.[55] However, with the collapse of war-inflated prices in the fall of 1920, there was a revival of interest in a strong growers' organization. The dramatic story of what resulted must be left to the next volume of this history.

Summary

In this chapter we have observed how during the period from 1896 to 1920 dairy farmers, grain growers, livestock producers, and raisers of cotton and tobacco turned increasingly to cooperative organization. The outstanding feature of these developments was the way in which these organizations expanded in scope from local to area operations, and devised practical cooperative techniques for accomplishing their aims. In the next three chapters we shall examine how the trend toward cooperation expressed itself among growers of fruits, vegetables, nuts, and other special crops.

Chapter XIII

THE FIRST INTEGRATED COOPERATIVE MARKETING SYSTEM—

The California Fruit Growers Exchange

The substantial progress made by California citrus fruit growers in cooperative marketing in the late 1880's and early 1890's was briefly described in Chapter IV. This was further intensified in the next 25 years under the leadership of the Southern California Fruit Exchange and its successor organization, The California Fruit Growers Exchange, now Sunkist Growers, Inc.[1] The highly significant pathfinding experience of this remarkable cooperative marketing association is examined in this chapter.

The Executive Board, 1893-1895

The "Organization and Marketing Plan" adopted by the Southern California Fruit Exchange on August 29, 1893, was the embryo of the Southern California Fruit Exchange, incorporated on October 3, 1895. Under this plan the various district exchanges were to be coordinated through the creation of an Executive Board chosen from the "boards of managers" in the respective districts. The Executive Board was to meet as often as necessary to adjust prices, regulate the distribution of fruit, or transact any other proper business. The Executive Board under the direction and approval of the several district exchange boards was to establish branch houses for the sale and distribution of the fruit embraced by the several districts. The expense of maintaining the branch houses and representatives in the East was to be borne pro rata according to the oranges shipped during the season.[2]

Under this plan the Executive Board immediately began to hold

237

weekly meetings in Los Angeles open to all interested citrus growers. It proved impossible to establish branch sales offices in the East as many growers had had "vexing experiences" with consignment sales and "were clamorous for an f.o.b. market." Yielding to this demand, the Executive Board employed the f.o.b. method for marketing during the two crop years 1893-94 and 1894-95. Under this scheme it set an f.o.b. California price on oranges about twice a month. This procedure soon proved unsatisfactory since opposing interests took advantage of the Board's price quotations.[3]

Thus, "there was no positive accepted plan adopted by the growers as a whole to govern the marketing proposition" prior to November 21, 1894, when the Executive Board with the prior approval of the individual exchanges and the local associations adopted a definite system for marketing.[4] Under the new scheme "citrus products controlled [by the member district exchanges] were to be marketed in conformity to a general plan. . . ." This plan was to continue for one year, but it did not provide for the establishment of sales offices in the East. Its main object was to empower the Executive Board with greater authority over the district exchanges in the interest of working harmony.[5]

Formation of the Southern California Fruit Exchange

After two years of disillusionment with the f.o.b. method of sale—which had been largely responsible for a gradual defection of grower support—the Executive Board finally decided that little could be accomplished without exclusive selling agencies in the eastern markets. The adoption of a comprehensive plan for selling on a delivered price basis on September 4, 1895, combined with the formal incorporation of the Southern California Fruit Exchange on October 3, 1895, marked the establishment of a permanent marketing institution in a stronger form.

Branch sales headquarters were to be opened in various markets, "under the control of the Executive Board" which was authorized to determine "the amount of fruit required to fully supply the markets . . . from month to month . . ." The Executive Board was to have full charge of all diversions so as to "avoid over-stocking markets." It was to appoint "as many inspectors" as might be necessary "to establish uniform grades of fruit and packing . . ."

The general objective of the marketing plan was expressed as follows:

All possible encouragement [is] to be given to efforts made with the view of bringing the other fruit industries of the state under the system, thus adding force and influence to the movement—providing a more efficient force, reducing the expense, establishing a chain of branch houses that shall become famous for the distribution of California products and inaugurating a system that shall control and ultimately become the supreme factor in handling and marketing the fruit, vegetables, and other like products of the state.[6]

The decision to incorporate the central selling agency as the Southern California Fruit Exchange came almost simultaneously with the adoption of the new sales policy, as it was recognized that the program determined upon could not be successfully administered by an informal committee. Under its articles of incorporation, the Southern California Fruit Exchange was empowered "to engage in the general business of buying, marketing, and selling oranges ... and generally to transact, carry on, and perform all such other business operations as are germane or incidental to the purposes above mentioned." The authorized capital stock of the Southern California Fruit Exchange was fixed at $10,000 with a par value per share of $100.[7]

The new organization was confronted with many difficulties. The plan of delivered sale represented an innovation in marketing procedure and its value could not be determined until experience had been gained. Moreover, the plan short-circuited the local buyers and the established commission men, who naturally spared no effort to ruin its success. However, the Exchange dauntlessly moved ahead with its plan and immediately stationed some 20 agents "in eastern consuming centers to attend exclusively to Exchange business during the winter months," and in the following summer (1897) continuous employment of agents was begun on a year-round basis.[8]

The future character of the Exchange system was largely determined when it elected to sell on a delivered sale basis under which prices were quoted essentially as of the delivery date. This method of sale established control over distribution from the grower to the central markets and thus eliminated speculation in the handling of growers' fruit. Moreover, by providing for central control over the movement to market, it permitted, in later years, the effective development of a national advertising program. Looking back in 1919, G. Harold Powell, then the general manager, paid this tribute to the vision of the early pioneers when they decided on this course of development: "The industry's problem was met only when the producers systematized the delivery of their own fruit, eliminated speculation from its purchase and distribution, established their own sales office, and sold their products to the wholesale trade in the territory where the fruit was to be consumed."[9]

The Formative Years, 1895-1903

With the incorporation of the Southern California Fruit Exchange in October 1895 the basic mold for the exchange system of marketing was cast—with growers united into local associations which in turn were joined together in a series of district exchanges, federated together in one central exchange. Moreover, the way for permanent growth was paved by the adoption of the delivered sales plan. The road ahead, however, was not yet clear of serious obstacles. In fact the struggle for survival during the next few years was to test severely the strength of the exchange idea and largely shape its character as an institution.

One of the immediate problems was to rekindle the growers' enthusiasm for cooperation, since much of the initial interest had been dissipated by the inability of the Executive Board to satisfy fully all expectations. Moreover, advantages to be derived from cooperative action were temporarily less apparent since the Executive Board had injected a new element of competition into the market. The established fruit trade, bitterly resenting the intrusion into the market of the growers' own marketing agency, took advantage of the confused situation by charging that the Exchange officials were not only incompetent but lacking in personal integrity.

At this time the Exchange was plagued also by internal problems due to its weakness in central administration and lack of experience in harmonizing diverse views. This difficulty was partially removed with the appointment of President A. H. Naftzger as general manager in 1897, but the primary difficulty was due to the fact that the growers had not yet learned that self-discipline was required for effective cooperation. For illustration, the growers in the more favored producing districts strenuously objected to a plan which was designed to afford a market for all while the growers in the less favored districts insisted with equal vigor that they should be given equal opportunity on the market. For a time it appeared that these difficulties might lead to disintegration—with each district exchange going off on its own. As the exchange system gathered strength so as to provide a more effective marketing service the attitudes of the discordant groups were gradually harmonized.[10]

Fortunately it was fully appreciated by the Exchange leaders that little could be accomplished without the support of those whom it was to serve and from the beginning all decisions on policy were made only after careful deliberation and review by all concerned. In fact, as we have observed, the first meeting of the Executive Board in October 1893 was thrown open to all interested persons, a procedure that proved so popular and useful that it was adopted as a permanent feature of Exchange policy. This policy, which permitted growers to see how affairs were carried on, engendered a feeling of confidence. Moreover, the struggle of the Exchange to establish itself as a marketing organization encouraged team work, for the growers were quick to appreciate that they would "all hang separately" if they "did not hang together." The bitterness of the opposition toward the emerging exchange system only served to strengthen cooperative solidarity.

The Exchange leaders saw clearly that educational procedures to teach growers how to organize and work together cooperatively were the best weapons that could be used against those who were determined to bring about its failure. Thus from the beginning every effort was made to enlist voluntary support through providing members with information on every phase of the business of the Exchange.[11]

During these early years, while the Exchange was establishing itself, community spirit was so high that there was little need of an organized membership program to maintain the support of the growers. Most of the growers in the local associations knew each other intimately and it was a common occurrence to have all-day annual meetings with a picnic lunch where the growers and the employees of the local, district, and central exchanges came to view each other as partners in a common enterprise.[12]

In its formative years the Exchange movement was very fortunate in having such enlightened leaders as T. H. B. Chamblin, P. J. Dreher, and A. H. Naftzger, who appreciated that the development of a plan for marketing was not enough. They saw that permanent success in marketing was dependent upon the construction of strong local democratic organizations disciplined in cooperative techniques and harmonized through central organization, and they undertook to teach farmers their responsibilities as cooperators. The leadership of these men created a remarkable spirit of growers' solidarity which expressed itself in a determination to make the cooperative plan succeed.

By 1898 the central exchange was beginning to find itself as an organization. It was then serving as a central clearing house and unifying center whose primary function was the maintenance of central sales facilities. Each local association, however, retained its autonomy over grading, packing, inspection, pooling, etc., with its own grades and brands.

By this time the leaders in the Exchange had found that control over the market was an impractical ideal so they devoted their attention to the problem of providing a more efficient sales service for their members. The delivered selling plan had gained general acceptance and as a result of its benefits the Exchange was beginning to take pride in its record as a merchandising agency. The character that the Exchange was beginning to assume is reflected in the following statement made about this time by President A. H. Naftzger:

> We have what we believe to be the most thorough organization and system that has ever been organized for the handling of perishable products. The Southern California Fruit Exchange acts purely and solely as a marketing agent for the various local exchanges of which there are twelve. The local exchanges and associations connected with it determine all the questions of grading, packing, etc., and we have to do with the goods when they are put on board the cars ready to go forward. We have our own sales agents in the principal cities of the United States whose sole business is to sell our goods . . . this system enables us . . . to gauge the requirements of the different markets and distribute the fruit according to the wants of the different places.[13]

The Exchange had found that membership support could only be maintained through the rendering of efficient service. While "like-minded growers" were encouraged to affiliate voluntarily, little was done "to induce growers to connect themselves with the Exchange," although it was admitted that the program could be even more effective with a control of 80 to 90 percent of the crop. President Naftzger declared: "If he comes in voluntarily it is because he has confidence in the system, and if he were not convinced that the system was advantageous he would probably be more or less of a disturbing element if he came in."[14]

Despite bitter attacks of trade competitors the soundness and efficiency of exchange methods steadily gained recognition. By 1900 citrus growers were coming to feel a real sense of pride in their plan of organization which they saw as something "permanent—not for a day or a generation." While the papers were full of complaints that farmers were forming trusts, little complaint could be made against the Exchange on this score, since "no grower was excluded from membership," and "no attempt was made to force arbitrary prices."

The functions of the three parts of the exchange system now had become well articulated. Local associations were held responsible for grading, pooling, packing, and other local matters. Responsibility of the central exchange began with the delivery of fruit to the exchanges. As one observer noted in 1901: "As in the government of the United States, all the freedom consistent with good and equitable service is retained by the individual."[15]

At the turn of the century the central exchange had thus become a symbol of unity and organized strength. While it was still little more than a general selling agency, its board meetings were forums for the discussion of all kinds of industry problems, and clearing houses for the formulation of common policies. It was beginning to standardize practices of locals through decisions arrived at through conferences or committees, and it was finding places where it could perform desired services for locals which could not be performed by the locals themselves, such as collecting claims on fruit damaged in shipment.

The year 1901 was marked by the inauguration of a joint sales agreement by which the Exchange made its entire sales force available to the California Fruit Exchange for selling deciduous fruit. This plan lowered the selling costs on citrus fruit while it enabled the California Fruit Exchange to establish itself as a cooperative organization.[16]

In this year T. H. B. Chamblin, the acknowledged "father of the Exchange," was able to declare that: "The Exchange has not only reached the climax of success, but has placed itself in a distinct class as compared with similar institutions the world over. For maximum of benefits to participants the Exchange may safely challenge comparison with any commercial enterprise known in the annals of trade . . ."[17]

The California Fruit Agency Agreement, 1903-1904

Just at the time when the Exchange was becoming stabilized as an organization, it temporarily lost its sense of direction and embarked upon an experiment which almost jettisoned the accomplishments achieved with so much difficulty. This experiment was to test the moorings of the organization and serve as an object lesson never to be forgotten in the subsequent development of the exchange system.

To understand this situation it is necessary to realize that the citrus industry in early 1903 was confronted by a very difficult problem. An unusually large crop, following several years of steady expansion in citrus acreage, had resulted in a complete demoralization of prices. This had given rise to a demand for some kind of industry program to stabilize the market for citrus fruit. Obviously the Exchange alone was not strong enough to achieve the desired end, since only 43 per cent of the California citrus shipments were then under its control. At this juncture a remedy for the depressed condition of the industry was suggested by a prominent commercial shipper who proposed that the Exchange and the commercial shippers pool their marketing efforts so as "to eliminate ruinous competition, prevent glutted markets and provide equal distribution of the output throughout the United States."

After much discussion the manager and the directors of the Exchange agreed to go along on the proposal "if all the independents would join such a movement" and "almost overnight" this led to the grouping of the independent shippers in a federation, The California Citrus Union, which in turn joined with the Exchange in forming The California Fruit Agency. This arrangement brought some 90 per cent of the California citrus crop under one control for sales purposes.[18]

To achieve the ends desired the California Fruit Agency and the Southern California Fruit Exchange entered into an agreement on April 1, 1903, which was to continue until October 31, 1908, although it was subject to cancellation under certain conditions. Under this agreement the Exchange was to continue legally, but its identity was to be largely submerged. The Agency was given "the right and authority to sell, market and dispose of all oranges, lemons and grapefruit" controlled by the Exchange and was to become "its sole agent" for marketing. Thus the Agency was to absorb the terminal market sales facilities which had been developed by the Exchange. A most objectionable clause of the agreement, in effect, limited the Exchange to its existing membership. This read as follows:

> The Exchange shall have the right to have marketed for its account by the Agency, all of the fruit that may be owned or controlled by all of the present members of the various Exchanges and Associations, during the whole term of this agreement. Also provided that any association now connected with the Exchange *may* during any year of this agreement *add new members with acreage and production equal to its losses by withdrawals*, provided such new members are not growers whose fruit was marketed by the Agency for other packers than the Exchange the previous year. And provided also that the Exchange and its associations may also have marketed by the Agency for its account, the citrus fruit from acreage not now bearing nor now owned by present members of the Exchange, *to the extent of 40 percent* of all such new acreage. . . .
>
> And the Exchange agrees that *it will not allow any increase in present membership of any Exchange or association* connected therewith, except as herein provided, *without the consent of the Agency* (Italics added).[19]

While the leaders in the Exchange who participated in the formation of the Agency were unquestionably sincere in their opinion that the resulting sacrifice of autonomy was justified by economic conditions, there is evidence that they exceeded their authority in entering into this combination. The Agency, with the Exchange manager serving as its manager, had already commenced business before the agreement providing for its establishment was sent to the district exchanges for their ratification. In fact, one of them refused to ratify the agreement and even filed notice of withdrawal on this account. Moreover, this district exchange had previously addressed a resolution to the Southern California Fruit Exchange which requested it to "quickly return to those sure principles upon which the organization . . . was based."[20]

As the anticipated benefits from the Agency agreement failed to materialize—despite the strenuous efforts of the Agency's management to make the plan work—the local and district exchange organizations began to demand that the Exchange withdraw from the agreement and proceed on its original course as a strictly growers' organization. In particular, the restriction on cooperative independence, inherent in the plan, had caused widespread dissatisfaction within the membership of the Exchange. Finally convinced that these two diverse groups could not harmoniously work together, the officers of the Agency, on May 20, 1904, agreed to terminate the agreement as of September 1, 1904.

On the day that this decision was announced, the Board of Directors of the Southern California Fruit Exchange issued a statement which declared that it would resume active business on September 1, 1904, "with such changes in policy and plans . . . as the growers through the local exchanges may dictate."

A second statement issued on June 10, 1904, made it clear that the Exchange was reverting immediately to its first principles and was determined to stand again on its own feet. This statement declared:

> Our crops are now so large that all markets should be constantly supplied with their full quota of fruit in order to consume the output. This distribution can be better accomplished by those most directly interested—the growers themselves. . . . Believing that in cooperation with each other, the best net results to the growers can be obtained, we appeal to the present Exchange members . . . to put forth every effort to secure as large a membership as possible in our associations and exchanges.[21]

Thus ended an arrangement which "did violence to the principle of local democratic control upon which the Exchange was formed."[22] The way was now clear for constructive growth.

Stabilization and Amplification, 1904-1908

The decision to terminate the Agency Agreement and go back to the original plan of independent marketing was a landmark in Exchange history, for after this action there was no turning back. The long-espoused idea of joining with the trade so as to achieve a dominant control over the supply had been tried and found unworkable. This experience had taught the growers that their interests could best be served only through their own organization under their complete control.

However, resumption of independent activities was not without its difficulties, for much bitterness had accumulated as a result of the Agency experience. For a time it appeared doubtful whether the Exchange could recapture the momentum which had been temporarily forfeited. For a brief period there was even danger that the exchange system would disintegrate.[23]

Nevertheless, the thousands of growers and their leaders who had built the Exchange were determined that it should not fail. The general manager who had served as manager of the Agency was replaced by W. A. Woodford, a man who had the respect of the growers as well as of the trade, and within a short time the way was cleared for definite progress.[24]

In resuming operations in 1904, the Exchange was determined to keep control in the hands of the growers themselves. The assumption of power by the manager and the directors in entering into the Agency Agreement had left as a heritage the determination on the part of the growers to maintain control so as to avoid the possibility of any similar action in the future. The new manager was sympathetic to this point of view and he was careful to get full acceptance of the growers—through their elected representatives—on any decision affecting their interests before it was placed into effect.

At this time the citrus industry was beginning to expand rapidly especially in the central part of the state and new local associations and district exchanges were being formed to serve the growers in this area. The Exchange assisted in this development. According to its minutes for November 30, 1904, J. S. Edwards was employed "at the expense of the Exchange in the work of forming new associations and working up membership in the associations generally."

When these new associations were admitted into the exchange system it was obvious that the name of the central exchange was no longer appropriate and so the Southern California Fruit Exchange was reorganized to become the California Fruit Growers Exchange. While this involved little more than a change in name, since the articles and by-laws adopted by the Southern California Fruit Exchange in 1895 were little altered, it was significant in that the new name got away from the old name clouded by participation in the Agency. Moreover, the new name reflected a broader conception of the Exchange as a cooperative organization in that it included the word "growers," a change of organic significance since it implied that the Exchange was designed to serve *growers* and to be subject to their ultimate control. The inclusion of the word "growers" also had a practical advantage in that it distinguished the Exchange from the California Fruit Exchange (Sacramento) which was then becoming prominent as a fresh fruit marketing organization.

Thus under new management and with a new name, the Exchange became a reformed and revitalized organization. The first meeting of stockholders under the name "California Fruit Growers Exchange" occurred on April 12, 1905.

At this time the Exchange was still little more than a sales agency for the local associations which were joined together in the district exchanges. In the next few years there was to be a great broadening of exchange functions in response to the pressure of its member associations for assistance on production and marketing problems. As these new functions were all essential to the more effective performance of the sales function they represented an amplication and improvement of sales efforts rather than a change in the basic objectives of the Exchange as an organization. Thus whenever any problem arose in which there was a common interest—such as the need for more complete market information, the control of citrus pests or diseases, the improvement of pooling methods, the collection of freight claims, the high cost of packing materials, etc.—it was quickly brought to the attention of the central exchange and steps were taken to solve the problem. The exchange meetings served as a general congress for growers and their associations where policies and methods could be worked out to make the whole exchange system more effective. As a natural development the Exchange was more and more called upon to provide certain services that could be effectively and economically provided only by a large-scale overhead organization. For example, in 1905, "a uniform cooperative agreement" was drafted for the guidance of local associations. This was designed to bring about a gradual standardization of local marketing agreements. The need for legal service led the Exchange to establish a legal department in 1909, and partly due to the advisory assistance of this department there gradually developed a considerable degree of uniformity in various documents used for marketing or organization. In this way the central exchange signally strengthened its position as the coordinating agency for its local and district organizations.

The years immediately following 1905 were noteworthy also in that they saw the development of a practical philosophy of cooperation within the exchange system. As the local and district exchanges, learning from one another, steadily improved their business and cooperative practices, they increasingly turned to the central exchange for help on problems beyond their control. The Exchange, on its part—under the direction of a competent manager and staff and directors who believed in the democratic process of development—responded only when it was obvious that the local associations required assistance that only it could perform. The Exchange took the position that it was the servant and instrument of the local associations rather than their master, and it was scrupulous in restricting its operations so as to maximize and safeguard local autonomy.

Market information service. The way in which the services of the central exchange grew can be shown by the way in which the market information service expanded. Under the exchange plan of marketing the local associations and the district exchanges required accurate information on market conditions as a basis for directing their shipments so as to obtain highest returns. It was natural for them to turn to the central exchange for this essential information since the broad sales contacts of the central exchange throughout the United States and Canada provided a fund of information on market conditions that could easily be made available through daily market reports. By providing these reports the central exchange emphasized its ability to serve a common need and broadened the concept of it as an organization that could do more than provide joint selling facilities and services.[25]

Traffic service. Another overhead service that developed rapidly grew out of the need of local associations for assistance in collecting freight claims. As early as 1895 the Exchange directors had appointed a committee to help local associations on this problem. By 1904 it had become so apparent that this work could best be performed by trained employees that a special department was established. The benefits from this service soon caused local associations to call for assistance on other traffic problems with the result that the claim department was soon helping local and district exchanges in all ways that would enable them to move fruit to market most expeditiously with a minimum of expense. This broadening of transportation service was further recognized in 1910 with the establishment of a complete traffic department.

Improvement in local handling. When the Exchange resumed marketing operations in 1904, there was little uniformity in the quality of fruit offered for sale by the member associations. Each local association had its own grades and standards and there was little control over the way fruit was picked and delivered for packing at associations. Just at this time a great industry-wide effort to improve quality was stimulated by an investigation into the cause of orange decay. This investigation— made by the U.S. Department of Agriculture under the direction of G. Harold Powell—soon proved conclusively that the heavy losses from decay in transit, then costing California producers about $1,000,000 annually, were largely attributable to the way in which the fruit was picked and handled at the local packing houses.

The organized citrus growers were quick to see that the problem uncovered by this study could not be remedied by the producers as individuals, since under the pooling method of marketing there was no practicable way in which the cost of losses, due to carelessness in picking or handling, could be charged back to the individual grower.[26] As a result of the findings of this investigation the local associations, with the encouragement of the directors of the central exchange, quickly began to assume responsibility for having the fruit picked through the employment of specially trained picking crews, and within a very short time this practice was adopted by a majority of the associations. Another natural consequence of Powell's work was the appointment of a committee by the Exchange Board of Directors in 1906 to investigate the methods of handling fruit in the packinghouses and this in turn led to the employment of a trained man "to superintend installation of suitable machinery" and otherwise assist local associations in improving their local handling methods.[27]

This campaign to reduce losses from decay greatly strengthened and broadened the entire exchange system of marketing. It brought home to the growers that they must yield some of their independence if an efficient system of marketing was to be developed and that the marketing effectiveness of the central exchange was dependent upon the quality of fruit delivered to it for sale. Moreover, by making them responsible for the quality of fruit shipped the significance of the local associations was increased. Improvement of local handling methods thus led to more cooperation between growers and the local associations and between the local associations and the central exchange in the performance of marketing functions. It also served to teach grower members their responsibilities and relationship to the system as a whole.[28]

Inauguration of advertising program. In this period there came another development which was destined to have an incalculable influence on the whole exchange system of marketing. To understand this it must be realized that in the early 1900's the threat of over-production hung over the entire California orange industry. To F. Q. Story, the president of the Exchange, there was only one solution—an advertising program "to get people to eat more oranges." For years Story had tried to get the directors of the Exchange to undertake an advertising program but without success, for some of the directors felt that the Exchange could not afford to incur an expense for advertising since its benefits admittedly could not be confined to Exchange members. Despite this skepticism, an appropriation of $250 was made in 1905 for the purpose of advertising Exchange fruit in England and Continental Europe and two years later under Story's persistent persuasion the Board appropriated $10,000 to test the possibilities of advertising oranges in Iowa.[29] This experiment proved conclusively that the demand for oranges could be expanded through advertising. It also demonstrated that an effective advertising program required the use of an attractive trademark. This led to the adoption of the "Sunkist" brand for Exchange advertising purposes in 1908. From this small beginning the advertising program was steadily expanded until within a very few years the word "Sunkist" had become a world-wide synonym for citrus fruit marketed through the California Fruit Growers Exchange.[30]

As the advertising program of the Exchange grew, it strengthened the whole exchange movement, for to get the benefits of advertising the Exchange had to form itself into a strong disciplined organization. Prior to the inauguration of the advertising program every local association had its own brands and there was no standard trademark for Exchange fruit. When it became appreciated that no program could be effectively developed without centralized administration over the quality of fruit to be shipped under the advertised trademark, the Exchange set up rigid grading requirements as a condition for its use. The adoption of the Sunkist label also resulted in a common industry effort for quality improvement and this served to heighten the prestige of the Exchange with the locals.

The advertising program also began to exert an influence on the thinking of Exchange leaders. In striving to please the public and gain acceptance of its product the logical necessity of building public good-will and the good-will of wholesalers and retailers became increasingly apparent. The Exchange came to recognize that its function primarily lay in distribution of the crop to terminal markets, and that a partnership was essential with those agencies which carried the fruit on to the ultimate consumers.

Although some of the local associations which had built up reputations for their own brands on certain markets were at first hesitant to participate in the common program, they gradually came to realize that their fruit could be sold more readily under the Sunkist trademark.[31] Moreover, this did not require them to give up their own individual brands for the Exchange permitted the use of the Sunkist label as long as the fruit came up to certain required specifications.[32]

The cost of introducing the advertising program was assumed by the Exchange as a general expense. However, a policy was soon established under which special funds for advertising were obtained through assessments charged on various types of fruit shipped through Exchange facilities. A separate assessment for advertising made it possible for growers to compare roughly benefits with cost, and segregation of advertising costs also permitted more precise measurement of other marketing costs. The assessment was made irrespective of whether the fruit was sold under the Sunkist trademark on the theory that the benefits from advertising would accrue to all local associations in proportion to their volume of marketings. The local associations were thus given an incentive to prepare their fruit so that as much as possible could be shipped under the Sunkist label.[33]

Early work in public relations. On the theory that any improvement to the citrus industry would benefit its affiliated growers, the Exchange had early encouraged any measure that would benefit the entire citrus industry. As the Exchange grew in influence it was called upon increasingly to represent the interests of its affiliated citrus growers on matters of common concern such as the encouragement of research on citrus cultural problems, the establishment of desirable railroad rates and customs tariffs, and on other questions affecting the "upbuilding of the industry." As such problems (which were often extraneous to the basic marketing objectives of the Exchange) called for the unanimous support of all interests in the citrus industry, the Exchange in 1906 joined with other elements in the industry to form the Citrus Protective League as an agency which could represent the citrus industry as a whole on such matters. The active support given to this common program by the Exchange made it clear that the Exchange as an organization was willing to support any program of benefit to all elements in the citrus industry and this increased the good-will of the entire citrus industry toward the California Fruit Growers Exchange.

Inception of supply purchasing program. These developments were designed to improve the efficiency of marketing. However, we have noted how the Exchange—with the acceptance by the growers—gradually came to interpret marketing in a very broad sense—maximization of returns from the crop—with the result that it became more and more concerned with helping growers on their cultural and other industry problems. An illustration of this was the way in which the Exchange came to assist in the problem of cooperative purchasing. Although the articles of incorporation of the Southern California Fruit Exchange in 1895 authorized the Exchange to engage in cooperative purchasing, little was done in this direction by the Exchange until the supply problem became so acute in 1907 that the Exchange could not resist the demand for such service. The way in which the Exchange undertook to help on this problem through the formation of a sister organization— the Fruit Growers Supply Company—is left for discussion in Chapter XVIII. Here it is only important to point out that the Exchange found a way to organize this activity so as to harmonize it with its general marketing program.

Expansion and Clarification, 1908-1912

By 1908 the exchange system was functioning with a minimum of internal friction. As one observer noted, "an air of simplicity marks the working basis of the organization . . . The growers . . . through a well-defined channel govern themselves and have complete supervision of the entire organization."[34] As the exchange system grew, its methods became more and more systematized and standardized. However, this does not mean that it became bureaucratic, for the changes made were designed to perfect cooperative procedures. In theory and practice, the growers through their local associations retained full autonomy. They delegated to the district exchanges and the central exchange only certain broad functions which they were not in position to perform for themselves. By this time the efficiency of the Exchange as a marketing agency was rapidly attracting adherents, for, as its volume grew, its costs for marketing fell, while its services in marketing were improved. By 1908, the Exchange had become the dominant force in the California citrus industry. It was then handling 56 per cent of all shipments from the state.

The reports of the general manager during the next few years disclose how the central exchange was increasingly called upon to expand its functions to meet the needs of its member associations. No new exchange function was undertaken, however, until power to perform such function was granted to it by the growers through their elected representatives.

1907-1908. In the report for the year ending August 31, 1908, the general manager called attention to the great improvement which had occurred in the methods of picking, packing, and shipping fruit through the Exchange during the preceding four years. He attributed much of the Exchange's progress to the support which had been given to it by the local and district exchanges. He also called attention to the fine teamwork which was developing within the exchange system. By this time the relations of the Exchange with the industry and with the trade had become less militant and more cooperative.

1908-1909. Further progress in gaining growers' support was disclosed in the manager's report for the following crop year. The Exchange was now marketing over 59 per cent of the California citrus crop, and its various services were being steadily strengthened with improved facilities and better selected and trained personnel. It was becoming appreciated that the maximum results from advertising were dependent upon the uniformity and quality of the product advertised. While the manager was proud of the accomplishments of the Exchange, he noted with apprehension a growing spirit of complacency, and cautioned: "You must not rest content thinking you have reached the top and that you will remain there indefinitely without great enterprise and effort on your part."

1909-1910. During this year the functions of the claim department were broadened so that it became a traffic department. By this time the educational efforts of the management to encourage improvement in picking and packing operations were showing results. The sales services of the Exchange had been strengthened with the opening of new agencies. The manager declared: "Every possible market will be reached by you in the coming year and the maximum amount of fruit put into consumption."

1910-1911. Although the Exchange in 1911 was confronted with the largest crop yet marketed in California its program of extensive advertising and wide market distribution enabled it to handle over 61 per cent of the crop "at attractive prices." In his report for the year the manager declared: "You have undertaken a much larger field of operation than formerly . . . [with] great benefit to Exchange growers and to the industry." The manager reported progress in the perfection of service by all departments, particularly in advertising where "each year shows a great success." Arrangements for sales service in all of the metropolitan markets now had become well established and a plan of bonuses had been adopted in order to increase the efficiency of the sales personnel. While the manager fully realized that the system could operate more efficiently if the central exchange were given more control over the methods of the local associations he recognized that the primary strength of the exchange system consisted of the willingness of the local associations to cooperate voluntarily with the central exchange.

Prior to 1911 little had been done by the Exchange to acquaint the industry and the general public with its methods and accomplishments. About this time Exchange leaders began to realize that its far-flung operations subjected it to public scrutiny under anti-trust laws. The general manager in a report to the Board of Directors, June 7, 1911, recommended that "business . . . be conducted upon a strictly legitimate basis so that in case of investigation—the Exchange can lay all of its records open for inspection," although he pointed out: "This always has been the policy." It was now seen that a more positive public-relations policy would give a greater stability to the organization by building up good-will for its efforts, and a circular was designed for general distribution with the significant title, "The California Fruit Growers Exchange and Its Relation to the Citrus Industry." This publication made an aggressive bid for public recognition which marked a transition in the thinking of the Exchange. From this time on, the necessity of keeping the public fully informed with respect to its methods, functions, and accomplishments was increasingly recognized.

1911-1912. In this year the Exchange successfully met a difficult crop marketing condition which, according to the manager, afforded an excellent illustration of one of the "cardinal principles of the exchange system—the desirability of keeping the growers so fully posted that they were in the position to get the benefit of all the desirable conditions to offset the bad." The adverse crop conditions of the preceding year had also emphasized the need of giving more attention to the improvement of quality. This was evident in the manager's comments with reference to advertising:

> It is surely true that the advertising campaign has made millions of dollars for California citrus fruit growers since it was inaugurated. . . . As before suggested in these reports any method of supervision that will result in more uniformity in the quality of the fruit put out under advertising brands will greatly increase the advantage you now have in the markets through advertising.

It had been found desirable to strengthen the sales organization through the rearrangement of its sales offices. As of July 1912 its sales territory was divided, in the northern and western states, into four grand divisions (to be followed two years later by the creation of southern and northwestern divisions) with division managers in charge. From 1904-1905 to 1911-1912 the number of salaried employees had increased from 90 to 241.

In view of the fact that he was then retiring, Mr. Woodford felt called upon to give his views on the significance of the general manager in the exchange system:

Your general manager is the mouthpiece of the board of directors. Upon him rests the responsibility of successfully carrying out whatever general business policies are agreed upon and this responsibility he can in no way avoid or transfer to another. With the loyal support of the whole body of Exchange growers your general manager can lead a successful fight against a whole world of adverse outside influences scheming for the downfall of the Exchange. ... The key to the whole situation lies in the loyalty of the growers themselves compared with which all other factors are relatively of small importance.

In the period from 1902-1912 the citrus growers had learned how to weld their local cooperatives into an effective large-scale marketing institution. They had found out how they could yield certain powers to the central exchange on such matters as grading, packing, and inspection without giving up their essential local autonomy or control of the system as a whole. They had found out how to devise workable contracts and how to make their pooling methods more effective so as to knit their local units into one integrated system. While much progress had been made in these directions by 1912 there was still much opportunity for improvement.

Integration and Articulation, 1912-1920

When G. Harold Powell became general manager of the California Fruit Growers Exchange in the fall of 1912 the structure and general policies of the Exchange were largely formed, although it was far from being the center of a well-integrated and well-articulated system such as it was to become in the next 10 years under Powell's capable administration. Its sales plan was well developed, its advertising program effectively launched, and its purchasing program under the Fruit Growers Supply Company working well but the central exchange was still little more than a brokerage and clearing house agency for its member district exchanges.

Although Powell admitted at the time that the Exchange "was the most scientific marketing system yet developed," it was still rather loosely organized. The local associations were willing to yield a considerable amount of autonomy on matters pertaining to marketing to their district exchanges and to the central organization but they were hesitant to entrust the central exchange with broad responsibilities through fear that this would jeopardize their independence. In the next 10 years the powers granted to the central exchange were amplified in almost every direction as such suspicions were increasingly allayed.

Powell was well suited to serve as manager of the Exchange at this juncture. He was known nationally as an exponent of scientific procedure in marketing and as the outstanding authority on the marketing of fruit, both cooperative and otherwise. His work with the Department of Agriculture had given him national experience and standing and he was well known and respected throughout the citrus industry for his valuable studies which had brought about changes in packing and handling methods that had largely stopped losses due to decay in transit. Moreover, since 1910 he had served as general manager of the California Citrus Protective League, a vantage point which permitted him to keep in close touch with the problems of the Exchange and its member associations. Thus he was respected both by growers and by the trade, as well as by educational institutions and government officials. Moreover, he was gifted with an unusual capacity for leadership as an executive. He was thus the ideal man to assume the management of the Exchange at this time when new problems were calling for the broadening and strengthening of Exchange operations.[35]

Powell deeply appreciated the character of the responsibilities which were entrusted to him as general manager of the largest cooperative organziation in America. Writing in 1910 he had held that a successful manager "must have a high order of business ability, sterling integrity, unusual tact and judgment in handling men, and unrestricted energy."[36]

While he considered an effective board of directors indispensable to sound cooperative operation, he realized that "a Board of Directors cannot manage a cooperative agricultural association."[37]

Powell came to his new position with a definite idea as to how the various elements in the exchange system could be harmonized so as to achieve exchange objectives better. In his book *Cooperation in Agriculture,* which was published almost simultaneously with his assumption of the managership, he said:

> ... it is fundamental that a central federation shall be formed so as not to destroy the initiative and individuality of each locality, or of different groups of farmers who may be associated for a common purpose in the same locality.... To amalgamate farmers into one large central organization will kill local pride and ambition. It is fundamentally wrong in principle ....
> The central organization, however, should cooperate .... in building up the cooperative spirit among the members. It should assist in the organization of new associations.... It should cooperate with the local associations in establishing the most approved methods of management, of accounting, and other details of operation. It should be given authority by the directors to place experts in the field to help in the standardization of the handling, grading, and preparation of farm products for market so that there may be established standard grades that have a definite meaning with the trade, and it should have the authority to advise and assist the local associations in every way that builds up the cooperative movement.[38]

Powell conceived of the Exchange as an instrument for giving leadership to the entire citrus industry. He saw that the individual citrus growers must come to have an understanding of, and an appreciation for, not only the work of the local associations but of the district exchanges and of the central organization. He saw that the strength of the exchange system depended upon the voluntary support of the citrus growers, but he appreciated that the problem of educating the citrus growers so that they would understand the importance of the work being undertaken by their cooperative organizations had to be also a responsibility of the central organization. Thus, the major achievement of Powell's administration was in the integration of the system so as to achieve the benefits of local democratic control and voluntary participation while obtaining the additional advantages of coordination through centralized administration.

Under Powell's administration, the annual reports of the Exchange soon became a very important device for membership and public education. They provided information on current operations and achievements and explained fully the difficulties encountered each year. They served as a means of showing the direction in which the Exchange was moving, in the light of economic conditions confronting the industry. They increased the knowledge of the growers with respect to the economic problems of the citrus industry and gave them a better basis for assisting in the development of broad policies for the exchange system.[39]

The way in which the exchange system unfolded during these years can best be shown by setting down certain developments chronologically.

1913. Soon after Powell became general manager, the strength of the entire exchange system was severely tested by a frost which resulted in a loss of 60 per cent of the estimated shipments for the year. This situation gave Powell an immediate opportunity to demonstrate his leadership capacity, for by taking energetic steps, the Exchange was able to reduce its expenses in line with the anticipated loss in revenue and to maintain intact its essential framework. Moreover, the initiative displayed by the Exchange in protecting the quality of fruit shipped under its advertising brands greatly enhanced the prestige of the Exchange in the business community as well as with the growers.

Experience in meeting the abnormal crop conditions in 1913 convinced the directors in December that the time was ripe for taking a step which had been contemplated for several years—the establishment of a "field organization department" through which the central exchange could work more directly with local associations and growers in improving the quality of fruit delivered for sale. By this time results in national advertising had fully demonstrated that effective marketing could be achieved only when the Exchange had sufficient control over grading and handling practices to guarantee the delivery of a uniform product.

While the department's immediate aim was to provide a uniform inspection service that would effectively protect the quality of fruit shipped under the advertising brands, its establishment was justified on the grounds that it would assist "in improving the methods of organization in the Exchange and its associations" and that it would "bring more money to growers by eliminating decay and other perishable losses." In inaugurating the new department, the directors of the central exchange made it clear that the fundamental objective was to help the local units to "handle more effectively their own local problems," and that its procedures were to be "cooperative in spirit rather than directive."[40]

The new department had an immediate effect on the Exchange for it afforded a mechanism for knitting the entire exchange system together. Before this time the functions of the central exchange and of the local associations were distinct and separate and the locals had jealously resisted any encroachment of their prerogatives in fear of domination. From a marketing standpoint, the field organization department enabled the central exchange to improve greatly its merchandising efficiency, for through the continuous contact of field representatives with local associations the central exchange kept in better touch with crop conditions thus furthering effective marketing.

1914. With the organization of the field department, the Exchange made rapid progress in improving the quality of fruit sold under advertised trademarks which resulted in a much greater efficiency in advertising efforts. This in turn greatly strengthened the position of the central exchange in the exchange system for it gave prompt evidence that an effective advertising program could be administered only by a strong central organization. By owning the trademarks and controlling their use, the central exchange was in a position to regulate the quality of fruit handled under its trademarks.[41]

As the grading rules of the Exchange were gradually tightened to improve the quality of fruit going to market, it became apparent that some salvage arrangement was essential for the efficient disposition of cull fruit—for it was difficult to maintain the market for good fruit as long as there was no satisfactory method for utilizing culls. The general manager of the Exchange called attention to this fact in his annual report for the year ending August 31, 1914, by saying: "There must be an improvement in the average standard of the fruit that leaves the state, both in grade and in keeping quality. This makes it imperative to develop the manufacture of the lower grades into by-products."

To meet this problem the Exchange in January 1915 formed the Exchange By-Products Company to carry on its by-products disposal work. Under its plan of organization which was patterned on that of the Fruit Growers Supply Company, the interested local lemon shipping associations acquired the capital stock of this corporation by permitting the Exchange to deduct fixed amounts per box from market proceeds due them on their lemon shipments. This arrangement enabled the Exchange to provide lemon growers with a needed service without becoming involved in what might be considered a speculative manufacturing operation. Moreover, under this plan the burden of supporting this service was placed on the local associations who were to be directly served.[42]

The first effort of the Exchange in by-product disposal was restricted to lemons since advertising had proved effective in finding market outlets for the expanded orange crop. It was less possible to expand lemon consumption by advertising and in years of heavy production only close grading could keep the abundant crop from demoralizing the market. Moreover, it was logical to undertake work in by-product utilization of lemons since the foundation for such work had been laid by the U. S. Department of Agriculture, which had established a citrus by-product laboratory in Los Angeles as early as 1911 to carry on investigations on a semi-commercial scale.[43] The Exchange was compelled to enter this field since there were no commercial concerns in position to serve the full needs of the industry. While it was appreciated that benefits from a by-products program could not be confined to Exchange members, it was recognized that the benefits which would accrue to Exchange members—as in advertising—would be greater than the cost to them. It was also appreciated that the significance of the program to Exchange members would grow as the relative volume of Exchange shipments increased.

By this time the Exchange was coming to realize that the success of its advertising efforts in moving constantly increasing quantities of fruit into consumption at satisfactory prices required more close cooperation with the retail dealers who distributed the product to the ultimate consumers. In 1914 the Exchange began to work more closely with wholesalers and retailers to break this bottleneck which was restricting consumption. This was done by establishing a dealers' service section in the advertising department, which was designed to help retailers more profitably move large quantities of citrus products to consumers.[44]

The workers in the dealers' service section soon found that valuable suggestions could be offered to dealers on such problems as display and arrangement. It was found that one of the heavy costs of retailing citrus fruit came from spoilage due to overstocking, or from irregular buying, or from weaknesses in selling methods. It became clear that retailers could make greater profits in merchandising oranges if they would order in smaller quantities at more regular intervals and handle them on a smaller margin as this would improve the quality of the product offered for sale and increase turnover. Through this activity the Exchange became in effect the partner of the retail merchant for both had as a common objective the expansion of sales volume.[45] Moreover, by making the product as advertised more widely available to consumers, dealers' service work greatly increased the value of the Exchange advertisements. The dealers' service section thus inaugurated market research work for the Exchange. According to Don Francisco, who developed this program: "A man with experience as a grocer was put on the road studying whole-sale and retail margins, turnovers, odd-cent prices, different types of fruit displays, importance of the fruit department in attracting business to the store, etc. We could easily prove that the store with the best fresh fruit and vegetable department gained an edge in competition. We also could easily prove the value of mass orange displays and odd-cent prices."[46]

1915. The work of the field organization department was firmly rooted when the manager reported for the year ending August 31, 1915. He then declared: "No permanent progress can be made by any associa-tion in correcting the details of fruit handled without the proper packing-house and field discipline and organization." He also declared that: "Our advertising policy . . . must be firm and constant."

Prior to 1915 the Exchange, in its advertising work, had placed great emphasis on premiums. At that time the name was not imprinted on the fruit itself and the only identification was the wrapper. The premium offer was a device for giving the wrappers a value that would keep them on the fruit. At first an orange spoon was offered for 12 wrap-pers and 12 cents, but eventually the line of premiums was increased to a complete set of more than 100 pieces including coffee pots, etc.[47]

Although premiums had contributed an important function in estab-lishing the Sunkist trademark, they were subject to abuse by those who could obtain the Sunkist wrappers without buying oranges and their use had become very unpopular with retailers. In the light of this situation—which had been disclosed by the studies and contacts of the dealers' service section—the premium offers were abolished and advertising emphasis was directed to the building up of consumer preference by stressing the qualities inherent in the product advertised. This led the Exchange to sponsor scientific research with regard to the health values of citrus fruits. Powell's correspondence of this period indicated that a Philadelphia research bacteriologist was commissioned to search the scientific literature, and investigate "the germ-killing properties of lemons."[48]

1916. A significant change in legal structure came in 1916 with the reincorporation of the Exchange as a non-capital stock membership corporation. In view of the passage of the Clayton Act in 1914 which gave governmental endorsement and certain privileges to cooperative associations when set up with the non-profit, non-stock form of organization, it seemed desirable to change the legal form of the Exchange to make it "what in substance it [had] always been . . . a cooperative non-profit, non-capital stock horticultural association."[49] It was thought that this action would dissipate any confusion as to the true character of the Exchange as a non-profit organization and gain for it any advantages that might accrue under the federal statute.[50]

The reincorporation of the Exchange as a non-stock association had little effect on its character as a cooperative organization, for up to this time it had functioned on strictly non-profit lines and all benefits had gone to its producer members in accordance with their use of the organization. Only a few thousand dollars of outstanding capital stock had been issued and this had been held by the district exchanges as evidence of their membership interest.

However, the change in organization was of more than formal significance since the new articles and the accompanying by-laws emphasized the fact that the exchange system was purely cooperative in every regard. Moreover, the new documents of organization completely overhauled the old articles and by-laws—which had been altered little since 1895—so as to set forth in a precise way the interrelationships of the various parts of the exchange system. While conforming closely to the spirit of the old, the new articles and by-laws reflected a much broader conception of the central exchange as the planning and administrative center for the system as a whole. Thus the new articles and by-laws formalized and unified the exchange structure as it had evolved up to this time.

Prior to 1916 the exchange system had been quite simple in organic structure. The local associations had been loosely federated together in the district exchanges and these in turn were loosely federated to form the central exchange. After 1916 the district exchanges served more as regional field offices for the central exchange although they still served as intermediary or liaison agencies for both the central and local associations. As the central exchange had grown in importance, the significant role of the district exchanges had been somewhat diminished for greater uniformity of decision making was required for the efficient operation of the system as a whole. As in the evolution of our national government there had been a gradual tendency toward centralization as the locals entrusted greater authority to the district and then to the central organization under what might be called a "citrus growers' welfare power."[51]

The central exchange was also strengthened during this year by the transfer of the advertising department from Chicago to Los Angeles. This change greatly increased organizational teamwork for it enabled the directors and officers of the Exchange to become more familiar with the character and significance of the advertising program, while it gave those in charge of advertising more cognizance of growers' problems.

At about this time the advertising department began to see the possibilities of expanding orange consumption through popularizing the use of orange juice as a healthful drink.[52] The first efforts in this direction were directed toward getting soda fountains and restaurants to use more fresh oranges in making orangeade, but the dealers' servicemen soon found that such distributors were not disposed to use fresh oranges in making such drinks due to the difficulties of extracting the juice.[53]

This problem led the Exchange to promote the development of an electrical juice extractor. For several years the Exchange continued to encourage juice consumption, but significant progress in increasing consumption was delayed until suitable extracting equipment was finally devised in 1920.

1917. With an excellent crop, the manager was able to report "the largest annual shipments in the history of the Exchange." At this time the Exchange was shipping 60 per cent of the total number of boxes of citrus fruit shipped from California.

The work of the field department was proving increasingly useful in standardizing field and packinghouse operations. The manager maintained that through the "advisory inspection work of this department the shippers were getting their full benefit of Sunkist advertising." The field department was also yielding "marked results . . . along membership lines."

The Exchange also was finding that it could help the member associations through giving them assistance on their accounting problems. Pooling of fruit requires accurate bookkeeping and there was gradually developing a demand that the Exchange recommend a uniform system of bookkeeping. The Exchange welcomed this demand since more uniform bookkeeping would enable the local associations to compare better the efficiency of their operations. In the beginning the accounting assistance given by the Exchange was more or less informal. As the Exchange began to work more closely with the associations through its field department it was given a greater opportunity to assist in standardizing accounting and auditing service.

The advertising department continued to use magazines, newspapers, and similar media aggressively. During the year its dealers' service representatives had personally assisted over 20,000 dealers in increasing their sales through merchandising advice. The Exchange now recognized that the benefits from advertising were cumulative in that its effect increased from year to year as the product advertised gained recognition.

Up to this time the central exchange had made no special effort to keep its grower members continuously informed with respect to its operations. Seeing the need for this, the advertising department in 1918 began the publication of a little magazine, *The Sunkist Courier,* to "regularly and directly advise the producers of the important happenings in the industry and in the markets which affect their interests and to keep them better and correctly informed of the policies, activities, and accomplishments of the growers' organization." Primarily, *The Sunkist Courier* was designed to educate citrus growers on the advantage of using the facilities of their own organization.[54]

The Exchange By-Products Company was by this time beginning to prove its value in providing "a certain outlet for lemons which it does not pay to ship." During the season it had handled over 5,100 tons of unmerchantable lemons or about 6 per cent of the Exchange's volume for the year. The excellent record of the Exchange By-Products Company had emphasized the need for a somewhat similar program to help salvage cull oranges. To help on this problem a group of local associations, affiliated with the Exchange, had conceived, with the encouragement of the central exchange, the idea of mutualizing an established orange marmalade manufacturing concern—the Orange By-Products Company—through the acquisition of its capital stock. This development was supported by the general manager of the Exchange in his annual report: "Arrangements are now being made by the Exchange shippers generally to join in a move mutualizing the marmalade company and making it the nucleus to develop a by-product business to utilize the orange and grapefruit culls."

1918. Due to a heat wave in June 1917 the total citrus shipments for the year ending August 31, 1918, were reduced to about 38 per cent of the previous year. This compelled the Exchange to adjust operations so as to lower expenses and the total average operating cost of the Exchange marketing service, not including advertising, was kept to 1¼ per cent of gross sales. This remarkable achievement again demonstrated the organization's ability to adjust its operations to unusual crop conditions without impairing its efficiency.

The severe curtailment of the crop also emphasized the importance of the work of the field department. The management maintained that the field department "has strengthened the entire Exchange movement by devoting extra attention to associations whose fruit has not given satisfaction in the markets [and by] assisting the directors and managers in improving their working organization and methods." Attention was also specifically directed to the advantages that had accrued to the Exchange from the membership work of the field department. "The growers and shippers who are not members have had the advantages and facts concerning the organization placed fairly before them where before most of their information regarding the Exchange came from those unfriendly to it." This was bringing a steady stream of new members into the exchange system.

Although the abnormally short crop reduced the immediate need for advertising, it was appreciated that it would be unwise to curtail advertising expenditures since "10 years of continuous education publicity ... could not be interrupted for an entire year except as an eventual sacrifice." Encouraged by the enactment of national prohibition, the Exchange was now beginning to stress orange juice as a beverage in its advertising, and it was working with an inventor to perfect an electric juice extractor suitable for soda fountains and similar dispensing outlets. In this year the advertising department issued a moving picture on the production and distribution of citrus products through the Exchange, designed to acquaint its members, its trade customers, and the public with its methods. It was recognized that the short crop was only temporary and that every effort must be made to attract new users and induce present consumers to use citrus fruits in greater quantities.

1919. With better crop conditions for the year ending August 31, 1919, the Exchange shipped 33,174 carloads, or 72.3 per cent of the total citrus fruit shipments from the state. With the greater volume the total average cost of Exchange marketing service, including advertising costs, was reduced to 1.62 per cent of the delivered value of the fruit (with advertising costs excluded it was but 1.04 per cent). The general manager declared this to be "the lowest known marketing cost of any perishable food in America," and he attributed this record "to large volume of operations made possible through organization." At this time the prestige of the organization among the growers and with the trade stood very high and methods were being examined and improved in almost every direction.

In recognition of its growing importance in membership and public relations work, the field department was "reorganized on a broader basis." In commenting on this departmental change the general manager declared: "The success, strength, and permanency of the cooperative movement is dependent primarily upon the efficiency with which the business of the local associations is handled. . . . The field department will continue to make a systematic study of every local association with a view of developing greater efficiency in the operations of each." In the words of Paul Armstrong: "The Exchange had no formal membership program or policy until the establishment of a Grower's Service Bureau as a subdivision of the Field Department in 1919.[55]

At this time the advertising program was expanding in almost every direction. The Sunkist brand had become one of the country's best-known trademarks and it was becoming recognized that the consumer demand for this brand and the trade confidence vested in it were assets of incalculable value to every citrus grower—both in or out of the exchange system. All major mediums of advertising were being used—magazines, newspapers, trade periodicals, billboards, streetcar cards, movies, posters, window displays, and mail literature. The dealers' service program which had been curtailed during the war had been revivified. One of its activities had been a study of existing methods of retailing fruit (carried on in 65 markets in 24 states) designed to provide a basis for recommending better retail sales methods.

To further develop the use of fresh lemons and oranges in popular beverages an expert on beverages had been employed to work with soda fountains and other beverage dispensing establishments. To obtain complete data for developing this work, two experimental beverage stores, selling orange, lemon, and grapefruit drinks were being operated by the advertising department. The importance of beverage promotion had been stimulated by the intense competition of other soft drinks with the coming into effect of national prohibition.

1920. The year 1920 was another year of good crop conditions with high prices. Although advertising was doing a very effective job it was becoming increasingly clear that additional outlets were necessary for lower grades. This led the Exchange to embark on a research program to find new uses for citrus products.

Perhaps the most significant Exchange development in 1920 was the establishment in April of a research department to serve primarily as a basis for the scientific development of its by-product operations. The need for a real research program in by-product utilization had been emphasized by the unfortunate experience of the Orange By-Products Company, whose stock had been acquired by the member associations of the Exchange, as a means of mutualizing its operations.

Formed without preliminary research work the Orange By-Products Company had not found it possible to manufacture immediately marmalade of uniformly high quality. Moreover, the Exchange had developed no special facilities for marketing a manufactured product of this type which could be effectively distributed through its regular fresh fruit sales outlets. Even though the marmalade was sold under the Sunkist label, this could not gain for it consumer acceptance and, in fact, the unsatisfactory quality of the product was injurious to the prestige of the Sunkist name. An even more serious objection came from the fact that marmalade manufacture did not afford a significant outlet for cull oranges. Thus the Orange By-Products Company found itself producing a product (with unusually heavy marketing costs) which required large expenditures for sugar and containers and which contributed little to the solution of its cull orange problem. This experience gradually disclosed that any effective program for by-products' utilization of oranges required the discontinuance of marmalade manufacture and the development of a program based on more intensive research.[56]

With the establishment of a research department the Exchange became a well rounded modern industrial enterprise.

Appraisal—1920

By 1920 the California Fruit Growers Exchange had become the outstanding illustration of cooperative marketing accomplishment in the United States—if not in the world. It had demonstrated over a long period that agricultural producers could organize themselves efficiently for marketing. More than any cooperative agency in the United States the Exchange was showing what could be accomplished cooperatively. By serving as a model for the formation of other cooperative associations it was having more influence on the character of the entire American cooperative movement than any other single cooperative organization.

At this time the exchange system had largely achieved maturity. It then consisted of some 10,000 growers grouped in some 200 local autonomous associations which were joined together in some 20 district exchanges which in turn were federated in the central exchange. Each of these three layers of organization had its own functions well delineated. The local associations were responsible for handling, packing, pooling, etc. The district exchanges served the local associations as their clearing houses for information and as their sales agencies. The capstone of the structure was the central exchange which coordinated the operations of the district exchanges and handled all functions of an overhead nature which were delegated to it by the district exchanges and the local associations.

While each part of the exchange system performed an indispensable function the whole plan was activated by the central exchange. Without it the system would have had no guidance, consistency, or cohesiveness. As Cumberland aptly observed, the central exchange was the "amalgam" which held the entire system together and gave it "power and efficiency."[57]

The growers in the exchange system had found a way for obtaining the advantages of large-scale operation through a generally democratic form of organization. Cumberland went so far as to say: "There is no feature in the Exchange system which is not strictly cooperative—growers, associations, district exchanges, all have an equal standing and equal opportunity in the Exchange."[58]

The central exchange was a fine illustration of an organization which had been built from the bottom up and not from the top down. As Teague has said, it was a "federated democracy in the purest sense of the word with a clearly defined channel of representation running from the individual grower to the central organization."[59] He also pointed out: "as in any federated democracy, the central exchange has no jurisdiction over local administration."[60]

Although the basic concept of cooperation as expressed in the exchange system of organization in 1920 had not changed appreciably over the years, its structure and methods of organization had gradually come to have a more stable character. It would be difficult to say when the Exchange became a mature organization in the sense that its basic structure was largely formed, but it would probably be around 1918 since the non-stock membership form of legal structure was then adopted.

By 1920 the exchange program had become well rounded. Its research activities were then established; its advertising program was recognized as outstanding; its machinery of marketing, based on complete market information, was thoroughly organized; its standard of personnel efficiency and the morale of its working force was unexcelled by any business organization. By this time the Exchange had solidified its position with the public and its business reputation was beyond question. Moreover, with growth in business power it had steadily improved in cooperative effectiveness. The individual grower in the system retained his individual freedom but, with the growth of understanding, there was a high degree of self-imposed discipline which directed the efforts of all the growers toward the achievement of common ends.

The exchange system was rendering service to the industry as well as to its own members through its advertising, supply purchasing, by-product utilization, and similar programs. These advantages would not have been possible except through an industry-wide organization. The efficiency of the system and the satisfaction given growers was indicated by the fact that its volume had steadily grown. Its costs for marketing service were less than half those of competitive agencies.

The whole exchange plan was responsive to the needs and directions of the grower membership. As Cumberland pointed out, "The Exchange did not sell fruit, it provided the facilities through which the growers marketed their own products."[61] It simply facilitated the flow of marketing information and opened up sales outlets so as to permit the most efficient sale.

In 1920 the exchange system of marketing was working smoothly. It provided a mechanism for distributing the fruit of its members to various markets of the United States so as to achieve the best adjustment of supplies to demand. Each local association through its district exchange had access to the markets in all parts of the United States and could regulate its own sales so as to take advantage of favorable regional price situations. The exchange plan in effect distributed all fruit produced so as to get maximum returns for it. By having a free flow of information, shipments were diverted to those markets where prices were highest, and this tended to maintain the best possible standard of prices throughout the United States, since both gluts and shortages were minimized. The exchange system provided facilities for selling which were available to all local associations and district exchanges on the same basis. Thus each local association and district exchange could have the same selling possibilities on the available markets. Cumberland used the term "competitive cooperation" to convey the significant idea that all parts of the exchange system were in organized competition with each other.[62]

The principal economic function performed by the Exchange was the development of market outlets, the adjustment of supplies of fruit to be marketed in accordance with the demands of consumers, and the sale of the fruit. It was recognized that it would be useless to attempt to control sales or fix prices. In character, the Exchange was thus not a trading agency but an organization which provided market accessibility. It could advise but it could not control.[63] It could, however, exert an influence on demand levels through widening and deepening the market by advertising and dealers' service work.

The success attained by the Exchange in its advertising efforts had enabled it to market constantly increasing crops at prices satisfactory to the grower. It is inconceivable that the citrus industry in California could have expanded so rapidly without the aggressive advertising efforts of the Exchange. Moreover, by its dealers' service work it had found ways to help jobbers and retailers expand their sales volume of oranges and other citrus fruit. Cumberland called this an "innovation in the field of fruit and produce marketing—a procedure utterly inconceivable for an unorganized industry."[64]

The Exchange could not be considered a monopoly in any sense, for it had no power to control production. Its primary function was to assist member growers in finding the most profitable market outlets. In fact, all the elements in the system were in competition with each other. It was this situation which caused Cumberland to refer to the process as "competitive cooperation." Erdman had the same thought in mind when he referred to the Exchange plan as a device for achieving working harmony among competitive groups.[65]

The Exchange stood for a program of free competition and was opposed to all types of control. It did not attempt to fix production in any way since it considered its role to be one of marketing the crops produced by its members. While it endeavored to increase consumption of citrus products through advertising, it recognized the fact that excessive supplies would have to be sold at lower prices.[66]

Although the Exchange did not endeavor to control production it did endeavor to provide a system of marketing which would tap the consuming markets so as to get the highest possible price for the fruit shipped by its members. Poe pointed out in 1913 that the Exchange did not try to obtain the profits "which a trust gets from fixing prices." He maintained, however, that the Exchange "acquired the profits of controlled prices by as even and wide a distribution of fruit as possible. No market is glutted and no market is undersupplied."[67] It was appreciated that the Exchange could not exercise arbitrary control over the crop even had it desired to do so—since the crop was perishable. All the Exchange could do was to get together all the available information on supply and demand and to furnish this to every separate local association. The determination of when to pack and sell was the responsibility of the individual. The central exchange could, however, provide advice as to market trends and help the local associations in most intelligently taking advantage of their market opportunities.

The system of sales offices and information service was designed to apportion shipments so as not to demoralize certain markets with excessive supplies. While the Exchange did not undertake to regulate the amount of fruit produced by its members it did successfully attempt—through its grading and by-product programs—to draw off or eliminate inferior fruit so as not to weaken the market for sound fruit.

The Exchange's theory of marketing was also expressed in its methods of financing. Assessments were levied on district exchanges for services rendered and these assessments were collected as proceeds were received from the sale of fruit. Its advertising program was also financed by the use of current assessments to cover costs. In this way costs for maintaining the services of the Exchange were obtained through deductions levied against the fruit as it was marketed. If surpluses were accumulated from assessments greater than the actual costs, they were annually prorated back to the district exchanges in proportion to their shipments. Thus as the Exchange made no profits, received no dividends, and accumulated no surplus, no permanent capital was required for carrying on its marketing operations. It functioned primarily as a service agency and its costs for rendering service were borne proportionately by its member organizations as the services were rendered.

By 1920 the exchange system could claim many remarkable achievements. It had eliminated speculation in the local handling of fruit;

it had broadened markets through advertising and by-product disposal; it had reduced marketing costs; it had improved quality and lowered costs of citrus production; it had secured advantageous freight rates which meant millions of dollars in savings to growers; and it had done many other commendable things.

The Exchange had gradually become more than a marketing agency. It was then the responsible representative for the organized citrus growers on all matters affecting their interests as producers. Whenever any problem arose which afforded an opportunity for collective action, the Exchange was called upon for guidance and assistance. No cooperative institution had gained such a position of leadership among the growers of any crop. It was significant that the Exchange had grown in cooperative consciousness, as it developed technical methods and business procedures necessary for the performance of its functions.

It would be difficult to evaluate the full benefits which were derived from the existence of the Exchange in 1920. By injecting higher standards into the non-cooperative parts of the citrus industry, competitive concerns were forced to give comparable service to that offered by the Exchange if they were to remain in business. Thus the standards of the whole industry were improved by the presence of the Exchange. It can almost be said that the Exchange was responsible for much of the prosperity of the entire citrus industry, for the Exchange through its advertising program and quality improvement efforts was largely responsible for the constant increase in consumption of citrus fruits. Cumberland, in 1917, estimated that the Exchange had brought a "hypothetical saving" to all citrus growers in California of about $100,000,000 during the 22 years since the Exchange was organized in 1894 as the Southern California Fruit Exchange.[68]

Thus by 1920 the Exchange had achieved an enviable position. It was recognized as a strong business and cooperative institution. Its costs of distribution were unusually low. Its personnel was excellent and it had retained its character as a democratically controlled organization. Its methods were systematized through the use of business contacts which clarified all functional relationships.

How can this success be explained? The answer probably lies in the fact that there was a happy conjunction of intelligent farmers and unusual leaders who were confronted by a unique situation responsive to a program of cooperative action. The plan developed was so logical and so in keeping with the sense of equity of its participants that its growth was both natural and swift. Moreover, the system devised was both flexible and self-renewing so that it could easily be adapted to new conditions as they arose.

By 1920 the exchange system was firmly established. Its objectives were well determined and its policies well outlined. It is not surprising that it has continued to operate with little substantial change down to the present.[69]

Chapter XIV

OTHER SIGNIFICANT COOPERATIVE
MARKETING PROGRAMS

While the California Fruit Growers Exchange was perfecting its form of organization and methods of operation, a number of other "model"[1] cooperative marketing associations were being formed in California and elsewhere by growers of fresh fruits, vegetables, and nuts. The nature and significance of their contributions to the concept and practice of cooperative marketing is important.

The Grand Junction Fruit Growers Association

The leading fruit marketing association outside of California in 1900 was the Grand Junction Fruit Growers Association, formed in 1891. After a full-time manager was employed in 1897, this association grew with the rapidly expanding fruit industry in the western slope region of Colorado.

Under the plan developed by this Association, each member sorted and packed his peaches, apples, or other fruit according to prescribed regulations. The fruit was then delivered to the Association's nearest loading platform where it was examined by an inspector who gave the member a receipt showing the number of boxes of each variety and grade. The fruit was then consigned to sales representatives who were located on the principal eastern markets. Returns were pooled so that each grower received the average price for fruit of the same variety and grade shipped within specified periods.

As the Association early recognized that effective marketing was dependent upon the cost and the quality of production, assistance was provided members on their pruning, spraying, and other cultural problems, and an extensive side-line purchasing service was developed. Following the precedent of the California Fruit Growers Exchange which packed citrus fruit in boxes, the Association introduced box packing of apples, peaches, and pears in place of the prevailing method of barrel packing. Box handling not only facilitated inspection but also provided a package more suitable for shipment and for use by consumers.

The heyday of the Grand Junction Fruit Growers Association was reached about 1906 when its carload shipments totalled 1,036 with a sales value of $565,499. These shipments went to 24 states scattered from California to Massachusetts and to Canada and Mexico. In 1910 the Association had some 800 members and was marketing about 75 per cent of all the fruit grown within its operating territory. This support was obtained entirely on the Association's ability to provide effective services as no membership pledge was required.[2]

As the achievements of the Grand Junction Fruit Growers Association became known, others were rapidly formed until there were some 30 fruit and vegetable associations operating in the state by 1906. Although the federation of these associations for more effective marketing and purchasing was strongly advocated, leadership adequate to break down the individualism of the local groups was not forthcoming and little was achieved in this direction.

Most of these early associations were organized on a capital-stock basis with all savings being returned to shareholders in proportion to their ownership of stock. As long as stock was well distributed among growers, savings were roughly shared on the basis of their use of the organizations. After the stock became concentrated in the hands of a few individuals—who were more interested in profits for themselves than in the maintenance of the Association—the support of the growers essential for permanent success was undermined. As a result, this promising cooperative development had largely evaporated by 1920.[3]

The Hood River Apple Growers Union and Efforts Toward Federation

For many years the model fruit marketing association in the Pacific Northwest was the Hood River Apple Growers Union of Hood River, Oregon. This association, formed in 1902 on a capital-stock basis, followed in the footsteps of two earlier fruit marketing organizations, the first of which had been formed in 1893. Along with apples, the Union handled pears, cherries, strawberries, raspberries, and blackberries. Under exceptionally able management the Union soon became famous throughout the entire Pacific Northwest. By 1907 it controlled "approximately 90 per cent of the fruit of the Valley."[4]

The constitution and by-laws of the Apple Growers Union gave its board of directors "exclusive and unqualified power to market all apples grown by any of its members." To implement this provision, each member was required to sign a simple contract with the association providing for the delivery of all fruit produced.[5]

Like the Grand Junction Fruit Growers Association, the Apple Growers Union held that the production of a high quality product was essential to efficient marketing. Great stress was placed on honesty in packing and in uniformity of packed fruit.[6]

All shipments were strictly supervised under the by-laws which stated: "The directors may refuse to receive for shipment under the brand of the Union any package of fruit not considered prime for any cause." Each grower's fruit was sold by type and quality although pooling was not attempted. In this way each grower was made aware of the importance of having a product of good quality since the price he received was dependent on the quality of his fruit. Owing to the strict enforcement of the association's grading and packing rules, apples from Hood River soon gained both a national and international reputation.[7]

The influence of the Hood River Apple Growers Union in the years from 1906 to 1912 was heightened by the missionary spirit of its general manager, E. H. Shepherd who, as founder and editor of *Better Fruit*, spread far and wide the gospel of organization as practiced by the Union.[8]

With increasing plantings and heavy crop production the Apple Growers Union was absorbed in the Hood River Apple Growers Association which was formed in 1913. This new association was set up on a capital-stock basis to provide adequate financing for cold-storage houses which were required for the better adjustment of supplies to the needs of the market. Since that time the Hood River Apple Growers Association has continued to be outstanding among the successful apple-marketing cooperatives in the United States.[9]

Federation efforts. The rapidity with which apple growers' associations were formed in the Pacific Northwest following the conspicuous example of the Hood River Apple Growers Union, is shown by the fact that there were about 50 associations in Oregon and Washington by 1910. As these associations grew in number there was a tendency for them to band together and this sentiment was encouraged through the editorial columns of *Better Fruit*. However, the need for federation was not widely recognized until 1910 when the apple market began to waver under the pressure of heavy production. As pessimism expanded,

growers increasingly called for more "intelligent marketing" to counter
"over-production" and sentiment began to gather for a strong regional
marketing organization which could do for the Northwest apple industry what the California Fruit Growers Exchange was doing for
the organized citrus growers of California.[10]

In response to this rising demand, the Oregon State Horticultural
Society called a convention of fruit growers and associations in January
1911 "to consider the organization of a fruit growers' central selling
agency."[11]

As a result of this meeting which was attended by delegates from
the three northwestern states, a plan was worked out almost identical
to that of the California Fruit Growers Exchange in that it provided
for district exchanges throughout the Northwest to be federated in one
central selling agency. However, when this ambitious plan was taken
to the local associations for their approval, their support was not generally forthcoming, primarily because many feared that they would be
forced to give up some of their local autonomy. As a result the plan had
to be abandoned.[12]

This unfortunate experience left a heritage of bitterness among the
local associations which made difficult other efforts to bring them together. However, plan after plan for achieving coordination through
federation was attempted in the next few years, although none proved
workable.

One ambitious attempt in this direction was the formation of the
Pacific Northwest Fruit Distributors as a mutual corporation in 1912 to
embrace all of the fruit marketing associations in the Pacific Northwest.
At first this organization "appeared to be a brilliant success," for it
included within its membership associations that controlled about 50
per cent of the output of the four northwestern states, but it soon began
to break up as "the old jealousies among the various districts began to
reappear."[13]

Following this disastrous experiment, the Bureau of Markets made a
careful study of the needs for federation and, on the basis of this work,
an attempt was made to federate the locals in an organization called
the Fruit Growers Agency. This organization had an immediate success
and was credited "with standardizing the entire fruit pack of the Northwest." It might have succeeded had not the government prematurely
withdrawn support. These experiments disclosed a desire for federation
but no leadership arose capable of fusing the discordant elements.[14]

In August 1919 the problem of achieving coordination was approached in a different way—by the formation of a centralized or-

ganization which would embrace all growers of fruits and vegetables. The sponsor of this plan was Aaron Sapiro whose advice had been sought by a group of influential fruit growers who were concerned with the problem of better marketing. The association devised by Sapiro ... the Oregon Growers Cooperative Association ... was largely based on his experience in forming centralized associations in California, although it departed from the California principle, later espoused by Sapiro, that growers should be organized along commodity lines.[15] The Oregon Growers Cooperative Association was organized on a non-stock basis with membership running direct from the producer to the central association. Each member was required to sign a long-term binding contract. The association was to have complete jurisdiction over marketing and was to arrange for warehouses and other facilities at both local and central points. According to Ellison, the Oregon Growers Cooperative Association was "the most complete and purely cooperative body organized on state-wide lines that had been undertaken so far in the Northwest."[16]

Although the Oregon Growers Cooperative Association was at first so successful that it was "watched by fruit producers of the entire Northwest," it gradually disintegrated under the pressure of declining prices following 1920. It had unwisely invested in plants and equipment when costs were at their peak and its attempt to handle all types of fruits and vegetables in one organization proved impracticable.

The experience of the Pacific Northwest fruit growers in attempting to establish regional sales agencies was quite different from that in California where federations or centralized associations had come into being almost as naturally as local organizations. In the Northwest the move toward federation arose after the locals were well established. It then proved impossible to get the bulk of them to accept the discipline involved in a larger group effort. At the time when federation was most needed, the movement had been split into discordant local groups which could not be harmonized by the available leadership. The inability of the fruit growers of the Northwest to establish large-scale marketing organizations under generally favorable conditions thus emphasizes the extent of the accomplishment during the same period by the fruit growers of California.

The California Fruit Exchange

While the California Fruit Growers Exchange was establishing itself in the citrus industry, a somewhat similar type of organization was being developed by California growers of deciduous fruits. This organization, the California Fruit Exchange—formed in 1901 at Sacramento under the name "California Fresh Fruit Exchange"—culminated a series of unsuccessful efforts to develop a comprehensive cooperative marketing plan for such fruits as grapes, cherries, and plums. The word "fresh" was dropped from its name in 1903.[17]

The California Fruit Exchange was incorporated under the California Cooperative Law of 1895 as a non-stock membership association with a fee of $5 per member. As "practically all of the local associations which had been formed in the preceding 20 years had disappeared," the new organization proceeded to establish affiliated local packinghouse associations and shipping agencies. However, the shipping agencies were discontinued "as soon as a local association was formed and affiliated with the Exchange."[18] With the growth of the local affiliated associations the Exchange took on the appearance of a federation although the method of electing the board of directors by direct membership vote was continued.[19]

The early success of the Exchange in establishing itself was largely due to the joint sales arrangement which was entered into with the Southern California Fruit Growers Exchange—later the California Fruit Growers Exchange—by which the latter organization made available the services of its experienced sales staff on the eastern markets (see Chapter XIII). This plan, inaugurated in 1901, proved of incalculable advantage to the new organization and greatly contributed to its progress.[20]

Burdened with a large debt in 1907, incurred in the attempt to develop rapidly affiliated associations, the Exchange on the insistence of its bankers, reorganized on a capital-stock basis. The authorized capital was set at $100,000, divided into 1,000 shares of $100 each, and "to eliminate the danger of control by a few persons, no individual or organization was allowed to own more than 10 shares." Under the plan local affiliated associations were expected to buy at least one share of capital stock. (In 1920 the number of shares owned by any individual or organization was restricted to two.)

The new plan of organization provided for the payment on capital stock of 6 per cent dividends plus one-half of the remaining net earnings after provision for a fixed reserve fund. The other half of the remaining net earnings was payable in patronage refunds. As this arrangement resulted in very high dividends on stock (32.5 per cent in 1908), changes were made in 1909 and 1910, which gave common stockholders a flat payment of 10 per cent of the net earnings and returned the balance of net earnings in the form of patronage refunds after 10 per cent of the net earnings had been deducted for reserve.[21]

As the Exchange took a fixed handling charge for its services, its steady growth in volume gradually built up a substantial reserve fund. The ease with which this fund was accumulated encouraged the Exchange leaders in 1917 to devise a revolving fund plan for permanent financing somewhat similar to the one adopted a few months earlier by the Fruit Growers Supply Company (see Chapter XVIII). The plan as it was developed placed all savings after capital-stock payments in a "Capital Withholdings Repayable Fund," which was subject to repayment at the discretion of the directors. The revolving process was started by refunding contributions to the reserves which had been withheld during the years 1907 to 1911. With large volumes of sales during the war years, the Withholdings Repayable Fund expanded from $351,000 in 1918 to $790,000 in 1920. Although some changes have been made in the plan, it has continued to serve as the basis for financing down to the present.

Although less significant than its big sister organization—the California Fruit Growers Exchange—the California Fruit Exchange effectively demonstrated that the principles of federation could likewise be used under the more varied conditions of the fresh fruit industry. In 1921 with a marketing volume of $12,721,000, the California Fruit Exchange had become "the largest handler of soft fruit in the cooperative world."

The American Cranberry Exchange

One of the most interesting early experiments in large-scale cooperative organization came with the formation of the American Cranberry Exchange in 1907. Prior to this time the cranberry growers in Massachusetts, New Jersey, and Wisconsin had formed semi-cooperative organizations, but these had proved ineffective (see Chapter IV).

In 1906 the stage was set for the creation of a strong growers' organization. Due to bumper crops, cranberry prices were below cost of production and no relief from over-production was in sight.[22]

Confronted by this situation, the cranberry growers in Wisconsin formed a strong state-wide association of the pooling type—the Wisconsin Cranberry Sales Company. Membership was open to any cranberry grower living in the state willing to abide by the company's regulations. All berries of each principal variety were marketed in separate annual pools, the grower receiving the average price of the season on the fruit placed in each pool. The importance of careful grading and sorting was stressed as a basis for efficient marketing.[23]

"The outstanding accomplishments of . . . this company in distributing . . . on the cooperative plan during the disastrous year of 1906," encouraged growers in New Jersey and Massachusetts to form state associations modeled on it in 1907.[24] These three state associations then, together, formed the National Fruit Exchange as a "non-profit" central sales organization with each state organization represented on its board of directors in proportion to the acreage which each controlled, with no state being allowed a majority.[25] In 1911 this organization became the American Cranberry Exchange through a merger of the old Growers Cranberry Exchange and the National Fruit Exchange.

While the individual members of each state association also became members of the American, the organization functioned as a federation since all contacts with growers were maintained through the state organizations which were largely autonomous. The American was thus primarily a sales agency to which the state organizations delegated full responsibility over sales. The state associations operated and financed their own pooling plans, employed field inspectors, and performed all local receiving and handling functions.[26] The central took control of the product after the berries were loaded in the cars and then arranged for transportation, warehousing, sales, advertising, and related services.

The state companies and the central exchange were financed out of an assessment of 7 per cent on the selling price of berries f.o.b. shipping point. Of this, 2 per cent was retained by the state company, the remaining 5 per cent going to the American. Any savings made on this charge were refunded to the state associations in accordance with patronage, and the state associations in turn returned any savings to their grower members in accordance with individual patronage.

In effect the American therefore served its three member associations in much the same way that the California Fruit Growers Exchange served its contiguous district and local associations, except that it carried the principle of federation even further by joining together for marketing purposes cranberry associations in three widely scattered areas.

The American Cranberry Exchange and its member state associations can be given credit for their accomplishments in improving cranberry marketing methods. By shrewd management, supplies of cranberries were adjusted to consumers' demands so as to obtain the highest possible returns for growers while demand was expanded by advertising so as to relieve pressure of supplies on the market. The sound price policy adopted by the Exchange early in its history was well expounded by its general manager at the first session of the American Institute of Cooperation. He declared:

> I think one of the secrets of our success . . . has been our price policy. It is very definite and very clear . . . At the beginning of the season, our exchange earnestly endeavors to determine an average price, in relation to the season's estimated total production, and such probable consumption as will eanble us to distribute the entire crop over the whole marketing season and maintain a stable market. The starting price from the producer, at the beginning of the season's movement is of prime importance, and it is our aim to quote on our first shipments of the season a price that in our opinion the market will sustain and that will permit a normal movement of the crop.[27]

It should also be recognized that there was a continuing increase in cranberry production following the founding of the American Cranberry Exchange. If this production were to be moved without demoralizing prices, it was necessary to have an expanded demand. Appreciating this fact, the American in 1918 embarked on an aggressive national advertising program under the "Eat Mor" trademark.[28] This trademark was used for all berries marketed through the American regardless of their local brands. To carry on this advertising program, special assessments were levied on the state companies and any amounts not used were returned to them. The foundation of the American's advertising program was its quality improvement work which was begun with the formation of the state companies. It should be stressed that there had been a continuous improvement in the quality and uniformity of cranberries through better agronomic practices, and by better grading, packing, and inspection methods initiated by the state companies and the American. Well-printed and informative annual reports also helped build grower support.

The effectiveness of the work of the American Cranberry Exchange and of its related state companies is shown by the growth in volume of Exchange marketings, and by the prices paid to growers. From 1907-1908 to 1919-1920 its annual shipments increased from 143,643 barrels to 321,374 barrels, and in the latter year this represented about 70 per cent of the entire American cranberry crop. During this period the price per barrel increased from $6.33 in 1907-1908 to $7.86 in 1919-1920.[29]

By 1920 the accomplishments of the American Cranberry Exchange were quite remarkable. According to the careful analysis of Hobson and Chaney, the Exchange could then be given credit for (1) improving quality through establishing and maintaining uniform grades and packs; (2) distributing market risks equally among all members of the association by means of pooling systems; (3) expansion of consumption through advertising sufficiently to care for increased production; (4) stabilization of market prices through coordination of distribution from the three producing districts; (5) moving the entire supply at the highest possible average price for growers through careful study of market factors; and (6) reducing greatly the costs of marketing.[30]

Eastern Shore of Virginia Produce Exchange

For many years the Eastern Shore of Virginia Produce Exchange was held up as the outstanding example of cooperative accomplishment by vegetable growers.[31] Prior to its formation in the fall of 1899, the potato and truck growers in the two peninsular counties of Virginia were handicapped by an "almost unbelievably bad system of marketing" which "absorbed any profits" from their farming operations. This condition attracted the attention of a New York produce dealer who had farming interests in this region. Under his leadership a series of growers' mass meetings were held throughout the territory to consider how marketing conditions might be improved through cooperative action. This led to a general meeting at Olney which resulted in the election of a committee empowered to draw up a constitution and by-laws for a growers' marketing agency. The organization thus designed—The Eastern Shore of Virginia Produce Exchange—was incorporated on January 26, 1900, under a special charter granted by the general assembly of Virginia as there was then no statutory authority which provided for the incorporation of cooperative associations.[32]

The Charter declared that "the general objectives and purposes" of the corporation "shall be the buying and selling of produce *as agent of the producer*, the consigning of produce *as agent of the producer*, inspecting all produce it may handle, owning and operating storage warehouses and packing houses for produce, and generally all other lawful things customarily connected with the trade known as the produce business" (Italics added). The capital stock which was "not to exceed $50,000" was to be composed of $5 shares, and to insure widespread ownership no member could hold more than one-tenth of the stock outstanding. The value of shares was made low, $5 per share, so as to make membership attractive to all growers, and a farmer could become a member by paying down 25 cents with the balance to be paid in installments as he received returns from his crops marketed during the year.

To launch the Exchange a few responsible growers in each community jointly endorsed an association note. In this way some $5,000 was raised to meet organization expenses, and little additional capital was needed to begin with as sales were made largely on consignment. As the Exchange established itself, its membership capital grew from sales of stock and its reserves were built up from margins taken for services rendered.

The Exchange began operations in the spring of 1900 under the managership of the dealer who had advocated its formation. This proved an advantageous arrangement since his excellent business connections in the produce trade gave the Exchange an immediate standing.

The Exchange functioned primarily as a shipping and sales agency. Growers were bound by the by-laws to deliver their produce to Exchange representatives with the understanding that the Exchange would sell it as advantageously as possible on the various terminal markets and return all proceeds to the growers less a fixed handling charge. With few exceptions, all sales of produce were made by the Exchange through its own salesmen in principal markets or through brokers where markets could not be served by such salesmen. The returns from sales for produce of like grade and quality were averaged daily and the grower was paid this average pool price at his local shipping point after all expenses for marketing and transportation attributable to his shipment had been deducted.

General control of Exchange operations was vested in the board of directors elected by stockholders as organized in local autonomous divisions. Thus, while the Exchange was centralized in legal form in that the officers including the general manager were elected at the annual meeting of stockholders, it was federated in general character.[33]

The Exchange represented something of an innovation in cooperative organizational structure. It indicated how an association could be designed to secure the advantages of centralized administration over a wide area, while giving individuals a high degree of control over local arrangements for service. Much of the success of the organization came from this recognition of the need for community participation.

The general manager was held responsible for all business operations except inspection. He selected and supervised the sales and other personnel although the local shipping agents were selected by the local divisions subject to his approval and removal. Thus the local agent acted as an intermediary between the individual member and the central exchange.

The chief inspector who was appointed by the board of directors was made independently responsible for inspection service as it was recognized that inspection work should be divorced from management so as to insure the rigid and impartial enforcement of quality standards. Moreover, an effective inspection service was deemed essential as there was then no federal or state inspection service.

The Exchange did not employ membership contracts to maintain the support of its members but it accomplished somewhat the same end by its refusal to handle the products of any member who shipped outside of the Exchange for the year during which such shipment was made. Moreover, the Exchange would grant permission to sell outside the Exchange if regular commission charges on such sales were paid to the Exchange. In effect, this was an application of the maintenance fee technique then being employed by many farmers' elevators in the Midwest (see Chapter IV).

In order to develop as much support as possible from tenant growers, the Exchange adopted in 1910 an ingenious plan whereby growers could obtain "shipping privileges upon the payment of one dollar." This device in effect gave all rights of membership except voting. It permitted extension of service to Negro farmers without upsetting the social customs of the area.[34]

When the Exchange was first formed it was bitterly opposed by the commercial dealers in the area since it threatened their lucrative operations. However, with good management, the Exchange was able to establish itself, and soon the organization's excellent business methods gained the respect of members of the produce trade and of bankers and businessmen of the area as well as of growers. Its equipment, sales methods, and inspection methods were of "the latest and most efficient type." Its employees were carefully selected and those who handled money were bonded. Its business forms and accounting records were well adapted to its needs and its books were audited annually by certified public accountants.[35]

The progress made by the Exchange was phenomenal. This is shown by the fact that the number of packages of produce handled increased from 552,000 in 1901, to 2,021,000 in 1910. By 1917 the Exchange was marketing over 65 per cent of the produce grown in its territory with gross sales valued at $10,833,000. With early postwar prosperity gross sales reached a value of $19,270,000 in 1920. By this time the Exchange was recognized as one of the leading cooperative-marketing associations in the United States.

Cooperative evolution. In the beginning the Exchange was primarily a farmers' stock company in which all benefits in the form of savings were limited to those who held stock,[36] but as its business volume expanded, the Exchange became steadily more cooperative in character. The weakness of the stock company form of organization soon became apparent as the immediate success of the Exchange enabled it to pay huge stock and cash dividends. For example, in the fall of 1901, the directors paid a 10 per cent stock and a 50 per cent cash dividend and in the following fall, a 50 per cent stock and a 20 per cent cash dividend was declared. While these substantial dividend payments served an important purpose through demonstrating "in a concrete way that the organization was a success" they disgruntled many supporters of the enterprise who felt that savings should be returned to growers in accordance with their patronage. To meet this growing complaint, the directors in 1903 restricted the dividend on stock to 6 per cent and prorated the balance of savings to "loyal growers" in accordance with their shipments. Stevens held that: "From this time on, the Exchange was a purely cooperative enterprise, and less like an ordinary stock company."[37]

For several years, however, no further patronage refunds were paid as the growing business of the Exchange demanded that all savings be husbanded for use as operating capital. The Exchange, therefore, placed all savings in surplus—after paying a 10 per cent cash dividend on stock, with the result that by 1910 its surplus of about $80,000 gave the Exchange an "impregnable" financial foundation.[38]

Although this plan of building surplus was quite acceptable as long as the association needed operating capital, there were increasing complaints as the surplus grew in amount and no further patronage refunds were declared. This situation led to so much dissatisfaction among the growers that to placate them a plan was adopted in 1910 under which one-half of the savings, after payment of stock dividends, was to be returned to growers in patronage refunds while the other half was to be added to surplus. Under this new arrangement refunds to growers during the six years from 1912 to 1917 aggregated $186,000 while the surplus continued to expand until by 1917 it stood at $230,189.[39]

Even though the Exchange had become more cooperative in character through its method of returning savings in patronage refunds, it remained vulnerable to the charge that a minority of stockholders could control the organization. In 1917, for illustration, a tabulation of shareholdings indicated that 4,023, or almost half, of the 8,328 shares outstanding were held by 112 shareholders who each held 11 or more shares, while 3,084 of these shares were held by 48 stockholders who each held 25 or more shares. The remaining 4,305 shares were held by 2,287 shareholders who each held 10 or less shares. As the shareholders voted in accordance with shareholdings, control was thus vested in the hands of a small group of influential farmers.[40]

While it was held that this arrangement maintained the stability of the organization on the grounds that the large shareholders were "public-spirited" individuals who had the "best brains" in the area served, it was also true that it gave no assurance that the large shareholders would not come to have a greater interest in their ownership rights than in providing a true cooperative service.[41] The weakening of the Exchange was largely the result of this basic weakness which curbed the maximum development of membership support.

Altogether, the Eastern Shore of Virginia Produce Exchange made a significant contribution to the advancement of cooperative marketing technique. By showing what could be done cooperatively it paved the way for other associations more strictly cooperative in basic structure.[42]

Michigan Potato Growers' Exchange

The Michigan Potato Growers' Exchange was the first vegetable-marketing federation of any significance. This organization was formed in 1918 as a sales agency for local warehouse associations following "a feverish state of discontent" over the poor returns received by Michigan potato growers from their 1917 bumper crop.[43] Under the plan of organization, which was devised by a field agent of the U. S. Bureau of Markets, growers signed marketing agreements with local associations which in turn were bound by contracts to sell through the central exchange.[44] The plan of organization was admittedly planned roughly on that of the California Fruit Growers Exchange although less control over grading was delegated to the central organization. Moreover, the local association members of the Exchange were not single purpose organizations as were the member associations of the California Fruit Growers Exchange. Many of the Michigan associations "handled one or more other commodities such as grain, hay, cream, fruit, and kept on hand a stock of feed, salt, coal, etc., for the convenience of their members."[45] Even though the Michigan Potato Growers' Exchange was little more than a "commission sales agency" it served the immediate needs of its member cooperative associations and rapidly gained strength. When it was formed it had 28 local associations. Within two years the number exceeded 100 and its sales volume was over $5 million.

The California Nut Associations

Like the California Fruit Growers Exchange, the California Walnut Growers Association got its start with the formation of local associations which grew up almost spontaneously as a means of remedying an unsatisfactory marketing system under the control of brokers, speculators, and commission men. The first of these groups was formed as early as 1890 in Los Angeles County. In 1905, the need for collective action among the local associations then formed led to the creation of an informal organization known as the Executive Committee of Southern California Walnut Associations. The Executive Committee "performed only a few limited functions such as purchasing bags for its members, handling matters involving the general welfare of the industry, and meeting prior to harvest time to discuss market conditions and prices that growers might reasonably expect . . . ." Experience soon indicated that a stronger organization was needed "if better distribution and market stabilization was to be attained."[46]

While this matter was under consideration, the managers of two local associations began to experiment by offering a pack of high-grade walnuts direct to wholesale grocers and fruit jobbers. Their success soon attracted the attention of the other associations and led to the organization of the California Walnut Growers Association in 1912, with three charter member associations.

In general, the new organization followed closely the federation plan already well developed by the California Fruit Growers Exchange. However, at first each local association retained the right of selecting its own broker, and this resulted in friction and price cutting among the associations. To remedy this condition, the California Walnut Growers Association was empowered to make all brokerage arrangements, and in 1914 the Association set up its own sales organization to sell direct "to the wholesale trade through brokers located in the consuming markets of the country."[47] In the following year the Association registered its "Diamond Brand" for use on its best walnuts, and so laid the basis for its well-known national advertising program.

For some time after the central association was formed, some of the locals resisted selling in a common pool on the grounds that their product was better than that of the other local associations. This made impossible an effective sales policy, and tended to "demoralize the market for all walnuts, good or bad." After considerable argument a "common pooling system" was eventually adopted in 1918 under which the California Walnut Growers Association received all walnuts and returned payments to growers in accordance with grade, size, and quantity, after expense deductions.

Another development of an integrating nature grew out of the problem raised by cull walnuts which, when sold to peddlers were frequently resold as good walnuts, thus injuring the reputation of the

Association's standard products. This condition gradually led the central association to require its member associations to place all walnuts, including culls and kernels, under its control. The central built its first cracking plant to handle the culls of locals in 1915, and in 1917 all growers were required to deliver all walnuts to locals in orchard-run form. This ended culling on the ranch and all culls thereafter were delivered to the central for cracking and handling.

As the Association improved and integrated its services, its place in the industry expanded until by 1920 it was marketing over 75 per cent of the California walnut crop.

The California Almond Growers' Exchange. To some extent the experience of the almond growers paralleled that of the walnut growers. The earliest local almond growers' association was formed in 1897 in the Sacramento Valley. In 1910, the nine associations then in operation established the California Almond Growers' Exchange as their joint sales agency. The exchange was organized as a non-stock membership corporation with each local having one representative on its board of directors. At first, there was no contract running between the Exchange and the grower, although the members of local associations were required to sign by-laws which empowered the locals to market their almonds through the Exchange.[48]

Although this arrangement represented a great improvement over the uncoordinated system of marketing that prevailed prior to the formation of the Exchange, it was felt by many that the central exchange did not have sufficient control over the product to provide adequately for the construction of essential processing facilities, or for the financing of the crop while in the process of marketing. This view led to a reorganization in 1921 whereby the individual growers gave the central exchange full control over the marketing of their crops through contracts running direct from the grower to the Exchange. Through this change the Exchange acquired the operating character of a centralized association, although its structure retained the general form of a federation. Its voting control remained in the local associations, which also continued to handle local affairs such as the operation of the local receiving warehouses.

By 1920 the California Almond Growers' Exchange had attained a position of leadership in the almond industry and was marketing over 75 per cent of the California almond crop.

With aggressive and competent direction and management, these two California nut growers' associations have flourished to the present day.

Summary

In this chapter we have examined the experience of several influential cooperative marketing enterprises to see how the concept of cooperative marketing was being broadened and sharpened under the impact of diverse situations and problems. In general these associations arose because of unsatisfactory local marketing conditions which convinced groups of growers that their welfare as agricultural producers depended upon their ability to organize and operate marketing associations efficiently. In the beginning these cooperatives were often crudely devised and operated. However, as experience was gained they became more and more responsive to the needs of their members and more professional in their business methods.

While these pioneer associations at first differed considerably in form of organization and methods of operation, they gradually came to have many features in common. From trial and error there was emerging the understanding of principles and techniques essential to efficient, cooperative performance. By 1920 the following lessons generally had been learned:

1. That the stock company form of organization—with control and benefits largely dependent upon ownership of shares of stock—was unsuitable for permanent cooperative growth. More and more associations had found it desirable to restrict control and benefits to members through organizing as membership cooperative corporations or by the adoption of the one-man, one-vote principle with return of savings as patronage refunds.

2. That efficient marketing by an association required some sacrifice of growers' independence. However, it was found that pooling systems and membership agreements could be devised and used so as to achieve strong marketing organizations without jeopardizing the essential freedoms of the individual.

3. That maximum efficiency in marketing a given crop required that the growers over a considerable area be organized together, either through a federated or centralized form of organization. Only through such arrangements could maximum efficiency in selling and cost reduction be secured.

4. That no cooperative organization could long succeed without competent business administration. By 1920, it was becoming well appreciated that cooperative marketing associations—while unique in their provisions for democratic control and for the equitable sharing of

benefits—could not long succeed unless they were efficient in business administration.

Up to this point we have centered our attention on cooperative marketing associations which were mainly concerned with ways of improving the efficiency of the marketing process, and in methods of reflecting the benefits of such increased efficiency to members in the form of greater returns for their crops. In the next chapter we will examine the growth of a new emphasis in cooperative marketing which was beginning to take shape during this same period. This new emphasis focused attention on methods of obtaining control over a substantial portion of the supply of an agricultural product as a means of achieving maximum returns for producers.

Chapter XV

THE CENTRALIZED COMMODITY
MARKETING EXPERIMENTS

The preceding chapters have shown how marketing cooperatives expanded through federation so as to embrace wide areas of territory.[1] We now turn to a new development in large-scale cooperation which grew out of various attempts by groups of California producers of special crops to achieve a form of organization that would insure marketing control. This gave rise to a new philosophy of cooperative marketing quite different from that represented by the California Fruit Growers Exchange. The advocates of the new philosophy made *control of the commodity* the dominant motive for organization, while the exponents of federation placed their primary attention on methods of achieving a more efficient marketing process.[2]

The idea of forming cooperative associations to achieve a monopolistic control over the supply of an agricultural crop comparable to that achieved by industrial monopolists had long been attractive to farmers. This theory was the basic premise of the American Society of Equity and the Farmers' Union crop-holding movements in the early 1900's (described in Chapter X), which held that concerted action by a mass organization of farmers could achieve the goal of higher market prices. As we shall see in this chapter these crude efforts were refined by the California experiments in a number of ways. The form of organization was centralized to achieve stronger administrative control; effective membership contracts were devised to insure collective action; and emphasis was placed on methods of merchandising the crop as well as on market control. As Herman Steen said: "It is probably true that most of these practices originated outside of California but it was in the Golden State that they were perfected, correlated, and demonstrated . . ."[3]

The way in which this conception of "commodity marketing"—which was to have a dominating effect on the character of American cooperative development during the 1920's—was nourished and delineated under the favorable conditions of California special crop production is shown in this chapter. This new trend in cooperative marketing theory was first given effective direction by the Lima bean growers of California.

The Lima Bean Growers Association

As early as 1897 the Lima bean growers of Ventura County, California—an area of concentrated production—had succeeded in forming an association with some 90 per cent of the growers as members. However, this association proved to be "a miserable failure for the simple reason that it . . . placed itself in a position of absolute dependence upon the Lima bean dealers."[4] Discouraged by this experience, no further attempt at organization was made until March 1909 when the bean growers met together in protest against the low prices being received and concluded that cooperative organization afforded "the only way to meet the big buyers."[5]

This soon led to the formation of the Lima Bean Growers Association, as a centralized capital-stock organization designed to serve producers in the several Lima bean growing counties of southern California as an outright pooling association.[6] This organization entered into contracts with its member growers under which it obtained control over their crops for marketing purposes. One of the original contracts is here quoted in full:

> I hereby agree to deliver and turn over to the Lima Bean Growers' Association, a corporation, . . . [part of] my crop of lima beans when threshed, the Association agreeing to sell same to best advantage for our mutual benefit, and pay me for same when sold.
> I understand that these beans are to form part of a pool or pools, and that I will share in the pro rata payment the same as other growers who are putting their beans into the same pool or pools.[7]

The Lima Bean Growers Association was the first successful "commodity marketing" organization to be formed in California on centralized lines.[8]

While the Association was becoming established in the fall of 1909, its leaders urged growers, whether or not members, to hold their beans for a price which was set somewhat higher than that being offered by the large commercial buyers. To maintain this price, some of the wealthier growers loaned funds to the Association to enable it to buy beans of non-members, and more funds were secured to buy beans of non-members by borrowing on the security of the beans delivered or purchased.[9] Through this purchasing plan the Association gained control over a significant part of the crop with the result that prices soon rose above the Association's holding price.

Although it was realized that the practice of buying up beans of non-members was subject to criticism under the anti-trust laws, this general procedure for supporting prices was continued until June 1912 when it was discarded in favor of a pooling plan more exclusively related to the needs of its members.[10]

Under the revised contract the association was authorized, for a one-year period, to commingle the beans of its members for purposes of sale and to return to them the average net price received.[11] However, the contract authorized the Association to use one-fourth of the proceeds of the sale of members' beans in order to buy beans from non-members.

Although this revised contract was designed to establish the legality of the Association's methods, the Attorney General's office continued to take the position that pooling in and of itself was illegal.[12] It was held that "the only rights that growers could exercise in pooling their products was to make reasonable resistance to combinations by brokers formed against them."[13]

Thus, even after the marketing agreement had been completely overhauled in June 1912, there was still some concern as to whether the Association was originally set up on the best possible basis to achieve its objectives. To meet this problem, Attorney George E. Farrand, at the request of the directors, presented for their consideration a membership plan of organization in November 1912. He pointed out that the use of the non-stock form of membership organization would give the bean growers a more complete control over their association. He said: "It is possible for the bean growers to form a non-profit cooperative association so that membership could be restricted to bean growers only and in which each grower would participate according to the tonnage of beans marketed or pooled by him through the association." Under the plan proposed, the "association would not have capital stock and its business would not be carried on for the benefit of the association as such but any profit realized from the activities of the association would belong to its members, all of whom would be poolers, and would be credited pro rata to such poolers according to their several interests therein and according to the terms of any marketing agreement which might be adopted by the association."[14]

Although the membership form of organization would have corrected a basic weakness in the capital-stock form of organization which permitted control by a few large stockholders,[15] it was apparently received with little enthusiasm and within a year or two the old association discontinued operations. By this time many growers had lost confidence in the possible revitalization of the Association. The efforts of the Association had improved the position of the growers and many forgot that conditions would quickly worsen in the absence of the Association. Then, again, the supporters of the Association had grown tired of holding up prices for the benefit of nonmembers.[16]

The demoralization of bean prices which followed the collapse of the old association soon led to a demand that a new association be formed on a more practicable basis. In response to this pressure, Farrand in November 1915, presented a plan patterned closely on the organizational structure of the California Walnut Growers Association.[17] By this time he had become convinced that the needs of the bean growers could best be met by a federated form of "non-profit, non-capital stock" marketing organization in which growers would "pool their brains as well as their beans."

Under the new plan of organization, strong local receiving and handling associations were established and these were federated together for marketing purposes in a central association—the Lima Bean Growers Association. Members entered into marketing contracts with the local associations and they in turn entered into marketing contracts with the central association. In this way the central was granted full authority for selling the beans of growers embraced by the system of organization. As it was hoped that the new plan would attract the majority of bean growers as members, less importance was attributed to control than to the establishment of an efficient system of marketing. Thus the experience of the bean growers led them to turn from centralized capital-stock organization to federated membership organization.

Although the bean growers contributed materially to the development of the conception of "commodity marketing," it is significant that they turned to federation as a means of maintaining membership support at the same time the centralized form of organization was being most vigorously promoted by the State Market Director of California (see Chapter IX).

The California Associated Raisin Company

Although the first significant attempt to achieve marketing control by contract was that of the Lima bean growers, the first effective demonstration of the idea was made by the California Associated Raisin Company in the years from 1913 to 1920.

The formation of the California Associated Raisin Company in 1912 culminated a series of unsuccessful attempts to achieve permanent organization for the raisin growers which dated back to the 1890's.[18] In that year the growers' morale had reached the lowest point in the history of the industry, since they were unable to recoup their costs of production. This was blighting the business prosperity of the entire raisin-growing region.

The initiative for the new plan came from a group of Fresno packers and businessmen, who saw that their economic welfare was tied up with the plight of the raisin growers. This group undertook to form an association—the California Associated Raisin Company—strong enough to obtain control over the marketing of a large fraction of the raisin crop.[19]

To achieve this end a marketing agreement was devised under which growers were to pledge their crops for marketing by the association for a period of three years, subject to renewal by the association for two more. It set a fixed schedule of minimum prices that would be paid to the grower upon delivery of his raisins. These agreements were not to be in effect until 60 per cent of the state raisin acreage was signed up under the association's control. On April 1, 1913, when the campaign closed, 76 per cent of the raisin acreage was covered by such contracts.

As the California Associated Raisin Company became the first "successful" commodity marketing association of the centralized type, its plan of organization is of special interest. It was set up as a capital-stock organization with 10,000 shares having a par value of $100. The ownership of stock, however, was not restricted to raisin growers and much of it was sold to merchants, packers, and others as dividends of 8 per cent were payable on the stock.[20]

The voting trust plan. A unique feature of the plan of organization placed control in the hands of 25 trustees under the terms of a "Subscription and Voting Trust Agreement." Under this agreement the prospective stockholder authorized the trustees to hold and vote his shares of stock—although actual management was to be vested in a board of seven directors responsible to the 25 trustees. The justification of this arrangement was stated in the agreement: "It is deemed to be vital to the interests of the subscribers hereto that a voting trust be created with the shareholding body of said corporation [the proposed association] as beneficiaries thereof in order that the stock of said company *shall not be bought up for speculative control and to secure safe and prudent management of said corporation in the interests of the whole number of stockholders. . . ."* (Italics added)

The desperate situation of the raisin growers in 1912 largely accounted for their willingness to accept a corporate dictatorship of this type. They hoped that this device which had been used so successfully by big business corporations might yield similar results for themselves.[21]

Although the voting trust plan was under criticism from the beginning as representing an unfortunate departure from sound cooperative practice,[22] there was no question of its effectiveness. Without this plan it is doubtful whether the organization could have so quickly become the dominant force in the raisin industry.

Development of marketing methods. The California Associated Raisin Company lost no time in establishing itself as a marketing organization. With control secured over a large part of the tonnage,[23] and with able and aggressive management, steps were immediately taken to provide for packing either through leased or purchased facilities or through exclusive packing arrangements made with private companies. Immediate sales service was obtained from packing companies or brokers but with the definite understanding that the association would have the right to sell direct if it should elect to do so.[24]

The success of the California Associated Raisin Company was almost spontaneous and within a year it had become the dominant factor in the industry. Prices paid growers rose from an average of $61.17 per ton in 1912 to an average of $72.19 per ton in 1913.[25]

It was appreciated from the beginning that the demand for raisins would need to be expanded if the production was to be moved at satisfactory prices. The company therefore lost little time in embarking upon an advertising program based on careful grading and this was intensified with the adoption of the "Sun Maid" trademark in 1916.[26] Expenditures for advertising expanded from $120,000 in 1914 to $373,000 in 1919. In 1920 they jumped to $1,250,000.

Whether or not advertising was the main cause contributing to the increased demand—for the curtailment of foreign raisin shipments during World War I improved export outlets for the California crop and reduced imports into the United States—California raisin production rose from 71,500 tons in 1913 to 182,500 tons in 1919, while prices to growers increased from $72.19 per ton to $228.21 per ton, although in the latter year prices were abnormally high because of war conditions.[27]

As the original three-year contract gave the association an option permitting renewal for two additional years, it actually expired with the 1917 crop.[28] The new contract which likewise ran for three years with the privilege of renewal by the associations for two more, differed from the old in two important respects: (1) It contained a provision under which members who failed to deliver their crop would pay stipulated liquidated damages. (2) It provided that all savings after payment of stock dividends of 8 per cent and payments to surplus could be distributed either in the form of stock or cash. This latter provision was designed to increase the ownership interest of growers so as to make the organization more truly cooperative in character.[29]

The success of the association in marketing a steadily expanding volume at generally satisfactory prices enabled it to sign up 87 per cent of the estimated production under the new contract. Fortified with this support the association in 1918 embarked on a more ambitious program of marketing, exclusively via brokers direct to the trade, an arrangement which was continued until 1921 when the association established its own sales force.

Government restriction of monopoly power. Almost from the date of its organization the association had been bitterly attacked by hostile trade interests as the "raisin trust," and continuing demands had been made for its investigation under the anti-trust laws. These demands which were quieted during the war when prices were fixed by the U. S. Food Administration were quickly resumed in 1919 when the price of raisins rapidly rose with the termination of price control. The price-fixing power of the association was so apparent that the Attorney General on September 30, 1919, requested the Federal Trade Commission to determine whether the association was "obtaining and maintaining more than fair and reasonable prices for its products," and "to make recommendations for the readjustment of the business of said corporation in order that the corporation may hereafter maintain its organization, management, and conduct of business in accordance with law."

Relative to the first instruction, the Commission in its report of June 8, 1920, said:

> Between 1912 and 1918 the success of the company was tested by the expiration of its three-year contracts with its growers. It appears that the company has, during the greater portion of this time steadily maintained its control of crop acreage, which indicates satisfaction on the part of the growers with the operations of the company. The argument that the marked advance in 1919 is justified by a comparison with prices charged for other dried fruits in California, upon which the Raisin Company very largely defends the 1919 price, does not control the question of the reasonableness of price. In the absence of a showing of a greater increase in the cost of production, there having been

no diminution in production, but rather a slight increase over 1918, after considering the diminishing purchasing power of the dollar, our conclusion is that the price fixed by the Raisin Company for the 1919 crop was in excess of a fair and reasonable price (p. 185).

With regard to the second instruction the Commission advised as follows:

To conform to the legal requirements of an agricultural or horticultural organization instituted for the purpose of mutual help, the Raisin Company must take the necessary legal steps to accomplish the following results:
(a) The elimination of capital stock and the substitution, therefore, if necessary, of a non-profit sharing basis of providing financial resources.
(b) The elimination of profit to the corporation or to its stockholders as profit on the operations of the corporation.
(c) The restriction of membership or beneficial interest in the corporation of those whose interests are identical, i.e., to actual growers of raisin grapes (p. 189).

The Commission concluded: "With an amended charter, capital stock retired, and a membership constituted solely of grape growers under delivery contracts, the Raisin Company would be in structural conformance with the Clayton law" (p. 190).

In the meantime the Department of Justice had brought suit in District Court, September 1920, to dissolve the Company as a means of stopping certain of the monopolistic practices disclosed by the Federal Trade Commission's study. This suit resulted in a court decree under which the company agreed to make certain changes in its selling policy and contracts.[30]

In compliance with this situation, the California Associated Raisin Company—which had changed its name in 1922 to Sun Maid Raisin Growers to take advantage of the popularity of its well-known "Sun-Maid" trademark—reorganized in June 1923 as a non-stock membership corporation. This gave direct control to the members and thus terminated the voting-trust agreement.

In endeavoring to curb the abuse of the monopolistic power of the California Associated Raisin Company, the government thus effectively prescribed the channel for the later growth of cooperative commodity marketing. This is shown by the fact that most of the large centralized associations formed after 1920 were organized as non-stock membership corporations so as to insure ownership and control by those served.[31]

The significance of the raisin growers' experience. The career of the California Associated Raisin Company up to 1920 represented a remarkable achievement. Within a period of eight years this association had become the dominant force in the raisin industry; and no one could deny it had brought prosperity to the growers of raisin grapes in a way unparalleled in the history of American agriculture. Naturally such dramatic success led other groups of agricultural producers to emulate its methods for achieving monopoly power.[32]

Thus the early experience of the raisin growers had a great effect in spreading the doctrine of commodity marketing before the weakness in this philosophy of organization had become apparent.[33]

During these eight years the California Associated Raisin Company had shown how a strong centralized marketing organization could be formed. Its membership contracts were strengthened and its market outlets were highly developed. Moreover, certain principles were being established: that organization on a membership basis was superior for the purpose of centralized commodity marketing than organization on a capital-stock basis; that the trust agreement plan of administration divorced the membership from vital democratic control which was essential if intelligent membership interest was to be sustained. In this manner, the experience of the raisin growers did much to fashion the technique and theory of "commodity marketing."

The California Peach Growers, Inc.

When Harris Weinstock became State Market Director of California on November 20, 1915, a large fraction of the year's dried peach crop had not been harvested due to "deplorable market conditions," and growers' dissatisfaction had expressed itself in the formation of a Peach Growers Association Organization Committee. At the request of its chairman, Weinstock met with this committee on his first day in office and declared, "It must be evident that unless you follow the lines so successfully demonstrated by the raisin growers there can be little or no hope for the future of the California dried peach industry."[34]

To develop confidence in the plan adopted by the peach growers' association—which was patterned in detail on the California Associated Raisin Company—Weinstock suggested the desirability of having a "public" representative on its board of directors as an assurance of governmental interest and as a guarantee of adequate supervision.[35]

The California Peach Growers, Inc., proved immediately successful, as evidenced by Weinstock's statement in his second annual report:

> In view of the fact that my first activity (taken on the day of my first inauguration as State Market Director of California) was in going to the assistance of

the Peach Growers, then in the throes of an effort to organize, it is with no small degree of pleasure that I now report that it ranks among the leading marketing associations of the state, with a strong financial status, control of the bulk of the production of drying peaches, and efficient business management and salesmanship. It has rescued the California peach grower from insolvency and despair and has placed this great industry on a sound and prosperous basis—all within a remarkably short period of time.[36]

Two years later Weinstock called attention to the fact that the association in its fourth year had marketed over 75 per cent of the dried peaches in the state. Its business volume then totalled about $10 million, its membership stood at 6,000 and its paid-up capital and surplus amounted to $1,203,810. There was much point in Weinstock's declaration that "this sturdy association has revolutionized the industry.[37]

California Prune and Apricot Growers, Inc.

Although the prune growers of the Santa Clara Valley had formed cooperative associations in the 1890's,[38] little progress was made before January 1916 when Harris Weinstock, as State Market Director, gave his support to the formation of an association for the marketing of prunes and apricots patterned on the plan of the raisin growers' association. After a comprehensive organization campaign, which was bitterly opposed by the well-entrenched prune packers, the California Prune and Apricot Growers, Inc., was launched on May 1, 1917, under the management of H. G. Coykendall, a popular producer and packer. The association was promoted as a "preparedness measure" for it was apparent that the rapidly increasing production would soon demoralize prices without a comprehensive marketing program.

The California Prune and Apricot Growers, Inc., was organized on a centralized capital-stock basis with each member taking $100 in stock for each 10 acres of prunes or apricots. However, stockholding was restricted to growers, a measure designed to correct one of the weaknesses of the plan of the raisin growers. Under the plan each grower entered into a contract which gave the association complete control of his dried prunes and apricots for a period of five years. As in the case of California Associated Raisin Company, the management was vested in a board of directors under the control of trustees, but the provision for a public director was designed to protect the rights of the individual member.

The method of operation required the grower to deliver his product to local packinghouses under the control of the association, and at first most of the packinghouses were leased by the association. As this method proved unsatisfactory, the association in 1919 took control of all packing facilities through the formation of a subsidiary corporation, the Growers' Packing and Warehousing Corporation. This arrangement enabled the association to keep its packing and warehousing operations distinct from its marketing operations and it also enabled the association to obtain capital for facilities from the investing public through the issuance of preferred stock.[39]

The immediate merchandising accomplishments of the California Prune and Apricot Growers, Inc., soon gave it a national reputation as a model centralized commodity marketing association and within three years its annual sales volume had reached $25 million. However, in the fall of 1920, the stability of the association was severely tested by an abrupt drop in prune prices as the association had in many cases advanced more than could be obtained on the market. Although "the organization survived this ordeal," the experience disclosed weakness in the plan of organization which led to the association's reorganization in 1921 as a non-stock membership association. The new plan arranged for the retirement of the original capital stock, and made provision for a revolving fund plan of financing under which each member contributed operating capital in proportion to the extent of his marketings through the association.[40]

The Poultry and Egg Associations

Among the other organizations which were set up in California on "commodity principle lines" in the years from 1912 to 1920, none achieved greater success than the regional poultry and egg marketing associations. The way in which these associations developed is therefore of particular interest.

The Poultry Producers of Central California. Prior to the organization of the Poultry Producers of Central California in 1916, little progress had been made in the effective marketing of eggs cooperatively. While a number of egg circles had been formed in the Midwest, often as a sideline activity of cooperative creameries, these did little more than assemble eggs for sale to dealers, and most of them expired within a few years.[41]

The Poultry Producers of Central California was built upon a considerable amount of preliminary experience, as poultry producers of Sonoma County had experimented with three cooperative marketing plans since 1908.[42] With the rapid growth of commercial poultry production in this area there was need for a more comprehensive marketing program and this was brought to the attention of Harris Weinstock after he assumed office as State Market Director in December 1915.[43]

After sending out a questionnaire to poultrymen which disclosed that there was a sincere desire for organization, Weinstock held a number of conferences with leading poultrymen which finally led to the formation of a promotion committee charged with the development of a satisfactory program. This committee, with the assistance of Weinstock's office, devised a centralized plan of organization based on two related documents: (1) a Subscription Agreement and (2) a Produce Sales Agreement. Weinstock considered these forms to be "a model for this form of organization" and he included them as an appendix to his first annual report.[44]

The Subscription Agreement provided for the incorporation of the Poultry Producers of Central California with a capitalization of $250,000 divided into 25,000 shares of $10 each, after *bona fide* subscriptions amounting to $10,000 were procured. Shares were to be restricted to poultry producers who agreed to purchase them "at the rate of one share for every thousand hens ... the minimum subscription ... being one share." There were to be 11 directors, of whom 10 were to be elected annually from among the shareholders so as adequately to represent the producing districts. The eleventh director was to serve as a representative of the public and was to be named by the State Market Director. Actual management was to be entrusted to an executive committee of five of whom one was to be the public director. Under the terms of the subscription agreement the subscribers agreed to enter into "agreements with the corporation for the sale of their products by the said corporation."

The arrangements for marketing were fully set forth in the Produce Sales Agreement under which producers respectively agreed to deliver their eggs and poultry to the association for marketing for a three-year period and to pay stipulated amounts as liquidated damages in the event of non-compliance. On its part, the association agreed "to use its best efforts" in selling such eggs and poultry delivered to it and to return proceeds to producers after deductions for transportation costs and for costs of selling "not to exceed 2 cents per dozen for eggs and 50 cents per dozen for poultry." The association was also authorized "to deduct 1 cent per dozen for eggs sold and 10 cents per dozen for poultry sold to be credited and applied on the account of the respective seller toward the purchase of additional shares of capital stock," until the authorized capital stock was "paid for." The association was given full authority over pooling, warehousing, and standardization. The Produce Sales Agreement was to become effective only if owners of one million hens subscribed to its terms by January 1, 1917.

The organization campaign which started in July was directed by a representative of the State Market Director and on October 30 it was declared that the conditions set forth in the two agreements had been fully met. The Poultry Producers of Central California was thereupon incorporated on October 31, 1916.

In beginning operations, the association attempted to sell the eggs of its members through the facilities of the San Francisco Dairy and Produce Exchange. This method was discarded after a one-year trial and from then on the association proceeded to develop its own marketing outlets.

At first many poultrymen had been skeptical of the new venture in view of their disappointing experience with earlier associations. These hesitating producers joined the association as it began to demonstrate that it was soundly conceived and well managed. By 1919, the association was doing a volume of business of $4,500,000 and handling over 50 per cent of the eggs passing through the San Francisco market.[45] Moreover, the provision for raising capital by an automatic deduction from marketing proceeds had enabled the association to develop a capital-stock fund of $25,000. This gave the association an excellent financial standing and sufficient capital to establish a number of branch warehouses to facilitate the assembly of eggs and poultry.

Other centralized poultry associations. While the Poultry Producers of Central California was being formed, the State Market Director was assisting in the organization of a somewhat similar association for the poultrymen in the Los Angeles area.[46] This association—the Poultry Producers of Southern California, Inc.,—was incorporated on December 15, 1916. The plans of these two associations soon attracted the attention of other poultrymen on the Pacific Coast who quickly formed the following organizations of a similar type: Poultry Producers of San Diego, 1917; the Washington Cooperative Egg and Poultry Association, Seattle, 1917; and the Pacific Poultry Producers at Portland, 1920. All of these associations were direct membership organizations of the centralized type with marketing centered in the central organization by means of membership agreements.[47] Much of the incentive for their development was the rapid expansion of the poultry industry on the West Coast following World War I. If markets were not to be demoralized, outlets had to be found in the East and this required strong regional marketing organizations capable of enforcing quality standards. How this led to the federation of their sales efforts in 1922 will be explained in Volume II of this history.

Summary

In this chapter we have shown how the concept of "commodity marketing" grew out of the experience of several associations which were formed to meet the special needs of groups of California agricultural producers. In other words, the theory of "commodity marketing" as perfected and nationally expounded by Aaron Sapiro in the 1920's was largely a rationalization of the practices which were found useful to meet a particular type of California marketing situation.

As we shall see in the second volume of this history, the commodity marketing doctrine—as thus incubated—was to have a great influence on the subsequent development of cooperative marketing institutions throughout the nation.

Part Four

THE DEVELOPMENT OF
COOPERATIVE PURCHASING

Parallel with the progress of cooperative marketing in the years from 1897 to 1920 came a striking development in cooperative purchasing. In this period rapidly changing economic and social conditions provided a new inducement for this kind of cooperative organization.

In Part Four we will see farmers turning from all-purpose buying associations to organizations specializing in providing bulk supplies used in agricultural production and marketing operations—feed, seed, fertilizer, coal, lumber, box shook, and packing materials.

Of special interest is the way in which the Fruit Growers Supply Company demonstrated that cooperative purchasing is of correlative importance with cooperative marketing. This organization pioneered in buying according to specifications, and the efficiency of its methods provided a yardstick for measuring competitive operations and prices. Of particular significance was its revolving fund plan devised to finance its box shook manufacturing operations. Its demonstration of the value of this method of financing for cooperatives was primarily responsible for the widespread adoption of revolving financing plans by cooperative marketing and purchasing cooperatives after 1920.

In Part Four attention is also directed to the distinctive ways in which two other large-scale supply purchasing associations arose to meet the particular needs of farmers—the Eastern States Farmers Exchange and the Cooperative Grange League Federation Exchange. These pacesetting organizations were destined to have great influence on cooperative purchasing developments in the United States. They were only well started by 1920 but this record will show that they were built on strong democratic foundations.

Chapter XVI

THE NEW MOTIVATION IN COOPERATIVE PURCHASING

During the years from 1896 to 1920 farming was transformed from a largely self-sufficient occupation until it had become a modern business, organized on a scientific, capitalistic, commercial basis. This change placed a new emphasis on the farmers' buying problem which had a marked influence on the growth and character of farmers' purchasing associations. Prior to 1896 the production supply needs of farmers were not of material consequence and, in fact, up to this time farmers generally were more concerned with the cost of staple consumers' supplies such as flour and sugar than with the cost of supplies for production. Farm machinery was then used with moderation. Feed and seed were largely raised on the farm, and few farmers, except on the Atlantic Seaboard, then used commercial fertilizer. Even as late as 1900, the total amount of farmers' purchases for all materials and equipment required for carrying on farming operations did not exceed $1 billion a year.

In the next 20 years—with little new land available for expansion—farmers were forced to buy substantially larger amounts of machinery and production supplies so as to produce crops more efficiently in order to meet the needs of a growing home and export market. Consequently, the burden of expenditures for equipment and supplies essential to efficient farming grew steadily until they exceeded $4 billion by 1920.

This condition gave a new motivation to cooperative purchasing as a means by which farmers could obtain supplies of the right type and quality at the lowest possible cost. As long as only a few farmers in a neighborhood purchased feed or fertilizer, the possibility of purchasing these commodities to advantage by cooperative action was negligible. When a large proportion began to require such supplies in considerable amounts it became more logical for farmers to combine their purchasing efforts. Furthermore, conditions were not favorable for the efficient operation of purchasing associations until there were sizable groups of farmers having similar needs.

The change that occurred in agriculture in the years from 1900 to 1920 was reflected in a general growth of agricultural output of 27.8 per cent. This increased output was made possible by more scientific farming methods and more abundant use of capital, either in the form of machinery and equipment or in production supplies such as fertilizer and feed.[1]

Some idea of the progress of farm mechanization during these years is given by the fact that the value of implements and machines on farms rose from $750,000,000 in 1900 to $3,596,000,000 in 1920. This represented an increase in the value of implements and machinery on farms of from 89 cents to $3.76 an acre. Although a large part of this increase was due to the higher level of prices brought on by World War I, the fact remains that the use of machinery and equipment was steadily growing in importance throughout this period.

The Growth of Farming Expenditures

The growth of farmers' expenditures for farm machinery is reflected by the fact that the value of farm machinery produced for domestic use increased from $89 million in 1899 to $122 million in 1909, and to $260 million in 1919. Moreover, these figures do not include the value of farm tractors produced for domestic use, since tractor production did not become important prior to World War I. In fact, the value of tractors produced, both domestic and for export, was only $18 million when first reported for 1914. However, in 1919, the value of tractors produced for domestic consumption alone amounted to $144 million. The actual extent of farmers' expenditures for farm machinery and tractors was considerably greater since these figures on manufacturing output did not include freight and distribution margins.[2]

Farmers' expenditures for fertilizer also expanded rapidly as farming became more intensive. While total expenditures for fertilizer in 1899 amounted to only $53 million they had reached $326 million by 1919. Not only were many more farmers using fertilizer but it was being used more generously.

The increase in expenditures for feed was even more striking. In the decade from 1909 to 1919 such expenditures rose from $300,000,000 to $1,098,000,000, or by about 375 per cent. While a substantial fraction of this increase was due to the upward trend of war-time prices, most of it represented substantial growth in tonnage of feed consumed by the expanding dairy and poultry industries.

The improvement in farm buildings and homes which came with a higher degree of agricultural prosperity also occasioned an expansion in farm expenditures for lumber, cement, roofing, paint, and other building supply materials. From 1900 to 1920 the value of farm buildings per acre rose from $4.24 to $12.02. Much of this increase represented better farm buildings and homes, along with higher valuations for farm property. Many other farm production supplies, such as insecticides, fungicides, and sprays, grew in importance as agriculture became more specialized.

While the rising level of prices, especially during the war years, accentuated the increase in expenditures for production supplies, the fact remains that farmers quadrupled their expenditures for materials required in farm production and farm maintenance in this score of years. By 1920 it was true that farmers, like other manufacturers, were purchasing raw materials in order to turn out finished products.

The effect of World War I on farm expenditures. While the expansion in farm expenditures was well under way by 1910, the period of rapid increase came during the next decade as the result of the pressure to increase agricultural production exerted by World War I. This is shown by the annual expenditures of farmers for specified farm supply and capital equipment items for the years from 1910 through 1920 as estimated by the Bureau of Agricultural Economics. Such detailed information on farmers' expenditures is not available for the years before 1910.

During this 10-year period the annual feed expenditure increased from $426,000,000 to $1,254,000,000. The expenditures for petroleum products, which were negligible in 1910, amounted to almost $300 million by 1920, and practically all of this expansion occurred in the years from 1915 to 1920.

Expenditures for capital equipment in the form of buildings, machinery, equipment, and motor vehicles also expanded rapidly during these years, and particularly after 1915. Such expenditures, which amounted to about $846,000,000 in 1910, had increased to $1,927,000,000 by 1920. Here it is of particular interest that the expenditures for motor vehicles increased from $32 million in 1910 to $392 million in 1920.

Much of the rapid expansion of expenditures for supplies used in farm production came during the war years when materials of all kinds were abundantly used to whip up agricultural output. While expenditures for capital equipment also increased, they were more limited by war shortages.

Although the increase in expenditures for farm supplies and equipment was nation-wide, it was more pronounced in the northern, central, and western states. In 1919, as shown by the Census, feed expenditures per reporting farm amounted to $435 while in the southern states such expenditures amounted to only $158 per farm. The greatest concentration of fertilizer consumption in 1919 was in the northeastern and South Atlantic states where it amounted to $183 per reporting farm. Except for the growers of specialty crops on the Pacific Coast, few farmers west of the Mississippi River then purchased fertilizer.

Growth of Monopolistic Control over Farm Supplies

The fact that farmers were buying more supplies for use in their farming operations made them conscious of the need for economizing on such expenditures, and this naturally inclined them toward cooperative buying. This tendency was increased by the belief then prevalent among farmers that they were paying exorbitant prices for supplies, due to the monopolistic practices of large corporations and industrial combinations. There was considerable justification for this feeling. Even before 1900 there had developed a high degree of concentration in the industries which served farmers' needs. As it was obvious that individual farmers were not strong enough to buy advantageously from these powerful concerns, a demand arose for sturdy organizations which could match on the buying side the power of organized industry on the selling side.

The situation in the fertilizer industry was fairly typical. Here even before 1900 two large industrial combinations had achieved a high degree of control over the manufacture and distribution of fertilizer. The first giant combination in this industry had been formed with the organization of the Virginia-Carolina Chemical Company in 1895, and by the end of the century "only two or three establishments of first rank in the southern region remained outside the combination." The second giant organization, the American Agricultural Chemical Company, was formed with a capital of $50 million in 1899 to acquire "some 24 of the largest fertilizer plants in the northern and eastern states."[3]

The Federal Trade Commission in its report on the fertilizer industry for 1916, found that seven corporations were then selling over 58 per cent of the total domestic consumption of fertilizer. Moreover, the Commission found that several of the largest companies controlled many so-called independents. The Commission found the "concealment of the connections of the controlled companies with the parent company" to be particularly objectionable. The Federal Trade Commission's 1923 report on the fertilizer industry for 1921 found that these seven concerns were then selling 65 per cent of the total fertilizer domestically used.

Concentration in the manufacture of farm machinery was also well established by 1900, and after 1902 the International Harvester Company "found itself in virtually monopolistic control of the harvesting machinery field."[4] Farm machinery lent itself to sale by dealer agencies and this enabled the dominant manufacturers to control the methods of retail distribution. This made it difficult for cooperatives to enter into the field of farm machinery distribution since they were not yet strongly enough organized to undertake manufacturing which required large amounts of capital if the economies of large-scale manufacturing were to be obtained.

Although the same degree of concentration found in the fertilizer and farm machinery industries did not develop in the commercial feed industry, there was a definite trend after 1895 toward large-scale organization and control.[5] Such control was particularly noticeable for certain by-products—corn gluten, molasses, etc.—which were produced by a few concerns. A few large flour mills early in the century also were becoming very powerful concerns in the feed industry. Nevertheless, there was less concentration in the manufacture and distribution of feed, since feed consumption was more widely scattered and the sources of feed supplies were more varied. While there was less opportunity for monopolistic developments, yet there was a tendency for large firms to develop as the consumption of commercial feed grew in importance, and by 1915 a few large concerns were dominant leaders in the feed industry.

Such growing concentration in the fertilizer, farm machinery, and commercial feed industries was paralleled in other industries serving the supply needs of farmers, such as coal, lumber, and salt. On all sides industrial combinations or "trusts" were dominant and the quality and price of supplies were subject to their control. As Powell observed, "everything that [the farmer] . . . buys—food, wire, nails, twine, fertilizers, transportation, the telephone—is purchased from organized capital, often operating as an unregulated monopoly."[6]

Along with these strong corporate manufacturing or processing organizations there had grown up an allied distributing system with a vested interest in the *status quo*. In many instances this system was highly inefficient as indicated by the large margins taken for the performance of retail distribution service and the ineffectiveness of the service provided. There was much evidence to show that many of the supplies required by farmers were under the control of a few large industrial concerns and the local dealers who were in league with them. Moreover, farmers were dissatisfied with the type of supplies obtained. They felt that in many instances they were forced to pay high prices for inferior products. Thus as farmers were forced to buy more and more supplies as a means for increasing their efficiency, they were increasingly dissatisfied with the type of supply service which they were receiving from commercial concerns. In many communities farmers were served by several farm supply dealers who kept prices high enough to permit them to grow rich with little obvious evidence of competition. The farmers knew that they were maintaining these "parasites" in the prices they paid for such supplies. In many cases farmers were forced to accept services that they did not desire. For example, they were encouraged to buy on credit when more economical service could have been provided on a cash basis.

The farmers saw that the only remedy for this general situation lay in counter-organization. Their experience in establishing elevators and milk-bargaining associations in the face of the organized opposition of the grain and dairy trades gave them much confidence. They saw no reason why they should not pool their buying power so as to deal directly with wholesalers and thus cut out the local retailer. As the leaders in the farmers' elevator movement declared about 1910, "We whipped the grain trust; now we will turn to the coal, lumber and other trusts."

As we shall see in the chapters that follow, the farmers first began to pool their buying power locally so as to take advantage of any competition between wholesale supply firms. As their local organizations became stronger, buying federations were formed which permitted them to deal directly with manufacturing concerns. By 1920 one major regional purchasing association was demonstrating that manufacture of box shook and other supplies could be well performed cooperatively, while other regionals were getting into position to move forcefully into the manufacture of feed and other products.

Influence of Cooperative Marketing Achievements

Cooperative purchasing during this period was greatly encouraged by the demonstrated ability of cooperative marketing organizations to ·establish themselves. As farmers gained experience in cooperative marketing they turned naturally to cooperative purchasing, for if the principles of cooperation could be used in marketing it was obvious that they could be applied as well in purchasing. Thus cooperation in marketing nurtured cooperation in purchasing.

The way in which cooperative achievement in marketing spread its influence to purchasing is well illustrated by the way in which the Fruit Growers Supply Company was formed by the California Fruit Growers Exchange in 1907 "to combat the lumber trusts." The citrus growers had proved the power of organization in marketing, and when the need arose they turned without hesitation to organization for buying (see Chapter XVIII). Supply purchasing came naturally with the development of cooperative marketing as it increasingly became clear that efficient marketing required efficient procurement of goods required in production and marketing operations.

In fact, as we shall see in the following chapter, many purchasing associations developed as auxiliary activities of marketing associations. In many cases the substantial growth in supply side-line purchasing business was largely dependent upon the prior growth of cooperative marketing associations. Although farmers organized first for marketing objectives, they soon added as an objective the cooperative purchasing of supplies. Moreover, sideline operations often contributed to the effectiveness of cooperative marketing associations through enabling them to reduce overhead costs to the advantage of their members.

Many of the first specialized purchasing associations were dependent upon cooperative marketing associations for initial support. The early purchasing regionals, especially in the Midwest, could not have established themselves without the volume of side-line business contributed by cooperative elevators or other cooperative marketing enterprises. The Fruit Growers Supply Company could not have developed its highly specialized regional purchasing service if it had not been based on the well-established marketing structure of the California Fruit Growers Exchange. Moreover, the strong marketing organization developed by the Dairymen's League made possible, as we shall see in Chapter XX, the rapid development of the Cooperative Grange League Federation Exchange.

The way in which the struggle to establish cooperative marketing organizations increased the spirit of farmer solidarity is well illustrated by the growth of feed purchasing associations in the eastern states following their successful attempts to form milk-marketing organizations. The struggle of farmers to establish cooperative elevators, creameries, fruit marketing associations, dairy cooperatives, etc., made them militant and gave them a determination to apply the power of cooperation wherever benefits might be derived. Farmers became aware of their power of organization through marketing. Finding that effective marketing required effective organization they saw that similar unification was essential in buying.

Cooperative purchasing was also influenced by the progress of cooperative marketing in many other ways. The methods of organization perfected for marketing strongly influenced the pattern of organization for cooperative purchasing. For example, the successful federation of local marketing cooperatives provided experience for the formation of similar federations for cooperative purchasing. Moreover, interest in cooperative-marketing organizations largely developed the legal framework which was necessary for the development of cooperative purchasing associations. The enactment of early legislation providing for the payment of patronage refunds which facilitated the rapid development of purchasing cooperatives was due to the pressure of the cooperative marketing associations. Experience with cooperative marketing organizations also gave farmers experience in cooperative behavior, and trained them as cooperative citizens, for the lessons learned by farmers in supporting and managing marketing organizations were as applicable to cooperative purchasing. Moreover, cooperative marketing associations were a training ground for cooperative managers, where many of the early managers of a purchasing cooperative "cut their eye teeth" in cooperative work.

The purchasing movement also drew on the cooperative-marketing movement for many technical ideas, such as the conception of pooling as applied to expenses, and the revolving fund method of finance. Cooperative marketing, by emphasizing the importance of quality of product sold, also encouraged purchasing cooperatives to handle supplies of high quality "as cheaper in the long run." These and many other ideas were directly or indirectly taken over from the marketing associations.

Summary

In this chapter we have examined the influence of three factors that explain much of the impetus given to cooperative purchasing during the years from 1896 to 1920: (1) the growing burden of supply expenditures, (2) the helplessness of farmers due to the domination of firms handling farm supplies, and (3) the example set by cooperative-marketing enterprises in proving that farmers could together solve their economic problems. In the following four chapters we shall show how farmers fashioned purchasing cooperatives to reduce their costs of farming, in a manner similar to the way in which they had formed marketing cooperatives to reduce their costs of marketing.

Chapter XVII

THE NEW GROWTH IN COOPERATIVE
FARM SUPPLY PURCHASING

The incentive and opportunity for cooperative farm supply purchasing was greatly increased with the spread of intensive farming after 1896 which required much larger expenditures by farmers for supplies and equipment. During the next quarter century cooperative farm supply purchasing was to gain a strong foothold. This development came from two directions: (1) the expansion of informal buying groups into local farm supply purchasing associations, and (2) the growth in importance of side-line purchasing operations of cooperative marketing associations.

The Development of Independent Purchasing Associations

As shown in Chapter I, it was not uncommon for farmers to pool their buying power before the Civil War. The Grange and Farmers' Alliance movements of the 1870's and 1880's kept group buying alive and further developed it. Such activity began to grow again in the early years of this century with the reactivation of the Grange and after 1902 it was fostered by the Farmers' Union, the American Society of Equity, the Missouri Farmers Association, and like organizations. Many farm clubs, not related to a farmers' organization, also carried on group buying as a major activity from about 1910 on. The early county agents also found group buying popular with farmers and assisted it through farm clubs or county Farm bureaus. By 1920 the practice was widespread throughout the nation, as evidenced by cooperative publications.[1]

These local buying groups generally obtained their supplies from wholesale dealers in nearby cities, often with the assistance of state agents of the Grange, Farmers' Union, or other farm organization. Most of the local groups simply assembled orders for a car of coal, feed, fertilizer, lumber, or other supply used in bulk quantities and then arranged for its division among the individual purchasers at the local point. Payment was made either in advance or at time of delivery. The whole arrangement was a neighborhood enterprise designed to save a little money by working together. In this way farmers obtained experience in the art of cooperative business and learned that cooperation paid in savings obtainable. These operations also engendered competition in the local communities, for they taught local merchants that farmers would take cooperative action in self-defense should prices charged be too high or services unsatisfactory.

The greatest weakness of the buying groups was their impermanence and the irregularity of their service. They often found it difficult to procure supplies of satisfactory quality from wholesale dealers who preferred to sell to established local merchants who provided regular service and priced goods at a margin over costs. As the buying groups operated on a cost-of-service basis, wholesale dealers were afraid that they would lose their regular outlets if buying groups took over the local business.

It gradually became clear to farmers that group buying, while helpful, was not the final answer to their supply purchasing problem. They found from experience that an effective supply service could only be performed with a warehouse and someone to buy and handle the supplies required. The logic of selling at market prices and returning savings in patronage refunds also gradually became apparent since this would enable them to obtain supplies more readily from wholesale sources. This method of operation also provided a purchasing incentive to farmers while making possible the accumulation of funds for working capital and facilities.

In time, many of the informal buying groups evolved into local supply purchasing associations, although group buying continued to be an important method of cooperative purchasing in many states as late as the 1930's[2]. The transition from group buying to warehouse operation was relatively easy for a warehouse could usually be rented at little cost and only a minimum stock of supplies was needed since most bulk supplies could be purchased on the basis of advance orders and delivery could be made at the car door. A small amount of capital, that could be built up from savings, was generally ample to stock required merchandise and pay for the part-time services of someone to attend the warehouse.

The first local purchasing associations. As late as 1910 there were few local farm supply purchasing associations operating with a manager and place of business on a year-round basis. However, this type of cooperative association was to gain a foothold in the years from 1910 to 1920. During this period farmers had to learn from experience that cooperative stores handling general merchandise would not serve their needs as a source of supplies needed in farming operations. Although many cooperative stores were formed, often under the auspices of general farm organizations, their record of performance and survival was poor. On the other hand, farmers' experience in buying basic farm supplies cooperatively through car-door groups or through simple warehouse associations was generally good. As Clarence Poe summed it up: "Cooperative buying is good; cooperative merchandising may or may not be." He went on to say:

> There is one fact that we would emphasize, and that is that buying ordinary groceries and dry goods is nowhere the big and significant form of cooperation to which our farmers must give attention. Consequently, if you and a group of neighbors buy a little stock of calico, plug tobacco, western side meat, and granulated sugar, and hire a manager to sit down and wait for customers, don't fool yourself into thinking you have then started the best form of cooperation.

Poe emphasized his views by saying:

> To make my position perfectly clear, I think I ought to repeat that I believe every farmer should participate in cooperative buying, but I should not say at all that every farmer should participate in cooperative merchandising. Ordering together certain definite supplies you need in farm work—this may be a very different proposition from buying a miscellaneous assortment of goods and hiring a man to sell them to a miscellaneous body of people...In any case, farmers should join together to buy their fertilizers, feedstuffs and machinery, whether bought through a local merchant or through a distant dealer.[3]

While English and European experience was widely cited in the early 1900's to promote cooperative stores on the Rochdale pattern, such experience was also drawn on to promote specialized farm supply purchasing associations. In England such organizations had long been known as "requirements societies" in view of the fact that they were set up to provide farmers with supplies required in farm production operations. However, few Americans knew of the English and European supply societies before 1908 when C. R. Fay's book, *Cooperation at Home and Abroad,* attracted the attention of influential farm leaders. This was the year when the Country Life Commission was calling attention to the need of American farmers for cooperation in both buying and selling. Fay favored cooperative stores for purchasing consumers goods for both town and rural people but he did not think them so essential for farmers as supply associations. He said:

> The economies of the cooperative supply of the materials of agriculture are parallel with the economies of the town store ... It happens indeed in some cases that the agricultural supply society deals in general provisions as well as in raw materials, but this department is always a later adjunct, never the *raison d'être*. Whereas the town store represents for its members the sum total of cooperation, the agricultural society, whatever it may supply, is but one point, generally the starting point, in a series of cooperations in the direction of production and sale.

Fay made a clear distinction between producers and consumers cooperation. He classified cooperative stores, whether urban or rural, as consumers' societies and farm supply and marketing cooperatives as producers' societies.[4]

G. Harold Powell's book, *Cooperation in Agriculture* (1913), also did much to gain recognition for cooperative farm supply purchasing as being of equal importance with cooperative marketing. Powell opened a chapter devoted to "Cooperation in the Purchasing of Supplies" with this sentence: "One of the most important functions of a cooperative is to purchase the supplies used on the farm and in the handling and marketing of the crops." He held that a supply company could be formed either as a department of a cooperative marketing association or "as a separate cooperative corporation." However formed, he maintained that "a well-managed supply company" should be able to furnish fertilizers, coal, lumber, nails, twine, spraying materials, tools, and machinery at a lower cost than the farmer pays when he buys them from the local merchant at the prevailing retail prices." Powell gave his support to the sale of supplies at regular retail prices, with return of savings in patronage refunds, rather than on a cost-of-service basis. He said:

> It protects the local dealers against ruinous price-cutting which they must do if the cooperative association sells the supplies at cost; it protects the wholesale dealers and manufacturers who are more likely to give favorable quotations when they know that their goods will not be sold at less than the prevailing retail prices; it tends to increase the membership among the non-members who learn of the dividends received by their neighbors; and the dividend at the end of the year has a peculiarly favorable psychological influence on the cooperative members which does not occur when the equivalent of the dividend is distributed over the purchases throughout the year ..."[5]

When Powell wrote his book there were few separately incorporated farm-supply cooperatives. An example was the Fruit Growers Supply Company operated in conjunction with the California Fruit Growers

Exchange which Powell then managed. This company, to be described in Chapter XVIII, was used as an example of what could be accomplished.

One of the first to recognize the need for local farm-supply purchasing associations was Alexander Cance, professor at the College of Agriculture of the University of Massachusetts. Cance, as an informed student of cooperatives, was aware of the importance of farmers' cooperative supply buying in Europe and the British Isles, and it was obvious to him that many of the informal buying groups common in New England could well expand to become cooperative farm-supply purchasing associations, or exchanges—as the associations were then called in New England. His thinking was congenial to Herbert Myrick, Editor of the *New England Homestead*, an advocate on all forms of agricultural cooperation, and largely through Myrick's efforts Massachusetts enacted a law in 1913 which authorized the formation and operation of "agricultural, dairying, or mercantile" businesses on the cooperative plan. With this law for support, the Massachusetts State College, through its embryonic Extension Service, was in position to give encouragement to the formation of cooperative organizations. As a foundation for this work the College issued an Extension Service Bulletin in 1914, prepared by Cance which, as we shall see in Chapter XIX, was to have a pronounced influence on the development of cooperative purchasing institutions in New England.[6]

From its establishment in 1913, the Office of Markets and Rural Organization of the U.S.D.A. gave significant encouragement to the organization of local purchasing cooperatives. In the 1914 *Yearbook*, Thomas Nixon Carver, then associated with the Office, pointed out in an article on "The Organization of a Rural Community" that there were three methods of providing farm supplies cooperatively: (1) joint order with delivery from the railroad car, (2) joint order plus a warehouse, and (3) cooperative store. He advocated beginning with the joint order method and then after experience was gained, adding a warehouse, should this be desirable. The operation of a store was "only to be undertaken after the most careful consideration on the basis of actual experience."

The first comprehensive statement of the U. S. Department of Agriculture on cooperative purchasing was made in an article on "The Cooperative Purchasing of Farm Supplies," by C. E. Bassett, Specialist on Cooperative Organization of the Office of Markets and Rural Organization. This article, issued as a 1915 *Yearbook* separate, brought nation-wide attention to the subject. Bassett began his article with this sentence, "A careful examination of the methods of a large manufacturing establishment shows that the success is due largely to the ability to buy its raw material at the lowest prices ..." He then went on to say, "The average individual farmer is a small manufacturer, working with the forces of nature to produce certain farm products." It followed logically that cooperative purchasing was to be recommended as a method for reducing farm production costs.

Bassett favored the use of a joint buying group—which "handles no money . . . , extends no credit, and orders no goods except for cash in the bank" as the "safest and most economical" purchasing plan. However, he recognized that such groups should acquire warehouses when the business grew large enough to warrant it. In such cases he favored selling supplies at regular retail prices and dividing savings according to patronage at the end of the year. But he urged caution in moving forward. "As the child learns to walk before it runs, so a community should be satisfied to begin working together in the simplest ways and should undertake more elaborate plans only as their cooperative strength and confidence is developed" (p. 82).

Bassett was skeptical with regard to cooperative stores as farm-supply handling agencies. He said: "Attempts of consumers, both rural and urban, to establish cooperative stores have been quite common in this country for many years, and in a small proportion of cases they have met with success . . . They should be attempted only after a most careful survey of local conditions and then only when sufficient capital and high-grade management are available" (pp. 80-81).

When Bassett wrote this article cooperative stores were being promoted vigorously in most parts of the country and many believed that this form of cooperation should be encouraged by the Office of Markets and Rural Organization. This pressure led the Office to make in 1915 a "disinterested survey" of about 60 representative cooperative stores to provide guidance to stores in existence "or those that might be formed." This study did not examine these stores as supply purchasing organizations for farmers. Rather, it analyzed them from the standpoint of their business efficiency. The general conclusion reached was that "the majority of the cooperative stores established are unsuccessful in achieving their main object—saving on purchases to members and a reduction in the cost of living."[7]

To help the cooperative stores improve their management efficiency, a separate bulletin was issued.[8] This bulletin gave attention to the improvement of cooperative store statements, reports, and operating records—an area of weakness for all types of cooperative associations at this time.

It cannot be said that public agencies, both federal and state, did not endeavor to assist the cooperative store drive at this time. While they were sympathetic with cooperative store objectives, they found that their success was dependent upon conditions beyond their control.[9]

During the years from 1915 to 1920 farmers gradually lost confidence in cooperative stores and increasingly gained confidence in farm supply purchasing through group buying, specialized purchasing associations, or through side-line operations of cooperative marketing associations.[10] There was one good result from the struggle to make a success of the cooperative stores. Farmers learned a great deal about the importance of management and business efficiency through the operation of cooperative stores. They also found out that more specialized buying organizations were needed to help them as farm operators. The lessons learned cleared the way for the development of strong independent farm-supply purchasing associations during the next decade.

The Growth of Cooperative Side-line Purchasing Operations

While independent farm supply purchasing cooperatives were slowly developing, cooperative purchasing began to grow as a side-line operation of cooperative marketing associations. The term "side line" implies that it was not considered the principal activity of a marketing cooperative but something that could be carried on along with the regular business. Even before 1896 some cooperative marketing associations engaged also in cooperative purchasing but up to that time such business was of little significance. In the years from 1896 to 1920 side-line purchasing was to become of major importance and have a significant influence on both cooperative marketing and cooperative purchasing. It first became important with fruit marketing cooperatives.

Side-line operations of fruit marketing cooperatives. Most of the early fruit marketing cooperatives described in Chapter IV found it essential to purchase packinghouse materials required for their marketing operations. As they gained experience in purchasing packinghouse supplies they extended this service to growers on fertilizers, insecticides, and other orchard supplies. Conditions were favorable to success in handling such items. The members were located near each other and they had common needs for substantial quantities of specific supplies.

Moreover, the fruit growers as a group were intelligent and responsible farmers. Their considerable investments in orchards gave them a business outlook and made them quick to see the advantages of group purchasing. They recognized the importance of having supplies available when needed and were thus willing to place orders in advance to enable their associations to make favorable buying arrangements. Cooperative purchasing was also favored in the fruit marketing associations by the fact that many employed marketing contracts which welded the growers into a cohesive unit for purchasing as well as marketing. From the beginning, the supply operations proved successful. It was found that substantial orders could be assembled easily for supplies required in bulk quantities which could be obtained at greatly reduced prices. Since the cost of supplies could be charged against amounts due growers for products marketed this tended to integrate marketing and purchasing operations.[11]

Many of the local citrus associations in California had carried on purchasing operations from the time of their formation. By 1897 such purchasing had grown to such an amount that the Southern California Fruit Exchange was asked to provide a purchasing service to meet the needs of the local associations. How this developed into a major farm supply purchasing association is explained in Chapter XVIII.

The deciduous fruit growers in California followed the lead of the citrus growers and handled supplies as a matter of course. As this volume grew, the California Fruit Exchange established a supply department in 1902 which steadily grew in importance over the years.

One of the pioneer fruit marketing associations to make an outstanding success in cooperative purchasing was the Grand Junction (Colorado) Fruit Growers Association which began to handle supplies upon its organization in 1891. In fact, the supply operations enabled this organization to establish itself. Will Payne quoted one of the original incorporators as follows in the *Saturday Evening Post* of July 16, 1910: "On this matter of supplies, however, we were successful from the start, saving money by cooperative buying."

Most of the major fruit marketing associations formed in the early 1900's also handled packinghouse and grower supplies. For example, the Apple Growers Union of Hood River, Oregon, undertook to handle supplies after its formation in 1902 and its success in this operation spread the practice to fruit-marketing associations throughout the Pacific Northwest.

The fruit and vegetable marketing associations set up in the eastern states also found it desirable to handle packinghouse and growers' supplies. The Monmouth County Farmers Exchange in New Jersey, formed in 1908, had its own fertilizer mixing plant, and for many years distributed over $100,000 worth of "no filler" fertilizer annually. It claimed that savings on fertilizer amounted to $3.00 per ton.

As early as 1910, G. Harold Powell said in an article in the *U.S.D.A. Yearbook of Agriculture*, "The cooperative method has brought about large economies in the purchase of supplies, in the cost of preparing the fruit for shipment, and in the charges for distribution and sale." He maintained that there should be "a division for the purchase, sale or manufacture of supplies of every kind used in the production, packing, handling, shipping and marketing of the crop" in every cooperative association.[12]

The first national survey of agricultural-cooperative associations, made during the years 1914-1916, found that "box shook, paper, nails, spray materials and general growers' supplies" were being handled by practically all of the fruit-marketing associations which then numbered 871. The report on this survey pointed out that the "handling of supplies has been found a profitable business to both the company and the grower, and that when once begun, the practice is seldom discontinued."[13]

Farmers' elevator side-line development. The success of the well-known Rockwell Cooperative Society in handling coal as a side-line activity, reported in Chapter IV, encouraged other farmers' elevator associations to follow its lead with the result that there were scores of farmers' elevators providing a side-line purchasing service by 1900. From this time on it was common for newly-formed farmers' elevators to take such names as "Farmers' Grain and Coal Company" or "Farmers' Grain and Supply Company." By 1903, when the farmers' elevator movement entered its period of rapid expansion, the handling of coal and other side lines was considered a natural function.

There is little information available on this early period of elevator side-line development. As the problem of getting an elevator started consumed most of the energies of the sponsoring farmers it is probable that side lines were not energetically promoted until the marketing operations were fairly well established.

The farmers' elevators undertook to handle supplies as a side line for various reasons. In general, high prices charged for supplies by private concerns forced them to find out if savings could be derived by joint buying. In some cases, competing private elevators handled side lines and it was essential that the farmers' elevator offer the same type of service. As side-line supply business was seldom looked upon as being of major importance, it grew up quietly in the shadow of the grain marketing operations. It was a commonsense activity since the location of the elevators alongside the railroad made them suitable depots for handling bulk supplies at little cost. As the elevators began to feel their power they reached out for other services to perform and as one elevator after another demonstrated that supplies could be advantageously handled, the movement spread from community to community. Coal was the first item to attract attention, as farmers required it in substantial amounts. As experience was gained from handling coal, they naturally took on other lines where there was a large operating margin. A main incentive for expansion came from the elevator managers who were quick to see that a good supply service would attract grain trade, lower overhead costs, and increase savings so as to permit payment of higher salaries for their services.

In the beginning, the farmers' elevators restricted their operations to farm supplies used in bulk quantities. They were not interested in handling a supply item unless it could be done with little additional help or capital expense. Coal was an item that met this requirement, for farmers could shovel the coal from the car. Moreover, the farmers were not anxious to stir up general business opposition. They knew that only a few merchants would complain if they handled coal or some other similar bulk item, while all the merchants in towns would resent it if they handled a general line of merchandise. Moreover, the elevators were not handicapped in handling bulk supplies direct from the car at the elevator siding. On the other hand, they were in no position to handle general merchandise which would require a location uptown and trained salespeople. Furthermore, while substantial savings could be made on items purchased in quantity where little expense for handling was required, it was feared that this advantage would be largely frittered away if an attempt were made to handle a general line of merchandise. On the whole, farmers' experience in cooperative merchandising had been discouraging. Many knew from participation that cooperative stores could suffer heavy losses from inability to control inventory or from over-extension of credit without good management.

In fact, the marked success of the farmers' elevators in establishing themselves was largely due to their singleness of purpose. They were set up to handle grain, and supply activities were undertaken only if this benefited the main purpose. Thus, no side lines were handled unless there was assurance that this service could be performed for the advantage of the enterprise as a whole.

In time, as savings were realized on a few supplies, farmers demanded

service on other supplies. As a result, the number of side-line items began
to expand until many elevators were performing a rather complete supply-
purchasing service for their patrons. As this business grew in volume it
became necessary to carry some merchandise in stock and coal sheds and
stores to accommodate it were erected alongside the elevators.

Prior to 1902, elevators had sprung up more or less spontaneously to
meet local farmers' demands as there were no central organizations to
direct and promote their development. This situation changed as the
state grain dealers' associations came into being, for they provided organizing centers for the elevators. From the first, these associations
encouraged the elevators to handle coal and other bulk supplies. They
assisted side-line purchasing in several ways. In starting a new elevator,
model articles of incorporation and by-laws were drafted which made the
handling of supplies an expressed objective. These associations also
brought together the officers and managers of various elevators and this
popularized the idea of supply buying through exchange of experience.
Such matters as desirable side lines to handle, best sources of supplies,
and preferred methods for handling side lines were discussed at these
conferences. The state farmers' grain dealers' associations thus did much
to spread the side-line gospel and get it effectively implanted in sound
operating procedures.

With the establishment of the *American Cooperative Journal* in 1905
to promote the interests of farmers' elevators, information was increasingly
disseminated on side-line experience, and this further encouraged the
practice. Then as the importance of supply operations grew, industrial
concerns began to cater for the side-line business by advertising in the
Journal, and this emphasized the fact that side-line business was important.

Nothing did more to impress farmers with the value of side-line business
than the Interstate Commerce Commission's investigation in 1906 of
alleged abuses in grain buying and shipping, in compliance wth a Senate
resoluton sponsored by Senator Robert LaFollette. Evidence presented
in the hearings called attention to the achievements of farmers' elevators
in getting higher prices for the farmer on his grain and lower prices on his
farm supplies. The secretary of the Iowa Farmers' Grain Dealers Association, in a widely distributed pamphlet, maintained that the investigation
had proved "that a farmers' elevator inevitably raises the price of grain
from 2 to 6 cents per bushel and lowers the price of coal from 50 cents
to $2.00 per ton." In view of such striking claims, it is not surprising
that most of the cooperative elevators as they were formed undertook to
handle coal and, in some cases, lumber and other supplies.[14]

Thus, as farmers' elevators established themselves in their marketing operations they became more interested in side lines. As they gained experience and power they naturally expanded the number of side lines handled. Moreover, as they began to employ better managers on a year-round basis, the desirability of reducing overhead costs by handling supplies during slack periods of the year became obvious. At this time farmers' elevators were confronted by a serious competitive situation owing to the animosity of the grain commission firms. Farmers' elevators were compelled to do anything that would help them lower costs and extend the range of their services so as to strengthen membership support.

By 1909 the desirability of handling side lines by farmers' elevators had become well established throughout the Grain Belt. In that year B. H. Hibbard noted in an article in the *Encyclopaedia of Agriculture* that two-thirds of the cooperative elevators in the United States were handling coal at a saving to the consumer of from 50 cents to $1.50 per ton, while many were handling twine, oil, tile, feed, seeds, lumber, and similar commodities. The farmers, through their elevators, had won a hard-earned victory over the elevator combines, and they were convinced that joint buying through their elevators could be just as effective in meeting the power of the large industrial concerns which largely dominated the coal, farm machinery, and other industries in the farm supply field.

About this time the importance of side-line elevator business attracted national notice when Will Payne reported in the *Saturday Evening Post* of March 12, 1910, that side-line purchasing was a significant feature of the rising cooperative elevator movement. He said: "Practically all of the farmers' companies sell coal as well as buy grain, some of them selling lumber, farm implements and binder twine, while a few handle salt and flour." Payne found that the regular grain dealers did not take kindly to these purchasing activities but he observed that the unfriendliness of local merchants was dying down, since the farmer companies "confined their merchandising to a very few staple articles." He observed that it was even becoming appreciated by them that a farmers' company attracted "more grain to a town and more business for the local merchants."

Payne also found that the farmers' elevators were shifting to the practice of selling supplies at market prices. Since most of the elevators were then organized on a stock-company basis this meant that savings were being added to general revenue and returned to farmers in accordance with their shareholdings. Payne pointed out that the practice of paying patronage dividends was just coming into use and that even when patronage refunds were made they were paid on the amount of grain delivered and did not reflect savings on supplies. As Payne said: "In selling coal, lumber . . . the companies operate like any strictly private concern, simply selling the merchandise at a certain price to members and non-members alike. There is no attempt to extend the cooperative principle by dividing profits . . ."

As long as farmers' elevators were organized on a capital-stock basis the large savings made on grain and supply operations went to stockholders in accordance with their shareholdings. This led to a scandalous situation in the years from 1909 to 1911 when promoters set up several manufacturing and wholesaling companies to supply farmers' elevators with farm machinery, fence, tile, coal, and other supplies. These concerns exploited the spirit of money making that was beginning to infest the farmers' elevators. Huge dividends were promised to investors and even some of the officials in the state farmers' grain dealers associations were swept up in the contagion. An advertisement for one of these ventures in the *Cooperative Journal* aroused vigorous criticism causing the Farmers Grain Dealers Association of Illinois to pass a resolution at its 1910 convention making it clear that the advertised company did not have its endorsement. This "diabolical" development was condemned in Iowa by such stalwarts in the farmers' elevator movement as Reuben Holman of the Rockwell Society and, in 1911, the Iowa Association was reorganized to obtain directors not connected with the manufacturing concerns.[15]

As none of these enterprises was soundly conceived or efficiently managed all soon failed with heavy losses to the investors. Although their failure gave cooperative manufacturing and wholesaling a black eye, it taught farmers a needed lesson—that no effective cooperative organization could be formed on a capital-stock basis. Those who were interested in farmers' elevators as agencies to serve farmers saw that they must reorganize on a basis that would return savings to farmers in accordance with their patronage—both on grain and supplies. Thus, this episode had a beneficial effect and cleared the air for real progress.

The manufacturing scandals focused attention on a situation that had been building up for a long time. It made clear that influential farmers and local businessmen had gained a large degree of control over many farmers' elevators because of their capital-stock form of organization so that there was little difference in character between them and those owned by general investors. This perversion of the aims of the farmers' elevator movement was not accepted without protest by the great mass of farmers who had contributed to their establishment and this led to a growing demand that the farmers' elevators be reorganized to make them more truly cooperative. It had become obvious that the return of savings in the form of patronage refunds was the only sound basis for cooperative operation. With the encouragement of the farmers' grain dealers associations, a number of farmers' elevators revised their by-laws to make this possible. However, it was recognized that no permanent solution to this problem could come without state laws to provide for the incorporation of cooperative associations along Rochdale lines. As a writer in the *American Cooperative Journal* (October, 1911) biblically expressed this: "Ye cannot put new wine in old bottles!" He went on to say: "The ordinary corporation law contains elements that will explode any cooperative institution." He advocated a cooperative law that would permit voting "on a manhood basis" and distribution of savings "according to services rendered."

This steadily mounting pressure from farmers led to a drive for state cooperative laws which resulted in enactment of Rochdale-type laws in most of the grain-producing states during the years from 1911 to 1916. These laws not only revitalized the cooperative elevator movement; they also gave great encouragement to the side-line purchasing operations of the cooperative elevators, for the payment of patronage refunds provided farmers with a direct incentive to buy their supplies from their elevator associations.

This changeover from stock company to real cooperative form of organization did not come all at once, for many stockholders were loath to give up their proprietary interest in the earnings of the elevators. However, as new elevators were organized and old elevators were reorganized under the new laws, the patronage refund practice became established. By 1920, the majority of farmers' elevators were paying patronage refunds.

This change was facilitated by the marked improvement in bookkeeping and business practices, sponsored by the Office of Markets and Rural Organization and the agricultural colleges, which came with the reorganization of the farmers' elevators. Prior to 1916, few farmers' elevators had maintained patronage records. In that year the Office of Markets and Rural Organization issued a bulletin which said: "The principle of patronage dividends has been understood by students of cooperation from the beginning, but has only lately been making itself felt among the rank and file of the great body of intending cooperators of America." This bulletin pointed out that it was not difficult to set up records to "show the total business transacted between the elevator and each of its patrons." It pointed out that the dividend could be determined by "allotting a certain amount per bushel to the transaction in grain and a certain percentage of the value of the goods sold to the merchandise transaction."[16] With improved records it was possible for the elevators to show savings separately for grain and side-line operations, and this gave emphasis to the value of farm supply purchasing.

Another factor that stimulated the spread of the patronage refund method of distributing savings was the adoption of the 16th Amendment in 1913 which provided for federal income taxes. Under the early income tax laws and regulations of the Bureau of Internal Revenue, farmers' marketing cooperatives were largely exempted from federal income taxes if they distributed savings in accordance with patronage. Although the exemption did not immediately apply to savings on supplies handled, it encouraged farmers' elevators to get their marketing operations on a patronage refund basis.[17] This fact was noted by Black and Robotka in 1919: "The provision of the federal income tax law exempting patronage dividends from taxation is proving a great benefit ... and many [grain] companies have recently amended their constitutions so as to limit stock dividends."[18]

Side-line purchasing by other marketing cooperatives. Although other types of cooperative marketing associations engaged in supply purchasing, this practice did not generally fit in so well with their marketing operations. Jesness and Kerr in the first national survey of cooperative associations found that supplies were often handled by cotton warehouses, creameries, and livestock shipping associations but not as commonly as by farmers' elevators and fruit marketing associations.[19] They pointed out that the handling of supplies may not interfere very much with the work of the elevator manager but "it would be an unsatisfactory arrangement to have the butter maker divide his energies between making butter, or loading lumber, or shoveling coal." They noted that the elevators were located along the railroads which made it convenient for them to unload supplies, while creameries were often located at some distance from the railroad and lacked proper storage space for supply handling (p. 31). Likewise, they found that the livestock shipping associations were not so favorably located to handle side lines, as few had permanent places of business suitable for such work, and there was generally an elevator in the neighborhood already performing such service. As a matter of fact, many of the livestock shipping associations were themselves side-line enterprises of the cooperative elevators. Thus, prior to 1920, the total extent of side lines handled by cooperative marketing associations, other than by the fruit and grain associations, was not extensive.

The Midwest Farm Supply Purchasing Federations

With the expansion of cooperative purchasing in the Midwest through buying clubs, stores, and side-line departments of farmers' elevators and other cooperative marketing enterprises, there came a corollary interest in developing organizations to provide these agencies with wholesale services. This was manifested in the ill-fated effort to set up farm supply manufacturing enterprises to serve the supply needs of the farmers' elevators.

The first wholesale associations to establish themselves grew out of the purchasing agencies started by the Nebraska and Kansas state farmers' unions in 1914. The Farmers Union State Exchange of Nebraska, the outstanding illustration of this trend, deserves a brief description.

This organization got its start in 1914 with the formation of a purchasing department in the newly established Farmers Educational and Cooperative State Union of Nebraska. At first its business was done largely on a mail-order basis with individual members or secretaries of farmers' union locals. As volume rapidly grew, with the development of local farmers' union stores, farm supply warehouses, elevators, and livestock shipping associations, the purchasing department was separately incorporated (1916) "so as to get away from unlimited liability." However, the character of the business did not change, as all of the stock was held by the state farmers' union and the directors of the union constituted its board of directors. A thorough reorganization in 1919 set up the exchange as a cooperative association "on its own feet" with an independent board of directors.[20]

The Farmers' Union State Exchange was organized as a state-wide association with individual stockholders, as the Nebraska law did not then permit the formation of a federation of local cooperatives. With the amendment of the law shortly afterwards to permit cooperatives to hold shares in other cooperatives, the Exchange took on the character of a federation of cooperatives with farmers' union stores, purchasing associations, cooperative elevators, and livestock shipping associations as stockholder members.

The business operations of the Exchange proved successful from the beginning, with volume steadily growing from $60,000 in 1914 to $320,000 in 1915; to $1,000,000 in 1916; to $1,800,000 in 1917; to $2,720,000 in 1918; and to $3,000,000 in 1919. The bulk of this business was comprised of mill feeds, flour, tankage, coal, fence posts, wire, binding twine, apples and other commodities that could be handled on a car-lot basis.[21]

The Exchange sold supplies at cost plus a small margin to cover expenses and provide capital for expansion. By March 31, 1919, its capital stock, reserves, and surplus amounted to $179,000. When it was reorganized as a separate corporation to take over the business developed by the state union on June 30, 1919, it sold stock amounting to $715,375.

Just as the organization was finding itself, the deflation of 1920 wiped out most of the gains made. The fact that the Exchange weathered this period and re-established itself shows how strongly the cooperative idea was implanted in this area.[22]

Summary

In this chapter we have shown how farm supply purchasing co-operation achieved a high degree of independent status during the years from 1896 to 1920. In this period one large-scale farm supply purchasing association came into being and demonstrated what could be done. The evolution of this organization will be examined in the following chapter.

Chapter XVIII

THE FIRST REGIONAL FARM SUPPLY PURCHASING ASSOCIATION—

The Fruit Growers Supply Company

The first significant regional purchasing association—the Fruit Growers Supply Company—was organized to serve as the purchasing arm for the citrus associations affiliated with the California Fruit Growers Exchange. The character of this relationship had a direct influence on the way in which the Fruit Growers Supply Company was developed.

Early Purchasing Operations

One of the stated purposes of the Southern California Fruit Exchange, when it was formed in 1895, was the handling of packinghouse and grower supplies. It was apparently thought that the Exchange would engage not only in marketing but in handling packinghouse materials, fertilizers, and other merchandise. Moreover, it was contemplated that the association might "acquire factories for the manufacture of boxes" or otherwise engage in general manufacturing operations.[1]

Although the Southern California Fruit Exchange gave its first attention to the development of its fruit marketing operations, it was soon called upon to assist member associations on their supply buying problems. As early as April 7, 1897, the board of directors gave consideration to a resolution from the San Diego County Exchange which expressed the view that the Exchange "should immediately take up the matter of securing fruit boxes from Maine by water." In offering this suggestion the San Diego Exchange said: "We understand Coast factories have entered into a combination and put the price of boxes up two or three points. We believe there is no better way to break the combination than a move like this. . . ." In compliance with this recommendation the board of directors instructed its secretary to obtain information from box manufacturers in Maine, and on June 23, 1897, the secretary was appointed a committee of one to carry on negotiations for the procurement of boxes from the Atlantic Seaboard. At this same meeting the Exchange was requested by the Ontario Fruit Exchange to take "immediate steps to secure commercial and other fertilizers for the use of exchange members at wholesale rates . . . and to ascertain what special benefits to each member can be obtained in the matter of fumigating."

During the next 10 years—pending the formation of the Fruit Growers Supply Company—the exchange system was in continual conflict with the box shook manufacturing interests and, as early as 1900, contracts were made to provide a supply of box shook to meet the needs of its member associations. Moreover, on many occasions during this period the board of directors of the Southern California Fruit Exchange or its successor organization, the California Fruit Growers Exchange, gave consideration to the procurement of fertilizer, paper labels, and other supplies required either by its member associations or by their individual grower members. Here it is of interest that as early as 1901 the board considered the advisability of purchasing a plant for the printing of fruit wrappers. In 1902, a contract was made under which nails were obtained for the local packinghouse associations. In such early contracts the Exchange simply obtained special prices on specific supplies for any of its local associations that might wish to be served under its contracts. The Exchange assumed no responsibility as a wholesaler but simply facilitated the purchasing efforts of its local member associations.

The Formation of the Fruit Growers Supply Company

The gradual expansion of Exchange supply purchasing activities was abruptly hastened in April 1906 by an "adventitious" event—the San Francisco fire. The great demand for lumber required in the rebuilding of San Francisco gave the well-organized lumber interests an opportunity to greatly advance their prices for all lumber products—including box shook. For many years box shook prices had averaged around 13½ cents a box. The new price fixed by the major producers of box shook—who were joined together in a common sales agency—was 21 cents a box, and purchasers were required to buy all their supplies from members of the agency if they were to be served even at this price. While some price increase would have been willingly accepted, in view of the abnormal situation, the extent of this advance was considered extortionate, for it represented an increase in packing costs for Exchange shippers alone of over $500,000.

As could be expected, this ultimatum caused intense resentment among the citrus growers in view of their extensive box shook needs. As a result, there quickly arose a demand for counter-organization strong enough to meet the power of the organized box shook manufacturing interests, and naturally growers looked to the California Fruit Growers Exchange as the one agency that could bring relief from this intolerable condition. Confronted with this demand the Exchange immediately attempted to find sources of supply which were not controlled by the box shook group and it was found possible to make contracts so as to meet most of the needs of its member associations for the current season without paying the prices asked by the so-called box shook trust.

Experience during the 1906-1907 season showed clearly that the Exchange would need to have its own lumber resources and box shook mills if it were to afford any permanent protection to the local packinghouse associations. This raised a question as to how the Exchange could best organize itself to meet this need, for a large amount of capital would be required for the program contemplated; whereas, it had been possible to carry on the marketing operations of the Exchange with practically no invested capital. This problem also raised the question as to how manufacturing operations could be handled so as not to upset the essential marketing activities of the Exchange. These questions were eventually settled through the decision to form a separate sister corporation which could administer all supply purchasing activities for the member associations of the exchange system. The natural consequence of federation for marketing was thus federation for purchasing.

In launching the new company in 1907, the Exchange first negotiated agreements with the local associations whereby they agreed to permit the Exchange to deduct 3 cents from the sales proceeds of each box of fruit shipped through the Exchange for a period of five years, and to apply the funds so created toward purchase of capital stock in the Supply Company. This ingenious plan thus provided for a fund of fixed capital contributed in accordance with the use made by the local associations of the Supply Company, since each association was subject to an assessment for capital in accordance with its estimated interest in the new enterprise. This automatic method of financing on a pro rata basis of marketings was unique at this time. It enabled the Supply

Company to get started during the hard times of 1907 and 1908 when the direct sale of stock would have been impossible.

In organizing the Supply Company as a distinct corporation, it was appreciated that some arrangement was necessary to insure that it would develop its operations in harmony with the marketing service of the Exchange. Such necessary coordination was achieved by having the directors of the California Fruit Growers Exchange serve also as the directors of the Supply Company, an arrangement designed to insure that the primary concern of the directorate would always be "the destiny of the marketing organization."[2]

The plan of organization of the Supply Company differed in one important respect from that of the Exchange in that it was set up as a purchasing federation for the local packinghouse associations without the use of the district exchanges as intermediary purchasing agencies.[3]

While the Supply Company was formed primarily for the purpose of meeting the acute box shook problem, its articles of incorporation clearly show that it was conceived along much broader lines. Among other things the company was empowered "to manufacture, buy, sell and deal in supplies of every kind or nature necessary or incidental to the packing, shipping, and marketing of fruits and fruit products and all other agricultural products."[4]

Early Box Shook Manufacturing Operations

With the selection of a general manager in the late fall of 1907, the Supply Company proceeded to investigate sources of timber supply. These investigations disclosed that there was much good timber land in California owned by small box shook manufacturing companies—not members of the box shook selling agency—who could take care of the needs of the Exchange members if they were promptly rendered financial assistance. In view of this situation the Supply Company decided to provide financial assistance to these smaller box shook manufacturing enterprises and postpone entry into the box shook manufacturing field. This was looked upon as a temporary measure for the board was determined that timber land should be purchased—even if not operated— "in order to make our position in the future secure." In accord with this general policy, the manager of the Supply Company proceeded vigorously to line up supplies of box shook through negotiating agreements with various small mills by which the Exchange would receive specified quantities of box shook in return for direct loans. In doing so the Supply

Company took the significant position that the funds advanced were "not to be regarded in any other light than as investments," in view of the "contingency of eventual ownership." By assisting several small mills through loans, the Supply Company was able to provide its local member associations with an adequate supply of box shook during the 1907-1908 season at a price of approximately 13½ cents per box.

Confronted by this situation the box shook combination reduced its prices on box shook to 11 cents in an attempt to break down the solidarity of associations federated in the Fruit Growers Supply Company. The struggle which followed, known in the area as the "box shook war," came to a climax in early 1908, with a clear-cut victory for the Supply Company. The blandishments offered to the members of the Supply Company proved unavailing, as the local associations realized fully that effective support to their own organization was their only means of protection. Moreover, the plan devised for financing the Supply Company had wisely given all members a financial stake in its success.

The final victory over the "box shook trust" came in 1910 when the Supply Company found it necessary to acquire full ownership of one of the mills being financed, in order to protect its investments in the enterprise. When the contingency of eventual ownership of a mill became a fact, it proved to be a very fortunate development in that the ownership of the mill immediately strengthened the bargaining position of the Supply Company in the box shook industry. Realizing that the Supply Company was now entrenched, the members of the box shook combination extended service to the Supply Company more or less on its own terms.

In taking over the mill the Supply Company made it clear that it was doing so only to safeguard the box shook needs of its members, and that it had no intention to manufacture all of its shook requirements if supplies were available at reasonable cost. Steps were immediately taken to make the mill a model low-cost plant as it was appreciated that the mill had to be organized and operated on a highly efficient business basis to perform properly this yardstick function in negotiating contracts for additional supplies.

With the acquisition of its own mill and timber properties the Supply Company was in an excellent position to determine the reasonableness of box shook prices as it could produce its own requirements if prices got out of hand. However, in negotiating contracts with box shook suppliers, the Supply Company followed a policy of allowing manufacturers a fair margin of profit, since it was realized that a policy of striving for the lowest possible price might drive out of business the small manufacturers and thus bring about a condition where supplies would need to be purchased from a more tightly concentrated industry.

At this time the Supply Company saw no advantage in acquiring more than the one mill since this was adequate to regulate competition. Moreover, at this time, the Supply Company did not have financial resources sufficient to provide for timber holdings and milling facilities adequate to supply the full shook needs of all of its member associations. In fact, the Supply Company desired to conserve its own timber holdings as far as possible for use in times of great emergency. As we shall see, this policy of insuring for future needs proved of incalculable importance when the Supply Company was forced to operate its mill at full capacity to meet the strains imposed by World War I.

Expansion of Supply Services

Although the Supply Company made the solution of the box shook problem its first consideration, service was provided almost immediately on other packinghouse materials. In his report at the end of the first year, Manager P. C. Daniels called attention to significant savings made in purchasing paper wraps and nails for the benefit of the member associations and referred to a promising investigation which had been started relative to the benefits which might be obtained through collective purchasing of fertilizer and cyanide. The annual report for the second year likewise was largely devoted to the various box shook undertakings although the local associations were urged to estimate their requirements in advance to permit "delivery of packing materials at lowest cost and expenses." The report for the third year disclosed that the company was beginning to extend its services into the field of growers' supplies. During this year such incidental items as fire equipment, building tools, gloves, and oil stoves were handled to the extent of $50,000. By this time the company had become "recognized generally as a jobber—making it possible to save money for members on sundry merchandise"—and it was declared that "the Supply Company stands ready at all times to take up and secure prices of any item of which its members may be in need."

The annual report for the fourth year (1911) indicated that volume had grown to $2,109,000. There had been a significant expansion in the sale of packinghouse materials (other than box shook) and of orchard supplies—from $75,000 the preceding year to $387,400. During this year the company had obtained 600,000 pounds of vetch seed for its members direct from Germany. On this the manager reported, "We are able to supply your requirements independent of the local markets at greatly reduced prices." One of the major activities undertaken during this year had been the development of fertilizer service and by the end of the fiscal year orders for fertilizer had totaled $166,000. Prior to this time it had been customary for dealers—who worked together under a general undertaking—to take a margin of about $6 a ton. The entry of the Supply Company into this field quickly reduced this margin by about $3 a ton to the benefit of all purchasers of fertilizer, whether members or non-members. The Supply Company also introduced the idea of sale according to plant food units, thus making possible more intelligent and economical usage.[5]

At this time the company was giving consideration to the complaints of local associations with regard to the quality of service received and the price paid for cyanide. For some years the price of potassium cyanide which was used then in large quantities as a fumigant had been maintained at 28½ cents a pound and all efforts to get lower prices had been unavailing. In 1911, the Supply Company met this situation by boycotting the American producers and by contracting with an English firm for a supply of sodium cyanide on consignment to be paid for as used. An interesting problem arose in connection with this transaction for sodium cyanide had not been used up to this time as an orchard fumigant in California. Although it was charged by the dealers that this cyanide would not work, it was successfully introduced into the market following investigational work carried on by the agricultural college at the instigation of the Supply Company. By the end of the year the new product was being successfully used and the manager of the Supply Company expressed the view that there was every reason to believe that domestic manufacturers would now be willing to deal with the Supply Company— a view that was substantiated the following year when a contract was negotiated with domestic manufacturers through which an adequate and satisfactory supply of sodium cyanide was obtained at 23 cents a pound. Since the members of the Exchange then required over one million pounds of cyanide annually this represented a direct annual saving to them of over $50,000.[6]

By the end of the fourth year the Supply Company was becoming well established. Its large volume of purchases and its ability to pay cash were bringing results in the form of contracts entered into directly with manufacturers and importers, and this made possible the virtual elimination of both wholesale and retail margins for the benefit of grower members. Moreover, the willingness of the Supply Company to enter actively into manufacturing or to make deals direct with foreign sources of supply whenever this was necessary to protect the interests of its members, was not being overlooked by the major producing firms. Moreover, handling costs were kept to a minimum by direct shipment of supplies to the local packinghouses without the use of an intermediary central warehouse. With the exception of small warehouses for the storage of fertilizer, no special facilities for handling supplies were required at the local packinghouses.

The progress being made in handling packinghouse materials (other than box shook) and orchard supplies was greatly intensified during the fifth year which closed in the fall of 1912. While there had been a decrease in the number of boxes sold due to a light crop, the sale of packinghouse materials other than box shook totaled $460,000 while sales of orchard supplies reached $575,000. This great expansion called attention to "the constantly increasing use made of the Supply Company by its members and growers." During the year fertilizer sales had grown to $318,000 while 500 tons of vetch seed had been imported "at prices much below the prevailing market." It is also of interest that the Supply Company had been giving the subject of orchard heating serious consideration with the result that 2,500 heaters had been purchased for members, a step which was to prove of almost immediate advantage.

All in all the Supply Company now was well established as a supplier of packinghouse materials and orchard supplies. The manager declared in the annual report that the company had become "a most important part of the Growers Cooperative Organization, performing for them in the purchasing of their supplies what the Exchange does for them in the marketing of their fruit. Operated as it is for the exclusive benefit of its membership, with its low cost of maintenance amounting to but 77 cents per $100 on the volume of business transacted the past season, its members are rapidly coming to realize the value of cooperation in buying as well as in selling."

The foresight of the Supply Company in providing its members with orchard heaters during 1912 was rewarded when the big January freeze in 1913 destroyed a large part of the crop; these heaters greatly reduced the loss to members. This accomplishment, however, was dwarfed by the remarkable achievement of the Supply Company in getting heating oil to its members during the freeze, an achievement which gave the Supply Company an opportunity to prove its usefulness in a dramatic way. A graphic description of this incident follows:

When the growers were in a pinch for oil to keep their orchard heaters going, that cold week in 1913, they called in the Supply Company and the Supply Company was not found wanting. It delivered the goods. The morning following the first freeze, even before the frantic appeals for oil had begun to come in, the Company had men out buying up all the oil in sight and long before night two special trains each hauled by two passenger engines with right of way over everything were speeding with the precious fluid to the aid of the growers. Eight hundred cars of oil were sent out during the freeze. Oil even went out on the back end of passenger trains. The railroads were only too glad to help save the crop. The citrus crop was their biggest business. During the entire cold spell, there were men on duty night and day at the office of the Supply Company. A regular dispatchers office was organized. The oil trains were sent out and each car was traced to the hands of the tank wagon men who delivered the oil in the groves. When the freeze was over all the oil was gone and the last that had been sent out was little better than tar. The big organization with plenty of money and power saved many a crop from the freeze that week.[7]

While the great loss in the citrus crop caused by the January freeze reduced the quantity of packinghouse materials handled during the year, there was an increase in the value of orchard supplies handled of 76.6 per cent for the year. A large part of this increase was accounted for by the heavy demand for fuel oil during January and by the subsequent demand for heaters to safeguard against the possibility of a similar disaster in the future. When the general manager made his report some 500,000 heaters had been ordered from the Supply Company for fall delivery and by the end of the next year over 1,000,000 heaters had been distributed to growers. From then on the orchard supply service of the Supply Company was considered of equal importance with the packinghouse service.

This involved a broadening of scope for the Supply Company in that box shook and other packinghouse supplies were purchased by local managers as part of the packinghouse service, while orchard supplies were purchased by the local managers only in response to the orders of individual members. Such volitionary transactions were dependent upon the satisfaction of the individual growers.

In handling orchard supplies the local associations in effect acted as the distributive agencies for the Supply Company. Members were required to transmit their orders in advance to the local association and the local association in turn forwarded them to the Supply Company. The local associations then distributed the supplies to the local growers. All collections were made by the local associations and since the local associations could deduct amounts due from proceeds due growers on fruit marketed there was no possibility of loss from bad debts. This method of operating could be carried on with the minimum of expense since no special personnel or facilities were required. Practically all the savings from such purchasing could therefore be made available to participating members.

Influence in Quality Improvement

During its formative years the Fruit Growers Supply Company had no direct means of contacting growers or local associations on their supply purchasing problems. A change in this situation occurred in 1914 when the California Fruit Growers Exchange established its field organization department to represent both the Supply Company and the Exchange in working with growers. In its work the field organization department quickly came to realize that the quality and cost of fruit produced was largely dependent upon the ability of the growers to obtain essential supplies of good quality at the lowest possible cost. The considerable expansion of orchard supplies distributed through the Supply Company in the years from 1914 to 1920 reflected the encouragement which the field service workers gave to the development of cooperative purchasing.

The role of the Supply Company as purchasing arm for the Exchange system was emphasized in 1917 when the Exchange entrusted it with the job of raising the level of fruit quality production in the state. To understand this development it is necessary to realize that for several years there had been growing among citrus growers an appreciation that the quality of citrus fruit was dependent upon "the type of trees in the orchard." This fact had been emphasized by the studies of the Bureau of Plant Industry carried on by A. D. Shammel who, since 1909, had been making tests to determine the best type of citrus trees for California conditions. These studies proved that citrus production could be increased and its quality much improved "by re-budding to improved stock." After considerable study the Exchange leaders concluded that the Supply Company was admirably designed to put these findings into practice for the benefit of the entire citrus industry and, as a result, a department of bud selection was set up within the Supply Company in May 1917 to develop a supply of tested budwood which could be made available at cost to citrus growers whether or not they were members of the Exchange system. This program carried on as joint activity with the field department of the Exchange demonstrated the interest of the Supply Company in industry betterment. Under the pattern developed, the Supply Company secured budwood from superior performance record trees and it was then distributed to cooperating propagators. This broadly conceived program could not have been made effective so rapidly except in a highly organized industry.[8]

Restriction of Supply Service

While the Supply Company was endeavoring to establish itself the member associations and, in turn, their members, had been encouraged to buy almost everything through the Supply Company. By 1913, the rapid increase in such purchases was beginning to give trouble. The general manager in his annual report for that year said:

> There appears to be an increasing tendency among the members to include in their purchases a larger number of minor articles. These minor articles are not handled in such quantities by the Supply Company as to effect a substantial saving. It would seem a wise policy to have our members restrict their purchases as far as possible to the larger and more important articles or materials that are used generally by all associations and their members. . . . The Supply Company operates as a buyer's agent and devotes its effort to securing the supplies in most common use by its members in their packing houses and orchards only, as distinguished from a shopping agency handling any and all petty purchases. *It is therefore, strongly recommended that the orders for these minor articles be confined to the minimum* (Italics added).

In response to this plea the value of such purchases declined by 60 per cent in the following year and during 1915 they were almost eliminated. By this time the Supply Company had developed a definite philosophy with regard to its proper field of service. According to the general manager:

> The Supply Company does not elbow its way into new fields; it waits until enough members demand additional service. The country is strewn with cooperation wrecks whose officers began to branch out, to go into all kinds of new lines, before the mass of members was ready to follow. . . . the Fruit Growers Supply Company is not a shopper, it is a shopper's agent. It handles practically everything that is used by the growers in common and in sufficiently large quantities to make the saving worth while. But the company does not handle personal supplies, which properly belong to the retail units and should be handled for the individual grower through the packing houses. Our trade includes only those commodities whose cheapening will reduce the cost of production and marketing.[9]

This type of business never again became important though for many years it had to be continuously discouraged.

Development of Pricing and Patronage Refund Policies

The distributive procedures of the Supply Company were very simple as long as the principal activity was procurement of box shook to meet the needs of the member associations. The entire operation could be handled as a pool with each local association paying its proportionate share of the cost of the shook obtained. In practice, the Supply Company attempted to set a price on shook purchased by the local associations that would simply cover the cost of box shook and the incidental expenses of the Supply Company.

The price, however, was set high enough to provide an adequate margin to meet costs and estimated expenses since it was appreciated that any surplus could be easily refunded to the member associations after full costs and expenses could be determined. Thus the practice of paying a patronage refund arose naturally as a means of returning overcharges.[10] The second annual report of the Supply Company shows that a refund of 3/10 of 1 per cent was paid on box shook operations in 1908-1909. The extent of such refund for 1909-1910 amounted to $17,000. The practice of sale at market prices with return of savings in patronage refunds was given further encouragement when the Supply Company became a shook manufacturer. Clearly the company could not sell its own product to its members at lower prices than those paid by the Supply Company for shook from the industry. It seemed advisable to bill all shook distributed at prevailing prices and to return any savings from manufacturing or distribution in the form of patronage dividends. Moreover, in its lumber operations, the Supply Company was forced to dispose of higher grades of lumber on the open market, since it required only the lower grades usable for shook. Any savings from such lumber operations were reflected in lower box shook procurement costs, or in patronage refunds to members.

As the Supply Company widened its operations to include other supplies, the same general procedure was followed. Each supply was handled as a separate pool and the price to local member associations was set to cover costs and incidental expenses, and any surplus was returned as a patronage refund.[11] However, as costs and expenses under this method of operation could be largely determined in advance, amounts paid as patronage refunds were negligible.

As experience was gained the disadvantage of reflecting the full benefits of group purchasing in price at time of sale became apparent. Suppliers were naturally unwilling to give the Supply Company advantageous terms which were immediately reflected in demands for price concessions throughout the industry. Moreover, this method did not provide a tangible inducement to cooperation, for the advantage in lower prices was not fully appreciated when such advantage was evidenced in small amounts at time of sale. To meet this problem the directors in 1914 authorized "the withholding of a portion of the advantageous prices secured, when found advisable, for refund to members at the close of the season."

As a result of this change in policy, patronage refunds of $48,000 were paid for the year 1913-1914. This represented an increase in such dividends of 183 per cent over the preceding year. In reporting on this matter, the general manager pointed out that such refunds had "been accumulated largely through the concessions in prices secured from manufacturers and wholesalers upon the understanding that such additional concessions would not be billed out to members in the first instance." At this time the Supply Company was still making part of its purchasing advantage available to members in the form of lower prices, and part in the form of patronage refunds.

The report for 1914-1915 shows that the policy of returning savings in the form of patronage refunds was becoming well established as the amount returned in patronage refunds had increased to $140,000 or by 195 per cent over the preceding year. This new policy was having two obvious advantages: (1) It was enabling the company to get concessions in lower prices which would have been unavailable if the company had not agreed to withhold them at the time of sale to members; and (2) it was giving member associations a more tangible measure of benefits derived from the company's operations.[12]

As the company began to return a larger share of savings in the form of patronage refunds a special problem arose in connection with the proper way of distributing the refund on orchard supplies since such purchases were made by the local associations upon the order of the individual members. Up to this time any savings of this type were generally paid out by the local associations in accordance with members' stockholdings, a procedure which was neither equitable nor wise since there was no direct relationship between the ownership of stock and the amount of purchases made by the stockholders. It was clear that the savings should go to those who made them possible by contributing patronage, and that this would also tend to build up the volume of such operations.

To remedy this condition the directors of the Supply Company passed a resolution on September 29, 1915, which recommended to all associations that refunds on orchard supplies should "be returned by them to the individual growers who had contributed the purchases." As the logic of this recommendation gradually became appreciated, this practice became standard among the local associations.

The manager's report for 1916 showed a steady increase in the volume of orchard supply business which reflected a more "extended and increased" use of the Supply Company "as a purchasing medium by the growers." By this time the Supply Company was charging "more nearly the prevailing price rather than cost."[13] This was protecting the advantage-ous prices made to the company by suppliers and it was resulting in additional concessions in prices received. Moreover, the increase in amounts returned as refunds was encouraging members to give the company their full patronage.

In his report for 1917 the manager stated that all savings were being reflected either in lower prices at the time of purchase or in refunds. It was pointed out that all markets had become sellers' markets and that the policy of charging the market price was favored since this increased patronage refunds.

Another significant change in patronage refund policy came in No-vember 1917 when the manner of paying patronage refunds on orchard supplies was refined by the board so as to make possible the return of actual savings to the individual purchasers on a more precise basis. This was done by authorizing the immediate segregation of orchard supply items into different classifications so as to show actual savings made. Prior to this time all savings on orchard supplies had been grouped and returned to member associations at a common rate of patronage refund. While this practice caused no objection when used for packing-house supplies—since such refunds on packinghouse supplies simply reduced the per unit cost for packing—it was obvious that it was not strictly equitable when applied to orchard supplies which represented voluntary purchases of individual growers. On some supply items, the margins of savings were quite high while on other items they were much lower. A flat rate of patronage refund on various orchard supply items thus did not reflect to individual purchasers the savings made possible through their patronage.

The new plan presupposed that these segregated refunds on orchard supplies would be paid to the local associations, and that they would be passed on to individual growers in accordance with the policy that had already been recommended. This new policy corrected a source of com-plaint on the equity of the refund practice then followed and at the same time it gave growers a greater direct incentive to purchase such orchard supplies through their local associations.

Operations During World War I

Fortunately, the operating methods of the Supply Company were well established prior to the advent of World War I. Supplies of all essential materials required for production and marketing became abnormally scarce and prices were quick to reflect the situation. The fact that the Supply Company had established satisfactory business relationships now proved of incalculable importance. The concerns which had served it in the past appreciated that the large volume of business represented by Supply Company purchases was worth keeping even though this entailed sacrifice of short-term profits in the seller's market which then prevailed.

It is doubtful whether the Supply Company could have maintained its supplier contacts during this period under its discarded procedure of reflecting the cost of merchandise purchased in direct prices charged. By charging its member associations prices in line with those charged by the industry to non-members the Supply Company did not upset the competitive situation, while its members could be given the full advantage of its savings from large-scale purchasing through patronage refunds. The market situation during the war period thus reacted to the direct advancement of the Supply Company, for the availability of supplies and large patronage refunds made possible by higher market prices greatly increased the incentive of growers and their associations to use the Supply Company as their purchasing agency.[14] The conditions occasioned by the war thus afforded a spectacular demonstration of the value of the Supply Company. It not only provided an assured source of supplies of good quality but it also provided such supplies at the lowest possible cost. Moreover, its large volume of purchases stood as a standing threat that it would go to other suppliers or engage in processing if this should be necessary to serve its members' needs. An outstanding proof of this fact came in box shook.

Expansion of box shook operation. Following the acquirement of its own mill, the Supply Company had little difficulty for several years in procuring box shook at a reasonable cost, and since it was deemed advisable to conserve the timber supplies for emergency use no attempt was made to operate at full capacity. The mill had fulfilled its main purpose by making possible the negotiation of favorable contracts on box shook from independent suppliers.

With the abnormal expansion of demand for timber during World War I it became increasingly more difficult to obtain adequate supplies of shook from outside sources and the Supply Company found it necessary to operate its mill at full capacity. This situation emphasized again the advantage of mill ownership for without the mill the cost of box shook to member associations would have become exorbitant and, moreover, their needs could not have been so effectively supplied.

The conditions resulting from World War I thus compelled the Supply Company to re-examine the adequacies of its timber supply and box shook manufacturing facilities. In the decade since the Supply Company was formed, there had occurred an enormous expansion of the California fruit industry and this had called for ever-increasing supplies of box shook for packing purposes. This augmented demand for box shook was greatly intensified by the heavy usage of lumber of all types due to the war. As a result, the Supply Company was compelled to operate its own mill at full capacity, and its timber reserves were greatly reduced. This situation would have occasioned no great alarm if there had not been a steadily increasing concentration of ownership of timber resources. By 1918, it was apparent that the Supply Company was in jeopardy unless it could increase its timber reserves and box shook manufacturing operations.

It was obvious that there was only one solution for this problem—an expansion in timber holdings and in box shook manufacturing facilities. After a careful survey, a large tract of timber near Susanville, suitable to meet the long-term needs of the Supply Company and its member associations, was purchased and plans were made for the construction of a modern mill and box factory. This expansion of the box shook manufacturing enterprise called for an investment of several millions of dollars, to be obtained through bank loans with the understanding that they would be liquidated through increased deductions from marketing proceeds under an ingenious revolving fund plan, which became effective November 1, 1918.

The Revolving Fund Plan

Under the original financing plan of the Fruit Growers Supply Company, each local member association had agreed to contribute capital by permitting the California Fruit Growers Exchange to deduct 3 cents per box on all fruit shipped for a five-year period.[15] In return for the proceeds so collected the Supply Company issued stock to the associations (in $10 shares) in proportion to their contributions. Although this novel plan proved very satisfactory as a painless way of raising capital without the sale of stocks or bonds, it was soon found to be defective in one important regard. While it had been intended that each member association would contribute its share of the invested capital, no arrangement had been provided that would keep the capital contributions of the local associations proportionate to their current use of the

Supply Company. This would have occasioned no serious problem if the industry had been static but changes in the acreages of grower members had gradually distorted the relationship of stock holdings to shipments.[16] Although interest was paid on capital stock, this did not correct the fundamental lack of balance between member shipments and their stock holdings.

The desirability of finding some method which would more equitably relate financial investment by the local associations to the services that they received from the Supply Company had been discussed for a number of years by the leaders in the Supply Company, but no workable remedy was found prior to 1918, when a comprehensive revolving fund plan was adopted.[17]

This new plan was apparently conceived in the fall of 1916 when the board of directors of the Supply Company were giving consideration to a plan proposed by the manager which was designed to permit the stockholding associations to better "utilize . . . their investment . . . without the possibility of placing control of the company in the hands of interests not affiliated as shippers of the California Fruit Growers Exchange."[18]

The proposed plan might have been accepted had it not been strenuously opposed by one of the directors, J. S. Edwards, who as a member of the original committee on Supply Company finances, had become "an indefatigable searcher for . . . [some plan] . . . that would coordinate investment and benefits, and also remove from the Exchange the inconvenience and possible embarrassment contingent upon the purchase of the stock of retiring members."[19] With the encouragement of the board of directors, George E. Farrand, as general counsel, undertook the task of working out a comprehensive revolving fund plan that would achieve the objectives sought.[20] This led to the development of the plan in the form of a carefully drawn legal document which became known as the "Revolving Fund Agreement No. 1."[21] This agreement which became effective on September 1, 1918, in fact provided for the "permanent mutualization of the company through the sale of stock by the oldest owner of record to current shippers in proportion to the number of boxes shipped through the Exchange marketing agency."[22]

The technical details of this agreement are of much interest. The parties to the agreement were the Fruit Growers Supply Company, the California Fruit Growers Exchange, the local stockholders' associations of the Supply Company, and the district exchanges of the California Fruit Growers Exchange. The agreement was to become effective when signed by local associations holding 100,000 shares of the Supply

Company's capital stock and it was to continue in force until 1927 unless mutually terminated before that date.

The general objective to be served by the agreement was carefully set forth as follows:

> Whereas . . . subscriptions to the capital stock of the Supply Company were originally made in proportion to the number of packed boxes of citrus fruit marketed by its subscribers through the Exchange, the benefits derived by the stockholders of the Supply Company in purchasing from it said supplies are, generally speaking, in proportion to the number of packed boxes of citrus fruit which they now market through the Exchange, and consequently the benefits of the Supply Company are no longer enjoyed by them in proportion to their ownership of stock therein, *the associations desire to bring about a readjustment of their holdings of stock in the Supply Company so that the distribution of stock among them shall ultimately be proportioned as nearly as may be to the number of packed boxes of citrus fruit which they market through the Exchange.* . . . (Italics added)

The agreement was designed therefore with the expressed objective of bringing about a readjustment in the holdings of the Supply Company's stock so as to provide for the maintenance of its ownership "more nearly in proportion to the benefits derived by its stockholders."

Additionally, the agreement was also designed to furnish more capital since, under its terms, each of the associations agreed to purchase as many shares of capital stock as could be purchased through a deduction of 1 cent on all packed boxes of citrus fruit shipped by it through the Exchange until the authorized capital of the Supply Company was subscribed and paid for. The clause setting up the revolving fund procedure read as follows:

> To bring about and to maintain the desired readjustment in the ownership of the stock in the Supply Company each of the associations agrees to pay to the Exchange the further sum of one cent (1¢) per packed box for each packed box of citrus fruit marketed by it through the Exchange until the present authorized capital stock of the Supply Company is subscribed and paid for and after that time . . . to pay to the Exchange the sum of two cents (2¢) . . . the total amount of such payments to be placed by the Exchange in a fund . . . to be called the "Revolving fund."

To carry out this arrangement each of the associations authorized the Exchange to deduct the specified amount to be contributed from sales proceeds of fruit marketed by it through the district exchanges. On its part, the Exchange agreed "to pay the amount so collected . . ." for capital stock in the Supply Company, and to place the remainder in the "Revolving Fund" to be used in purchasing Supply Company stock in the order of priority in which it was issued. The Supply Company agreed to issue stock to the local associations as it was thus paid for.

The Exchange was to hold all of the stock issued to the member associations in escrow and was to issue to the associations a receipt for shares of stock received from the Supply Company "on account of their subscriptions to the capital stock or to the Revolving Fund." (As a matter of fact, the stock really represented the ownership interest of the individual grower members, as each local association maintained a record of individual equities represented in its collective holding.) It was furthermore agreed that each subsequent purchaser of stock would become a party to the agreement and that no association could dispose of stock except in accordance with the terms of the agreement. The agreement contained many other technical provisions which were designed to cover all administrative and legal contingencies. According to Farrand: "Some of the verbose language of the agreement which was designed to preclude any possibility of misinterpretation or misunderstanding was due to peculiarities in our then constitution and statutory law concerning corporations."[23] However, the revolving fund plan as developed gave immediate satisfaction and it has continued in use with little modification down to the present.[24]

The adoption of a revolving fund plan by the Fruit Growers Supply Company was of great significance since it was the first carefully devised plan of this type to be employed by a large cooperative corporation.[25] While the idea involved was not strictly new, its application to the needs of cooperatives had not as yet been widely recognized. The revolving fund plan of the Supply Company dramatized the idea and provided a model that could be used by cooperatives in devising similar plans to meet their own needs. It was ingenious also in that it provided for the financing of a cooperative purchasing organization through current deductions due members from the proceeds of a related marketing organization.[26]

Evaluation of Supply Company Experience (1920)

In this chapter we have shown how the organized citrus growers of California fashioned the Fruit Growers Supply Company as an organization for purchasing supplies essential for their production and marketing operations, and how its program evolved one step at a time out of experience.

By 1920, the Supply Company was as important in the field of purchasing as the California Fruit Growers Exchange in the field of marketing. In that year the volume of business of the Supply Company totaled $8,758,223. Of this, box shook amounted to $4,876,356; other packing materials such as paper wraps, etc., to $1,458,118; and orchard and miscellaneous supplies, particularly fertilizer, insecticides, and oil for heaters to $2,390,820.

The fact that the California Fruit Growers Exchange was already organized provided the Supply Company with a ready-made organizational structure suitable for its evolving needs. This joint relationship with the Exchange thus provided the Supply Company with a basis for intensive large-scale purchasing operations and freed it of administrative detail and the necessity of maintenance of a separate set of local organizations. Thus the Supply Company could channel its purchasing efforts so as to make them most useful to the Exchange members.

It is significant that the Supply Company came into being in 1907 as a protest against the "box shook trust," which then threatened the economic foundation of the citrus industry. Success in meeting this problem soon established the fact that growers when organized on a large scale could combine their volume so as not to be victimized by strongly organized selling interests. The early experience of the Supply Company also made clear that the California growers had to have an organization strong enough financially so that it could acquire basic sources of supply and manufacturing facilities if this should be necessary to provide desired service at a reasonable cost. It was, moreover, found desirable to have the financial structure equitably supported by all the growers and maintained by them in proportion to their use of the association. The development by the Supply Company of the revolving fund method of finance to achieve this dual aim was a landmark in American cooperative development.

The Supply Company soon found that its large volume of purchasing power gave it other advantages. If California suppliers were not giving a satisfactory service the Supply Company could negotiate with outside suppliers and bring additional supplies into the market. In fact, the mere threat that the Supply Company might do this often sufficed to bring better price offers and membership service from existing suppliers. The large volume of Supply Company purchases also enabled it to protect its members in times of emergency. Through the employment of technically trained men the Supply Company could anticipate supply situation scarcities and make plans to meet them. Moreover, through the Supply Company the growers were in position to mobilize themselves so as to obtain and conserve supplies when necessary.

The Supply Company also found that a large volume made possible specification purchasing. It could determine the amount of particular supplies needed by its members and then negotiate to get them at the best prices and delivered most conveniently to meet the growers' needs. As the operations of the Supply Company expanded, it also became apparent that to growers the quality of supplies was of equal importance with price. By laboratory testing the Supply Company could insure provision of quality supplies that would yield maximum advantages in production. The program of bud selection was an outstanding illustration of how this fact was recognized.

When the Supply Company was formed it had few definite operating policies and there was little comparable experience to draw on. Actual operations soon disclosed the weakness of giving members the economies of mass buying in lower selling prices at time of purchase and this led in time to the practice of selling at regular prices and returning savings as a patronage refund. At first the Supply Company had looked upon the refund as a price adjustment device. Later it came to look upon the refund more properly as a means for providing growers with an incentive to purchase cooperatively. As experience was gained, the method of paying refunds was refined so as to relate refunds to savings on specific orchard supply items.

The Supply Company also found from experience that it was desirable to confine its purchasing efforts to those supplies required in volume for production and marketing operations since the local associations were not in position to handle miscellaneous supply items economically, and the extension of such service tended to involve the Supply Company in competitive conflicts with local business firms so as to impair good-will toward the Exchange system of marketing. The Supply Company was not interested in making a profit out of its purchasing service for it was designed to perform a function of procurement, so as to increase the efficiency of its members as citrus producers. By confining its program to a few basic items consumed in quantity by its members the Supply Company was able to achieve an extremely low cost of operation. Expense for distribution could be kept at a minimum, for outlets were already available in the packinghouse associations required for marketing.

While the organized citrus growers affiliated with the Supply Company in the Exchange system derived the maximum benefits in savings, in quality, and in protection, these could not be entirely restricted to the membership. The Supply Company, by exerting a strong competitive interest in behalf of its members, raised the quality and lowered the cost of supply service for the benefit of all citrus growers.

Chapter XIX

THE INCEPTION OF THE EASTERN
STATES FARMERS' EXCHANGE

The Eastern States Farmers' Exchange was the outgrowth of two streams of influence: (1) the independent growth of cooperative purchasing throughout New England, and (2) the rural improvement movement which centered in the Eastern States Exposition.

In the early years of the century cooperative purchasing was favored by special agricultural conditions in New England in the same way that cooperative marketing was encouraged by special but somewhat reversed agricultural conditions in California. While large urban centers in New England provided nearby market outlets, the supplies required by farmers for producing crops had to be largely imported from other areas. Therefore farmers were more directly interested in means for lowering the cost of feed, fertilizer, and other supplies which were essential to efficient production than they were in finding a market for their products.

The problem of purchasing supplies required for farming needs had become important in New England by 1900, and this had led to the development of three kinds of farmers' purchasing organizations. In many towns there were Grange cooperative stores which handled farm as well as domestic supplies. In localities not served by Grange stores, group-purchasing clubs often served as adjuncts of local Granges or of similar local organizations. Such clubs usually flourished where crop conditions required special types of machinery or supplies. In some communities, associations were formed to obtain trade discounts on farm supplies and consumer goods required in bulk quantities such as sugar, tea, and flour.

As cooperative purchasing in New England expanded it began to attract the attention of state Granges. However, according to Ford, "up to 1907, cooperation within Granges was still in an early experimental stage. It was chaotic, local, and of slight significance." There was no single direction, and supplies were obtained from any available concern. About this time a movement for federating this activity occurred, with the result that by 1908 "cooperative supply associations for the wholesale purchase of grain and fertilizer were to be found in every northeastern state." In the next three years, from 1908-1911, there occurred "the most significant advance in the practice of cooperative distribution" that New England had yet seen.[1]

In the beginning, these wholesale associations were primarily state Grange purchasing agencies. Their principal function was to place orders of local groups with reliable manufacturers and wholesale concerns. By 1910, these various state purchasing organizations were moving toward federation into a New England-wide organization when this trend toward unification was hit a hard blow by the failure of the Patrons Cooperative Association in Massachusetts in 1911, due to ineffective organization and weaknesses in operation. On the other hand, its failure hastened indirectly the process of interstate federation, for it indicated the desirability of having one organization capable of serving all of the New England states.

About this time support for cooperation began to come from outside the Grange. The principal source of inspiration was the *New England Homestead,* published by Herbert Myrick, long an exponent of all forms of cooperation.[2] The *Homestead* saw the need of cooperative organization in New England and effectively promoted the idea throughout the area. Another important source of support came from the Massachusetts Agricultural College under the enlightened presidency of Kenyon L. Butterfield. It will be recalled that the Massachusetts Agricultural College was the first land-grant institution in the United States to offer a course in agricultural cooperation, and that Professor Alexander Cance who gave this course was a strong advocate of cooperative organization as a means of improving the condition of New England farmers. He promoted the formation of cooperative associations not only in his classroom but through outside lectures and writings.

The organization of Rochdale-type cooperative associations in New England was given great encouragement in 1913 by the enactment of a cooperative law in Massachusetts,[3] and within a few years similar laws had been enacted by most of the other New England states.

In 1913, the Massachusetts Agricultural College employed an extension man to assist farmers in the formation of cooperatives and, in 1914, it issued a bulletin written by Professor Cance, *The Farmers'*

Cooperative Exchange, which was designed "to serve as a guide to farmers desiring to form cooperative societies for buying agricultural requirements ..." This bulletin pointed out that "perhaps the most easily organized form of cooperation is the cooperative exchange for the purchase of supplies; probably also it is one of the most necessary in Massachusetts." It called attention to the fact that many groups of farmers in New England were then buying their fertilizer, feed, spray materials, boxes, barrels and crates, and coal in quantity lots. It saw no reason why this should not be done in any community where a number of farmers were using somewhat the same sorts of fertilizers, or feed, or spraying materials. The bulletin declared that the organization of buying societies

> is simply accomplished by pooling the purchases of the members, appointing one man who has some business ability to do the bargaining and order the supplies, and paying the necessary cash into his hands or into a local bank. The buyer purchases the supplies, has them shipped to the nearest railway depot, inspects the shipment, pays the wholesale firm, and notifies the members who have purchased to come to the railway station and haul home their orders of supplies. (p. 17)

While it was admitted that "this method of buying does very well for a season" it was not recommended as a method of permanent organization. Therefore, farmers were urged to form cooperative societies with capital stock "for the purpose of purchasing all their agricultural requirements in common." Under this plan supplies would be warehoused and sold to members at a reasonable profit over cost, and savings would be returned in the form of patronage refunds. Professor Cance commended "this form of cooperation most heartily to the farmers of Massachusetts," holding that "these societies can be very easily formed and that the results will be almost always satisfactory."

During the five years from 1913-1918 more than a hundred of such purchasing associations were formed in the various New England states. Some were rather large and well established, others were little more than car-door buying clubs.

The Eastern States Exposition Movement

As the local exchanges and buying groups grew in number, various proposals were made for their federation so as to obtain the advantages of mass buying power. However, the job of mobilization into one unified system seemed to be beyond the power of the local isolated groups. At this juncture support began to come from an unexpected quarter—a group of industrial leaders who recognized that the welfare of New England's industry was dependent upon a healthy condition of its agriculture. Led by Horace A. Moses,[4] these leaders in 1913 incorporated the Hampden County Improvement League at Springfield, Massachusetts, with such broad objectives as the following:

> To acquire and disseminate information regarding modern agricultural activities; to increase the productivity of farms; to bring about cooperation in producing and marketing farm products ... To encourage and promote the federation and cooperation of all community forces in the adoption of long term policies ...

Well financed by its businessmen backers, the Hampden County Improvement League employed as manager, John A. Sherley, a man already recognized throughout New England for his achievement in developing cooperation between businessmen and farmers at Bennington, Vermont. Sherley quickly gathered specialists who could assist farmers on their specific farming and livestock problems and a strong organization was soon built up among the farmers of Hampden County.

The work of the League proved so successful that within a year several similar leagues were formed in other New England counties. *The New England Homestead,* of February 29, 1914, declared "No movement for rural uplift ever caught the popular fancy more strongly than these county farm leagues." On April 9, 1914, the *Homestead* found "that there is hardly a county that is not interested in league work." The establishment of such leagues or similar bodies was given much encouragement by the passage of the Smith-Lever Act in May 1914 since to obtain federal and state funds for county agent extension work it was necessary that local supporting organizations be formed.

While enthusiasm for the county farm leagues was at its peak it was apparent to some that they might become over-expanded and impractical. As the *New England Homestead* declared in an editorial: "The great danger is in trying to do so much that nothing is done completely." It was the view of the *Homestead* that this work must reach the "pocket nerve" of farmers: "It must cut out out preaching and get down to the job of helping farmers in their own business affairs."

During this period the *Homestead* stressed the importance of real business cooperation for farmers. It wanted to see cooperation develop "up from the people instead of down from a few." For that reason it gave its support to boys' and girls' club work as a means of training young people "in associated and community effort" (Dec. 5, 1915).

Encouraged by the immediate success and popularity of the Hampden County Improvement League, its sponsors proceeded to form, as a non-profit corporation, the Eastern States Agricultural and Industrial Exposition as a means of stimulating dairy and livestock production in the 10 northeastern states.[5] The activity of the Exposition was centered on the holding each year of a great agricultural and industrial fair, but this was not to be its sole function. It was formed "for the purpose of encouraging agricultural and horticultural advancement by all proper means including the holding of agricultural fairs and expositions ..."[6]

The Exposition soon was having a significant influence on New England agriculture. By energetic action its sponsors succeeded in bringing to Springfield the National Dairy Show in 1916, thus establishing Springfield as "agricultural headquarters for the New England states."

While the enthusiasm for the forthcoming dairy show was intense the Exposition leaders undertook to build up a sentiment for rural-urban cooperation by holding a New England Town and Country Conference in Springfield on September 15 and 16, 1916. Although the call for this conference emphasized the necessity of better methods in agricultural production the conference deliberations which were attended by some 300 rural and urban leaders from all parts of New England quickly disclosed that the primary interest of the group lay in better marketing and better rural organization.[7]

The upshot of the conference was a declaration of general principles favoring a broad program for rural and urban cooperation throughout New England and the appointment of an organization committee to develop a detailed program for putting these plans into effect. A fund of $14,000 was subscribed by the industrial sponsors of the conference to get the program under way but it was understood that the program envisaged would eventually be supported by farmers themselves and their local organizations.[8]

In a resolution adopted on November 8, 1916, by the organization committee it was recommended that the new organization "adopt a permanent definite policy of promoting the forward movement in the agricultural and rural life of the Eastern States." The following program was projected in outline form:

> Cooperate with existing agricultural organizations, or promote such other effort as inquiry proves to be desirable and feasible, including:
> a. Better marketing of farm products.
> b. Better methods of farming.
> c. Better farm finance.
> d. Boy and girl work.
> e. Home economics.
> f. Closer cooperation between farmers and other business men.
> g. Provide a program and funds for carrying out these purposes.

During the early months of 1917 the Exposition leaders quickly proceeded to carry these ambitions into effect by the establishment of a "field committee" to encourage and direct various kinds of rural improvement programs throughout New England. The broad public spirit of the Exposition leaders was gradually coming to be better understood and it was becoming appreciated that they had no ulterior motives in endeavoring to assist the farmers. The initial aim was to spread throughout New England the type of work then being carried on by the Hampden County Improvement League, and John A. Sherley of the Hampden County League was drafted to direct the program. The program was patterned on the work of the Hampden County League. It was contemplated that the "field committee" would have a number of bureaus to be headed by specialists in marketing, home demonstration work, girls' and boys' club work, etc.[9] As assistance in marketing was recognized as of primary importance this type of work was given first attention and in September 1917 a marketing bureau was established with Howard W. Selby, a former employee of the U.S.D.A. Bureau of Markets, as manager.

As a basis for developing a working program for promoting better marketing organizations throughout the New England States, Selby immediately began to study the marketing problems of New England with special reference to poultry and poultry products. These studies soon disclosed that New England farmers were only mildly interested in any broad plan of cooperative marketing while they were deeply interested in some means of improving their joint purchasing efforts through overhead organization. In view of this more vital concern with cooperative purchasing, Selby recommended that emphasis be first directed to this problem. This led the Exposition leaders to form a purchasing committee in October to work with Selby to devise a purchasing organization suitable for the needs of New England farmers. As the membership of this committee was comprised of several important business leaders as well as the managers of several of the leading farmers' purchasing organizations, it brought to bear on the problem some of the best available business and agricultural brains in New England. Moreover, the committee was assisted in its deliberations by representatives of the agricultural colleges and extension services of the New England states and state departments of agriculture, as well as of the Bureau of Markets of the U. S. Department of Agriculture.

After several weeks of study the committee brought in a plan for the formation of a cooperative purchasing organization to be called the Eastern States Farmers' Exchange. Although the proposed Exchange was to be authorized to engage in cooperative marketing, it was designed to give immediate and particular attention to the problem of cooperative purchasing.

The purchasing committee foresaw that central control for the new organization was essential—at least during its formative period. While it was designed to serve, and work through, the local associations it was not conceived so as to be solely responsible to them. The Exposition leaders were to retain direction over the enterprise by a provision that members of the Eastern States Farmers' Exchange would initially consist of representatives of the field committee of the Exposition equal in number to representatives from the local organizations. From this panel of members a board of directors and an executive committee were to be selected. This arrangement was designed to place control, during the organization period, in the hands of the field committee of the Exposition.

For some time it had been apparent to the field committee of the Exposition that its broad program for rural improvement could best be carried on through the formation of a separate organization. Thus while plans were going forward for the formation of the Eastern States Farmers' Exchange plans were being made for the transfer of the functions of the field committee to a new organization designed to take over this work as its sole activity—the Eastern States Agricultural and Industrial League. The two organizations, therefore, were formed concurrently so that the control of the Eastern States Farmers' Exchange could be placed in the League.

With the field committee of the Exposition thus converted into the Eastern States Agricultural and Industrial League the market bureau of the Exposition became the market bureau of the League. During the next few years Selby served both as manager of the market bureau for the League and as manager for the Eastern States Farmers' Exchange. As the objectives of the market bureau of the League were executed through the Exchange, this did not involve a serious overlapping of responsibilities. However, it did have one disturbing effect. Since the League was more interested in the promotion of marketing than purchasing it forced Selby to devote a considerable amount of attention to matters which otherwise might have been considered extraneous to the work of the Exchange. The constant attempt to involve the Exchange in marketing programs during the next few years was no doubt partly due to this general relationship. On the other hand, the attempt to provide marketing services through the Eastern States Farmers' Exchange provided valuable experience through showing the danger of having divided objectives. Also, it made the Exchange the promotional center for all cooperative activities in New England. By centering attention on the Exchange as the cooperative planning center state boundary lines were broken down.

The Organization of the Eastern States Farmers' Exchange

The purchasing committee was originally comprised of members of the League who were most interested in the possibilities of such service, and this group invited others into its membership as they showed a specific interest in the objectives of the committee. The committee membership eventually embraced a dozen or more—made up of business leaders and managers of the strongest county exchanges.

In its deliberations the purchasing committee was advised by officials of the Bureau of Markets of the U. S. Department of Agriculture and state representatives of the agricultural colleges and extension services. At first the committee visualized the organization of a federation of existing county or local exchanges, but it gradually became apparent that the existing local or district exchanges were not themselves strong enough to establish and support a strong organization formed on the federated plan.

The purchasing committee took a very practical view of what might immediately be done. It was primarily concerned with providing some kind of central organization which could pool the buying power of the local and county exchanges so as to get for them the advantages of large-scale buying both in quality of supplies and in lower prices. The committee realized that the plan should not be too ambitious at the start but one that could be altered and broadened as cooperative purchasing in local communities grew in significance. The emphasis was thus directed toward the development of a workable, simple plan that would be largely self-supporting and flexible enough to provide for its adaptation to changing conditions.

It was therefore decided that the proposed purchasing organization should be formed independently of the county and local exchanges although designed to serve their specific needs. Control of the proposed organization was to be vested in the Eastern States Agricultural and Industrial League until the county and local exchanges were themselves strong enough to assume control.

The plan for the new organization was embodied in the by-laws for the Eastern States Farmers' Exchange which was incorporated on January 28, 1918. These by-laws set forth the objectives of the Exchange as follows:

1. To encourage, introduce and apply improved business methods in agriculture and to promote cooperation with national, sectional, State, county and local organizations, which are engaged in the work of developing agricultural interests concerned in cooperative buying and selling.

2. To encourage, introduce and apply better and more economical methods in the purchase of farmers' supplies and products.

3. To secure efficient and economical methods in the grading, packing, transporting, marketing and advertising of farm products.

4. To effect economical methods of distribution.

5. To develop business cooperation among agricultural interests and to encourage a cooperative spirit on the part of the public.

6. To encourage and promote a close mutual relationship between agricultural interests and industrial interests and the consuming public, and a better understanding of the problems pertaining thereto.

It will be observed that these broad objectives did not limit the Exchange to the field of cooperative purchasing. Although it was anticipated that the cooperative purchasing phase of the program would be first developed it was then believed that the Exchange would eventually serve both as a marketing and purchasing organization.

No provision was made for financing the organization in the by-laws since it was understood that the Eastern States Agricultural and Industrial League would provide such initial financial assistance as might be necessary.[10] The by-laws simply stipulated that the Exchange would have "no capital stock" and would "conduct business for the mutual help of its members and without profit."

The plan, as set forth in the by-laws, provided for two classes of members. Members of the first class were to be "representatives of existing or subsequently to be formed national, sectional, state, county, or local organizations which have for their purpose the development of cooperative marketing of supplies or products." Members of this type were to be "recognized and sanctioned by vote of the directors of the Exchange." Such representatives were to be elected annually and were to be producers of farm products. It was also provided that no organization of this type would have more than two representatives. The balance of the membership or the members of the second class were to be representatives appointed by the Eastern States Agricultural and Industrial League, and it was also stipulated that they were to be agricultural producers. The number of such members was restricted to 50, but this number could be increased when the number of members in Class 1 exceeded 50, the object being to maintain an equal number in both classes of membership. When the Exchange was set up, its membership consisted entirely of representatives appointed by the League and of these only three could be strictly classified as farmers, although the others had farming interests. It was, however, anticipated that there would be a rapid expansion in the number of members of the first class.

The original board of directors was composed mainly of the members of the purchasing committee who had drawn up plans for the organization, but in the future directors were to be named by the members at annual meetings. The problem of getting business services started was largely entrusted to Selby, who was promptly appointed General Manager.

The preliminary study of the purchasing committee enabled the Exchange to get started promptly with a definite plan of action. It was understood that the immediate task was to provide a brokerage service for the existing county and local buying groups. Good business practices were established from the beginning, no doubt due to the presence on the board of directors of several very able and progressive business leaders. The directors took the position that it was better to go slow and be sure. Rather than scatter their efforts they proceeded to first develop an effective service on feed of good quality.

At the first meeting of the board of directors on February 4, 1918, these two definite policies were adopted: (1) to make the Exchange "self-supporting as far as possible," and (2) "to work closely with the League." At this first meeting, Selby offered three significant recommendations, all of which were adopted: (1) that a bulletin be prepared to set forth the plans and methods of the Exchange; (2) that immediate buying operations be confined to feed and grain with service on other items to be added only as experience should show that savings could be provided; and (3) that buying relations should be established with Boston brokers with the understanding that as soon as the volume of the Exchange should warrant, contracts would be arranged "as near the source of production as is practicable."

Selby immediately made arrangements for opening a business service through Boston brokers, and detailed plans were worked out for handling and financing such transactions so that within six weeks the Exchange was ready for business.

The financing plan. In forming the Eastern States Farmers' Exchange on a non-stock membership basis it was realized that initial working capital would need to be created by some other means than through the sale of stock. This was not considered to be a difficult problem since under the proposed plan of brokerage operation no storage facilities were required, and it was anticipated that actual expenses could be met through commissions charged for services rendered. The main problem was to provide enough working capital to cover cost of merchandise bought until it could be paid for by the county and local exchanges as shipments were received. To meet this problem an independent trust fund was established to make loans to the Exchange as operating funds were required. Thus, a relatively small fund of capital could be used over and over again.

Although the Eastern States Agricultural Trust was not incorporated until February 19, 1918, it was designed as an essential part of the Exchange plan of organization.[11] The charter of the Eastern States Agricultural Trust declared that:

> The primary purpose of this Trust is to furnish credit for and render financial assistance to the Eastern States Farmers' Exchange ... at such times, under such circumstances and under such conditions as in the discretion of the Trustees seems warranted and provided the said Trustees in their discretion are further satisfied that the said Eastern States Farmers' Exchange is engaged in commercial activities which have for their purpose the development of the agricultural interests of the 10 North Atlantic states.

The charter also provided that "all payments for interests [shares] in this Trust shall be made by promissory notes payable on demand without interest and in amounts of $100 or multiples thereof ..." It gave the Trustees "full power and authority to use in their discretion the promissory notes received by them under this Trust ... for the purpose of borrowing money for the operation of the Trust."

Furthermore, it stipulated that "the Trustees shall invest such funds as from time to time they may be possessed of in the promissory notes of the Eastern States Farmers' Exchange, at such times in such amounts and under such conditions as in their discretion they may deem advisable, but provided, however, that said Exchange is not engaged in the business of dealing in futures."

Under the Trust plan, Horace Moses, with a few of his League associates who were deeply concerned with the success of the Exchange, each signed promissory notes payable to the order of the Trust. These notes could then be used by the Trust as collateral for borrowing funds from banks which in turn could be loaned to the Eastern States Farmers' Exchange. As John A. Sherley said in the *Eastern States Magazine* of September, 1919, "Thus a few individuals loaned their credit and through their trustees gave a trust note using the individual notes as collateral to furnish the credit needed by the Exchange in its purchasing operations."

Under this plan promissory notes were immediately pledged to the amount of $42,500, thus providing collateral for use in borrowing about 75 per cent of this amount. This gave the Exchange a working capital of approximately $30,000 which could be used over and over again as funds were needed and transactions were consummated.

First Operations

The bulletin which was prepared in accordance with instructions of the directors to set forth the objectives, plan, and methods of the Exchange was issued early in April. It made clear that plans were definite although objectives and policies were still in flux. Although purchasing was to be its first major activity, it was equally interested in promoting cooperative marketing. This is shown by the following statement:

> *Economical methods in the purchasing of farmers' supplies and products together with efficient economical methods of grading, packing, transporting, marketing, and advertising of farm products of the Eastern States is a summary of the big, broad program proposed by the Eastern States Farmers' Exchange.*

However, emphasis was to be placed on the immediate establishment of purchasing service: "In the beginning it is proposed that the Exchange organization shall develop on the basis of buying grains and feedstuffs . . ." It was also held that the great need of farmers was a plan which would combine the volume of the local purchasing organizations into one central pool. The bulletin said: "There is a great need existing in the eastern states for an organization which will federate the present existing local and county associations in order to increase the buying power and to employ specialists . . . to handle the buying of supplies and the selling of products on a large eastern states basis."

The bulletin then described in detail how the Exchange was to operate as a buying-brokerage agency. The manager was "to secure quotations on the supplies—needed by the members and representative organizations at the most attractive prices attainable. . . . These commodities will be placed on the quotation list of the Exchange and orders will be accepted from regularly recognized associations or exchanges." For this service a small commission was to be charged to cover the cost of operation and any surplus was to be returned to the various exchanges on a prorata volume basis, "provided the amount of the saving is more than one percent of the gross business handled in any one year."

At the meeting of the Executive Committee on March 19, Manager Selby set forth in detail the manner in which the Exchange would provide "quotation order-buying service." Quotations were to be limited to feeds, fertilizers, and seeds. If special requests were made for farm implements, the Eastern States would quote "but assume no responsibility." At this time the Executive Committee was anxious to enlist promptly the full cooperation of the existing county exchanges, and the policy was established of working "as far as possible with the county exchanges" and of urging "farmers in local exchanges to organize and federate into county exchanges."

With this platform Selby undertook to build up support from the various county and local exchanges scattered throughout New England. It is significant that the whole plan was largely developed before active operations were begun on March 26, 1918, when the Exchange sent out its first quotation letter.

The first purchasing operations through the Exchange were very simple. The local or county exchanges placed their orders for feeds with the Exchange and the Exchange assembled these orders and purchased feed as cheaply as possible to meet this demand.

When the Executive Committee met on May 1, Selby pointed out that "the propaganda work preceding the organization had left the impression that the main advantage to be gained was in cash savings," and that "too little consideration had been given to the principle involved." By this time the organization was already beginning to demonstrate what could be accomplished.

During the next few months Selby worked energetically to obtain the support of the existing county organizations while actively promoting the formation of new exchanges. Within a few months the program was becoming well established. Purchases of feed through the organization increased from three cars in April and four in May to 25 in August. No attempt was made to do more than could be promised and the volume of business expanded month by month.

During the first few months while the Eastern States was financially subsidized by the Eastern States Agricultural and Industrial League it was appreciated that the rapid building up of business volume would be discouraged if commission rates were set high enough to meet all expenses. By August 1918, the Exchange was beginning to find itself. The job of getting its services established had been well performed and "the most representative and most active farmers' cooperative organizations of New England" were now affiliated with the Exchange. Cooperative buying—which had been intensified by the establishment of the Exchange—was now expanding rapidly throughout New England.[12]

The Exchange was already beginning to find out from its experience that many of the local exchanges were endeavoring to render comprehensive services with inadequate margins and that the most economical type of local distribution was car-door delivery. The manager of the Exchange saw that the county exchanges—if they were to hold their own—would need to work out a plan "whereby the car will be unloaded upon its arrival and the goods not handled or rehandled several times unnecessarily." This method of operation had the advantage of eliminating speculation through holding commodities for sale, and it had the further advantage of avoiding the extension of credit which increased operating costs and tied up operating capital.

Up to this time the Exchange had limited its services to a few brands of feed and many of the county exchanges were pressing the Exchange to handle more brands. The Exchange was resisting this pressure on the grounds that its opportunity for savings depended upon the restriction of its feed services to a few standard brands. The manager declared: "The aim of the Exchange is to test various feeds and offer a line of four to six brands." He promised that "an attempt will soon be made to settle upon a standard dairy ration which will bear the trademark of the Eastern States."

The Exchange was also endeavoring to standardize its service on other commodities. It took the position that no item should be handled unless a real saving could be effected for its membership. It determined to limit its field of service in commodities and varieties handled until its program could be more thoroughly established.

With the job of initial organization largely completed and its major working policies established, the Exchange was now in position to perfect and broaden its services.

When the Board met on September 21, 1918, the organization was beginning to gain support as evidenced by the fact that there were a dozen applications for membership awaiting attention. To expedite action on these the manager recommended that a committee of three be appointed with power to accept them prior to the annual meeting. He also urged that a uniform policy be adopted in accepting membership applications with membership being restricted to county exchanges as far as possible. In order to make clear the policy of the Board with regard to the basis of organization, Selby also proposed that county exchanges be recognized as "the unit through which business is conducted."

At this board meeting Selby declared that "superior quality products has been the first aim of the Exchange—savings to the farmers the secondary aim." To assure supplies of good quality Selby saw the need of a committee on standardization of feeds which could "determine on an analysis which will as nearly as possible and practical meet the needs of the average New England dairyman for an honest product at the most economical cost" and "reduce to a minimum the cost of milling." The appointment of this committee established standardization as a policy of the Exchange.

With personnel increased, the manager was relieved of burdensome detail and as its methods of operation were smoothed out, steady progress was made during the next six months. With larger volume it was possible to buy at better advantage, and as it bought to better advantage its volume grew. By the end of the first year the Exchange could justifiably claim that it had largely consolidated the buying power of the various county and local exchanges existing throughout New England. It is also significant that revenue from operations was then sufficient to cover all expenses involved in the purchasing program of the Exchange.[13]

Gaining Experience

On February 3, 1919, when the Exchange held its first annual meeting, operating revenues from commissions were already largely covering direct operating costs, and the plan of organization was giving satisfaction. Some 50 persons were in attendance, half of whom represented the Eastern States Agricultural and Industrial League and half the "county and local" exchanges.

Up to this time the Exchange had dealt only with county exchanges where such county exchanges were formed. If no county exchange was serving farmers the Exchange provided service through local exchanges or local car-door buying clubs. The county plan was favored "because county-wide organization furnishes adequate volume of business to make it practical to place a capable man in the field on a full-time basis to serve as manager." Under the county plan—it was claimed—the farmers in each shipping point community could be organized so as to achieve about the same purpose "as if there was a separate independent organization at each station." The Exchange had made no effort to promote a standard pattern of county organizations for it was considered desirable that each "maintain its own distinct characteristics and independence."

The Exchange advocated that local operations be conducted on the most simple lines. Emphasis was placed on sale for cash and car-door delivery as a means of avoiding overhead cost and speculation. Ownership of warehouses and performance of retailing was actively discouraged as involving unnecessary service. "It has been everlastingly insisted upon that the Exchange is not a service institution in the sense that that word is generally used."

Thanks to its organizational efforts the number of county and local affiliated exchanges had steadily increased until at the end of the first year they made up a network of some 30 organizations scattered throughout New England. Of these, one-half were formed on the county plan while several others were regional cooperative marketing associations.

While the Exchange had, given major emphasis to the formation of county exchanges it had also succeeded in getting its purchasing services for them fairly well established. During its first five months of active operation it had handled feed and other supplies to the value of about $200,000, and a volume of $1,000,000 was anticipated for the year ahead. The Exchange was pleased with its record in effecting savings estimated at $2.00 to $14.00 per ton on feed, and from 5 to 25 cents per bushel on grain. As added volume could be expected to yield further advantages in purchasing opportunities and lower administrative costs, great savings in 1919 were anticipated. The Exchange was also proud of the fact that its price quotations—by having a competitive effect on the market—was saving money for all New England farmers, whether or not they were served directly through the Exchange.

It was appreciated that the immediate need of the organization was "the creation of a feed and grain department—with a competent man in charge." A sales department also was proposed "for the promotion of organization loyalty and sales," since "many sales are lost because of the lack of more intensive field work." It was believed that the proper functioning of these two departments would enable the general manager to promote the formation of more county exchanges and advance the establishment of a fertilizer department, while devoting the major part of his time to getting the marketing plan into operation.

Up to this time the manager had been able to devote little time to the advancement of cooperative marketing, which was considered by many to be of much greater importance than cooperative purchasing. Now it was hoped that cooperative marketing work could soon be undertaken in a vigorous way. While the thinking of the Exchange with respect to cooperative marketing methods was not yet formulated its experience in working with the county exchanges was convincing it that cooperative marketing should not be directly undertaken by the county exchanges —but through specialized marketing organizations which would look to the Exchange for information on production and market demands.

During the spring of 1919 purchasing service continued to expand month by month. Although feed and grain continued to be the principal commodities handled there was a growth of service in fertilizer, seeds, and insecticides. In April, as the program grew, an "organizational specialist" was employed to work directly with the local and county exchanges in strengthening their organizational and operating methods and in getting their support, for it was fully appreciated that the Eastern States Farmers' Exchange was dependent upon a strong body of supporting local organizations.

Until now, the Exchange had been primarily concerned with getting its brokerage service established. It was now possible to embark on a more ambitious program under the leadership of the general manager. Reporting to the board of directors on May 7, 1919, Selby pointed out that the volume of the Exchange had been built on local savings made possible by a more efficient system of retail distribution. Declaring that "efficiency is the only factor which reduces costs to farmers" he asserted that it was now necessary "to overcome the inefficiency of the manufacturers and wholesalers." To do this he proposed "a central storage and feed mixing plant with an elevator located west of Buffalo with milling and mixing in transit privileges." He believed that it was "entirely feasible to enlist the orders of farmers through their county exchanges for their winter needs and to purchase at the season of the year when prices were generally at the lowest ebb and store at a central plant for shipment as needed in either straight or assorted cars." As a foundation for eventually getting a program of this type established he proposed an arrangement—for which tentative plans had been made—with a commercial milling company in New York under which supplies would be "purchased on order for our affiliated organizations to be held for deferred shipment."

At first the Exchange had devoted its attention to the problem of getting its feed service established. The only other commodities handled in any quantity were fertilizer, seeds, and insecticides—all of which could be handled like feed on a brokerage basis. Now the county and local exchanges were beginning to request that the Exchange handle "implements and other items which call for various degrees of service." While the Exchange had been inclined "to shun such items" Selby now felt that the time was ripe to determine whether service on such commodities could be economically provided. On the basis of preliminary studies he thought that it might be desirable to handle some standard line of implements under an agency agreement.

Selby completed his report by recommending the appointment of two committees. The first was to develop a marketing plan for the Exchange "now that the purchasing plan had been carried into effect."

The second committee was to study the feasibility of constructing a mill to be operated by the Eastern States Farmers' Exchange, and to consider the plan recommended for immediate adoption whereby feed would be purchased on order for the affiliated exchanges and stored until required by them during the fall and winter months.

Selby's recommendations were largely accepted by the Board in its meeting on June 7, 1919, and committees were appointed to develop plans for marketing service and determine the feasibility of a feed mill. Moreover, the establishment of a feed and grain department with a qualified manager in charge was authorized so as to permit the general manager to have time for more general responsibilities.

With the establishment of the feed department the Exchange was able to strengthen greatly its feed service, and by the end of the year contracts had been made with mills at Oneonta, New York, and St. Johnsbury, Vermont, under which feed and grain could be stored and service provided on assorted cars so as to meet the needs of most of the county and local exchanges in New England. With mill connections made, the Exchange was in position to develop standardized lines of feed in accordance with the growing demand that the Exchange have its own brand of feed and flour. The Directors took a definite step forward in this matter on November 8, 1919, when they voted to establish a brand for feed and flour with the character of the brand to be determined by a committee of three. At this time the Directors voted that "there be marked and printed on the container of the feed the ingredients and list of contents without stating the amount of each."[14]

The quotation letter of December 26 announced that an Eastern States dairy ration was now available. In offering the feed it was pointed out that the formula was owned by the Exchange, and that its manufacture was under its absolute control. Moreover, this feed was claimed to be "as good as the average proprietary feed—while its cost was less." However, the use of this ration was optional and as it was never aggressively pushed, no real "open formula feed program" was, in fact, undertaken by the Exchange prior to the spring of 1922.

With the feed service on its feet the Exchange began to make very substantial progress. In an official bulletin issued in September 1919, it was claimed that "the plan of cooperative buying of farm supplies is spreading rapidly throughout the Eastern States" and that "more co-operative business enterprises" had been established by farmers "in the past 18 months than in the preceding 18 years." It was also claimed that "practically every cooperative agency in the six New England states" was affiliated with the Eastern States Farmers' Exchange in its plan "to accomplish for agriculture in the East what big business organization has accomplished for industry." The record of the Exchange in volume of supplies handled was becoming impressive. Within 18 months, it had distributed 485 carloads of supplies having a value of $700,000. The bulk of this volume represented feed and grain, but it also included 1,699 tons of fertilizer, a considerable quantity of seed, and some 26,000 pounds of spray material. The Exchange was then anticipating that specialized departments similar to the department already established for feed would be established to handle fertilizers, seeds, and implements.

With the expansion of volume, costs had been reduced to approximately 1-1/2 per cent, and the immediate goal was "to make the business entirely self-sustaining on the basis of 1 per cent commission charge." In boasting of its accomplishments the Exchange stressed the fact that they were beyond the reach of individual farmers or small groups of farmers and were made possible only by the cooperation of the whole New England rural community. It was held that the success of the general program "depended on the strength of the county exchanges and the local organizations all working together for the common good of each other."

By this time the Exchange was becoming more and more conscious of itself as a purely farmers' cooperative organization. The Exchange bulletin declared "We are in business as a farmers' organization directed by farmers and working on the truly cooperative non-stock, non-profit plan."

The preceding discussion indicates that the management of the Exchange had become increasingly aware of the fact that the strength of the Eastern States Farmers' Exchange was dependent upon the loyal support of a body of strong county and local farmers' exchanges. Although the Exchange had been able to help these organizations on their business problems to some extent, it was not in a strong enough position financially to give them the assistance they required on their accounting and other technical problems.[15]

Seeing that such assistance was essential to the sound development of county and local cooperatives John Lawrence, a wealthy businessman who had become interested in one of the county exchanges, proposed that the Exchange set up an "accounting service" for the assistance of county and local associations with the understanding that he would underwrite costs in getting this work established that could not be covered by charges for services performed, up to $6,000. Although this proposal was accepted by the Exchange in the fall of 1919, several months were required to find a man with the abilities and training suitable for this work.

Ready for Expansion

At the start of 1920 leaders of the Exchange had every reason for optimism. Economic conditions had been favorable for its method of operation. Farmers were enjoying postwar prosperity and the high margins taken by farm supply dealers afforded an opportunity to provide farmers with service at substantial savings. In less than two years the Exchange had become the recognized buying agency for most of the cooperative exchanges in New England. Its feed department was well established, and substantial progress had been made in departmentalizing its fertilizer operations.

The weakest link in the Exchange program was the service provided at the local distribution point by the county and local exchanges, since substantial volume operations required strong supporting local organizations. It was hoped that this phase of the program would be strengthened with the establishment of the accounting service department then being organized. Another weakness—little perceived—lay in the tendency toward overdiversification and expansion of extraneous activities. While the Exchange had given its major attention to the purchasing function, it was becoming increasingly involved in cooperative marketing responsibilities. The Eastern States Agricultural and Industrial League, then at the peak of its popularity, was demanding continuously broader services from its market bureau—which was under the direction of the general manager of the Eastern States Farmers' Exchange.

The interesting story of how the Exchange met its marketing and other difficult problems in the 1920's must be left for consideration in the second volume of this history. The significant fact to record here is that foundations for a strong regional purchasing cooperative had been laid by 1920.

Chapter XX

THE ORIGINS OF THE G.L.F.

In earlier chapters we have shown how economic and social conditions in agriculture became more favorable to the formation of farm
supply purchasing associations after 1900. In this chapter we will observe how these conditions gave rise to the formation of the Cooperative Grange League Federation Exchange, better known as the G.L.F.[1]
—destined to be for many years the largest cooperative purchasing
organization of this type in the world. In 1963, the G.L.F. and the
Eastern States Farmers' Exchange merged to form Agway, Inc., with
headquarters in Syracuse, New York.

Until 1912, the interest in agricultural cooperation in New York was
sporadic and intermittent. Some support was given by the state Grange
but this was a program only for Grange members and it was of little
general effect. The situation changed rapidly after 1912 with the growth
of organized support from the state department of agriculture, the state
agricultural college and extension forces, and the county Farm Bureaus.

State Encouragement—1912-1915

The growing importance of cooperation in New York was significantly recognized by the New York State Agricultural Society in its
annual meeting in January 1912 when a resolution was passed which
instructed its president to call a conference of "delegates of producers'
and consumers' organizations" for the purpose of bringing producers
and city consumers into closer relation by cooperative methods.

At the conference held in New York City on April 19, a State
Standing Committee on Cooperation was set up under the chairmanship
of John J. Dillon, Editor of the *Rural New Yorker*, "to encourage cooperative action between consumer and producer." Although little was
accomplished during 1912, the chairman of the standing committee was

able to report significant achievements when the New York State Agricultural Society held its annual meeting in 1914. In his report he declared: "For nearly two years we have worked to lay a foundation for a comprehensive cooperative structure, and we believe that we are now ready to raise the timbers." He then pointed out that: "During the preceding year we have succeeded in securing laws for the organization of cooperative purchasing and selling associations and credit unions. We also secured the appointment of an assistant commissioner in the Department of Agriculture to promote and help organize cooperative work in the State."

A serious obstacle to cooperative advancement at this time was a growing friction between organizations interested in cooperative development. In particular, the leaders in the Grange were apprehensive that the emerging Farm Bureaus, which were rapidly spreading and getting into full swing, would set up independent cooperative associations and thus interfere with Grange-sponsored cooperative activity. There was also a conflict of interest and viewpoint between supporters and advocates of producers and consumers cooperative organizations.

Sensing this sentiment the Superintendent of the Bureau of Cooperation called a conference of cooperative associations at Utica, New York, in July 1914. In a statement to this conference Dillon, the Chairman of the State Standing Committee on Cooperation, maintained that ultimately "the local associations must have a central organization to furnish information and execute the orders and transact the wholesale business of both selling and buying for the local associations."

However, the conference discussion disclosed that the various groups were not yet ready for a comprehensive plan of federation. One faction, composed largely of urban consumer cooperatives, favored giving support to a consumers' wholesale society then being formed. Grange representatives, on the other hand, maintained that the state Grange purchasing agency was in position to serve farmers' needs adequately. According to the Master of the state Grange, "its perfect success" was "only dependent upon cooperation."

Although the conference refused to endorse any plan for federation, it passed the following resolution which shows that the concept of federation was gaining adherents: "Resolved, that it is the sense of this meeting that considerable saving can be made by a federation of the cooperative associations of this state for the purpose of ordering supplies collectively directly from the producers and shippers, preferably on specifications and analyses by contract."

At the meeting of the New York State Agricultural Society in January 1915 the report of the Committee on Cooperation indicated that many marketing and purchasing associations had been formed and were operating "with a very large degree of success." The Farm Bureau movement had taken hold—and county agents were aggressively promoting cooperative associations. M. C. Burritt, the state extension leader, maintained: "Nowhere is education and assistance more sorely needed than along the lines of cooperation in the purchasing of farm supplies and in the marketing of farm products ... No feature of Farm Bureau work is more important than this."

The spirit of the times was reflected in an address by Dean Beverly T. Galloway, the new Dean of Agriculture in Cornell University.[2] He declared: "If agriculture is to continue to prosper under a democratic form of government, if we are to be a nation of freemen of the soil, if we are to avoid coming to what all the older nations have come to—an agricultural peasantry—we must organize our industry, and that means cooperation."

The Influence of the Farm Bureaus, 1914-1917

In 1913, a new force in support of cooperative organization among farmers in New York was beginning to make itself felt—the county Farm Bureau associations. These organizations were formed to facilitate the work of county agents, and they soon became recognized as the county groups of farmers cooperating with the agricultural college and the Department of Agriculture in carrying on county agent work. This relationship is indicated by the fact that the county agents were then commonly called "Farm Bureau managers."[3]

While the first county Farm Bureau associations were conceived of as educational organizations through which farmers could improve their efficiency in production, it was soon realized by the county agents that "the better application of scientific and modern ideas to production" required the organization of farmers into groups of associations for cow testing, herd, seed or soil improvement, or some similar purpose. Through such organizational activity the farmers came to look to the county agents for assistance in organization as well as for direct instruction on scientific agricultural practices. Work in organizing farmers to improve their methods of production led almost immediately to demands for help in organizing purchasing or marketing associations as a means of meeting their most pressing economic problems.[4]

The way in which the interest of county agents and county Farm Bureau associations shifted from production to economic problems is

shown by the following passage from a novel which portrays the conditions that led to one man's support of the Dairymen's League in the
milk strike of 1916. The county agent is explaining his position to a
group of farmers:

> Two years ago, I came down to the county, happy and enthusiastic that at
> last I was in position to do something worthwhile for farmers. I had great
> dreams.... I saw the fields that needed drainage, the buildings that needed
> repairing, the crops that needed improvement. I saw what could be done with
> lime to make the clover grow and with spraying and pruning to rejuvenate the
> orchards, so I began to ride your hills and valleys and to talk with you at
> meetings, in your barns and in your lots about the gospel of better farming.
> But something was wrong....I finally saw what was the matter...These
> many years all of us have been emphasizing and working to make two blades
> of grass grow where one grew before, without even trying to sell the first
> blade at a profit....We should use better seed; we should study varieties;
> we should spray our orchards; we should weed out poor cattle...But none
> of these things touched the greatest of all our problems, that of marketing....
> It is our lack of study of our selling problem that has put farm people into
> the control of middlemen and is losing us our much vaunted independence.[5]

As a result of the pressure by farmers for assistance, much of the
work of the county agents and county Farm Bureau associations from
1914 on was concerned with helping farmers organize and operate
cooperative marketing and purchasing associations. Writing in 1927,
E. R. Eastman declared:

> The influence that the extension men and the county agents have had upon
> the rural social and economic life of the past decade is immeasurable. Many
> of these county agents recognized that the first problem of rural life was an
> economic one and they have been of invaluable service to farmers in helping
> to spread information about cooperative organizations, in encouraging organi-
> zation and in helping farmers to get better markets for their products.[6]

Looking back in 1922, M. C. Burritt, New York leader, County
Agricultural Agents, 1914-1916, and New York Director of Extension,
1917-1924, said: "The greatest immediate demand for the application
of the County Agent's organization and leadership abilities has proved
to be that of cooperative buying and selling."[7]

The support and encouragement which the county agents and county
Farm Bureau associations gave to farmers' cooperatives was bitterly
resented by private business establishments which were naturally opposed to farmers doing business for themselves. Their principal criticism was that it was improper for county agents, as government employees, to participate in business activities on behalf of farmers.

Those in charge of county agent work recognized the force of this
argument and soon established the policy that it was proper for county
agents to provide farmers with information and advisory assistance in

organizing and operating cooperative associations, but improper to take an active part in their management or direction.

Although a conscientious effort was made by state officials to enforce this policy it was difficult to do so, for assistance to farmers on their production problems led directly to marketing or purchasing responsibilities which could not be divorced easily from the county agent's office. Farmers demanded that the county agents help them in pooling orders for feed, seed, and fertilizer and it was difficult, if not impossible, for the county agents to disassociate themselves from such activities. This situation gradually convinced extension workers and county agents of the need for farmers' cooperative associations which could operate as independent organizations. It then became the established policy of the county Farm Bureau associations in New York to encourage the formation of cooperative marketing or purchasing associations—but not to carry on cooperative marketing or purchasing as a Farm Bureau business activity. Thus the county agents and county Farm Bureau associations played a highly significant role in fostering the organization of farmers into marketing and purchasing associations.

However, there was one important commercial activity—in seed distribution—that could not be easily divorced from the educational activities of the Extension Service since no other agency was in position to render the service that farmers required if they were to produce efficiently.

This major exception to the rule of non-participation in commercial enterprise developed out of natural circumstances. To understand this situation one must realize that when the county agents came on the field one of the greatest handicaps to efficient production was the inability of farmers to get reliable seed. The importance of good seed was then being stressed by the agricultural college, but the farmers were unable to get from their local dealers the type and quality of seed being recommended. In 1913, H. E. Babcock,[8] then county agent for Cattaraugus County, recognized this problem by forming a seed committee among the farmers in his county Farm Bureau association which soon became known as the "Farm Bureau Seed Committee." This committee, with the assistance of the county agent, proceeded to pool the seed orders of its members and obtain them from a reliable source. The beneficial results in yields obtained from this experiment soon led to the formation of similar Farm Bureau seed committees and, in view of the close relationship of this program to the work of the college and county agents, it was natural for them to turn to the state office of the Extension

Service for assistance in establishing a source of supply. Within a few years this had grown into a sizable volume of seed business.

Since the Extension Service was interested in this program only as a means of helping farmers obtain reliable seed, it was embarrassed as it grew in commercial scope. A way out of this difficulty came in late 1918, with the establishment of the State Grange Exchange to serve as a state-wide purchasing organization for local cooperatives. The task of acquiring seed to meet the pooled requirements of the farmers in the Farm Bureau seed committees was then entrusted to this organization. Thus, the State Federation of Farm Bureaus through the Better Seed Committees, and the Grange through the State Grange Exchange, entered into partnership to conduct this cooperative activity. This partnership strengthened the better seed committees and maintained the interest of the Federation of Farm Bureaus in state-wide purchasing service.

The Demand for Better Feed

The economic factor that had the most effect on the formation of cooperative purchasing associations in New York was the commercialization of the dairy industry. During the years from 1900 to 1910, there was a considerable expansion in the production of dairy products to meet the growing requirements of New York City and other urban markets. Within a few years a number of strong feed manufacturing concerns had grown up to meet farmers' needs and these provided service through retail feed dealers. If the service provided by the feed manufacturers and feed dealers had been satisfactory there would have been little opportunity for cooperatives to develop. But the service was not satisfactory. Dairy farmers came increasingly to the opinion that prices charged for feed were too high and that the quality of feed furnished was too low. In many instances, dairy farmers preferred to obtain their feed ingredients and mix them themselves, and they naturally turned to the New York State College of Agriculture for information on how they could provide for themselves mixed feeds of reliable feeding values.

The Department of Dairy Husbandry of the New York State College of Agriculture was responsive to these requests, and students and farmers were given instruction in the art of "scientific feeding," and in the practice of "home mixing."

The Open Formula Feed Plan

Starting about 1900, certain manufacturers had begun compounding feeds in the form of balanced rations which farmers could use without mixing. Supported by vigorous advertising the mixed feed industry had flourished and rapidly spread. As the sale of mixed feeds grew, the colleges found it increasingly difficult to instruct students in the nutritional values of feeds made up in closed commercial formulas. This situation led Professor E. S. Savage, animal husbandryman at New York State College, to conceive the idea of open formula feeds—which would provide full information on the content of the ingredients in the feed sold.

As Savage worked on the problem from 1912 to 1914 he became convinced that the existing method of selling proprietary brands of feed was detrimental to the sound development of the dairy industry. He saw that dairymen could not buy mixed feed intelligently unless they knew the amount and quality of the various ingredients combined in a "brand" of commercial feed.

There were a few feed manufacturers who were interested in Savage's theories and through their influence he was invited to present his views at the Sixth Annual Meeting of the American Feed Manufacturers Association in Chicago on May 22, 1914. Savage's talk, "The Attitude of the Teacher to the Mixed Feed Industry," which launched the idea of "open-formula feeds," proved to be the feature of the meeting. In his talk Savage pointed out the difficulties involved in trying to teach students how to feed most satisfactorily when the ingredients in a compounded feed were not known.

> My point is this, [said Savage] I want to bring out just how I wish to teach my students—how shall I do it—to choose their feeds. That is what they are up against. Any farmer or student or any man handling cattle goes into a local feed store. The local feed dealer may have ten straight by-products and three or four mixed or compounded feeds on hand. The problem right before that farmer is how to select the four or five feeds that he may mean to mix together to make his ration or, which one of those compounded feeds will he select as his ration, if he doesn't want to mix his feed himself.

Realizing that he was treading on delicate ground Savage asked that his ideas be examined with open minds. He declared that his only wish was "to help in bringing together the manufacturer and the consumer so that one may sell his product at a fair price, at a good profit, and the farmer purchase his necessary feeds as cheaply as possible."

Savage asked the manufacturers this question, "Why not guarantee a certain formula on every bag of feed sold so that I may teach all of my students to compute exactly the total nutrients in a ton of compounded feed. . . . Then, as a feeder, when I see this feed at a feed dealer's I can compute its digestibility and check up closely whether I

want to buy it or not." Savage granted the honesty of the feed manufacturers but he insisted, "We cannot study your compound feed in
any other way."

Such views were heretical to the assembled feed manufacturers
and they were actively challenged in the discussion which followed.
Roger W. Chapman, President of the American Feed Manufacturers
Association, maintained: "This mixed feed business is on a sufficiently
stable basis for the agricultural colleges ... to experiment with, to know
their uniformity and place them on their regular teachings."

The immediate resistance to his proposal convinced Savage that
there was little reason to hope that the established feed manufacturers
would adopt the "open formula" method. Although he endeavored to
find feed manufacturers who would give his idea a trial he recognized
that the idea went against established practices and that the only real
solution to the farmers' feed problem would come when the farmers
organized to provide themselves with the type of feed service that they
required. As Savage himself remarked many years later, "from that day
on ... I determined to do all I could to see that farmers had the opportunity to buy their feeds cooperatively."[9]

Unable to attract the interest of the commercial feed manufacturers
and distributors, Savage finally persuaded the New York State Grange
Purchasing Agency (to be described later) to try out his idea, and in
1916 this agency began to market an "open formula feed" using a formula provided by Cornell University. This gave the idea wide publicity
among farmers and demonstrated its practicability.

The Feed Industry Attack on Cooperative Buying

The support given cooperative purchasing by the federal and state
governments, and especially by the Farm Bureaus, gave great concern
to the established feed manufacturers and distributors. This matter
came to a head in May 1916 when *Flour and Feed* published a four-
page editorial under the title: "Feed Dealers Now Must Fight Uncle
Sam on Direct Buying Proposition." This editorial quoted Secretary
Houston of the U. S. Department of Agriculture as saying:

> The Department considers it a legitimate function of the County Agent to
> aid the farmers in organizing associations for the cooperative purchase of
> farm commodities. The agent is expected to assist in an advisory way such
> associations in purchasing their farm supplies upon the best possible terms.

The editorial also complained of a letter which had been sent out in February 1915 to county Farm Bureau presidents and managers by M. C. Burritt, State Director of Farm Bureaus in the State of New York. Burritt had said: "Farm Bureau Managers may furnish information as to where lime, fertilizer, seeds and other supplies may be secured and if asked to do so, may quote wholesale and retail prices ... But the Managers should never personally take or transmit to shippers orders or money for supplies."

Flour and Feed was very critical of this declared policy:

> Feed dealers, manufacturers and jobbers don't care a whoop whether or not the agent actually handles the money in direct buying transactions. This is incidental to the main proposition. The trouble lies in the fact that the farm bureau man is expected to promote direct buying associations.

Maintaining that Secretary Houston's statement constituted a "dangerous menace to the feed dealers'· business," feed dealers were urged to carry on a strong campaign to protect their interests, and during the next few months they waged aggressive warfare on the work of the county agents. In the June issue of *Flour and Feed* an editorial declared: "Feed dealers must not be satisfied with any halfway success in this campaign against the activities of the farm bureau managers ... There can be no halfway stand." This same issue carried the annual address of the president, C. H. Chapman, of the American Feed Manufacturers Association. Chapman found promotion of cooperative buying associations to be both "*economically* and *morally*" unsound.

In 1917, the organized feed trade was placed on the defensive by the report of the Wicks' Committee—which disclosed that it had gone beyond reason in its attack on cooperative buying. This official report found conditions in the feed trade so unsatisfactory that it urged farmers to protect themselves through the formation of their own buying associations. How this committee came to be formed is of interest.

In the fall of 1916 the successful milk strike of the Dairymen's League had "welded into one solid block" the dairy farmers of New York. Aroused by the struggle of the dairymen for fair prices the Senate and Assembly of the State of New York had set up a joint committee under the chairmanship of Senator Charles Wicks to investigate marketing conditions for dairy products, poultry and eggs, and livestock. This committee—known as the Wicks' Committee—sought to determine, among other things, whether the distribution of milk and butter, eggs, poultry and livestock was "controlled by combination and monopoly of dealers and manipulation of prices ..."

The carefully prepared report of this committee which was transmitted on February 15, 1917, gave much encouragement to the development of cooperative marketing and purchasing organizations in New York. It was the judgment of the committee that "cooperative agencies ... are economic factors of great importance and should be permitted" and that "legalized cooperation, publicly controlled, should be equally beneficial to producer, distributor, and consumer." The report frankly declared that "the milk industry at the present moment needs to be handled through cooperative effort."

However, the part of the report that aroused the most interest had to do with the quality of feed service then available to New York dairymen. It is doubtful whether any similar state legislative committee has ever been more outspoken in its criticism of conditions and practices found. Significant passages in the report are here quoted:

> A wide field for fraudulent operation exists in the selling of concentrated feeding stuffs to the dairymen of this state ... It is not going too far to assert that many thousands of dollars are yearly paid out by the dairymen of the State of New York for dirt, dust, straw and rubbish permitted to be sold under some high-sounding name as a valuable cattle food, sure to increase the production of his dairy.[10]

Much of the blame for the conditions described was attributed to the feed dealers' associations which were singled out for special censure:

> An examination of the record of these feed dealers associations discloses the most abhorrent and immoral practices, aims, and methods ... They sought by a system of black-listing to frighten and terrorize all millers and wholesale dealers in grains from dealing in any way with the local grange, a co-operative society, or an individual dairyman ... Coercion and libel were two of the instrumentalities used by the Association to attain its ends ... This little group of men with a relatively insignificant capital sought to impose tribute on all the great dairy industry of the state of New York and made it difficult for the dairymen to do business except under their direction and control.[11]

The Dairymen's League Feed Plan

By calling attention to the conditions under which New York farmers were forced to buy feed, the report of the Wicks' Committee supported the efforts of Professor Savage who had been trying for years to get the feed manufacturers to prepare feed rations on an open formula basis. By showing dramatically that farmers had no way of protecting themselves except through organization it made organization imperative. The fact that the Dairymen's League was already in the field as a militant champion of their rights in marketing led the farmers to insist that it assume the responsibility of leadership in providing them with the kind of feed service they required.

This mandate could not be ignored and the president of the

League, R. D. Cooper, called for assistance from H. E. Babcock, then State County Agent Leader and Secretary of the State Federation of Farm Bureaus, and Professor E. S. Savage. Together, these men hammered out a plan for providing feed service under the auspices of the Dairymen's League. The main feature of the proposed plan was that feed of a definite quality was to be manufactured under contract by reputable commercial feed concerns in accordance with specifications set by Cornell University. Distribution was to be effected through approved local dealers who were to serve as local representatives of the League on a fixed service charge basis.

Since the Dairymen's League was not in position to manufacture feed, it was essential that arrangements be made with reliable manufacturers to have feed manufactured in accordance with an agreed-upon formula for distribution under the League plan. It was also essential that arrangements be made for distribution through regular feed merchants since the League had no local feed distributing facilities of its own. To work out such arrangements the League officers called a conference to present their proposed plan to interested feed manufacturers and distributors.

With the apparent endorsement of important elements in the feed industry the League undertook to make arrangements for manufacture and local distribution. A contract was signed with one firm, and negotiations were begun for similar contracts with other manufacturers.

However, the plan was vulnerable from the standpoint of its workability and arbitrariness. If the League had been a strongly entrenched organization it might have been able to compel acceptance through power of boycott—but the League then had no strong local organizations or strong central power. It was not a plan attractive to manufacturers or to local dealers for it was a period of rising prices and dealers saw little advantage from a fixed margin agreement. These difficulties might have been overcome if the cooperation anticipated from the manufacturers and feed dealers had been forthcoming. However, almost immediately *Flour and Feed* vociferously condemned the plan in a long editorial entitled, "Prussianizing the Feed Business." This editorial charged that the scheme was "wholly atrocious and contrary to sound economic practice." It declared that dealers should oppose this "most brazen attempt to deliberately Prussianize a big element in our business life . . ."

With the powerful feed trade stirred up in bitter opposition against the plan—which in reality was quite innocuous—it was impossible to make adequate local arrangements for getting the plan under way.

Whether or not H. E. Babcock was right in believing that the New York State Retail Feed Dealers Association had "sprung a mouse-trap play" there is no question that they sabotaged the plan. According to him most of the members of this association when they got the feed "(1) talked it down, (2) offered other so-called better feed cheaper, or (3) hid it in the back of their warehouses."[12]

This ambitious program thus collapsed almost as soon as it was launched. However, the League's leadership was not willing to call the chapter closed. From then on it gave active support to the Grange and Farm Bureau in their efforts to establish a workable feed program.

The State Grange Exchange

Cooperative purchasing by the Grange in New York in the 1870's and 1880's had never completely died out. It began to grow again in the early 1900's. In March 1912, the Committee on Cooperation of the New York State Grange recommended:

> That the New York Grange enter into a contract with some reliable parties to conduct a business of supplying members of the Grange, through a representative selected by a subordinate or Pomona Grange, or a regularly organized Grange "cooperative association," with farm supplies that can be handled in car lots on a cash basis, and to be delivered to any railroad station in the State.

A few weeks later an agreement was worked out whereby the firm of Godfrey and Sloan would "carry on a supply purchasing business under the name of the New York State Grange Purchasing Agency." This was little more than a Grange-endorsed private agency and it was widely felt that a stronger type of organization was needed to meet effectively the needs of local Grange members. A new plan was approved by the Executive Committee in August 1913. It proposed that "Cooperative Societies be organized and incorporated in every locality producing for market any considerable quantity of farm produce, or buying for the farm and house feeds, fertilizers, and other supplies in considerable quantities." These local societies were to be federated to form a central selling and buying organization, and all dividends were to be credited to the local societies in accordance with "the volume of business done by them through the central organization."

However, no serious attempt was made to carry out this ambitious Grange cooperative program, in view of the fact that it would have supplanted the State Grange Purchasing Agency which then had the support of influential Grange leaders.

The ineffectiveness of the State Grange Purchasing Agency was emphasized in late 1916 by the success of the Dairymen's League milk strike, and in early 1917 by the report of the Wicks' Committee which disclosed that farmers were being victimized by feed manufacturers and distributors. Just at this time a special committee of the Grange found that the State Grange Purchasing Agency was taking an excessive profit in handling flour, and the support of the Grange was withdrawn.

The time was ripe for action and S. J. Lowell, Master of the New York State Grange, focused attention on the problem in his address at the annual meeting in January 1917.

> No one thing receives so much discussion and in no one thing has there been less accomplished than in real cooperation. It is time we developed a plan of true cooperation. Our purchasing agency has done some good work, but it is time this valuable factor were enlarged and brought into a full plan of cooperative buying, and later selling for every Grange member who desires to become one of its members. I am firmly convinced that the time has gone by for talking only, and that action must now be taken....It is OUR duty ...I rely on your calm deliberation over this subject at this session.

Later in the meeting a resolution presented by the Committee on Cooperation proposed the formation of a stock company, "to give to the members of the Grange such purchasing power as will supply the members with their supplies desired direct from the manufacturer at the lowest price possible." Consideration of this resolution led to the appointment of a committee which concluded in its report on September 2, 1917, that "the time is opportune for starting such an enterprise ... without unnecessary delay." The Committee unanimously recommended "the organization of a limited liability stock corporation ... to be known as the New York Grange Exchange." The plan as developed was unanimously approved at the next annual meeting of the Grange (February 1918) and after several months of organization work, business offices were established at Syracuse under the management of Richard Hall.

Although the New York Grange Exchange was very much a "Grange affair" this was not a serious drawback since a large percentage of New York farmers were then active in Grange work. The emerging county Farm Bureau organizations at this time were of the opinion that the Grange Exchange could facilitate their own efforts in promoting cooperative purchasing by serving as a central purchasing agency, especially for seed. Moreover, at this time the Dairymen's League was disillusioned by its efforts to establish its own feed buying plan and saw in the Grange plan definite possibilities for serving the Dairymen's League members. Thus, *The Dairymen's League News,* in describing the new plan (October 1918) said, "It is in reality the first state-wide opportunity offered the farmers for the purchase and sale of their farm supplies and products . . . under their own control."

According to the newly designated manager, the Exchange was to be "a bureau of concentration." He pointed out that "this is really the first state-wide effort that has ever been attempted to affiliate the various agricultural interests." He proposed "to proceed step by step with the utmost conservatism" with the idea of laying "at least the foundation for the building up of an organization that would eventually have the full confidence of the people at large, not only the producers but consumers as well."

The Farm Bureau better seed committees welcomed the opportunity to use the newly formed State Grange Exchange as a central source of supply. Therefore, as soon as the Grange Exchange was formed an arrangement was worked out whereby it procured seed to meet their pooled requirements and, in general, the program gave satisfaction. Thus, by this joint operation the state Grange and the State Farm Bureau Federation laid a cornerstone for their later cooperation within the G.L.F. Moreover, the Dairymen's League also participated in this project since many local League branches likewise pooled orders for seed through the State Grange Exchange.

From the beginning, the New York Grange Exchange was handicapped by lack of capital, for its initial paid-in capital amounted to only $3,000, a sum entirely inadequate for its ambitious objectives. Since its capital was so limited it could operate only on a brokerage basis. At first it simply purchased supplies to cover orders from its members, most of which were assembled through the local granges. The only way it could obtain merchandise was to arrange for it to be shipped on a sight draft bill of lading basis. Even with this handicap, the Grange Exchange succeeded in obtaining supplies from a number of reputable concerns.

However, the power of the organized trade was soon demonstrated in the case of feed. When the Grange Exchange began operations it had entered into an informal agreement with a concern under which feed was to be manufactured on an open-formula basis and sold as Grange Exchange Dairy Feed. Almost immediately the regular dealer customers of this concern boycotted it with the result that it had to terminate its deal with the Grange Exchange so as to continue in business. The same sort of opposition came in obtaining fertilizer, farm machinery, or other supplies.

The Grange Exchange, although well supported by the state

Grange, the Farm Bureaus, and the Dairymen's League, thus met with immediate difficulties in getting its plans into operation due to the bitter opposition of competing private organizations. It was extremely difficult to obtain supplies of feed, fertilizer, and other needed supplies from manufacturers who were fearful that dealing with the Grange Exchange would cause private dealers to boycott them and leave them with no certain outlet except the not well-established Grange Exchange.

Notwithstanding such difficulties in arranging for sources of supply, the volume of Grange Exchange business steadily expanded. The attitude of many farmers in New York toward the venture was well expressed in an editorial, "We Must Support the Grange Exchange," in the *Dairymen's League News* of March 1919. This editorial declared:

> As might be expected, it [the Grange Exchange] is meeting with bitter opposition from dealers and others. We understand that many of the wholesale feed dealers are refusing to sell feed to this farmers' organization. This is simply a revival of what the organized feed dealers have tried to do before; that is, to make it impossible for farmers to buy grain or obtain supplies cooperatively. The fact remains, however, that it is impossible for the dealers to succeed, providing the farmers stand by themselves, that is, by organization. Not only every granger, but every farmer in New York State should get solidly back of the New York State Exchange and stay back of it.

Although the State Grange Exchange had begun to establish itself by early 1920, there was a widespread belief that it was not set up on a basis that would attract full support of all New York farmers. The catalytic agent for bringing about unification was the Conference Board of Farm Organizations.

The Conference Board Achieves Coordination, 1918-1920

The pressure of events had been gradually forcing the various farm organizations of New York to work together on common problems. The Dairymen's League had needed the support of the Grange and the Farm Bureau on milk marketing and feed buying plans; the Grange had found that its cooperative marketing and purchasing efforts could not be restricted to Grange members and be effective; while the State Federation of Farm Bureau Associations, in view of its partial support by state and federal funds as an educational agency, needed the backing of all farmers, regardless of their other affiliations.

Although these state-wide organizations of farmers had much in common, prior to 1918 there was little coordination of effort and as a result "it had become established technique in the New York State Legislature for legislative leaders to line up one farm organization

against another and then say to farmers, 'We can't give you any legislation because you aren't agreed as to what you want.' "[13]

The need for some kind of coordinating center had long been obvious, but it took a direct problem to bring one into being. In the winter
of 1918, John J. Dillon, publisher of the *Rural New Yorker*—disgruntled
by the unwillingness of existing organizations to accept his leadership—
undertook to establish the New York Federation of Agriculture to
supersede all other farm organizations in the state. This aroused the
existing state organizations to action and led in May 1918 to a meeting
of their leaders in New York City where it was decided to form a body
which subsequently became known as the New York State Agricultural
Conference Board. The original members were the New York State
Grange, The Dairymen's League, Inc., The New York State Federation
of County Farm Bureau Associations, and the New York State Horticultural Society. As the primary object of the Conference Board was
to promote the common interests of its member organizations it was
agreed that it would "speak for its members only when they were
unanimous in their opinions."

During the next two years the Conference Board integrated the
support of the various farm organizations on many problems of common
concern, and it was this body—rather than its constituent member
organizations—which actually brought about the establishment of the
Cooperative Grange League Federation Exchange in 1920.

Shortly after the annual meeting of the Grange Exchange in February 1920, W. L. Bean, the newly-elected president, called upon H. E.
Babcock, then secretary of the New York State Federation of Farm
Bureau Associations, to enlist his support on a plan designed to make the
New York Grange Exchange a state-wide purchasing association for all
farmers in New York—whether or not Grangers. Babcock was not immediately impressed with the soundness of the proposal. He later said: "I
found so many holes in the plan that I talked him out of it and also
thoroughly convinced myself of the folly of any such idea."[14] However,
Babcock's "cold water" did not discourage Bean. In fact, it stimulated
him to develop his idea more realistically, which he did with the assistance of W. G. Morse, the attorney for the Grange Exchange.

Although the revised plan did not entirely convince Babcock, he
saw its possibilities and agreed to call up the proposal for discussion at
the spring meeting of the Agricultural Conference Board. Before this
meeting was held Babcock became convinced that Bean's idea was
sound and he became an earnest advocate.

The real beginning of the G.L.F. thus came with the meeting of the Conference Board at the Yates Hotel, Syracuse, in late April 1920. At this meeting Bean's proposal was carefully considered and a decision was made to form a state-wide purchasing cooperative designed to attract the support of all farmers in New York. The imagination and foresight of the group was displayed in three vital decisions made at this meeting.

1. It was agreed that the authorized capital would be set at $1,000,000. This was a "bold stroke," for it served notice that the organization was to be "no piddling affair."

2. It was agreed that the new organization would be named the Cooperative Grange League Federation Exchange, a name which would show that the new organization had behind it the New York State *Grange*, the Dairymen's *League*, Inc., and the New York State *Federation* of Farm Bureau Associations. The G.L.F. was a natural nickname and it soon took hold.

3. It was agreed that responsibility for raising the capital required would be vested in H. E. Babcock with the understanding that he would devise such plans for this purpose as he might deem necessary.

With these decisions made, the Grange Exchange was in position to work out a plan acceptable to its stockholders for turning over its assets to the proposed new organization. Thus the G.L.F. was launched. How it overcame its problems to become one of the major cooperative organizations in the world will be examined in Volume II of this history.

Part Five

THE EXPANDING
COOPERATIVE UNIVERSE

While cooperative marketing and purchasing was progressing rapidly from 1897 to 1920 other forms of cooperative enterprise were gaining strength. During these years farmers made increasing use of cooperatives for crop and livestock improvement, and for insurance, irrigation, and telephone services. In fact, wherever farmers had an economic problem they turned to cooperatives for its solution.

Of particular interest in this period was the experience of cooperative stores in serving the needs of consumers, and the efforts made to establish regional and national wholesale associations. Little was achieved, other than the formation of The Cooperative League of the U.S.A., but many lessons of future usefulness were learned.

It was during these years that the mutual form of cooperative organization became well established in life insurance, savings banks, and building and loan associations. Businessmen also found that they could advantageously use cooperatives to meet many problems. For example, retail grocers, druggists, and hardware merchants—confronted by strong competition from mail-order houses, department stores, and chain stores—found it desirable to set up cooperative wholesale firms, later to be known as "retailer cooperatives." Bankers also found it practicable to use the cooperative form of organization in the operation of clearing houses, and all kinds of mercantile establishments turned to the nonprofit form of organization in setting up credit rating bureaus. Moreover, newspapers developed the greatest news gathering association in the world on cooperative lines. Thus, the cooperative form of enterprise was employed as a supplement, or partner, to other forms of business organization whenever it could perform services not otherwise available.

Chapter XXI

THE COOPERATIVE STORE MOVEMENT

By 1897, organized labor had lost interest in cooperative workshops, and it was placing its confidence in the power of collective bargaining. It had found "self-employment through the self-governing or cooperative workshop . . . a snare and a delusion,"[1] . . . although it continued to give support to the formation of cooperative stores.

During the next quarter century the cooperative store movement was marked by vigorous experimentation as it attempted to adapt itself to a rapidly changing business environment. The nation was steadily becoming industrialized and urbanized, and there were growing up new forms of mass merchandising—mail-order houses, department stores, and chain store systems.[2]

In this chapter we will trace cooperative store developments as they unfolded in three almost unrelated regions—New England, the Midwest and the Far West. As a background it should be noted that cooperative store activity was almost dormant as the nineteenth century drew to a close. As Sonnichsen has pointed out, this form of cooperation then "seemed dead. Nowhere was there any sign of an expansive propaganda with social ideas, with a general program."[3]

Trial and Error in New England

When the Cooperative Union collapsed in 1899 (see Chapter II), the propaganda work of the *American Cooperative News* was soon taken over by the *American Cooperator,* a journal which for several years published enthusiastic articles on all things cooperative. This journal was the organ of a little group headed by Bradford Peck, the owner of a department store at Lewiston, Maine, and the author in

1900 of *The World a Department Store—A Story of Life under a Cooperative System*.[4] Owing to Peck's efforts there was organized in 1900 a body known as the Cooperative Association of America, which proceeded "to begin the cooperative organization of industry upon a small scale and extend its scope gradually through all fields of industry."[5]

Somewhat dissatisfied by the slow acceptance of this plan, the promoters of the Association in 1904 proceeded to establish the Cooperative Exchange of Boston with two departments, one "to build up retail cooperative societies," and the other "to organize the wholesale and jobbing field so that there will be the least possible waste between the manufacturers and consumer."[6] The plan in reality envisaged a combination of private and cooperative stores in a purchasing federation. This is shown by a statement of the Exchange's secretary: "We wish to have as many cooperative stores as possible for members of the 'Exchange' and shall systematically encourage the conversion of private owned stores into cooperative stores."[7] Although some cooperative stores were formed, the plan did not meet with hearty response and apparently collapsed some time after 1913.[8]

The immigrant impulse. While the Cooperative Association of America was striving to establish the Cooperative Exchange of Boston, a more substantial "grass roots" development was springing up among the various immigrant groups in New England. As was pointed out in Chapter V, there was a large influx of immigrants into the United States which came to full flood about 1890, and many of these first settled in New England. In general, these immigrants came in groups from their home countries and retained for a period a high degree of social cohesion favorable to cooperative organization. Like the frontiersmen who banded together for protection against the Indians, these newcomers banded together to set up cooperative stores to protect themselves from economic exploitation. Moreover, some of them, especially those from England, had already acquired cooperative experience which they could apply in their new environment.

In many instances the cooperative stores formed by these groups were closed organizations, comprised of immigrants from a common country. An exception was those formed by English workingmen, who were less handicapped by language barriers and customs in the process of assimilation, and who generally opened their associations to any interested persons. By 1900, there were a number of "immigrant" cooperative stores, and during the next dozen years their number greatly expanded. James Ford's study, *Cooperation in New England,* in 1913, found some 30 store associations in New England which had been founded by English, German, Swedish, Belgian, French, Italian, Polish, Lithuanian, and Finnish groups.

The clannish character of many of these early cooperatives precluded much interest in federation except on nationality lines and, even here, this was made difficult by the scattered character of the settlements. However, there was one highly significant experiment in federation undertaken by the Finnish groups in eastern Massachusetts that deserves mention. In 1910, five Finnish stores in this area established a wholesale depot at Maynard, Massachusetts. The success of this venture made the Finnish stores outstanding among the workingmen's cooperatives in New England. Their solidarity was further increased in 1911 by the formation of the Eastern Finnish Cooperative Educational League—possibly patterned on the Pelervo Society in Finland—which carried on a campaign of cooperative education among the Finnish settlements.

Following a period of flourishing growth during the war years, six of the leading Finnish cooperatives—located at Maynard, Fitchburg, Quincy, Norwood, Gardner, and Worcester—proceeded to unify further their movement by pooling their capital and properties in an organization incorporated as The United Cooperative Society of New England. This organization was designed to achieve lower wholesale prices through quantity buying and more efficient supervision over local operations. To achieve this end the local societies allowed themselves to be almost completely merged in the new organization. As one observer said: "From all intents and purposes, it was a chain store in character for it owned and controlled the properties and capital of its members."[9]

This ambitious plan soon disclosed serious weaknesses. For one thing "the consolidation of properties caused friction between wealthier and poorer societies." There were also "factional quarrels over political issues." With the severe price drop in 1920 the organization was dissolved and its capital was apportioned back to the original member societies.[10]

Although the collapse of this experiment retarded the unification of cooperative effort in New England, it at least cleared the air for subsequent developments in federation. It taught the Finnish cooperators that the control of their local societies must remain in their communities, and that the control of any cooperative federation must remain in its local societies.

Efforts in the Midwest

During the years from 1897 to 1920 the Midwest was a center for experiments in cooperative store development. In the first part of this period cooperative stores were advanced to a large extent by the efforts of one man, N. O. Nelson—a self-made St. Louis manufacturer—who had become nationally known in the 1880's for his successful experiments in profit-sharing.[11]

Convinced of the need for a national organization of cooperative store societies, Nelson worked tirelessly toward that end. In 1898, after a visit to the well-known Johnson County Cooperative Association at Olathe, Kansas, we find him commenting as follows: "There are many small stores scattered through Kansas and Missouri but the absence of a Union prevents active movements."[12] In 1902, he wrote to all cooperative stores of record, inquiring whether they would be interested in joining either a national or a state federation and of the 192 stores that reported, about half replied "affirmatively."

The desirability of a national cooperative federation, as advocated by Nelson, was recognized in June 1904 at a national cooperative convention held in St. Louis during the World's Fair. This meeting brought together representatives from most of the important groups interested in promoting cooperative stores, and they immediately adopted the Rochdale-type system for organizing cooperative associations throughout the United States. They then organized a national association, "The National Cooperative League," which was to carry on educational and organizational work.[13] While nothing came of this "paper organization" Nelson continued energetically to promote the organization of cooperative associations on the Rochdale plan, and the improvement of their business methods. Nelson next became associated with the efforts of the Right Relationship League (described in a following section) and in 1909 he served as an associate editor of its publication, *Co-operation*.

Disillusioned at last by the slow growth of Rochdale cooperative stores, Nelson in 1915 struck out on new lines in an experiment which was designed to prove that it was not necessary to operate on Rochdale lines to achieve Rochdale ends. "Believing the bayou region around New Orleans, Louisiana, to be one of the most impoverished and backward areas of the United States, he undertook to establish there, with his own money, a chain of stores, which should eventually pass into the control of the customers."[14] For a time this enterprise, incorporated as the Nelson Cooperative Association, grew rapidly until it included

"61 retail stores, four meat markets, a large bakery, a milk pasteurizing plant, a coffee factory, a condiment factory, and a 1,500 acre farm," and claimed sales of "between two and three million dollars per year."[15]

Nelson aimed to demonstrate the advantages of large volume turnover as a basis for "inviting the main capital subscriptions from consumers," and to increase sales volume he sold at the lowest possible margin over cost of goods, his goal being to reduce all expense to 10 per cent of sales. The basic weakness of the plan came from this pricing policy which not only did not permit the accumulation of capital through savings, but brought on price wars. As Kallen pointed out:

> [Nelson] omitted one technic which establishes consumer cooperation as consumer cooperation. For some occult reason, Nelson did away with the dividend on purchase . . . Customer control subsequently could only come about through the investment of share capital in the company's stock. But the dividend on purchase was the only way in which the farmers and workers, especially of the bayous could ever secure any capital to invest.[16]

With his working capital finally absorbed in over-expanded operations, Nelson filed a personal petition for bankruptcy in 1918. This brought to a close Nelson's 30-year campaign in behalf of cooperation.[17]

The influence of the Right Relationship League. While Nelson was evangelically promoting cooperative stores, support came from an unexpected quarter—a group of businessmen. To understand this development, it is essential to realize that many retailers in the closing years of the last century were alarmed over the increasing growth of mass merchandising institutions, particularly the department stores and mail-order firms. These retailers saw the necessity of cooperation for their own protection through the formation of cooperative wholesale associations with retailers as members.[18] Some of them even became interested in the possibility of turning over their stores to their customers for operation on a cooperative basis.

The genesis of the Right Relationship League came from the formation of the Associated Merchants, USA, of Chicago, in the middle 1890's, to serve as the cooperative buying agency for a group of retail stores. In 1900, the company was reorganized as the Cooperating Merchants Company of Chicago under a plan which provided for equal shareholdings of $1,000 per store and, at the same time, an allied propaganda organization—the Right Relationship League—was formed to assist local merchants to convert their operations to a cooperative basis.[19]

Under the League plan, a painless revolution was to replace private stores with cooperative stores. The plan was simple. In the event that the private owner wished to transform his store to a cooperative basis, the League would undertake to organize an association which would buy him out and, if mutually agreeable, employ him as manager. The associations were to obtain funds for buying out existing stores through sale of $100 shares of stock to individuals. No individual was to own more than one share and each stockholder was to have one vote, without the privilege of proxy voting. Business was to be conducted on a cash basis, and goods were to be sold at market prices. Net profits were to be distributed annually among the members according to the amount of their patronage, after providing for 8 per cent interest payment on shares, depreciation, educational, and other reserves. The plan evidently had an appeal, for in 1905 about 20 of the 450 members of the Cooperating Merchants Company were then operating as cooperative stores.[20]

As the League gained experience in converting private stores into cooperatives, its plan became more and more independent of the Cooperating Merchants Company. In 1907, it broke away entirely and established its own offices in Minneapolis, for interest in cooperative development in the Northwest was becoming intense. The real life of the League as a cooperative store-organizing force dates from this action. Within a short time it succeeded in establishing several cooperative stores and, in 1909, it started the publication of an informative journal, *Cooperation*, which carried contributions from prominent cooperators. The League also issued large quantities of pamphlet literature spreading the gospel of "True Cooperation—the real thing."[21]

The control of the League was largely vested in its founders, although an effort was made to achieve democratic operation. The funds for carrying on the work of the League came largely from commissions paid by merchants from the proceeds of the sale of their stores to the cooperatives which the League organized, and from the sale of its publications, as all members of cooperative stores set up by the League were required to subscribe to *Cooperation*. Another source of revenue was the fees charged for auditing and similar services. The organizing methods of the League have been described as follows:

> Its organizers would go to a private merchant (usually in a farming locality) who, for some reason or other, was willing to turn his store over "to the people," and would enter into a contract with him, to the effect that if the organizer succeeded in forming a cooperative store company in the locality, the merchant was to sell his store to the new organization at a certain approved price and give the League a commission (varying from 5 to 7 per cent of the appraised value of the stock of merchandise) for its trouble in completing the organization work. Frequently the former owner of the store continued to manage the business for the cooperative company.[22]

Under this plan the amount of stock sold depended upon the size of the establishment to be taken over, the customary amount ranging from $5,000 to $30,000. Moreover, the cooperative company did not assume control until a sufficient amount of capital had been raised.

The League plan of "True Cooperation," known as The American Rochdale Plan of the Right Relationship League, contemplated

> a store and shipping department owned exclusively by local people, in every leading community, by which means the entire buying and selling power of many communities may be eventually concentrated through their Cooperative Wholesale and Terminal Societies. This store allows the redistribution of the wealth produced by profits and saving, among those who actually create it and who assume the responsibility of ownership.[23]

As the League program developed, it was soon found that one of the greatest weaknesses of cooperative stores lay in their accounting methods. The League thereupon devised a set of accounting books and report forms and, in 1908, an auditing department was set up to assist cooperatives on their accounting problems.

From the beginning, the leaders of the League had recognized the desirability of uniting the League stores in a cooperative wholesale federation. However, an effort to establish a wholesale with League stores as members, undertaken in 1907, with the advisory assistance of N. O. Nelson, proved premature and did much to blight further efforts along this line. As a result of this experience, the League concentrated its efforts toward the building up of a network of strong local associations as a necessary preliminary step for the formation of a cooperative wholesale. In June 1914, the position of the League with regard to the advisability of forming a cooperative wholesale was fully expressed in an editorial in *Cooperation,* entitled "Taking the Next Step." It was maintained that the cooperative stores of the Northwest must "solve and solve right" three principal problems "before they may expect to be successful in inaugurating a wholesale cooperative." (1) Membership must be educated to appreciate efficient business principles. (2) Each store must increase its membership and capital. (3) Credit business must be cut out *in toto.*

As an organizing force the League had five fundamental defects:

1. Its plan encouraged the formation of weak stores through the payment of commissions to "organizers." As would be expected, the organizers were little concerned with the success of a store after it had been set up. The plan also resulted in collusion between the organizers and the store owners, who were glad to have an opportunity to unload unsuccessful stores.

2. Few of the previous store owners who were employed as managers

made good cooperative managers. It was not practicable to expect them to change the habits of a lifetime overnight and be sympathetic advocates of the cooperative method of operation. Moreover, few store owners who were competent as managers were attracted by the scheme.

3. After the organization stock was sold to buy out a store it was found impossible to sell additional stock to provide capital for expansion. Dry rot set in after the initial capital was used up.

4. The League had no control over the widely scattered stores established. It was a promotional body rather than a federation and without democratic backing no policy for improvement could be enforced.

5. The League had no clear objectives. It lost its position of leadership as it became more and more opportunistic. In the words of Albert Sonnichsen it "attempted to straddle two steeds that will not pull together: consumers' cooperation and agricultural cooperation."[24]

Although these weaknesses eventually brought on the League's collapse in 1915 it can be given much credit for its accomplishments in organizing many successful cooperatives and promoting better cooperative business practices.[25] For six years (1909-1914), its propaganda flooded the Northwest and much of it lodged and took root in successful cooperative enterprises.

The Central States experience.[26] In the early 1900's, several cooperative stores were formed among the miners of southern Illinois. These early societies were nourished by the propaganda efforts of N. O. Nelson and the Right Relationship League, fused with a growing spirit of miners' solidarity following their organization in District No. 12 of the United Mine Workers.

The success of some of these early miners' societies paved the way for a more intensive development which commenced about 1912, when Illinois leaders in the United Mine Workers began to turn their full energies to the promotion of cooperative stores as a means of lowering the cost of living. In 1913, four cooperative stores were opened, and these were followed by 7 in 1914 and 18 more in 1915.

Sensing the need for a central promotional and coordinating agency to serve the rapidly growing interest in cooperation, John H. Walker, President of the Illinois Federation of Labor, and Duncan MacDonald, Secretary of District No. 12, United Mine Workers, called a convention of cooperative representatives to meet at Springfield on March 22, 1915. This meeting brought forth the Cooperative Society of Illinois which was designed to "encourage and assist local societies in combining their purchasing power through some centrally located buying agency."

When the Cooperative Society of Illinois held its next convention, in July 1916, attention was directed to the problem of finding "ways and means of forming a wholesale," but no definite program of joint buying was achieved. However, at this meeting the Society adopted the name "Central States Cooperative Association."

When the Central States Cooperative Association held its annual convention in September 1917, the avowed purpose was "to agree on the basis of establishment of a cooperative wholesale department." The number of individual cooperative societies established by the miners had increased to 50, while there were perhaps as many other cooperative stores formed by farmers and other workers' groups in the state.

The sentiment of the 1917 convention was expressed in a remark of one of the delegates: "Start doing something and not be forever discussing the proposition," and plans for a wholesale to be formed under Illinois cooperative law were devised. The wholesale was to be a federation of stores affiliated with the Central States Cooperative Association, with shareholdings limited to five $100 shares for each society. To begin with, a committee was appointed to negotiate with wholesale houses for collective buying and arrangements were made for the employment of a salesman to solicit orders from local cooperative stores.

The program of joint buying became a reality in February 1918 with the employment of a sales agent. An arrangement was worked out with a wholesale firm for a 5 per cent discount on the wholesale price of groceries, and miners' tools were obtained from another firm at jobbers' prices. This program gave immediate satisfaction, and in June a second salesman was employed to serve the rapidly growing demand for this service.

The Central States Cooperative Association held its next convention (September 1918) in a spirit of jubilation. The growth of stores had continued unabated, the plan of joint buying was at last under way, and sentiment was strong for the immediate formation of a cooperative wholesale. This spirit was furthered by the launching of the National Cooperative Wholesale at the first convention of the Cooperative League (described later) which was held in Springfield immediately following the convention of the Central States Cooperative Association. On December 5, the Central States Society commenced wholesale operations with the purchase of a warehouse at East St. Louis, with Robert McKetcham, the sales agent, as manager.

However, the new plan did not immediately "catch on." Only 7 of the 55 eligible Rochdale societies joined during December, and sales for the month totaled little more than $5,000. When little additional support came in January and February, the officials of the Society forsook their plan of federation in favor of a centralized plan, with branch store operations.

The American Rochdale Chain Store Plan.[27] This new plan soon became popularized as the American Rochdale Chain Store Plan and for the next three years it was the dominant form of cooperation among Illinois miners. This plan was not conceived as a whole, but grew piece-meal out of local conditions. Its start came in February 1919 when an arrangement was effected "whereby the Central States Cooperative Wholesale Society sold goods in bulk to [a local] union at [Herrin] Illinois, a miners' committee undertaking the task of distribution." The idea worked and soon resulted in the establishment of a full-time distributing station. This branch undertook to sell on a cash-and-carry basis at the wholesale cost plus 9 per cent, a margin which was considered adequate to cover expenses and provide a 3 per cent profit to the wholesale.

The simplicity of this arrangement, coupled with its apparent success, led to an insistent demand for similar branches in neighboring mining towns and by July 1919, when the society held its convention, four stores were in operation. At that meeting the manager gave a glowing report of accomplishments and contrasted the branch store plan favorably with the slow results which had been obtained before the plan had been tested. To force the independent retail stores to support the wholesale, it was decided that branch stores would be opened wherever the local Rochdale stores did not give the Wholesale at least 80 per cent of their business.

In November 1919, the American Rochdale plan reached full flower with the adoption of a constitution for the Central States Cooperative Wholesale Society. Membership was to be open to cooperative societies, labor unions, and individuals upon subscribing to five shares of stock ($100 par value) bearing 4 per cent interest. Control was to be vested in a board of directors of 10 men who were to meet once every three months. Auditing was to be done by three elected auditors. In time of strike, goods were to be sold at cost to unions holding shares in the society.

With 15 branches opened by the end of 1919, "cooperative sentiment throughout Illinois was rapidly shifting from its previous straight Rochdale bias," and the movement was becoming more and more a union activity. Large investments began to come in from local unions and the district miners' organizations.

The American Rochdale plan by now had become formulated into a definite pattern. Local unions desiring a store were expected to invest prescribed amounts in the share and loan capital of the Central States Cooperative Wholesale Society, ordinarily 25 per cent in excess of the amount of goods required at the retail branch. The Wholesale furnished a manager and a stock of goods to the new branch. Goods from the Wholesale were billed to the retail branch at the Wholesale's cost; plus 10 per cent. This percentage was to cover expenses of the Wholesale, the freight, the salary of the store force, and provide a reserve for the Wholesale. The local branch store was to add 2 per cent to this cost (or 4 per cent if the store delivered) to cover rental and miscellaneous local expenses. No provision was made for patronage refunds on the theory that this plan would give the customer "his dividend in the basket."

The rate of growth of local branches accelerated from 15 on January 20 to 30 on March 16, and to 40 on May 3. By February 26, 1921, there were 70. In March, the enthusiasm of Manager McKetcham and of the other leaders knew almost no bounds. McKetcham predicted: "Before the year is out we will have stores in every labor center in Illinois ... I believe that the American Rochdale plan will be running in every town in the United States before five years." This enthusiasm was shared by Professor Gordon Watkins of the University of Illinois who wrote to the leaders of the Wholesale: "I believe you have started something that is going to be one of the biggest things on the American continent."[28] For the six-month period ending June 30, 1920, sales totaled $1,068,635, and sales were steadily increasing with each month.

When the Society met for its annual convention in September 1920, President Walker characterized its growth during the preceding year as "a magnificent accomplishment" and he claimed that the system had saved $200,000 for its membership. However, unmistakable signs were beginning to appear that the organization was riding the tide of inflation. There was no adequate system of management control, and without effective supervision the branches were recklessly extending their operations into paints, hardware, and meats. Local management at the branches was steadily deteriorating as shown by tardy daily reports, overemployment of help, overstocking of merchandise, and careless extension of credit. The auditors who were to serve as district supervisors proved totally unsuited for their function, as most were "political appointees" selected for their loyalty to the District Mine Workers. As President Walker remarked, "As auditors, they would make excellent ditchdiggers."[29]

To make matters worse, the central office was overworked and poorly equipped to provide adequate supervision and direction. The manager was torn between his responsibilities as organizer, wholesale manager, and supervisor of local stores. Advancing prices also brought on extravagance and speculation. To obtain goods, it was necessary to buy certain merchandise on future contracts which threatened heavy loss should there be a rapid decline in price. In one transaction during the summer of 1920 involving the advance purchase of sugar, a loss of $36,000 was suffered. With the drop in prices during the fall of 1920, the unemployment of miners made matters worse, and during this time private and chain stores "fearing for their existence" waged price-cutting wars "against the American Rochdale plan enterprisers." Managers of the local branches complained that they could not meet close competition with the prices charged by the wholesale.

At the 1920 convention in September, the enthusiasm of the advocates of the American Rochdale plan had become tempered by a realization that all was not going well. By this time the postwar boom had broken, and a sober view of prospects was prevalent. The fears of many were voiced by Dr. James P. Warbasse, President of the Cooperative League of America (since 1922 named "The Cooperative League of the United States of America, Incorporated") who challenged the chain store plan by saying: "You are really stretching a point to call an American Rochdale store a cooperative store ... The right name is a trade union store." President Walker was unconvinced. He maintained that "the check-off system applied to cooperation will get us the finances of the indifferent ... and help ... to build up the great cooperative movement."

Following the convention, conditions went from bad to worse. Prices steadily declined with increasing inventory losses, and discontent among the branches swelled. The central office was inundated with complaints that the prices of the wholesale were out of line.

There is no need to prolong the description of the gradual decline and eventual failure of the American Rochdale plan of the Central States Cooperative Wholesale Society. Even with transfusions of capital by the unions and a drastic reorganization, the initial momentum could not be recaptured. After October 1920 its life was one "of lingering death."

In passing from this brief description of the highly publicized American Rochdale Chain Store Plan, mention should be made of the significant lessons that were derived from this experience. These were well set forth by Colston E. Warne, as follows:

> First, workers have come to realize the need of local interest in cooperation, which is possible only with local control. Second, the cost-plus system of retail pricing has shown itself unworkable under the prevailing conditions. Third, the necessity is more clearly seen of divorcing cooperation from union-

ism, thus finding relief from the political antagonisms and inefficiencies which are grafted onto the movement by such affiliation. Fourth, a better appreciation of the need for accounting control has been brought home to co-operators. Finally, the movement presents at once a fair picture of, and a challenge to, democracy. Leaders were blind, and the followers were blind. Consequently in the attempt to build the structure to the sky, success was not forthcoming. Cooperation must of necessity move slowly, groping its way through new problems. A bold sally toward a changed order cannot move faster than the managerial technique employed.[30]

The Tri-State Cooperative Association. Another interesting organization of a somewhat similar character developed in the area around Pittsburgh during 1917. At that time there were several local cooperative associations, mostly composed of miners, operating in western Pennsylvania, eastern Ohio, and northern West Virginia. With these as a nucleus, the Tri-State Cooperative Association (formed under the energetic leadership of Dalton T. Clark, a young lawyer who gave up his practice to devote all of his attention to cooperative expansion) began to open retail branches, with the intent of later converting them into *bona fide* independent Rochdale societies. Ownership of these stores was vested in the collective membership of the association, and their management was placed in the hands of the Tri-State Board of Directors, officers, and central operating forces assisted by local committees.

To finance its operations, the Tri-State issued two kinds of stock, "permanent" and "ordinary," paying interest at the rate of 6 and 5 per cent respectively. The latter was, in effect, loan capital as it was withdrawable on 90 days' written notice. Members were required to pay $1 membership fee, and purchase at least five $10 shares, of which two were to be for "permanent" stock. Already established independent cooperative stores could become branches by taking Tri-State stock for the value of their net assets, and turning this stock over to their members so that each member would have at least two shares of permanent and three shares of ordinary stock.

All of the retail branches were operated as a unit through a "retail" department which supervised all accounting and auditing work, provided for local management, and returned—if made—a uniform dividend to all local societies irrespective of their individual efficiency. A bonus was also payable to employees on their salaries at the same rate. In April 1920, twenty-two branches were operating. Independent retail cooperative stores could become members of the wholesale department through purchasing $200 worth of permanent stock, and such stores were paid patronage dividends on the basis of their patronage. Some 20 stores of this type were connected with the Tri-State in April 1920.[31]

Overexpanded and inefficiently managed, the Tri-State Association was unable to weather the economic crisis of 1920-1921.

The Cooperative Wholesale Society of America. Building upon the work of the Equity, the Right Relationship League, and other promotional groups in the Northwest, the Cooperative Wholesale Society of America was formed in the autumn of 1917, with central offices at St. Paul. Its aim was to serve both as a wholesale buying and marketing agency for farmers' cooperative stores and associations in Minnesota, Iowa, the Dakotas, Montana, and the Pacific Northwest. It was first capitalized at $10,000, but within a year this was increased to $1,000,000. Any cooperative organization subscribing to the Rochdale plan of operation could become a member through purchasing $1,000 worth of capital stock. There were 28 member associations in early 1920, with a combined membership of 5,000.

Buying and marketing operations were carried on through separate departments. In its wholesale buying department, goods were handled at current wholesale prices, and retail savings were paid to member associations in proportion to their purchases, while non-member associations were paid savings at one-half the rate of dividend paid member associations. Employees of the Cooperative Wholesale Society were also paid a bonus on wages.

The Cooperative Wholesale Society ceased to function in 1921 when it was unable to weather the prevailing economic depression. The cause of its failure lay in overextension of credit and similar weaknesses which showed up when economic conditions became difficult.[32]

Cooperative Central Exchange. The only regional cooperative to mature later in the form of a strong cooperative wholesale society was started in 1917 by a group of Finnish cooperative stores in the area centering on Superior, Wisconsin. To understand this development, it is necessary to know that a high proportion of the foreign-born Finns living in this country were then concentrated in the Lake Superior district of Minnesota, Michigan, and Wisconsin. Most of these immigrants were employed as miners or lumberjacks, although in Finland they had been farmers.[33]

At first, these Finns got their supplies from company stores, but the company stores soon gave way to private merchants who charged monopoly prices for supplies of inferior quality. This fact soon led the Finns to band together for their own protection by forming cooperative stores on the Rochdale plan. As the local Finnish cooperative stores gained experience, they felt the need of a central wholesale organization and, on July 30, 1917, seventeen societies came together at Superior,

Wisconsin, and launched the Cooperative Central Exchange which changed its name in 1931 to Central Cooperative Wholesale. Within a month a warehouse had been acquired and business begun. From then on, the organization steadily gained ground, its sales increasing from $132,287 in 1918 to $409,591 in 1920, while the number of member associations rose from 17 to 44.

The Cooperative Central Exchange appreciated the need of trained personnel from the beginning and it inaugurated in 1918 the first American cooperative training school for employees. As a result of its conservative policies and good management, this organization was able to weather the economic depression of 1920-21.[34] (In 1964, the Central Cooperative Wholesale became part of Midland Cooperatives, Inc., Minneapolis, Minnesota.)

The West Coast Developments

In the closing years of the nineteenth century, cooperative stores began to spring up in a number of rural communities in central California as a means of lowering living costs. Representatives of these stores and others interested in the possibilities of cooperation came together in Oakland on November 7, 1899, for the purpose of launching a strong cooperative movement in California. This meeting resulted in the formation of the Pacific Coast Cooperative Union and a cooperative wholesale association which opened for business in San Francisco as a buying agency on January 1, 1900, as the Rochdale Wholesale Company. Since it was recognized at the outset that more cooperative stores would need to be organized if the wholesale were to be adequately supported, the Cooperative Union was established as a promotion department for their formation.

The plan of organization provided that local member associations would have an "equal ownership, equal vote, and equal share" in the wholesale society. As the stores were set up under a common "Rochdale" pattern, they became known as Rochdale stores and together these stores became known as the "Rochdale family." They did not represent a true federation in the sense of a coming together of locals, since the plan was developed from the top down.

The minimum membership stockholding in each local Rochdale store was set at $100, of which $10 was required upon entrance. The Rochdale Wholesale Company in turn required each member association to subscribe for a $1,000 share of stock, with $100 being required as a down payment. Profits were to be divided in the case of both the wholesale and the retail associations on the volume of purchases after tne payment of interest on the amount of paid-up shares.

During the first few years, the Rochdale family apparently prospered. In 1901, the formation of stores and encouragement of cooperation was facilitated by the publication of an effective eight-page monthly organ, *The Cooperative Journal*. By 1902, the steady increase in business made a move to more spacious quarters necessary.

By 1905, the progress of the Rochdale family was beginning to attract national attention. In a comprehensive study, *The Cooperative Store in the United States*, Ira B. Cross then asserted: "It is safe to say that in no place is the cooperative movement so strong or so successful as it is upon the Pacific Coast. The principles of cooperation have been sown far and wide throughout these states while the organization for the establishment and operation of cooperative stores has been made almost perfect."[35] Cross reported for 1905 that there were 64 cooperative stores in California, of which 51 were Rochdale companies. The Rochdale Wholesale Company was then doing an annual business of $260,000.

The volume of the Wholesale continued to grow modestly during the next few years but this did not indicate a gain in real strength. By 1911, many of the local stores had failed while others were showing serious weakness. Professor Cross had become somewhat disillusioned and in an article on "Cooperation in California" in the *American Economic Review* for September 1911 he found that only 23 of the 51 Rochdale stores engaged in business in 1905 were still in existence. Cross commented: "Truly a most unsatisfactory showing for the success of this branch of cooperative endeavor."

What had happened to the fond hopes of the Rochdale family enthusiasts? For one thing, business conditions affecting farmers had improved and they were less interested in the small gain that could be derived from cooperative effort. Then again, competitive service from private stores had improved, and it was less easy to show cash benefits. Like all movements of this kind which have been rapidly developed, insufficient attention had been given to the maintenance of capital and the conduct of business operations. Many of the associations failed on account of overextension of retail credit or through incompetent management. The members of the Rochdale family had grown up like a succession of Topsies and there was lacking any comprehensive plan of overhead supervision. While some of the stores gave their full support to the Rochdale Wholesale Company, many used it as a chisel to pry better deals from private wholesale firms. Although outside factors also contributed to the declining condition of the Rochdale family, the primary difficulties were internal. The stores had been hurriedly formed, and they were weak in financial and business stamina.

The California Rochdale Company. It had become apparent by the summer of 1910 that vigorous action would need to be taken to save the movement and the wholesale company. After considerable deliberation, a plan was devised for the unification of the movement as a whole. G. D. Rice, the principal advocate of the new plan, said: "I am convinced that what we need today is a general manager to travel and inspect the stores. I believe all locals should be under one management because such concentration in buying would give them a great advantage in the market." There was to be "one supervising manager, one auditor, one set of buyers for the entire chain."

To effectuate the new plan of "consolidated cooperation," a new organization, the California Rochdale Company, was set up with Rice as manager, designed to strengthen the Rochdale Wholesale Company, which was to serve as the source of supply for the branches of the California Rochdale Company.

The California Rochdale Company immediately proceeded to organize branch associations in local communities and nine were formed within as many months. Each branch was to be supervised by an assistant manager who would work under the general supervision of the manager of the Rochdale Company. Under the plan individual members of the California Rochdale Company were to have an equal interest in all of the branches. It was believed that they would thus be concerned with the efficiency of the system as a whole.

Though an effort was made to insure business stability, the plan disclosed weaknesses from the beginning. The scattered branches made supervision difficult and the plan of pooling all operations weakened local initiative and responsibility. With better administration, the plan might have survived, for one who observed the experience of the California Rochdale Company later commented:

> The plan had a good deal to recommend it and might have succeeded
> if it had been consistently pushed. The Federation, however, was very limited
> and ineffective and the management loose and lacking in efficiency. Unfor-
> tunately ... the new stores were not run on a cash basis, the educational
> work was almost nil, and buying was scattered in all directions. New stores
> were opened rather too rapidly to be properly established [and there was]
> insufficient capital to pay for the large stocks carried by most of the stores."[36]

Within less than two years, the California Rochdale Company could go no further, and its 10 cooperative stores were closed. By this time, the total number of local Rochdale stores had dwindled to 30, and most of these were on the verge of failure. If the Rochdale Wholesale Company

—which was suffering greatly from lack of volume and loss of money from defaulting stores—was to survive, a more ingenious remedy was required.

The Pacific Cooperative League. At this juncture a group of determined cooperators undertook to salvage the remnants of the old Rochdale movement by establishing the Pacific Cooperative League (1913) as a "propaganda and sustaining organization."

The League was organized with two kinds of members, "associate" and "full." Associate members paid five-dollar admission fees and were given the privilege of buying goods direct at wholesale prices. This plan was designed to give immediate cooperative benefits while relieving such members of any fear of future liability. The full members, who were required to pay $105 ($5 for entrance fee, $100 for membership), controlled the organization on the basis of one vote for a full member. Under this arrangement, the full members, who were the founders, established a protective dictatorship for the organization during its formative period. They shared alike in the responsibilities of management and in financial support.

At the beginning the League was a kind of mail-order scheme, tied to the Rochdale Company. The League took the orders from members and had them filled and shipped direct to the members by the Wholesale Company. The plan developed slowly, but gradually gained support. Buying clubs of League members began to form near San Francisco and some of these eventually grew into League stores. Haunted by the memory of the Rochdale Company's failure, the League was at first very conservative. It discouraged the use of the name "Rochdale" which had fallen into disrepute, and every effort was made to popularize the advantages and safety of the League idea.

In the first few years, the sales of the League, mostly of coal, sugar, and groceries, were very modest, being only $39,393 in 1914; $57,746 in 1915; and $61,074 in 1916.[37] When, in 1917, the League began to organize local stores, care was taken to establish each store on a secure basis. The first store, for example, was opened only after 40 individuals had paid up $25.00 each on full membership shares, as the management had set 40 members and $1,000 as a minimum requirement (later, the requirement was increased). Provision was made for a local board of directors elected by the members to act as a "management committee," but the store manager was selected and supervised by the central management.

The success of the first League store soon caused others to be formed and by October 1919 there were some 32 branches in California and

Arizona, either organized or being organized. This growth continued during 1920 with the extension of branches into Oregon, Washington, Idaho, Nevada, New Mexico, and even western Texas. By mid-summer, E. O. F. Ames, the president, claimed that the League had become a "sort of western states union" with himself "a sort of general manager for the western states." The League had already taken over the cooperative wholesale at San Francisco and district offices were being planned for Los Angeles, Portland, and Spokane. In March 1921, it claimed 47 member stores and a business volume running at the rate of $4 million a year.[38]

With the growth of the Pacific League system it became more and more a combination of centrally supervised stores. Although the president of the League maintained that the system "preserved the utmost of local autonomy with the efficiency of central supervision" the degree of control exerted by the League left little independence to the individual store. It is true that each store was permitted to declare its own dividends, but buying, management, financing, bookkeeping, and educational work were all centrally directed.

Several factors were responsible for the collapse of the League. Perhaps the main cause lay in the boom conditions that followed World War I. Within a short time many stores had been established over a wide territory with insufficient capital and without adequate preliminary work. Moreover, the promotional growth of the organizations diverted the attention of the management from close business supervision. Another cause of failure was the war waged by the Cooperative League of America on "centralized" cooperatives, which caused disruption within the local branches. This situation reached a climax in November 1920 when the delegates of the Pacific League were refused recognition at the National Congress of the Cooperative League. At this meeting, Dr. James P. Warbasse, President of the Cooperative League, declared: "It is quite correct to say that suspicion is growing against the Pacific League ... Complaints against the League accumulate so fast that I cannot keep track of them all. Much of the so-called educational work of the Pacific League is not education but advertising, aimed to sell stock. This policy results in flagrant misinterpretations ..."[39]

The Pacific Northwest labor development. While most of the cooperative stores on the Pacific Coast were drawn into the Pacific Cooperative League, there were a number which maintained their independence. Most of these were concentrated in the state of Washington, where cooperative stores in considerable numbers had been formed prior to the war. The period of most rapid development, however, came with the growth of a militant labor movement during World War I. As a contemporary writer described the situation:

> Out around Puget Sound is where things cooperative happen overnight. There it is all a question of months. [The Puget Sound area] is dotted with cooperatives, each possessed of the acute energy characteristic of the Seattle cooperators. A federation has been formed . . . which has behind it the drive of all the labor elements of the state. "The Big Idea" they call it, and as such it is known to all, without further description.[40]

For a time the outstanding cooperative in this area was the Cooperative Food Products Association of Seattle, which was formed in February 1918 by a group of militant labor leaders. Within a few months this organization had opened several branch stores and markets, and was doing a volume of business running at the rate of over $1 million a year. It was, however, a product of boom times. With the decline in prices and employment (especially when the shipyards closed down) after the war, it began to disintegrate. Its assets were finally taken over, in 1923, by the Associated Grange Warehouse—now the Grange Cooperative Wholesale.

The Drive Toward National Organization

With embryonic wholesale cooperatives springing up in several parts of the country during 1917-1918, it is not surprising that a sentiment was generated for a national cooperative wholesale association. This idea had a natural appeal to the imagination of cooperative leaders —one national wholesale similar to the powerful Cooperative Wholesale Society in England.

It is significant that the doctrine of consumers' cooperation was at this time just beginning to attract adherents in the United States.[41]

Under this philosophy all economic activity was to be under the control of consumers through local consumers' stores or associations which, in turn, were to federate to form regional and national organizations that were to undertake manufacturing and other essential services.[42] The principal proponent of this idea was The Cooperative League of America which had been launched in 1916, with Dr. James P. Warbasse as president.[43]

Imbued with this philosophy that consumers should be organized on a national basis with the League as the coordinating center, Dr. Warbasse undertook to bring together representatives of most of the "consumers' cooperatives" then in existence for the express purpose of launching a national cooperative wholesale society. The first Congress of the

Cooperative League, held at Springfield, Illinois, in September 1918, represented a culmination of these efforts.

When this Congress convened, Dr. Warbasse immediately appointed a committee on cooperative wholesale, saying: "I regard [this] as the most important committee which can grow out of this convention. The committee is made up of men who have given time and thought to the problem of a national wholesale. If this convention adjourns without setting on foot the measures to establish the national wholesale, it has failed in its most important possibility.[44]

The Committee on Cooperative Wholesale brought together the key figures of the various cooperative wholesale movements: Duncan Mac-Donald (Central States Cooperative Society), Dalton T. Clark (Tri-State Cooperative Society), John Nummivuori (Central Cooperative Wholesale), Carl E. Lunn (Washington State Society), C. F. Lowrie (Cooperative Wholesale Society of America), and Ernest O. F. Ames (Pacific Coast League).

Considering the later variation in the development of the groups represented, it is surprising that the members of the committee were so unanimous in the report that they presented to the Convention. However, at this time Rochdale thinking was still in the ascendancy—the centralized or chain store plan of organization not becoming popular until early 1919. The report of the committee was brief and general in character. It recommended that "a national cooperative wholesale association be inaugurated by this convention," and it proposed a detailed plan for putting this recommendation into effect.

This report was unanimously adopted by the League convention and those who had served on the committee were elected to serve on the temporary board of directors. The Board immediately named Dalton T. Clark, president, and C. F. Lowrie, secretary, and proceeded to take steps toward perfecting the organization.

The implementation of the plan proved more difficult than had been expected, for existing cooperative wholesales were reluctant to throw in their lot with the new organization. For example, the Central States Cooperative Society which was just on the point of establishing its own wholesale could not be persuaded to merge its efforts with those of the national. A somewhat similar situation developed among the Finnish cooperatives around Superior who had just formed their own Central Cooperative Wholesale. The Cooperative Wholesale Society of America at St. Paul, which had hoped to be the nucleus for the national organization, also stood aloof. The other two regional organizations of promise —the Pacific Cooperative League and the Tri-State Cooperative Society—

while willing to affiliate, were unwilling to convert themselves into branches of the national.[45]

On April 21, 1919, the National Cooperative Association (Wholesale) was finally incorporated under Wisconsin law with a capitalization of $1 million (10,000 shares at $100 each). The membership was restricted to Rochdale cooperative stores which were required to buy one share for each 100 members and would have one vote regardless of shareholdings. However, unions and individuals were invited to supply loan capital.

Confronted by the unwillingness of the existing organizations to merge in the national effort, the officers of the National Cooperative Association decided to set up chains of retail stores which were to be served by branches of the wholesale to be located at Chicago and other centers. The first branches were opened in Hoboken and Seattle in October, the Chicago branch not being opened until November 1919.

At each of these points, separate chain store organizations were formed as adjuncts of the regional wholesale offices. The way in which this system worked can be best illustrated by describing the methods followed in the Chicago area. Here the chain store organization was named the National Consumers' Cooperative Association. Under the plan devised, individual consumers became members of a retail branch store by paying a $3.00 membership fee and purchasing from two to five non-withdrawable $10.00 per value shares which drew 6 per cent interest. The members of the retail branches elected their own directors who in turn selected delegates to represent the branch at the quarterly meetings of the National Consumers Cooperative Association. The Board of Directors of the NCCA was composed of a director from each branch.

The close relationship of the National Consumers Cooperative Association to the National Cooperative Association was clear from the requirement that 25 per cent of the stock subscriptions of individuals in the NCCA were to be reinvested in shares of the National Cooperative Association. Moreover, the leaders in the two organizations were practically identical. T. Dalton Clark and C. F. Lowrie served as president and secretary respectively for both organizations.

The chain-store program was launched with an abundance of promotional energy. High-pressure organizers went "out in all directions" where, through "whirlwind campaigns ... people were stampeded into subscribing to shares in the association." To assist with propaganda, the National Consumers Cooperative Association in November started the publication of *The Cooperative News* which almost promised that the new plan would bring in the millennium.[46]

The progress of the organizational campaign after five months was shown by an audit as of March 31, 1920. On that date 5 stores were operating, while 20 were being developed. Paid-in subscriptions for stock amounted to $55,387, and unions and individuals had loaned $3,861. The operating record was depressing. Even though organization and development expense of $19,898 was carried in the assets, there was an operating loss of $4,355, and this covered a period of rapidly increasing prices. By early summer, pessimism with respect to the future of the plan was general. By then, paid-in stock subscriptions stood at $87,441, but organization expense had already absorbed a large portion of this. There were then 10 stores in operation and 7 of these were operating in the red. The loss for the system for the three months from March 31 to June 30 totaled $10,052.[47]

Control over the system was proving impossible and local management was steadily degenerating. This condition could not go on long, and a drastic reorganization was undertaken in July which attempted to achieve complete control over the branches. Unfortunately this action came too late to prove very effective, especially since prices had already begun to fall rapidly. Although strenuous efforts were made to tighten up by closing weak stores and by improving supervision, it was not possible to re-establish confidence in the plan. After a few more months of struggle, the 17 stores then in the system were placed in the hands of a receiver on February 19, 1921. "Thus the National Consumers Cooperative Association passed out of existence, 7,000 members losing their investment of $115,000."[48]

The situation in the Hoboken and Seattle areas largely duplicated that of Chicago. In these areas the chain-store plan was likewise oversold and inefficiently administered and few successful stores were ever placed in operation. The Seattle branch of the National Cooperative Association was forced to close as early as August 1920. The Hoboken experiment collapsed in December. Since the National Cooperative Association had placed its full confidence in the practicability of the chain-store plan and had developed little support from independent Rochdale retail stores, there was no possibility of continuing the experiment after the chain-store plan had failed.

In retrospect, it is easy to see how the National Cooperative Association made its mistakes. It must be appreciated that its organizers were caught up in a whirl of economic and social forces that were beyond their control. On paper, their plan was not so bad as their execution of it.

The experiment was commenced in a time of abnormal optimism which affected the thinking of the entire business community.[49] Like many private ventures in this same period, this effort collapsed with the drastic fall in prices. It is thus doubtful whether this experiment can be looked upon as a legitimate test of the principles involved in the plan attempted. Under different conditions and with different leadership, it might have succeeded.

It is of interest that Dr. Warbasse was one of the first to recognize the defects in the plan. Until December 1919, he had gone along eulogizing the cooperative chain store trend. Then he abruptly expressed his concern over this trend in a leading article in *Cooperation*, which was entitled "Centralization—Warning." He said: 'There is one and only one sound way to organize a cooperative wholesale society. It must represent a stage in the line of progress from the individual consumer toward the sources of supply." He attacked centralization by saying: "Such a central organization proceeds to create societies for its own good." From then on he waged an unrelenting war on the chain-store plans of the Tri-State Society, the Pacific Cooperative League, and the National Cooperative Association. The peak of this attack came at the second Congress of the Cooperative League, held in Cincinnati in November 1920, when the representatives of the National Cooperative Association and the National Consumers Cooperative Association were expelled from the Congress. After the National Cooperative Association was finally forced to close, Dr. Warbasse wrote the epitaph of the chain-store experiment, saying: "Thus closed a chapter in the history of cooperation in the United States which will be one of its unfortunate memories but a lesson of incalculable value."[50]

The Status of Cooperative Stores in 1920

Cooperative stores were fairly common in much of the United States in 1920, as shown by a comprehensive survey of the Bureau of Labor Statistics for this year.[51] There were then 2,600 cooperative buying societies (cooperative stores and buying associations) although many were farm supply purchasing associations, or purchasing departments of cooperative marketing associations.

Of the 1,009 cooperative buying societies for which data were collected, only 728 were classified as "strictly consumers' societies" or as buying associations made up only of consumers. Cooperative buying by cooperative marketing associations was excluded. The total business volume as reported by 650 of these consumers' societies in 1920 amounted to about $65 million, an average of nearly $100 thousand per society. However, more than two-thirds of the societies had annual sales below this average. Over two-thirds of the reported business by "strictly consumers' cooperatives" was done in the Eastern and North Central states, and most of these organizations were largely supported by farmers and were located in small towns (see comments on farmers' cooperative stores in Chapter XVII). Only 76 were found in cities with populations over 100,000. The combined share capital of the reporting societies amounted to about $11 million, an average of about $17,000 per society.

Summary

From 1896 to 1920 there was a gradual increase in the number of cooperative stores, but by 1920 their number was not impressive nor were they generally strong business organizations. It was a period of experimentation in retail and wholesale cooperation during which much was learned of value for the future, while little of a tangible nature was accomplished.

During these years various efforts were made in regional promotion and integration which culminated in the formation of the Cooperative League of America and a national cooperative wholesale society. However, the wholesale and its regional counterparts were not able to survive the postwar depression of 1920-1922. This experience provided many lessons, but none more important than that sound cooperative associations must be built with strong membership support.

The theory of consumers' cooperation which brought with it the conception of a cooperative commonwealth was just coming into prominence as this period closed. In the decades ahead it was to widen the goals of cooperative buying, attract many adherents, and be of significant influence as an educational and unifying force in retail and wholesale cooperative organization.

Chapter XXII

THE EXTENSION OF THE COOPERATIVE IDEA

In Part I we followed cooperative enterprise as it developed informally among farmers and how it spread in the form of mutual insurance and irrigation institutions down to 1896. In the next quarter century these forms of mutual effort were greatly amplified while cooperative enterprise entered new areas of service. Before going on to examine how the cooperative idea gained wider acceptance during this dynamic period of national economic development let us briefly see how existing cooperative organizations were extending their operations.

The Proliferation of Neighborhood Cooperation

From colonial days, as we observed in Chapter I, farmers found that they could do many things together better and more economically than by themselves. Cooperation of neighbors in house and barn raising, in threshing, and in other activities which could be performed better by several persons than separately were commonly established customs throughout the nation in 1896. In the next 25 years there was a proliferation of such cooperation—encouraged by new means of communication in the form of better roads, automobiles, free mail delivery, and telephones; by expanded educational efforts carried on by farmers' clubs, farmers' institutes, farm organizations, and extension service workers; and by the Country Life Movement which gave cooperation in all forms its blessing and encouragement.

Stimulated by rising prices for their products farmers had an immediate interest in joint efforts to improve their efficiency as producers. This was manifested in the formation of cow testing associations for dairy herd improvement, breeding associations for all varieties of livestock, and other associations to achieve greater and cheaper agricultural production.[1]

Cow testing associations. Of striking importance was the development and rapid expansion of cow testing associations which were also commonly called "dairy herd improvement associations." The first organization of this type was established in late 1905 in Michigan. By 1910, there were 40 associations of this type and by 1917 there were 459 in operation.[2] The principal purpose of a cow testing association was to ascertain the profitable and unprofitable cows in a farmer's herd by means of cooperative weighing and testing of milk and weighing of feed. Henry E. Erdman has described the method of operation of a typical cow testing association as follows:

> According to the usual plan, from twenty to twenty-six men agree to hire a man to test their cows for them, each to contribute a nominal sum, usually about $2.50 per month, to make up the salary of the tester. In addition, each man agrees to furnish board and lodging for the tester for at least one day each month, and to convey him to his next place, or to stable and feed his horse, while he is staying at the farm in lieu of furnishing such transportation. The tester spends one day at each farm each month.

Erdman pointed out the beneficial influence of cow testing as shown by increasing production at a typical association where milk production per cow went up from 5,793 to 6,855 pounds, while average production of butterfat went up from 289.9 to 345 pounds. Moreover, he pointed out that the association enabled farmers to locate and sell their poor cows.[3]

Powell recognized the great importance of cow testing associations by saying: "The value of a cow testing association to a dairy community is incalculable. It leads to more economical feeding, better herds, and better general management. The cooperation is thoroughly practical. It furnishes a striking example of a method by which a great industry can be built up by the adoption of a cooperative plan where the individual has failed."[4]

Breeding cooperatives. The quality of livestock could not be greatly improved by individual farmers working alone, for it was clearly uneconomical for each farmer to have a bull or stallion of high quality for his own limited farm needs. Getting rid of the scrub bull became a necessity. As Clarence Poe expressed this:

> The use of scrub sires has been a bane of American agriculture. We cannot expect proper interest in stock-raising until our farms have animals in which they can take pride and which have been bred for profit-making

along certain definite lines. Nor can we ever have this if each individual farmer must purchase worthy sires for his own herds and flocks ... Every farmer should have an interest in some royal-blooded stallion, bull, boar or ram that he will feel proud to name as the sire of his colts, calves, pigs or lambs. Talk this matter over with your neighbors as one of the surest methods of starting cooperation.[5]

The first cooperative bull association was started in Michigan in 1908. By 1919 there were 78 associations of this type in 27 states. The object was to have better and fewer bulls. The typical bull association was composed of from 15 to 20 farmers who together owned five bulls. The cost of operation was low and there was a quick return on the investment. It was generally agreed that the educational value of a bull association in stimulating livestock improvement was more important than the cash savings.[6]

Similar associations for horse and hog breeding were to be found in most agricultural states by 1920. It should be remembered that before the coming of tractor farming horses were the principal source of farm power. These early breeding associations were the prototypes of the large artificial insemination associations of the present day, which will be described in the second volume of this history.

Seed improvement associations. The interest of farmers in higher returns from their crops led them to cooperation for crop improvement. The significant contribution of the one-variety cotton improvement associations to cotton production and marketing was described in Chapter XII. A comparable development for corn arose in Illinois where as early as 1899 the Illinois Corn Breeders Association was formed as an outgrowth of the efforts of A. D. Shamel, who was studying corn breeding at the experiment station. Results were so satisfactory that by 1911 similar associations had been formed in 14 states. Powell, in 1913, said: "The immense increase in the yield of corn in recent years in the Central West is attributed primarily to the use of better strains of seed that have been developed and grown and sold by the members of the corn-breeders' associations." He recommended that "this kind of local cooperative effort should be applied to the improvement of all kinds of farm crops."[7]

Better farming associations. The urge for higher agricultural productivity also led to the formation of associations for better farming under such names as "soil" or "crop improvement" associations. One of the first associations of this type was the DeKalb County (Illinois) Soil Improvement Association formed in 1912. This organization concerned itself with both soil and crop improvement and its success soon brought a chain reaction of similar associations in other Illinois counties. These organizations provided the foundation for early county agent work in Illinois and, like other associations common in most states by 1919, made the matrix for the national Farm Bureau movement.[8]

Other new cooperative enterprises of farmers. Following the report of the Country Life Commission farmers were increasingly alert to ways in which they could apply the cooperative idea to their needs. An interesting example of a new service was the organization of a cooperative laundry in Minnesota to utilize the churns and equipment of a cooperative creamery. The success of this venture led to the fairly widespread adoption of this idea.[9] Another interesting new cooperative enterprise was the organization in 1917 of a cooperative motor truck route to take produce from two local communities in Halifax County, Maryland, to Baltimore and to return with supplies. This was the forerunner of the extensive trucking operations of farmers' cooperatives today.[10]

Cooperative Telephone Companies

Although farmers began to provide themselves with crude neighborhood telephone service as early as 1880 it was not until 1893 that they began to organize their own telephone lines. This step was encouraged by Bell and other telephone companies who saw it as a means of extending service. The first rural telephone associations arose as neighborhood projects. The story of their evolution has been well presented by a contemporary writer:

> In those communities where the farmers have built their own telephone lines, the original form of organization has been purely mutual. Construction has been a cooperative work, and the association of the farmers the most primitive type ... A group of farmers who lived within a reasonable distance of one another ... would meet together and arrange to establish a telephone system ... The work involved in constructing such system would be so divided that each member of the association would contribute an equivalent part of the material and labor. If the country was wooded, the farmers making up the association agreed to cut and supply the poles and to haul them to the places where they were needed ... The farmers' boys and the farm hands did the work of setting the poles and putting on the cross-arms ... The wire and the insulators, the switchboard and the instruments would have to be bought, and so a cash assessment would be levied on each member to make these purchases.[11]

In time, these local cooperative lines were connected with Bell or some other system and, as they became better established as business organizations, they gradually took the corporate form.

Although a few mutual telephone companies were formed before 1900 the great period of expansion came in the years from 1905 to 1912. They were started for two main reasons: (1) to obtain telephone service where it was otherwise unavailable, and (2) to obtain low cost and satisfactory service where available service was too expensive or unsatisfactory. By 1920 there were some 20,000 telephone mutuals and cooperatives serving about half a million farmers. However, only about 4,000 of these were providing exchange service. The remainder were farmer-owned "switch lines." The mutual companies provided telephone service to thousands of farmers who could not have obtained it otherwise. By doing so they provided an important mechanism for breaking down rural isolation and for furthering other forms of community cooperation. Rural sociologists who observed the coming of the rural telephone attributed great importance to its beneficial influence on rural social activities. As Dwight Sanderson said, "The telephone has made possible a degree of organization hitherto impossible."[12]

Amplification of Farmers' Mutual Insurance and Irrigation

In Chapter IV we observed how farmers' mutual fire insurance companies spread throughout the United States after the Civil War until by 1896 they were serving the fire insurance needs of most farmers. Likewise, mutual irrigation companies had continued to grow in number and strength as more farmers turned to irrigation with the settlement of the West. In the next 25 years these developments were to be amplified.

Mutual fire insurance. In 1895 the mutual fire insurance companies were to become a cohesive national force through the formation of the National Association of Mutual Insurance Companies to serve as a clearing house for mutual fire insurance problems and as an agency to represent the interests of such companies in national legislation. Writing in 1923, Valgren said:

> Since 1900 the farmers' mutual fire insurance movement has continued to grow by the enlargement of existing companies, even more than by the formation of new ones. Most of the companies organized since that date are to be found either in the newly developed states west of the Missouri or in some of the states of the South. In the older states ... relatively few companies of this kind have been organized during the past two decades. In some localities they have decreased in number by the consolidation of small companies ... With the improved means of communication ... a county

or even several contiguous counties can now be covered by a farmers' mutual as conveniently as could a township in the days when this movement began."[13]

By 1920 about 15 per cent of the farmers' mutual fire insurance companies had broadened their coverage to offer so-called protection against loss or damage from wind as well as from fire and lightning. Another development during this period was the beginning of re-insurance plans whereby the mutuals could diversify and share risks. The need for this kind of intercompany cooperation led to the establishment of the Iowa Farmers' Mutual Re-insurance Association in 1909. The number of farmers' mutual fire insurance companies in 1920 totaled nearly 2,000 and their risks in force totaled over $8 billion. Their great success gave encouragement to all forms of cooperative enterprise.[14]

Cooperative irrigation. Mutual irrigation associations also greatly improved their business practices and services during the period from 1896 to 1920. The importance of these associations was stressed in 1913 by G. Harold Powell who devoted a chapter to them in his book, *Cooperation in Agriculture.* By 1920 about one-third of all irrigated land was served by mutual irrigation associations.[15]

Mutual Insurance for Everybody

During the period under review—1896 to 1920—the mutual insurance idea steadily gained adherents in all forms of insurance—fire, casualty, and life. By 1920 the logic of the mutual form of cooperative insurance was accepted throughout industry and commerce, and by people in general.

Mutual fire insurance for industry and commerce. In earlier chapters we noted how factory owners made use of the mutual fire insurance idea, especially after the Civil War. By 1896, factory mutual fire insurance was well established. Other class mutuals—so-called because they confined their operations to a certain class of industries—were also becoming established for grain dealers and millers and for lumbermen. During the next quarter century all of these forms of mutual fire insurance company were to thrive and expand in importance, while similar class mutuals were to be formed for hardware merchants, druggists, and grocerymen. Thus, by 1920, mutual fire insurance had become well established in both the agricultural and industrial world. By and large, these mutual fire insurance organizations were made up of individuals or groups who maintained close control through voting supervision. Unlike the mutual life insurance companies, few became so large as to lose their sense of cooperative personality.[16]

Mutual casualty insurance. Prior to 1900, mutual casualty insurance had been little developed, for in 1900 total mutual casualty premiums amounted to only $403,000. The Mutual Boiler Insurance Company of Boston, founded in 1877, was the first genuine mutual casualty insurance company. Shortly afterwards, in 1880, the Mutual Plate Glass Insurance Association of Shelby, Ohio, began to offer plate glass insurance coverage. In 1883, the Commercial Travelers Mutual Accident Association of Utica, New York, was established to furnish accident insurance for traveling salesmen. By the close of the century two dozen other forms of casualty coverage were being offered by stock or mutual companies, but the lines of casualty insurance—workmen's compensation and automobile—to have the greatest potential were just "looming on the horizon." During the next 20 years mutual insurance was to become well established in these areas although the great growth of mutual automobile insurance was to come after 1920.[17]

Mutual life insurance. In 1896 the mutual life insurance companies were competing vigorously with stock companies for volume. They were going through a period of aggressive cut-throat competition, for ruthlessly ambitious men had gained control of the major companies, both mutual and stock. These tycoons took "authority into their own hands, selected trustees, determined all the major policies of their companies, and made a cult out of sheer size. Bigness became the goal toward which they all worked—and with success."[18] To attract business they developed ingenious deferred dividend plans under which the insured received no dividend until a stipulated number of years elapsed— at first 5 years, but gradually this was extended to 20. Even a well-established mutual company like the Mutual Life Insurance Company was swept up in the ruthless spirit of the times. When the annual salary of its president reached and exceeded $100,000 and the amounts returned in dividends went down as the amount of insurance business went up, the term "mutual" lost much of its appeal.

The scandalous situation in the whole life insurance field got so bad in the early 1900's that something had to be done about it. The matter was brought to a head in July 1904 when *Everybody's Magazine* began serial publication of Thomas W. Lawson's *Frenzied Finance.* As Lawson was a highly respected Boston financier his views carried great weight. "He damned a system of life insurance which resulted in heavy lapses, condemned marketing methods, and exposed many of the investment syndicates which had resulted in profits to insurance officers."[19] In July 1905, largely as a result of the disclosures in this book, the Assembly and Senate of the State of New York concurred in a resolution which called for a thorough investigation of the business affairs of life insurance companies doing business in the State of New York in order to provide a basis for a thoroughgoing revision of New York life insurance laws. The committee set up to represent both the Assembly and Senate under State Senator William W. Armstrong was fortunate in obtaining the services of Charles Evans Hughes as counsel, for his competence and character were unquestioned. The Armstrong Committee began hearings in September 1905 and submitted its report in February 1906. No stone was left unturned in the investigation—nepotism, rebates, excessive salaries, dominating management, questionable methods of operation, and relationship to politics. The investigation "threw a lurid light on some wrongful practices" and the report of the committee brought about an extensive revision of insurance law not only in New York but in all other states as well.[20] The Armstrong report terminated the abuses under the deferred premium plan, it stopped rebating, it curtailed nepotism, afforded members of mutual companies a greater voice in the management, prohibited contributions to political campaigns, and gave teeth to state supervision and regulation of all life insurance companies.

The main result of the Armstrong investigation was to impose reform on life insurance companies. As Clough said: "The Armstrong investigation and the insurance legislation of 1906 changed profoundly the operations of life insurance companies..." He called attention to three long-term effects: "(1) life insurance companies were henceforth to restrict their activities definitely to the life insurance business, that is, were to stop other entrepreneurial functions; (2) life insurance was after 1906 to be conducted in all its branches on a conservative basis; and (3) a new code of business ethics was to be adopted by the industry."[21]

Although mutual companies were found guilty of most of the malpractices of stock companies the committee recognized the value of the mutual idea and sought to correct it of abuse. As a result, the state law was amended to facilitate mutualization of stock companies by providing for the liberalizing of elections so as to give policyholders an opportunity to nominate candidates for vacancies on boards of directors. Significantly, three of the largest stock companies immediately reorganized on the mutual plan, and several more adopted the mutual form of organization by 1920.[22]

The effect of the Armstrong investigation proved salutary to the life

insurance business, as evidenced by the growth of life insurance in force
from $8.5 billion in 1900 to $42 billion in 1920. By 1914 Myron Herrick,
a good friend of cooperatives, could say: 'The New York Life, the Mutual
Life,... are cooperative except for the one point that voting may be
done by proxy. With their hundreds of thousands of policy holders and
hundreds of millions of assets they are not only the greatest cooperative
institutions but are also among the greatest and soundest and in actual
results the most benevolent institutions in the world . . ."[23]

Mutual Savings Banks and Building and
Loan Associations

After 1896, mutual savings banks and building and loan associations
continued to grow, although they increasingly came to resemble other
financial institutions. They retained the mutual feature of returning
savings to stockholders but membership—although it continued to represent voluntary participation—ceased to have any significant meaning.
They became cooperatives operated *for,* rather than *by,* or *of* those who
were served.

The first building and loan associations had been established to
serve members in towns and cities. In the early 1890's an attempt was
made to set up national building and loan associations but this resulted
in a fiasco which brought a return to restricted forms of area organization. Although some of the mutual savings banks became very large
organizations they generally confined service to a city and its environs.[24]

From 1893 to 1918 the number of building and loan associations
increased from 5,578 to 7,484, while their membership increased from
1,000,000 to 4,000,000 and their assets from $473,000,000 to $1,898,000,000.
The mutual savings banks also prospered during these years of business
growth. Their savings deposits reached $3,419,000,000 in 1911 and $5,050,-
000,000 in 1920.

Although building and loan associations and mutual savings banks
were not generally classified as true cooperatives they were commonly
accepted as a modified form of cooperative organization. In calling
attention to the widespread operations of "cooperative financing institutions" in the United States "far exceeding all credit societies in Europe,"
Myron T. Herrick in 1914 said: "The building and loan associations are
organized for thrift and a specialized kind of credit based upon urban
real estate, and the mutual savings banks for thrift and for credit not
necessarily accorded by preference to members." However, Herrick

admitted that the depositors of mutual savings banks could hardly be considered members "for most of the mutual savings banks are managed by self-perpetuating boards of trustees." But, however, he added: "There is very little difference in spirit and business methods between [the Schultze-Delitzch and Luzzati banks in Europe] and the American mutual savings banks." At another point he said: 'Building and loan associations deal in cooperative credit only in a restricted sense, since they do not require members to obligate themselves in any way for borrowers. They are formed for collective saving—quite a different thing from cooperative credit—and for investing the accumulated savings by preference in mortgages and of home buildings."

Herrick made the important point that "The progress already achieved by the United States in mutual and cooperative finance, and other forms of cooperation, is frequently overlooked." He maintained that "it proves that cooperation and mutuality are congenial to the spirit of the American people, and may be applied in their most complicated forms to the ordinary affairs of life.[25]

Roy F. Bergengren also called attention to the cooperative importance of the building and loan associations. He said: "The building and loan associations have kept their light under a bushel. . . . The possibilities of cooperative banking are being demonstrated in most practical fashion by this development." He held that a credit union and a building and loan association had much in common, in that both had "a most democratic form of organization" and both "appealed to the small saver," and "encouraged small savings through an installment share plan." Moreover, he found that both operated with low overhead and were managed, for the most part, under the supervision of state departments of banking.[26] Although mutual savings banks and building and loan associations were but semi-cooperative, they were significant manifestations of the way in which the cooperative idea could be employed to the problems of business.[27]

Cooperative Enterprise for Businessmen

The cooperative form of business enterprise can be used by individuals or business concerns. It is available to any organization that wishes to join other like organizations to accomplish common economic objectives. We have seen how industry and commerce have made use of the mutual idea in insurance operations. In this section we will examine how groups of independent business enterprises have adopted the idea to meet their own needs.

Retailer-owned cooperatives. Cooperative retail merchandising groups date back to the late 1880's. The first to establish itself was the Frankford Grocery Company of Philadelphia (now the Frankford-Quaker Grocery Company), formed in 1888 by a group of about 100 grocers, milkmen, and butchers who were primarily interested in developing an improved method of collecting bills. It soon undertook cooperative buying for its members and long operated from a rented room. In 1906 it purchased an old mill for headquarters and incorporated. In 1910 it built a warehouse which was enlarged in 1918. The experience of the few other retailer cooperatives formed before 1910 was similar. At first they operated informally as buying clubs. "Often, the organization lacked a warehouse, and merchandise was divided among the members right at the dock or depot after the products were received from the manufacturer. Originally the items handled were confined to staple merchandise, but with the acquisition of warehousing facilities, the inventory was expanded to include other supplies. At this point, the organization began to take on the structure of a formal enterprise..."[28]

The real development of retailer-owned cooperatives came with the rise of the chain store system of retailing after 1910.[29] "At this point the chain store organization began to emerge as a real threat to the future of independent retailing. The wholesaler-owned stores could be manipulated to provide the wholesaler with a continuing steady influx of orders which enabled him to operate his warehouse facilities with the maximum efficiency of the times. This tie-up of retail outlet with wholesale source also produced a merchandising entity which, with its tight control over pricing, advertising, and personnel, functioned as a vengeful force in the competitive arena.[30] In their predicament independent retailers began to join together for protection through membership in retailer-owned cooperatives.[31] By 1920 there were about a dozen associations of this type, although their record at first was not impressive. However, a foothold for this type of cooperative had been gained.

The first cooperative of retail drugstores dates back to the formation of a buying club in 1887 which became the New York Consolidated Drug Company. Several other associations of drugstores were formed by 1910, and in 1915 the Federal Wholesale Druggists Association was organized to correlate the activities of the dozen or so associations then in existence.

The first cooperative of retail hardware stores was formed in 1910. The principal cause for the forming of all of these associations was to pool merchandising experience and carry on group buying as a means of meeting competition from mail-order firms or chain stores.

The Associated Press. The cooperative method of organization can be used in any situation where a group of individuals or organizations can join together to perform economic services that could not otherwise be obtained—even at high cost. A good illustration is the case of the Associated Press (AP), the largest news-gathering organization in the world.

Like all early news services, the Associated Press—organized in New York City in 1848 by a few leading newspapers—was cooperative in form. It was set up to pool the resources of the member papers for gathering domestic and foreign news. It flourished from the start and soon became a national organization. However, in the 1880's some of its officers took selfish advantage of their positions and this led to an investigation of its affairs by a committee representing the newspapers served, under the chairmanship of Victor Lawson, Editor of the *Chicago Daily News*. This investigation disclosed some shocking instances of corrupt management, and brought about the reorganization of the Associated Press in 1893 as an Illinois non-profit corporation whose members were to supply each other with news from their areas of publication. In 1900 the association was reorganized as a New York corporation with headquarters in New York City. From this time on, the Associated Press has functioned as a true cooperative organization. In December 1965, Paul Miller, President of the Associated Press, declared: "The greatest strength of the Associated Press lies in the cooperative form of its organization and the diversity of news represented in it."[32]

Clearing house associations. Commercial banking, to operate efficiently, must have some system through which checks drawn on a great number of banks can be balanced. Clearing houses to facilitate the settlement of claims of banks against each other date back to the beginnings of commercial banking. The first American clearing house association was established in New York City in 1853, and such associations for local clearings now are found throughout the United States. Clearing house associations are simply cooperative associations designed to improve the welfare of the member banking institutions by eliminating "competitive evils" so as to strengthen commercial banking practices: According to Walter E. Spahr:

> The modern clearing house is defined in law as a voluntary association of banks to simplify and facilitate the exchange of such items as checks, drafts, bills and notes, and to serve as a medium of united action upon all questions affecting their common welfare. Most of them are unincorporated, cooperative associations and derive their authority over their members through their written assent to their respective constitutions.[33]

The coming of the Federal Reserve System in 1913 greatly simplified the process of settling clearing house balances for each of the 12 Federal Reserve banks now acts as a clearing house for banks in its district, and clearings between Federal Reserve banks are effected by means of a central clearing fund in Washington, D.C.[34]

Summary

In this chapter we have seen cooperative enterprise moving into new areas of service with a rapidly changing economic environment. By 1920 cooperative enterprise had penetrated many areas of industry and commerce although its center of strength was still in agriculture.

Chapter XXIII

THE END OF THE BEGINNINGS—

Accomplishments, Lessons, Prospects

In preceding chapters we have seen how cooperative enterprise grew step by step from local experimentation and experience. The lessons from the days of colonial settlement were picked up and adapted in the early mutual fire insurance companies, in the Mormon irrigation cooperatives, and in other forms of joint effort. With the coming of the Grange and the Farmers' Alliance local enterprises had the benefit of guidance and encouragement from a widespread general farm organization. This was influential in securing the passage of cooperative statutes in half a dozen Midwest states and in California. The process of development was hastened by the great changes in our economic and social life in the years from 1897 to 1920. By the latter year we can say that the basic character of American cooperative enterprise was formed. It had reached the end of its beginnings.

Prior to the Civil War, cooperative undertakings received a strong impetus from factory workers and townsfolk—including consumer groups. But the growth of industrial corporations from the 1880's on diverted this worker interest into trade unionism. In agriculture, cooperatives provided a method of economic organization uniquely adapted to the needs of farmers, for the agricultural industry was comprised of millions of individual small business units that could be best coordinated for productive efficiency by means of the cooperative form of organization. Through cooperative associations farmers found they could obtain for themselves the operating advantages available to large-scale commercial concerns. As Edwin G. Nourse observed in 1922: "Agricultural cooperation offers to the inherently decentralized industry of agriculture a workable and expansible scheme of organization . . . It seeks to organize such a range of activities as can be effectively integrated and to distribute the economic benefits of this efficiency so broadly and equitably as to ensure the prosperity of the whole body of family-farm operators."[1] Thus agriculture provided an ideal laboratory for trying out and developing cooperative ideas.

Cooperative enterprise in agriculture had been growing rapidly during and following World War I and it was booming as the year 1920 opened.[2] In the first national survey of farmers' cooperative business organizations made by the U.S. Department of Agriculture in 1915 there were found 5,424 associations doing a total business volume of $635 million. The next comparable survey for the year 1921 recorded 7,374 associations with a volume of business of $1,256 million. It is therefore reasonable to assume that the volume of business of farmers' marketing and purchasing associations was about $1 billion by 1920.

Most of the cooperatives formed before 1920 were local in character, for large-scale or regional-type associations were then just becoming prominent. From available information it is clear that the total business volume of large-scale organizations did not then exceed $200 million. Of this, two-thirds represented the business of the California Fruit Growers Exchange (now Sunkist Growers, Inc.), the California Associated Raisin Growers (now Sun-maid Raisin Growers of California), and other important regional cooperatives in California.

Information on membership of farmers in cooperatives is not available for 1920 but the census reported for 1919 that over 600,000 farmers were engaged in cooperative marketing or purchasing activities. Moreover, the census figures did not include the large number of farmers who obtained insurance, irrigation, telephone, or other business services from cooperatives.

Some Lessons Learned by 1920

The preceding chapters have made clear that by 1920 farmers and other cooperators had learned many lessons on how cooperatives could serve them, on what cooperatives could and could not accomplish, and on how to form and operate cooperative associations. Although much was yet to be found out on how cooperatives could be expanded, perfected, and developed, the record of progress in understanding was impressive. Some of the more significant of these lessons can be grouped in three broad categories: general, organizational, and operational.

General

In general, it was learned that:

1. The cooperative form of business organization can be advantageously employed by any group of persons or firms having a common recognized economic need.

2. Cooperative membership increases the dignity of individuals by giving them a sense of ownership and participation in the economic organization that serves them.

3. Participation in cooperative operations provides farmers and citizens with training in business and community affairs.

4. Cooperative associations engender competition in the market. Their yardstick competition has been an important contribution—beneficial to the activation and preservation of the free competitive system of private enterprise.

5. Farmers through group action in cooperatives can promote improved methods for marketing their products and in purchasing supplies needed in their farming operations.

6. Cooperatives provide farmers with a choice of markets and free them from dependence on sale to a single dealer. By federated action—as demonstrated by the California Fruit Growers Exchange—farmers could develop market outlets throughout the United States and Canada.

7. Many economic and social problems can not be met by political measures but require cooperative action of the individuals most concerned. The Farmers' Alliance and other early organizations made cooperatives subservient to political objectives. It took time to teach cooperatives that politics and business operations would not mix.

8. Efficient cooperatives can only be built and maintained where there is an economic need for the function to be undertaken. Cooperatives must be able to provide a service of value to participants to merit their support.

9. General farm organizations such as the Grange and Farmers' Union can best help farmers by educational and promotional activities, and by helping them obtain legal statutes and legislation to enable them to operate efficiently. It was found wise to divorce farm organizations from management control of cooperatives, thus permitting the cooperatives to stand on their own feet.

10. Public support and approval of cooperatives requires an understanding by the public of the objectives and methods of cooperatives and the value of their benefits to all citizens. As a corollary, cooperatives found that they must keep the public informed and must operate in such a manner as to warrant public respect.

11. Government, both state and national, can properly provide help in the form of education, research and credit to farmers and other citizens for organizing and operating cooperative associations. On the other hand,

cooperatives were beginning to learn that they could not become dependent upon government for financing, leadership, or in other ways without losing their independence and vitality.

12. Farmers can fashion cooperative marketing and purchasing organizations strong enough to achieve economic power. Experience indicated that cooperatives could obtain the personnel, management, and capital essential to cope with strong competitors. The California Fruit Growers Exchange demonstrated how this could be done through federating local cooperative associations. Centralized marketing organizations provided an alternative method of organizing growers through direct members and contractual arrangements.

Organizational

Organizationally, it was learned that:

1. There is need for a community of interest among members of a cooperative—in types of products marketed, in kinds of supplies or services purchased, and in the size of the areas served.

2. Effective cooperatives cannot be built on idealism alone, nor based upon a glorified conception of human nature. If cooperatives promise too much, disillusionment will soon set in. Cooperatives require an informed membership that is willing to accept responsibilities. Advance planning is necessary so that services can be adequately financed and management and facilities provided for. It was found that cooperatives can not run before they learn to walk; that slow initial progress usually contributes to later strength.

3. Democratic control, limited returns on capital, and return of financial benefits on the basis of each member's participation are basic ingredients of cooperative structure and operation.

4. Cooperatives can best be formed on the one-man, one-vote basis in which each member has voting power without regard to the amount of capital supplied or the amount of business done through the association. It was found that organized otherwise, jealousy and dissension soon destroyed the harmony among the membership.

5. Organization on a capital-stock basis destroys a cooperative unless dividends on stock are limited and the amount of stock held by any individual member is restricted.

6. Cooperatives can be organized on a non-stock, or membership, basis so as to get away from the capital-stock form of organization. Under this form of organization proceeds after deduction of operating costs are returned to members in proportion to their participation.

7. It is wise to build large-scale regional-type organizations from the bottom up with assured strong membership support rather than from the top down. It is difficult to infuse cooperative spirit and understanding into an organization after it has been set up.

8. Large regional cooperatives can be built effectively by federating already strong local cooperatives. This achieves democratic control and maintains membership support.

9. Subsidiary corporations for manufacturing, financing, or for other purposes can be employed to segregate risks, promote management flexibility, and otherwise further the objectives of a cooperative.

10. Membership agreements can be used advantageously by marketing cooperatives to establish predictable volumes of product and behavior and thus assure effective administration and operation.

11. By-laws to govern the operations of an association must be carefully drawn and revised when conditions change.

12. Cooperative associations should be incorporated under cooperative statutes to provide them with legal status and give limited liability for members.

Operational

Operationally, it was learned that:

1. Cooperation, as a method of business organization, requires concentrated attention on business performance. Cooperatives found that there is no place for dissension because of politics, religion, race, or nationality in performing an economic service.

2. Members must be kept thoroughly informed so as to maintain their interest and confidence in their organizations and understand their problems. Loyalty to objectives requires knowledge of them and appreciation of the problems involved in achieving them.

3. Accounting systems and business records of cooperatives must be maintained in an efficient and orderly manner. Cooperation is a form of business that calls for the tools used by all good business organizations.

4. Like other forms of business, cooperatives must have conservative practices such as annual audits, and reserves for losses and bad debts. They must be vigilant to detect dishonesty of employees, avoid nepotism or favoritism in any form, and obtain the best employees for all positions.

5. Good management is indispensable to effective administration and cooperatives must pay competitive wages for management ability.

6. Competent directors are an essential part of effective management. It was found from costly experience that competence of directors has

many elements besides popularity and likability—including character, capacity, experience, and good judgement.

7. Responsible financial planning to supply needed capital and provide for adequate reserves is necessary to maintain efficient service and build a sound financial structure. In the revolving fund method of financing, farmers had found a way of keeping controlling equity capital in their cooperatives in the hands of current users of the cooperatives' services.

8. Educational programs and membership relations work are required to develop and maintain adequate membership interest, support, and understanding.

9. Research, or analytical study of methods to find better ways of applying them, is essential to cooperative progress.

10. Pooling provides an equitable method of distributing marketing risks and can be used in effectively merchandising products and in the distribution of returns to members.

11. The safest form of cooperative procedure, particularly for purchasing and service-type associations, is along Rochdale lines—with provision for sale at prevailing market prices and return of savings as patronage refunds in proportion to individual member participation. Where the Rochdale method is found not so applicable, marketing cooperatives can be set up on a pooling plan, under which all participants receive pro rata shares of all proceeds from sales over costs of operation.

12. Cooperatives can best price goods for sale at prevailing market prices, and then return savings over costs to patrons in the form of patronage refunds. This practice avoids price cutting and helps cooperatives build up financial reserves. It gives members returns based upon the efficiency of their cooperatives and sustains their interest in cooperative performance.

13. Cooperatives can improve the quality of products produced for market by reflecting the value of high-quality products in returns made to producers.

14. Directors must not be permitted to interfere in the everyday operations of an association. Managers must be given freedom to hire and fire employees, and otherwise carry on operations. Board interference makes it impossible for a manager to perform his functions. The job of the directors should be to lay down broad policies, select the manager, and make sure that operations are properly maintained.

15. Benefits derived from cooperatives are dependent upon scale of operations. Larger volumes make possible improved marketing and purchasing efficiency and achieve lower overhead and operating costs.

16. The development of grades, brands, and standards that equitably

reflect the sales value of products back to producers in marketing returns is essential to the effective marketing of farm products, and to the establishment of quality standards essential to attract consumer support. Likewise, quality standards are essential to the success of purchasing and service cooperatives for the quality of supplies and services furnished can not be dissociated from the prices charged for them.

17. Cooperatives cannot control supplies of products on markets and regulate prices. Early crop holding efforts made clear that control of supply is impossible to achieve through voluntary action of producers. As cooperatives learned how to use membership contracts effectively this helped them strengthen their market power in selling to best advantage under supply and demand conditions.

A captious critic may say that many of the lessons enumerated were but inadequately learned by 1920; and that cooperative failures still result because these lessons are not yet fully recognized. This may be admitted, for learning is a process that must be continued by succeeding generations. However, in broad terms the lessons here outlined were being stressed in 1920 by close students of the cooperative form of organization[3] and they were being increasingly accepted. It was because these lessons were to a large extent learned by 1920 that rapid progress was to ensue during the next decade.

A Glimpse into the Great Advance After 1920

In closing this volume it is appropriate that we look forward to see how trends apparent by 1920 worked out in the years that followed. While much had been accomplished by cooperative organizations prior to 1920 the period of great advancement was still to come.

In the next few decades cooperative marketing and purchasing cooperatives were to gain nation-wide acceptance as a method of economic organization suited to the needs of agriculture. Fishing and forestry cooperatives were to be set up as conditions made them practicable. Cooperative electric associations, undeveloped in 1920, were to become the means of "lighting up" rural America. Mutual insurance companies were to expand markedly in automobile liability insurance. Bull rings were to give way to artificial insemination associations.

While the bastion of cooperative strength continued to be in agriculture,[4] significant progress was made by cooperatives in urban areas. Credit unions, which were just getting under way in 1920, were to become important in urban consumer financing. Housing cooperatives—not started until 1927—were to become highly important. Although consumer cooperatives providing groceries and household goods and services did not attain the goals set by their early enthusiasts many cooperatives of this type gained a strong position. Moreover, cooperative organizations of business firms expanded greatly.

Now, let us look a little more closely into these developments.

Although cooperative purchasing and marketing associations were strongly established in agriculture by 1920 they then represented only a foretaste of their development in ensuing years. At that time such organizations were doing a total business of approximately $1 billion. They were mostly small community organizations supported by less than one million farmers whose investments in them represented less than $50 million. By 1967, there were about 8,000 marketing and purchasing associations with total memberships running to over 6.5 million, with a total net business volume of over $16.5 billion.[5] Farmers' investments in these organizations by 1968 amounted to $3.9 billion. Many of these cooperatives have become highly integrated regional and national organizations with operations covering one or more states. A significant number do annual volumes in excess of $50 million annually and five were large enough to qualify in the list of 500 major industrial concerns reported by *Fortune Magazine* in June 1968.[6]

The great development of agricultural cooperation after 1920 has been furthered by the growth of federal credit agencies operated in partnership with farmers and their cooperatives. The Federal Land Banks, established in 1917 under the Federal Farm Loan Act of 1916, provided a model for the creation of the Federal Intermediate Credit Banks, Production Credit Corporations, and Banks for Cooperatives. All of these agencies became parts of the Farm Credit Administration in 1933. These credit organizations were started with government capital but provision was made for its repayment so that they would eventually be owned by the farmers and cooperatives served. By December 31, 1968, these credit institutions supervised by the Farm Credit Administration had repaid all government capital. The total net worth of the Farm Credit System now held by farmers and their cooperatives is nearly $2 billion.[7]

It may be said that the rural electric cooperatives built on the early experience of the rural telephone cooperatives. The great development of these associations came with the financial and technical assistance provided by the Rural Electrification Act of 1936, which was patterned somewhat on the Federal Farm Loan Act of 1916. Rural electric cooperatives—distribution, generation, and transmission—as of January 1, 1968, numbered about 920 and served some 5,300,000 farm families and other rural consumer members. These associations had some 33,000 employees and total assets of $4,863 million. The financial interest held by members amounted to $1,279 million, or 26% of the total assets. The rural electric cooperatives provide electric power to about one-half of the farmers and other consumers living in rural areas.[8]

The numerous rural telephone lines of 1920 were operated mostly by small and informal associations. With the financial and technical assistance provided after 1949 by the Rural Electrification Administration such cooperatives have grown in financial and operating strength. By January 1, 1968, there were about 230 rural telephone cooperatives, with about 3,400 employees, serving some 632,000 members. The ownership or net worth interest of members in these associations amounted to $31.6 million, or about 7.8% of their total assets of $4,072 million.[9]

The credit union movement which was only well started by 1920 has grown to great dimensions. By January 1, 1968, the number of credit unions—urban and rural—exceeded 23,000. These organizations had over 19 million members and represented members' savings of over $11 billion.[10]

Consumers' cooperative stores were endeavoring to gain a foothold in 1920. While this form of cooperative enterprise has not grown spectacularly there are today 826 associations of this type, serving 572,000 members and doing a business volume of $754 million. Fifty-six of these are "supermarkets" in that they do annual volumes of business of over $1 million. Most of these consumer cooperatives obtain their supplies from seven full-line cooperative grocery wholesale warehouses, which in turn are served by a national purchasing organization.[11]

In 1920 retail merchants were just beginning to form cooperative wholesale organizations to serve their needs. With the great growth of chain stores and supermarkets the independent retail food stores increasingly joined wholesale cooperatives as a means of meeting their competition. Such retailer-owned wholesale organizations now number 135 and have a combined net worth of approximately $100 million. The thousands of independent merchants who are members of these associations do a total business of approximately $18 billion, or about one-quarter of the retail food business in the United States.[12]

Other forms of cooperative association, highly important today, were non-existent in 1920. Cooperative housing, for example, has grown enormously with the urbanization of America. Presently, it represents a large and potentially significant part of cooperative enterprise. There are now about 680 housing cooperatives with 173,000 individual members and they have a revenue of $240 million annually.[13]

The concern for health has also resulted in the development of health care associations. There are now 180 cooperative group health organizations serving some one million members. The annual operating revenue is about $400 million. Some of these organizations, such as the Group Health Association of Washington, D. C., serve many thousands of members and provide complete medical care and hospital service.[14]

Cooperatives also provide nursery schools, babysitting services, funeral arrangements, or serve the varied needs of students. Altogether, cooperatives of all types now serve tens of millions of people, both rural and urban.[15]

The progress of cooperative enterprise since 1920 has not come easily. The significant fact is that so much progress has been made in the face of so many obstacles. The ability of cooperatives to root themselves and then grow has evidenced their capacity to adjust to a dynamic and changing environment. Like broadly educated persons, cooperatives have been able to learn from cumulative experience. To a large extent they have been self-renewing and flexible, able to reproduce themselves in stronger forms to meet new requirements. Lessons of the past have not proved to be dogmas that have arrested development. Rather they have served as logical working principles.

In the next volume of this history—*The Advance of American Cooperative Enterprise*—the progress of cooperatives as they expanded during the years from 1920 to 1970 will be carefully examined. This will provide a basis for exploring the future potential significance of American cooperative enterprise.

Notes

NOTES

Chapter I

1. "We, whose names are underwritten . . . solemnly and mutually in the Presence of God, and one another, covenant and combine ourselves together into a civil Body Politick, for our better Ordering and Preservation and Furtherance of the Ends aforesaid . . ." From the Mayflower Compact (signed by 41 men), as given by Henry Steele Commager, *Living Ideas in America* (New York: Harper & Brothers, 1951), pp. 111-112.

2. George E. NcNeill, "Cooperation in Massachusetts," *Eighth Annual Report of the Massachusetts Bureau of Statistics of Labour* (1877): "Any attempt to treat of cooperative efforts in Massachusetts without commencing with a reference to the Pilgrim Church, the township, and the fisheries, would be like a record of the Revolution with Samuel Adams, Lexington and Concord left out" (p. 55).

3. Percy W. Bidwell and John I. Falconer, *History of Agriculture in the Northern United States, 1860-1920* (Gloucester, Mass.: Peter Smith, 1941), p. 21. See also Sumner Chilton Powell, *Puritan Village* (Garden City, N. Y.: Doubleday & Company, Inc., 1965), pp. 18-20.

4. Bidwell and Falconer, *op. cit.*, p. 34.

5. *Ibid.*, p. 164. This fact greatly impressed Frederic J. Turner in his classic study, *The Frontier in American History* (New York: Henry Holt, 1921): "This power of the newly arrived pioneers to join together for a common end without the intervention of governmental institutions was one of their marked characteristics. The log rolling, the house-raising, the husking bee, the apple paring, and the squatters' associations whereby they protected themselves against the speculators in securing title to their clearings on the public domain, the camp meeting, the mining camp, the vigilantes, the cattle-raisers' associations, the 'gentlemen's agreements,' are a few of the indications of this attitude" (pp. 343-44, 358). Daniel J. Boorstin in *The Americans—The National Experience* (New York: Vintage Books, 1967) points out that "of all American myths, none is stronger than that of the loner moving west across the land." As a matter of fact, settlement was a group enterprise. "People moving these great distances into an unknown landscape, threatened by numerous nameless dangers, banded together; not because they especially loved their neighbors or had inherited any ties to them, but because they needed one another. Westward-moving pioneers everywhere found group travel and group living normal" (Chapter 8, "On the Continent-Ocean: Men Move in Groups," pp. 51-57).

6. Reuben Gold Thwaites, *Early Western Travels, 1748-1846,* Vol. V, p. 282, as quoted in Bidwell and Falconer, *op. cit.*, p. 164.

7. Chester W. Wright, *Economic History of the United States* (1st Ed., 1941):

"The outstanding feature that characterized colonial agriculture was the fact that the greater portion of the products was for the family's own consumption ... This relatively self-sufficing economy meant that most farmers raised a considerable variety of products, in short engaged in general farming, and that commercial agriculture, that is raising crops chiefly for sale in the markets, played a relatively small part in the farm organization in most sections. Moreover, the amount of capital employed in the way of tools and equipment was relatively small and the labor used was generally limited to that supplied by the family; so the problems of finance and labor were distinctly less difficult than today and the farmer thus more independent of the market conditions for these factors of production" (pp. 89-90). Victor S. Clark, *History of Manufactures in the United States, 1607-1860*: "Household industries are of two kinds—those in which families use their own materials to make goods for general sale, and those in which they receive materials to work up for employers. Both types existed in the colonies, but the first was the earlier and at the beginning of the Republic was the more common ... Many minutemen of 1776 were summoned to arms from workbenches, where three generations of ancestors before them had manufactured hats, boots, chairs, and other articles for general markets" (pp. 440, 443).

8. Bidwell and Falconer, *op. cit.*, p. 133. Compare also the following observations on colonial methods of marketing. Wright, *op. cit.*: "The marketing organization and methods that were developed for carrying on trade during the colonial period were naturally very simple and crude as compared with those of today. In the country districts, about the only individual who could be said to have specialized in trade, except for the Indian trader of the frontier, was the keeper of the country store, and even he was apt to be a farmer as well" (p. 130). Ralph M. Hower, *History of Macy's of New York, 1858-1919* (Cambridge, Mass.: Harvard University Press, 1943): "The undifferentiated nature of trade in this country before 1800 was especially evident in the settled but sparsely populated country districts and at the frontier, a fact which continued to hold true as the frontier moved westward during the course of the nineteenth century. Whether one was trading with Indians or meeting the needs of outlying agricultural communities, circumstances made it necessary to handle a variety of staple goods such as cotton and woolen cloth, gunpowder, kitchenware, sugar, rum, axes, drugs, and trinkets. Generically there is little difference between the trading post, the general store, and the pedlar so far as merchandise sold is concerned. Furthermore, the same merchant commonly conducted wholesale as well as retail operations in the same store if any wholesale trade existed in the region" (pp. 77-78).

9. The community responsibility for fire protection was recognized in New Amsterdam as early as 1656 by the appointment of fire wardens. See Charles W. Burpee, *A Century in Hartford*, pp. 93-96.

10. Benjamin Franklin was by nature cooperatively minded. In his *Autobiography* he records how as a young man he had formed "a club of mutual improvement ..." Later in 1730 he had organized for "common benefit" a subscription library, "the mother of all the North American subscription libraries, now so numerous."

11. See pamphlet, *Franklin and Fires*, The Philadelphia Contributionship for the Insurance of Houses from Loss of Fire, 1906, pp. 4-6.

12. That Franklin was justifiably proud of the Union Fire Company is indicated by the following passage from his *Autobiography*: "About this time I wrote a paper (first to be read in Junto but it was afterward published) on the different accidents and carelessnesses by which houses were set on fire, with

cautions against them, and means proposed of avoiding them. This was much spoken of as a useful piece, and gave rise to a project which soon followed it, of forming a company for the more ready extinguishing of fires, and mutual assistance in removing and securing of goods when in danger. Associates in this scheme were presently found, amounting to thirty. Our articles of agreement obliged every member to keep always in good order and fit for use, a certain number of leather buckets, with strong baskets (for packing and transporting of goods) which were to be brought to every fire; and we agreed to meet once a month and spend a social evening together, in discovering and communicating such ideas as occurred to us upon the subject of fires, as might be useful in our conduct on such occasions.

"The utility of this institution soon appeared, and many more desiring to be admitted than we thought convenient for one company, they were advised to form another, which was accordingly done; and this went on, one new company being formed after another, till they became so numerous as to include most of the inhabitants who were men of property, and now, at the time of my writing this, tho' upward of fifty years since its establishment, that which I first formed, called the Union Fire Company, still subsists and flourishes. I question whether there is a city in the world better provided with the means of putting a stop to beginning conflagrations."

13. See report of *Centennial Meeting of the Philadelphia Contributionship for the Insurance of Houses from Loss by Fire* (1852) with printed insert, June 1, 1939 designed to present "conclusive evidence that Benjamin Franklin is entitled to the credit for supplying 'the motive power' in the organization of the Philadelphia contributionship" (p. 26).

14. This historic document, written on fifteen feet of parchment, is available for inspection at the office of the company. Franklin's name is also recorded at the top of the list of the first board of directors, but he was not active in the early work of organization and management. The prime mover in the actual development of the enterprise apparently was John Smith, the first treasurer of the company. See *Centennial Meeting of the Philadelphia Contributionship*, pp. 24-26.

15. It is significant that the Philadelphia Contributionship adopted as its mark four hands united, while the Amicable mark was two clasped hands. It is possible that the Philadelphia group also may have studied the plan of a mutual fire insurance company founded in Charleston in 1736, which apparently succumbed to the Charleston fire in 1741 which destroyed some 300 houses. Burpee, *op. cit.*, pp. 98, 101-02.

16. As adapted from address of Horace Binney, *Centennial Meeting of the Philadelphia Contributionship*, pp. 30-31.

17. *Ibid.*, p. 33. Horace Binney maintained that the important principle of using premium accumulations in insurance was first recognized in this action.

18. For a history of the Philadelphia Contributionship from 1852-1938 see N. S. B. Gras and Henrietta M. Larson, *Casebook in American Business History*, (Cambridge, Mass.: Harvard University Press, 1939), pp. 149-161.

19. See S. S. Huebner, "Fire Insurance," *Encyclopedia of the Social Sciences*, pp. 235-39.

20. Hamilton referred to "a vast scene of household manufacturing" and urged measures to promote manufacture for a home market. Tenche Cox in 1787 "had estimated that less than one eighth of the population was engaged in manufactures, fishing navigation and trade, a category so broad that it includes nearly everything save agriculture." Willard L. Thorp, *The Integration of*

Industrial Operation (U. S. Department of Commerce, Census Monograph III), p. 24.

21. In advertising this venture in the Philadelphia *Aurora* of April 28, 1806, the journeymen maintained that they had been compelled "to resort to this undertaking as the only expedient left them to maintain themselves and families from the most abject dependence," since the alternative was to submit to employers "who could take away or lessen their wages whenever their caprice or avarice might prompt them." The journeymen promised to "spare no pains to give satisfaction to such as may favour them with their custom. Their work shall be made of the very best materials and sold at the most moderate prices." Unfortunately, no information is available on the degree of success attained. John R. Commons, and others, *History of Labor in the United States* (1918), Vol. I, p. 129.

22. Hower, *op. cit.*: "Between 1800 and 1860 America saw the rapid development of intense specialization (by both function and merchandise), and retailing took on differentiation with a vengeance.... It is practically impossible to find a specialized retail store in America around 1800 ... but in 1850 the cities were full of them . . . ." (pp. 82-83). See also N. S. B. Gras, *Business and Capitalism* (Cambridge, Mass.: Harvard University Press, 1939), p. 197; and Solon J. Buck and Elizabeth Hamilton Buck, *The Planting of Civilization in Western Pennsylvania*, Ch. 13.

23. Commons, and others, *op. cit.*, pp. 466-68.

24. John R. Commons and Helen L. Sumner, *Documentary History of American Industrial Society*, Vol. V, p. 368.

25. As quoted in Commons and Sumner, *op. cit.*, Vol. VI, p. 299.

26. Harold G. Moulton, *Financial Organization and the Economic System* (1938): "The original form of building and loan association was little more than a home-builders' club, where each individual paid into the common treasury a certain sum of money each month. The purpose was to secure enough members so that a moderate monthly payment by each would provide every month a fund sufficient to build a house for one of the group. For example, if there were one hundred members and each paid into the association twenty dollars per month, every month one member could begin the building of his house, to cost two thousand dollars; and at the end of one hundred months each would have a two-thousand dollar home. The club required each house-builder to give a mortgage on the home as security in case he failed to continue his monthly payments after receiving a loan from the association. When each member had acquired a house, the association, having accomplished its purpose, was dissolved" (p. 457).

27. Alexander Block and Horace F. Clark, "Building and Loan Associations", *Encyclopedia of the Social Sciences*: With the passage of time, however, they have lost much of their mutuality in control, although the benefits are still confined to members. "The early institutions were all local just as they were terminating—not on principle, but because it was natural for an organization to be joined by people who had specific needs and who were bound by neighborhood ties" (p. 49).

28. Charles Barnard, in his book *Cooperation as a Business* (1881), was exceedingly proud of these associations as an American cooperative invention, pp. 1-66. Albert Shaw, "Cooperation in the Northwest," *History of Cooperation in the United States* (Johns Hopkins University Studies, Vol. VI), Baltimore (1888), said: "The form of cooperative enterprise that has attained far greater results in the United States than all others combined is that of the well-known and almost invariably successful 'building and loan association.'"

29. Bidwell and Falconer, *op. cit.*, pp. 184-85. See also Wayne D. Rasmussen (Ed.), *Readings in the History of American Agriculture* (Urbana, Ill.:University of Illinois Press, 1960), pp. 41-45.

30. Bidwell and Falconer, *op. cit.*, p. 191.

31. *Ibid.* p. 193.

32. W. A. Lloyd, *The Agriculture of Ohio*, Agricultural Experiment Station Bulletin No. 326, pp. 83-84.

33. Bidwell and Falconer, *op. cit.*, pp. 249-50, 294.

34. The real introduction of cooperative marketing did not come until after 1860, although a number of interesting sporadic trials were made in the fifties. For example, a cooperative elevator built in Madison, Wisconsin, by the Dane County Farmers' Protective Union in 1857, was not able to survive the dishonesty of the manager followed by a fire (from Chastina Gardner, *Beginnings of Cooperative Grain Marketing* [Mimeo.], Federal Farm Board, 1932). More successful were the dairymen in "associated dairying," following the lead of Jesse Williams of Oneida County, New York who in 1851 began to unite the milk from several neighboring dairies for manufacture at one place (from Chastina Gardner, *Beginnings of Cooperative Dairy Organization* [Mimeo.], U. S. Department of Agriculture, 1927).

35. See Victor N. Valgren, *Farmers' Mutual Fire Insurance Companies in the United States* (Chicago: University of Chicago Press, 1923), p. 11. For general historical background, see Burpee, *op. cit.*

36. For a full description of the early methods of the company and its history to the present, see Burpee, *op. cit.*

37. For a full account of the early history of the factory mutuals see John Bainbridge, *Biography of an Idea: The Story of Mutual Fire and Casualty Insurance* (Garden City, N.Y.: Doubleday & Company, Inc.), pp. 92-107. See also Valgren, *op. cit.*, p. 7.

38. Sheppard B. Clough, *A Century of American Life Insurance: A History of the Mutual Life Insurance Company of New York, 1843-1943* (New York: Columbia University Press, 1946), p. 32. This book provides an invaluable history of life insurance in the United States.

39. *Ibid.*, p. 35.

40. Joseph B. MacLean, *Life Insurance* (New York: McGraw-Hill Book Company, 1957), pp. 503-4.

41. It should be realized that the social customs of the period were not unfavorable to such efforts, as the practice of joining together to promote a common interest was well established. This fact generally impressed de Tocqueville, who observed: "Americans of all ages, all conditions, and all dispositions, constantly form associations . . . As soon as several of the inhabitant of the United States have taken up an opinion or a feeling which they wish to promote in the world, they look out for mutual assistance; and as soon as they have found another out they combine" (from Alexis de Tocqueville, *Democracy in America* [1835], Pt. 2, Bk. 2, Ch. V, "Of the Use Which the Americans make of public associations in Civil Life").

42. Frank Podmore, *Robert Owen, A Complete Exposition of His Life and Work* (1906), pp. 289-290. See also G. D. H. Cole, *Robert Owen* (1925).

43. Podmore, *op. cit.*, pp. 292-293.

44. *Ibid.*, letter of William Owen to Robert Owen, October 1825, p. 292.

45. *Ibid.*, pp. 301-302.

46. *Ibid.* pp. 323-335. The whole experiment represented a loss to Owen of approximately $140,000. or about four-fifths of his fortune.

47. From "Explanation of the Design and Arrangements of the Cooperative Magazine, Mechanics Free Press, Aug. 9, 1928" in Commons and Sumner, *op. cit.*, Vol. V, p. 126.

48. *Ibid.*, Vol. V, pp. 129-33. See "Constitution of the Philadelphia Labour for Labour Association."

49. See Commons, and others, *op. cit.*, pp. 96-97.

50. The story of this experiment is fully told in the *Second Biennial Report of the Wisconsin Bureau of Labor and Industrial Statistics, 1885-1886*, pp. 193-206. "It would hardly be possible to test any ideal scheme of cooperation under circumstances more favorable than those enjoyed by the Ceresco Fourierites ... They chose one of the finest and richest counties in the West ... Those who joined the community were educated, intelligent, and inured to frontier life; all were American born and thoroughly imbued with American ideas, as well as anxious to succeed in this new experiment" (p. 204).

51. Commons and Sumner, *op. cit.*, Vol. VII (1840-1860), p. 264.

52. *Ibid.*, pp. 267, 268-69. For a more complete statement of the conditions leading to failure, see the *Second Biennial Report of the Wisconsin Bureau of Labor and Industrial Statistics*: "Although the members of the Phalanx were clothed, fed, housed and enlightened better than the average ... one or two of the more aggressive males had an itching for speculation in lands, town-sites, etc., and by persistent effort succeeded in disintegrating the association ... Those who accomplished the most work had a right to more compensation, yet to grant it to them caused more trouble than to treat all alike—giving the slothful as much as the industrious ... Workingmen should avoid the teachers of such balderdash, and when formulating practical schemes of co-operation ... entertain no idea of at once revolutionizing society ... or making of each community a Heavenly Utopia" (p. 205).

53. Vernon L. Parrington, *Main Currents in American Thought*, 1928, Vol. II, p. 347.

54. The communal structure of the Mormon colony was clearly influenced by the New Harmony plan of Robert Owen. (See L. H. Creir, "Mormonism," *Encyclopaedia of the Social Sciences*, pp. 14-17). While the Mormon Church has always espoused cooperative methods, the most significant cooperative contribution was in irrigation. According to Wells A. Hutchins, *Mutual Irrigation Companies in California and Utah*, Bulletin No. 8, Farm Credit Administration, 1939: "The major activities of these (early Mormon) communities were on a highly cooperative basis. Irrigation was and always has been one of their major activities; it is one of the four original industries remaining essentially cooperative and giving no indication of receding from that principle" (p. 15).

55. George Thomas, *The Development of Institutions Under Irrigation*, 1920. pp. 18, 33.

56. *Ibid.*, pp. 19, 35.

57. A survey in 1937 found that 95 of the existing mutual irrigation associations had been formed by 1860. Of these, 92 were in Utah and 3 in California. Farm Credit Administration, *A Statistical Handbook of Farmers' Cooperatives*, Bulletin No. 26 (1938), p. 255.

58. The period during which the Protective Union store movement flourished (1845-57) was characterized by rising prices and business optimism. By this time the specialized retail store for groceries, hardware, dry goods, boots and shoes, furniture, and so forth had largely replaced the general store except

in rural areas. Hower, *op. cit.*: "The main influence at work was certainly the Industrial Revolution, which began to exert its full impact upon America after 1815. Machines began to pour forth a swelling stream of goods, resulting not only in an increased quantity of the wares that men had used in the past but also in a greatly expanded variety. Trade grew in volume and complexity ... Of course, the transfer of a substantial amount of production out of the household into the factory necessarily added to the quantity of goods which had to pass through the retailer's hands" (pp. 85-86).

59. Even prior to 1840 it had been common for labor organizations to obtain price reductions for their members by pledging their members to exclusive trade with a store. See *Cooperation in New England*, a report written by George E. McNeill, included in the *Eighth Annual Report of the* (Massachusetts) *Bureau of Statistics of Labor*, 1877, p. 58. This report contains a full account of the Protective Union Store movement based upon material obtained from original sources and participants. See also Florence E. Parker, *The First 125 Years: A History of Distributive and Service Cooperation in the United States, 1829-1954* (Chicago: Cooperative League of the U.S.A., 1956), pp. 4-8.

60. A rather complete abstract of the Constitution of the Workingmen's Protective Union is included in Commons and Sumner, *op. cit.*, Vol. III (Labor Movement), pp. 267 ff.

61. McNeill, "Cooperation in Massachusetts," *op. cit.*, pp. 63-66.

62. *Ibid.*, pp. 68-81.

63. Ira B. Cross, *Twelfth Biennial Report of the Wisconsin Bureau of Labor and Industrial Statistics* (1905-06): "If the Civil War had not occurred just at this time and thus hastened, if not actually caused the downfall of these stores, it is safe to say that the cooperative movement would be much further advanced than it is today. True, the methods which were then in use would not be fitted to our modern trade conditions, but the methods of cooperative stores evolve as do the methods of other mercantile enterprises" (p. 11).

64. James Ford, *Cooperation in New England*, p. 16.

65. Shaw, *op. cit.*, pp. 332-33.

66. Jonathan Periam, *The Groundswell—A History of the Origins, Aims, and Progress of the Farmers' Movement* (1874), p. 202. For full discussion, see Ch. XVI, "The Movement Toward Cooperation," pp. 196-206.

67. *Ibid.*, pp. 203-206.

Chapter II

1. For illustration, the Bessemer steel-making process introduced from England in 1864 revolutionized the steel industry. Among the more important industrial inventions of the period were the following: the Westinghouse air-brake (1869), the typewriter (1873), the refrigerator car (1875), the telephone (1875), the electric dynamo (1876), and the incandescent electric light (1882).

2. The corporation form of business enterprise was in bad repute up to the time of the Civil War and was little used in manufacturing and commerce. It began to be generally employed in the sixties. Trusts and other forms of business combination also rose rapidly after 1880. By 1900, when the Census first reported data on corporations engaged in manufacturing, it was found that corporations accounted for 59 per cent of the total gross volume of products manufactured. See William Z. Ripley, *Main Street and Wall Street* (1927), pp. 23-24; Alfred L. Berhheim (Ed.), *Big Business—Its Growth and Its Place* Twentieth Century Fund, 1937,

pp. 12-13; Chester W. Wright, *Economic History of the United States*, p. 669; Ida M. Tarbell, *The Nationalising of Business, 1878-1898: Twelfth Census of the United States* (1900), Vol. VII, *Manufactures*, Pt. I, p. lxvi.

3. See Paul H. Nystrom, *Economics of Retailing*, Vol. I, pp. 90-99; George Burton Hotchkiss, *Milestones of Marketing* (1938), particularly Ch. VI, "The Rise of Large-Scale Retailing," pp. 184-202.

4. Quoted by Edward W. Bemis, "Cooperation in the Middle States," *History of Cooperation in the United States*, Johns Hopkins University Studies (Sixth Series II-III), 1888, pp. 141-42.

5. See John R. Commons, and others, *History of Labour in the United States*, 1918, Vol. II, Pt. 1, pp. 39-41.

6. *Ibid.*, p. 53. William H. Sylvis, the leading spirit of the Molders' Union declared in the summer of 1867: "Cooperation is taking hold upon the minds of our members, and in many places very little else is talked about."

7. John R. Commons and John B. Andrews, *A Documentary History of American Industrial Society*, Vol. IX, p. 138.

8. *Ibid.*, pp. 148-49.

9. Commons, and others, *op. cit.*, pp. 53-57, 111. It was at this time also that the Minneapolis coopers began their famous kind of cooperative workshop which was to be continued for some 30 years. However, little was known of this experience nationally until it was dramatized in the middle 1880's by the Knights of Labor, Albert Shaw, and Professor Richard T. Ely. See Albert Shaw, "Cooperation in the Northwest," *History of Cooperation in the United States*, Johns Hopkins University Studies, 1888, pp. 199-242.

10. See E. G. Nourse, *Legal Status of Cooperation*, 1927, pp. 39-41.

11. Commons, and others, *op. cit.*, p. 79. It is of interest that "in 1869 and 1870 the Grand Lodge of Massachusetts made a vigorous effort to secure from the legislature an act of incorporation for the purpose of conducting cooperative stores for purchasing supplies . . . In 1870, the New York State Grand Lodge recommended to its subordinate lodges cooperative workshops. These cooperative shops became numerous after 1870, and there were established also between thirty and forty cooperative stores, which soon, however, went to pieces."

12. The cooperative plank of the National Labor Union was expressed as follows in 1867: "*Resolved,* that in cooperation, based upon just financial and revenue laws, we recognize a sure and lasting remedy for the abuses of the present industrial system, and that until the laws of the nation can be remodelled so as to recognize the rights of men instead of classes, the system of cooperation carefully guarded will do much to lessen the evils of our present system. We, therefore, hail with delight the organization of cooperative stores and workshops and would urge their formation in every section of the country, and in every branch of business." Commons and Andrews, *op. cit.*, Vol. II., p. 182.

13. The Philadelphia Industrial Cooperative Society (Ltd.), organized on the Rochdale plan in 1874, thrived for many years. Its sales in 1888 were reported at $171,238 and patronage dividends at $6,066. The non-members received a dividend of 3 per cent on purchases while members received from 3 to 8 per cent in addition to 6 per cent dividends on stock holdings. For an interesting description of this significant early organization, see Bemis, "Cooperation in the Middle States," *op. cit.*, pp. 143-44.

14. For a complete discussion of the Sovereigns, see Edward W. Bemis, "Cooperation in New England," pp. 37-52. See also George E. McNeill, "Cooperation in Massachusetts," *Eighth Annual Report of the Massachusetts Bureau of Statistics of Labor*, March 1877, pp. 98-113; Ira B. Cross, "The Cooperative

Store in the United States," *Twelfth Biennial Report of the Wisconsin Bureau of Labor and Industrial Statistics* (1905-06), pp. 24-26; James Ford, *Cooperation in New England—Urban and Rural,* 1913, pp. 21-27; Commons, and others, *op. cit.,* pp. 171-75; Florence E. Parker, *The First 125 Years: A History of Distributive and Service Cooperation in the United States, 1829-1954* (Chicago: Cooperative League of the U.S.A., 1956), pp. 18-21.

15. Bemis, "Cooperation in New England," *op. cit.,* p. 39.

16. *Ibid.,* pp. 43-45. According to Bemis, who had access to first-hand sources of information, "Directors were elected, and managers and clerks in the various branches of the store were chosen who knew nothing of the business . . . Never . . . did any two directors or auditors . . . find any way of balancing the accounts. . . Contrary both to the constitution and the orders of the directors . . . thousands of dollars worth of goods (were) sold for credit and never paid for . . . Whatever economy was attempted was in the wrong direction. One thousand dollars were paid to the manager, but many thought even that too high. A mistake was made in attempting too many kinds of business."

17. *Ibid.,* p. 47. John Orvis had been a member of the Brook Farm Community. (See Commons, and others, *op. cit.,* p. 173.) Thomas Phillips, the organizer of the first Rochdale store in 1862, also became an organizer for the Sovereigns in the late 1870's (p. 40).

18. *Ibid.,* pp. 49-50. The total trade in 1876 was estimated by President Earle at not less than $3 million, with savings of 14 per cent.

19. Ford, *op. cit.,* p. 22. In 1913, Ford found that "five of the most prominent cooperative stores in New England today date from the Sovereigns of Industry movement."

20. The general conditions of the time have been portrayed as follows: "That year (1878), the fourth since the Panic, found many laboring men in what they felt an almost intolerable position, and yet one that was growing worse. In all the great cities, from Boston to Omaha, crowds of workless and hungry men tramped the streets, hung disconsolately about the public squares, and joined in parades and mass meetings of protest." (From Allan Nevins, *The Emergence of Modern America, 1865-1878: A History of American Life,"* Vol. VIII Macmillan, 1927, pp. 384. See also pp. 303-304.

21. Bemis, "Cooperation in New England," *op. cit.,* p. 51. "Although not fully recognized at the time, this cause is now held by the old leaders of the movement to have caused the downfall of the national organization".

22. Ford, *op. cit.,* p. 27. According to Ford, the modern period of cooperation in New England started with Sovereigns. "The Sovereigns" stores mark the transition from workingmen's joint-stock to cooperative companies to workingmen's Rochdale cooperative societies."

23. The philosophy which motivated the Knights of Labor movement has been precisely outlined as follows: "The Knights were clearly proceeding upon the assumption that no fundamental disharmony of interest obtained between employers and workers as such and that the interests of all workers were basically the same. The real conflict was between the producing and the non-producing classes. Only on this assumption would the deprecation of strikes, the emphasis on education and political methods, and the ignoring of the separate trade interests be regarded as consistent. It was a plain-people crusade, based upon the premise of an abundance of opportunity to be shared among all workers of hand and brain; the mission of the producing classes was to regain for themselves, and to protect, this opportunity." Harry A. Millis and Royal E. Montgomery, *Organized Labor* (1945), p. 68,

24. T. V. Powderly, *Thirty Years of Labor—1859-1889*, (1893). See chapter entitled "Cooperation under Difficulties." Powderly was Grand Master Workman during the effective life of the order from 1879 to 1893.

25. Commons, and others, *op. cit.*, pp. 351, 431, 437. For several years the Knights unsuccessfully labored to make this venture successful. After they had invested $20,000 in land and equipment and mined $1,000 worth of coal, they could not get the railroad company to connect their switch with the main track. The mine was sold in 1885.

26. Quoted by Commons, and others, *op. cit.*, p. 436, from *Philadelphia Journal of United Labor*, April 25, 1886.

27. Millis and Montgomery, *op. cit.*, pp. 66, 70. See also Parker, *op. cit.*, pp. 17-18.

28. Commons, and others, *op. cit.*, p. 438.

29. Bemis, *op. cit.*: This attitude was also reflected at this time in a growing enthusiasm for "partial cooperation" in the form of various systems of profit-sharing. Many concerns started such schemes as a method of improving relations with workers. The Pillsbury Mills of Minneapolis adopted a plan of this type in 1882, and there were many functioning in 1888 when the Johns Hopkins University Studies were published: (pp. 107-25, 168-82, 255-62). Some employers also encouraged co-operative stores for their employees. Many years later Andrew Carnegie told of his interest in a venture of this sort. *Andrew Carnegie Autobiography* (1920): " The remark about high prices charged set me to thinking why the men could not open a cooperative store. This was also arranged—the firm agreeing to pay the rent of the building, but insisting that the men themselves take the stock and manage it. Out of that came the Braddock Cooperative Society, a valuable institution for many reasons, not the least of them that it taught the men that business had its difficulties" (p. 250).

30. Charles Barnard, *Cooperation as a Business* (New York: G. P. Putnam's Sons, 1881): "In the cooperative store, the member claims interest on his money and a dividend on his purchases. This is as it should be. Capital can do nothing without the consumer. It is the consumer's money that moves the business, and he deserves both a rate and a dividend" (p. 140).

31. A more complete list of publications is given by Herbert Myrick, *How to Cooperate* (1891), p. 345. The work of this Society is described in the *Second Biennial Report of the Wisconsin Bureau of Labor and Industrial Statistics, 1885-1886*, pp. 117-119.

32. See Bemis, "Cooperation in New England," *op. cit.*, pp. 73-75. For an interesting and detailed study of this influential cooperative up to modern times see N. S. B. Gras, *Harvard Cooperative Society: Past and Present, 1882-1942*, Cambridge, Mass.: Harvard University Press, 1942. Many well-known Harvard Professors, including Frank W. Taussig and W. B. Munro, took an active part in its affairs.

33. It was also issued as Part I of the *Seventeenth Annual Report of the Massachusetts Bureau of Statistics of Labor* (1886), pp. 51-119. Wright later became United States Commissioner of Labor.

34. Publications of the American Economic Association (1887), Vol. I, "Cooperation in a Western City" by Albert Shaw, "Cooperation in New England," by Edward Bemis. Vol. II, "Three Phases of Cooperation in the West," by Amos G. Warner.

35. See Herbert Myrick, *How to Cooperate—A Manual for Cooperators* (New York: Drange Judd Company, 1891). See Ch. I, "What Cooperation Is and Is Not."

36. *Ibid.*, p. 253. Myrick's American optimism and Yankee caution were combined in the following paragraph: "With past experience in this country and England combined with the superior energy and enterprise of the American people,

cooperation is destined to make far greater progress on the American continent than it has in other countries. This statement is predicated on the idea that our people will be satisfied to undertake cooperation in a small way instead of beginning at the top, as has been the characteristic of the efforts in this direction heretofore."

37. Ford, *op. cit.*, pp. 78-79. See also Edward W. Bemis, "Cooperative Distribution," *Bulletin* of the United States Department of Labor, Vol. I, 1896, pp. 626-27.

38. See Cross, *op. cit.*, p. 31.

39. For a first-hand description of these events, see Ray Stannard Baker, *American Chronicle*, 1945.

40. Bemis, "Cooperative Distribution," *op. cit.*, pp. 610-11.

41. See *Ninth Annual Report of the Commissioner of Labor*, p. 15.

Chapter III

1. N. B. Ashby, *the Riddle of the Sphinx* (1890), pp. 211-12.

2. For a comprehensive discussion of these and other factors, see Louis Bernard Schmidt, "The Agricultural Revolution in the United States, 1860-1930," *Science*, Vol. LXII (1930), pp. 585-94; Everett E. Edwards, "American Agriculture—The First 300 Years," *1940 Yearbook of United States Department of Agriculture*, pp. 221-66. For a more general interpretation, see Leverett S. Lyon, Victor Abramson, and associates, *Government and Economic Life*, Vol. II (1940), particularly Ch. XXIII, "Agriculture," by E. G. Nourse, pp. 864-77.

3. It is true that farmers politically supported the "soft money" Greenback movement in the 1870's in the belief that this would increase prices and thus lower their fixed debt burdens. However, farmers did not become generally conscious of the adverse effects of deflation on their industry until it was emphasized by Alliance and Populist leaders in the late 1880's and early 1890's. Bryan's famous "Cross of Gold" speech in 1896 came near the end of the long period of price decline.

4. For a farm leader's analysis of the farmers' grievances, see Jonathan Periam, *A History of the Origin, Aims, and Progress of the Farmers' Movement* (1874), pp. 196-99.

5. The farmer's concept of organization did not preclude its use in political action. The farmers, through the Grange and Alliance, sponsored many reforms for abuses that could only be remedied by legislation.

6. For a full discussion of the political, social, educational, and other manifestations of the Granger movement, see Solon Justice Buck, *The Granger Movement*, Harvard University Press, 1913. While the intention here is to focus attention on the Grange's economic enterprises, it should be realized that all aspects of the movement were interrelated. An excellent interpretive account of Grange cooperative activities is given by George Cerny, "Cooperation in the Midwest in the Grange Era, 1869-1875, *Agricultural History*, October, 1963.

7. O. H. Kelley, *The History of the Patrons of Husbandry* (1875), pp. 14-15. For a profile of Oliver Hudson Kelley by Theodore Saloutos see *Great American Cooperators* (Joseph G. Knapp, and associates, Washington, D.C.: American Institute of Cooperation, 1967, pp. 7-9).

8. One of Kelley's disciples wrote him as follows in 1867: "To secure the attention of the masses, it must be made to apear that one of the legitimate consequences

of being a member of the Order, will be to promote the pecuniary interests of those who belong to it." *Idem*, p. 35.

9. Kelley, in organizing Granges in Minnesota in the fall of 1868, had advocated "a business agent in each Grange, to be established by ballot, who shall keep a record of such articles outsiders wish to purchase, thereby saving our members valuable time in hunting up customers for their produce. We can secure discounts to Grangers on purchases of books, implements, etc." The first request made of the state business agent was for the purchase of a jackass. When this was brought to the attention of Kelley, he facetiously observed: "This purchasing business commenced with buying jackasses; the propects are that many will be *sold*." At that time, the national officers of the Grange were indisposed toward cooperation, so the state business agent was appointed by the Minnesota state Grange without their blessing. *Journal of Proceedings of the Seventeenth Session of the National Grange of the Patrons of Husbandry* (1883), pp. 18, 180, 183.

10. O. H. Kelley, *op. cit.*, p. 303.

11. *Idem*, p. 361.

12. *Proceedings of the Sixth Session of the National Grange*, 1873, pp. 5-6.

13. An Iowa Granger explained this as follows: "Our first plan of cooperation was to pay cash and offer our whole trade to one man in a town, provided he would sell at a small profit, say ten per cent. We had no trouble in finding merchants who would agree to that. But we soon found trouble, for other merchants were not going to be outdone, so they would put their goods down below our price, and then some of the Grangers would go there and buy. This soon broke up our boycott business." See Albert Shaw, *Cooperation in the Northwest*, Johns Hopkins University Studies (1888), pp. 336-37.

14. The most complete discussion of Grange business agencies is given by Buck, *op. cit.*, pp. 239-55. See also A. E. Paine, *The Granger Movement in Illinois*, Univ. of Ill., Vol. I, No. 8, Sept. 1904, pp. 37-41; and B. H. Hibbard, *Marketing Agricultural Products*, pp. 201-03.

15. The farmers in settling new country needed large amounts of household goods as well as farm machinery and equipment. Sewing machines, stoves, carpets, furniture, dishes, guns, clocks, and similar articles were in demand as well as cloth, boots and shoes, sugar, spices, tobacco and items for more personal use. At that time barbed wire, binding twine, fertilizer, and grain sacks were just coming into demand. Feed and seed were largely locally produced, and there was little need for petroleum except for lighting and grease, or for coal, since wood was still generally available.

16. "Mr. Ward started this business in 1872 and his best patrons at the start were the Grangers of Illinois and adjacent states. For many years the catalogue bore the title, 'The Original Grange Supply House.'" Letter from F. W. Jameson of Montgomery Ward and Co., April 23, 1945. A multigraphed history of the firm furnished by Mr. Jameson states that: "For many years Montgomery Ward and Co. was recognized as the official Grange Supply House." This history also shows that Mr. Ward in founding the company was in accord with the Grangers' contention that "many merchants charged unjustly high prices . . . In his contact with rural communities, Mr. Ward sensed a growing dissatisfaction with existing conditions. He was covinced that the merchandising practices of that time were wrong, and the information he obtained from his associates in the small cities and on the farms added to his conviction that a radical change should be made in existing trade methods. He fully realized the obstacles which lay in the path of the revolutionary merchandising movement that he had in mind. He believed, however, that if goods could

be bought in large quantities at a close margin over the manufacturers cost, by selling these goods direct to the consumer and eliminating the profits and expenses of middlemen, large sums would be saved for the consumer."

17. Buck, *op. cit.*, p. 244. In Illinois "large reductions were secured by this system and afford ample proof that the middlemen were making unusual profits or were conducting their business in a reckless or extravagant manner. In either case the farmer had suffered unnecessarily. Reapers for which the middlemen charged $275 were secured by the Grangers for $175. Threshers were reduced from $300 to $200, wagons from $150 to $90, sewing machines from $75 and $100 to $40 and $50, and other articles in like proportion. Thus, for a few years, the members of the Grange probably saved at least 33-⅓ per cent on such purchases." Paine, *op. cit.*, p. 40.

18. Buck, *op. cit.*, pp. 267-68. The high price of farm machinery—which was indispensable to low-cost farm production—was a constant complaint of farmers at this time. Even in the 1860's farm machinery manufacturers were developing a controlled system of distribution through their own exclusive agents, and prices were largely fixed at what the traffic would bear. Each farm machinery company thus had a limited monopoly, and in view of the tremendous demand for any machine that promised more efficient farming operations, prices were abnormally high. Farmers saw no real relief except through their own manufacture.

19. See Amos G. Warner, *Three Phases of Cooperation in the West,* Johns Hopkins University Studies, 1888, pp. 386-87.

20. See Buck, *op. cit.*, pp. 268-69.

21. *Ibid.*, p. 269. The Executive Committee in its report for the year 1874 said: "The disposition among our members to inaugurate manufactories and to increase the products of the soil, the forest, and the mine, in the different sections of our country is well known. The wisdom of such a policy is evident. To facilitate the progress of such worthy enterprises we have employed much of our time in visiting the machine-works and mill-works of New England and other sections of the country, obtaining estimates of the cost of machines for such manufactories as we know are suited to our people, and desired by them, valuable statistics in this connection; making terms for mill and other machinery, as we have heretofore done for farming implements; negotiating with skilled mechanics, operative artisans; presenting to capitalists in the East information of the great undeveloped resources of the West and South, inviting them to at least 'come and see'; in which we trust we have benefited our Order, and laid the foundation for a much larger benefit in the future." *Journal of Proceedings of the Ninth Session of the National Grange of the Patrons of Husbandry* (1875), pp. 21-22.

22. In Texas, for example, the Grange entered into a partnership for the purpose of making plows and farm implements, adapted to the various regions of Texas, with a George A. Kelley who owned the plant for manufacturing plows and stoves and who was also a patron in good standing. Under the plan a joint-stock company was organized with an authorized capital stock of $250,000, with shares of $25 each which could be held by subordinate granges or members. Kelley was issued stock equal to the value of his plant, and was sole manager under a directorate elected annually by the State Grange. While a considerable amount of stock was sold, this proved insufficient capital in the opinion of Kelley, and moreover "he apparently found the undertaking irksome under a dual management." In 1878 he was released from his contract under an arrangement by which he returned every dollar subscribed in capital by members of the order plus 10 per cent per annum for the use of the money. See R. L. Hunt, *A History Of Farmer's Movements in the Southwest, 1873-1925.*

23. *Proceedings of the Seventh Session of the National Grange of the Patrons of Husbandry.* 1874, pp. 14, 80.

24. *Journal of Proceedings of the Ninth Annual Session of the National Grange,* 1875, pp. 93-100.

25. When comparison is made with the Rochdale rules, the Rochdale paternity is apparent in almost every paragraph. To a considerable extent the same arrangement and phraseology was employed. The principal difference lay in the fact that the Grange proposed to use the Rochdale plan in marketing their produce, as well as in purchasing their requirements.

26. D. Wyatt Aiken, "The Grange: Its Origin, Progress, and Educational Purpose," U. S. Department of Agriculture, *Special Report No. 55* (1883).

27. *Journal of Proceedings of the Tenth Session of the National Grange of the Patrons of Husbandry* (1876), pp. 144-52. According to Aiken, who had been a member of a special committee appointed to examine the matter: "This proposal was not rejected from any patriotic motive, but it was not entertained because the executive committee were not competent to control the purchases or sales of a single subordinate grange." Buck attributed the failure of this scheme for "international cooperation" to the inability of the Grange to raise the required amount of capital. Buck, *op. cit.,* p. 260. For a full discussion of this interesting plan, see *Proceedings of the National Grange of the Patrons of Husbandry,* 1875, pp. 8-19, 25-27, 48-67, 124-130, 144-52, 167-69, 172; 1877, pp. 12-13.

28. *Journal of Proceedings of the Eleventh Session of the National Grange of the Patrons of Husbandry,* 1877, p. 17.

29. Buck, *op. cit.,* pp. 263-64. See also Herbert Myrick, *How to Cooperate—A Manual for Cooperators* (New York: Orange Judd Company, 1891), p. 115

30. *Nineteenth Biennial Report of the Kansas State Board of Agriculture* (1915), pp. 208-12. See also Myrick, *op. cit.,* pp. 114-21.

31. An unsuccessful attempt was made in 1880 to establish a cooperative wholesale house in Cincinnati for the Grange stores of Ohio, Indiana, Kentucky, and West Virginia. After several years of struggle this organization was finally liquidated in 1886.

32. *Second Biennial Report of the Wisconsin Bureau of Labor and Industrial Statistics, 1885-86,* p. 160. Cooperative writers of the 1880's were enthusiastic in their praise of this organization. "The Texas Cooperative Association has reaped the greatest success in this country in distributive cooperation." Randal, Johns Hopkins University Studies (1888). "The Texas Cooperative Association ... is much like the English and Scottish Wholesale." *Report of the Wisconsin Bureau of Labor ...* 1887, p. 158. Myrick in 1891 referred to it as a "conspicuously successful society," *op. cit.,* pp. 121-25. For a more sober analysis, see Hunt, *op. cit.,* pp. 20-25.

33. For complete by-laws, see Myrick, *op. cit.,* pp. 287-90.

34. See Hunt, *op. cit.,* p. 23.

35. *Proceedings of the National Grange,* 1885, p. 96.

36. This early interest was described as follows by D. W. Adams, as master of the Grange: "When the first subordinate granges had been organized, one of the first and most proper subjects for discussion was, how to make two blades of grass grow where one grew before. During these discussions, the fact soon became prominent that how to sell crops was fully as knotty a question as how to grow them. The solution of this problem soon became a leading idea in the Order." *Proceedings of the Sixth Session of the National Grange of the Patrons of Husbandry* (1873), p. 13.

37. Buck, *op. cit.*, p. 271. For further discussion of marketing activities of the Grange, see E. C. Nourse, *Fifty Years of Farmers' Elevators in Iowa*, Iowa State College Bulletin No. 211, pp. 236-41; E. G. Nourse and J. G. Knapp, *Cooperative Marketing of Livestock*, pp. 10-11; Hibbard, *op. cit.*, pp. 207-09; Newell H. Comish, *Cooperative Marketing of Agricultural Products*, pp. 133, 374-76.

38. *Journal of Proceedings of the Tenth Session of the National Grange of the Patrons of Husbandry*, (1876), p. 154.

39. The Farm Credit Administration found in 1936 that 460 mutual fire insurance associations formed during the years 1870-79 were still in operation. *Statistical Handbook*, p. 268.

40. The total number of Granges declined from 21,697 on January 1, 1875 to 19,007 on October 1, 1875 and to 15,127 by July 1, 1876. The membership which had stood at 758,767 on October 1, 1875 (about the time that the Rochdale plan was accepted) fell to 588,525 by July 1, 1876. Buck, *op. cit.* (see table inserted between pp. 58 and 59). The membership continued to decline gradually until by 1880 there were only about 125,000 members, and it continued on about this level for the next decade. In 1900 the membership had increased to 187,000, and by 1920 it was 541,000. See Edward Wiest, *Agricultural Organization in the United States*, pp. 395-96.

41. This is vividly presented by John B. Hicks, *The Populist Revolt*, The University of Minnesota Press, 1931, See Chap. III, "The Grievances." See also Theodore Saloutos, *Farmer Movements in the South*, 1865-1933, University of California Press, 1960, especially Chapter III, "The Farmers' Alliance: Economic Activities." See also Carl C. Taylor, *The Farmers' Movement, 1620-1920* (1953), especially the discussion of economic projects of the Farmers' Alliance, pp. 234-243.

42. A large portion of the farmers of the South were in the same "fix," due to the impoverishment which followed the Civil War. While farmers in the East were more secure, they also were drastically affected by the competition of more cheaply produced products in the West, and the resulting lowering of land values.

43. Claim or "squatters" associations similar to those set up in the 1840's in Iowa and Wisconsin moved westward with the frontier in the 1850's and 1860's. With the prevalence of horse and cattle stealing in the 1860's and 1870's many protective associations were organized "to assist the civil officers in maintaining law and order." Many of these were organized as "alliances" and this led to the formation of state alliances. In Texas, the Alliance adopted a special livestock brand for protecting the rights of members, and had special signs and signals for detecting thieves and notifying the sheriff. See N. A. Dunning, *The Farmers' Alliance History and Agricultural Digest* (1891), pp. 13-14. Hamlim Garland in *A Son of the Middle Border* (1923) tells of similar protective associations which were operating further north at this time: "During these years [early 1870's] the whole middle border was menaced by bands of horsethieves operating under a secret well-organized system. Horses disappeared night by night and were never recovered, till at last the farmers, in despair of the local authorities, organized a Horse Thief Protective Association which undertook to pursue and punish the robbers and to pay for such animals as were not returned. Our county had an association of this sort and ... my father became a member. My first knowledge of this fact came when he nailed on our barn-door the white cloth poster which proclaimed in bold black letters a warning and a threat signed by 'the Committee.'—I was always a little in doubt as to whether the horse-thieves or ourselves were to be protected, for the notice was fair warning to them as well as an assurance to us. Anyhow, very

few horses were stolen from barns thus protected" (pp. 146-47). In a way, these early protective associations were a product of the same sort of conditions which led to the rise of the vigilante societies of the Far West.

44. Information on the "barbed wire trust" is largely drawn from Shaw, *op. cit.*, pp. 344-49. For a more recent and complete study, see Earl W. Hayter, "An Iowa Farmers' Protective Association: A Barbed Wire Patent Protest Movement," *Iowa Journal of History and Politics*, October 1939, Vol. 37, pp. 331-62. For a discussion of the importance of barbed wire in the settling of the West, see Earl W. Hayter, "Barbed Wire Fencing—A Prairie Invention," *Agricultural History*, October 1939, pp. 189-207.

45. "Then came the Alliance ... Like Topsy, it 'just grew.' In numerous backwoods communities widely scattered over the country, between 1874 and 1886, Alliances, Unions, Wheels, and whatnots sprang up spontaneously. Each of these became a mother order, multiplying into neighboring communities, counties, states, meeting each other, amalgamating, and thus developing almost unconsciously into a great nation-wide movement." A. W. Arnett, *The Populist Movement in Georgia*, 1922, p. 76.

46. Hicks, *op. cit.*, p. 121.

47. Dunning, *op. cit.*, pp. 356-57.

48. For a description of Texas Alliance experience in marketing cotton, see O. W. Hermann and Chastina Gardner, *Early Development in Cooperative Cotton Marketing*, F. C. A. Circular No. C-101, pp. 3-5.

49. Dunning, *op. cit.*, p. 52. For a profile of Charles W. Macune by Theodore Saloutos see *Great American Cooperators* (Knapp, and associates, *op. cit.*, pp. 10-12).

50. *Idem*, p. 52.

51. Clarence N. Ousley, "A Lesson in Cooperation," *The Popular Science Monthly*, Vol. 36 (April 1890), pp. 821-28.

52. Dunning, *op. cit.*, pp. 84-85. In his address to the Texas State Alliance in August 1888 Macune said: "We have been talking cooperation for twenty years. Now we have an aggressive movement . . . It saved us last year from one to five million dollars on our cotton; it saved us forty per cent on our plows; thirty per cent on our engines and gins; sixty per cent on sewing machines; thirty per cent on wagons; fifty to seventy-five per cent on buggies; thirty to forty per cent on reapers and mowers, and by the reduction of prices of all other commodities in every county, city, town and hamlet of the entire state, aggregating beyond any possibility of doubt millions of dollars saved on our purchases. In spite of all this, the question today is: Shall we endorse the aggressive movement? . . . Will you cease an aggressive effort that promises certain relief, simply because the opposition howl and curse?" W. S. Morgan, *History of the Wheel and Alliance and the Impending Revolution*, 1899, p. 313.

53. An expert employed by the Alliance found that the failure was due principally to lack of paid-in capital, high costs of doing business and low margin pricing policy. See Ashby, *op. cit.*, pp. 376-77. For a critical case study, see Ousley, *op. cit.*, pp. 821-28. Ousley pointed out that the management of the Exchange during 1889 was conservative and judicious, and "under other circumstances, he (the manager) would doubtless have made it a successful enterprise, but it was too heavily encumbered, and the confidence of the order in it had been sacrificed."

54. Dunning, *op. cit.*, p. 69.

55. The Georgia Exchange was credited with saving its patrons $200,000 on

fertilizer alone during the first year of its existence. See Arnett, *op. cit.*, pp. 80-81.

56. The plan of organization is given by Dunning, *op. cit.*, pp. 367-68.

57. For more complete information on this early experiment, see Ashby, *op. cit.*, pp. 368-71. In 1890, the company claimed "the largest business of any implement house in the state of Dakota."

58. See Myrick, *op. cit.*, p. 209.

59. A copy of the constitution and by-laws of this organization is available in Myrick, *op. cit.*, pp. 298-301.

60. The State Business Agents Association in 1890 claimed that member State Exchanges and agents were doing a business of 10 million dollars. At that time State Alliance exchanges or business agents were apparently functioning in Georgia, Alabama, Kentucky, Tennessee, Louisiana, North Carolina, South Carolina, Arkansas, Florida, Texas, Nebraska, the Dakotas, Kansas, Minnesota, Missouri, Iowa, Indiana, Illinois, Virginia, Wisconsin, Maryland, New York, Indian Territory, California, Washington. See Hicks, *op. cit.*, p. 139, and Dunning, *op. cit.*, p. 369.

61. Nourse and Knapp, *op. cit.*, p. 105.

62. Hicks, *op. cit.*, p. 133. For an account of Alliance insurance experiences in Iowa and other states see Ashby, *op. cit.*, pp. 380, 385.

63. Dunning, *op. cit.*, p. 84 (Italics supplied). See also Morgan, *op. cit.*, p. 307.

64. Macune was not impressed by the working of the Rochdale system in Texas as illustrated by the unfortunate Texas Cooperative Association. At that time, while there were many vestiges of Grange-Rochdale cooperation in the state, the Grange itself was discredited and looked upon as an old-model form of organization, not capable of dealing with the mass problems of the Texas farmers. The very fact that the Grange had adopted the Rochdale idea thus carried little weight with the Alliance leaders in their attempt to fashion a program capable of attracting farm support in meeting the acute farm problem of that day. Then again there was a bitter rivalry between the Texas Cooperative Association and the Texas Alliance, which made the Alliance leaders anxious to show that their plan was different.

65. Dunning, *op. cit.*, pp. 364-66.

66. The Alliance thus anticipated the "commodity marketing" approach which became widespread in the 1920's. However, the Alliance was thinking more of the whole industry than of specific commodities. The state exchanges handled various products and also engaged in purchasing, insurance, and other activities. Saloutos maintains that Macune, the leader of the Alliance, "might easily have been employed by any of the cotton-pooling associations of the 1920's, or might even have gone to work for Alexander Legge and the Federal Farm Board" as he "believed that the farmers should avoid mass political action and concentrate 'in buying and selling, in producing and consuming.' The larger the business unit the more effective it would be; in fact he anticipated the construction of enterprises that would transcend state lines and encompass entire regions. Moderation and a slow, seasoned growth was almost foreign to his thinking; only a mammoth program of agrarian purchasing and selling... made sense to him." Theodore Saloutos, *Farmers' Movements in the South*, pp. 90-91.

67. It is of interest that "the Farmers' Alliance is supposed to have been active in the formulation of [the California non-stock law of 1895], which marked a new departure in cooperative legislation in America." See E. G. Nourse, *Legal Status of Agricultural Cooperation*, pp. 44, 59. Nourse says: "These laws

(the 1895 and 1909 California non-stock laws) represent a distinct departure from the structure developed under the Rochdale movement. The membership clause . . . shows that instead of a 'company' of stockholders the idea becomes that of an 'association' of persons, engaged in a like undertaking, specifically qualifying for membership and accepting the discipline of the association" (pp. 61-62).

68. See Hicks, *op. cit.*, pp. 115, 123. See also Dunning, *op. cit.*, pp. 111-12.

Chapter IV

1. X. A. Willard, *Practical Dairy Husbandry* (1872), pp. 213 ff. and pp. 261-62, as quoted by Chastina Gardner, *Beginnings of Cooperative Dairy Organization,* U. S. Department of Agriculture (Preliminary Report, mimeo., 1927), p. 6. For an incisive analysis of this early experience and its significance to cooperative development, see H. E. Erdman, "The 'Associated Dairies' of New York as Precursors of American Agricultural Cooperatives," *Agricultural History,* April 1962, pp. 82-90.

2. George Williams, "Organization of Factories," *First Annual Report of N. Y. State Cheese Manufacturers' Association,* 1864, p. 49, as quoted by Gardner, *op. cit.*, p. 11. George Williams was the son of Jesse Williams, the "father" of associated dairying.

3. X. A. Willard, *Sixteenth Annual Report of the Secretary of the Maine Board of Agriculture,* 1871, pp. 73 ff., as quoted by Gardner, *op. cit.*, p. 13.

4. It is of interest that the highly successful plan of cooperative dairy marketing developed in Denmark was influenced by a study of the American system in 1876. According to Herman Steen in *Cooperative Marketing—The Golden Rule in Agriculture* (1923), "Danish commissioners to the Centennial Exposition at Philadelphia discovered successful cooperative creameries in Orange and Dutchess counties in New York, and prepared a report on them that was distributed to the agricultural schools of their country. Stiller Andersen, a student at Tune, learned from this report that the American creameries were succeeding by a plan fundamentally different from that under which some Danish cooperatives were formed in 1866 to 1875, only to fail. Andersen was fired with the idea of transplanting the American system of cooperation to his native land, and in 1882 he established at Hjedding the first successful co-operative creamery in Denmark . . . The New York creameries were independent of each other; each fixed its own standards of manufacture and sold its own product. The Danes followed this plan at first, but in 1899 improved materially upon it by federating to manufacture a standard product; a few years later a central selling agency was created . . ." (pp. 142-43).

5. Herbert Myrick, *How to Cooperate,* pp. 146-47, 153.

6. Fred A. Shannon, *The Farmers' Last Frontier* (1945), p. 137. See also pp. 257-58.

7. B. H. Hibbard and Asher Hobson, *Cooperation in Wisconsin,* Univ. of Wis. Agr. Exp. Station Bull. 282, p. 41. These authors estimated that some 1,500 creameries were promoted at a cost to the farmers of about $5,000 per plant. "The agents representing the promoter companies, were well chosen and well trained. They were clever talkers. They took groups of farmers to plants already installed, and convinced them that things were running splendidly . . . Probably not less than 75 per cent of the money put into these promoted projects was wholly wasted . . ."

8. According to Herman Steen, in *Cooperative Marketing—The Golden Rule in*

Agriculture, "This is one of the most constructive pieces of pioneer work contributed by any agricultural college to the co-operative marketing movement" (p. 146). See John W. Dysart, "T. L. Haecker—Father of the Cooperative Creameries," in *Great American Cooperators* (Joseph G. Knapp, and associates, Washington, D. C.: American Institute of Cooperation, 1967, pp. 13-14).

9. For an excellent discussion of the conditions leading up to the promotion of cooperative fluid milk associations, see Henry E. Erdman, *The Marketing of Whole Milk* (1921), particularly Ch. V, pp. 134-55. For New York developments, see also J. F. Booth, *Farmers' Cooperative Business Organization,* Cornell Univ. Agr. Exp. Bull. 461 (1928), pp. 19-21.

10. Erdman, *The Marketing of Whole Milk, op. cit.,* pp. 138-39, 140-41.

11. *Ibid.,* pp. 140-41. "Late in 1891, for example, the Union won a case in which it charged the New York Milk Exchange with being a combination which had "unlawfully assumed to control the milk market by arbitrarily fixing prices and other means to the detriment of the producers and consumers." The New York Milk Exchange had been organized in 1882 by milk dealers primarily for the purpose of fixing the price paid to producers. "Forfeiture of stock in the Exchange was the penalty for violation of the price agreement by any member." The Exchange was finally dissolved in 1895.

12. *Ibid.,* pp. 144-45. Other associations formed prior to 1896 were Milk Producers' Union, Cleveland, 1887; Milk Producers' Union, Pittsburgh, 1889; Milk Shippers' Union of the Northeast, Chicago, 1887. The Milk Shippers' Union, Chicago, 1896, continued operations until 1912.

13. The Clayton Amendment to the Sherman Anti-trust Law in 1914, which established labor's right to bargain collectively, also legalized farmers' associations when established on a non-stock membership basis. The Capper-Volstead Act extended "legislation" to cooperative associations established on a stock basis. See E. G. Nourse, *Legal Status of Agricultural Cooperation,* pp. 252-61. In 1895, a Chicago milk producers' association had been declared to be in restraint of trade. For a discussion of this case, see pp. 222-24.

14. For a full discussion of the control which railroads had over elevator operations in the 1860's, see Henrietta M. Larson, *The Wheat Market and the Farmer in Minnesota, 1858-1900,* "Studies in History, Economics and Public Law," Columbia University, Vol. CXXII, No. 2, Whole Number 269, pp. 55-117. According to Harold S. Patton, "While the railroads frequently undertook the construction of transfer and terminal elevators they found it necessary as a means of speeding up the loading of cars at country points to offer special inducements to private concerns to provide elevator facilities along their lines . . . Rebates on the combined elevator and freight charges were often allowed to members of wheat rings who agreed to buy grain at company stations" ("Grain Elevators," *Encyclopaedia of the Social Sciences*).

15. For a description of a ring which dominated local wheat marketing in Minnesota about 1870, see Larson, *op. cit.,* pp. 84-86. "The wheat ring appears, therefore, to have been a combination of agents against mutual competitors in the wheat trade . . . The ring was in a position to pay higher prices for wheat than small scalpers or independents could. Its rebates cut transportation costs considerably. By the consolidation of buying on the whole road under one management, expenses could be cut further. The ring was also able to avoid risks which had to be carried by others, because its close relations with central markets gave it an advantage in regard to market information, storage and sales. It also had more capital and could secure loans more easily. And, lastly, the ring was given special elevator privileges by the railroads."

16. "Even though no cooperative law was available at the time, most of the

essentials of cooperative practice were introduced ..." E. G. Nourse, *Fifty Years of Farmers' Elevators in Iowa*, Iowa Agr. Exp. Sta. Bulletin No. 211 (1923).

17. "The quality of management ... was one of the weakest points in the Grange elevator efforts. There was a very inadequate understanding of the grain business or appreciation of the necessity for business skill and experience. Rivalry for office was keen and 'Grange politics' altogether too much a factor. Only too often, as a result, the position of manager went as a plum to some farmer who was a good Granger, but a very poor grain man." *Ibid.*, p. 240.

18. *Ibid.*, p. 241. A somewhat similar early development had occurred in Minnesota where agitation for cooperative elevators began in 1869—although a group of Scandinavian immigrants had engaged in joint marketing a few year earlier. Little apparently was done, however, until the middle 1870's when "a number of elevators and mills were started . . . by Grange organizations." Most of these "were eventually closed or sold to individual proprietors [due to] difficulty in securing managers and capital," and "unfavorable discrimination on the part of railroads. By 1878 all had discontinued operations." It is of interest that at one time: "The possibility of forming a farmers' wheat pool was even suggested, the plan being to pool the wheat of the northwestern states through the Grange in such a way as to 'corner' their own wheat." See Larson, *op. cit.*, pp. 103-05.

19. "A 'line' is a group of country elevators, sometimes having storage at primary points, which is under one entire management. The buyers at the individual elevators receive definite instructions from the central office, where all matters of policy, price, grading, weights, charges for storage and handling, shipping and selling in the primary market are determined. The local buyers are merely agents of the line and as such are obliged to follow instructions." *Ibid.*, p. 139.

20. "From the very first the railroads in the state [Minnesota] had considered it their business to provide storage, but toward the middle of the seventies a change occurred in this respect. The Granger movement severely criticized the participation of railroads in the grain trade, and the courts had upheld the attack. The railroads had, moreover, suffered financially as a result of the panic of 1873 and were forced to retrench. Meanwhile the capital and the entrepreneurship necessary for carrying on the wheat trade had developed locally. The control, therefore, of the trade passed from the railroads to local middlemen, the stronger of whom became line operators." *Ibid.*, p. 139.

21. While Miss Larson felt that the "monopolistic features of the association" were perhaps exaggerated by farm leaders, she concluded: "It must be recognized that its vast business gave great commercial power, which was further increased by special rates, exclusive elevator privileges, and favoritism in the assignment of cars—favors which eventually destroyed a free market." *Ibid.*, pp. 151-57.

22. *Ibid.*, p. 219.

23. *Ibid.*, p. 193.

24. *Ibid.*, pp. 195-96.

25. *Ibid.*, pp. 215-18.

26. Nourse, *op. cit.* pp. 242-43.

27. *Ibid.*, p. 242.

28. *Ibid.*, p. 244.

29. The significant influence of the "maintenance clause" on the structure of American cooperative law is carefully presented by E. G. Nourse, *op. cit.*, pp. 173-83, 279 ff.

30. Nourse. *Fifty Years of Farmers' Elevators in Iowa, op. cit.*, p. 244. For an interesting historical sketch of the Rockwell Society written by one who was intimately

associated with it during much of its early life, see Reuben A. Holman, *Forty Years of Cooperation—A History of the First Successful Cooperative Grain Elevator in the United States,* 1931.

31. Holman, *op. cit.,* p. 9. The protection afforded elevators under this clause has been well described by Oscar N. Refsell in "The Farmers' Elevator Movement," *Journal of Political Economy,* Vol. 22, "Under this arrangement the farmers' company would not be so greatly tempted to bid a high price against a competitor when doing so would probably involve a loss. Neither could the company be ruined by the high prices paid by a competitor, even though these high prices would prevent the farmers' company from securing any grain. The income of the company would still continue to be as great as before, while its expenses would be slightly reduced. In reality, its condition would be improved by its being outbid by its competitor for the grain marketed by its own members" (p. 891).

32. *Ibid.,* pp. 891-92. See also Josiah B. Kenkel, *The Cooperative Elevator Movement,* p. 22.

33. There is another interesting parallel with the Rochdale Society; the Cooperative Wholesale Society of England developed under Rochdale auspices. In a like way, the Rockwell Society was the mother of the Iowa Farmers' Grain Dealers' Association, which was formed at Rockwell in November 1904 to federate the elevator movement in the state. See Nourse, *Fifty Years of Farmers' Elevators in Iowa, op. cit.,* p. 244; Holman, *op. cit.,* pp. 23-24; Refsell, *op. cit.,* p. 969.

34. Holman, *op. cit.,* p. 14.

35. According to Holman, "Though organized under corporate laws, the intent of the [Rockwell] Society's organizers was to give farmers the benefit of every dollar possible at the time of each transaction. However, the volume of business transacted resulted in some remarkable dividends being paid, not regularly, but, as the society found itself in possession of surplus." *Ibid.,* p. 30.

36. Myrick, *op. cit.,* p. 227.

37. *Ibid.,* pp. 229-39.

38. *Ibid.,* pp. 239-40.

39. There were many other fruit and vegetable associations formed by 1896, mostly of a local character. Typical of these were (1) the Catawba Dock Company in Ohio, 1878; (2) the Grand Junction (Colorado) Fruit Association, 1887. For information on these early associations, see Chastina Gardner, *Beginnings of Cooperative Fruit and Vegetable Marketing,* USDA (Preliminary report), 1928. Miss Gardner remarks: "Search has disclosed more associations of this type than had been anticipated."

40. *Ibid.,* pp. 2-3.

41. Myrick, *op. cit.,* p. 211.

42. H. D. Phillips, *Cooperative Marketing in the Chautauqua-Erie Grape Industry,* Cornell Univ. Agr. Exp. Sta. Memoir 28 (1919), p. 32. This publication gives an excellent account of the growth of the grape industry in this region which is essential to a full understanding of its cooperative development.

43. *Ibid.,* p. 32. The similarity of this "penalty" bylaw to the "maintenance clause" bylaw of the Rockwell Cooperative Society has been noted by Nourse, *The Legal Status of Agricultural Cooperation, op. cit.,* p. 183.

44. Phillips, *op. cit.,* pp. 32-33. See also comments on pooling, p. 34.

45. *Ibid.,* p. 27 (Italics added).

46. *Ibid.,* p. 52. Although the association was set up on a stock company basis

as required by the New York State Law, an ingenious method for giving growers direct control was developed. See p. 51.

47. Gardner, *Beginnings of Cooperative Fruit and Vegetable Marketing, op. cit.*, p. 9.

48. *Ibid.*, p. 10. It is of interest that the plan of the Florida Exchange had a direct influence in stirring up sentiment when the California Fruit Growers Exchange was beginning to take form. This is shown by the following quotation from the *California Fruit Grower* of June 10, 1893: "The Florida Fruit Exchange has been so well and ably managed for several years that it has given a high degree of satisfaction and has steadily gained ground among Florida growers and shippers. ... It is possible that some organization may be formed in California to handle fruit on a large scale, but it has not yet appeared. At present we may well copy its methods and rejoice in its successes."

49. It is of interest that the committee on organization "sought to enlist support ... by calling attention to the [somewhat similar] plan of organization of the Florida Fruit Exchange, which had been established in February, 1885." The Florida plan embraced both deciduous and citrus fruit producers. In California the citrus growers preferred to have their own organization, although they favored working together to mutual advantage, an arrangement which was eventually to materialize in an organized way. See Erich Kraemer and H. E. Erdman, *History of Cooperation in the Marketing of California Fresh Deciduous Fruits*, Univ. of California, Bulletin 557 (1933), pp. 15-29.

50. *Ibid.*, pp. 24-25.

51. *Ibid.*, pp. 21-22.

52. *Ibid.*, p. 21.

53. *Ibid.*, footnote, p. 26.

54. Myrick was apparently impressed by the opportunity of the Union to expand this service for he summed up his description of the Union (in 1891) by saying: "The main thing to regret in this wonderfully successful effort is, that the net profits are not utilized as a fund for the establishment of a State wholesale exchange to furnish supplies direct to local stores and individuals. The members would get far more benefit out of the money used in this way than from the comparatively small driblets divided among them in the shape of rebates." Myrick, *op. cit.*, pp. 215-16, 221.

55. In 1893, "the Union's returns to shippers amounted to about $34 per ton of packed fruit," and "it was perhaps only natural that shippers should blame the management." Kraemer and Erdman, *op. cit.*, p. 28.

56. *Ibid.*, pp. 28-36.

57. For an interesting contemporary account of the experience of the California Fruit Union, and its cooperative significance, see Edward F. Adams, *The Modern Farmer in His Business Relations*, 1899, pp. 452-57.

58. A. W. McKay and W. Mackenzie Stevens, *Organization and Development of a Cooperative Citrus-Fruit Marketing Agency*, U. S. Department of Agriculture, Bulletin 1237 (1924), pp. 2-3.

59. Rahno Mabel MacCurdy, *The History of the California Fruit Growers Exchange* (1925), pp. 9-10.

60. *Ibid.*, p. 13.

61. *Ibid.*, pp. 11-12. The similarity of this scheme for maintaining the organization to the famous "maintenance clause" adopted by the Rockwell Farmers Society in 1891 is apparent. Any surplus from this payment was to be distributed at the

end of each year, "each receiving such proportion of the surplus as the whole amount paid by him bears to the whole amount paid by all."

62. *Ibid.*, p. 13.

63. Although the Union was revived in 1890, it was disbanded again in 1893. See McKay and Stevens, *op. cit.*, p. 9; MacCurdy, *op. cit.*, p. 13.

64. *Ibid.*, p. 14. See also McKay and Stevens, *op. cit.*, p. 9.

65. MacCurdy, *op. cit.*, p. 16. The association was incorporated in 1892 "without capital stock" under the Benevolent Corporation Act of 1892.

66. *Ibid.*, pp. 16-17.

67. *Ibid.*, pp. 17-19.

68. *Ibid.*, p. 19 (Italics added).

69. *Ibid.*, pp. 22-24.

70. The economic conditions of the California orange industry at this time, and the need for a better marketing system, is well presented by McKay and Stevens, *op. cit.*, pp. 6-8.

71. *Ibid.*, p. 10. The plan as adopted provided for local associations, district exchanges, and an executive board. (See pp. 49-50.) For interesting detail with reference to the adoption of this plan, see MacCurdy, *op. cit.*, pp. 26-35. See also William W. Cumberland, *Cooperative Marketing* (1917), Ch. III, pp. 41-55. For incisive contemporary account of the formation of the exchange system as "an Orange Trust, designed to embrace all producers," see Adams, *op. cit.*, pp. 505-16.

72. McKay and Stevens, *op. cit.*, p. 10. The situation soon stabilized and from then on the exchange system steadily grew with the industry.

73. Adams, *op. cit.*, pp. 458-69. See also Gardner, *Beginnings of Cooperative Fruit and Vegetable Marketing, op. cit.*, p. 14.

74. Adams, *op. cit.*, pp. 437, 473-74.

75. "Especially they disliked the idea of pooling their fruit with that of their neighbors: almost everyone was of the opinion that his fruit was better . . . and that he would somehow lose if he allowed it to lose its identity." *Ibid.*, pp. 474-75.

76. *Ibid.*, pp. 475-76.

77. *Ibid.*, p. 488. A list of California cooperatives compiled by Adams for the U. S. department of Agriculture in 1898 listed also a winemaking cooperative, and a beekeepers' exchange. He also found some Granges and farmers' clubs purchasing for their members. He estimated that the marketing cooperatives in 1898-99 had aggregate sales of over $5 million and a membership of something less than 7,000. See also pp. 602-05.

78. E. J. Wickson, writing in 1923, attributed much of California rural prosperity to the "benign influence of cooperation." He held that: "Unquestionably the most principal agency for advancement in the quality of rural life in California during the last two decades has been cooperation." *Rural California*, p. 78.

79. Adams, *op. cit.*, p. 439. "The California societies are instances in which people of intelligence and sufficient means, although usually greatly indebted, have organized with no great display of altruistic spirit, in the main upon commercial lines, for the promotion of commercial ends." He supported this sentence with the following footnote: "The salaries paid indicate this. The salary of the president of the Raisin-growers' Association is $500 a month." This was a high figure in those days.

80. See E. G. Nourse and Joseph G. Knapp, *Cooperative Marketing of Livestock* (Washington, D. C.: The Brookings Institution, 1931), p. 12.

81. Chastina Gardner, *Beginnings of Cooperative Livestock Marketing* (mimeo. preliminary report), U. S. Department of Agriculture, pp. 8-9.

82. O. W. Hermann and Chastina Gardner, *Early Developments in Cooperative Cotton Marketing*, Farm Credit Administration Circular No. C-101 (1936), p. 2.

83. *Ibid.*, pp. 3-7.

84. Letters from John T. Downs in historical files of Farmer Cooperative Service, U.S.D.A. Mr. Downs attended his first meeting in 1864.

85. *American Cooperation*, Vol. 1, 1925, p. 60.

86. A photograph of this store, and the arrangement of the first two floors is given by Myrick, *op. cit.*, pp. 228-235.

87. *Ibid.*, pp. 227-37.

88. Holman, *op. cit.*, pp. 11-12, 18.

89. *Statistical Handbook of Farmers' Cooperatives*, Farm Credit Administration Bulletin No. 26 (1938), Table 226, p. 255.

90. Wells A. Hutchins, *Mutual Irrigation Companies in Utah*, Utah Agr. Exp. Sta. Bulletin 199 (1927), pp. 24-25. It is significant that the early district organizations which were of a mutual character were "almost invariably succeeded sooner or later by one or more incorporated mutual companies" (p. 23).

91. Wickson, *op. cit.*, pp. 320-23. In effect, the Wright law was a forerunner of the idea of "compulsory cooperation" which was to be advocated in the 1920's, and applied to some extent by the Agricultural Adjustment Administration in the 1930's. It may also be said that the first early Mormon irrigation enterprises had an element of compulsion applied by the Church, which at first also had the power of a state.

92. See Wells A. Hutchins, *Organization and Operation of Cooperative Irrigation Companies*, FCA Circular No. C102, "Comparison of the Mutual Company and the Irrigation District," pp. 3-5. According to Hutchins, "The principal difference between the mutual company and the irrigation district is that the former organization is private and voluntary; whereas, the district is public and involuntary, and is a political subdivision of the state" (p. 3). "The highest courts in the land have held that irrigation is a public benefit and that the district is a constitutional instrumentality for conferring this benefit" (p. 4).

93. *Statistical Handbook of Farmers' Cooperatives, op. cit.*, Table 245, p. 268.

94. "The movement for this form of rural cooperation during the last half of the century was encouraged in one state after another by the enactment of liberal laws governing the organization and management of farmers' mutuals." Victor N. Valgren, *Farmers' Mutual Fire Insurance in the United States* (1924), p. 15.

95. Victor N. Valgren, *Problems and Trends in Farmers' Mutual Fire Insurance*, FCA Bulletin No. 23 (1938), p. 2. For more complete discussion of these laws, see Valgren, *Farmers' Mutual Fire Insurance in the United States, op. cit.*, pp. 15-20.

96. Valgren, *Problems and Trends in Farmers' Mutual Fire Insurance, op. cit.*, p. 42.

97. For a full discussion of the legal evolution of cooperative business during the period under review, see Nourse, *The Legal Status of Agricultural Cooperation, op cit.*, particularly Ch. II, pp. 25-50.

Chapter V

1. Louis Bernard Schmidt. "The Agricultural Revolution in the United States, 1860-1930," *Science*, Vol. 72, pp. 585-94. See also Everett E. Edwards, "Ameri-

can Agriculture—The First 300 Years," *U.S.D.A. Yearbook of Agriculture, 1940*, pp. 221-366.

2. E. G. Nourse, "The Outlook for Agriculture," *Journal of Farm Economics,* January 1927, p. 23.

3. "The improvement in business conditions that started in the latter half of 1897 was destined to usher in a period which for widespread and long-continued prosperity was scarcely equalled in the history of the country . . . In this period the rapid increase in the world output of gold, chiefly that from the South African mines, was a factor of major significance. A rapid and world-wide rise in the price level ensued." Chester W. Wright, *Economic History of the United States,* p. 876.

4. "Industrial development in the United States caught up with the overstimulated agricultural development of the free land period, with a resultant increase in the ratio at which agricultural products exchanged for manufactures." E. G. Nourse, *Agriculture and the European Market* (New York: McGraw-Hill Book Company, 1924), p. 38.

5. *U.S.D.A. Yearbook of Agriculture, 1912*, pp. 11-12.

6. See E. R. Eastman, *These Changing Times* (1927); Kenyon L. Butterfield, *Chapters in Rural Progress* (1908).

7. "With the industrial revival of the late 90's . . . the drive to consolidate competing business took on the proportions of a tidal wave." E. G. Nourse and H. B. Drury, *Industrial Price Policies* (1938) p. 158. This volume gives a good account of the rise of big business from 1897 to 1920.

8. See G. H. Powell, *Cooperation in Agriculture* (1913), Ch. I.

9. As James Ford pointed out: "Many conditions of the immigrant's life in America make cooperation on racial lines desirable. Newly arrived immigrants are unfamiliar with American goods and prices, have difficulty in understanding and making themselves understood in trade, and when unorganized are often the victims of fraud. Co-operation is frequently resorted to in self-protection". . . (*Co-operation in New England* (1913), p. 34 and Ch. III.) Various illustrations of cooperative action among immigrant groups are given in U.S. Immigration Commission, *Immigrants in Industries,* (Pt. 24, "Recent Immigration in Agriculture"), Vol. I, pp. 72-75, 117-20, 206; Vol. II, pp. 50-51, 107. These volumes were prepared under the direction of Alexander E. Cance.

10. This is well shown by L. C. Kercher in his analysis of the social and cultural foundations of the Finnish industrial cooperative movement in L. C. Kercher, V. W. Kebker, W. C. Leland, Jr. (R. S. Vaile, Ed.), *Consumers' Cooperatives in the North Central States* (1941), pp. 18-32. See also Frank Aaltonen, *Maynard Weavers* (1941), pp. 13-21. "Many of these immigrants left their native Finland at a time when a surging wave of cooperative interest swept that country; and although very few may have been active members of cooperatives in Finland, practically all of them had been touched by the movement's educational and missionary activities before coming here."

11. The price of the Model-T touring car fell steadily from $950 in 1909 to $360 in 1916. A high proportion of the 2,146,362 automobiles on farms on January 1, 1920, were Model-T's. Henry Ford, *My Life and Work* (1923), p. 145.

12. For detailed information on the history and significance of power farming in the United States, see Eugene G. McKibben and R. Austin Griffin, *Tractors, Trucks and Automobiles,* Works Progress Administration (Studies of Changing Techniques and Employment in Agriculture), December 1938; and Eugene G. McKibben, John A. Hopkins, and R. Austin Griffin, *Field Implements,* Works Progress Administration (Studies of Changing Techniques and Employment

in Agriculture), August 1939. A briefer treatment is that of Harold Barger and Hans H. Landsberg, *American Agriculture, 1899-1939; A Study of Output, Employment and Productivity*, National Bureau of Economic Research (1942), pp. 201-22.

13. Powell, *op. cit.*, p. 89. "The spirit that leads the people to meet these rural problems collectively rather than individually is quickened in such a community with a resulting impulse to every movement that leads to a better rural life."

14. Charles L. Dearing, *American Highway Policy*, p. 46.

15. *Ibid.*, p. 266.

16. Eastman, *op. cit.*, maintains that the development of strong cooperative associations would have been impossible without the automobile. (pp. 7-13).

17. "Except possibly the automobile, no other factor had done more for country life than the rural mail service. It has brought the city to the country ... and helped to put the farmer in closer touch with his markets ... the mail carrier is the farmer's agent and office." Eastman, *op. cit.*, pp. 20 ff.

18. See W. J. Spillman's famous pioneer article, "Systems of Farm Management in the United States," *U.S.D.A. Yearbook of Agriculture, 1902*, pp. 343-64.

19. See Fred Shannon, *The Farmer's Last Frontier* (1945), pp. 372-76.

20. See J. F. Abel, *Consolidation of Schools and Transportation of Pupils*, U. S. Department of Interior Bulletin No. 41, 1943, pp. 13, 17, 19.

21. "Where conditions have forced rural organizations for production, protection, or marketing, some form of centralized school has developed at the same time or followed shortly after. Given the need or the desire for community solidarity, the consolidated school develops, being strengthened by and in turn strengthening the feeling which brought the school about." *Ibid.*, p. 35.

22. Alfred Charles True, *A History of Agricultural Extension Work*, U. S. Department of Agriculture, 1785, 1923, Misc. Pub. No. 15, 1928, pp. 10 ff, 32.

23. To get a full understanding of the cooperative demonstration plan as it expanded, and an appreciation of its significance, see the book by Knapp's disciple, O. B. Martin, *The Demonstration Work* (1926). The volume contains many excerpts from Knapp's speeches which show how the plan grew under his leadership. See also Joseph Cannon Bailey's valuable biography, *Seaman A. Knapp* (1945), esp. Part 2, "The Founding of the County Agricultural Agent System"; Russell Lord's interpretative history of agricultural extension, written under the title, *The Agrarian Revival* (1939); and Alfred Charles True, *op. cit.*

24. The interesting story of the inception and growth of home demonstration work is well told by O. B. Martin, the principal sponsor of this program, in *The Home Demonstration Work*. For an interesting account of this development by a pioneer state home demonstration agent, see Jane S. McKimmon, *When We're Green We Grow* (1945). This volume shows how various forms of community cooperation developed naturally from home demonstration work.

25. See True, *op. cit.*, p. 100.

26. Lord, *op. cit.*, p. 100.

27. "The advantages of community breeding have been emphasized to the boys ... with the result that in many counties one breed of hogs has been adopted as the standard of the county ... This emphasizes to the boys the advantages of co-operation, and after the one experience, as boys, it will doubtless be much easier to get cooperation among the members after they become men than it has been with the grown folks of the present day." See W. F. Ward, *The Boys' Club Work, U.S.D.A. Yearbook of Agriculture, 1915*, pp. 180-81.

28. For full information, see Rufus W. Stimson and Frank W. Lathrop, *History of Agricultural Education of Less than College Grade in the United States* (1942), U. S. Office of Education, Vocational Division Bulletin No. 217.

Chapter VI

1. E. G. Nourse, "The Place of Agriculture in Modern Industrial Society," *The Journal of Political Economy*, Vol. XXVII, No. 7, July 1919, p. 565.

2. The best sources of information on the inception and character of the Country Life Movement are the books by its principal leaders. In *The Rural Life Problem of the United States* (1910), Sir Horace Plunkett argued that "the city has been developed to the neglect of the country." He maintained: "There must be better farming, better business, and better living. These three are equally necessary, but better business comes first. For farmers, the way to better living is cooperation, and what cooperation means is the chief thing the American farmer must know" (pp. 3 and 173-74). In *The Country Life Movement* (1911), Liberty Hyde Bailey declared: "The country-life movement is the working out of the desire to make rural civilization as effective and satisfying as other civilizations . . . It is a world-motive to even up society as between country and city." The social character of the rural life problem was emphasized by Kenyon L. Butterfield, *Chapters in Rural Progress* (1908). See also Carl C. Taylor's essay "The Rural Life Movement" in the *Encyclopaedia of the Social Sciences*.

3. Samuel Eliot Morison and Henry Steele Commager, *The Growth of the American Republic*, Vol. II (1937), p. 366. See also pp. 334-44. For a full discussion of this epoch, see Harold Underwood Faulkner, *The Quest for Social Justice, 1898-1914*. (1941).

4. I have had the privilege of interviews with two members of the Commission: Chairman Bailey in Ithaca, N. Y., on November 30, 1945, and Gifford Pinchot in Washington, D. C., on October 15, 1945. Both Bailey and Pinchot stressed President Roosevelt's keen interest in the work of the commission. Bailey recalled that in addition to his own efforts as chairman, the two who contributed most to the work of the Commission were Butterfield and Wallace, although all members gave conscientious service. Bailey stated that he had made but one stipulation in accepting the chairmanship—the appointment of his former student, Butterfield. According to Pinchot, the influence of Bailey was paramount among the commissioners.

5. See Earle D. Ross, "Roosevelt and Agriculture," *The Mississippi Valley Historical Review*, December 1927.

6. *Wallace's Farmer*, May 14, 1909, p. 710. For an enlightening account of Plunkett's relationship to Roosevelt see Margaret Digby's biography: *Horace Plunkett*, especially Chapter VI, "Roosevelt and the Country Life Commission," (Oxford: Basil Blackwell, 1949), pp. 117-43.

7. No appropriation was made for the Commission's expenses. Its traveling expenses were defrayed by the Russell Sage Foundation. The Census Bureau cooperated by analyzing the data so assembled.

8. An interesting account of the formation, character, and methods of the Commission is given by Henry Wallace in *Uncle Henry's Own Story*, Vol. III (1919), pp. 100-04. See also Ch. 61, "Calling All Farmers" in Gifford Pinchot's autobiography, *Breaking New Ground*, (New York: Harcourt, Brace and Company, 1947), pp. 340-344.

9. This formula: "Better farming, better business, better living," which Sir Horace generously referred to as "Roosevelt's formula," had been coined by Plunkett to epitomize his philosophy as it was then being applied in the rural renaissance of Ireland. Plunkett's pamphlet, *Noblesse Oblige*, published in Ireland in early 1908 (before the Country Life Commission was appointed) contains a full statement of the *three betters:* "There must be rehabilitation of rural life; and this includes three things, all equally essential. First, the small farmers must be taught the best methods of farming, so that each may make the best possible use of his land. Second, they must be united in business associations, because when thus banded together they can obtain those advantages of capital, of machinery, of transport, of buying and selling on a large scale, which are inaccessible to them singly, and which, to meet the competition of their foreign rivals, they must in some way secure. Third, they must have in the country something corresponding to the social and intellectual improvements which have been introduced into the modern city . . . This threefold scheme of rural advancement through *better farming, better business* and *better living*, is admitted to cover the ground" (see pp. 12-15).

10. *Report of the Country Life Commission*, 60 Cong. 2 sess., S. doc. 705, p. 7. The Report is available in book form from the University of North Carolina Press (1944).

11. In an interview with the author on November 30, 1945, Bailey recalled that he prepared several drafts of the report prior to its general acceptance.

12. "Theodore Roosevelt's Country Life Commission," *Agricultural History*, October 1960, p. 168.

13. Powerful interests did not agree with the Commission's view that: "We must arouse the country folk to the necessity for action, and suggest agencies which, when properly employed, will set them to work to develop a distinctly rural civilization." President Roosevelt laid the suppression of the report to the fact that it provided "a mass of information so accurate and so vitally important as to disturb the serenity of advocates of things as they are, and therefore it assured the opposition of the reactionaries" (*Autobiography*, pp. 415-16). It is to the credit of enlightened business leadership that the report was soon published by the Spokane Chamber of Commerce.

14. See Ross, *op. cit.*, pp. 308-09.

15. For more complete information see Clayton S. Ellsworth, "Theodore Roosevelt's Country Life Commission in *Agriculture History*, October 1960, pp. 170-171.

16. According to Dean Bailey, Plunkett had privately protested to President Roosevelt that the report did not place enough emphasis on the solution of the business problems of farming through cooperative organizations. However, Plunkett's protests had no effect "on the statements affecting co-operation as they came after the Report of the Committee had been written and had become the voice of the membership." (Interview of November 30, 1945 and letter of December 14, 1945). No doubt Plunkett was assuaged by President Roosevelt's strong endorsement of business cooperation in his special message transmitting the report.

17. See Sir Horace Plunkett, *The Rural Life Problem*, pp. 155-74.

18. See Charles W. Holman, "Sir Horace Plunkett's Cooperative Philosophy and Contribution to American Cooperation," *American Cooperation*, 1937, pp. 14-15. See also Digby, *op. cit.*, pp. 137-142.

19. A full discussion of the formation, methods, findings and influence of the American Commission's report is given in Chapter VII.

20. Interview with Charles W. Holman, October 10, 1945. See *Wallace's Farmer*, April 18, 1913. For additional information on these conferences see my profile

of Charles W. Holman in *Great American Cooperators* (Joseph G. Knapp, and associates, Washington, D. C.: American Institute of Cooperation, 1967, pp. 227-229).

21. The foreword of the *Proceedings of the Fourth National Conference on Marketing and Farm Credits,* 1916, declared: "The 1916 volume . . . marks the transition in economic thought from the theoretic to the functional."

22. See Charles W. Holman, "The Rise of the Dairy Cooperative," *American Cooperation,* II, 1925, pp. 12-13.

23. *Proceedings of the Fourth National Conference on Marketing and Farm Credits,* p. 496.

24. For a discussion of the work started, see Charles W. Holman, "First Aid to Farming Business," in *Proceedings of Fourth National Conference on Marketing and Farm Credits,* pp. 477-91. Mr. Holman, who was secretary of the Society, later wrote: "Plunkett desired to see the funds [obtained from the American Agricultural Organization Society] used . . . to establish a series of community experiments. [Charles] McCarthy and I felt that the first big job was to lay the legal basis in various states for the development of the cooperative movement." *American Cooperation,* 1937, p. 15.

Chapter VII

1. See John D. Hicks, *The Populist Revolt* (Minneapolis: University of Minnesota Press, 1931). pp. 23-35m, 81-95.

2. *Farm Policies of the United States, 1790-1950* (New York: The Twentieth Century Fund, 1953). p. 145.

3. Claude L. Benner, *The Federal Intermediate Credit System* (New York: The Macmillan Company, 1926), pp. 3-23.

4. According to his biographer, "He equipped himself with the rosters of State and subordinate Granges, Farmers Associations, business organizations, with press and congressional directories, and compiled a regular mailing list of some fifty thousand names." Moreover he did this out of his own pocket. Olivia Rosetti Agresti, *David Lubin: A Study in Practical Idealism* (Boston: Little, Brown and Company, 1922). pp. 272.

5. The Southern Commercial Congress was formed in 1908 by commercial organizations in the South to promote the economic welfare of the region. See official proceedings of the Congress held in Washington, D.C., December 7-8, 1908.

6. *Ibid.,* p. 274.

7. "The Federal Land Banks" in *Great American Cooperators* (Joseph G. Knapp and associates, Washington, D. C.: American Institute of Cooperation, 1967, p. 552).

8. The Progressive Party platform also promised to foster the development of agricultural credit and cooperation and the reactivation of the Country Life Commission. For planks of the three parties, see Norman L. Wall, "Agricultural Credit" in *The Story of Agricultural Economics* by Henry C. and Anne Dewees Taylor (Ames, Ia.: Iowa State College Press [now Iowa State University Press], 1952), p. 920.

9. Herrick had long been interested in the rural credit problem. Prior to his appointment as Ambassador, he had been President of a large savings society in Cleveland, Ohio. In 1910, following a trip to Europe he had given a talk on cooperative land-credit systems of Germany at a meeting of the American

Bankers' Association. In November 1911, he brought up a resolution before the American Bankers' Association which instructed a committee to investigate the general subject of rural finance in the United States. Taft's interest in rural credit agencies in Europe was directly stimulated by the activity of the American Bankers' Association promoted by Herrick. Much of the material assembled for the 1912 report was published in book form by Myron T. Herrick and R. Ingalls, *Rural Credits—Land and Cooperative,* (New York: D. Appleton and Company, 1914). In 1917, when Herrick was back in Cleveland as President of the Cleveland Society for Savings, he employed a young man, by the name of Murray D. Lincoln, to build business among farmers and this relationship exerted an important influence on Lincoln's distinguished career as a cooperative and business leader. See autobiography of Murray D. Lincoln as told to David Karp, *Vice President in Charge of Revolution* (New York: McGraw-Hill Book Company, 1960), especially pp. 44-58.

10. President Wilson was no doubt advised by Walter Hines Page in making his appointments to the United States Commission. Page had been a member of the Country Life Commission and was imbued with its spirit. See Carl R. Woodward, "Woodrow Wilson's Agricultural Philosophy," *Agricultural History,* October 1940, p. 131. Dr. John Lee Coulter, who served as secretary of the United States Commission, held that it was a definite follow-up of the Country Life Commission with many of the same people behind it. According to Coulter, Butterfield and Bailey kept up a constant pressure for a European Commission to study cooperation, and the United States Commission would have been appointed regardless of the organization of the American Commission. Interview with John Lee Coulter, October 29, 1945.

11. *Marketing and Farm Credits,* 1913, pp. 205-9.

12. For a brief history of the Federal Reserve Act by its principal author, see H. Parker Willis, "Federal Reserve System," *Encyclopaedia of the Social Sciences.* Senator Carter Glass, then Chairman of the House Committee on Banking, helped frame the Federal Reserve System and sponsored it effectively in the Congress.

13. John D. Black, *Agricultural Reform in the United States* (New York: McGraw-Hill Book Company, 1929), p. 452.

14. E. G. Nourse, *Agricultural Economics* (Chicago: University of Chicago Press, 1916). p. 713.

15. Woodward, *op. cit.,* pp. 134-135.

16. The Second National Conference on Marketing and Farm Credits, April 1914, declared in a resolution: "Great interests which have already controlled the marketing of industrial securities are now striving to gain control over rural credit . . . We favor the basic cooperative principles in dealing with the question of farm credit, as well as in all other matters of farm organization."

17. Robert B. Tootel, "The Federal Land Banks" in *Great American Cooperators* (Knapp, and associates, *op. cit.,* pp. 552-53).

18. Myron T. Herrick, "Suggestions for Rural-Credits Legislation," *Marketing and Farm Credits, op. cit.,* p. 403.

19. *Marketing and Farm Credits, op. cit.,* p. 509 (Italics added).

20. As quoted by Tootel, *op. cit.,* p. 553.

21. Woodward, *op. cit.,* p. 136.

22. *The Federal Farm Loan System* (New York: Orange Judd Company, 1916), Foreword.

23. One observer at the time said: "By the Farm Loan Act American farmers

have been blessed with twin credit babies . . . The fundamental difference in the characteristics of these two youngsters leads me to believe that sooner or later one of them will kick the other out of bed." Attributed to Herbert Quick by Carl Herbert Schwartz, Jr., *Financial Study of the Joint Stock Land Banks* (Washington, D. C.: Washington College Press, 1938), p. 13.

24. "The Federal Farm Loan Act," *American Economic Review* (Supplement), March 1917, p. 118. Herbert Myrick, a strong advocate of the Act, held that: "There is a large field of usefulness for these joint stock institutions among farmers who for various reasons may not care to join with the federal system . . ." He saw rivalry between the two systems as desirable, saying: "to encourage legitimate competition in better service to agriculture, is not the least beneficial purpose of the federal farm loan act." *The Federal Farm Loan System, op. cit.*, pp. 156-57.

25. *Ibid.*, pp. 121, 123.

26. "The Federal Farm-Loan Act," *The Journal of Political Economy*, February 1917, pp. 139-141.

27. Nourse, *op. cit.*, p. 713.

28. *Marketing and Farm Credits, op. cit.*, pp. 7-16.

29. *Ibid.*, pp. 507-08.

30. See Circular No. 2, "How Farmers May Form a National Farm Loan Association" (March 20, 1917), and Circular No. 5, "The Farm Loan Primer" (Fourth Edition, October 1, 1917).

31. The first loan under the new system was made by the Federal Land Bank at Wichita on March 12, 1917. No joint-stock land bank was organized to make loans during 1917.

32. Claude L. Benner, "Federal Farm Loan System," *Encyclopaedia of the Social Sciences*.

33. According to Roy F. Bergengren in an essay on "Credit Unions" in the *Encyclopaedia of the Social Sciences,* the purpose of a credit union "is to supply its members with a ready system of saving from which they can borrow at currently fair rates of interest, and net earnings are to be returned to the members as dividends on their savings." For a full description of how credit unions work today, see Jack Dublin, *Credit Unions—Theory and Practice,* (Detroit, Mich.: Wayne State University, 1966). The term "credit union" for cooperative credit societies has been used in Europe since 1848, or earlier.

34. Alphonse Desjardins, "Rural Cooperative Credit," *Marketing and Farm Credits, op. cit.*, pp. 81-82.

35. Alphonse Desjardins, *The Cooperative Peoples Bank* (New York: Russell Sage Foundation, 1914), as quoted by Roy F. Bergengren, *Cooperative Banking— A Credit Union Book* (New York: The Macmillan Company, 1923), pp. 50-51.

36. This law provided a pattern for similar credit union laws in other states. It also did much to popularize the term "credit union" which was adopted to distinguish such credit associations from building and loan associations which were then called "cooperative banks."

37. See G. Harold Powell, *Cooperation in Agriculture*, 1913, pp. 274-277. C. W. Thompson of the U.S.D.A. reported in 1915 that the Jewish Agricultural and Industrial Aid Society had organized 18 credit unions in New York, New Jersey, Connecticut, and Massachusetts, *Marketing and Farm Credits, op. cit.*, p. 29.

38. For detailed information on how this program was developed, see R. O. Moen, *Rural Credit Unions in the United States* (Privately published), Raleigh, North Carolina, 1931; see also Bergengren, *op. cit.*, pp. 55-59, 171-223.

39. For a review of the U.S.D.A.'s early studies of rural and urban credit unions, see U.S.D.A. Circular 197 by V. N. Valgren and E. E. Englebert, issued in October 1921.

40. See Richard Y. Giles, *Credit for the Millions* (New York: Harper & Brothers, 1951), pp. 84-86.

41. See the annotated bibliography on "Cooperative Credit" issued as Bulletin No. 5 of the Russell Sage Foundation Library, June 1914. See Bergengren, *op. cit.*, pp. 265-267.

42. For a full report on credit union progress up to 1920, see *Ibid.*, Ch. III, "Credit Union Development in the United States."

Chapter VIII

1. The titles of articles in the Agricultural Yearbook for 1896 afford an excellent barometer of the Department's major concerns at that time: *The Use of Steam Apparatus for Spraying, Extermination of Noxious Animals by Bounties, Potash and Its Functions in Agriculture, The Feeding Value of Corn Stover, Olive Culture in the United States, Methods of Programming the Orange and Other Citrus Fruits,* etc.

2. As a matter of record the Department issued a Farmer's Bulletin (No. 62), *Marketing Farm Produce* (by George H. Hill) as early as 1897. However, this publication did not attempt to discuss "the present organization of the trade, but rather [took] the trade as it is [and gave] . . . to the producer and shipper the benefit of such information as [could] be obtained at the market end" (p. 6). The first significant work of the Department in marketing did not come until it ceased to accept "the trade as it is," and began to examine analytically the whole marketing process. For a detailed review of the early work of the U. S. Department of Agriculture in marketing and cooperation, as well as in farm management, see J. T. Horner, "The United States Government Activities in the Field of Agricultural Economics Prior to 1913," *Journal of Farm Economics,* October 1928, pp. 429-60.

3. *U.S.D.A. Yearbook of Agriculture, 1908,* pp. 184-86.

4. For an intresting discussion of the background of the first bills to establish a Bureau of Markets, see James C. Malin, *Agricultural History,* Vol. 6 (July 1932).

5. Caroline B. Sherman, "The Legal Basis of the Marketing Work of the United States Department of Agriculture," *Agricultural History,* October 1937.

6. U.S.D.A., Office of the Secretary, Report 98, (1913). (Prepared in the Bureau of Statistics under the immediate supervision of George K. Holmes, statistical scientist.)

7. Sherman, *op. cit.*, pp. 289-301.

8. *Ibid.* p. 293.

9. Stat. L. 37 (1): 854. The House Committee on Agriculture had submitted the following explanation for this appropriation: "In response to many appeals made to this committee by various organizations of citizens of this country for the establishment of a division of markets in the Department of Agriculture, this item is inserted in the bill to enable such work to be done by the Department of Agriculture along the lines indicated, that Congress may be able to decide as to the feasibility and desirability of establishing at some future time the division of markets as requested." *Ibid.*, p. 293.

10. *Ibid.*, p. 294.

11. *Organization and Conduct of a Market Service in the Department of Agriculture,* discussed at a Conference held at the Department on April 29, 1913, pp. 1-2. (Unnumbered publication)

12. *Ibid.,* pp. 7-10.

13. Sherman, *op. cit.,* Interview with Brand, October 15, 1945.

14. It was understood that there was to be close cooperation between the work in rural organization and in marketing, but according to Carver "it was not made clear just what my relation would be to the study of marketing." Letter of T. N. Carver, October 29, 1945.

15. Carver held that he probably went further in his support of cooperation and rural credit improvements than was desired by the General Education Board, although the program of work had been agreed upon in advance. Although Carver returned to his professorship at Harvard, he continued to assist Brand during 1914-15 as a special adviser. Letter of Oct. 29, 1945.

16. See Carver's articles "The Organization of a Rural Community," *U.S.D.A. Yearbook of Agriculture, 1914,* and "The Work of Rural Organization," *Journal of Political Economy,* November 1914, pp. 521-844. To Carver, business cooperation was only one form of necessary rural organization. The work of the department in *the field of rural sociology* largely dates back to the stimulus given by Carver and C. M. Thompson whom Brand selected to head up the rural organization work. It is also of interest that Carver's emphasis on the need for "local organization of working farmers" foreshadowed the later growth of the Farm Bureau Movement. See Gustav A. Lundquist and Thomas Nixon Carver, *Principles of Rural Sociology* (1927), p. 363.

17. Carver records that he traveled some 55,000 miles in the United States "promoting cooperation in marketing crops, buying supplies, and in farm finance, including insurance. I found that I had to spend a good share of time discouraging badly planned projects that were doomed to failure . . . I had to keep warning farmers that a few conspicuous failures would set the cooperative movement back a generation. I had to teach the farmers that there were certain fields and certain conditions under which a co-operative organization might succeed *if well* managed, and other fields and conditions under which it could not succeed, no matter how well managed." During this year Carver and Bradford Knapp, then in charge of extension work in the South, also made a survey of cooperative marketing and credit in European countries. Letter of October 29, 1945.

18. Report of the Chief of the Office of Markets, *Annual Reports of the Department of Agriculture,* 1914, p. 317.

19. Annual report of the Department of Agriculture for the year ended June 30, 1913, pp. 20-21.

20. *Ibid.,* pp. 24-25.

21. Report of the Chief of the Office of Markets, *op. cit.,* pp. 320-21.

22. *Agriculture Appropriation Bill* for year ending June 30, 1915, Hearings before House Committee on Agriculture on H. R. 13679, 63 Cong. 2 Sess., p. 131.

23. Report of the Chief of the Office of Markets and Rural Organization, 1915, pp. 363-64.

24. Sherman, *op. cit.,* p. 298. The Appropriation Act for the fiscal year 1916 provided $484,050 for the Office of Markets and Rural Organization.

25. The considerable influence of this model law on cooperative legislation and development is discussed by E. G. Nourse, *Legal Status of Agricultural Co-*

operation, pp. 78 ff., esp. p. 88 and pp. 405-06. The full text is given in App. C., pp. 457-69.

26. Charles J. Brand, "Fertilizer History Connected with World War I," *Agricultural History,* April 1945, p. 107.

27. Brand, *op. cit.,* p. 109.

28. Brand stated that the county agents "induced 2,156 communities or organizations of farmers to purchase fertilizer co-operatively. The reported value of the fertilizer so purchased was $3,630,000 and it was estimated that a saving of over $532,000 was effected. Exclusive of nitrate of soda, more than 64,000 tons of fertilizer and lime were involved in the purchases in which county agents assisted. . . From the close of the war until 1923, there was constant agitation that the Department resume its activities along this line. Large appropriations were proposed for the purpose." *Ibid.,* pp. 109-10, 12.

29. Brand had spent his youth in the cooperative atmosphere of Minnesota and South Dakota. One of his first jobs was as weigher-in, sampler, and bookkeeper of a cooperative creamery. Livingston, his successor, was more vitally interested in the administration of laws affecting the marketing of farm products such as the U. S. Grain Standards Act and the Warehouse Act. For a profile of Charles J. Brand see my essay, "Cooperative Facilitator," in *Great American Cooperators* (Joseph G. Knapp, and associates, Washington, D. C.: American Institute of Cooperation, 1967, pp. 84-87).

Chapter IX

1. For more complete information on the first work of the agricultural colleges in marketing and cooperation see Henry C. Taylor and Anne Dewees Taylor, *The Story of Agricultural Economics in the United States,* 1840-1932, especially Ch. 20, "Marketing Work in Agricultural Colleges Prior to 1921," pp. 547-566.

2. U. S. Department of Agriculture, Office of Experiment Stations, Circular 115, 1912.

3. Letter from Alexander E. Cance, September 14, 1945.

4. At this time Irish experience was being widely drawn on by American co-operative leaders. In a series of articles in *The Outlook* during 1909, Sir Horace Plunkett espoused a program of agricultural cooperation for the United States based upon achievements in Ireland. These articles formed the basis for his timely book, *The Rural Life Problem in the United States* (1910). With the publication of John Lee Coulter's book, *Cooperation Among Farmers* (1911), American books suitable for instructional use began to appear—the two most significant being G. Harold Powell's substantial treatise, *Cooperation in Agriculture* (1913), and Clarence Poe's guide book, *"How to Cooperate and Double Profits* (1915).

5. Letter of September 14, 1945. Cance attributed the enactment of the "second co-operative law" largely to the influence of Herbert Myrick, the author of *How to Cooperate* written in 1891, then editor in chief of the *New England Homestead.* Cance said: "Myrick worked with me very zealously for a number of years in an endeavor to increase the prosperity of farmers through co-operative action." (Letter of September 27, 1945)

6. Letters of Professor Whiton Powell, August 13 and November 21, 1945.

7. Letter to Professor Whiton Powell of November 21, 1945. Dean Bailey also wrote me as follows on the same date. "So far as my own ideas were con-

cerned they had been growing on me for many years before the Commission on Country Life was established."

8. Letter of Whiton Powell, December 10, 1945.

9. See Charles McCarthy, *The Wisconsin Idea* (1912). Ex-President Theodore Roosevelt in the foreword declared: "That state (Wisconsin) has become literally a laboratory for wise experimental legislation aiming to secure the social and political betterment of the people as a whole . . . All through the Union we need to learn the Wisconsin lesson of scientific popular self-help, and of patient care in radical legislation."

10. The enactment of the Wisconsin Cooperative Act of 1911 was attributable to the efforts of the American Society of Equity and the Right Relationship League. See E. G. Nourse, *Legal Status of Agricultural Cooperation.*

11. See Edward A. Fitzpatrick, *McCarthy of Wisconsin* (1944). See also the profile of Charles McCarthy by Marvin Schaars, in *Great American Cooperators* (Joseph G. Knapp, and associates, Washington, D. C.: American Institute of Cooperation, 1967, pp. 293-300).

12. *The Nineteenth Century and After,* Vol. 77, p. 1344.

13. Sinclair report, Pt. I, pp. 91-94.

14. Fitzpatrick, *op. cit.,* pp. 151-52.

15. Dr. Taylor had been striving since 1900 to build a Department of Agricultural Economics at the University of Wisconsin. The rising Country Life Movement in 1908 gave the "outside push" necessary for its establishment in that year.

16. Interview with Taylor, October 26, 1945. See also profile of Benjamin H. Hibbard by Marvin Schaars, in *Great American Cooperators* (Knapp, and associates, *op. cit.,* pp. 205-212).

17. In the preface to this pioneer study, which was published in April 1913 under the title *The Marketing of Wisconsin Cheese* (Wisc. Ag. Exp. Sta. Bul. No. 231) under the authorship of H. C. Taylor, W. A. Schoenfeld, and G. S. Wehrwein, Director H. L. Russell set forth the position of the University with regard to cooperation in the following way: "In the spring of 1912 the Wisconsin State Board of Public Affairs requested the College of Agriculture to undertake a thorough statistical study of the processes of marketing the various Wisconsin agricultural products with the view of having accurate information to serve as a basis for any future legislation. Much interest is being manifested at the present time in the subject of cooperation, but this is only one of the phases of the problem of marketing and distribution. Before any rational plan can be proposed that will aid in the development of the cooperative idea, an accurate picture of the entire marketing process is necessary. In this preliminary bulletin, Professor Taylor and his assistants have drawn the picture as it relates to the American or cheddar cheese problem. It is hoped that similar studies can ultimately be made on other leading agricultural products of the state."

18. See also Fitzpatrick, *op. cit.,* p. 249.

19. Interview with Henry C. Taylor, October 26, 1945. See his book *Agricultural Economics* (1919), pp. 357-65.

20. L. D. H. Weld, *Statistics of Co-operation among Farmers in Minnesota in 1913,* Minn. Agr. Exp. Sta. Bul. 146 (1914). The introductory paragraph of this bulletin explained how this study came to be made: "In 1913 the Minnesota Legislature enacted a law requiring the Department of Agriculture of the University of Minnesota 'to collect statistics and information in reference to cooperative associations among farmers and the management and methods of conducting such associations.' It was enacted that it should be the 'duty of all

cooperative associations to report annually to said department on blanks provided for that purpose.' The carrying out of this law was entrusted to the Division of Research in Agricultural Economics which set about to . . . secure the reports." (p. 3)

21. Letter of H. C. Filley, August 25, 1925. Filley had been a member of a cooperative elevator since 1907, and as a member of the Nebraska State Legislature, he had worked for the passage of the Nebraska Cooperative Law of 1911.

22. Letter from Dean Thomas Cooper, April 22, 1946.

23. North Carolina was the first state to undertake such work, with the establishment of a Division of Markets and Rural Organization in 1913. South Carolina also began such work in the same year with a Bureau of Marketing. In Oregon the Board of Regents of the Oregon Agricultural College set up a Bureau of Organization and Markets in 1914. Idaho, New York, California, Alabama, Michigan, Vermont, and Texas started marketing divisions in 1915, and they were followed by Kentucky, New Jersey, and Virginia in 1916, and by Arkansas, Florida, Georgia, Maine, New Hampshire, Ohio, Oklahoma, South Dakota, Washington, and West Virginia in 1917. A brief description of the early work of these first state marketing divisions is given in U. S. Bureau of Markets, *Results of a Survey of State Marketing Activities throughout the United States,* 1916.

24. This pioneer organization did not survive the war. However, in 1920 the National Association of Marketing Officials was formed along similar lines.

25. A number of state agricultural colleges then were beginning to give research and extension assistance to cooperatives. This often led the state marketing divisions to center their attention on regulatory work and on market news service although in some states there was no clear-cut division of functions.

26. Weinstock's interest in agricultural marketing dated back to about 1885 when he and his half-brother, David Lubin, were partners in a mercantile business at Sacramento and in a nearby vineyard. As noted above Weinstock in 1886 had persuaded the California Fruit Union to adopt the auction method of sale on eastern markets. In 1894 he was the leader in the formation of the California Fruit Growers and Shippers Association, and its president until it discontinued operations in 1901. Weinstock was also a member of the American Commission sent to Europe in 1913 to study cooperatives and rural credit. For a profile see Grace H. Larsen's essay, "Harris Weinstock; Innovator in Marketing Service," in *Great American Cooperators* (Knapp, and associates, *op. cit.,* pp. 524-30).

27. Carl C. Plehn, "The State Market Commission of California," *American Economic Review,* Vol. VIII (1918), p. 5.

28. Nourse, *op. cit.,* p. 94.

29. *First Annual Report of the State Market Director,* pp. 89-91.

30. Plehn, *op. cit.,* p. 11.

31. However, Weinstock in 1917 publicly disclaimed the charge that he favored 100 per cent control: "I have never advised that there should be more than 70 or 75 per cent. And why? Because 100 per cent of the growers would spell monopoly, and I am 'agin' monopoly." (Proceedings of the 49th Convention of California Fruit Growers in the Monthly Bulletin of the California State Commission of Horticulture, Vol. VI, No. 5, p. 175.) Moreover, in 1919 he held that producers' organizations "even when they are strongly organized cannot arbitrarily lift the price of their product," saying, "The good of organizing lies in this: they can get . , . every penny they are entitled to on the price

established by the law of supply and demand." (Proceedings of the 51st Convention of California Fruit Growers in the Monthly Bulletin of the California State Commission of Horticulture, Vol. VIII, No. 7, p. 415).

32. *First Annual Report of the State Market Director*, p. 10.

33. At the meeting for incorporation, a resolution was passed which provided that the corporation would not begin business until $600,000 had been subscribed and 75 per cent of the dried peach acreage of the state signed up. At this meeting, 25 trustees were elected by the stockholders. This arrangement for trustees who in turn were to select directors, was directly copied from the plan being followed by the raisin growers. *Ibid.*, p. 14.

34. This idea was copied in the early 1920's by many of the large "commodity marketing associations" promoted by Sapiro in other parts of the country. The Bingham (Sapiro) Co-operative Marketing Act of Kentucky (1922) provided that "the by-laws may provide that one or more directors may be appointed by any public official or commission or by the other directors selected by the members or their delegates. Such directors shall represent primarily the interest of the general public in such associations." (Par. 12)

35. Sapiro was the protege of Weinstock. Their connection dated back to about 1911 when Weinstock helped Sapiro obtain a position as secretary of the Industrial Accident Commission following his graduation from the Hastings Law School of the University of California. Their association increased when Weinstock himself became a member of this Commission in 1913. From 1911 to 1915 Weinstock and Lubin, often joined by Sapiro, had given much time and study to the problem of marketing California crops. It is of interest that Sapiro has claimed: "I established in Weinstock's mind, as well as generally, that the one distinction between successful cooperation ... and futile attempts ... was organization by commodity as contrasted with organization by locality. In 1913 I first convinced Weinstock of that, and established thereby the parallels of industrial commodity organization. This is my one contribution of the early days—articulating the experience in successful cooperation" (Nourse, *op. cit.*, p. 98n). The main facts of Sapiro's early life are given in a "success story," by Merle Crowell entitled, "Nothing Could Keep This Boy Down," *American Magazine*, April 1923. See also Grace H. Larsen and Henry E. Erdman, "Aaron Sapiro: Genius of Farm Co-Operator Promotion," *The Mississippi Valley Historical Review*, September 1962, pp. 242-68. For a condensed version of this article see Grace H. Larson, "Aaron Sapiro: Cooperative Evangelist," *Great American Cooperators* (Knapp, and associates, *op. cit.*, pp. 446-454).

36. Weinstock had long been a proponent of the "clearing house" idea. He had sponsored "bureaus of information" as early as 1894. Erich Kraemer and H. E. Erdman, *History of Cooperation in the Marketing of California Fresh Deciduous Fruits*, Univ. of Cal. Agr. Exp. Sta. Bulletin 557 (September 1933), p. 33.

37. See remarks of J. F. Nagle, general manager of the California Fruit Exchange, speaking at the California State Fruit Growers Convention, November 1916: "I have never known an institution to work out successfully that started from the top and worked downward. God knows we have slaved for years to build up and lay a foundation for our institution ... we are purely cooperative, organized and operating solely for the benefit of the industry ... it does not appear to be that with this record we need a guardian appointed by the state of California." *The Monthly Bulletin of State Commission of Horticulture*, May 1917, pp. 170-71.

38. As Plehn pointed out, Weinstock, with the sanction of the governor, had "established a market commission, instead of any commission markets. It is

obvious that a commission market is just as different from a market commission as a chestnut horse is from a horse chestnut." *op. cit.*, pp. 9-10.

39. Nourse, *op. cit.*, pp. 95-96.

40. In view of the fact that most of the associations which had been set up by Weinstock had public directors appointed by him, there was some apprehension that the proposed organization would be too much under the control of the State Market Director. The Federation idea languished with the establishment in 1919 of the California Legislative Committee which attracted most of the important California cooperatives into membership. This committee in 1933 assumed the name "Agricultural Council of California." The State Cooperative Councils now found in many states were largely patterned on its experience.

Chapter X

1. Edward Wiest, *Agricultural Organization in the United States* (Lexington: University of Kentucky, 1923), p. 500. Isaac Newton Gresham, the founder, had been an old Alliance organizer. Many of those active in the early days of the Union had been trained by the Alliance. However, the Union was more successful than the Alliance in maintaining its political independence. While the Union supported various measures of interest to agriculture, it never became engulfed in a political crusade. See Commodore B. Fisher, *The Farmers' Union* (Lexington: University of Kentucky, 1920), pp. 52-66; and Wiest, *op. cit.*, pp. 475-502.

2. "The minimum price" for 1904 was set at 10 cents per pound. The inability of such holding plans to maintain prices caused the Union in 1907 and 1908 to urge drastic acreage reductions. The failure of this campaign in 1908 caused the Union then to sponsor a 10 per cent plow-up campaign.

   The Union's holding plan was greatly influenced by the crusade of Colonel Harvey Jordan, who in 1900 had organized the Southern Cotton Growers Protective Association "to persuade growers to reduce the quantity of cotton produced and to hold their crop for an established price." This program was very popular with growers in the eastern cotton-producing states in 1903 and 1904. After 1905, when the name of the association was changed to the Southern Cotton Association, its program calling for crop reductions was overshadowed and absorbed by the more vigorous efforts in the same direction of the Farmers' Union. See O. W. Herrmann and Chastina Gardner, *Early Developments in Cooperative Cotton Marketing*, Farm Credit Administration, Circular C-101, 1936, pp. 8-13. See also Charles P. Loomis, "The Rise and Decline of the North Carolina Farmers' Union," *North Carolina Historical Review,* July 1930, p. 307.

3. R. L. Hunt, *A History of Farmer Movements in the Southwest, 1873-1925,* (Privately published, no date), pp. 116-17.

4. Herrmann and Gardner, *op. cit.*, pp. 15-16.

5. Mr. Charles J. Brand who reviewed this chapter in an early draft commented on this sentence as follows: "The idea of a U. S. Warehouse Act arose from this background" (Letter of June 27, 1946).

6. For plan in full see Charles Simon Barrett, *The Mission, History and Times of the Farmers Union* (Nashville, Tenn.: Marshall and Bruce Company, 1909), pp. 131-34.

7. Hunt, *op. cit.*, p. 128.

8. *Ibid.*, pp. 126-128.

9. In 1909, Eubanks bitterly commented as follows on the business departments of other states: "Most of them have made a failure ... through several causes. Some very active men have been placed at the head of some ... with ambition much ahead of their ability to accomplish, lacking either in financial backing or business training. Some of them, being more optimistic than practical, spent time and money on impractical theories, in place of taking hold of things they could have done for the people ..." Barrett, *op. cit.*, pp. 147-50.

10. Little information on these early "joint-stock" manufacturing plants is available other than that given by Barrett, *op. cit.*, pp. 124, 153-55, 217, 293, 301.

11. Charles P. Loomis, "Activities of the North Carolina Farmers' Union," *North Carolina Historical Review*, September 1930, p. 449. An excellent discussion of cooperative activities of the Union in North Carolina at this time is given by Loomis. He concluded: "Besides helping to secure legislation desired by the farmers, fostering economic cooperation, and conducting a worthwhile social and educational program in North Carolina, the Farmers' Union has left the farmers of the state with more knowledge about the problems involved in organization. Building upon the experience accumulated by those affiliated with the Grange and Alliance, the Union has contributed knowledge about the mechanics of organization, which future farm organizations in the state will use" (p. 462).

12. The first local Farmers' Union in the Pacific Northwest was established at Waitsburg, Washington, in April 1907. With the rapid formation of other locals, a state Union was formed in June 1908. The Union had as its primary objective the improvement of grain marketing, and at the annual convention in 1909, a plan was developed for marketing through a state Farmers' Union agent. "Under the plan . . . local country houses were not required to sell through the agent, but were to pay a fraction of a cent per bushel for his support whether they sold through him or not. The arrangement proved unsuccessful because too many of the local houses failed to pay their assessments. By 1911, membership in the Farmers' Union had spread to the wheat growing areas of Oregon and Northern Idaho and the number of local farmers' companies had grown rapidly. In that trend the encouragement was found to launch the Tri-State venture." Letter of A. C. Adams, September 13, 1945. For further information, see E. F. Dummeier, *Cooperation in Marketing Washington Farm Products*, Agricultural Experiment Station Bulletin 194, State College of Washington (1925) pp. 98-99.

13. The following situation gave rise to this interesting development. "For some time ... a great deal of effort had been put forth to consolidate further the support of local farmers' companies into the Tri-State, and to strengthen Tri-State's control over the movement of the crop from the country. Tri-State officers and Farmers Union leaders shared the belief that Tri-State's effectiveness in maintaining stable markets was too often dissipated by the indiscriminate selling practiced by local farmers' companies. Repeatedly the trade requirements of a Tri-State competitor were supplied by a local manager at prices below the level of market possibilities conceived by Tri-State. Frequently these local sales to its competitors occurred while Tri-State was negotiating with the same competitor and Tri-State's reputation for knowledge of sound market values was discredited." The president of the state Union who had heard Sapiro expound the philosophy of commodity marketing through membership contracts in California believed that this plan was adaptable to the wheat marketing problem in the Northwest. Letter of A. C. Adams, September 13, 1945.

14. For an interesting account of this experience, see Paul T. DeVore and Don H. Phipps, "A. C. 'Doc' Adams—Cooperative Sage of the Northwest," *Great Amer-*

ican Cooperators (Joseph G. Knapp, and associates, Washington, D. C.: American Institute of Cooperation, 1967, pp. 21-26).

15. Letter of A. C. Adams, September 13, 1945.

16. For a discussion of Farmers' Union developments in Nebraska prior to 1920, see Maurice H. Weseen, "The Cooperative Movement in Nebraska," *Journal of Political Economy,* Vol. 28 (1920), pp. 477-98. For description of the Farmers' Union cooperative development in Kansas, see Theodore Macklin, *Cooperation Applied to Marketing by Kansas Farmers,* Kansas State Agricultural Experiment Station Bulletin 224 (1920), pp. 8, 13, 47-61.

17. See E. G. Nourse and J. G. Knapp, *The Cooperative Marketing of Livestock,* (Washington, D. C.: Brookings Institution, 1931), pp. 109-16.

18. See Robert H. Bahmer, "The American Society of Equity," *Agricultural History,* January 1940, p. 39. The way in which Everitt's plan gradually took shape is presented in this article, pp. 35-39.

19. J. A. Everitt, *The Third Power—Farmers to the Front* (Privately published, Indianapolis), 1903, pp. 246-266.

20. *Ibid.,* pp. 1, 28.

21. *Ibid.,* pp. 5-6.

22. *Ibid.,* p. 9.

23. *Ibid.,* p. 59.

24. *Ibid.,* pp. 240-43.

25. *Ibid.,* p. 69. It is of interest that Everitt's economic views antedated Sapiroism by nearly 20 years. The concept of "orderly marketing" is clearly discernible in the following passage: "The farmers' organization must be strong enough and general enough to regulate the marketing. The question is not one of holding products, but of selling them. The proposition is that they shall be held only for the purpose of securing a fair price. In a word, the farmers must make a seeking market, instead of dumping their fine, valuable products without system, like in the case of bankrupt stocks." He also said: "The farmers can prevent a large visible supply by keeping the produce back on the farm and let it come forward gradually during twelve months" (pp. 75, 87).

26. *Ibid.,* p. 246.

27. *Ibid.,* p. 99.

28. *Ibid.,* p. 253. Everitt was apparently afraid that espousal of cooperative purchasing might arouse resistance from local businessmen and thus endanger support for his holding plan. However, writes Bahmer, "If Everitt hoped to encourage the good will of local businessmen and to prevent the rise of class antagonisms, he was doomed to disappointment" (*op. cit.,* p. 40). It may be that Everitt's ownership of a feed and seed store in Indianapolis also influenced his thinking on this matter.

29. Everitt, *op. cit.,* pp. 127-28.

30. "The Equity price bulletins and propaganda did more perhaps than all other factors to establish the 'dollar wheat' fixation in the minds of Northwestern wheat farmers." Balmer, *op. cit.,* p. 43.

31. *Ibid.,* p. 48.

32. *Ibid.,* pp. 48-49.

33. *Ibid.,* pp. 50-51.

34. The way in which the American Tobacco Company dominated the industry is well described by Theodore Saloutos, "The American Society of Equity in Kentucky: A Recent Attempt in Agrarian Reform," *The Journal of Southern*

History, August 1939, pp. 347-49. Tobacco purchased for foreign consumption was likewise controlled through the "Regie" buyers and the Imperial Tobacco Company formed in 1901. While no collusion between these interests was ever proved, there was little evidence of competition between them. Anna Youngman, "Tobacco Pools of Kentucky and Tennessee," *Journal of Political Economy,* January 1910, pp. 34-38.

35. "In this excessively capitalized company was centralized the control of the numerous corporations which composed the trust, with total assets of approximately $200,000,000 and with earnings of 17 or 18 percent...In 1911 the Supreme Court declared the Corporation to be a combination in restraint of trade and ordered its dissolution." John P. Troxell, "The Tobacco Industry," *Encyclopaedia of the Social Sciences.* The completeness of the domination of the American Tobacco Company was shown by the Report of the Commissioner of Corporations on the Tobacco Industry, Part I, "Position of the Tobacco Combination in the Industry" (1909), pp. 1-41, and Pt. III, "Prices, Costs, and Profits" (1915), pp. 1-29.

36. "An evidence of the growing success of the organization is the fact that at its inception it controlled only 40,000,000 pounds of the crop of 1904, whereas it was enabled to obtain about 80,000,000 pounds of the crop of 1907." Youngman, *op. cit.,* pp. 41-42. See also Saloutos, *op. cit.,* pp. 351 ff. The Planters' Protective Association was overshadowed by the more powerful Burley Society after its formation in 1907. Although the two organizations continued independently, they were part of the same movement, and followed the same tactics of holding for agreed-upon prices.

37. Just prior to the formation of the Burley Society on January 2, 1907, The Equity had carried on a "forty-day whirlwind campaign" to pledge growers not to sell their stored crops at the trust prices. Of the estimated planted acreage, 58 per cent was pledged to the association when the association was formed. At the organization meeting, Everitt, the president of the Equity, was praised as "the Moses who had pointed out the way." Saloutos, *op. cit.,* p. 353. See also Youngman, *op. cit.,* p. 41.

38. For text of this law, with changes made by amendment of 1908, see E. G. Nourse, *Legal Status of Agricultural Cooperation,* Appendix M. The emergency character of this legislation was indicated by the following clause: "Whereas, many persons of this commonwealth now desire to combine their respective crops of tobacco, wheat, corn, and other farm products, an emergency is now declared..." This act was upheld by the Kentucky Court of Appeals in 1908. However, it was declared unconstitutional by the Supreme Court in 1914. For a full discussion of the significance of this act in the development of cooperative law, see Nourse, *op. cit.,* pp. 159-60, 309-10, 350 ff.

39. Saloutos, *op. cit.,* p. 355.

40. Youngman, *op. cit.,* pp. 45-47. For a more flamboyant account of this episode, see H. Clyde Filley, *Cooperation in Agriculture,* pp. 248-50. Filley states (p. 250) that, "Up to February 1908, the actual property loss was $50,000,000. It was necessary to keep militia in many places."

41. The preliminary agreement read as follows: "The American Tobacco Company has bought seventy-five percent of the 1906 pooled tobacco at scheduled prices and seventy-five per cent of the 1907 pooled tobacco at graded prices to average seventeen cents." The value of tobacco then sold amounted to 12 million dollars, at a price about double the prices originally offered by the American Tobacco Company. Saloutos, *op. cit.,* p. 360. Soon after the price agreement had been reached between the Burley Association and the American

Tobacco Company, the Planters' Protective Association was able likewise to sell its pooled tobacco at "a good price." See H. Clyde Filley, *op. cit.*, p. 251.

42. This idea had the sanction of economists. Anna Youngman came to the conclusion that organization of growers into a disciplined body "would be a logical step forward in the general combination movement . . . Why . . . should not the individualistic and reactionary farmer be drawn into the trust form of organization" *op. cit.*, pp. 48-49. This type of thinking provided a seedbed for the reorganization of the burley district in 1921 under the stimulus of the "commodity marketing" movement led by Sapiro.

43. Letter from Dana G. Card of the University of Kentucky, August 28, 1945.

44. B. H. Hibbard, *Marketing Agricultural Products*, (New York: D. Appleton and Company, 1921), p. 236. It is of interest that this statement was made just before the burley growers were again reorganized under the aegis of Aaron Sapiro.

45. Bahmer, *op. cit.*, pp. 46-47.

46. *Ibid.*, pp. 53-54. About 1908 Tubbs became secretary of the Wisconsin Society of Equity, a position which gave scope to his cooperative philosophy.

47. *Ibid.*, p. 56. See also Wiest, *op. cit.*, pp. 526, 531.

48. Balmer, *op. cit.*, pp. 57-58. However, in 1910 the Equity had adopted a plan whereby local Equity unions would establish cooperatives in accordance with Rochdale principles, and this led to the organization of "dozens of Equity cooperative creameries, cheese factories, elevators, and grist mills."

49. Theodore Saloutos, "The Wisconsin Society of Equity," *Agricultural History*, April 1940, p. 81.

50. A representative of the Society maintained in 1915 that: "What the merchants and manufacturers' association, the retail lumber and hardware dealers' associations, the bankers' associations, and the federation of labor are to their members, the Wisconsin agricultural cooperative societies, federated into the Wisconsin Society of Equity, are to their constituents." Charles A. Lyman, *Marketing and Farm Credits*, 1915, p. 39. See also B. H. Hibbard and Asher Hobson, *Cooperation in Wisconsin*, Univ. of Wisconsin Agr. Exp. Sta. Bulletin 282 (1917), pp. 4-7.

51. Hibbard, *op. cit.*, p. 237; Saloutos, "The Wisconsin Society of Equity," *op. cit.*, p. 95.

52. Hibbard, *op. cit.*, p. 238. "The extent to which the Equity influenced the development of cooperative purchasing in Wisconsin can scarcely be overemphasized . . . It is significant that 25 per cent of the supply associations in Wisconsin in 1935 showed definite signs of Equity influence during this early period of operation." Rudolph K. Froker and Joseph G. Knapp, *Farmers Purchasing Associations in Wisconsin*, Farm Credit Administration Bulletin No. 20, 1937, p. 7.

53. Nourse, *op. cit.*, pp. 45 ff.

54. In the 1907 campaign it was claimed that 30 million bushels were signed for the pool in Minnesota and the Dakotas. Herman Steen, *Cooperative Marketing: The Golden Rule in Agriculture*, 1923, p. 212.

55. Theodore Saloutos, "The Rise of the Equity Cooperative Exchange," *The Mississippi Valley Historical Review*, June 1924, p. 44. At the organization meeting there were present the secretaries of the Minnesota and South Dakota state unions of the Equity, the head of the grain growers department of Equity, and other Equity officials. *Ibid.* p. 31.

56. In 1915 the paid-up capital amounted to $75,000 divided among 1,200

stockholders. See J. M. Anderson, "Problems of a Cooperatively Owned Terminal System," *Marketing and Farm Credits*, 1915, pp. 283-84.

57. Saloutos, "The Rise of the Equity Cooperative Exchange," *op. cit.*, pp. 46-47.

58. Anderson, *op. cit.*, p. 284.

59. "Amateurish, crude, ill-informed, and impolite as they were, they [The Equity leaders] saw the need and proceeded to tackle the problems of distribution before our institutions of learning had started to stir." Saloutos, "The Rise of the Equity Cooperative Exchange," *op. cit.*, p. 45.

60. "This philosophy of organization was not destined to promote good relations between the American Society of Equity and the Equity Cooperative Exchange ... The Equity Cooperative Exchange was interested solely in the problems of the spring wheat producer, while the American Society of Equity was interested in all farm products . . . The former was more realistic and opportunistic, the latter more idealistic and altruistic" *Ibid.* p. 46. While wheat was the principal interest, the Exchange had established a livestock department at South St. Paul in 1916. A second unit was established two years later at Chicago. The annual volume of livestock handled at St. Paul reached a peak of $5,000,000 and that at Chicago $4,000,000. "As the general Equity influence declined, it had to merge with the Farmers' Union group (1922) in order to avoid complete extinction." See Nourse and Knapp, *op. cit.*, pp. 106-09, 114.

61. See H. Bruce Price, *Farmers Cooperation in Minnesota, 1917-1922*, Minnesota Agr. Exp. Sta. Bulletin 202 (January 1923), pp. 34-35 and *Marketing of Farm Products*, p. 101.

62. Wiest, *op. cit.*, p. 533. See also Theodore Saloutos, "Charles Orrin Drayton— Rural Organizer," in *Great American Cooperators* (Knapp, and associates, *op. cit.*, pp. 15-17).

63. The interesting early history of the Missouri Farmers Association is well presented by Ray Derr in *Missouri Farmers in Action* (Columbia, Mo.: Missouri Farmer Press, 1953), pp. 6-71. See also Jack Hackethorn, "Bill Hirth— Equality for Agriculture" in *Great American Cooperators* (Knapp, and associates, *op cit.*, pp. 213-219).

Chapter XI

1. For a general discussion of the influence of the Grange in bettering rural conditions, see Edward Wiest, *Agricultural Organization in the United States*, pp. 399-431.

2. *Proceedings of the National Grange*, 1897, p. 125.

3. *Proceedings of the National Grange*, 1905, p. 69.

4. *Proceedings of the National Grange*, 1919, pp. 151-53.

5. *Proceedings of the National Grange*, 1920, p. 159.

6. *Ibid.*, pp. 160-161.

7. *Ibid.*, p. 161.

8. *Organizations among Ohio Farmers*, Ohio Agricultural Experiment Station Bulletin 342, 1920, pp. 129-30.

9. Ford, writing in 1913, referred to this development, "as the most significant advance in the practice of cooperative distribution that New England has yet seen." James Ford, *Cooperation in New England—Urban and Rural*, p. 95.

10. Ford maintained that an interstate federation in New England was "especially

desirable because of the smallness of the six political divisions which constitute New England, and also because of their similarity in industries and in general social constitution." *op. cit.*, p. 111. For complete discussion of "the movement for federation among Granges," see pp. 103-11.

11. For more complete information on the formation and experience of the New York Grange Exchange, see Joseph G. Knapp, *Seeds That Grow—A History of the Cooperative Grange League Federation Exchange* (Hinsdale, N. Y.: Anderson House, 1960). pp. 24-28.

12. Richard Pattee, *My Personal Word,* (Baltimore, Md.: The Lord Baltimore Press, 1927), pp. 65-66.

13. M. C. Burritt, *The County Agent and the Farm Bureau* (New York: Harcourt, Brace & Co., 1922). p. 161. The story of this embryonic development has been well told by O. M. Kile in *The Farm Bureau Movement*, pp. 94-99. The Binghamton Chamber of Commerce became interested in a program for agricultural betterment as a method of solving the abandoned farm "problem" in southern New York State—which had been emphasized in a statement made by Secretary Wilson after a visit to that area in 1909. Further interest was aroused by the report of the Country Life Commission in 1910. The concern of the Chamber led to appointment of a committee on agriculture which included representatives of New York State College of Agriculture, the United States Department of Agriculture, and the New York State Department of Agriculture. "Following a tour of the area, the party returned home convinced that the time was ripe for someone to take the initiative in opening to all farmers the opportunities afforded through modern science and practice of agriculture." This led to the establishment of the "bureau" in the Chamber of Commerce. The decision to carry on the work of rural betterment through the appointment of a county agent was taken upon the recommendation of W. J. Spillman, in charge of the farm management work of the United States Department of Agriculture. See also Alfred C. True, *A History of Agricultural Extension Work in the United States, 1785-1923,* U. S. Department of Agriculture Misc. Pub. 15 (1928), pp. 77-80.

14. Gladys Baker, *The County Agent,* (Chicago: The University of Chicago Press, 1939), p. 16. For a full discussion of the early development of Farm Bureau programs in various states as an ancillary of the county agent plan see True, *op. cit.,* pp. 76-100.

15. Baker, *op. cit.,* p. 16.

16. Kile, *op. cit.,* p. 101-02.

17. True, *op. cit.,* p. 154.

18. *Ibid.,* pp. 154-55.

19. "In 1916 some of the farm bureaus in Illinois undertook a more elaborate enterprise which was to have a far-reaching influence on the status and work of such organizations throughout the United States." *Ibid.,* p. 155.

20. *Ibid.,* p. 249 (Italics inserted).

21. *Ibid.,* p. 160.

22. Kile, *op. cit.,* p. 114.

23. *Ibid.,* p. 114.

24. B. H. Hibbard, *Marketing Agricultural Products,* pp. 262-63.

25. Kile, *op. cit.,* p. 115.

26. True, *op. cit.,* p. 161.

27. Quoted by Kile, *op. cit.,* p. 123.

28. Each state farm bureau was obligated to pay into the National Federation 50

cents for each member in a county farm bureau. This gave the National Federation an income of $137,344 in 1920. True, *op. cit.,* p. 162.

29. The letter here quoted was prepared for Secretary Houston's signature by Charles J. Brand, chief of the Office of Markets, in response to a "bitter complaint (from the National Implement and Vehicle Association) . . . against the assistance that was being given farmers in educational ways to promote co-operative organization." According to Mr. Brand (letter of October 19, 1945), this letter "contains the first official declaration of the Department of Agriculture's policies for cooperatives." A photostatic copy of the Secretary's letter, along with a copy of the original draft as prepared by Mr. Brand has been inspected by the writer. At this time much pressure was being applied on the Department of Agriculture by various business interests who were opposed to the work of the newly established Office of Markets in assisting farmers to form and operate cooperative associations. For an elaboration of the department's position by Secretary Houston on the business activities of county agents, April 4, 1916, see True, *op. cit.,* p. 153.

30. Kile, *op. cit.,* p. 110.

31. Burritt, *op. cit.,* pp. 11-12.

32. *Ibid.,* p. 13.

33. "The Relationship of Agricultural Extension Work to Farmers' Cooperative Buying and Selling Organizations," *Proceedings of the 31st Annual Convention of the Association of American Agricultural Colleges and Experiment Stations,* November 1917.

34. True, *op. cit.,* p. 153. It should here be observed that under the government's plan for nitrate of soda distribution by the Bureau of Markets, the county agent was made the active officer for carrying out the program in each county. This forced the county agent to perform business functions as a war measure.

35. *Ibid.,* p. 153.

36. W. A. Lloyd, *County Agricultural Agent Work in the Northern and Western States,* U. S. Department of Agriculture, Circ. 5, Ext. N (1917), p. 7.

37. One cannot be too dogmatic on this. As we shall see later in this chapter, the county Farm Bureaus in California, a state then famous for its cooperative development, early undertook cooperative functions. However, here the county Farm Bureaus undertook to perform services which were then unobtainable through existing cooperative associations.

38. L. R. Simons, *Farm Bureau Organization Plan,* U. S. Department of Agriculture, Circ. 4, Ext. N (1917), p. 1. See also Burritt, *op. cit.,* pp. 252-531.

39. "While we may not have thought of the farm bureau particularly as a cooperative organization, it represents in my judgment, the most highly developed and the most comprehensive system of cooperation among farmers so far developed in this country. I say this because the farm bureau, as we understand it in Illinois, is conceived in the idea that it shall represent all farmers, and have as its object the improvement of agriculture and rural life in all of its phases. It is limited in its aims and activities not to any special interest or line of production nor to any special phases of agriculture as a whole . . . It represents a sane, deliberate, constructive movement, in which several hundred of the most progressive farmers in a county have organized themselves not only to make their own farm business more profitable and their individual farm life richer, but to improve, in its various aspects, the farming and community life of their county as a whole." Walter F. Handschin, *The Relation of the Farm Bureau and the Farm Adviser to Cooperative and Commercial Activities* (address at winter conference of farm advisers), January 1919, p. 8.

40. For more complete information see Chapter XX. The full story of how the G. L. F. came to be formed is given by Knapp, *op. cit.*, pp. 3-29.

41. Charles L. McNeil, "The Farm Bureau Set-Up and System of Operation in Mississippi," *American Cooperation 1933*, pp. 185-86. See also "Cooperative Marketing in Mississippi Through County Agents," Mississippi Extension Bulletin No. 15 (1920), pp. 3-7.

42. E. D. Tetreau, *The Objectives and Activities of the California Farm Bureau*, Univ. of Cal. Agric. Exp. Station Bull. 563, November 1933, pp. 8-9.

43. In fact, the need for co-ordinating the cooperative efforts of the county Farm Bureaus was one of the factors which led to the formation of the state Farm Bureau federation. Tetreau, *op. cit.*, pp. 11, 60 ff. See also E. G. Nourse and J. G. Knapp, *Cooperative Marketing of Livestock*, pp. 203-10.

44. For an intimate account of how the Farm Bureau movement came into being and rapidly gained adherents in Illinois, see John J. Lacey, *Farm Bureau in Illinois* (History of Illinois Farm Bureau) Bloomington: Illinois Agricultural Association, 1965.

45. True, *op. cit.*, pp. 89-90.

46. Handschin, *op. cit.*

47. True, *op. cit.*, pp. 11-12.

48. Handschin, *op. cit.*, pp. 13-14.

49. C. V. Gregory, "A Brief History of the Illinois Agricultural Association," *Illinois Agricultural Association Annual Report*, 1925, pp. 6-7.

50. *Proceedings of the Fifth Annual Meeting of the Illinois Agricultural Association*, January 13-14, 1920, pp. 4-5, 55.

51. *The Nation's Agriculture*, July-August 1938, p. 7.

Chapter XII

1. The growth of the centralizers was stimulated by the adoption of the centrifugal cream separator which permitted the farmer to skim practically all the cream from his milk and retain the skimmed milk for feeding of livestock. The centralizers were also favored by technological improvements, particularly in refrigeration and pasteurization, which made possible a better standardized product more suitable for large-scale methods of distribution. For information on the growth and economic importance of the centralizers, see Theodore Macklin, *A History of the Organization of Creameries and Cheese Factories in the United States*, University of Wisconsin doctoral thesis (1917), Ch. 9.

2. L. D. H. Weld in 1916 pointed out that the Minnesota Cooperative Dairy Association had contented itself with selecting wholesale receivers. Although he recognized that some benefits had been derived in lowering transportation costs, he believed that: "Much greater benefits might accrue from such an organization if it had a system of inspection and perhaps of grading and handling, and it might possibly undertake a supervision of business and accounting methods of the creameries." Weld was doubtful with regard to the advantage of the association selling through its own distributing houses in the east. *The Marketing of Farm Products* (New York: The Macmillan Company, 1916), pp. 420-421.

3. The conditions leading to the formation of this association are described by A. M. McGuire in *The Report of the National Dairy Marketing Conference*, May 1921, pp. 74-ff. It is of interest that this association was largely formed through McGuire's tireless efforts as extension dairy specialist for the University

of Minnesota. In addressing the American Institute of Cooperation in 1925, McGuire said: "I feel that if it were not for the educational work of the United States Department of Agriculture, and the State Departments, experiment stations, agricultural colleges and the county agents, that this great cooperative movement would not have gotten across the first track."

4. For detailed information on the development of this organization, see Paul E. Quintus, *Operating Methods of Challenge Cream and Butter Association*, U. S. Department of Agriculture Circular C-119, May 1940.

5. "[The cooperative centralizer] is really a hybrid institution, having the advantage of the feature of pure cooperation combined with the large scale production advantages of the old line centralizers." See Francis A. Flood, "Cooperative Centralizers in Nebraska," *Wallace's Farmer*, July 21, 1925.

6. The rise of competing commercial centralizers had created a scramble for cream at local points, and in some communities each of several centralizers had its own cream station—usually an agency in a country store. This situation sometimes resulted in gentlemen's price agreements among the centralizers. To meet this problem, the local dairy producers began, about 1910 to organize cream shipping associations, patterned on their experience in organizing livestock shipping associations, for the purpose of collectively selling their cream to the centralizer which would pay the highest price. A considerable number of such associations were operating in the Dakotas and Nebraska by 1920. With the establishment of cooperative centralizers, many of these associations became local assembling stations for them while others were formed expressly for the purpose of serving the cooperative centralizers. For more complete information on the significance and methods of cooperative cream shipping associations, see Alva H. Benton, *Marketing Dairy Products*, North Dakota Agr. Exp. Station Bulletin 182 (1924).

7. For more complete information, see O. B. Jesness and W. H. Kerr, *Cooperative Purchasing and Marketing Organizations Among Farmers in the United States*, U.S.D.A. Bulletin No. 547 (1917), pp. 46-47. Herman Steen, *Cooperative Marketing*, pp. 163-65; and Carl Haberlach, "History of the Tillamook Cheese Industry," *American Cooperation* (1927), Vol. II, pp. 206-13.

8. See Theodore Saloutus, "Henry Kumrey—Promoter and Organizer" in Joseph G. Knapp, and associates, *Great American Cooperators*, Washington, D.C.: 1967, pp. 270-272.

9. See Theodore Macklin, *Marketing by Federations*, Wisconsin Agricultural Experiment Station Bulletin 332 (1920). The author maintained that: "Wisconsin farmers have within their home state a federation of notable success. What it is doing for the producers of American cheese, a similar federation could easily do for the producers of foreign cheese. Still other federations could be created by combining as separate groups local cooperative creameries, livestock shipping associations, fruit marketing concerns, and the other farmer marketing companies . . . Instead of being obliged to search in distant states and countries for plans of organization and for advice, Wisconsin cooperators may now examine the Cheese Federation which is well adapted to their needs" (pp. 7-8, 9-10).

10. Statement by John D. Miller in Report of the National Dairy Marketing Conference, Chicago, May 3-4, 1921, p. 14.

11. *Ibid.*, pp. 14-15.

12. *Ibid.*, p. 16.

13. According to John D. Miller, who as general counsel of the Dairymen's League, largely wrote the membership contract for the reorganized League: "Our objective was to have a financing system so elastic that capital could be increased or

decreased at any time to meet changes in business conditions. Upon careful study it was found that the revolving fund method of financing then being promoted by the U. S. Bureau of Markets met this objective in a practical way." Letters from John D. Miller, June 26 and August 14, 1945.

14. See H. E. Erdman, *The Marketing of Whole Milk* (New York: The Macmillan Company, 1921), pp. 155-182.

15. Statement of Richard Pattee, in *The Report of the National Dairy Marketing Conference*, Chicago, May 3-4, 1921, p. 25.

16. For an interesting account of the origin and significance of the base-surplus plan, see I. W. Heaps, *Twenty Years of Cooperative Milk Marketing in Baltimore* (Baltimore, Privately Published, 1938), pp. 34-37. Mr. Heaps, as the manager of the Maryland State Dairymen's Association, which later changed its name to Maryland Milk Producers Association, largely devised the plan and insured its successful operation. See John D. Black, *Dairy Marketing and the A.A.A.* (Washington, D.C., Brookings Institution, 1936), p. 197; and also Roland W. Bartlett, *Cooperation in Marketing Dairy Products* (Springfield, Ill.: Charles C. Thomas, 1931), p. 211.

17. More complete information on the early experience of dairymen in devising and operating base-surplus plans is given by Hutzel Metzger in *Cooperative Marketing of Fluid Milk*, U.S.D.A. Tech. Bul. No. 179, (1930). See also Erdman, *op. cit.*, pp. 102-117.

18. For the detailed history of this development see the 1920 *Annual Report of the Twin City Milk Producers Association*.

19. This legislation was embodied in the Capper-Volstead Act of 1922. The steps leading up to the enactment of this act will be more fully discussed in Volume II of this history.

20. E. G. Nourse, *Fifty Years of Farmers' Elevators in Iowa*, Iowa Agr. Expr. Sta. Bul. No. 211 (1923), p. 246.

21. Farmers who endeavored to by-pass the local elevators by directly loading grain in railroad cars for shipment to terminal markets were called "scoopers" or "scoop shovelers." Although handicapped by lack of cooperation from the railroad companies which were often in league with the elevators, a considerable volume of grain was so handled from about 1885 to 1905.

22. For more detailed information with documentary evidence on how the boycott was applied, see Federal Trade Commission, *Report on Grain Marketing*, Vol. 1 (1920), pp. 86 ff. See also Nourse, *op. cit.*, p. 247; Joseph B. Kenkel, *The Cooperative Elevator Movement* (1922), pp. 24-26; and Lawrence Farlow, *The Farmers Elevator Movement in Illinois* (1928), pp. 21-34.

23. Farlow, *op. cit.*, p. 34.

24. For information on the formation of the Nebraska association see H. Clyde Filley, *Cooperation in Agriculture* (1929), p. 63-64. See also *Early Struggles of the Cooperative Movement in Nebraska*, a pamphlet issued by the Nebraska State Historical Society in 1918, pp. 26-50. The birth of the Illinois association is described by Farlow, *op. cit.*, pp. 34-39. Nourse comments as follows on the beginnings of the Iowa association: "The founders of the state association saw that there must be some agency for assisting farmers who wanted to handle their own grain business to organize on right terms, to adopt suitable by-laws and to follow methods of day-to-day operation which would be both commercially sound and successful . . ." *Op. cit.*, p. 248. This philosophy was expressed in the objectives of the Iowa association as stated in the preamble to its constitution: ". . . to advance the commercial interest of the cooperative organizations of the state engaged in the handling of grain, to inculcate just and equitable principles of trade; to acquaint, present and disseminate valuable business

information; and to encourage frequent intercourse and consultation among its members for the promotion of their common interests." It is of interest that the Rockwell Society called the meeting which led to the formation of the Iowa association—partly as a measure of "self-preservation." See Reuben A. Holman, *Forty Years in Cooperation* (1931), p. 23.

25. In the first issue under the direct control of the state grain dealers' associations the trustees declared: "The Journal will be placed on a broad cooperative basis ... We need an organ baptized in the font of true cooperation to cry 'Wolf, Wolf' to distinguish the true from the false, the friend from the foe . . . Such a Journal should be more than a news gatherer. It should be the head and heart, the voice and soul of the cooperative movement. We recognize the credit due to the former owners of the Journal for the work of establishing the first successful paper in the farmer elevator field. However, there is a vital difference between a cooperative paper used for private profit and a cooperative paper owned and published by the farmers and its profits used in the interest of the entire body of cooperators ... The dairymen, the livestock farmer, the fruit and truck growers, the worker in packing and wire and mercantile establishments are awakening to a realizing sense of the power for the common good in cooperative organization and the Journal will gladly make room for them as members of the growing cooperative family." (August, 1911, pp. 963-64.)

26. Its circulation in early 1920 was 68,000. The *American Cooperative Journal* became the *Farmers' Elevator Guide* in 1924.

27. A "national managers' association of Farm Cooperative Companies" was promoted by the *Journal* in 1911. There was a considerable opposition to the formation of this association on the grounds that this would tend to weaken farmer control in the movement. (See *American Cooperative Journal*, April and May 1911). In 1916 the *Journal* editors began publication of the *American Cooperative Manager*, for "directors and managers."

28. Holman, *op. cit.*, p. 32. The rise, significance, and gradual eclipse of the maintenance clause as a device for integrating cooperative activity is fully examined by E. G. Nourse, *Legal Status of Agricultural Cooperation* in the chapter, "The Evolution of the Members' Contract" and in pp. 279 ff. After 1913, the legal position of the clause was questioned by court decisions which held that such clauses were "in restraint of trade." Unfortunately many of the early maintenance clauses were so drawn as to give the impression that they were more "aimed at competitors" than designed to ensure "maintenance and upkeep" of an association. However, it is doubtful whether this would have made any difference in view of the prevailing attitude of the courts at that time. For a time such decisions imperiled the use of "Liquidated damages" clauses in marketing agreements, but cooperative statutes passed since 1920 have expressly authorized "associations to include in their contracts and by-laws provisions for liquidated damages," and these provisions have been upheld by the Supreme Courts of many states. See L. S. Hulbert, *Legal Phases of Cooperative Associations*, Farm Credit Administration Bulletin No. 50, 1942, pp. 181-82.

29. See Nourse, *Fifty Years of Farmers' Elevators in Iowa, op. cit.*, pp. 238-39.

30. *Cooperation in Agriculture*, p. 42.

31. These laws are generally referred to as being of the Rochdale pattern since they generally gave "specific recognition to the three cooperative fundamentals identified with the Rochdale movement, namely, limitation of capital holding, democratic voting, and dividends on patronage." The model law of this type was passed in Wisconsin in 1911 although a somewhat similar law was enacted in the same year in Nebraska. Laws of this general type were passed in Michigan, Minnesota, Indiana, Colorado, South Dakota, New York, Kansas, Washington, and Massachusetts in 1913, in Virginia in 1914, in Iowa, Wyoming, North

Dakota, North Carolina, South Carolina, and Oregon in 1915, in Rhode Island in 1916, Florida in 1917, Kentucky in 1918, and Oklahoma in 1919. Nourse, *The Legal Status of Agricultural Cooperation, op. cit.,* pp. 43-50.

32. Kenkell, *op. cit.,* p. 39.

33. The weakness of the business organization and practices of the farmers' elevators was immediately recognized by the newly formed Office of Markets. After a study of the problems involved, a system of accounts for farmers' elevators was tested by a number of elevators located in seven states. The plan was then recommended for general adoption in U.S.D.A. Bulletin No. 236, "*A System of Accounts for Farmers' Cooperative Elevators*" (1915), and within a few years its use was general among cooperative elevators. The elevators also drew heavily on the advice given in U.S.D.A. Bulletin No. 178, "Cooperative Organization Business Methods" (1914); and more particularly in U.S.D.A. Bulletin 411, "Patronage Dividends in Cooperative Grain Companies" (1916).

34. For a full discussion of the conditions that motivated the livestock shipping association movement, see E. G. Nourse and Joseph G. Knapp, *The Cooperative Marketing of Livestock* (1931), pp. 39-54.

35. The first livestock shipping association in Minnesota was formed by the supporters of the successful cooperative creamery at Litchfield in 1902. For many years the creamery manager served also as the manager of the shipping association. After a visit to this association, Clarence Poe remarked "One form of cooperation usually leads to another." *How Farmers Cooperate and Double Profits,* 1915, pp. 98-99. "Other examples of successful cooperative business were also before the eyes of livestock producers" in the form of creameries, cheese factories, and breeders' associations. The movement was also given much initial encouragement by the American Society of Equity and the Farmers Union." For more detail see Nourse and Knapp, *op. cit.,* pp. 10, 18.

36. This description is admittedly too limited even for the simplest associations since the operations were far from being automatic. *Ibid.,* pp. 55-67.

37. Some associations adopted "maintenance clauses" in their by-laws, designed to increase the solidarity of their efforts. However, the "maintenance clause" never took hold as it did among the early farmers' elevators, possibly because the livestock shipping association problem was not strictly analogous. Unlike the cooperative elevator, the shipping association ordinarily had little invested in physical plant, and there was no fixed salary charge as the managers were customarily paid on a commission basis. It is, however, significant that the famous legal decision that blighted the use of the maintenance clause concerned a livestock shipping association (*Reeves* v. *Decorah Farmers' Cooperative Society,* 160 Ia. 194, 140, N.W. 844 (1913). After 1920, marketing contracts were employed by Iowa associations to obtain the same general objectives, but these were supported by new cooperative laws which provided expressly for this use. See Nourse and Knapp, *op. cit.,* pp. 74-79.

38. An attempt was made in 1919 to form a national federation of state shipping associations, similar in form to the national association of state farmers' grain dealers' associations. This plan which was sponsored by the *American Cooperative Journal* gave way to the industry-wide livestock marketing schemes which were launched the following year under the auspices of the newly formed American Farm Bureau Federation.

39. This organization was a fine illustration of "bottom up" development out of the experience gained in working together first in local shipping associations. See Nourse and Knapp, *op. cit.,* pp. 116-20.

40. "Much of the emphasis laid by the state federation upon points of efficient management centered around questions of market analysis designed to reveal

the most profitable sales outlet for the particular association at a given time or for a certain class of stock." *Ibid.*, p. 95.

41. *Ibid.*, pp. 106-09.

42. Those interested in the sound development of agricultural cooperation were skeptical, from the beginning, of the possibilities of cooperative packing plants. One of the first efforts of the National Agricultural Organization Society, when it was formed in 1916, was to make a careful examination of the so-called cooperative packing plants. In reporting on this study, Charles W. Holman disclosed how a number of these organizations had taken advantage of the farmers and he urged that farmers proceed cautiously in the development of such enterprises without "stepping blindly into the snares spread by the J. Rufus Wallingfords." See "Cooperative Packing Plants," *Marketing and Farm Credits,* 1916, pp. 286-301. See also, L. B. Mann, *History of Cooperative and Farmer Owned Meat Packing Enterprises in the United States,* U.S. Department of Agriculture, Farm Credit Administration Report No. 72, May 1944.

43. See "Cotton Improvement on a Community Basis", *U.S.D.A. Yearbook of Agriculture, 1911,* pp. 397-98, 409-10.

44. In 1911, Brand devised a project for the study of cotton handling and marketing problems as Physiologist in Charge of Farmers Cooperative Cotton Handling and Marketing. It is significant that this project served as a model for the early work of the Office of Markets when it was created in 1913, and that Brand's work on the cotton project demonstrated his fitness for appointment as chief of the new office.

45. "Improved Methods of Handling and Marketing Cotton", *U.S.D.A. Yearbook of Agriculture, 1912* pp. 443-462.

46. Wells A. Sherman, Fred Taylor, and Charles J. Brand, *Studies of Primary Cotton Market Conditions in Oklahoma,* U.S.D.A. Bulletin No. 36 (1913). A prefatory note states that "the market survey here described was planned and supervised by Mr. Charles J. Brand, while Physiologist in Charge of Farmers' Cooperatives Cotton Handling and Marketing, Bureau of Plant Industry."

47. See O. W. Herrmann and Chastina Gardner, *Early Developments in Cooperative Cotton Marketing,* Farm Credit Administration, Circular No. C-101 (1936), pp. 17-19; and Clarence Poe, *op. cit.,* pp. 137-141.

48. Robert L. Nixon, "Cotton Warehouses; Storage Facilities Now Available in the South," USDA Bulletin 216 (1915), pp. 5-11. See also Poe, *op. cit.,* pp. 100-112.

49. See O. W. Herrmann, *Development of Cooperative Cotton Ginning,* Farm Credit Administration, Circular C-112 (1939), p. 8. However, a significant attempt to operate a joint-stock cotton gin on true cooperative lines was made in 1913 by a group of Farmers' Union members at Rule, Texas. This association which was set up with 92 members undertook to distribute savings on a basis of volume contributed.

50. See Nourse, *Legal Status of Agricultural Cooperation, op. cit.,* pp. 68-72. See also Herrmann, *op. cit.,* pp. 8, 9, 20.

51. The leader in this movement was W. W. Cole, who as a member of Farmers' Alliance of Texas had organized an unsuccessful cooperative gin in 1887, and who in 1907 assisted as a member of the Farmers' Union of Texas in the formation of a joint company gin. *Ibid.,* pp. 3, 7, 21. See also C. E. Bowles "Father of the Cooperative Gins" in *Great American Cooperators* by Joseph G. Knapp, and associates (Washington, D. C.: American Institute of Cooperation, 1967), pp. 122-126.

52. A. M. Dixon "The Place of Cooperative Gins in a Cooperative Cotton Marketing Setup," *American Cooperation,* 1933, p. 458.

53. The farm price of cotton fell from 31.8 cents on October 1, 1918 to 24 cents on March 1, 1919. It had climbed back to 29.5 cents by June 1, 1919.

54. See Charles D. Bohannan and D. P. Campbell, *The Preliminary Study of the Marketing of Burley Tobacco in Central Kentucky*, Kentucky Agricultural Experiment Station, Bulletin 202 (1916).

55. The average price of burley increased from 16.68 cents in 1916 to 32.06 cents in 1918. See Verna Elsinger, *American Cooperation*, Vol. II (1928), p. 509.

Chapter XIII

1. In 1952 the California Fruit Growers Exchange changed its name to Sunkist Growers, Inc.

2. For the plan in full see A. W. McKay and W. McKenzie Stevens, *Organization and Development of a Cooperative Citrus-Fruit Marketing Agency*, USDA Bulletin 1237, 1924, pp. 49-50.

3. Rahno Mabel McCurdy, *The History of the California Fruit Growers Exchange*, Los Angeles, California, 1925, p. 33.

4. *Ibid.*, p. 30.

5. For example, one provision of the plan read as follows: "No exchange, association, or corporation signing this agreement, shall employ any agent, traveling man, or solicitor for the sale of its fruit independent of those employed by the said executive board." See McCurdy, *op. cit.*, pp. 71-76. Prior to this, competition among the exchanges was unbridled. See A. W. McKay and C. H. Lane, *Practical Cooperative Marketing* (1928), p. 260.

6. The plan given in full by McCurdy, *op. cit.*, pp. 33-35, indicates that at this date there was still sentiment in favor of using the Exchange as a system for marketing various California agricultural products.

7. For complete articles of incorporation and the by-laws of the Southern California Fruit Exchange, see *Ibid.*, pp. 77-82.

8. *Ibid.*, p. 56.

9. *The California Citrograph*, February 1920.

10. See Edward F. Adams, *The Modern Farmer in His Business Relations* (1899), pp. 512-13.

11. Soon after the Southern California Fruit Exchange was organized in 1894, a committee was appointed to design a circular for the purpose of offsetting charges designed to weaken growers' support. In the following year a committee was appointed "to formulate some plan of repudiating incorrect statements." At about this time a resolution was passed by the representatives of the local member asociations which declared that "the interests of this organization demand a more direct medium of communication with the growers..." and in compliance with this request the Exchange issued the *Fruit Exchange Review* from September 1896 to June 1897, its first attempt at a continuing effort in the member-grower field. John William Lloyd, *Cooperative and Other Organized Methods of Marketing California Horticultural Products* (1919), pp. 46-47.

12. P. J. Dreher, one of the Exchange pioneers, later pointed out that these meetings, semi-social in character, welded the various elements of the exchange system into an enduring partnership. See "Early History of the Co-operative Marketing of Citrus Fruits," *California Citrograph*, October 1916.

13. See Adams, *op. cit.*, pp. 514-16.

14. *Ibid.*, pp. 514-16.

15. See *California Cultivator,* October 11, 1901. In a way the early history of the Exchange was similar to that of our federal government. At the start of our national life there was a period when the states were dominant which can be compared to the incipient period in the life of the Exchange when the district exchanges were dominant. Then there was a period when informal coordination of the states was achieved under the Articles of Confederation, a period which compares with the experience of the Exchange under the Executive Board. With the failure of informal organization "a more perfect union" under the Constitution was formed in 1789. Similarly, the district exchanges found it necessary to replace the Executive Board with an incorporated organization—the Southern California Fruit Exchange—the prototype of the California Fruit Growers Exchange.

16. For full information on this unique cooperative partnership which continued to 1940, see Kelsey B. Gardner, *Joint Use of a Sales Organization by Two Cooperative Associations,* USDA Circular No. 10 (1927).

17. *California Cultivator,* February 1, 1901. See also comment in *California Cultivator,* October 10, 1902, that the Exchange was coming into its years of "maturity."

18. For the most complete discussion of the inception and operation of this plan see Lloyd, *op. cit.,* pp. 52-62. See also McCurdy, *op. cit.,* pp. 46-48; William W. Cumberland, *Cooperative Marketing,* pp. 55-58; and McKay and Stevens, *op. cit.,* pp. 12-13.

19. For the complete agreement see McCurdy, *op. cit.,* pp. 83-84.

20. A. W. McKay and W. McKenzie Stevens, *op. cit.,* p. 12. See also Lloyd, *op. cit.,* pp. 58-59.

21. See McCurdy, *op. cit.,* pp. 49-50.

22. McKay and Stevens, *op. cit.,* p. 12. Charles C. Teague, later president of the California Fruit Growers Exchange, referred to this arrangement as an "unholy alliance." According to Teague, "It represented an attempt to amalgamate two interests with diametrically opposed philosophies and viewpoints ... It was like trying to mix oil and water." *Fifty Years a Rancher* (1944), p. 80. G. Harold Powell well characterized the Agency as being an "incongruous combination of producers and dealers." *U.S.D.A. Yearbook of Agriculture, 1910,* p. 405.

23. An editorial in the *California Cultivator* of August 5, 1904, which was entitled "Whither" referred to the "desperate onslaught on the Southern California Fruit Exchange which threatens its destruction." C. C. Teague has observed that: "Even after the California Fruit Growers Exchange in 1905 succeeded the Southern California Fruit Exchange ... there ensued a long era of considerable uncertainty marked by periods of low prices, dissatisfied growers, and withdrawals, and an irregular and fluctuating membership. This was largely due I believe to the fact that the exchanges did not handle a sufficient percentage of the California citrus output to regulate shipments effectively and to stabilize the markets." *Op. cit.,* p. 79.

24. The fact that Mr. Naftzger had been one of the principal architects of the Agency plan, as well as the general manager of the Agency, made essential the employment of a new general manager for the Exchange. See Lloyd, *op. cit.,* p. 63.

25. Manager Woodford said, "This gathering and distributing of information is one of the most valuable things the exchange does. I have no doubt it helps very much to bind the members together." Will Payne, "Cooperation: The Small Man's Salvation," *Saturday Evening Post,* March 26, 1910.

26. In fact, Powell found that the cooperative method of handling was often "responsible for a large amount of rough handling," since there was little

incentive for the grower to handle his fruit with unusual care as long as it was pooled with the fruit of other growers who might handle it carelessly. G. Harold Powell, "The Decay of Oranges While in Transit from California," USDA Bulletin No. 123 (1908), p. 29. It is of interest that Powell in conducting his study carefully examined the methods then being used by the Limoneira Association. This association, then managed by C. C. Teague, through care in picking and local handling, had been able to reduce greatly the loss from decay. Powell's study scientifically proved that the future of California citrus industry was dependent upon the widespread adoption of such methods. The minutes of the Exchange from 1906 to 1908 contain many references to the significance of Powell's findings.

27. McCurdy, *op. cit.*, pp. 52-53.

28. According to McKay and Stevens, the improvements in local handling following Powell's study "served perhaps more than any other single factor to place the cooperative marketing of citrus fruits upon a stable basis." *Op. cit.*, p. 40.

29. This initial advertising campaign was developed in cooperation with the Southern Pacific Railroad which assumed half the cost. The Southern Pacific was interested in developing California agricultural production so as to increase east-bound traffic and realized that wider sales outlets for California crops were necessary. This cooperation overcame much of the initial objection that Exchange growers would pay all of the costs of advertising but share in benefits to be derived. For more complete information on the origin of the advertising program see McCurdy, *op. cit.*, pp. 59-64. See also President Story's account in *The California Citrograph*, March 1920, p. 143.

30. The minutes of the Exchange Board of Directors indicate that the Sunkist name was recommended as the trademark "for our best grade of fruit" on April 8, 1908. Steps were officially taken by the Board to copyright the Sunkist trademark on August 12, 1908.

31. The way in which the Sunkist trademark gradually established its general superiority over local brands has been described by C. C. Teague, manager of a prominent local association at that time: "As the Sunkist trademark became established we had to decide which should be most prominently printed on the boxes and wraps, the associations' brands or Sunkist. Both were permitted. Our own brands had become well known because of our many years of careful handling and packing. It was hard for me to believe that Sunkist could be more valuable to us. Finally a house-to-house canvass was made in Lincoln, Nebraska, where Limoneira brands had been sold for many years. It established the fact that Sunkist was better and more favorably known than were our own brands. After that I was quite willing that Sunkist should have the greater prominence on the boxes and wraps." *Op. cit.*, pp. 87-88.

32. Don Francisco, Advertising Manager for the Exchange 1914-20, points out (letter of November 22, 1948) that "the Association's label was on the end of the box and the Sunkist trademark on the wrappers . . . The Association's brand [thus] acquired a reputation with the trade . . . [while] the name 'Sunkist' . . . became familiar to the public. This method of branding was one example of what we called 'competitive cooperation.' Growers who put up a better pack . . . developed a special trade acceptance. Thus the associations competed to see which could produce the best quality but they cooperated in the process of marketing."

33. Cumberland, writing in 1917, pointed out "The privilege of using the Sunkist brand is another inducement to growers and associations to improve the quality of their fruit so as to have as large a percentage as possible of their total shipments admitted to the advertised brands." *Op. cit.*, p. 165. It should be noted that the

advertising program was started on a permissive basis as the Exchange authorized the use of the Sunkist trademark only where fruit met certain specified standards.

34. *California Cultivator,* January 9, 1908.

35. Since Powell came to the organization as general manager when great decisions were forcing themselves on the Exchange he has perhaps been accorded undue credit for accomplishments that would have come naturally. Without doubt Powell was fortunate in having at hand an excellent Board of Directors to work with and good operating personnel which made rapid progress possible. He was especially fortunate in having Earl Dezell as assistant general manager throughout his administration. Dezell, having started work with the Exchange in 1896 as a messenger boy, had a complete and unexcelled grasp of operating problems and methods. He was a perfect balance wheel for Mr. Powell since his ability to handle the operating functions of the Exchange freed Powell for the things that he liked to do and could do best. While Powell was the front man, Dezell operated quietly behind the scenes, knitting the operations together. It is of interest that Dezell succeeded Powell as general manager upon the latter's death in 1922.

Powell's function was that of catalytic agent who brought out the best from all elements in the system. This valuable ability was recognized by his close associate, C. C. Teague, in a public assessment of Powell's contribution: "Mr. Powell understood, as few do, how to build up a great organization. He realized fully that one man, no matter how able, can accomplish little by his own efforts, but can accomplish much by the development of able lieutenants. . . . He never failed to give credit where credit was due. . . . Is it any wonder that such a man should have built up such a great spirit of loyalty and teamwork among his assistants and among all the employees of the great organization which he so ably managed. . . . Whenever any controversial question was being discussed, he never took a position hastily; but, when he took a position, he was firm, but always considerate of the position of others. The great confidence which the membership had in his good judgment, ability, and fairness went far in smoothing the way." *The California Citrograph,* May 1922, p. 234.

36. *U.S.D.A. Yearbook of Agriculture, 1910,* p. 396.

37. *Ibid.,* p. 397. It is of interest that some of the Exchange Board of Directors feared that Powell might be too theoretical in his approach to Exchange problems. This objection was soon overcome as Powell demonstrated his practical ability. In fact, later students of cooperative enterprise have expressed the view that Powell's outstanding contribution consisted of his demonstration of the importance of sound business management. According to Charles W. Holman, "Powell gave a positive business turn and business standards to the cooperative movement." *American Cooperation,* 1932, p. 62. E. G. Nourse has pointed out that "Powell did an enormous service to the cooperative movement by expressing in persuasive business-like terms the distinctive character and distinctive ideals of cooperation as a different form of business." *Ibid.,* p. 69.

38. G. Harold Powell, *Cooperation in Agriculture,* pp. 68-69.

39. The Exchange annual reports also encouraged the local associations and district exchanges likewise to issue reports, and thus more complete information on the affairs of the cooperatives in the exchange system became more generally available to the members.

40. Annual report, 1914.

41. The way in which the Exchange used its trademarks to regulate quality standards can be shown by the following illustration: For some time the salability of California oranges had been handicapped by the quantity of immature fruit offered for sale. To meet this problem the U.S. Department of Agriculture recommended that no fruit be shipped which did not come up to what was

known as the "8 to 1" maturity standard (8 parts solid to 1 part acid). Although the soundness of this recommendation was widely recognized it was resisted by certain growers who were hesitant to apply a rigid standard to their own fruit shipments unless all growers were bound by it. The Exchange had a weapon to use in getting enforcement of this standard, for it could require that no local association would use its Sunkist or Red Ball trademarks on fruit which did not come up to the 8 to 1 standard. The leadership taken by the Exchange quickly resulted in the widespread adoption of the recommendations of the Department of Agriculture. See Cumberland, *op. cit.*, p. 165.

42. The Exchange By-Products Company, unlike the supply company, had its own separately elected board of directors. Its operations were coordinated with those of the Exchange through an arrangement whereby the Exchange selected 2 of the 17 directors, of whom one was the manager of the Exchange's lemon sales department.

43. The Exchange fully recognized the value of the Department's research efforts. This is shown by a letter of General Manager G. Harold Powell (Jan. 22, 1915) to Dr. C. L. Alsberg, Chief of the Bureau of Chemistry. Powell wrote: ... The Department work has stimulated a good deal of interest in the utilization of cull fruit.... [However] we have felt the question might be stabilized through the organization of a company *controlled by the producer himself and not entirely for the profit of anyone, except the producer* (italics added).... We feel that if the Department can continue its experimental work and extend it much more widely, the organization for the handling of the question by the producer ... will make much more effective the results of the investigations of the Department. ... We have felt for a long time that the by-product business could only be established by making it an incident to the fresh fruit shipping business and that if it were conducted for the profit of the corporation, it would fail because the supply is not large enough to warrant a profit concern to conduct the business continuously. ..."

In reply to this letter Dr. Alsberg said: "I am very glad to know that you contemplate handling the by-products in this way, thus avoiding speculative promotion." For more complete information on the scientific work underlying this program, see article by C. P. Wilson in the *California Citrograph*, February 1921.

44. This work was started through the initiative of Don Francisco, a young employee in the advertising department, whose curiosity had led him to inquire into the way citrus products were sold by retailers. His informal studies had disclosed that the methods of retailing citrus products greatly restricted their consumption and that much benefit would be derived from a program which would help retailers increase the efficiency of their merchandising methods. The logic of these findings appealed to the advertising department. Upon the death of the advertising manager a year later, Francisco was made manager of the advertising department. (Letter of Don Francisco, February 9, 1948.) For further information on how this program was initiated see Joseph G. Knapp, "Paul S. Armstrong—Sunkist Salesman" *in Great American Cooperators*, by Joseph G. Knapp, and associates, (Washington, D.C.: American Institute of Cooperation, 1967), pp. 31-32.

45. Cumberland referred to this program of cooperation with the distributing trade as "an innovation in the field of fruit and produce marketing—a procedure utterly inconceivable for an unorganized industry." *Op. cit.*, p. 167.

46. Letter from Don Francisco, February 17, 1948.

47. Letter from Don Francisco, February 17, 1948.

48. Letter from Paul S. Armstrong, January 6, 1949. Sunkist advertising began to refer to vitamines (now spelled vitamins) during the 1921-1922 season.

49 Annual report for 1916.

50. George E. Farrand who, as attorney for the Exchange drafted the new organization papers, has informed me that he recommended the change as a matter of cooperative business strategy. He deemed the change desirable "in view of the peculiar language of Sec. 6 of the Clayton Act which purported to grant certain exemptions to certain organizations—'instituted for the purpose of mutual help and not having capital stock or conducted for profit...'" He "thought it worth while to make the recommendation [which led to the retirement of the capital stock] as there was a possibility that the exemption for whatever it was worth was given only to cooperatives which did not have capital stock." Mr. Farrand doubted whether the change would have been made just at this time "had it not been for Section 6." (Letters of Aug. 28, 1945, and May 29, 1947.)

51. This analogy can be carried even further. The locals, like the citizens and states in our federal government, reserved certain powers so as to maintain their ultimate authority. Any expansion in the Exchange's power was expressly granted by the locals and such power was withdrawable by the locals.

52. One of the first advertisements of this type which was carried in the *Woman's Home Companion* for March 1916, showed a baby being fed orange juice. The copy read: "All good doctors recommend pure orange juice for babies as well as grown-ups."

53. The surveys of the dealers' service section found that soda fountains and similar outlets were reluctant to serve orangeade or lemonade because it was "bothersome, messy, and time-consuming."

54. Annual Report, 1917. Two years later the Exchange entered into an arrangement with the *California Citrograph* under which *The Sunkist Courier* became a department in the *Citrograph* under the complete control of the Exchange. This arrangement whereby the Exchange bought subscriptions of the *Citrograph* brought to each grower member of the exchange system a well-edited magazine devoted to the welfare of the citrus industry and brought to the attention of all citrus growers a discussion of the service and problems of the Exchange. Letter from Paul S. Armstrong, February 24, 1947.

55. Letter from Paul S. Armstrong, January 24, 1947.

56. The Orange By-Products Company suspended operations on June 1920 with a net loss to stockholders of approximately $175,000. In 1921 a new company with the same name was formed on the pattern of the Exchange By-Products Company to develop a real by-products program for cull oranges and grapefruit based on substantial laboratory research work carried on by the Exchange research department. This company reconverted the marmalade manufacturing plants to meet its needs, and soon established itself as a valuable adjunct of the exchange system.

57. Cumberland, *op. cit.*, p. 131.

58. *Ibid.*, p. 146. In broad terms Cumberland was correct. There was, however, one anomalous feature in the Exchange set-up eventually to be corrected as will be reported in Volume II of this history. While the great majority of citrus growers served by the Exchange were members of the local associations there were some large shippers and others who obtained packinghouse service through privately owned and operated packinghouses which marketed through the Exchange and enjoyed the same membership status as local associations. This arrangement had become fixed in the early days of the Exchange and had never been corrected. McKay and Stevens called attention to this condition as not being in accord with "strict cooperative principles." *Op. cit.*, pp. 15, 22-23, and chart p. 32.

59. Teague, *op. cit.*, p. 82.

60. *Ibid.*, p. 83.

61. Cumberland, *op. cit.*, p. 167, See also Powell, *Cooperation in Agriculture, op. cit.*, pp. 171-172.

62. Cumberland, *op. cit.*, pp. 13, 183.

63. *Ibid.*, p. 167.

64. *Ibid.*, p. 167.

65. H. E. Erdman, *The California Fruit Growers Exchange: An Example of Cooperation in the Segregation of Conflicting Interests*, American Council of Pacific Relations, 1933. Erdman made the significant point that the Exchange system of control by the growers through their local and district associations was "just the reverse situation from that found in commercial life, where holding companies usually own and dominate the various units in a group" pp. 14-15.

66. This philosophy has been well expressed by a later general manager: "The management accepts neither the credit for success in the case of a high price level nor the blame for a low price level if that exists because of reasons beyond their control. I think that this is a fundamental point in the social and psychological set-up of the California Fruit Growers Exchange." Paul Armstrong, *American Cooperation*, Vol. 1 (1928), p. 107.

67. Clarence Poe, *How Farmers Cooperate and Double Profits* (New York: Orange Judd Company, 1915), pp. 133-134.

68. Cumberland, *op. cit.*, pp. 147-151.

69. Although there has been no great change in basic structure or in cooperative procedures, there has been an enormous change in scope, governmental relations, and in business organization with the growth and spread of the industry. Some of these changes will be discussed in Volume II of this history.

Chapter XIV

1. The term "model" is used here to indicate that these associations were widely used as models for other groups of growers in fashioning similar associations. These model associations were not perfect in any permanent sense for, like the Ford automobile "model," they were in continuous evolution.

2. For more information on this pioneer association, see W. Paddock, *Fruit Growers Associations*, Colorado Agricultural Experiment Station Bulletin 122 (1907); E. K. Eyerly, "Successful Cooperation Among Fruit Growers," *Journal of Political Economy*, February 1909, pp. 92-95; and Will Payne, "Cooperation—Colorado Apples; Virginia Potatoes; Retail Stores," *Saturday Evening Post*, July 16, 1910, pp. 17-18.

3. See comments of Charles W. Holman on cause of failure of the Grand Junction Fruit Growers Association. He said: "If the organization operates for profit it tends inevitably to become a middleman and not a cooperative." *American Cooperation*, Vol. 1 (1925), p. 167.

4. See C. I. Lewis, *The Apple from Orchard to Market*, Oregon Agricultural Experiment Station Bulletin 94 (1907), p. 39.

5. For significant provisions of this contract see *Better Fruit*, March 1907, p. 4.

6. There is good reason to believe that the Union was greatly influenced in its methods by those of the Grand Junction Fruit Growers Association. The manager of the Union referred to the Grand Junction Association as "the most ably managed of any association that I know of." *Ibid.*, August 1906, pp. 11-12.

7. "This association has made Hood River famous the world over for the excellence of the grading and packing of the apples grown in the Hood River Valley." G. Harold Powell, *Cooperation in Agriculture*, 1913, pp. 221-26. For a full description of the methods of this association, see Lewis, *op. cit.*

8. The first issue of this attractive and well-edited magazine was published in July 1906. Its interest in organization was well expressed by an article in March 1907, "How to Form Fruit Growers Associations." In this article the editor declared *"Better Fruit* took up the work of fruit associations and has kept at it insistently since its initial number. The ground has been so well covered in the way of information as to the importance, necessity, and benefits of associations that there seems to us that the next thing in line necessary is information about constitutions, by-laws, contracts, etc. and we therefore publish in this issue constitutions and contracts of some of the large associations that are successful."

9. The Hood River Apple Growers Association changed its name to Diamond Fruit Growers in 1964.

10. At the 1910 annual meeting of the Oregon State Horticultural Society its president inquired, "Is there peculiarity in climate of California that makes such business organization impossible to apple growers of the Pacific Northwest?" See Joseph Waldo Ellison, "The Cooperative Movement in the Oregon Apple Industry, 1910-1929," *Agricultural History*, April 1939, p. 79.

11. *Ibid.*, p. 79.

12. According to Ellison, this plan—"the first sincere effort to establish a great cooperative association in the Northwest fruit industry—was dashed on the rocks of individualism, local jealousies, and possibly hostile trade interests." *Ibid.*, pp. 79-84.

13. *Ibid.*, p. 85.

14. *Ibid.*, pp. 84-87.

15. Herman Steen, however, held that the "commodity principle" was followed. "They took a leaf out of California's book and decided to organize by commodity, but because their fruit is so diversified they grouped it all together . . ." This was certainly a broad interpretation of the commodity marketing doctrine. *Cooperative Marketing* (New York: Doubleday, Page and Company, 1923), pp. 77-78.

16. Ellison, *op. cit.*, p. 92.

17. See Erich Kraemer and H. E. Erdman, *History of Cooperation in the Marketing of California Fresh Deciduous Fruits*, University of California, Agricultural Experiment Station Bulletin 557, 1933, p. 42.

18. *Ibid.*, pp. 43-44.

19. After the reorganization of the Exchange in 1907 on a capital-stock basis, the directors were elected by the stockholders who were in effect the members. However, provision was made whereby each local association not represented on the board would be represented by an "associate director" who would have all privileges except voting. McKay and Lane classified the organization as "primarily a federation of local associations" but they admitted that "ownership of stock by individuals is unusual in a federation." A. W. McKay and C. H. Lane, *Practical Cooperative Marketing* (New York: John Wiley & Sons, 1928), p. 230.

20. For a complete analysis of the plan, see Kelsey B. Gardner, "Joint Use of a Sales Organization by Two Cooperative Associations," U.S.D.A. Circular No. 10, 1927. The plan was continued until 1942.

21. Kraemer and Erdman, *op. cit.*, p. 61. This was later reduced to a flat 8 per cent in compliance with the provisions of the Capper-Volstead Act of 1922.

22. "It was the disastrous year of 1906 which actually brought about the formation

of a central cooperative selling association.... On top of the demoralized state
of the trade came one of the largest crops that had been produced up to that
time and the country simply would not consume it. Prices fell as low as 70 cents
a barrel and carloads of berries were never shipped because they would not
bring enough to pay freight charges... In addition there were prospects of a
large increase in production of cranberries. Newly planted bogs would soon come
into bearing and growers realized that unless something was done the cranberry
industry would soon be wiped out from lack of profits." Asher Hobson and J.
Burton Chaney, *Sales Methods and Policies of a Growers National Marketing
Agency*, U.S.D.A. Bulletin 1109, January 1923, p. 6.

23. See Wisconsin State Board of Public Affairs, Report Upon Cooperation and
Marketing, Pt. 1, *Agricultural Cooperation*, 1912, p. 65. See also Vernon Goldsworthy, "Cooperative Marketing of Cranberries," *American Cooperation*, 1934,
p. 347.

24. A. U. Chaney, the co-founder of the Wisconsin plan, helped organize the New
Jersey and Massachusetts associations. This fact no doubt facilitated the later
formation of the central sales agency under Mr. Chaney's management. *Ibid.*, p.
347. Each of the state associations was organized originally on a capital-stock
basis. In 1919 all three of the state associations reorganized as non-stock membership associations so as to obtain the protection of the Clayton Act, but this involved no significant change in operating methods. The state associations did
not employ "specific membership contracts" but each grower member, under
by-law provisions, was required to deliver his entire crop. Seasonal pooling
was practiced in Massachusetts, as in Wisconsin, but in New Jersey the pre-
dominance of small growers who preferred "to choose their time of selling"
led to the use of weekly pools. See Hobson and Chaney, *op. cit.*, pp. 13-14.

25. This organization was incorporated as a stock company with an authorized
capital stock of $9,000. As stock was held by each state company in proportion to
acreage controlled, it was thus primarily qualifying membership stock.

26. The state associations were really locals as they operated in highly concentrated
localities of cranberry production. Some of the state associations developed
special revolving fund arrangements and made separate assessments for such
purposes. The funds so acquired were used for the acquisition of office buildings,
packing houses, etc. For a more detailed discussion of the way in which the
Exchange functioned in relationship to the member companies, see Hobson and
Chaney, *op. cit.*

27. A. U. Chaney, "Cranberry Price Policy," *American Cooperation*, Vol. 2 (1925),
pp. 521-22.

28. The first advertising experiments were tried out in 1916 following a period of
low prices largely occasioned by a bumper crop in 1914. The results of the test
convinced the American that a comprehensive advertising program was essential
to its success as a marketing agency. See Goldsworthy, *op. cit.*

29. For complete record see Hobson and Chaney, *op. cit.*, p. 9.

30. *Ibid.*, p. 9.

31. See Payne, *op. cit.*; John Lee Coulter, *Cooperation Among Farmers* (1911), pp.
152-58; Clarence Poe, *How Farmers Cooperate and Double Profits* (1915), pp.
113-22; O. B. Jesness and W. H. Kerr, *Cooperative Purchasing and Marketing
Organizations Among Farmers*, U.S.D.A. Bulletin 547 (1917), pp. 47-48; W.
MacKenzie Stevens, *The Eastern Shore of Virginia Produce Exchange* (type-
written report in files of Cooperative Research and Service Division, 1917); Federal Trade Commission, *Report on Cooperative Marketing* (1928), S. Doc. 95,
70 Cong. 1 ses., pp. 222-23, 434-73.

32. *Ibid.*, p. 435. See also Stevens, *op. cit.*, pp. 5-6.

33. Stevens held that "the exchange is built up on the federation plan . . . a large number of local divisions each with its local government and each of which elects a representative on the central board." *Op. cit.*, p. 13.

34. For a discussion of the significance of this arrangement, see Payne, *op. cit.*, p. 19.

35. Stevens, *op. cit.*, p. 63.

36. The effect of this arrangement was mitigated by the fact that the low cost of shares made them accessible to most growers.

37. *Ibid.* p. 8. As the Exchange was formed before there was knowledge or experience in cooperative techniques, it was necessary to graft cooperative practices onto a capitalistic plan. As Clarence Poe remarked, "The idea of patronage refunds was not abroad in the land at the time the Exchange was organized." *Op. cit.*, p. 12.

38. This surplus fund enabled the Exchange to finance shipments in transit and thus pay growers promptly as they delivered their produce. The fact that growers who sold through the Exchange did not have to wait for their money proved an excellent "talking point." Moreover, by restraining growers who needed their money from selling to cash buyers at low prices this method of prompt payment kept such sales from demoralizing the local price structure. Will Payne writing in 1910 referred to this feature of the Exchange as "unique among cooperative associations." He pointed out that the Exchange "found this surplus very useful . . . for more than once in order to maintain a price for its own product it has gone into the market and bought potatoes . . . and soon routed the bears." *Op. cit.*, p. 19. This is one of the earliest illustrations of a cooperative stabilizing operation.

39. See Stevens, *op. cit.*, p. 95.

40. As Stevens said, "In actual practice . . . about 100 members can control the organization of 2,400 members." *Ibid.*, pp. 19-20.

41. Stevens was of the opinion that the early success of the organization was largely due to the fact that control was held by a few "public-spirited" individuals in that the rank and file of the growers were incapable of successfully directing an important business enterprise. While something can be said for this view when we consider the state of growers' experience and education in the early 1900's, it is also true that the plan of control by stock ownership tended to become customary and finally outlived any usefulness that it may have had during the formative years of the organization when the public spirit of its founders was high. *Ibid.*, pp. 60-61.

42. The influence of the Exchange on the social life of the region served has been set forth as follows by a keen student of rural conditions: "Better farm buildings, more comfortable homes, attractive schools and churches built during this period [1899-1919] all bear eloquent testimony to the improved services rendered by this unique marketing organization." T. B. Manny, *Problems in Cooperation and Experience of Farmers in Marketing Potatoes*, U.S.D.A. Circular No. 87 (1929), p. 4. The Eastern Shore of Virginia Produce Exchange reached its position of greatest influence about 1920. Although subsequently reorganized on a one-man, one-vote basis it never recaptured its earlier prestige in cooperative marketing circles.

43. See H. L. Barnum, "The Michigan Potato Growers' Exchange," *American Cooperation*, Vol. 2 (1925), p. 466.

44. All of the original marketing agreements bore the statement "The agreement has the approval of the U. S. Bureau of Markets." *Ibid.*, p. 469.

45. *Ibid.*, p. 467. See also Federal Trade Commission, *op. cit.*, p. 218.

46. Charles C. Teague, *Fifty Years a Rancher* (Los Angeles: Anderson & Richie, 1944), p. 98.

47. *Ibid.*, p. 101.

48. See Federal Trade Commission, *op. cit.*, p. 212; Steen, *op. cit.*, p. 277.

Chapter XV

1. In a few instances—as in the case of Eastern Shore of Virginia Produce Exchange and the dairy bargaining associations—cooperatives were initially designed to cover wide areas with membership being direct rather than through local organizations. However, prior to 1920 federation was the prevailing pattern for large-scale cooperative development with the exception of the associations described in this chapter.

2. The difference in objectives represented largely a matter of emphasis. Monopoly power was the primary concern of the new philosophy but efficiency in marketing was also considered essential. On the other hand, the advocates of federation were primarily interested in achieving for growers the fruits of marketing efficiency, but they recognized that a substantial control over the crop to be marketed would be helpful to this aim. The first group felt that it was necessary to obliterate the importance of the local unit while the second held with G. Harold Powell, general manager of the California Fruit Growers Exchange, that this was "fundamentally wrong in principle" and contrary to "sound public policy." The differences between the two philosophies will become more apparent as we proceed.

3. Herman Steen, *Cooperative Marketing* (New York: Doubleday, Page and Company, 1923), pp. 6-7.

4. J. R. Gabbart, *The California Citrograph*, December 1915, p. 9.

5. Will Payne, "Cooperation—Prunes and Beans," *The Saturday Evening Post*, May 28, 1910.

6. Information supplied by R. L. Churchill, for many years secretary of the California Lima Bean Growers Association, letter of July 31, 1946.

7. As early as 1893 the Pachappa Orange Growers Association had employed a membership agreement and such "agency" agreements were in common use among the citrus associations by 1909. However, these agreements were not designed to serve as instruments for control of a given crop. While the raisin growers had used "holding contracts" as early as 1898 similar to those of cooperatives formed by the American Society of Equity in the early 1900's, these contracts were more in the nature of pledges than marketing agreements. The contract of the Lima bean growers, especially after it was revised in 1912, was the first significant contract, of the sale and resale type, designed to give complete marketing control to a cooperative association. For a complete discussion of the evolution of the membership contract, see E. G. Nourse, *The Legal Status of Agricultural Cooperation*, Ch. 8, and particularly pp. 189-90.

8. George E. Farrand (the attorney who, as counsel, drafted all of the organization papers and contracts for the Lima Bean Growers Association from 1909 through 1916), in a letter to the author of December 2, 1946, said: "In my opinion the bean contracts were the first contracts used in this modern era whereby the crop was pooled by a commodity throughout the area where produced. In making this statement observe that I used the words 'modern era' because some years before that some sort of plan had been adopted in the lima bean business but which blew up; and I think also that some raisin growers plan had been in

effect before that. . . . The bean association contracts with state-wide coverage, that is coverage as broad as the crop itself, long antedates the contracts which showed up in apricots and prunes and elsewhere. . . ." Farrand in a letter to Chris L. Christensen of March 30, 1926, explained how the raisin growers were influenced by the earlier experience of the bean growers. "When the Associated Raisin Growers were contemplating the organization of their company about 1912 . . . they came to Ventura County and discussed with us the form and set-up of the lima bean growers. . . . [Thus] the lima bean growers quite largely by their precedents furnished forms to the raisin growers though the raisin growers did not note some of the changes through which the lima bean growers were going at this time."

9. "The contract with growers gave the association full title over beans delivered and this permitted the association to store the beans and use the warehouse receipts so secured as collateral for borrowing funds to procure more beans which could be similarly warehoused and used as collateral for procuring more beans, and so on until the equities were exhausted." Letter from George E. Farrand, December 2, 1946. For a dramatic account of the first year's experience of this association, and its first year of operation, see Payne, *op. cit.*

10. With reference to this experience, Farrand said: "It was obvious that this expedient was but temporary and of doubtful validity. The plan was immediately attacked by hostile interests who complained to the Department of Justice about it. . . . Before their complaints could be considered . . . the value of the agreement had been obtained and there was no longer any necessity for its maintenance . . . When the matter came before the federal Department of Justice, a substitute plan had already been prepared and that disposed of the situation." (Letter of December 2, 1946.)

Will Payne pointed out, in 1910, that while the first year's operations "had furnished a striking object lesson, the cooperators hope to control a large part of the crop on a purely cooperative basis without having to adopt the unusual expedient of buying up for cash an important part of the output." *Op. cit.*

11. "We did not use the word 'pool' but used the word 'commingled' simply because at that time we were fearful that a pool was illegal. . . ." (George E. Farrand as quoted by Harry M. Creech in letter of March 17, 1926, to E. G. Nourse.) Significantly, the contract also maintained that the objective was more efficient marketing. "The association has been incorporated . . . for the purpose of more conveniently and economically handling and marketing the crops of lima beans to be grown, handled, or controlled by them and of establishing for the product, recognition as a standard commodity and for itself a reputation as a medium through which by fair dealing it may secure a closer relationship between the grower and the distributor or consumer and a more stable and extended market for such product. . . ."

12. "We had many discussions in Washington and elsewhere with the federal authorities endeavoring to sustain our rights as growers to form a uniform pooling contract and cooperatively market our crops and distribute them into the markets." George E. Farrand, as quoted in letter from Harry M. Creech to E. G. Nourse, March 17, 1926.

13. According to Farrand: "[The Dept. of Justice] was neither friendly nor unfriendly so far as I could tell at that time. They permitted us to form marketing pools as an offset to broker attack. . . You can see though that the so-called money pool [carried on under the 1909 contract] was quite different from the ordinary pooling contract. I was always dubious about its validity but it served its purpose. . . ." Letter of December 2, 1946.

14. Voting was to be in accordance with tonnage pooled so that "each member would have one vote for every ten tons of beans or a major portion thereof

marketed." There was to be a membership fee of $100 and the marketing agreement, as revised in June 1912, was to be used. It will be recalled that this agreement authorized the association to purchase beans on the open market equal to 25 per cent of the beans placed in the pool. Farrand's plan also ingeniously provided for "a reserve fund" and "an insurance fund" which were designed to provide necessary capital while strengthening membership support. (Letter from Farrand of December 2, 1946)

15. This plan is of interest in that it recognized that the membership form of organization had inherent legal and cooperative advantages two years prior to the enactment of Section 6 of the Clayton Act. If this was apparent from the experiences of the bean growers it could not have escaped the attention of representatives of the Department of Justice or of the Office of Markets. In fact, the new plan was no doubt devised with the thought that it would be acceptable to the Department of Justice.

16. See Gabbert, op. cit., pp. 9-10.

17. Significantly the organization papers of the walnut association formed in 1912 had also been drafted by Mr. Farrand.

18. For a colorful account of these early efforts, see Will Payne, "Cooperation—The Raisin Baron," Saturday Evening Post, April 30, 1910. In 1898 there was formed the Raisin Growers Association "which for six years dominated the situation controlling 75 to 80 per cent of the crop. Its form was simple. To join it a grower signed a contract agreement to turn his crop over to the association for three successive years. The association then sold the crop to the packers." This bargaining type of association had several weaknesses. There was no way of restricting benefits to members. M. Theodore Kearney, the leader of the association movement, maintained that the association thus "held the umbrella" for the non-member grower. Moreover, there was no practical way of compelling growers to live up to their contracts. To remedy this latter situation, the association devised what was known as the "New Jersey Lease," by which the grower "instead of merely contracting to deliver his crop to the association outlet, leased his land to the association becoming its tenant. This gave the association absolute control over his crop." Kearney realized that the association would be dependent upon the commercial packers until the association could develop its own packing facilities. To meet this problem, he devised a supplementary contract which authorized the association to "withhold $10 a ton of the price to form a permanent capital for the purpose of building and equipping its own packing houses." If carried out, this arrangement would have provided the association with a fund of a million dollars for this purpose within a few years. These devices might have enabled the association to establish itself in an effective way if it had not been for the erratic temperament of Kearney, whose dictatorial qualities earned for himself the sobriquet, "The Raisin Baron." In 1904 he alienated many of his followers by dumping raisins on the market in order to force non-cooperative growers to recognize the association's power. For a contemporary account of the old raisin growers association, see Edward F. Adams, The Modern Farmer in His Business Relations, 1899, pp. 458-69. It is of interest that Adams considered this association to be the first successful cooperatively formed "trust" (p. 440). Adams felt that trusts of agricultural producers were needed as an offset to the power of industrial trusts.

19. An interesting account of the formation of this association was given by Wylie Giffen, its president, in testimony on Authorized Associations of Producers of Agricultural Products, hearings before a subcommittee of the Committee on the Judiciary, U. S. Senate, 19 Cong., 1 sess., 1921, pp. 89-99.

20. The association adopted the capital stock form of organization in order to acquire capital for acquisition of packing house facilities. President W. M.

Giffen, later said, "We organized a stock company because . . . there was not any law of California by which we could organize a cooperative company on a strictly capital basis. We organized the only kind of company we could at that time, to have money, and we felt that money was absolutely necessary." Although Giffen admitted that sale of stock to non-members was probably a mistake from the cooperative standpoint, he called attention to the fact that this procedure did much to obtain the good-will of the business community. *Ibid.*, p. 98.

21. The president of the association admitted that "this plan of organization is a sort of benevolent autocracy . . . it is not democratic but it works." See Steen, *op. cit.*, p. 26. It was Steen's view that the company was "the only real 'trust' ever formed and operated by farmers." But he maintained that it is "unique" because it "never attempts to restrict production . . . ," (p. 22). The use of a voting-trust agreement of this type had been effectively employed by the Standard Oil Company and other early trusts of the agency marketing type about 1880. This form of industrial combination had been largely superseded by the holding company device, when it was resurrected in 1912 by the California Associated Raisin Company. See Jeremiah Jenks and Walter E. Clarke, *The Trust Company* (1929), pp. 30 ff. and 132 ff.

22. For example, one student of cooperative organization questioned the advantage "of having one large organization made up directly of individual growers who have no voice whatever in the affairs of the organization except at long intervals." John William Lloyd, "Cooperative and Other Organized Methods of Marketing California Horticultural Products," *University of Illinois Studies in the Social Sciences*, Vol. VIII, No. 1, March 1919, p. 92. As "trusts" were under vigorous public attack in the years following the organization of the company, the use of the trustee device made the company especially vulnerable to attack by hostile trade interests or others as "the raisin trust." To some extent, Col. Weinstock gave recognition to the danger in trustee control through his suggestion that a representative of the public should be placed on the board of directors of associations so organized (see Ch. IX).

23. When the company began operations in 1913, there was a large "hold-over" still in growers' hands. To keep this "hold-over" from disrupting its efforts, the company undertook to purchase it at a set price of two and one-half cents per pound. The association also undertook to increase its control of the new 1913 crop by offering to buy from non-members at an outright price of four cents per pound or a price three quarters of one cent higher than the advance guaranteed under the contract. Both of these actions were maneuvers designed to establish the position of the association on the market and were used only in the initial year. The president of the company later referred to them as a "mistake" and said, "I think any organization that tries to do both a commercial and a fraternal business . . . is going to eventually break up." Testimony of Giffen, *op. cit.*, p. 102.

24. *Ibid.*, pp. 100-01.

25. Fred K. Howard, "*History of Sun Maid Raisin Growers*," published by Sun Maid Raisin Growers, 1922, p. 43.

26. Soon after the association was established, a sales analyst was employed to find out what was wrong with the raisin industry. His report showed that the consumer was not eating raisins. The association thereupon proceeded to create a brand and establish standards (1914) and to follow this up with an aggressive advertising program designed to stimulate the desire of the consumer for raisins. H. Clyde Filley, *Cooperation in Agriculture* (New York: John Wiley & Sons, 1929), p. 210.

27. Federal Trade Commission, *Report on Cooperative Marketing,* 1928, p. 109; Howard, *op. cit.,* p. 43.

28. However, by refusing to renew its contracts with growers until 15,000 additional acres were signed up, the California Associated Raisin Company greatly increased its control over the 1916 and 1917 raisin crops. See *The California Citrograph,* March 1916, p. 9.

29. The president of the organization later declared: "We were trying . . . to remedy the weak point in our contract. . . . Under the first contract the grower could sell us his crop and not be a stockholder . . . so we required that every grower should take a small proportion of his pay for his raisins in the capital stock in the company." Giffen, *op. cit.,* p. 109.

30. For the main provision of this decree see Federal Trade Commission, *op. cit.,* pp. 106-07.

31. Although the raisin growers strongly resisted the government's efforts to change their form of organization, it was later generally admitted that the long-run results were beneficial to sound cooperative development.

32. In 1920 the association had about 90 per cent of the crop under its control. Up to this date, however, the monopoly power of the organization had not been fully exploited. See Jenks and Clarke, *op. cit.,* pp. 132-34.

33. Experience after 1920 soon disclosed that such plans could not be long effective without power to control production. During the years from 1920 to 1923 the association was fairly successful in maintaining prices but this success proved to be its undoing. Production expanded so rapidly that the association found it increasingly difficult to sell at remunerative prices. As a result many growers deserted the association leaving it with the impossible task of market stabilization.

34. *First Annual Report of the State Market Director of California,* 1916, p. 10.

35. As many of the dried peach growers were members of the raisin association, this was an implied criticism of the trustee device as used by that organization. Weinstock's suggestion was designed to meet a weakness inherent in the trustee system of control.

36. *Second Annual Report of the State Market Director of California,* 1917, p. 10.

37. *Fourth Annual Report of the State Market Director of California,* 1919, pp. 12-16. The testing time for this association did not come until prices collapsed in 1920-1921 when it became necessary to change the plan of organization.

38. In 1893 the Santa Clara County Fruit Exchange had been formed to market the fruit of several local drying associations. The object "was to obtain entire control of the products of that section." But little progress was made in achieving that goal. The exchange was a loose federation with no contractual power over individual growers. See Edward F. Adams, *The Modern Farmer,* 1897, p. 486.

39. According to Herman Steen, the prune and apricot association was the first cooperative to work out this double plan of organization on a large scale. Since the plan was largely devised by Manager H. C. Coykendall, it became known as the "Coykendall Plan." *Op. cit.,* pp. 33, 341-42.

40. Federal Trade Commission, *op. cit.,* pp. 99-100. See also Steen, *op. cit.,* pp. 35-36.

41. As late as 1915 the Office of Markets and Rural Organization issued a farmers' bulletin to promote the formation of community egg circles. A foreword declared that the bulletin "would be of especial interest at this time to farmers in the cotton belt who desire to diversify their farming because of the economic crisis which adversely effects the cotton crop at present." This bulletin provided a model preliminary agreement and constitution, with receipt forms for this form

of cooperative association. See C. E. Bassett and W. H. Kerr, *The Community Egg Circle*, U.S.D.A. Farmers Bulletin 656.

42. See A. V. Swarthout, *An Analysis of the Business of the Poultry Producers of Central California*, U.S.D.A. Circular No. 111 (1921), pp. 6-7. For the complete story see historical manuscript by Knox Bode in the files of the Poultry Producers of Central California, and J. H. Barber, *The Development of Poultry and Egg Marketing in the United States*, Transactions of the First World's Poultry Conference (1921).

43. J. H. Barber, chairman of the original promotion committee and first general manager, gave Weinstock full credit for getting the organization formed and into effective operation. "Without him perhaps all of our hopes would have fallen flat. Without him I doubt that we could have matched wits with the many jobbers and commission men who did not love us. Colonel Weinstock watched and warned us." *Nulaid News*, February 1937.

44. See the *First Annual Report of the State Market Director of California*, 1916, pp. 16, 92-95. It is of interest that Aaron Sapiro's first experience in drafting cooperative organization papers was gained in drawing up these documents. In preparing the produce sales agreement Sapiro was guided by the contract drawn up in 1914 by members of the Sonoma federation, as well as by the contract of the Associated Raisin Growers Company. See Bode, *op. cit.*

45. See *Fourth Annual Report of the State Market Director of California*, 1919, pp. 24-31.

46. See J. M. Tinley and E. A. Stokdyk, *Operations of the Poultry Producers of Southern California, Inc.*, University of California Agricultural Experiment Station Bulletin No. 516, 1931, pp. 32 ff.

47. The Washington Association did not adopt a membership agreement until 1920. The Pacific Cooperative Poultry Producers replaced the Oregon Poultry Producers Association which had been formed in 1919 as a federation of egg circles. By 1921, all of these organizations were operating in a similar manner. See J. H. Barber, *The Development of Poultry and Egg Marketing in the United States, op. cit.* For the early history of the Pacific Cooperative Poultry Producers, see "Twenty-Five Years of Cooperation," a booklet issued by the association in December 1945.

Chapter XVI

1. For detailed information by commodities see Harold Barger and Hans H. Landsberg, *American Agriculture, 1899-1933—A Study of Output, Employment, and Productivity* (New York: National Bureau of Economic Research, 1942), pp. 43-44, 251.

2. See article by Solomon Kusnets on *Agricultural Machine Industry* in *Encyclopedia of Social Sciences*. The figures on farm machinery include implements for cultivation, harvesting, etc., as well as farm tools, windmills, etc.

3. For more complete information see Victor S. Clark, *History of Manufacturers in the United States*, Vol. 3 (1893-1928), pp. 289-291.

4. Kusnets, *op. cit.*

5. See Larry Wherry, *The Golden Anniversary of Scientific Feeding* (Milwaukee: The Business Press, 1947), p. 31, Appendix I.

6. G. Harold Powell, *Cooperation in Agriculture* (New York: The MacMillan Company, 1913), p. 8.

Chapter XVII

1. For a description of group-buying activities in a fairly typical state in 1915 see E. Dana Durand and H. B. Price, *Cooperative Buying by Farmers' Clubs in Minnesota* (St. Paul: University of Minnesota Agricultural Experiment Station Bulletin 167, 1917). This bulletin gives detailed information on the buying procedures used by 50 individual clubs. Information on the extensive group-buying activities carried on in Ohio in 1920 under the auspices of the Grange, the Farmers' Union, the Gleaners, Farm Bureaus or independent farm clubs is given by H. E. Erdman, *Organizations Among Ohio Farmers* (Wooster: Ohio Agricultural Experiment Station, No. 342, 1920).

2. In the early 1930's the author, then an agricultural economist for the North Carolina Agricultural Experiment Station, found from an informal survey that a considerable amount of group buying was being carried on in North Carolina with the active encouragement and assistance of county agricultural agents and teachers of vocational agriculture.

3. Clarence Poe, *How Farmers Cooperate and Double Profits* (New York: Orange Judd Company, 1915), pp. 37-47.

4. C. R. Fay, *Cooperation at Home and Abroad* (London, P. S. King and Son, 1908), pp. 135-148.

5. G. Harold Powell, *Cooperation in Agriculture* (New York: The Macmillan Company, 1913), pp. 250-257.

6. Alexander E. Cance, *The Farmers' Cooperative Exchange* (Amherst: Massachusetts Agricultural College, 1914), p. 3. More information on the contents of this bulletin is given in Chapter XIX.

7. J. A. Bexell, Hector MacPherson, and W. H. Kerr, *A Survey of Typical Cooperative Stores in the United States*, U.S.D.A. Bulletin No. 394, 1916, p. 26.

8. J. A. Bexell and W. H. Kerr, *Business Practices and Accounts for Cooperative Stores*, U.S.D.A. Bulletin No. 381, 1916.

9. Many state college bulletins on agricultural cooperation gave information on cooperative stores from 1914 to 1920. The degree of success reported was not impressive. For example there is this statement on cooperative stores by John D. Black and Frank Robotka in *Farmers' Cooperation in Minnesota, 1913-19*, Bulletin 184 (1919) of the University of Minnesota Experiment Station: "It is a business that has many difficulties for the inexperienced, and more attempts at cooperation fail in this field than in any of the others thus far discussed." These were cooperative creameries, cheese factories, farmers' elevators, potato associations, and livestock shipping associations. See p. 37.

10. Many cooperative stores suffered severe losses with the abrupt drop in prices in the fall of 1920, and a number failed to recover.

11. See Wells A. Sherman, *Marketing Fruits and Vegetables* (New York: A. W. Shaw and Company, 1928), pp. 79, 101.

12. See "Cooperation in Handling and Marketing Fruit," *U.S.D.A. Yearbook of Agriculture, 1910*, p. 398.

13. O. B. Jesness and W. H. Kerr, *Cooperative Purchasing and Marketing Organizations Among Farmers in the United States*, U.S.D.A. Bulletin No. 547, 1917, p. 33.

14. See Reuben A. Holman, *The Romance of the Farmers' Grain Dealers Association of Iowa* (1947), p. 87.

15. See Laurence Farlow, *The Farmers' Elevator Movement in Illinois*, Farmers Grain Dealers Association of Illinois, 1928, pp. 50-52. Holman, *op. cit.*, pp. 90-91.

16. John R. Humphrey and W. H. Kerr, *Patronage Dividends in Cooperative Grain Companies*, U.S.D.A. Bulletin No. 371, 1916, p. 5-6.

17. For early history of federal income tax exemption see John H. Davis, *An Economic Analysis of the Tax Status of Farmer Cooperatives* (Washington, D.C.: American Institute of Cooperation, 1950), pp. 60-61. See also Joseph G. Kenkel, *The Cooperative Elevator Movement*, 1922, pp. 42-43.

18. Black and Robotka, *op. cit.*, p. 27.

19. Jesness and Kerr, *op. cit.*

20. Letter of L. S. Herron to author, December 12, 1946.

21. See H. C. Filley, *Cooperation in Agriculture* (New York: John Wiley & Sons, 1929), pp. 362-363.

22. For more complete information see Joseph G. Knapp, *Farmers in Business* (Washington, D. C.: American Institute of Cooperation, 1963), pp. 205-211.

Chapter XVIII

1. See articles of incorporation of the Southern California Fruit Exchange as adopted October 3, 1895.

2. See Paul S. Armstrong, *American Cooperation* (1938), p. 657.

3. However, the district exchanges were actually partners in the enterprise for they selected the directors of the California Fruit Growers Exchange, who, in turn served as directors for the Fruit Growers Supply Company. Thus the Supply Company simply used the mechanism of the Exchange as a basis for organization. In fact, the Supply Company was a part of the Exchange since its organization was predicated upon the existence of the Exchange. The two organizations served practically the same group of local associations although in the beginning a few associations who were not in the Exchange system were permitted to hold stock. With the adoption of the revolving fund plan of financing in 1918, described later in this chapter, only members of the Exchange could hold memberships in the Supply Company.

4. The articles of incorporation are quoted in full in G. Harold Powell, *Cooperation in Agriculture* (1913), pp. 254-56.

5. Walter V. Woehlke, "Buying for Sellers," *The Country Gentleman*, May 29, 1915.

6. *Ibid.*

7. D. C. Fessenden, *The California Citrograph*, August 1916.

8. A. D. Shammel has given unstinted credit to the leaders in the Exchange for facilitating his investigations and for making the results of his investigations effective for the benefit of the California citrus industry. He held that "the widespread use of the improved methods of bud selection and propagation could not have been so quickly and efficiently introduced commercially in the citrus industry without the active participation of the cooperative growers' organization, the California Fruit Growers Exchange." See "Cooperative Improvement of Citrus Varieties," *U.S.D.A. Yearbook of Agriculture* (1919), pp. 275 ff. This article describes fully the bud selection service as it was then being provided by the Fruit Growers Supply Company.

9. Woehlke, *op. cit.*

10. However, when the Supply Company was formed it was apparently intended that profits would be returned as dividends on stock. The minutes for December 11, 1907, state that "profits made or arising from the material supply department, if any, shall be paid from time to time to the holders of the subscribed stock of the company as dividends."

11. For example, all orders for nails were handled as one pool. The company purchased nails to satisfy the orders of the local associations and then charged the local associations a price which would cover all costs and overhead. In one early year the price of nails was not changed from the preceding season since the benefit of lower prices could more easily be made available through a change in the refund rate.

12. Woehlke, *op. cit.*

13. On November 26, 1916, the board had approved a recommendation of the manager "that hereafter goods be billed at prices that will include a profit adjustment to meet competition, and that such classified record be kept as will enable the management to make an equitable return of the profits to the members at the end of the year."

14. The demand for service from non-members caused the board on May 23, 1917, to restrict service to members. The policy was then established "to discontinue accepting and filling orders for supplies for the use of associations or individual shippers who are not members of the Supply Company."

15. From time to time the subscription agreements were extended to obtain capital contributions from new member associations. See minutes of Fruit Growers Supply Company, June 21, 1911, also June 28, 1911. See also minutes of August 11 and November 4, 1914. On September 29, 1915, the board approved a recommendation of the manager that all new associations to become members "be required to subscribe for stock 1 cent per box over 5 years."

16. George E. Farrand recalls that "for a long time it was quite apparent in Supply Company circles that the distribution of the stock of the Company among the locals was on an inequitable basis. Some groups which used Supply Company facilities a lot had little stock. Others who had a lot of stock used it only a little." It was believed that the harmonizing of financial investment with patronage would provide a stronger basis for permanent growth. (Letter of June 27, 1947)

17. As early as January 23, 1908, Director J. S. Edwards proposed that a readjustment of stock should be made "from time to time" and "that the readjustment shall be made, when it is made, in such a manner as will put the holders of stock on the basis of the shipments of the year in which adjustment is made." This proposal, which anticipated the adoption of the revolving fund agreement of 1918, failed of approval by a vote of five to eight.

18. See Rahno Mabel McCurdy, *The History of the California Fruit Growers Exchange*, Los Angeles, 1925, p. 55. The report of the manager of the Supply Company for the year ending August 31, 1916, contained the following comment: "The manager has submitted to the Board of Directors a comprehensive and flexible plan for the holding of the capital stock of the Supply Company by the associations. . . . If the plan is adopted by the stockholders, it will give them greater liberty in the handling of their investment . . . without impairment of their representative or voting rights."

19. *Ibid.*, p. 55.

20. On June 27, 1917, the board approved a motion "that we proceed to make an effort to work out the plan prepared by J. S. Edwards and attempt to fit it into the requirements of the Supply Company." On October 3, 1917, George E. Farrand reported "on his investigation of the capital stock readjustment plan submitted some time ago by Director J. S. Edwards, and he pointed out the necessary steps to be taken in order to bring about such a reorganization." This was made a matter of special order of business for a later meeting. On November 6, 1917, Farrand explained "the method of handling the Fruit Growers Supply Company stock on a revolving fund plan." The plan, after many meetings of discussion, was adopted in principle on March 20, to be

placed in operation on September 1, 1918. At this time Mr. Farrand was authorized to prepare the revolving fund contract with the assistance of the manager and the assistant manager, E. S. Dezell. The plan was further studied in several board meetings and the revolving fund contract was finally adopted on July 10, 1918, upon motion of J. S. Edwards, with the second of P. T. Dreher.

21. The possibilities of revolving fund financing had already intrigued the interest of Mr. Farrand and he was quick to appreciate that the problem of devising a plan for the Supply Company "was unique both from the standpoint of legal draftsmanship and of social objectives." When he set to work on the problem there were many theories as to how the plan might be developed and he patiently studied all suggestions in coming to his own conclusions. He recalls that his own conception of the plan passed through various stages and that at one time he thought of the plan as "a caterpillar plan because it picked up its track as it went along." Farrand saw that the idea was of more than incidental significance in that it could provide an impeccable legal procedure through which the members of a cooperative association could finance their organization in proportion to the utilization of its services. He thus gave the idea legal exactness and financial respectability and he presented the plan so succinctly that its practical significance could be immediately understood. In his opinion: "The equity of it was so simple that it did not take much talking to convince people that it was the right way to proceed." Farrand has never claimed that the plan as devised was original with him, although he admitted that he contributed "practically all of the language and phraseology and most of the basic thinking involved . . . While I did not just step out and create the plan . . . I did see a chance to apply some of the fundamental rules of equity to the law of corporations and put them in the form of a contract." Letters of June 16, June 28, August 28, and September 19, 1945; and of May 29 and June 12, 1947; and of August 17 and August 19, 1948.

22. McCurdy, op. cit., p. 55.

23. Letter of June 27, 1947.

24. See Irwin W. Rust and Kelsey B. Gardner, Sunkist Growers, Inc.: A California Adventure in Agricultural Cooperation, Farmer Cooperative Service Circular 27, 1960, pp. 77-78.

25. However, a less ambitious revolving fund plan was adopted by the shareholders of the California Fruit Exchange on January 8, 1918, while the Supply Company plan was still in process of development. It is probable that the California Fruit Exchange plan was modeled to some extent on the plan being then devised by the Fruit Growers Supply Company.

26. For a review of Sunkist's experience with revolving fund plans see Grace Larsen and H. E. Erdman, "Development of Revolving Finance in Sunkist Growers," Journal of Farm Economics, November 1959. For a more general history of revolving fund financing see Henry E. Erdman and Grace Larsen, Revolving Finance in Agricultural Cooperatives (Madison, Wisc.: Mimir Publishers, Inc., 1965.)

Chapter XIX

1. James Ford, Cooperation in New England—Urban and Rural (New York: The Russell Sage Foundation, 1913), pp. 95-111.

2. See Chapters IV and VII.

3. This law was actively sponsored by The New England Homestead and the State Grange.

4. For a profile of this interesting man see Kenneth Hinshaw, "Horace Moses: A Great Friend of Farm People" in *Great American Cooperators* (Joseph G. Knapp, and associates, Washington, D.C.: American Institute of Cooperation, 1967, pp. 353-357).

5. An article in the *New England Homestead* of May 9, 1914, points out that the project had been incubating for about eight months and that the plan was being fathered by the Springfield board of trade with the encouragement of the U. S. Department of Agriculture, state agriculture colleges, the Hampden County Improvement League, and similar organizations.

6. In an editorial, the *New England Homestead* (May 9, 1914) held that the "Exposition will be the most comprehensive and far-reaching fair in New England. ... This is to be no ordinary fair but a great exposition broad enough in its scope to cover every line of activity in agriculture, horticulture, forestry, education, domestic science, and recreation."

7. The cynicism of the *New England Homestead* on the stated objectives of the conference as expressed in an editorial entitled "Up the Wrong Tree" (Sept. 16, 1916) no doubt greatly influenced the direction taken by the conference itself. "These good folks who have called the New England Farm and Business Conference . . . are again on the wrong track. The call lays emphasis on 'increasing the production of foodstuffs' . . . there is not a word in the call that touches the most vital thing—that of better organization, better distribution, better marketing. . . . The true way out is to cut this cheap talk about increasing production and cooperate with the farmer for improved marketing. There are some points in common between the farmer and city businessman but crop production is not one of them."

It is of interest also that Herbert Myrick, the publisher of the *New England Homestead* gave the conference its key note by declaring "This conference should be primarily concerned with helping farmers to obtain a better price for what they already produce before urging increased production." The importance of cooperation as a means of providing better business organization for farmers was also emphasized at the conference by Theodore M. Vail, then chairman of the board of directors of the American Telephone and Telegraph Company. Vail held that "cooperation can do much to advance rural interests . . . it is the golden rule applied to commercialism and industrialism." (*New England Homestead*, Sept. 23, 1916.)

8. See *New England Homestead* of September 23 and October 14, 1916.

9. Sherley, in the *Eastern States Magazine* for September 1919, stated that the field division was set up "to reinforce all existing agencies." When the field department was started there were several agencies that worked in the field of rural organization—the Extension Service of the U.S.D.A., the colleges, and the Farm Bureaus. This work "called for earnest support to encourage cooperative purchasing of farm supplies and marketing of farm produce." Sherley pointed out that: "These and other matters of farm business which could not logically be undertaken directly by the organization responsible for the Exposition justified the establishing of a central agency."

10. At that time—as will be discussed later—an ingenious plan for providing working capital through the establishment of a trust fund was then being developed. While the services of the Exchange were being established, the salary of the manager and that of the secretary was paid by the League along with incidental expenses involved in local organizational work. The League also furnished office space, an arrangement which continued for several years.

11. According to Selby, the organizers of the Exchange contemplated the use of a trust fund when they adopted the non-stock plan of organization. "The develop-

ment of the Agricultural Trust and the Farmers' Exchange was parallel and complemented each other. The interest in getting the Exchange established was accompanied by plans for financing [through the Trust] and it was not a later improvision. The use of such trust funds for the purpose in mind was then well established in New England, and was facilitated by the laws of Massachusetts." (Letter of H. W. Selby, April 16, 1948)

12. See article by Howard Selby, *New England Homestead*, August 17, 1918.

13. Letter from Howard Selby, April 16, 1948.

14. The Board also voted to accept the services of E. S. Savage of Cornell University in connection with determining the ingredients of the proposed Eastern States dairy feed. It is of interest that the Directors voted also to extend the service of the Eastern States Farmers' Exchange into New York, where the G.L.F. had not yet been formed to perform a state-wide purchasing service for New York farmers.

15. At this time, such service was not generally available through state colleges, state departments of agriculture, or similar agencies.

Chapter XX

1. For a comprehensive history of the G.L.F. see Joseph G. Knapp, *Seeds That Grew—A History of the Cooperative Grange League Federation Exchange* (Hinsdale, N. Y.: Anderson House, 1960).

2. Dr. Galloway had come to Cornell following a distinguished career in the U.S.D.A. It is of interest that the early cooperative marketing studies of Charles Brand were made under his general supervision, as Chief of the Bureau of Plant Industry.

3. See M. C. Burritt, *The County Agent and the Farm Bureau*, pp. 170-71.

4. The work of the first county Farm Bureaus was determined largely by the desires of the farmers themselves, as there was little agreement among sponsors as to what they ought to do. The stated objectives of several of the county Farm Bureaus organized in New York in 1913 and 1914 show that farmers expected assistance in forming marketing and purchasing associations. For example, the first of the declared objects of the Farm Improvement Association of Broome County (formed on October 10, 1913) was "to foster cooperation in the buying and selling operations necessary to farming." Alfred Charles True, *A History of Agricultural Extension Work in the United States, 1785-1923* (1928), pp. 79, 82.

5. E. R. Eastman, *The Trouble Maker* (1925), pp. 19-20. Eastman was himself one of the pioneer county agents. In a companion novel, *Tough Sod* (1944), Eastman dealt with the complaints of farmers in buying farm supplies that led to the formation of the G.L.F. These novels catch the spirit of frustration and bitterness in rural New York from 1914 to 1920 that determined farmers to organize for their economic self-protection.

6. E. R. Eastman, *These Changing Times*, 1927, p. 156.

7. Burritt, *op. cit.*, pp. 78-79, 87.

8. For a biographical sketch see 'Howard Edward Babcock—A Renaissance Man" by Warren A. Ranney in *Great American Cooperators* (Joseph G. Knapp, and associates, Washington, D. C.: American Institute of Cooperation, 1967, pp. 42-49).

9. Excerpt from statement by E. S. Savage on *History of Open Formula Feeds*, October 17, 1946.

10. Preliminary Report of the New York Joint Legislative Committee on Dairy Products, Live-Stock and Poultry (Wicks' Report), pp. 784 ff.
11. *Ibid.*, pp. 790 ff.
12. Letter of July 1, 1946.
13. H. E. Babcock, "The G.L.F. Idea and Its Development" (a talk to G.L.F. employees), October 1937.
14. *Ibid.*

Chapter XXI

1. Selig Perlman and Philip Taft, *History of Labor in the United States 1896-1932*, 1933, pp. 3-4.
2. See Paul H. Nystrom, *Economics of Retailing*, Vol. 1 (1930 revised ed.).
3. Albert Sonnichsen, *Consumers' Cooperation* (New York: The Macmillan Company, 1919), p. 150.
4. This book, which no doubt drew inspiration from Edward Bellamy's famous book, *Looking Backward*, espoused the idea that all business activity could be organized as a world department store with each industry being organized cooperatively. The preface declared: "It is intended to unite producer and consumer through mill, farm, supply store, etc., into one combination, eliminating all waste and loss of energy, and for the benefit of all."
5. Ira B. Cross, *The Cooperative Store in the United States* (Twelfth Biennial Report of the Wisconsin Bureau of Labor and Industrial Statistics 1905-06), p. 36.
6. From a circular of the Association, quoted in *Ibid.*, p. 36.
7. *Ibid.*, p. 36.
8. James Ford, in referring to New England cooperative store federations, said: "There remains today only the Boston Cooperative Exchange which is now endeavoring to induce private retailers to adopt cooperative methods." *Cooperation in New England—Urban and Rural*, 1913, p. 81.
9. Letter of Charles W. Manty, April 22, 1946.
10. See Frank Aallonen, *Maynard Weavers*, 1941, pp. 33, 39.
11. See Nicholas Paine Gilman, *Profit Sharing Between Employer and Employee*, 1889, p. 303. Nelson had founded the N. O. Nelson Manufacturing Company in 1877. It became one of the largest concerns in the world engaged in the making of building and plumbing supplies. He had become interested in profit-sharing in 1886, and in 1890 he had founded a model community at LeClaire, near Edwardsville, Illinois. Here in 1892 he had established a cooperative store for employees, which for many years was a cooperative "show place." Nelson's interest in profit-sharing and cooperation took him to London in 1895 where he was active in the formation of the International Cooperative Alliance. *Proceedings of First International Cooperative Congress*, August 1895, pp. 185-86.
12. *American Cooperative News*, October 1898.
13. For a contemporary report on the formation of The National Cooperative League see Cross, *op. cit.*, pp. 37-39.
14. See Horace M. Kallen, *The Decline and Rise of the Consumer*, 1936, p. 249.
15. Emerson P. Harris, *Cooperation, the Home of the Consumer*, 1918, pp. 292-93.
16. Kallen, *op. cit.*, p. 249.
17. See the interpretative article on Nelson by Leo W. Stephens in *Dictionary of American Biography*, Vol. XIII.

18. The Frankford Grocery Company, organized in 1888, was one of the first efforts of this kind. See Wilford L. White, *Cooperative Retail Buying Associations* (New York: McGraw-Hill Book Company, 1930), pp. 14, 18-20.

19. According to Davis Douthit, the general manager of the Cooperating Merchants Company, Edward T. Keyes—inspired by accounts of the success of cooperative stores in Great Britain—"became obsessed with the idea" of converting member stores "into retail consumers cooperatives," and organized the Right Relationship League to further this objective. With the death of Keyes in 1905, the work of the League as an adjunct of the Company languished, and in 1908 the company itself disintegrated. *Nobody Owns Us—The Story of Joe Gilbert, Midwestern Rebel* (1948), pp. 66-70, 81-82.

20. Cross, *op. cit.*, pp. 33-34.

21. For a sympathetic account of the work and influence of the Right Relationship League in its heyday, see John Lee Coulter, *Cooperation Among Farmers,* 1917, pp. 261-269.

22. See V. S. Alanne, "The Right Relationship League," *The Cooperative Builder,* June 1, 1935, p. 5.

23. *True Cooperation,* a pamphlet issued by the Right Relationship League about 1910, p. 2.

24. Sonnichsen, *op. cit.*, p. 152.

25. See E. M. Tousley, "Putting Cooperation on a Business Basis," in *Marketing and Farm Credits,* 1915, pp. 50-56. Tousley, as the manager of the Right Relationship League, was a recognized cooperative leader.

26. For more comprehensive information see Colston Estey Warne, *Consumers' Cooperative Movement in Illinois* (Chicago: The University of Chicago Press, 1926).

27. For more comprehensive information see Warne, *op. cit.*

28. See Gordon S. Watkins, *Cooperation: A Study in Constructive Reform,* University of Illinois Bulletin, Vol. 18, No. 28, March 14, 1921, pp. 61-65.

29. Warne, *op. cit.*, pp. 59-60.

30. *Ibid.*, p. 94.

31. For more complete information on the methods and experience of this association, see Watkins, *op. cit.*, pp. 55, 60-61; Sonnichsen, *op. cit.*, pp. 158-59; Florence E. Parker, "Consumers' Cooperative Wholesale Societies in the United States," *Monthly Labor Review,* Vol. X (1920), pp. 957-58.

32. The flamboyant story of this organization is well told by Douthit, *op. cit.*, pp. 162-171. Douthit characterized it as "one of these cooperatives-in-a-hurry" which were organized at about this time "to get the world by the tail by Christmas." M. W. Thatcher (later general manger of the Farmers Union Grain Terminal Association) served as manager of the auditing department. For additional information see Watkins, *op. cit.*, pp. 56-57; Parker, *op. cit.*, p. 124.

33. See Leonard C. Kercher, Vant W. Kebker, Wilfred C. Leland, Jr., *Consumers' Cooperatives in the North Central States* (R. S. Vaile, ed.), pp. 22-23.

34. *Ibid.*, pp. 79 ff.

35. Cross, *op. cit.*, p. 33.

36. Ernest O. F. Ames, *The Cooperator,* March 1921, pp. 70 ff.

37. Harris, *op. cit.*, p. 290.

38. See Clinton F. Wells, *The Status of Consumers' Cooperation on the Pacific Coast,* Stanford Univ. Master's thesis (August 1920), pp. 32 ff.; Parker, *op. cit.*, pp. 951-953; Watkins, *op. cit.*, pp. 54-56.

39. For full discussion see *Proceedings of Second Convention of Cooperative League of America,* November 1920, pp. 35-37. For an interesting review of California cooperative store experience from 1860 to 1960 see Art Danforth, "This Is the Story of Consumer Cooperation in California," Berkeley, California, 1964. Processed copies available from Cooperative League of the U.S.A., Chicago, Illinois.

40. Sonnichsen, *op. cit.,* pp. 160-61.

41. Credit for formulating the theory of consumers' cooperation is generally accorded to Beatrice Potter (Mrs. Sydney Webb) who sketched out its main lines in *The Cooperative Movement in Great Britain* (1891). The first American book to present fully the theory was Albert Sonnichsen's *Consumers' Cooperation,* 1919. To Sonnichsen, "Beyond any doubt consumers' cooperation is an anti-capitalist, revolutionary movement, aiming toward a radical social reconstruction based on an all-inclusive collectivism." He contrasted consumers' cooperation with agricultural marketing associations which he maintained were "an integral part of the capitalist system" (pp. 171-184, 185).

42. The result envisaged by many advocates of consumers' cooperation was the eventual creation of The Cooperative Commonwealth. This conception was popularized in the United States by Leonard Woolf's persuasive book, *Cooperation and the Future of the Industry* (London: George Allen and Unwin, 1919), pp. 125-34.

43. The Cooperative League of America, with headquarters in New York City (now Chicago), was patterned on the Cooperative Union of England as a propaganda organization for consumers' cooperation. It distributed pamphlet literature and issued a journal, *Cooperation.* By 1918, the League had gained the interest of such liberal thinkers as Harry W. Laidler, John Graham Brooks, John Dewey, Frederick C. Howe, Florence Kelly, Walter Lippmann, and Helen L. Sumner. During its early years, the League was largely supported by Dr. Warbasse, a well-known surgeon who in 1919 retired from active practice to devote his life and property to the advancement of consumers' cooperation. The League later moved its headquarters to Chicago. For information on the formation and early history of the League, see Sonnichsen, *op. cit.,* pp. 155-156; Kallen, *op. cit.,* pp. 250-60. For Dr. Warbasse's own account of the formation and first days of the Cooperative League see his autobiography, *Three Voyages* (Chicago; The Cooperative League of the U.S.A., 1956), pp. 113-24.

44. Report of the *Proceedings of the First American Cooperative Convention,* Springfield, Illinois, September 25-27, 1918.

45. Warne, *op. cit.,* pp. 106, 394-95.

46. *Ibid.,* p. 118.

47. *Ibid.,* pp. 119, 202.

48. *Ibid.,* p. 128.

49. It was at this time that Harrison Parker floated his Cooperative Society of America, and other spurious cooperative schemes which cost investors millions of dollars, while doing much to destroy confidence in all cooperative programs. For an excellent analysis of Parker's methods, see *Ibid.,* Ch. XIV.

50. *Cooperation,* December 1921.

51. Florence E. Parker, *Consumers' Cooperative Societies in the United States in 1920,* U.S. Bureau of Labor Statistics, Bulletin No. 313, 1923. When this bulletin was issued the terms "consumers' cooperative" and "consumers' cooperation" were just coming into general use to describe any cooperative designed to serve individuals in their capacities as consumers. Cooperative stores thus came to be called "consumers' cooperatives." This bulletin, and other publica-

tions of the Bureau of Labor Statistics, did much to establish this terminology in American cooperative literature.

Chapter XXII

1. G. Harold Powell, *Cooperation in Agriculture* (New York: The Macmillan Company, 1923), pp. 87-88.

2. *Cow Testing Associations,* U.S.D.A. Farmers' Bulletin 1446.

3. Henry E. Erdman, *Organizations Among Ohio Farmers* (Wooster: Ohio Agricultural Experiment Station Bulletin 342, 1920), pp. 150-52.

4. Powell, *op. cit.,* pp. 89-93.

5. Clarence Poe, *How Farmers Cooperate and Double Profits* (New York: Orange Judd Company, 1915), pp. 13-14. See also Powell, *op. cit.,* pp. 92, 94-108.

6. For discussion of methods of organization and operation and for type of membership agreement used see *Cooperative Bull Associations,* U.S.D.A. Farmers' Bulletin 993 (1918).

7. Powell, *op. cit.,* pp. 109-19.

8. See John J. Lacey, *Farm Bureau in Illinois* (Bloomington: Illinois Agricultural Association, 1965), pp. 3-52. See also O. M. Kile, *The Farm Bureau Through Three Decades* (Baltimore: Waverly Press, 1948), pp. 24-46.

9. For a good description of this experiment see "Cooperation Number" of the Minnesota Farmers' Institute Annual, published by Superintendent of Farmers' Institutes and Agricultural Extension Division, University Farm, St. Paul, 1913, pp. 95-106.

10. For full information see H. S. Yohe, *Operating a Cooperative Motor Truck Route,* U.S.D.A. Farmers' Bulletin 1032, 1919.

11. From a census report quoted by Powell, *op. cit.,* pp. 300 ff. See also *Rural Telephone Service—U.S.A.,* Rural Electrification Administration, U.S.D.A. Miscellaneous Publication No. 823, 1960, pp. 3-4.

12. Dwight Sanderson, *The Farmer and His Community* (New York: Harcourt, Brace and Company, 1922), pp. 43-44.

13. Victor N. Valgren, *Farmers' Mutual Fire Insurance in the United States* (Chicago: University of Chicago Press, 1923), pp. 20-21, 98.

14. *Ibid.,* pp. 10, 86-94, 104.

15. For more detailed information see Wells A. Hutchins, *Organization and Operation of Cooperative Irrigation Companies,* Farm Credit Administration Circular No. C-102, 1936; and *Mutual Irrigation Companies in California and Utah,* Farm Credit Administration Bulletin No. 8, 1936. Hutchins defined a mutual irrigation company as "a community organization operated as a non-profit cooperative enterprise." He indicated that such companies financed themselves primarily from assessments against the stock owned by the water users.

16. The interesting story of how all forms of mutual fire insurance developed in the United States is well told by John Bainbridge, *Biography of an Idea: The Story of Mutual Fire and Casualty Insurance* (Garden City, N.Y.: Doubleday and Company, 1952).

17. For a full account of how mutual casualty insurance came into being and grew in scope and amount see *Ibid.*

18. Shepard B. Clough, *A Century of American Life Insurance—A History of the Mutual Life Insurance Company of New York 1843-1943* (New York: Columbia University Press, 1946), pp. 197, 200.

19. *Ibid.,* p. 218.

20. Henry Moir, "Life Insurance," *Encyclopaedia of the Social Sciences,* Vol. 9, pp. 466-467.

21. Clough, *op. cit.,* p. 228.

22. Of the 20 largest life insurance companies listed by *Fortune Magazine* in June 1968, 14 are organized as mutual companies. All of the five largest companies are mutuals.

23. Myron T. Herrick and R. Ingalls, *Rural Credits—Land and Cooperative* (New York: D. Appleton and Company, 1914), pp. 459-60. The authors continued with this interesting observation: "The cooperative feature of the administration and management of an institution, however, becomes correspondingly less as it increases in size, no matter how much care has been taken in making the organization perfectly cooperative. This is true of a bank or of any other kind of concern. The majority of the policy holders of the large American insurance companies do not exercise their voting privilege, have no personal acquaintance with their officers, and know very little about the principles of insurance or the ways in which their funds are invested, and thus through the lack of interest of the policy holders the cooperative spirit is weakened. This does not mean necessarily that their affairs are handled any the worse because of that fact. It simply shows that undiluted cooperation cannot be practiced except by relatively small groups of persons." Although there is much truth in this statement it is not true that cooperative organizations need to be small to be truly cooperative. Since Herrick wrote the above sentences many very large cooperatives have come into existence—without the loss of cooperative spirit or membership control.

24. Myron T. Herrick, long president of the Society for Savings of Cleveland, Ohio, described this mutual savings and loan association as follows: "The Society for Savings, with nearly one hundred depositors, is one of the largest of the mutual savings banks in the country. It has no capital stock; it is mutual in its organization, and was founded primarily for the purpose of encouraging thrift." See *Ibid.,* Preface.

25. *Ibid.,* pp. 458-460.

26. Roy F. Bergengren, *Cooperative Banking—A Credit Union Book* (1921), p. 236.

27. See Bayard Taylor, *Financial Policies of Business Enterprise* (New York: D. Appleton-Century Company, 1942), Chapter IV, "The Cooperative." Taylor held that building and loan associations and mutual savings banks had been built "on cooperative lines" but did not "behave as cooperatives in actual operations" in that membership was largely perfunctory (p. 82).

28. *The History of Retailer-Owned Groups,* a pamphlet issued by the Cooperative Food Distributors of America, about 1965. The Cooperative Merchants Association, of Chicago, mentioned in the preceding chapter, was an association of some 500 retail merchants in the Midwest formed about 1900 primarily to meet the competition of the fast growing mail-order houses. Each member merchant had a stock investment of $200, and orders for merchandise were pooled and placed with various wholesale houses. Davis Douthit, *Nobody Owns Us* (Chicago: Cooperative League of the U.S.A., 1948), pp. 66-68.

29. While the chain store type of retailing goes back to the establishment of the Great Atlantic and Pacific Tea Company in 1859, the growth of such organizations was slow until around 1900. See George Burton Hotchkiss, *Milestones of Marketing* (New York: The Macmillan Company, 1938), chapter on "The Rise of Large-Scale Retailing."

30. *The History of Retailer-Owned Groups, op. cit.*

31. To protect their businesses, wholesalers also sponsored group organizations under which retailers were given the advantages of large-scale buying and merchandising advice and services. As these organizations were not strictly cooperative in form they are not discussed in detail here. However, as they were financed by wholesalers they were able to make faster immediate progress than the retailer-owned cooperatives. See Wilford L. White, *Cooperative Retail Buying Associations* (New York: McGraw-Hill Book Company, 1930), pp. 1-18. White also pointed out that 17 large department stores set up in 1916 the Retail Research Association for the exchange of confidential information on store operations. In 1920 a subsidiary corporation, the Associated Merchandise Corporation, was formed to perform group buying.

32. "Truth Is Our Business," a Sigma Delta Chi Foundation Lecture, University of Michigan, December 1, 1965, *The Quill*, February 1966. In this lecture Mr. Miller pointed out that The AP membership then included 1,250 daily newspapers in the United States and more than 2,700 radio and television stations. "The governing body of The AP is a board of 18 directors elected for staggered three-year terms from among the total membership. The bylaws provide that large and small newspapers shall be represented on the board. The president of The AP is elected by the board of directors. All directors, including the president, serve without compensation. The board appoints the chief executive of The AP, a general manager: it delegates to him complete control over personnel and operations. For further information see *The History of AP*, multilithed, seven pages (provided by The AP); Frank Luther Mott, *The News in America* (Cambridge, Mass.: Harvard University Press, 1955), pp. 99-100; Richard Hooker, "The Newspaper's Changing Role," *The Yale Review*, Autumn 1950.

33. "Clearing Houses," *Encyclopaedia of the Social Sciences*.

34. For additional information see Harold G. Moulton, *Financial Organization of Society* (Chicago: University of Chicago Press, Third Edition, 1930), pp. 420-433.

Chapter XXIII

1. "The Economic Philosophy of Cooperation," *American Economic Review*, December 1922, pp. 594-597.

2. In the six years from 1915 to 1920, inclusive, there were organized 1,538 grain associations, 232 fruit and vegetable cooperatives, 471 cooperative creameries and cheese factories, and 424 livestock shipping associations. See R. H. Elsworth, *Development and Present Status of Farmers' Cooperative Business Organizations* (Washington, D.C.: USDA Bulletin No. 1302, 1924), p. 32.

3. See O. B. Jesness, *Cooperative Marketing* (Washington, D.C.: USDA Farmers' Bulletin No. 1144, September 1920). This publication, of which some 200,000 copies were printed in the early 1920's, expressed in positive and simple terms many of the lessons enumerated, and helped fix them in farmers' minds. Many of these lessons were also cogently stated by G. Harold Powell in *Fundamental Principles of Cooperation in Agriculture* (Berkeley, Calif.: University of California Agricultural Experiment Station Circular No. 222, October 1920).

4. Although agriculture has gone through a technological and economic revolution during the past half century, and the number of farms has been halved, it has remained primarily an industry of farm-family units although they have increased greatly in size and economic strength. No doubt, cooperatives have contributed to this result.

5. The total gross business volume amounted to $21.9 billion. The net figure eliminates business done between cooperatives.

6. Data for memberships and volume of business is from a USDA Farmer Cooperative Service press release on November 27, 1968. Information on farmers' investments in cooperatives is from *The Balance Sheet of Agriculture, 1968* (Washington, D.C.: USDA Agricultural Information Bulletin No. 334, January 1969).

7. See *Farmers Become Sole Owners of Farm Credit Administration* and *American Farmers Now Own $12 Billion Banking System—The Impossible Dream Comes True.* "After a half century in partnership with the Government, nearly a million American farmers and over 3,000 of their cooperatives now completely own the Cooperative Farm Credit System" (news releases of the Farm Credit Administration, Washington, D.C., December 31, 1968).

8. Information provided by Donald Cooper, Research and Information Consultant, National Rural Electric Cooperative Association, Washington, D.C., January 1969.

9. *Ibid.*

10. For more complete data see *International Credit Union Yearbook, 1968* (Madison, Wisc.: CUNA International, Inc., 1969).

11. For more complete information see annual statistical editions of *Co-op Report* (Chicago, Ill.: Cooperative League of the U.S.A., September 1968, pp. 10-11; September 1967, pp. 4-6). The nation's largest consumer cooperative, Greenbelt Consumer Services, Inc., which serves the Washington-Baltimore area had, in 1968, 26,000 members and did a business volume of approximately $43 million. It operates 20 supermarkets, 8 service stations, and 5 Scan Furniture Stores (*The Washington Post,* February 22, 1969).

12. Information supplied by Ray O. Harb, Executive Vice President of Cooperative Food Distributors of America, Park Ridge, Illinois (letter of February 1, 1969). See also Staff Report to the Federal Trade Commission, "Retailer Owned Cooperative Food Wholesalers," *Economic Inquiry into Food Marketing, Part I,* U.S. Government Printing Office, 1960, pp. 157-201. See also *Progressive Grocer,* April 1969, pp. 64-65. Certified Grocers (California)—the largest retailer-owned cooperative wholesale—reported sales of $471 million for 1968. *Ibid.* p. 85.

13. See annual statistical edition of *Co-op Report* (Chicago, Ill.: Cooperative League of the U.S.A., September 1968), pp. 10-11. In New York City some 50,000 families now live under cooperative housing arrangements. "Co-op City," now being settled in the Bronx, will provide homes for 15,382 families. It represents a total estimated development cost of $294 million. Such organizations—operated in accordance with Rochdale cooperative principles—are endeavoring to ameliorate the urban crisis by providing low cost housing to persons of all religions, races, and nationalities. For more complete information see *Co-op City Information Bulletin,* Riverbay Corporation, New York City.

14. Annual statistical edition of *Co-op Report* (Chicago, Ill.: Cooperative League of the U.S.A., September 1969), pp. 10-11. These statistics do not include such quasi-cooperative health programs as the Blue Cross and Blue Shield plans. See E. P. Roy, *Cooperatives: Today and Tomorrow* (Danville, Ill.: The Interstate Printers & Publishers, Inc., 1964), pp. 192-193.

15. It is difficult to estimate the total number of members in cooperatives for many individuals belong to several cooperatives. Many are not even aware of their membership. Since there are now 20 million members in credit unions (1969), besides many millions of members in other cooperatives who are not also members of credit unions, the total number no doubt exceeds 30 million. This figure does not include many millions who are members of mutual life insurance companies or other semi-cooperative or quasi-cooperative organizations. For more complete information see Roy, *ibid.,* pp. 34, 120-123, 192 ff.

Index

INDEX

DATE DUE

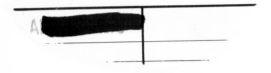